MASTERING

counselling skills

second edition

jennie lindon and lance lindon

palgrave
macmillan

First edition 2000
Second edition 2008

Published by
PALGRAVE MACMILLAN
Houndmills, Basingstoke, Hampshire RG21 6XS and
175 Fifth Avenue, New York, N.Y. 10010
Companies and representatives throughout the world

PALGRAVE MACMILLAN is the global academic imprint of the Palgrave Macmillan division of St. Martin's Press, LLC and of Palgrave Macmillan Ltd. Macmillan® is a registered trademark in the United States, United Kingdom and other countries. Palgrave is a registered trademark in the European Union and other countries.

ISBN-13: 978–0–230–53786–6
ISBN-10: 0–230–53786–3

This book is printed on paper suitable for recycling and made from fully managed and sustained forest sources. Logging, pulping and manufacturing processes are expected to conform to the environmental regulations of the country of origin.

A catalogue record for this book is available from the British Library.

A catalog record for this book is available from the Library of Congress.

10   9   8   7   6   5   4   3   2   1
17   16   15   14   13   12   11   10   09   08

Printed and bound in Great Britain by
Creative Print & Design (Wales), Ebbw Vale

Palgrave Master Series

Accounting
Accounting Skills
Advanced English Language
Advanced Pure Mathematics
Arabic
Basic Management
Biology
British Politics
Business Communication
Business Environment
C Programming
C++ Programming
Chemistry
COBOL Programming
Communication
Computing
Counselling Skills
Counselling Theory
Customer Relations
Database Design
Delphi Programming
Desktop Publishing
e-Business
Economic and Social History
Economics
Electrical Engineering
Electronics
Employee Development
English Grammar
English Language
English Literature
Fashion Buying and Merchandising
   Management
Fashion Marketing
Fashion Styling
Financial Management
Geography
Global Information Systems
Globalization of Business

Human Resource Management
International Trade
Internet
Java
Language of Literature
Management Skills
Marketing Management
Mathematics
Microsoft Office
Microsoft Windows, Novell Netware
   and UNIX
Modern British History
Modern European History
Modern German History
Modern United States History
Modern World History
Novels of Jane Austen
Organisational Behaviour
Pascal and Delphi Programming
Personal Finance
Philosophy
Physics
Poetry
Practical Criticism
Psychology
Public Relations
Shakespeare
Social Welfare
Sociology
Spanish
Statistics
Strategic Management
Systems Analysis and Design
Team Leadership
Theology
Twentieth-Century Russian History
Visual Basic
World Religions

www.palgravemasterseries.com

Palgrave Master Series
Series Standing Order ISBN 0–333–69343–4
(outside North America only)

You can receive future titles in this series as they are published by placing a standing order. Please contact your bookseller or, in case of difficulty, write to us at the address below with your name and address, the title of the series and the ISBN quoted above.

Customer Services Department, Macmillan Distribution Ltd
Houndmills, Basingstoke, Hampshire RG21 6XS, England

To **Nick Georgiades** and **Brian Wilkinson**
who set us on this path

Contents

list of figures

acknowledgements

We have learned a considerable amount from our colleagues and clients and the wide range of people from public services and business to whom we have taught counselling skills. It would be impossible to name everyone, so we would like to express our appreciation of the many ideas, suggestions and constructive feedback over the years.

As we were writing this book, the following individuals were generous with their time and further contacts: Sarah Johnston, Jessica Johnson, Diana Renard, Steve Rathborn and Kath Kelly. All the organisations mentioned in the book have been helpful over the telephone or in sending written material about their work. We would especially like to thank the Women's Nationwide Cancer Control Campaign (WNCCC), the Advice and Mediation Services at the National Foster Care Association, the Kingston Friends Workshop Group and the Samaritans.

The diagram of the counselling model (page 135) was adapted and developed from the idea of the four diamonds in Gerard Egan and Michael Cowans, *People in systems: a model of development in the human-service professions and education* (Brooks Cole, 1979). The diagram of themes and outcomes in work teams (page 190) was adapted from John Adair, *Effective leadership: a modern guide to developing leadership skills* (Pan, 1983). The diagrams of levels of communication (page 28), the communications process (page 30) and the listening and questioning funnel (page 47) have been adapted from material that has been available for some years among professionals working in the area of communication. Despite our efforts, we have been unable to identify the originator of these diagrams and would be pleased to make an appropriate acknowledgement in future editions. The illustration of two ears, two eyes and one mouth (page 34) was originated by Lance, who also developed and adapted the remaining diagrams. In addition, the authors and publishers would like to thank the following illustration sources: Steve Redwood for photographs on pages 8, 139, 261; Bill McKenzie for that on page 61; RNIB for that on page 81; Relate for that on page 82; Childline for that on page 111 and NCH for that on page 189. Other photos were supplied by Jennie and Lance Lindon. Every effort has been made to trace all copyright-holders, but if any have been overlooked the publishers will be pleased to make the necessary arrangement at the first opportunity.

JENNIE LINDON
LANCE LINDON

introduction

objectives and focus of the book

Many people within the caring professions are involved in helping relationships with the users of their service, whether short- or longer-term. This book is specifically designed for readers who are in the position of offering support to clients. Primarily these roles will be through information or advice and sometimes direct help through supportive conversations with individuals or through work with groups.

Use of skills in communication is essential for even the shortest exchanges with clients. Good communication can make a crucial difference in how clients then use, or choose not to use, your own or other services within an organisation.

The bedrock of effective daily communications within a service comes from the basic skills of counselling. As such, an understanding of counselling skills has become essential for the majority of workers in health, education, social services, careers advice and voluntary helping organisations. Professionals and volunteers in these settings need to understand and use counselling skills to improve their effectiveness even though they are not, nor are they intended to be, full-time counsellors.

a reader's guide

In response to the wide-ranging use of communication skills in helping professions, this book starts with general approaches to good practice in any setting and the important communication basics underpinning how to share information – both directly and through the Internet. Chapters 1–5 offer practical advice and explanation that is applicable to many settings. Chapters 6–8 cover more specific application of counselling skills to the caring professions. Chapters 9 and 10 cover working with groups. Chapter 11 highlights in brief a range of applications to different kinds of help or to groups of clients. Chapter 12 considers safe practice and personal well-being for helpers in any profession.

Links to further information are given in terms of readings, key websites and other published material.

The content of the book includes both information and explanation but also offers a wide range of suggested activities to undertake on your own, as well as in discussion with colleagues or within a team meeting, or with fellow students during a training course or session. In many cases each chapter is complete in itself, although Chapters 6–8 on counselling skills and 9–10 on group work are designed to be read in the given order.

terms used

Given the wide variety of readers, our choice of words and phrases was not straightforward. We decided to use the term 'client' as the recipient of counselling throughout rather than change the descriptor depending on the setting being used. Both clients and service providers may be female or male. We resolve this potential problem of style by using the plural, as in 'clients ... they'. Sometimes we use 'she' or 'he' and names are given in examples.

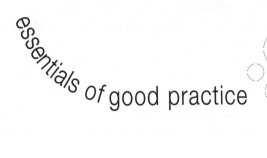

essentials of good practice

1.1 helping in context

helping services and organisations

A wide range of public services, commercial organisations and charitable groups offer some kind of help to their clients. For example:

- Health services may offer support and information to clients whilst some health centres make counselling services available. Health visitors make personal contact with families, and some health authorities are part of outreach services that offer advice and support. Specialist units and clinics deal with children, young people, adults and their families.
- A range of departments within local authorities offer information and advice, as well as direct client support through the social work system.
- Early years and school services recognise that parents welcome advice and information. Some settings operate home visiting schemes and some forms of early years provision, including developments like Sure Start, have aimed to blend family support with other types of service. Pastoral care systems, offering support to children and young people, have been effective in some schools for many years.
- Careers guidance for secondary school pupils and for college students combines information and advice.
- Youth services may also offer information, advice or group work to young people on the range of issues that concern them.
- Commercial companies sometimes offer support services to their employees, either as a regular part of the Human Resources function or in response to particular events, such as redundancy.
- Citizens' Advice Bureaux offer advice or information to people who visit or telephone.

- There are a considerable number of helping organisations, some with charitable status and some with a membership structure. Some offer a very broad base of help, while others have more specific concerns and therefore a more focused client base.

different types of help

There are broad differences between the kinds of help to clients that are covered in this book, although many of the same skills remain important.

information

Some organisations have a primary role in offering an information service. Some start with such information and then add further services as these are requested by clients. Information may be given through clear explanations to clients, for instance of the possible forms of child care or the implications of particular legislation. Information might also be offered about other individuals, groups or organisations who could help further. This can be delivered face to face, through print, CDs, DVDs, the Web, broadcast media or any combination of these.

advice

In some services clients reach their own decisions based on the information provided. However, other services help clients to weigh up the implications of this information. Advisers may suggest that one course of action would be more appropriate or realistic, given a client's wishes or needs, for instance between the possible options for child care. Similarly advice can assist a client approaching retirement to choose the best ways to manage a different set of financial circumstances, or a redundant employee to prepare a professional CV.

guidance

Use of information and advice plays a larger part in guidance than in less directive helping. Clients make their own decisions but help is offered with a view to the realities of a client's situation, for instance about study and careers choice or dealing with a serious health condition. Helpers use their expertise and experience to guide clients towards realistic options rather than leaving clients to discover these alone.

support

Some helping services aim to support clients so that they feel confident there is someone who will give them attention and empathy. Support may be offered through a sympathetic listener over the telephone or face to face, a friendly place to find company, or by providing a companion to attend a stressful meeting or consultation. Befriending services offer personal contact, face to face or over the telephone, and non-judgemental support. Some people prefer anonymity and hence may find email helping services or online counselling beneficial.

counselling

Genuine counselling includes an explicit offer of time and expertise to a client, which is accepted by the client without any pressure. The use of counselling skills is essential for many helping relationships – not just those of full-time counsellor and client. The counselling approach covered in this book depends on qualities of warmth, genuineness and empathy and includes effective skills of communication, positive and respectful challenge and joint problem-solving.

mediation or conciliation

This use of counselling skills is focused on helping people in conflict to reach a resolution in a non-confrontational way. Mediators provide a neutral place for clients, for instance couples in the process of separating, to discuss difficulties and reach important decisions without increasing resentment. Mediation skills have also been successfully taught to children.

advocacy

Support through advocacy represents more active involvement for helpers, since an advocate speaks up on behalf of clients. Advocacy supports clients who are sufficiently young, daunted by authority or unable to express their views and preferences so as to be heard.

self-help

Some services have an explicit objective that clients will be enabled to help themselves, and perhaps also to support others in a similar position. The services offered might include information so that clients can plan and act from a strong base, or groups in which clients help one another. An organisation might offer basic counselling or a group facilitator to support clients to the point where self-help is a realistic option.

clients' acceptance of help

Within the UK there has been a long tradition of asking for advice or support from within the family, from close friends, from the immediate local community and from respected figures such as the local priest or doctor. These sources of support have not disappeared, and some social and cultural groups still place a great deal of emphasis on dealing with difficulties within the family or immediate community without involving strangers. However, public services and specific organisations have increasingly developed to meet a need for help when people either feel they cannot speak with family or friends or are seeking information or advice that they cannot find from their personal circle.

Certain kinds of help have been socially acceptable in the UK for a long time. Advice and information on specialist areas, such as careers guidance, financial advice or health information, have generally been viewed as sensible consultation with experts. There has been considerably more reservation about seeking help for personal difficulties.

One source of resistance seems to be a cultural outlook that equates asking for help on personal problems as an admission of failure, though this is changing gradually. In contrast, the United States experienced a widespread acceptance of therapy and counselling long before the UK. Another source of resistance is the fear that talking will only make matters worse – a view summed up by the cliché 'least said, soonest mended'. The belief persists that even very distressing experiences will fade away and talking will only make matters worse. This view is not, of course, universal but is expressed in connection with seriously distressing experiences for children, young people and adults. There now seems to be rather more acceptance that talking through problems and difficulties can be useful and that it does not imply incompetence or mental breakdown. However, a level of wariness remains.

| ACTIVITY

Over several weeks, collect examples that highlight common views about seeking advice, information or help with personal problems. You could cut out items from newspapers or magazines. Or listen in to everyday conversation.

▷ What range of views are emerging?
▷ Can you see a different outlook depending on the type of help sought?

common misunderstandings about helping

A number of beliefs persist about the process of helping and such misunderstandings can affect both clients and inexperienced helpers, in any of the different types of help.

helpers always solve people's problems

Even very experienced helpers do not resolve all the issues put to them. Some queries or difficulties do not have an easy or quick answer. A helper should be able to draw on past experience to support the person currently seeking help. However, that experience does not provide a certain list of reliable solutions to common problems. Sometimes helpers enable clients to come to terms with the realities of their situation or to learn to live with a situation that cannot easily be changed.

helpers solve problems quickly

Swift answers do not work because the 'quick fix' approach depends on reducing clients' individuality and pushing them into a ready-made category, such as,

'It's a mid-life crisis' or 'Just like the housing problem I solved last week.' An effective helper uses skills of good communication, including listening, to understand what clients are expressing. Even relatively straightforward information or advice cannot be given effectively for a client unless you have listened and understood in the first place.

helping means telling people what to do or how to think – giving answers

A common belief about being helpful is that the apparently more experienced person tells the less experienced person what he or she should be doing or not doing. If you listen to everyday conversations, you will hear a lot of telling masquerading as help. Another kind of unhelpful telling is through premature explanations or forced interpretations. Comments may be made like, 'You know what this is really about' or 'I know you don't want to face it, but what's actually going on is . . .' The intended help is more likely to be experienced as patronising and intrusive.

in order to help other people, you need age and wisdom

Of course, age in increasing years does not necessarily bring wisdom. Sometimes it just brings a greater conviction of being correct, of having the right to tell younger people what to do and define their priorities. Genuinely effective helpers draw on appropriate skills, as well as experience gained over time. Furthermore, grown-ups are not the only helpers. Children and young people can be very supportive and genuinely helpful to each other.

you can't help unless you've been through the same experience

If this belief were true, the helping services would be very fragmented. Effective helpers listen, so that they can understand what this individual client has experienced, whether or not the helper has experienced something similar. Relevant experience can contribute both to the practical help that is offered and to an understanding of emotions, but the helper still has to draw on appropriate learned counselling skills.

in order to help other people you need lengthy training

Effective helping does require preparation and training. You need opportunities to practise and improve the skills needed for the kind of help that you will offer to clients. Some types of counselling and therapeutic intervention do have training courses that spread over years, but this type of study is not necessary for all kinds of helping intervention. Experienced helpers continue to learn and to take opportunities that extend their skills, as well as reflecting on their own approach and reactions.

helpers never have problems themselves

An enduring myth is that people who offer help or advice to others avoid any personal problems or doubts, but even very experienced helpers will have some difficulties in their own life. It can be especially hard if you experience personal difficulties in the very area in which you are a professional helper.

1.2 boundaries and objectives

Any service that offers help to clients needs to be organised with a clear understanding of the nature of the service.

› What kind of help is being offered?
› Is help on offer to anyone who makes contact or only to certain groups of people?
› Is it clear if your organisation offers a specialised kind of help and who might benefit?
› What are the boundaries of the service, in terms of the kinds of help or time available? Identifying boundaries is not a criticism of a helping service. All organisations will have some boundaries because help can never be limitless.
› How does the organisation ensure that potential clients understand what is offered and what is not?

Everyone within a team should be able to explain to clients, or to other agencies, in simple and accurate terms, what the organisation offers and its boundaries (what it does not do). So, a new team member has to be fully briefed during the early days and weeks to build common understanding and commitment. This induction period is equally important for volunteers, who are sometimes overlooked, but who are just as crucial as paid employees in promoting an accurate and positive view of the organisation.

Any team with a positive outlook will discuss the direction of the service: whether it continues to meet the needs of clients or should be adjusted in some way. Every service that offers help should give room for initiative and flexible response by individual practitioners, but some areas of what is offered and in what way will not be negotiable. Every team needs opportunities to talk and listen to each other, so that possible improvements and 'what if' scenarios can be covered.

review and change of direction

A healthy service is both open to review and ready to adapt in response to changing circumstances. Organisations which have been in existence for many years have often taken a constructively critical look at the reasons why they were originally started, the current request for services and changes in society as a whole, and adjusted accordingly. A change in focus or in the breadth of what is offered is frequently signalled by a change in name for an organisation.

For example, the organisation Relate was first established as the National Marriage Guidance Council in 1938 and changed in 1987. Relate developed from an organisation focused on marriage and associated values to one concerned more broadly with relationships. Their work also expanded to help clients with the breakdown of any relationship as much as supporting people, not always couples, to live together peaceably.

1 Explore the ways in which your own service or organisation promotes a shared understanding of your objectives and boundaries to team members. For instance, reflect on your experiences during your early days and weeks with this team:

   ▶ Looking back, what was most useful in the induction period?
   ▶ On the basis of your current experience, what would you add to, or take away from, the induction programme?

2 If your service or organisation has experienced a change in direction over the years, explore how this arose and how the change was managed:

   ▶ You could talk with team members who were involved in the discussions about change.
   ▶ You could also look at any written material about the refocusing of the service.

If you are part of a relatively new organisation, then you could look at written material from organisations of longer standing. Some have leaflets describing the life of the service. For example, Action for Sick Children, previously the National Association for the Welfare of Children in Hospital, covers the charity's history on its web page: www.actionforsickchildren.org/.

monitoring a service

Any service needs to be monitored, to check both the nature and extent of the service offered and the quality of the work. There are two broad approaches: making a service audit and quality assurance.

1 The aim of a service audit is to identify who uses a service and how resources are allocated within that service. An audit has to use methods of systematic data collection and analysis. This approach could include some socio-demographic details of service users, such as gender, ethnic group or self-described disability. This audit is typically designed to track the characteristics of clients. So clients' names may not be required and counselling services would not break confidentiality.

2 Quality assurance relates the service provided closely to established standards. The aim is to assess the extent to which the service meets those required standards. It is therefore essential that clear and specific standards have been agreed in the first place.

In your own service it may not yet be feasible to undertake a comprehensive audit or establish a specific quality assurance system. However, there will always be opportunities to monitor at least parts of your service and increasingly some kind of quality assurance is expected.

log of requests to your service

Do you have a system for keeping track of the kind of enquiries you receive? Effective monitoring requires simple and appropriate categories, for instance the different kinds of enquiry to a health information line or the numbers of pupils or students who ask about particular kinds of higher education courses. You can monitor your service in this way even when exchanges with clients are brief or over the telephone.

If your service is open to a wide spectrum of people, then it will be appropriate to keep track of the range of clients in terms of broad social and ethnic group categories. This kind of monitoring should be self-determined by clients because it is not your role to decide on a client's ethnic group or whether they consider themselves to be disabled. So the monitoring has to work by asking clients themselves to complete short information forms that ask for gender, ethnic group or any disability. This information can help you to address those not using the service and find possible reasons for the gap. You might need to make the service, or its publicity, more appealing to some groups, or work harder to reach them in the first place.

ask clients for their views

All services should be open to feedback from clients. You need to listen to what is said, even if clients do not express their comments in a flattering way, and learn from the feedback. A more organised survey of client views can be helpful so long as this is done with care. Clients need an accurate idea of why they

figure **1.1**   **interview with client**

are being asked and the likely result. Much like isolated customer charters, a regular canvassing of opinion about a service with no visible consequences tends to create cynicism. You might organise a questionnaire survey, perhaps followed by some interviews with clients. If your services are available to children and young people, make sure that you invite their opinions too, rather than just canvassing their parents.

Such consultation is a process through which both the service providers and service users influence each other with the joint objective of improvement. It is important that everyone recognises that they are involved – albeit in different ways – and that expectations as to what will happen and when are shared and made clear.

1.3 standards of behaviour

Any helping service should take an ethical approach to clients. This requirement means that everyone within the service must be clear about appropriate standards of behaviour towards clients.

the importance of trust

A valid helping relationship between clients and your service is based on trust. Trust is based upon truthfulness and delivering on promises made. Clients should be able to have confidence in your organisation, from a basic reliance on the information that you give, all the way through to a safe setting in which to confide very personal issues.

Genuine helping, even of the most short-term kind, needs to be based firmly in what clients ask or explain about their situation. Effective helpers stand back from their own assumptions and personal preferences about what people should do in similar situations. Any information or advice should be given in an even-handed way and not direct clients towards options in which the helper has any kind of vested interest, or personal or business involvement.

codes of practice

All helping organisations should have clear and public standards for the behaviour of anyone offering the help. These standards should be described in specific terms, so that it is possible for the team members and clients to recognise when standards are being met and when they are not.

In your organisation you may talk about standards, a code of conduct or good practice guidelines. You may refer to the ethics of the service or relate the expected behaviour of helpers to the underlying core values of the service. Regardless of the exact words or phrases used, any helping organisation should have a clear view, communicated throughout the whole team, about how you should all act: in some cases what you should do and some instances of what you definitely should not do.

Written codes of practice lay out a framework in which the service should be offered. They help to ensure that any actions are even-handed, objective and genuinely helpful. A set of standards or a code can guide a team, but cannot foresee and cover every possible situation or dilemma. For this reason, every team within a helping service should have opportunities to discuss issues or dilemmas that arise and to learn from them.

Clear ethical standards for behaviour can become especially important when you use counselling skills with clients or work with groups. Clients often draw on other life experiences to judge the quality of a walk-in information service and a telephone helpline. However, clients may be much less certain about suitable boundaries in a counselling relationship or within a group. Clients who are at a vulnerable point in their life are at risk from poor use of counselling skills or group work. Clients placed under inappropriate pressure, or who feel unsafe in a group, may doubt the validity of their concerns. Perhaps they feel their discomfort or distress is their own fault or that they have to experience this level of emotional pain in order to improve their life. Safe use of counselling skills can help clients to face areas of their life that they find hard to handle. However, neither the individual nor the group experience should make clients feel worse, nor should they create new distress and problems.

personal and professional

An effective helping relationship will be friendly but you are not forming a friendship. Neither short-term nor long-term help should be guided by how much you warm to the client. All clients should be treated professionally, which means with equality. Any problems that arise because of difficulties in forming an appropriate, courteous relationship need to be tackled rather than allowing your feelings of like or dislike to shape the amount and quality of help you give.

A close relationship can develop when you use counselling skills over several sessions, or run groups, but your relations with clients have to remain at a professional level. There is a need to balance genuine empathy for clients with a necessary professional detachment. It is contrary to codes of practice for counsellors or group leaders to become personally involved with individual clients. You will lose your objectivity if you become close friends or intimately involved with a client. There is also a serious risk of exploitation of vulnerable clients because, however well-intentioned the counsellor or group worker, the relationship is one of uneven power and privilege.

Given the large numbers of people involved, it is inevitable that some counsellors or group leaders will be personally attracted to an individual client. The only acceptable response is to postpone any personal involvement until the professional relationship is completely finished. Alternatively, if feelings are strong and appear to be reciprocated by the client, then the professional part of the relationship must end and, if necessary, the client be referred to someone else. Some organisations have a clear time span required between the end of a professional relationship and the beginning of a personal one.

Concerns are most often expressed about intimate relationships between a client and practitioner. However, any kind of non-professional involvement brings a risk of confusing the boundaries of the professional relationship. For example, it is unwise to enter any kind of business relationship with a client, such as buying a car or inviting the client's expertise for your financial affairs. You should talk in confidence with a colleague or supervisor if you face a blurring of the boundaries between personal and professional relationships with clients.

confidentiality

Few services will be totally confidential in the sense that what any client tells any helper will never go beyond that conversation. There must, however, be clear guidelines about any limits to confidentiality and these must be understood by all the team and communicated to clients. Such boundaries are just as important in information and advice services as in more personal counselling relationships.

clients' concerns remain within the service

Clients have the right to expect that their use of a service and any conversations are kept within professional exchanges inside the boundaries of your service.

› What clients have said, their questions, concerns and experiences should never fuel light conversation or be the source of 'good stories' exchanged with anyone else.
› Personal information about clients should not be repeated, as a kind of professional gossip, within an organisation.
› If you give examples within a training or workshop context, then these should be anonymous and with no detail that could possibly identify the individual client.
› This emphasis on confidentiality and honesty with clients applies in work with children and young people just as much as in work with adults. Children's confidences should never be routinely broken with the justification of 'the good of the child'. Your own issues and concerns for the child should be shared with them in appropriate language.

> Helpers may discuss a client with their supervisor or seek specific support from a colleague in dealing with a complex situation, but the boundary to confidentiality should be drawn clearly at that point. In services where support and supervision is an important part of working with individual clients, then those clients should be told at the outset that you may discuss their situation with your supervisor and the client's agreement should be gained before you do so.

The confidentiality guidelines apply to the providers of a service. If clients want to talk with friends or anyone else about what they have discussed or asked, then that is their decision. They have the right to discuss their situation or confide in anyone else, if they wish.

ethical problems and confidentiality

The only valid reason for breaking confidentiality is the genuine risk that the client is currently damaging or is likely to damage someone else, especially if this other person is young or for some other reason unlikely to be able to protect themselves.

All services share an obligation of safeguarding children and young people. These limits to confidentiality should be made clear in any written material about the service and directly to clients themselves. When children or young people disclose abuse, the helper has an obligation to support their young client but cannot agree to keep secrets that endanger that individual. This exception to the general rule of confidentiality also applies if an adult client discloses information that leads you to believe that a child or young person is at risk. Any helping services should already be familiar with contact details of the local safeguarding/child protection services. You do not delay until this difficult situation arises.

Services that work with clients under great stress, or who are very depressed, will face the dilemmas raised by individuals who sound suicidal or who express feelings and plans about self-harm. You must be clear about the approach that your organisation takes over such ethical dilemmas and should follow those guidelines. Additionally, you need access to support and supervision in order to discuss the strong feelings that can be aroused even in experienced helpers.

inappropriate requests for information

Your own organisation may have a clear understanding about your confidentiality, but you may have contact with other professionals who take a different view. For example:

> An employer asks you to give personal details of employees who have asked for advice.
> Teachers expect to be briefed on confidential pastoral or careers guidance sessions with pupils.

- Parents expect to be told about what their children or teenagers have discussed with you.

You can be placed in a difficult position by such requests, especially if you have not explained the situation beforehand. You may have assumed that your work will be confidential, but did not check the assumptions of other people involved. Perhaps the employer has paid you, or your organisation, and assumes that his or her briefing is part of the service. The teacher or parent has assumed that they have a right to know what is happening with the child or young person.

Good practice in confidentiality requires that you:

- Explore other people's assumptions about confidentiality when your service could be seen to have more than one client in the situation.
- Tell your clients of any limits to the confidentiality of what they discuss with you. It is crucial to be clear and explicit about what is, and what is not, confidential.

The situation regarding help for children and young people is uncertain. On the one hand, some legal principles, for instance the 1985 *Gillick* ruling, have established that under-sixteens can make medical decisions for themselves if they are judged to have sufficient understanding. On the other hand, adults like parents and teachers are responsible for children in their care. Genuinely caring individuals may benefit from understanding a child's problems and young people choose the person in whom they wish to confide.

The application of *Gillick competence* has been taken to mean that professionals are not required to tell parents if their adolescent has asked for information about contraception or other matters relating to sexual health. However, the situation is much less clear when young people seek specific advice and support for considering different options. The Children's Legal Centre recommends that practitioners should be cautious about situations in which they are effectively assuming a level of parental responsibility. Any readers who are involved in offering health, especially sexual health, support to young people are advised to be clear within their team about boundaries. A good starting point would be Carolyn Hamilton's book *Working with Young People: Legal Responsibility and Liability* (Children's Legal Centre, 2006, 6th edn).

inappropriate use of personal material

No detail of a client's situation, no matter if it appears very minor, should be used without their clear and informed consent. This limit applies to using examples in the written material of your service or if you write magazine articles or books. Clients should never be put in the position of having to agree to the use of their personal information in order to receive help. So it would be unacceptable to push clients into an agreement to:

- Be featured as a case study or training material.
- Take part in a research project or experimental trial.
- Be taped in audio or video either overtly or more covertly through devices such as a webcam.
- Accept the presence of trainees or students in a session.

Clients may sometimes agree to any of the above, so long as they are asked in a respectful way and the reasons or benefits to them explained. Clients should have time to consider the request and not be pressured with, 'It's alright if we … isn't it?' Clients have the right to refuse such requests and still receive the full service with no reservations.

EXAMPLES

In the following examples consider:

- How a team might explain their actions.
- The reasons that such situations are not good practice.

1 Alice went for help at her local child guidance centre because her eight-year-old son was refusing to attend school. In the first meeting, Alice was told that the clinic's policy was to video-record all guidance sessions for use as training material. She felt pressured to agree and was doubtful that any further help would be given if she refused. She attended one session with her son but felt very uneasy and did not return for the next appointment. Her son's school head telephoned the clinic and was told that there was no pressure and that Alice could have refused to be videoed.

2 Jake was taking his daughter, Siobhan, to the local out-patients' clinic for a minor health condition. After three visits, the condition appeared to be better but Jake was asked to make another appointment. When questioned, the doctor confirmed that there was no concern about Siobhan. However, the consultant was undertaking a research project on this condition and wanted to monitor any children who had been seen. Jake said that Siobhan could join the project, but that the researchers would have to visit her at home after school hours. The doctor said that was impossible; patients had to come into the clinic.

3 A group of first-year students agreed to complete a very personal questionnaire and were assured that the information would remain with a named college project. A year later they found that the questionnaire information was part of a large computer database to which many researchers had easy access. The group demanded a meeting with the original project leader who was unwilling to apologise, saying that they had overreacted and that this would block valuable research.

1.4 attitudes towards clients

what do you call clients?

Commercial organisations use the term 'customer' or 'end user'. Public services generally only use the word in reference to customer care and charters. Different service traditions have led to different terms:

- Originally coming from the legal profession, 'client' has been the preferred term in social work, for most counselling services and is often used in training and consultancy services.
- In educational services, one set of customers are called 'parents' and the second set may be called 'pupils', 'students' or 'children'.
- Medical services, and any therapy or counselling services with medical links, are most likely to refer to 'patients'.
- Some community and voluntary services have chosen the term 'service user'.

However, the word can carry negative overtones in services where there is a tradition of selecting people on the basis of defined need and priority. People who are believed to work the system, or to be manipulative, are said to use the service for their own ends.

TO THINK ABOUT

▶ What are the users of your service called? What are the associations of the word – positive and negative?

▶ Think about this issue yourself but also gather the opinions of colleagues and of some service users.

▶ When you are a service user, how do you feel about the term used to describe you? For example, how does it feel to be a 'patient'?

It matters what you call the users of your service because the term chosen conveys a message, which can be more or less positive. Some years ago one of us worked with a large educational day centre for young people with learning disabilities. The head had taken the decision that every young person was to be called a 'student', regardless of the programme of study followed or whether this led to any paper qualification. This positive term for the young people contributed to an atmosphere of learning and of respect.

customer charters

The 1990s saw an extensive development of customer charters within public services and a wide range of commercial organisations. Charters are grounded in the belief that users of any service have a right to accurate information about what they can expect from the service and how they will be treated. Charters do not in themselves create good customer service; they only work as part of an integrated approach.

If implemented well, charters can contribute to a positive relationship between the service provider and the user. However, charters, not surprisingly, raise expectations that clients will experience treatment consistent with the promises. Dashed expectations and dismissive treatment create resentment and cynicism. Clients, who were previously resigned to an indifferent quality of service, become angry and ready to take action. Irritation is further fuelled by heavy use of slogans in charters and related material or frequent use of the word 'care' by a service whose employees manifestly fail to show this quality. Similar cynicism sets in when people are invited to partake in more than one consultation regarding their views and little or nothing appears to follow from their efforts.

develop a positive outlook on clients

You need to see each client as an individual and, even within brief exchanges, to attend to what the client wants and may need. Various attitudes can block a respect for and valuing of clients and you may need to acknowledge and deal with your own personal outlook. However, dismissive attitudes can also develop within a service and they then become part of the working atmosphere and have to be tackled within the whole team.

Without a clear direction and positive supervision in helping services, a team may develop the negative outlook that short encounters do not deserve their attention. There may be a view of, 'What's the point, I never see clients again', a 'half-empty bottle' philosophy may be expressed as, 'If I had a lot more time, I could help.' Every team involved in helping needs to focus on what can be offered to clients and what can be done, with an outlook determined by respect for clients and the type of courteous treatment that you yourself would wish to receive.

address negative views

Clients will not be valued by a team who share firm views about how clients should behave, such as:

› Patients of a medical service should not question or express doubts. The ones who question are troublemakers.
› Parents whose children attend educational facilities should acknowledge that teachers have more expertise than parents ever could.
› Young people attending a drop-in facility should be appreciative and not criticise the behaviour of volunteers who are giving their time without payment.

A team, or an individual, with rigid views about how clients should behave can develop two approaches depending on whether these are 'good' or 'bad' clients. The good ones deserve attention, whereas the bad ones can be pushed through the service and out again as fast as possible. Overall negative outlooks about clients can develop: that they are difficult, manipulative or generally troublesome. Such attitudes are often developed from (and then justified by) a few bad experiences with clients. These experiences are then generalised to the whole group of clients. Experiences with clients that fit the stereotype are logged as further evidence. However, clients who do not behave in the expected negative way are seen as exceptions, perhaps as 'good' clients who stand out from the rest.

Finally, it can be that much harder to value clients if you feel seriously under-valued yourself. Organisations sometimes treat their staff poorly and yet still expect that this dismissive treatment should not affect the quality of service to clients.

expertise of clients

Sometimes clients are already knowledgeable about the area in which they are seeking some help. Certainly never assume that clients are inexpert. Clarify their level of expertise first. Clients may through necessity have become experts on their own health condition or that of a member of their family. Parents of disabled children can be very knowledgeable about the disability of their own child and how it affects him or her, as well as the reality of the condition for their family.

Practitioners in helping organisations can feel threatened by expert clients, particularly if those helpers have a firm belief that they should always know more than their clients. However, genuine help builds on joint problem-solving – which includes a recognition of clients' knowledge and skills. It is not helpful to believe (even if only privately) that clients will always be less knowledgeable and to resent or challenge any evidence to the contrary.

friendly but not friends – an example

A common misunderstanding is that customer service in helping organisations means getting to know clients very well as individuals. So, if your service offers short and irregular contact with clients, then good customer service is judged to be impossible.

This view was expressed to us during a conversation about possible improvements in how a walk-in library and information service team behaved towards clients. It would indeed have been difficult, if not impossible, to keep track of the many people who came and went during a week. However, the constructive criticism of some employees' behaviour was in no way linked to their making a close, personal relationship with clients.

Some of the team failed to greet clients in any way, left them waiting at the counter with no acknowledgement and chatted with colleagues while ignoring the waiting client. Some staff failed to make eye contact or say anything at all, if an exchange could be completed without words. None of the staff were actively rude in what they said, although the body language was often dismissive. However, the overall message was discourteous, that there was no point in spending time on people who were just passing through the service.

‣ In your organisation how have you clarified the difference between being 'friendly' and 'being friends'?

Technical advances in collection, storage and accessing of information have led to a society in which many people experience regular requests for personal information, often linked with a purchase or application for financial services. Some of the information requested is necessary for the commercial service, but a proportion is of benefit only to the organisation and not to the customer.

The result of this common experience is that many people answer a series of questions without resistance, until questions become very intrusive. However, another consequence is that, overloaded with unnecessary questions, some people have become more assertive, either asking for a rationale for the questions or refusing to answer beyond a point that seems appropriate to them.

ACTIVITY

Over a month, keep track of all the requests made to you for personal information: face to face, over the telephone or through the mail.

▶ What was the context and rationale for the questions?
▶ How far do you judge that answering the questions was of real benefit to you as a service user or purchaser?
▶ How did you feel about being asked very personal questions and were there any questions that you declined to answer?
▶ What reaction did you receive if you challenged someone's need to ask you?
▶ What have you learned that could be applied to your contact with clients?

Clients have a right to privacy on the personal information that you hold, specifically that:

▸ Their names, with or without details, are never passed to third parties without the explicit informed consent of the individual client – ideally their written consent
▸ Clients' data should not be added to other databases, unless you have their specific, informed consent.

This good practice holds even if you genuinely believe that the client could benefit from contact with another individual or organisation, from a book, pamphlet or any other product. Ask before you pass on a client's name. See also page 97 on referrals.

good practice in keeping records

Written records are only as good as the care taken in setting up a record and adding relevant information.

- Information must be accurate and any mistakes in personal details of clients should be corrected promptly.
- Care needs to be taken in hand-written records; these must be clear and legible. Entering information on a computer database needs just as much care to check that the information has been entered correctly.
- Any records should clearly distinguish facts from any opinions. Your opinions can be valuable but should always be supported by observations and reasons.

Any records should be stored securely. The nature of the records and the location of your service might necessitate higher levels of security, for instance if you are working in an area that has many break-ins. If your records are on computer then you need secure systems with password access only.

Written files and records should be easily accessible for practitioners to consult, but kept secure from people who have no right of access. Good practice often involves simple precautions such as putting files away when you have finished, never leaving a file on a desk or countertop and not leaving a client's file on the computer screen in full view of anyone who passes. These restrictions apply as much to fellow professionals who visit your service as to the general public. Other helping professionals must have a sound reason for consulting the records.

informing clients about records

Your organisation needs to establish and maintain good practice in collecting information on clients of your service:

- Be clear about your organisation's reasons for collecting the information that you request and explain the rationale simply to clients.
- Be ready, with no resistance or surprise, to answer specific queries from clients about details that you ask, any forms to be completed or the notes you make.
- Deal with clients' questions courteously, even if they ask in an abrupt or confrontational way. Clients may feel uneasy about challenging your information systems and this unease can emerge in an apparently unfriendly way.
- It is important that your entire organisation commits to a view that clients have a right to understand why information is requested. Clients are not being awkward, unduly anxious or paranoid. They are exercising a basic civil right to ask, 'What do you want to know that for?'
- Explain in a straightforward way how clients can access their own information, and the extent to which their information is available to others in the organisation.

clients' right of access

Policy, practice and the legal situation about written records has changed considerably since the 1970s. At that time, clients were very unlikely to be able to see their own records and a request to do so was likely to be met with surprise as well as refusal. The climate has changed towards a far greater recognition of everyone's basic right of access to their own records. Parents, and other adults *in loco parentis*, have right of access to records on their children. A series of legal changes established that access was good practice, for instance:

› The Access to Personal Files Act 1987 applied to Social Services and gave clients right of access to their own files.
› Since 1990 all parents of pupils under 18 years and all pupils of 16 years and older have right of access to the pupils' own education record held by the school.
› The Access to Health Records Act 1990 gave right of access to individuals of their own health records written after 1 November 1991. If these are not stored electronically, a fee of £50 may be payable to gain access.

It is accepted good practice to remove third party information, that is, letters or reports from professionals outside your service, before clients have access to their files unless those people have given permission. You would also remove, or make anonymous, any references to other individuals within a file. Some local authorities and organisations follow a policy, made explicit on all correspondence, that any material is open in a file to the person about whom the file is written, unless third parties make a specific request that their letters or reports are to be removed. Make sure you are clear about the policy of your service.

The Data Protection Act 1984 entitled individuals to be informed about the existence of records about themselves stored on computers and the right to inspect them. This is described as 'the right of public access'. A small fee may be required to access – typically £10 for electronically stored information. The Data Protection Act 1998 extended some of these rights. If an organisation holds personal data on computer, then, with few exceptions, it has to be registered with the Data Protection Registrar.

|FURTHER INFORMATION ON COMPUTER RECORDS

You can contact the Data Protection Registrar and get more information from Wycliffe House, Water Lane, Wilmslow, Cheshire SK9 5AF; information line 01625 545 745; or the website at www.direct.gov.uk/en/rightsandresponsibilities/DG_10028507.

descriptive personal notes

If you undertake work with individual clients or groups, there are advantages in keeping a descriptive record. Short notes are often appropriate because:

- Clients of some services may not be seen by the same professional each time. A written record should contain essential personal information so that clients do not have to repeat themselves each visit.
- Brief records of repeat telephone callers can be important if different people are likely to answer the help line.

Descriptive notes will be valuable if you use counselling skills with clients individually or in groups over a series of sessions.

- A written summary of a session can help you to identify themes, to organise your thoughts and to think ahead to the next session.
- If you are working with a number of individuals or groups, your written notes will be important in helping you to keep the work clearly separate.
- Keep records that are only as detailed as you need; the aim is not to produce large files that you rarely consult. Useful notes will cover the scope of a session and where the work finished. Notes for group work can additionally cover attendance, the objectives of a session, planned activities and how those activities were received by the group.
- You should write up notes promptly after working with an individual or group. You would not normally take notes during a session.
- Records also help you to monitor and evaluate your own work and can sharpen up your powers of reflection and observation.
- Records place your work in the context of the organisation to which you belong and help to make you more accountable.

You should let individuals or a group know if you keep notes and explain your reasons. You would not normally share your personal notes with an individual client or group. However, you should nevertheless ensure that any notes are either factual or are your well-supported opinions and do not contain offhand remarks about clients.

1.6 equality issues and anti-discriminatory practice

Any service has to ensure that every aspect of organisation and daily running meets the legal requirements of equality legislation and the implications of supporting guidance.

good practice

Laws affect the whole process of employment of team members, promotion of your service, physical access to your building and behaviour towards clients. There are several broad themes within the legislation relevant for equality.

the meaning of equality

Equality practice now applies to individuals' group membership as defined by gender/sex, sexual orientation, ethnic group/race, religion/faith, age and disability. The legal situation is slightly different across the four nations that comprise the UK. For further information please follow up the sources given at the end of this subsection. The following practice issues in no way offer any kind of legal advice to readers.

All clients, and potential clients, must be treated in an equal and even-handed way. Sound equality practice does not mean treating clients as if they are all the same. Respect for the diversity within your client group can appropriately lead to fine-tuning your service. For instance, unless you address physical access issues, then potential clients in a wheelchair or with limited mobility may literally not be able to reach your service.

anti-discriminatory practice

Practice must be free of direct discrimination towards any groups in society. Direct discrimination would be rejecting, or favouring, clients within your service on the basis of their group membership, for instance refusing to accept any Gypsy or Traveller clients. The same ruling applies to selection of any team members. It is acceptable to offer a service that is especially designed for specific groups within society, so long as the nature of the service is clear and is not judged to exclude potential users in a discriminatory way. A similar proviso applies to recruiting team members with specific and relevant skills, such as fluency in the home language of a new client group. The choice must be justified as a genuine occupational qualification (GOQ) for the role.

Services also have a legal responsibility to ensure that policy and practice is free of indirect discrimination, i.e. organising your service in such a way that it is more difficult for some groups to access and use. It is no longer acceptable for any service to say that the discriminatory effect was unintentional, for instance it was just habit that the leaflets were only placed in one of several local places of worship. It is expected that services actively explore the possible impact of long-standing policy or established ways of working, such as the publications used to place job advertisements. Equality legislation has also established that it is illegal to victimise or harass any individuals – clients, employees or volunteers – who have challenged their treatment as discriminatory.

It is illegal to segregate individuals on the basis of their group membership by offering them a very different service. The exception again is when the separation of individuals is a positive response to the needs that they present as clients. For instance, it may be a crucial part of the service for women who have experienced domestic violence from male partners that they have an all-women support group. However, you should consider how to meet the needs that arise from domestic violence meted out by women on men or other family members. Your response might be to know of a suitable local service.

promoting equality of opportunity

Increasingly, the focus of equality legislation and guidance has been to place a responsibility on services to promote equality of opportunity in an active way, as well as to avoid discriminatory behaviour of any kind. This strand of good practice usually means an effort to be proactive, to identify any groups who might struggle, for whatever reason, to hear about and then access your service. However, any such efforts have to be compatible with the transparent boundaries to your service: what you are competent to offer, in what way and to whom. Equality legislation certainly does not require any service to make promises that cannot be honoured.

Good practice within the team means that prejudiced actions, words or assumptions form no part of how the team works. It is, however, important to create an atmosphere in which it is possible to question assumptions and beliefs in a constructive way. The overall aim is that practitioners feel able to reflect on what they have said, rather than to defend their position and attack the comments of others. Listening is key, as everyone within a team, whatever their group membership, will have areas of ignorance or misunderstanding.

Tough dilemmas may arise, within your team or with regard to the responses of clients, when the deeply held beliefs of individuals include dismissal of others, solely on the basis of that person's sex, faith or other markers of group membership. Careful discussion, followed by informed decision-making, will be necessary to ensure that you do not act disrespectfully, or in a discriminatory way, towards an individual or group as the consequence of responding to firmly expressed views of someone else.

FURTHER INFORMATION

▷ Commission for Equality and Human Rights, Kingsgate House, 66–74 Victoria Street, London SW1E 6SW. Tel.: 020 7215 8415. Website: www.cehr.org.uk/

▷ Employment issues: Ministerial Correspondence Unit, Department of Trade and Industry, 1 Victoria Street, London SW1H 0ET. Tel.: 020 7215 5000. Website: www.dti.gov.uk/employment/discrimination/index.html

▷ Disability Rights Commission, DRC Helpline, FREEPOST MID02164, Stratford upon Avon CV37 9BR. Tel.: 08457 622633. Website: www.drc-gb.org/

how your service operates

As discussed earlier, some services are tailored to specific groups in order to respond to a defined need. Under these circumstances it is appropriate to guide some potential clients away from the service because it will not be right for them. Many other helping services are open to a much wider range of potential clients within the population.

Within the boundaries of the service, it is essential that team members remain open-minded about potential clients. Discriminatory assumptions or beliefs can mean that you fail to meet clients' needs. It will be important that:

› All your promotional material about a service makes clear the potential client base and any specific needs that are being addressed. The material needs to be produced in the main languages of the local community.
› Everyone on the team understands any boundaries and expresses these in a positive way to potential clients. You can suggest other possible services, when your own is not appropriate, but any referral should also be made on the basis of what you have learned about a client and not on assumptions.

Even in a service with a clearly defined client base, all the team still has to be open to discussion about their own assumptions and possible lack of knowledge. Such a discussion needs to be positive and constructive. Improvements in practice will not emerge from a team whose members only criticise each other with negative labels like 'racist', rather than listening and working through any assumptions or unchecked beliefs.

promotion of your service

What messages are given by any written material on your service? Does it imply that the service is for particular groups of people and is this accurate? Check out whether any case examples, descriptions and illustrations suggest inaccurate restrictions, for example that:

› None of your clients are ever disabled, when your service would be equally relevant for people with disabilities.
› Most of your clients are adolescents or young adults, when they could just as well be older. Of course, it would be unwise to imply your service extends to an age group when that is not the case.
› It is appropriate to check that any material is inclusive in terms of ethnic group diversity. However, it is unwise to use illustrations that imply a level or type of diversity that is far from visible in your local area. Such illustrations do not look authentic and appear more like an attempt to tick an equality box.
› Most of your team are female when you also have males working too, or vice versa.

reception and welcome to clients

What impression do clients form when they first walk into your building or make their first telephone call?

› What implicit message is given by any posters or pictures on the walls? Can clients see themselves in any illustrations?

- How easy is it for clients to get into your building or office if they have a disability that affects mobility? Or if a parent is visiting with young children and a buggy?
- Can a client in a wheelchair see you clearly, or is the view blocked by a high desk or a restricting access window?
- Does your service have a text telephone facility for deaf clients who cannot hear a voice at the end of the phone and need to write their inquiries? Do you offer text messaging for clients as well as voice messaging?
- In a service that anticipates clients with young children, are the baby changing facilities easily available to fathers as well as mothers?

Some clients may appreciate practical help at this early stage, for instance a client may be visually disabled. Useful help starts with questions such as 'How may I help?' or 'Would you like me to walk with you to the reception desk?'. It is discourteous to seize the arm of visually disabled clients without asking first or to start talking for them as if they are not present.

assumptions within the team

Unspoken assumptions affect the quality of service that you offer clients. Some assumptions will be offensive, but others may simply be an inaccurate generalisation that will reduce the help you offer to the client. For instance, there may be unchecked assumptions that:

- A physically disabled young woman will also have difficulties in communication. Much will depend on the source of her physical disability.
- A smart, well-spoken young man will not have any literacy problems when in fact he may be dyslexic.
- An older woman who is widowed will lack confidence in money matters, because her late husband will have handled the family finances.
- Young male clients know their way around computers and so will not need support in accessing information, whereas female clients will want help.
- Men are less likely to be distressed by bad news and so can be relied upon to calm their female partner who will get upset.
- A client of Asian origin will have to consult her husband before making a major decision.

Some of the above will prove to be the case in some circumstances. Good equality practice is to avoid acting as if they are firm predictions. You need to be open in checking your own assumptions and help to create a positive atmosphere in the team. Make it easier to explore beliefs and challenge assumptions in a constructive way.

- Describe what you have noticed in a specific way. You might ask, 'Are you aware that you addressed all the health care advice to Mrs Parkinson? You scarcely talked with her husband' Descriptions increase the chance that colleagues will listen and learn.

▸ Avoid guessing about underlying motives or applying critical labels. Colleagues are likely to defend themselves against blunt accusations such as 'That was a really sexist thing to say' or 'I would never have thought you'd be so crass about disability.'

▸ Raise issues as a matter of general concern within the team rather than putting the entire responsibility onto individuals. For instance, you might say, 'I think we should go further than simply putting up the multi-lingual welcome poster. Couldn't some of us learn how to say key phrases?' rather than, 'Why hasn't Marlene learned any Polish; she's on the front desk.' You might raise as a general issue, 'People keep saying "We have to treat gay clients the same as anyone else." I think in practice this means we don't acknowledge specific issues that bring some clients through the door.'

▸ Acknowledge positive changes within team practice or individuals; do not just speak up for negative observations.

dealing with assumptions of clients

Sometimes you will need to deal with unhelpful beliefs of the clients about who should help them and how. For example:

▸ Speaking with a female member of the team, the client assumes that a nearby male colleague of hers will be the more senior and can hence take the decision about the current disagreement.

▸ A white client is resistant to sitting down with a black team member and says, 'No offence really, but I'd rather speak with somebody who's English.'

▸ One of your team is in a wheelchair. Some clients look surprised when she moves out from behind her desk.

ACTIVITY

It can be valuable for a team to discuss a range of 'what if' scenarios. Work through the following examples, ideally with colleagues. Discuss and try to decide whether the requests are:

▸ Acceptable because . . .
▸ Unacceptable because . . .
▸ Would only be appropriate when . . .

1 Is it acceptable for a female client to express a preference to speak with a female practitioner rather than a male?

2 Is the reverse all right? Can a male client say he would be more comfortable speaking with another man?

3 A client, who is less confident in English than her home language, makes a request for a practitioner who is also bilingual.

4 An English-speaking client asks not to be assigned your Nigerian colleague in the future on the grounds that she and her child have difficulty in understanding the practitioner's accent. And if a similar request is made about your Irish colleague?

5 A client in his fifties asks to be passed on to someone with more experience. The current helper is in her twenties.

6 What if a black teenager asks if he can talk with a black practitioner? And if a white teenager expresses a preference for a white team member?

7 A client is changing places in the queue, apparently in order to avoid the next available help desk run by a disabled practitioner, who has one foreshortened arm and missing fingers on the other hand.

8 A gay client asks if you have a team member who is also gay. And if a heterosexual client wants to move on from the current helper on the grounds that the practitioner is gay? Does the sex of client or practitioner lead you to any different conclusion?

I TO THINK ABOUT

Meaningful equality and anti-discriminatory practice is part of continuing discussion and reflection in your work. There should never be any sense of, 'Right, we've fixed that then!'

For instance, during the second half of the 1990s there was some refreshing thinking about anti-sexism, including a challenge to the assumption that this approach should only focus on the needs of girls and women. You will find a good example of addressing the imbalance in *Let's Hear it for the Boys*, edited by Gill Lenderyou and Caroline Ray (National Children's Bureau, 1997). This report looks at the response of educational and youth services to supporting sex and relationships education for boys and young men. The report is a stimulating read whether or not you are involved in this area yourself. The contributors offer a full view of the services, including the image promoted by leaflets and posters, creating a positive setting, preparing and training staff, consulting with and learning from the boys and young men and informed group work.

effective communication

2.1 the communication framework

Communications by people in any kind of helping service need to convey acceptance and welcome to clients, a message of the genuineness of your response, a basic sense of empathy (fellow feeling) with the client and a respect for service users. These qualities are shown, or fail to be conveyed, through all aspects of your communication and cannot be faked.

levels of communication

Communication between people can be seen as a hierarchy (see the diagram below). As a helper you need to be aware of the subtle rules and levels of communication, many of which are influenced by cultural tradition.

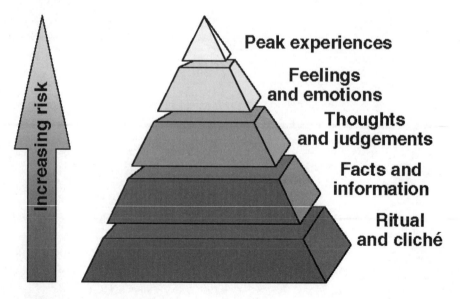

figure **2.1** **levels of communication**

At the most basic level, communication is in the form of ritual exchanges – even in such a diverse culture as that in the UK. For example, within some social groups the greeting of 'How are you?' is supposed to be followed by the response of 'Fine, thanks', 'All right' or 'Not too bad'. This ritual question is not supposed to be taken literally and followed by details of the other person's skin problems or family worries. Such ritual exchanges will vary between ethnic groups, age groups and social levels. We use ritual and cliché to acknowledge each other and not to convey deep meanings or personal concern. When people are genuinely interested in the details of 'How are you?', their additional words and body language flag this message. As communication moves up the levels, the level of risk also increases:

› An exchange of information or a request for facts is slightly more risky than ritualised communication. Some clients may be wary of showing that they do not know something or concerned that you will think them ignorant.
› Sharing thoughts entails a higher level of risk since someone else may disagree with either your way of thinking or your conclusions. As you get to know people better you are more likely to share your opinions and views yet still be wary about potentially contentious areas like politics or religion.
› Sharing emotions involves a greater level of risk since very personal inner feelings and reactions are communicated. People are unlikely to communicate at this level unless they trust the other person.
› Very important experiences, highs and lows in personal life, are the most risky kind of communication, since a negative response or use of cliché will be experienced as a deep rejection.

You will tend to move towards the upper levels of communication with people whom you know well and trust. Ritual and cliché will be more usual in trivial interactions with acquaintances. Some people will always be more private than others, some are more outgoing. Cultural and social traditions also affect beliefs about the appropriateness of expressing thoughts and feelings and to whom. In a helping relationship with clients you broadly move through the levels as clients feel more able to trust you. It will not be good practice to urge clients to move faster than they wish.

Clients may start at different levels of communication when they make contact and you need to match their level. At the information-seeking level, the risks are relatively low since the exchange is usually emotionally neutral, although clients can still experience good or poor practice in a service. When clients wish to share emotional issues then they are very likely to resent clichés in response because they will feel dismissed and their worries trivialised. Ritualised responses can provoke annoyance because they feel impersonal (see page 57).

In working with clients, it is crucial to base your work on facts and information communicated by the clients. This material forms the basis of shared understanding and provides the details of the query, problem or situation that you are helping the client to address. For many helping services covered by this book, the factual level of communication is the basis of the enquiry anyway. When clients become emotional, it is important to acknowledge and deal with the feelings so that they and you can better process the relevant information. You constantly return to the communication level of facts and information so that you can give objective and practical help.

the potential for misunderstanding

Even without any mismatch in levels, communication with others inevitably brings the risks of misunderstanding and misinterpretation. The diagram below sums up what can happen.

Communication is a social process. Inevitably, everyone starts to make sense of the communication of another person as soon as the exchange starts. Everybody interprets to some extent, fills in the gaps of what is implied, but not said, and starts to anticipate what may come next. If you are puzzled by what you hear, part of your attention is working through in your head some of the possibilities of what the other person means. You do not communicate with a completely blank sheet, because your past experience provides a set of expectations, assumptions and ways of making meaning out of the words you hear and the gestures you see. An advantage is that this *selective perception* helps

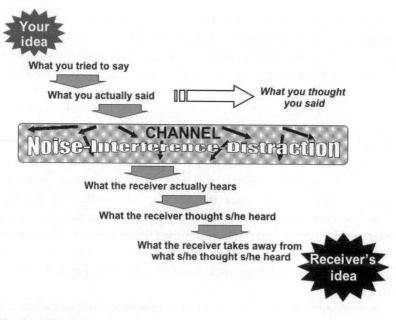

figure **2.2 the communication process**

you to focus your attention on key areas of interest. The disadvantage is that it can block important information outside your focus and/or which fails to support your own assumptions and views.

Because everyone works to make meaning from what they hear, there is always some scope for misunderstanding, even with people who know each other well. There is more to communication than just 'I send you a message' and 'You receive it'.

Any communication starts with an idea, however brief. Imagine that you are talking with a colleague:

- You have some idea of what you want to say, a message that you try to get across.
- You speak to your colleague or communicate in some way (the channel of communication).
- You have a memory of what you are sure that you said, which may be slightly or very different from what you actually said.
- The reception process of communication starts with what your colleague actually hears. This may not be everything that you said, because she was not listening to the beginning of your sentence, or there was a distracting noise.
- However, your colleague forms a clear thought about what she is sure that you said.
- Then she builds an understanding from what she is sure that she heard from you, becoming an idea in her mind as a result of your communication.

Sometimes the process of communication is very clear with few misunderstandings. More often a wider gap develops along the way between your original idea and the idea that has now lodged in the mind of the other person. The communication is easily shaped by:

- Your mood and that of the other person.
- All the expectations and assumptions that are based in past experience between the two of you and outside this relationship.
- Factors that block communication, such as a delay in starting to listen, other people talking and background noise.
- Lack of flexibility in either person, such as insisting that 'what I thought you said' definitely is 'what you said to me'.

The channel of communication also creates or blocks possibilities. Face-to-face communication offers the most information, since you have visual as well as auditory feedback. Telephone communication loses the visual element, although this loss is sometimes an advantage in allowing some information through for callers who do not wish to see the other person and their reaction, for instance, to bad news.

Any kind of one-way communication prevents immediate interaction and clarification of the message. Letters, email and voice mail offer the advantage of thinking about the communication and rephrasing it but also bring the disadvantage that miscommunications may not be known, since the person on the receiving end may not express confusions or misunderstandings to you.

2.2 the importance of attention

attending to others

Whenever you are in a discussion with someone else you effectively make a choice to give greater importance either to what you want to say or to what the other person is trying to communicate. When you attend fully to someone else, you are choosing to value that person and what she or he wishes to say to you. Full attention is crucial in your work with clients, at all levels of communication. Good attention involves both looking and listening:

▸ Awareness of the body language of your clients: what you can see in their behaviour.
▸ Awareness of your own body language: what they can see in your behaviour.
▸ Listening to what clients say and how they say it.

Without attention, a dialogue between two people fails to be a give-and-take exchange and works more like a double monologue, a parallel communication. It is almost impossible to make someone believe that you are really attending when you are not. Your lack of attention will show in two ways:

▸ Your body language will betray you. Your eye contact will wander or you will fidget; perhaps you will often glance at your watch.
▸ What you say in reply will demonstrate that you have not been listening. For instance, your words will show that you do not understand what has been said and are not trying to understand. Or what you say may bear little relationship to what you should have heard.

You cannot attend properly while half your mind and your eyes are interested elsewhere. The ability to look and listen is absolutely central to good practice in any of the helping services, including those in which your contact with clients is brief. If you attend well then:

▸ Clients feel respected. They feel that you are giving them time and attention and that their concerns matter to you.
▸ You will hear and be better able to understand the reasons why clients have come to your service, or have contacted your telephone help or information line.
▸ You will be in a much stronger position to provide clients with appropriate information or advice that meets their concerns in a way that will genuinely help them.
▸ You will be able to judge whether your service is likely to be able to help a client and, if not, to make sensible suggestions about who may be more appropriate.

In contrast, if you do not attend properly, then:

- You fail to show respect for the client as a person because you are unwilling to give appropriate time and attention.
- You cannot know what kind of help clients may require. You can only make broad assumptions. You are reduced to guessing what clients want or shaping their needs in the direction that suits what your service offers.
- You will be less helpful than you could be and may even be actively unhelpful. You may undermine the confidence of a client who found it hard to come and ask for help. Maybe you give misleading, inappropriate or plain wrong advice. Even worse, perhaps your lack of attention discourages clients from seeking help again, from you or other agencies.

Giving clients your full attention may lead to spending slightly more time with each client. However, in many short contact services your time per client will not be greatly extended. This avoids more work later because clients have been wrongly referred or have become irritated with the lack of proper attention.

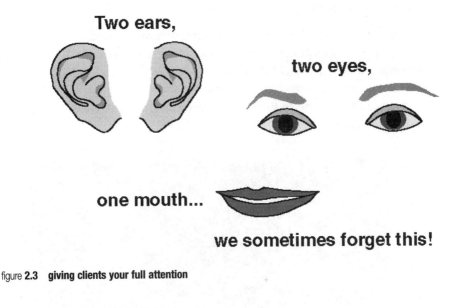

figure **2.3   giving clients your full attention**

⫶ **ACTIVITY**

How do you judge whether or not somebody is paying you full attention? Note down experiences over the next couple of weeks when:

- ▶ You felt that the other person was fully aware of you and listened well. What made you sure that you had his or her attention?
- ▶ You felt that the other person was not listening, or was distracted from what you were saying. What exactly led you to this conclusion?
- ▶ What can you learn for your own practice from what you noticed about other people's attentive behaviour, or lack of it?

Some people are probably better natural listeners than others but everyone can improve their listening skills. You need to:

- Value clients enough to give your time and attention. Valuing the client is just as possible, and important, in brief exchanges as in longer-term helping relationships. In a conversation as short as a few minutes, clients should feel confident that they have your undivided attention.
- Plan how to listen well in your setting and draw on those communication skills that you already have.
- Pay attention to what seems to distract you from listening well to clients and work to improve those areas within your control.
- Practise your listening skills.

focus on the client

Give clients your full attention, with your eyes and your ears. It is easier to listen well to another person when you:

- Are close enough that neither of you has to strain to hear.
- Face one another directly rather than looking from an angle. If you are sitting down, you should be able to look directly at each other.
- Maintain regular eye contact but do not stare. A friendly and attentive gaze is broken from time to time; an unwavering stare is likely to be experienced as intimidating.

figure **2.4** **listening skills**

- Are aware of your own body language and make changes towards greater attentiveness. Perhaps you need to stop hair, beard or jewellery twiddling, fiddling with your pen, drumming your fingers or crossing and uncrossing your legs. You are definitely not trying to be a robot, just peaceful and focused on the other person.
- Create a comfortable open space between the two of you, as far as your work environment allows. See also physical barriers on page 36.

See also physical barriers on page 36.

| ACTIVITY

Work with another person to explore the kinds of behaviour that help you to listen and those that do not.

> Decide who will be the talker (A) and who will be the listener (B). Person A talks about any lightweight topic for two minutes at the most. If you cannot think of a topic, pick one of the following: 'my ideal weekend', 'my worst holiday ever' or 'what I would do if I won the lottery'.

> For two minutes, person A talks. Person B says nothing but shows, in any way that makes sense, that she or he is *not* listening.

> Stop and talk over what has just happened. What did person B do and how did person A feel about it?

> Reverse the situation for two minutes: B now talks and A shows in any way that she or he is *not* listening.

Talk over what you have just experienced. What really got in the way? The opportunity to exaggerate poor listening behaviour often throws into relief the bad habits that are so easy to develop. By looking at the flip side, you can highlight what matters for you to listen.

Now spend the same short periods of time with some proper attention through looking and listening.

> Person B takes the first turn to talk, on the same topic as before, and person A listens. A says nothing but focuses on listening and showing that she or he is listening carefully.

> At the end of two minutes, B stops talking and A summarises as accurately as possible what has been heard: the facts and the feelings.

> Discuss the experience. If you were A, how did you show that you were listening? How did it feel for B? And how accurate was A's summary at the end of the two minutes?

> Reverse the situation – A talks, B listens.

> Then talk over what you have both experienced. What was it like to keep silent as a listener for two minutes?

Listening cannot be continuous silence because, after a short while, the person talking misses the lack of any kind of verbal feedback.

quieten your inner voice

| TO THINK ABOUT

The word 'listen' is an anagram for 'silent'. You need to still your inner voice, the one that drifts away with all your unspoken thoughts, as well as your voice that everyone else hears out loud.

Good listeners do not rush to interrupt or make their own points. There is a great difference between active listening and waiting for your turn to talk. In order to quieten your inner monologues, you have to switch your attention fully to the client. You need to put to one side other thoughts and actively ignore them. Sometimes these thoughts will be related to this exchange, but are not helpful if they crowd out your attention to the client. For instance, you cannot listen if you are busy thinking of:

  ▸ What you are going to say when it is your 'turn' in the conversation.
  ▸ All the suggestions you might make when this client takes a pause.
  ▸ A line of possible help stimulated by just a few words or phrases that the client has used.
  ▸ Premature worries about whether you will be able to help.

  Equally, you need to put to one side any concerns not related to this client:

  ▸ What else is happening in your work: meetings, paperwork or a message that you need to pass on to a colleague.
  ▸ Any personal issues, worries or domestic plans.

internal physical blocks

It is hard to attend if you feel unwell; for instance, you have to work harder to focus with a cold or headache. If your ill health is blocking your ability to listen, then you need to take some remedial action. Sometimes, this is an apology to clients about your cough or croaky voice, or you may need to take appropriate medication. If it really is not possible to work effectively with clients, then you need to take a break or stop this kind of work for the day. If you find it very hard to attend then your difficulty will be communicated to the clients, who may form a negative view of your interest and commitment.

handle interruptions

People do not believe that they are receiving your full attention if your focus is constantly broken. Clients should not be interrupted for you to answer the telephone or speak with a colleague. In some working circumstances a few interruptions may be unavoidable. Handle the interruption as swiftly as possible and apologise to clients.

  Clients should never feel that the telephone is more important than them. Any team should also ensure that bad habits do not develop in talking between colleagues. For instance, in some settings, practitioners routinely interrupt clients who are talking to a colleague, or talk across or even lean across clients, often without so much as an 'excuse me'. Clients will experience this kind of behaviour as discourteous, dismissive and as evidence that clients are a low priority in your service.

physical barriers to good listening

Large desks, glass screens and small speaking windows are blocks to communication and clients find them unwelcoming. If your service genuinely needs physical barriers because there is a real issue of personal security, then you have to work that much harder to show attentive behaviour.

- Your open gaze, smile, if appropriate, and careful listening need to counter-act the impression of the physical surroundings that clients have to be kept at a distance.
- Be close on the other side of a screen or window so that clients feel that the necessary distance is kept to a minimum.
- Ensure that clients can make themselves heard without having to lean across the counter and shout into a communication grill.

ACTIVITY

1 Keep a brief record of your experiences as a customer or client when the service has a physical barrier as above.

▷ How do you feel on the customer side of the barrier?
▷ In what ways does the service counteract any negative impact on communication?

2 Does your own service have some kind of physical barrier? If yes, then spend some time standing on the other side of your counter.

▷ What can you see and hear? What are your first impressions?
▷ Is communication clear and does the technical system work well?
▷ What does it feel like to be on this side?

TO THINK ABOUT

Read through the following excuses for not listening to clients.

▷ What kind of outlook is indicated by the statements?
▷ What is wrong with this attitude?
▷ What could be the first steps to tackling such a negative outlook?
▷ Which comments are most familiar from your own service?

1 'We're the experts. We know what's best for clients. What's the point in listening to them? They come here for us to tell them what to do.'
2 'I've heard it all before. In 30 seconds, I know what kind of problem we've got this time.'
3 'I don't have the time to listen to clients. It's all very well if you've got masses of time on your hands but I've far too many other things to do.'
4 'I'm not supposed to talk with clients, I'm not trained. I just write down their name and their problem and pass them on.'
5 'What's the point, you never see most of them again? You never get to know anybody, so what's the point in listening?'
6 'You have to keep clients in line. If you listen to their complaints, they think they can wheedle anything out of you.'
7 'I can't listen to clients going on in their own way. I have to ask them all these questions; I have forms to fill in.'
8 'I'd listen if they were pleasant to me. But clients come in here with their "I want this" and "What are you going to do about that?"'
9 'What is there to listen to? We get kids who just sit there. I'm lucky to get one word and a grunt out of most of them.'
10 'Why should I listen to clients? Nobody listens to me! We get treated like dirt in this organisation.'

listening on the telephone

With the exception of making eye contact, all the ideas discussed so far are equally important in listening to clients on the telephone. However, telephone exchanges lose the visual element, so you need to concentrate very carefully on what people say and how they say it. See Chapter 5 for a full discussion of helping over the telephone.

2.3 understanding body language

ways to communicate non-verbally

Well over half the meaning of any face-to-face communication is provided by the non-verbal messages, also called body language. You will be affected by the non-verbal communication of other people, even if you are not conscious of what you have noticed. Equally, other people are aware of your body language. So it is just as important to increase awareness of how you behave as to be aware of the sense you make of how others react non-verbally. Your objective is for clear communication, to give and receive messages with as little distortion as possible. So your body language needs to match your words and you need to be very aware of your clients.

Unspoken messages are sent through different parts of the body:

> The face and facial expression.
> Eye contact.
> Body movements and gestures.
> The distance between two people talking.
> The use of touch.

match and mismatch

Especially in a helping situation, your body language should match the positive message of your words. If there is a mismatch, then people usually believe the non-verbal message, although they may not easily be able to explain the source of their conviction. For example:

> The practitioners on the reception desk can say, 'How may I help you?', but the words are accompanied by a wooden expression and the practitioner continues to turn the pages of a newspaper. Clients are unlikely to believe that this person really wants to help.
> From the other perspective, a client who has recently been bereaved says to you, 'I'm fine; I'm coping.' You doubt the client's words because of her sad expression and the way in which she twists the folds of her skirt.

Practitioners in helping services are responsible for ensuring that what they say and how they say it are in accord. The first example arises when someone has been told to use a form of words, but has not been prepared to take a positive approach to clients as individuals. The person on the reception desk has little respect for clients and this outlook leaks through the body language.

It is not the responsibility of clients to ensure that their non-verbal communication matches their spoken words. It is your responsibility to be alert to this information so that you can understand and support clients. You have to decide how far and in what way you raise any mismatch with a client. In the second example, it would never be helpful to challenge the client with, 'You can't fool me! You're obviously not fine!' Depending on the circumstances in which you are offering help, you could approach the mismatch in several different ways:

› If you have an on-going relationship with the client, then it might be appropriate to say gently, 'Are you sure? You look rather down to me', or, 'You don't look to me as if you feel fine?' Do not make comments inviting a client to talk, unless you have time to listen immediately.
› If you are only having a short exchange with the client, you might say something that keeps a slight emotional distance but raises possibilities. For example, 'That's good. But you know there's always someone here to talk if you want', or, 'Yes, I know you can cope, but this is probably a hard time for you.'
› If you are in the position of easing the client on to spend time with another member of your team, you could alert your colleague to your observation with, 'Mrs Watson tells me she's "fine". But she looks very sad and under stress to me.'

awareness of your own body language

You cannot stop communicating non-verbally and you certainly should not try. However, an awareness of your own body language can mean that you use this form of communication productively – much like choosing better words to say. You can also work on any personal quirks that you realise may be unhelpful because they give the wrong messages.

facial expression

The muscles in the face are used, more or less consciously, to produce smiles, frowns, or puzzled or doubtful expressions. Your face can look more or less welcoming, open or closed. A smile is a typical welcome. An immovable, fixed expression seems uninviting and lacking emotion. On the other hand, marked, frequent changes in facial expression can be distracting for clients, who focus more on the messages passing across your face than on telling you what they wish to say. You need to aim for a calm and alert expression that is not wooden and adjusts appropriately to what clients say to you.

eye contact

The way in which you look at someone and how you hold or break a gaze add meaning to what you say.

> Looking directly at someone suggests that you are listening and are open to what they say.
> An unsteady gaze, looking away frequently or looking at some point in the middle distance all tend to suggest that your attention is elsewhere and you are distracted.
> A steady, unwavering gaze is experienced as a stare ('eyeballing') and is felt to be intimidating, challenging or aggressive.
> Friendly and inviting eye contact in a helping situation tends to be regularly looking at the other person, holding the gaze for a while and breaking the gaze, usually by looking down briefly.
> Be sensitive to how much the client looks at you. If clients seem uneasy, you might reduce the extent that you make eye contact. However, it is usual for listeners to hold more eye contact than talkers.

body movements

Your whole body communicates messages. If you sit or stand upright facing the client, then you will look attentive. On the other hand, a slumped posture or turning away from the client tends to communicate inattention or not caring. An upright position can be taken too far, of course. A rigid, bolt upright position may seem unwelcoming or perhaps provoke negative images of critical school teachers ready to pass judgement.

Your hands and arms create gestures that add meaning to your words. Gestures can be expansive and cover a lot of space or be more contained. Hand and finger gestures often convey quite specific messages that vary considerably between cultures. As a helper, it is usually best to keep your gestures simple and non-expansive. Especially avoid finger pointing and wagging, which is usually taken as a criticism and especially patronising when done to adults.

distance and touch

Non-verbal messages are also sent through the distance maintained between one person and another. Individuals may vary in their preferred personal space and less distance is often acceptable, and welcomed, between people who know each other well. The physical surroundings in which you work may place some limits on possible distance between you and clients. It is worth trying to reduce unhelpful barriers, such as large tables, in order to be able to speak at a comfortable communication distance. When you are seated and with no barriers, a distance of about two metres is about right for most people. Let clients create more distance if they wish.

Use of touch is another aspect of distance and of closing the gap between two people. Physical contact can be a strong message of affection, support or calming. But it involves a movement into the personal space of another person and should be used with great care in a helping situation, especially if you do not know the client well. There will be occasions when a touch, hand squeeze or an arm round someone's shoulders will be appropriate but apart from the handshake of greeting, such times are likely to be with clients whom you have got to know, or those in obvious distress. You may also need to consider how best to deal with situations in which a client prefers to sit more closely or to use touch more than you would prefer.

learning about your own body language

You have several sources of useful information:

) How clients react to you, either what they say or their body language.
) Feedback from your colleagues who see you in action.
) The opportunities of video feedback, perhaps on a course or workshop. You may feel uncomfortable about being on video but it is worth overcoming your resistance as it provides a unique chance to see yourself as others see you.

You can learn about your body language in such a way that you could make improvements. Perhaps:

) Until a colleague tells you, you were unaware that you hold a steady gaze, but that it is directed slightly to the side of the person with whom you are talking.
) What feels to you like a 'serious listening expression' appears more like a frown of disapproval to others. In a group discussion, two clients have commented, 'Is something the matter?', or, 'Don't you agree with me then?'
) You wondered if you smiled too much and should be more sober-looking, but a client says to you, 'I love your smile; it makes my day.'
) Until you watched yourself on video, you had no idea you so often fiddled with your hair.

feedback within communication

You need a positive working atmosphere within a team so that any useful work observations, not just about body language, can be shared in a constructive way. Unless colleagues trust one another, it will not be possible for the give and take of feedback to be of benefit. Helpful comments between colleagues are more likely to be:

) A blend, over time, of encouragement through positive comments as well as some constructive criticism. Find the time to tell a colleague how well you think she handles interruptions or manages to include children in a conversation with a parent and child. If you are on the receiving end of such a compliment, then accept it graciously.

- Specific examples rather than vague generalisations. People have a chance to do something about an observation like, 'I think you need to find a way to keep looking at clients as you fill in their form', rather than, 'You make clients think you're more interested in the paperwork than them.'
- Descriptions rather than labels – a colleague needs to understand what you have observed rather than just feel praised or criticised in a general way. It is more possible to react thoughtfully to an observation like, 'You don't smile a lot when you're with clients', rather than, 'You're cold.' Specific feedback also enables you to do something to change the behaviour of which you were unaware.
- Given in response to a request rather than imposed.
- Phrased so that the other person has a chance to consider rather than feel a defence is required straightaway. Often this means offering a suggestion of how the behaviour could be improved or developed.
- Made in circumstances when the other person does not feel exposed. The comments are better shared in a private conversation between colleagues or in supervision rather than in public.

If you are given feedback then your responsibility is to listen and to ensure that you understand by asking for an example or further explanation, not by arguing with your colleague. Reflect on the feedback you receive and consider changes you could make to improve your practice.

making sense of the body language of other people

What you notice about a person's body language and appearance will add to the meaning you take from the words you hear. In some cases body language will emphasise and support clients' words but, in other circumstances, their body language may modify the words or give a very different message.

cautious interpretation

You need to be aware of what you notice in clients' body language and be open-minded over what it means. For instance, a client who sits with firmly crossed arms is showing a closed body posture. This behaviour may mean that he:

- Doubts that you will be helpful.
- Wishes to defend himself non-verbally and not allow you through.
- Is angry with you or something else that has just happened.
- Is cold, since the room is chilly and he has no jacket.

A client who looks steadily at you may be:

- Genuinely interested in what you are offering.
- Trying to unnerve you by staring.
- One of those rare people who can hold an unblinking gaze and do not realise its impact on others.

> Reacting to feedback from a friend who has suggested that the client's usual pattern of looking away gives the impression of shiftiness.

The better you know someone, the more reliably you can interpret the meaning of his or her body language. Otherwise, there are no absolute rules so caution is advisable. A good rule of thumb is to verify your interpretation, either by asking the client when appropriate or through continued observation. For instance, a client who firmly crosses her arms may feel any of the emotions described earlier. However, if she crosses her arms every time you try to discuss her partner's serious ill health, you could read the movement as a likely self-protective gesture, indicative of her concern and anxiety with this topic.

social and cultural issues

Body language is not inborn; children learn patterns of non-verbal as well as verbal communication. The social rules and accepted variations are often only obvious when they are broken. For instance, young people or adults with a learning disability sometimes continue to use body language that is more associated with the behaviour of younger children. Children, young people and adults who cope with autistic spectrum disorder are insensitive to non-verbal clues, for instance about stopping talking or a give-and-take exchange with another person.

Further evidence that gestures and body movements are learned comes from the differences observed between males and females from a relatively young age. Within any culture, girls and boys learn some different ways to behave, either through observation of adults or specific instruction. For instance, within British culture you will notice that:

> Females generally take up less space than males. Boys and men often sit with legs apart or stretched out, perhaps with arms spread as well. On the other hand, females are more likely to sit with knees together, taking up less space than a male of the same size.
> Girls and women tend to touch their face far more than boys or men. Females put a hand to their mouth or cheek whereas males make this gesture far less often.

Differences between cultures, and sometimes within one culture's social or class groups, can be seen in:

> The expansiveness of arm and hand gestures.
> The meaning of gestures using the hand, fingers or thumb, which can be seriously different between cultures. An acceptable gesture within one culture may be very rude in another, or only appropriate for use with children and so discourteous when used with an adult.
> The use of touch to emphasise a point or to require attention. Some cultures use touch a great deal whereas others regard being touched, especially by relative strangers, as an invasion of personal space.

- Varying traditions of how close it is normal to stand to another person. Again, when people of different cultures meet, person A may feel slighted because person B keeps moving away, while B feels that A is imposing.
- The extent of eye contact. In some cultures, holding another person's gaze is regarded as discourteous. When cultures meet, polite behaviour in one culture may be seen as the reverse in another.

There are many group and individual variations within any culture, so it is risky to set rules about the body language of people from specific cultural backgrounds. You need to be conscious of potential differences without holding firm expectations.

2.4 using verbal communication well

the words

Spoken language is formed of many words and phrases and the sentences into which they combine. You have choices about using simple or more complex words and the length of your phrases and sentences. Everybody has an accent, although many people remain convinced that their speech is normal; other people are the ones with an accent. Even when the form of language is not so different as to be called a dialect, you will find many local variations in words and phrases from a shared language. You will not notice these differences until you talk with someone from a different geographical area to your own.

Verbal communication also gains meaning from how you speak:

- The tone of your voice, which can convey additional or even different messages from your words.
- The rhythm of how you speak and your use of pauses. Some people speak in short or single sentences, others will say several sentences before a break. The speed of speech varies and some people regularly speak faster than others.
- Spoken language varies in volume and some people habitually speak more loudly or softer than others.

You can modify any of these aspects of your speech. Everyone has developed a style in which they speak and you may be more or less conscious of your own. Personal styles can vary according to the situation in which you find yourself: the people with whom you are speaking, the formality of a situation or even your mood. It is useful to become aware of how you use your speech, so that you can adjust what you say and how you say it to improve communication.

Some appropriate ways to modify your language and delivery for clients could be to:

- Speak in simple words and phrases and in short sentences with a client with whom you do not share a fluent language.
- Simplify your language when speaking with children.
- Speak more quietly with a client who seems very ill at ease.
- Check more frequently that clients have understood or agree if their body language suggests to you that they are puzzled or resistant.
- Talk clearly and face to face with a client who has a hearing disability.

On the other hand, it would be inappropriate to:

- Raise your voice because a client is shouting. (See also page 257.)
- Talk loudly to a client who has a hearing disability. Raising your voice well beyond normal volume distorts communication rather than making it any clearer. Shouting makes it harder for someone to lip-read or to hear through the distortions entering supportive hearing equipment.
- Talk very slowly to a client with whom you do not share a fluent language, or to a child. Excessively slow delivery comes across as patronising or superior.

| ACTIVITY

Experiment with saying a short phrase like, 'How may I help you?' or 'What is your problem?' in different ways, to communicate:

- A genuine wish to help this client.
- The message that you are short of time and this had better not take too long.
- An expectation that this client is going to be awkward or difficult.
- The sense of unease that you will not be able to help this client.

Now try these variations just with the word 'Yes' and any body language that seems appropriate to the message:

- Try saying the word as a welcome, with a questioning tone.
- Experiment with snapping out the word to imply, but not say, 'Get on with it!' to a client.
- Say the word in a way that conveys the message that you are expecting this client to be trouble.
- Express doubt that you will be able to help this client.

You could experiment with taping your different versions. If possible, practise and experiment with a colleague. You will then be able to give each other feedback, especially on how your body language supports your words.

---

use of language in helping

Good listening is not achieved through total silence. The point that 'listen' is an anagram of 'silent' is a reminder that most people have to hold back on talking in order to improve their listening. You cannot listen effectively for long amounts of time and not say anything. If you have tried the activity on page 35, you may have experienced that the talker's need for some reaction from the listener usually cuts in well before two minutes. If you say nothing at all, the likely consequences are that:

- The person talking begins to doubt that you are listening. The social traditions of a communication exchange are that the listener says something, otherwise there is no interaction.
- The longer you stay silent, the harder and harder it becomes to interrupt the client's monologue.
- You will find your task of listening more difficult, because information will wash over you and disappear from your awareness. It is easier to listen if your verbal contributions are relevant to what the client is saying.

An effective helper, in even the shortest exchanges, is working for a positive balance between saying too much and saying too little. If you speak up after you have heard only a few sentences with anything other than a brief summary or request for clarification, then clients will have one of two reactions. Either they will think you want them to be quiet and listen to you or else they are likely to tell you, 'Be quiet and listen to me.' If you say nothing and clients talk on and on, then their reaction is likely to be a questioning 'Are you listening to me?'

Your use of communication skills within helping is different from having a conversation with a friend or a discussion in a team meeting. The combination of skills that support helping is sometimes called reflective or active listening and includes:

- Simple and brief words or sounds to show that you are listening.
- Reflecting back (paraphrasing) what a client has said.
- Use of short and accurate summaries of what you have heard.
- An open-ended use of questions.

These skills covered here are appropriate to short- and medium-length exchanges with clients. You will find more in Chapters 7 and 8 about using reflective listening with counselling skills. Most early conversations with clients will be at the facts-and-information level of communication. This kind of exchange works best when you follow a series of questions with paraphrases until a summary covers the main issues of the whole conversation. Questions start open-ended and can become more focused when you genuinely understand what the client seeks. Figure 2.5 sums up the process.

encouraging sounds and words

There are a range of simple words and sounds that can show a client that you are listening, often supported in face-to-face communication with appropriate nods and smiles. Possibilities include:

- Encouraging sounds such as 'aha' or 'mmm'
- Words like 'yes', 'right' or 'okay'
- Short phrases such as 'I see', 'I hear' or 'I know'.

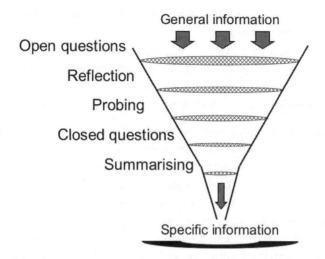

figure **2.5** **the questioning funnel**

Of course, any of these suggestions could be overused or made inappropri-ate if they do not match what the client is saying. Perhaps you have listened into a conversation, on a train or as you wait in a queue, and the person listening has repeatedly said 'I know' or 'right'. As an impartial observer, you have probably sensed that such constant repetition creates the impression that the person is not listening and that the words have become a ritual or cliché through over-use. If any word or phrase is overused by a listener, the result can seem patro-nising or as an impatient implication to 'hurry up'. Be sensitive to the client and adjust your simple responses accordingly.

paraphrasing and summarising

Another way to contribute effectively is to reflect back what the client has said or shown. Sometimes it makes sense to repeat the actual words, but usually you will rephrase using your own words. This paraphrasing or summarising supports the communication in two ways:

▸ It signals to clients that you have heard the points they just made.
▸ The brief summary helps you to register what you have heard and gives the client an opportunity to clarify any misunderstandings on your part and keep you both on the same track.
▸ Your focus on giving the client an accurate paraphrase or summary also helps you to avoid a focus on points you are tempted to make, but which may not be relevant to the issue.

Some examples of useful summarising could be:

▸ 'You'd like a work placement in something to do with the theatre.'
▸ 'You're really upset at the way you've been treated.'

- 'So, you've got two children at school and you'd like to know about after-school clubs around here.'
- 'You've had the tests and you're waiting for the results.'
- 'You sent your application in on the 5th and you haven't heard anything yet.'
- 'You've spoken three times with your neighbours about the loud music and they're not willing to turn it down.'

Occasionally, when you summarise, the client may react with, 'Yes, I've just told you that.' In that case, you can reply with, 'I appreciate that. I'm checking that I've understood you properly.' Or you can begin your summary with, 'I'd like to check that I'm clear about what you've told me.' It is often valuable to summarise at the end of a conversation so that a client feels confident that you have understood their main concerns or enquiry. You can link your summary to an explanation of what can happen next.

Like any potentially positive contribution in a helpful exchange, paraphrasing or summarising will be counterproductive if that is all you do. Questions can also be used in a positive way.

open-ended questions

The whole point about questions is that they should be asked only to help you to understand and respond more helpfully to the client. Questions should not be used just to satisfy your own curiosity. Generally speaking, open-ended questions are more useful than closed, especially at the beginning of an exchange:

- Open-ended questions are those which seek an answer of more than one word and encourage clients to share information with you in their own way. Closed questions are those which only invite replies of one word, often 'Yes' or 'No'.
- Open-ended questions tend to start with words like 'who', 'what', when' or 'how'. They are phrased in a way that opens the doors of communication rather than shuts them. Closed questions tend to direct a conversation and check facts. The most open-ended questions will be at the start of the exchange, for instance, 'How can I help?', or, 'What are you concerned about?'

You need to use questions with care because:

- Questions starting with 'why' tend to put clients on the spot, with the implication that they should justify themselves. 'Why' questions often provoke a reply that starts with 'because' and do not encourage clients to explore the issue.
- Some closed or leading questions may imply to clients that you want or advise them to take a particular direction. For example, 'So if I could get you this childminder, you'd accept her?' Clients who lack confidence may feel uneasy about questioning you or saying, 'That's not what I was after.'

▸ Overuse of questions, especially closed ones, shifts the balance of the conversation into one where you ask the questions and the client gives you answers. The consequence can be that a client goes quieter and just waits for your next questions.

Less helpful closed questions can be reworded, for example:

▸ 'Do you want a work placement in lighting?' (closed question) becomes, 'What parts of working in the theatre interest you?' (open question).
▸ 'Do you want a childminder from next week?' (closed) becomes, 'What practical details do we need to discuss about your child's care with a minder?' (open).
▸ 'Do you want a home help for your father?' (closed) becomes, 'What kinds of help would you like for your father?' (open).

You can reword 'why?' questions to encourage clients, for instance:

▸ 'Why are you upset about your noisy neighbours?' becomes 'What problems is the noise creating for you?'
▸ 'Why does Patty have these temper tantrums?' can become 'What do you think happens before Patty has her tantrums?' or 'What do you think Patty throws her tantrums for?'
▸ 'Why do you think . . .?' becomes 'What makes you think that . . .?' or 'What information made you reach that conclusion?'

Often it makes sense in working with a client to flag up the shift from listening actively to your asking some questions. You might say:

▸ 'Can I ask you about . . .?'
▸ 'It would help me to know about . . .'
▸ 'Do you mind if I check the details on . . .?'

Towards the end of a short helping conversation you might use closed questions to check final details for the client and ensure there is no misunderstanding. By now it will be appropriate to ask questions such as:

▸ 'When would you like your child to start at the pre-school?'
▸ 'So the two most important issues about your father's day centre are closeness to home and the costs of the care?'

a range of languages

You may work in an area where everyone, or almost everyone, is a first-language English speaker. However, many towns and cities have districts in which different languages, dialects and accents can be heard. If you do not share a language to the same level of fluency with the client with whom you are communicating, then it can be harder to offer a good service.

If you speak more than one language yourself, you will know that working to understand what has been said and replying takes that much longer in your second or third language.

You may also have experienced that you can have a good working vocabulary for some topics of conversation but dry up when you try to express yourself on another topic. Perhaps you sound fluent when you are buying in shops or joining in everyday conversation but struggle for the words to explain the symptoms of a sick child or your utter frustration about cockroaches in your kitchen.

If you and the client share fluency to some level in a language, then you may able to work reasonably well if you:

▶ Keep your language simple. Express yourself in short phrases and sentences.
▶ Take pauses to let your words sink in for the client.
▶ Use pauses and invitations like, 'Are you clear?', or, 'Shall I say anything again?', to encourage clients to ask questions or have you repeat anything they wish.

There are other practical options to consider, depending on the nature of the service:

▶ A service dealing with clients speaking a range of languages should seek more bilingual staff or volunteers.
▶ Staff can be given the opportunity to learn key phrases and some basic level of fluency in one or more local languages.
▶ Initially developed by Haringey Council in London, the Language Indicator Prompt System (LIPS) is designed to support the first contact staff in public services such as Housing or Social Services departments. The manual includes introductory questions in 22 core languages to help people to identify their language in written form. (LIPS is available from One Stop Shops, 40 Cumberland Road, London N22 4SG. Tel.: 0208 862 3914.)
▶ Services such as Language Line offer phone-based 24–7 rapid translation service in 100 languages on the phone from staff well-briefed in public service matters (www.languageline.co.uk/nonenglish/index.htm).
▶ Encourage clients to bring a friend who can interpret. If necessary, adjust your physical setting so that it is easy to sit and talk with more than one person. Include the client in your gaze and do not just speak and look at the interpreter.
▶ Check whether you have a local interpretation service and how you book their services. However, be aware that you cannot conduct a confidential longer-term helping relationship through an interpreter. You, or an alternative helper, need the relevant fluent language.
▶ Have some supporting written material in key local languages. A local authority translation and interpretation service should help you but check on any fees.

a positive approach

You and your colleagues should think about and talk about clients with respect. It is possible that your own team has a positive outlook, but that new members or volunteers in your service make thoughtless remarks.

A client should never be described as having 'poor English'; this comment is derogatory and overlooks the alternative perspective that you have 'poor Spanish' or 'non-existent Hindi'. It is more positive and accurate to say, 'Luigi's home language is Italian and he has some English', or, 'Rashida can communicate in three languages but she is least confident in English.' Clients speaking in a language that you do not understand should never be described as 'gabbling' or any similar offensive term. Practitioners who make this kind of unacceptable comment presumably do not classify their own conversations as 'gabble'.

three-way communication

Sometimes you cannot easily speak directly to the client. For example:

▸ A child or young person is accompanied by a parent who does most of the talking.
▸ Adult clients who lack confidence have a companion who speaks on their behalf.
▸ Clients need the support of an interpreter because they do not speak English with confidence and you do not speak their home language.
▸ Clients have learning disabilities which affect communication and understanding.
▸ Clients have disabilities that affect their hearing, their speech or both.

If you are involved in three-way communication, you need to make contact with the person who is the client. Sometimes, you may be uncertain who actually is the client, or the situation makes more sense if you see both people as your clients. You need to relate to parents and their child or teenager or to an adult and his or her elderly parent. At root, make sure that you include everyone in the discussion, paying at least as much attention to the client as to those who ease the communication. Several options are available:

▸ Use eye contact to include the person who is silent or talking considerably less.
▸ Ensure that you do not just look at the person who is speaking for a client.
▸ Definitely avoid talking about the child, young person or elderly parent as if she or he were not present. Find out their name and use it. Quieter clients may not talk but are listening. It feels demeaning to be discussed along the lines of, 'She wants to know about . . ', or, 'He can't cope with . . .'
▸ Invite the quieter client to join the conversation. You might ask directly, 'What would you like to tell me?', 'What do you think about . . .?', or, 'Your mother tells me that . . . How do you see it?'

- You may judge that the younger or less confident client could join the conversation if the more confident person would make that space. You may need to suggest courteously, 'I'd like to hear from your son now. Gerry, what bothers you about this situation?' If the parent, or other outspoken co-client, interrupts, you may need to insist, still politely, with, 'Mrs Baker, I'd like to concentrate on Gerry for the moment', or, 'I know you've told me about the . . . Mr Laurence, but I need to understand what your father thinks is most important.'
- Undoubtedly, third-party conversations are often less straightforward, since the others present (friends, members of the family and even professional interpreters) are not always accurate transmitters; sometimes they add meaning, interpretations and opinions which have to be (additionally) addressed by the helper.

2.5 responding to clients' feelings

Feelings are an upper level of communication (see page 28) and as such need to be acknowledged sensitively – with care. Feelings are communicated both through words and non-verbally. Within helping services, an awareness of clients' feelings or their possible feelings is important because:

- If you ignore clients' feelings, you are losing information and you could be less helpful than possible.
- Problems and concerns are rarely all logical and cannot always be resolved through giving information. If you ignore the emotional content of clients' communication, then you give the message that they should not have feelings, or should not have expressed them to you.
- Clients sometimes have strong feelings about the situation or how they have been treated by a service. Such feelings do not go away by being ignored; they tend to increase and be expressed in ways that are less easy to manage within a helping service.
- Feelings are powerful and drive everyone's behaviour. It is unwise to act as if emotions do not exist.

awareness of feelings

In short encounters with clients, your alertness to feelings will be at a basic level. You are not offering a service in which clients have time to express and explore deep feelings. However, your service will be of a poor quality if you insist on ignoring the fact that clients are people with feelings, perhaps treating them merely as 'cases'. For example:

- Clients appreciate a warm welcome that acknowledges them as valued individuals who have arrived to use your service or picked up the telephone to call.

- Even with short exchanges, it can useful to register that an individual client looks puzzled or uneasy. When you register these feelings, you can make adjustments to what you do. It might be as simple as offering, 'Would you like me to explain that part again?', or, 'You look uncertain, what can I do to help?'
- You may need to give some space to how a client feels about a recent health diagnosis and not focus entirely on medical options. The disease or condition can be medically treated but the whole illness needs emotional care.
- A client may have difficulty listening to all the logical possibilities for help with an elderly parent, if you avoid dealing with the clear message that she or he feels guilty about seeking outside help in the first place.

Some clients may be comfortable expressing their feelings directly, to say, 'I'm not happy about this', or, 'You're not taking my worries seriously', whereas other clients may never use 'I', saying 'you' or 'one' instead. Perhaps they say, 'It makes you feel unwanted', 'Anybody would be worried, wouldn't they?', or, 'I can take it but it really upset my child.' Sometimes feelings are expressed through denial, for example, 'I'm not really hurt by what he said', or, 'It's not exactly that I'm angry.' You need to be alert for feelings that are expressed in a way that would not be your own style.

You need also to allow for the fact that clients often have competing feelings. For instance:

- Parents who settle their young children into a care or play facility want their child to be happy and not be distressed at the parting. Yet, they would also like some sign that their child will miss them. Parents may also be coming to terms with the mixed emotions of pleasure that their child is growing and becoming more independent and yet feeling nostalgic for times past.
- A young person coming for careers advice may be excited about the prospects of a new course or job, but also be wary about the unknown or wonder if she or he will cope with a new situation.

a positive response to clients' feelings

In relatively short conversations it would not be appropriate for you to encourage clients to express their feelings in depth. However, clients may express strong feelings anyway and there are many opportunities between the two extremes of backing away from any acknowledgement and offering considerable time for clients to explore emotions. Many helping services are somewhere in between.

You can use the skills of reflective listening (see page 45) to recognise a client's expressed feelings and that they matter. Using these skills will show a client that you have heard and acknowledge what they have said. Your contribution to the conversation can be simple but consider the kind of comments that are helpful.

an example

A client comes to talk with you about local possibilities in care for elderly people. You have shown her some leaflets and begun to discuss a few possibilities. The client goes silent and then says, 'It's all very difficult. I should be the one looking after my father.'

You can acknowledge her feelings by reflecting back with comments like:

- 'You feel you ought to do it all yourself.'
- 'It feels difficult to come here and talk about getting outside help.'
- 'It's not always straightforward, I understand. You have feelings of responsibility about your father.'
- 'You have doubts about asking for some extra help.'

This kind of reply communicates to the client that you have heard her and recognise that her feelings are involved; it is not just a logical decision. In contrast you will deny her feelings with comments like:

- 'Come on now. You can't do everything yourself.'
- 'Don't think like that. He'll be fine in the day centre.'
- 'That's a silly thing to think. Women always take on too much.'
- 'Well, if you're so upset about it, you ought to talk to our counsellor.'
- 'Perhaps you should read one of our booklets.'

Later in the conversation it might be appropriate to reassure the client that her father could well have an enjoyable day at the centre or to suggest that she is not being selfish to want some help. Perhaps she would appreciate a chance to read the booklet or talk with someone else. However, if you come in prematurely with such comments, the client's feelings have been bypassed. You will lose credibility and trust by giving the message that you believe the client's feelings are irrelevant or should not have been expressed to you.

ACTIVITY

Imagine that you are speaking with a man who has undiagnosed prostate problems. He has been advised to go into hospital for an exploratory operation and you are explaining the practical details to him. He says to you, 'I think I understand what's going to happen. I suppose it'll be all right. But you hear such awful stories.'

Consider some possible responses below. How might the different comments affect this man, what might he feel? Which comments would be more appropriate:

- 'You sound concerned about this procedure.'
- 'Well, if you're so worried, I'll go through it all again one more time.'
- 'Perhaps it would help to tell me some of these stories.'
- 'You men, you're such hypochondriacs.'
- 'You don't want to listen to stories. People like to frighten you.'
- 'I'll get you another leaflet. We've got one on common worries about prostate problems.'

> 'You shouldn't think like that. What'll happen if you don't go into hospital?'

> 'It's all right to be wary. Are there particular questions you would like to ask me?'

> 'If you've got a problem with the operation, perhaps you'd better talk again with your GP.'

be aware of your own reaction

You also need to be aware of how you react to dealing with the emotional side of clients.

- How comfortable are you when clients express feelings? Are you concerned that, if you acknowledge any feelings at all, then the emotional floodgates will open? This consequence is unlikely; in most cases clients will express the feelings relevant to what you are discussing and no more.
- Do you gloss over clients' feelings because you do not want to hear anything that might distress you? You will not be helpful if you approach work in a highly self-protective way. See page 126 for a discussion of an appropriate blend of caring and detachment.
- Does it depend on the kind of client or the subject matter? Perhaps you feel uneasy if the client is a different sex to you or noticeably older? Such feelings belong to you and are your responsibility to handle. If an older client feels able to express feelings to you, then it is for you to feel complimented that he or she feels able to communicate with you. Give the client your full attention. The support and supervision system in any helping service should provide opportunities for you to talk about the kinds of clients with whom you feel less confident or more uneasy.
- How far are your reservations based on doubts about what to say, or a belief that there will be just one right comment to offer? There is rarely a single ideal contribution to make, but some are better than others.
- Do you tend to jump ahead of the client and make too much of feelings you hear or notice – for instance, that expressed doubts mean that clients are backing out or have changed their mind?
- On the other hand, if you are comfortable with listening to feelings from clients, you may need to be cautious that you do not encourage clients to speak at greater depth or for longer than you can genuinely handle in your helping situation.

| TO THINK ABOUT

Your personal experience will shape your reactions and is part of your learning to be a more effective helper. Like everyone else, you will have learned within your childhood about how to express feelings, or not to, and that some emotions are perhaps more appropriate to one sex than the other. Reflect one by one on the questions given above and help yourself towards a greater awareness of how you personally react to the expression of different feelings and by different clients.

first contact and short exchanges

3.1 clients' first impressions

Potential clients of your service will build up an impression of the whole organisation from what they have heard or read before their first visit, their perceptions of the first people they meet and how the physical setting strikes them.

the first contact

All organisations should value the first-contact members of the team. Unfortunately, the importance of initial-contact staff is often badly underestimated and there is no second chance to make a good first impression. First impressions are strong and shape how clients are likely to behave towards members of your organisation they meet later. A positive first impression helps clients to feel more open to your service because they feel valued. Of course, a positive first impression will not carry on if, after the first contact, clients feel poorly treated or dismissed by other staff within a service.

Negative reactions are more individual, so an offhand receptionist may provoke some clients into a more aggressive approach than others. Other clients may feel cowed and then be wary and unforthcoming. When potential clients are uncertain about using your service, an unwelcoming setting or first contact may be all that is needed to make some people back away from your service.

Some organisations may have receptionists whose main task is to greet clients and make a first-stage identification on what or who is wanted. Other organisations ensure that all team members operate as the first contact at some point. Sometimes first contact may be over the telephone. Other services operate in a situation where the very first contact person is not from your organisation, for instance where there is a general reception to your building.

courtesy and attention

The first contact from your service must always show courtesy:

▸ Clients should be greeted promptly when they arrive.
▸ If there really has to be a slight delay, because you are on the telephone or dealing with another client, then indicate by a friendly gesture and a few words that you will not be long. Clients feel awkward and increasingly irritated if they are left, obviously waiting for your attention, and it is not forthcoming.

Give the client your full attention, shown through a smile, eye contact and a few words of greeting. Your team may agree on a choice of greeting, perhaps that the first contact says 'Good morning' or the equivalent for the time of day and follows with 'How may I help you?' and some variations along that theme.

▸ Clients should continue to be given your attention until the conversation is complete. If some interruption is genuinely unavoidable, then you should apologise. You should not simply ignore the client in order to pick up the telephone or turn to a colleague.

initial greeting

Some services and organisations have established a regular greeting that is given to all clients, but this approach has definite drawbacks, especially if the greeting extends beyond a very short phrase. Standard greetings of several sentences, given to every caller, are likely to sound like a formula. If clients hear other people in the setting receiving exactly the same opening comments, they feel that the words are less genuine and are ritualised. The same feelings tend to be provoked if clients telephone more than once and hear an identical opening greeting. Clients do not feel treated as individuals. First-contact practitioners, who are less than careful, also tend to get lazy and bored by the repetitions. So they start to deliver the phrases in the same rhythm and tone each time and they become clichés. The impression given to callers can then be that the practitioner is being almost patronising, or making fun of the caller.

Any team in a helping service needs to discuss how clients are greeted and if there are particular words or a message that should be part of every greeting. In face-to-face communication, or over the telephone, you need something that falls between the two extremes of "Ello!' and 'Good morning and welcome to the free information and support line of the Kempton Advice Bureau for parents and carers on 0226 783401 this is Angela speaking how may I help you'. Your tone of voice and the level of sincerity that this implies carry more importance in the end than the precise words. Valuing each caller as a special individual is critical to avoid slipping into ritualised and rote phrases carrying no warmth.

appearances

Clients' first impressions are also formed from how you appear and dress as a first-contact person, or as any other member of the team. Suitable dress for work is a useful discussion to have within your own team, since a single dress code will not apply across all the helping services. Work cultures have their own codes, varying in degrees of 'smartness', with the requirement for a suit – particularly for men – on the decline as society dresses more casually. However, some assumptions still apply. For example, almost everyone would be surprised by visiting a bank manager who was dressed in a torn T shirt, jeans and sandals.

A good rule of thumb is that you show respect for clients by dressing smartly yet appropriately for your kind of work. Very tailored clothing for men or women may give a visual message that is too formal for some services. On the other hand, sloppy clothing can look as if you are ready to slouch around your own home rather than attend to clients. A smart casual style is often the best compromise; it looks as if you have taken care but are not overdressed. UK society today reflects a very wide range of cultural and social traditions and this diversity is mirrored in preferences about style of dress. A suitable balance in dress can be achieved through a range of styles.

Issues have been raised in recent years around chosen style of dress and whether there are legitimate reasons for requiring people to adjust. Two examples, with a very different underlying rationale, highlight that dress has implications whether the focus is on the clients or practitioners. The concern over hooded tops (hoodies) usually worn by young people has been largely couched in terms of security in public places. There has also been significant discussion around the chosen style of dress for some women who follow Islam and believe that the Muslim requirement of modest dress cannot be met unless their face is covered outside the home.

In our view, anything in dress terms that is likely to reduce the chance of open communication with clients needs to be discussed fully within the service. This discussion is about balancing respect for individual choice – and all cultural traditions involved – with the responsibility to remove blocks to communication to make the service as effective as it can be. There are additionally legitimate concerns about security for everyone. You may feel at ease with asking a potential client to push back a face-covering hood or remove a crash helmet as a first step on approaching your service. If the rationale is to ensure security, then at some point clients will challenge your policy if you fail to apply the ruling to other kinds of significant covering, such as a face veil. Many types of hat or head covering chosen by clients or practitioners raise no problems for security or ease of communication. A full face covering for a woman restricts information from her facial expression to her eyes alone. This limitation therefore makes it harder for other people fully to understand messages face to face; it reduces open communication between practitioner and client.

After careful consideration, we feel that practitioners who wish to cover their face, and continue to work face to face, are creating an inequality of communication – even of power – with clients, and that such practice is therefore unacceptable. The practitioner's right to follow her deeply held belief cannot but infringe on the right of the client to receive a full service. The practitioner in this situation has the option to seek work in which she can use her skills with the seclusion offered by telephone or email support and advice. When it is the client who wishes to cover her face, then (assuming there are no security concerns) then it makes sense to offer the requested service up to the point where the restricted visual communication has become a block on the helping relationship. At that point, probably having assigned a female practitioner and privacy, it will almost certainly feel acceptable to the client to remove the section of her dress that covers her face. The onus is upon the helper to put the client at ease so that communication can be full.

value the first-contact person

It can be hard to offer a quality service to clients if you do not yourself feel valued within the service. The task of some first-contact practitioners is made more difficult by being poorly appreciated by the rest of the team.

There are several ways that a helping service can show that the first-contact person is valued:

- Consider what the first-contact people are called. Do they have a job title and, if so, in what way does it affirm their importance to the service?
- Ensure that the front person is part of the team, involved in team meetings and with his or her experience clearly valued.
- Nobody in the team should push the front person into inappropriate gatekeeping or dishonesty, for instance by saying someone is out of the office when she or he is in.
- Look at how the front person's job is defined. What is the job description on paper and is this how the tasks work out in practice? What are his or her assumed priorities: to help clients, to pass them on as fast as possible, to head off inappropriate inquiries, to prevent exploitation of the service, to protect the 'more important' members of the team?
- Offer help and support to your first-contact staff. Talk with them and listen to what they have learned about clients and how the service works.
- Look at the possibilities for relevant training.

the physical setting

Clients' first impressions are also shaped by what they see and hear as they enter and walk through your building.

- Is your service easy to find: are there notices, arrows and places where clients can easily check for directions? Do clients regularly get lost?
- Is the outside of your building welcoming or unwelcoming? What are the hallways and corridors like? How may clients feel before they even reach you?
- How straightforward is it for clients in wheelchairs or with limited mobility? For clients with young children and buggies? For clients with visual disabilities or clients with limited literacy or fluency in a language other than English?
- If clients have children with them, are the surroundings safe and interesting?

What happens when clients reach your reception area?

- Are the waiting areas comfortable and spacious for the types and numbers of clients that your service usually experiences?
- Do clients have to wait? If so, for how long? How do you explain about waiting and any system of queuing or priorities for how clients are seen?
- How easy is access to the first-contact person? Can you see each other, can you hear without shouting, having to repeat yourself or leaning forward uncomfortably? Is there some level of privacy even to the first contact?
- Is the furniture comfortable and arranged to bring people together rather than form barriers between clients and practitioners?

figure **3.1** **Citizens Advice Bureau**

Try walking into your own place of work with fresh eyes, as if you were a new client:

▷ Is it clear to you where you should go to reach the service?

▷ How many gatekeepers do you have to pass from the entrance to the building to where the service is located?

▷ Is there anybody to ask if you are lost or uncertain?

▷ What strikes you about the setting: the decor, posters and other displays, information or warning notices?

▷ How are clients likely to experience the setting if they have young children with them? How easy is it for clients with physical or visual disabilities?

issues of security

Personal security may be a real concern for your service. Grills, safety glass, locked internal doors stating 'Staff only' and other such measures may achieve a level of personal security for the team but can give very negative messages to clients. Staff may say, with genuine conviction, that such measures are necessary because of the verbal and physical aggression from a minority of clients in this service. Unfortunately, few services who are concerned about the safety of their staff seem to have considered how the majority of their clients feel.

For example, in our local health centre there are two windows through which you talk with a receptionist. When we wrote the first edition of this book in 2000, each window and the adjacent notice board had an A3-sized notice that stated, 'Any patient who is aggressive or abusive to members of staff will be removed from the doctor's list. If necessary we will telephone the police.' There were no additional 'Welcome' notices or one saying 'Thank you to our patients who are courteous'. Nothing, therefore, that could balance the message that this medical practice expects trouble. Most of the staff working at the practice *are* friendly and courteous, but the three identical notices undermined this impression. And, as you wait, you have time to count such notices! In the intervening years, we have observed how such notices have multiplied and most still give an implied message to clients that they are expected to be troublesome. Few, if any, teams seem to have considered that such notices also give the impression to potential clients that here is a service in which serious confrontation is a frequent occurrence – not exactly a comfortable feeling on your first visit!

Any setting has to achieve a balance between welcome to clients, the safety of service providers and the provision of confidentiality to clients talking with practitioners. However, the impact on clients is especially high when poor treatment of clients is combined with unwelcoming physical surroundings and notices suggesting that all clients are a potential threat. The combination of a poor setting and poor behaviour of front-line staff almost invites clients to become awkward and argumentative.

3.2 positive short exchanges

A positive working relationship can be developed with clients even if you only have brief, one-off exchanges, rather than undertaking more extended work.

be realistic

It is essential that short contacts are seen positively and that you look at your work from what you can do ('half-full bottle') and not from what you cannot ('half-empty'). It is obviously unrealistic to hope to get to know clients very well in a short time. An appropriate goal is that clients should emerge from every short exchange with something extra, that your contribution should make a small difference. That difference may be in terms of:

‣ Clients feeling welcome here, with every right to seek advice or help
‣ Empathy for the client's tiring and frustrating search for help so far
‣ A friendly face and a listening ear to guide clients to what may be of help
‣ A specific referral to someone who will directly be able to help
‣ Useful direct information or a positive lead to someone or somewhere else.

find out what clients want

Positive short exchanges with clients use all the communication skills discussed in Chapter 2. Effective use of attention, questions and reflective listening will enable you to treat clients as individuals, avoiding assumptions about what clients want, need or already know. Even in a short exchange, your aim is to keep the conversation relatively open and exploratory, to avoid foreclosing on the client's expression of needs and concerns. Swift conclusions on your part can only be based on assumptions about this client or this 'type' of client or in pushing clients towards the range of services that your organisation has to offer.

The information about your service needs to be clear, through conversation and any supporting written material. The possibilities and options need to be discussed with a client in such a way that he or she can make an informed decision about what this means. If your service can meet this client's needs, then explain how and in what way and move on to the practicalities of how the client can take advantage of information, advice or help.

Perhaps you can meet part of what the client wants, but not all. You can still approach the situation positively by explaining:

> What you can offer, if the client wishes to take you up on it.
> What you understand the client is seeking that is not covered in your service. However, the client may find help from another (named) organisation, helpline or individual.
> That you can refer the client directly to another person or organisation. (See page 98.)

be personal

use your name

It is hard to offer a personal helping service if you do not use your name.

> If the first face-to-face contact is very short, then it may not make sense to introduce yourself to a client personally. You could instead have your name for them to see easily on a badge or nameplate.
> UK society is generally less formal now than in previous decades, so it is most likely that you would give your personal name, with or without your surname.
> If your service works partly or wholly over the telephone, then consider whether the first-contact person, and subsequent practitioners with the client, give their names. It could be standard practice that anyone who is on telephone duty gives not only the name of the organisation but also his or her own name.
> Sometimes it will make sense to offer or to repeat your name at the end of a short exchange, for instance, 'My name is Nneka. Please ask for me if you have any other questions.'
> Be prepared to say your own name more than once for clients who find it unfamiliar.

use the client's name

In many circumstances, you will need to find out and use the client's name. Some practical issues arise about formal or more informal ways of addressing clients:

> Your organisation may be informal, but you should respect a client's expressed wish to be known more formally, as Mr, Mrs, Ms, Dr, etc., if that is their preference. Some clients may introduce themselves as 'Miss Brewster', which suggests they might prefer a more formal mode of address. You should follow the client's lead.
> Some social and cultural groups may find an unchecked use of the personal name as discourteous. Additionally, some retired people within the older generation in the UK have lived and worked at a time when first names were not usually exchanged, except between friends. If you use their personal name without asking, older clients may feel that you are being presumptuous.

- If someone gives their name as 'Carol Brewster' or 'Miss Carol Brewster', you can ask, 'May I call you Carol?', or start by calling the client 'Miss Brewster' and wait to be invited to use her first name. It is unlikely to be felt as courteous to the client if you ask a leading closed question such as, 'It's fine to call you Carol, isn't it?'
- There is an essential inequality in a service that addresses the clients by their first name but the practitioners more formally. For instance, medical services have a rarely questioned tradition of calling patients by their first name but doctors as 'Dr Yousuf' or consultants as 'Mr O'Donnell'. As a client, it is hard not to feel that such a practice puts you in an inferior position as a patient.
- Be very cautious about calling clients 'dear' or 'my dear'. Some clients do not mind these terms and may even address you in this way. However, other clients will find it patronising, especially if females are called 'dear' and male clients addressed by their proper names.

| TO THINK ABOUT

There are different possible ways of asking for a client's name. Which of the following options might be better under different circumstances or in your own service? Are there any options that would be discourteous with any client group?

- 'My name is Ben and you are . . .?'
- 'Name?'
- 'Could I ask your name, please?'
- 'And who might you be?'
- 'I'd like to check your name now.'
- 'And you are?'
- 'Have I got your name?'
- 'Do you have a name?'
- 'What's the name please?'
- 'How about telling me who you are?'
- 'Who are you?'
- 'What was your name again?'

Use of the client's name adds a personal touch, so long as it is not repeated a great deal, because this can create a sense of personal intrusion and be over familiar. Names also should not be used to emphasise a criticism of the client, for instance, 'Now, Gaby, you started this problem, didn't you?' Nor should names be repeated in a patronising way, for instance, 'Daniel, Daniel, I don't think you're listening to what I'm telling you.'

uncertainty about names

When names are less familiar to you, ask rather than assume. You may have to ask clients how to pronounce their name and spell it. Ask courteously. This is far better than to continue saying the client's name wrongly, a pattern which will annoy people. Clients' names should never be described as 'odd' or 'difficult'. View the situation as one in which you find the name unusual or are having difficulties with pronunciation or spelling.

In work with families, bear in mind that every member of the family does not necessarily share the same surname. Partners may not be married, married women may not have chosen to change their surname, children may take either parent's surname and stepfamilies may have several names. If in doubt, ask, 'Do you all share the same surname?', or, 'May I ask, is Malcolm's surname Carpenter as well?'

The Western naming system of first name followed by more optional personal names and finally by a surname is not a universal system by any means. If you are in doubt, ask the client, 'Can I check please? Is this your personal name?', or, 'I'm not sure which is your family name.' The box below gives some examples.

> ### SOME EXAMPLES OF NAMING SYSTEMS
>
> ▸ Traditionally in the UK women have taken their husband's surname on marriage. In contrast, several mainland European countries have the tradition of making a double-barrelled family name from the two surnames.
>
> ▸ Chinese and Vietnamese tradition is to have a family name first, then a generation name, followed by the individual's personal name.
>
> ▸ Sikh and Muslim families do not traditionally have a surname, nor do some African ethnic groups. However, families sometimes take on a chosen surname to make life easier within the UK.
>
> ▸ Muslim males have a religious name, which often, but not always, comes before the personal or calling name. The family name is last.
>
> ▸ In the UK the use of the term 'Christian name' for people's personal name is the consequence of a cultural tradition of christening babies that arose from religious practice in some parts of the Christian faith. In a multi-faith society it is more accurate to refer to 'personal' names.

use of written material

All clients will not be equally confident in reading or writing. Dyslexic clients need longer to handle written material and may appreciate some help. Clients who are not dyslexic may still be uneasy with written material. A proportion of people emerge from their education with a limited grasp of reading and writing and a serious lack of confidence when trying to use their skills.

It would be unwise to approach all clients with the expectation that they will have difficulties with reading. However, you should be alert to signs that a client is not happy about completing paperwork. Young people may feel more confident to say, 'I'm dyslexic. It'll take me time to read this.' Older clients may have experienced schooling at a time when literacy difficulties were more often blamed on the child and adults can still be ashamed of their difficulties. You can offer help in a sensitive way:

- 'Would you like me to go through the form with you?' is a more positive question than 'Do you know how to fill in the form?'
- 'Shall I read it out to you?' could be the reply to a strategy of 'I haven't got my glasses', sometimes used by adults with reading difficulties. Of course, a short-sighted person may actually have forgotten his or her spectacles.
- It will sometimes be possible to offer, 'You're welcome to take the form [or leaflet] away with you.' This response may be appropriate when a client says, 'My spouse does all the paperwork in our family.' This comment may be true, but again it is a strategy used by some adults who have trouble with reading and writing.

endings

You need a proper closure even to a short exchange. Clients should never be left standing at a window or sitting looking at you, because they are not aware that as far as you are concerned the exchange is complete. You and the client need to finish at the same time and you can help this process:

- As the conversation moves to what feels like a close, you might ask, 'Is there anything else I can help you with?', or, 'Have we covered all you would like to know about . . .?'
- Your closing words might be, 'Thanks for coming to see us', or, 'Please call again if we can help.'
- If you have not been able directly to help the client, you might say, 'I hope that Sergio at the Careers Advice Office [your suggested and named organisation or individual] will be able to give you more information', or, 'I think you'll find the telephone helpline [named] will have some practical suggestions about how to help your child.'
- Leave clients with the option to take up your suggestions or not; it is their choice. So avoid the pressure of, 'You will call Sergio, won't you', or, 'Don't forget to call the helpline.'
- It is wise to avoid standard ending phrases as much as standard greetings. They are unlikely to sound genuine.
- If it feels appropriate, then say, 'Thank you for coming in', or, 'I'm glad you were able to drop by.' Say 'Goodbye', 'See you again' or 'All the best with . . .' as appropriate.

3.3 dealing with mistakes and complaints

All helping services need clear guidelines on how everyone should deal with common problems or difficulties.

Positive effort within a service can avoid complaints that need never have arisen or can prevent some developing from a minor irritation into something more serious:

» Be clear about what your service or organisation offers and, just as important, what it does not. At least some problems arise because callers have been given the wrong impression. The problem might be as simple as the belief that your publications are free when they are not.

» Ensure that commitments to a caller or personal visitor that 'someone will get back to you' are honoured. Your first-contact person should make a note and ensure that the request is passed on properly.

» If you have the opportunity, deal with problems early rather than letting them grow. Many people who are dissatisfied are still willing to accept an explanation. Dismissive or discourteous treatment pushes the most tolerant client towards serious complaint.

» Brief and train the whole team to understand the importance of courtesy and good communication skills with clients.

communicate courteously

listen

The best approach to difficult situations with clients is to hear what they have to say:

» Attend fully to clients and listen to what they want to tell you. Show courtesy and respect.

» Avoid redirecting them immediately, especially if they obviously want to talk with you. Clients may need to clarify their problem.

» Respect their right to tell you as much or as little as they want. Use open-ended questions to help you to understand the nature of the problem. You might ask, 'What happened?', 'Please tell me how things went wrong', or just, 'Tell me about it.'

» Make sure that you understand the nature of the problem from the client's point of view. You certainly do not have to agree with the complaint itself and it is unhelpful to start to justify the actions of your organisation.

» If you need to pass the client on to someone else, summarise the problem for your colleague so that the client does not have to repeat everything.

acknowledge feelings

Many clients, who want you to acknowledge that something has gone wrong, are not angry. They may be frustrated, puzzled or disappointed in a service that they had trusted. Clients may be ready to give you the benefit of the doubt, anxious about raising the issue or confident that you can resolve the problem once you know what has gone wrong.

Your role is to listen to clients' feelings and watch the messages of their body language. Make sure that you have recognised the expressed feelings. It is not your role to agree or disagree with what clients feel or the strength of the feelings. You can show empathy with clients' feelings by comments like:

 ▸ 'I appreciate that you want this mistake put right.'
 ▸ '1 do understand that cancelled appointments disrupt your arrangements.'
 ▸ 'I can see that this has made life very difficult for you.'
 ▸ 'I realise that you are very fed up about this whole business.'
 ▸ 'I understand how disappointed you are.'
 ▸ 'I can hear that you feel strongly about . . .'

Be cautious about using words to label clients' feelings that they have not used themselves. It is better to reflect back the same or very similar words and phrases. For example, a client who has said, 'I'm very concerned about . . .' is unlikely to appreciate being told that she or he is 'cross' or 'upset'.

Even relatively calm clients who are ready to listen to you will become irritated if their feelings are ignored. They will think you are rude if you use dismissive phrases like, 'You don't really mean that', 'You're only saying that because you're upset', or the patronising, 'Don't you think you're making too much of all this?' Even if clients are agitated, you should avoid blunt demands that clients 'should calm down' or, 'Don't raise your voice to me.' Remain calm yourself and keep your voice steady and low. Summarise the client's feelings to show that you have heard. (See also page 152.)

take appropriate responsibility and action

Make sure that you get a clear sense of what the client would like to have happen now. Clients are not particularly interested in your rules and system, your problems with the computer or other organisations who have let you down. Clients are interested in their concerns and problems and this is a very reasonable perspective for them to take. They want to know what you are going to do for them, not what other people have failed to do for you:

 ▸ Give clients information that is appropriate to how you will now help. They want to hear, 'I appreciate that you want your name spelled correctly on any letters. I'll follow this up with the person responsible', rather than, 'It's on the computer, it's all so complicated and they only put in corrections once a month.'
 ▸ Explain what you can do, or what you can now do through consulting someone else. Do not make promises, for yourself, or on behalf of colleagues, that may not be kept. Offer something that can be done and not a list of what you cannot do.

- If the person wants to take a complaint further, then explain their options and give the relevant written material for your organisation.
- Make a written note of the complaint, if appropriate. All services and organisations should monitor complaints or problems since patterns may show you how to improve the service.

It is wise to avoid routine and formula responses to clients at any stage, whether in face-to-face communication or over the telephone. Like any communication, an exchange dealing with a problem or complaint needs a closure, but clients will not feel personally treated if they realise that everyone is given an identical last sentence. Much like greetings (see page 57), you need a number of different ways, appropriate to this client, in which to bring the exchange to an end. Depending on the circumstance, you might say:

- 'I'm glad you told us about . . .'
- 'We'd much rather know when something has gone wrong.'
- 'Thanks for letting me put this right.'
- 'I'll get back to you before the end of the week with an answer on . . .'
- 'I will speak to you again on Friday about . . .'
- 'Again, I would like to say sorry about . . .'

| ACTIVITY

Think about a recent experience when you have been dissatisfied with service of any kind.

- In what ways was your complaint handled well or handled poorly?
- What did you want as a result of someone hearing your complaint?
- How could your treatment have been improved and what lessons can you take for your own service?

individual differences between clients

People complain in different ways and they have learned these behaviours:

- Some clients will complain quietly, especially if they realise that you are ready to listen. However, even clients who prefer to be courteous will have a breaking point if they are treated rudely.
- Some clients start at a loud and confrontational level. They believe that aggression is the best approach, or may have no idea how to complain in any other way. They may turn their complaint into a personal attack on you but you should not retaliate with personal remarks in return.
- On the other hand, some clients may be unduly apologetic. They may understate their concern, saying they do not want to make a fuss or create any trouble. However, what they have to say may be very important to your service or part of it, as well as to themselves. Unless you listen and follow up, you may miss a serious issue or alternatively leave such clients with a problem that worsens.

- Occasionally, clients continually change their story or seem to mislead. You can deal with this situation by comments like, 'Mrs Jones, I heard you say ... and then I heard you say ... Which is correct, please?' Avoid the challenge of saying, 'You're lying.'
- You are a representative of your service, so it is inappropriate to push the complaint away with 'I didn't do this' or 'Why are you blaming me?' You are not accepting personal responsibility for what happened; you accept responsibility on behalf of your organisation to deal with the problem now.
- Focus on the facts of the complaint and acknowledge the underlying message. You might ask questions like, 'What leads you to say that?', or, 'What exactly went wrong?'

| ACTIVITY

- Select a number of complaints or problems that arise within your service and consider the best and worst ways of handling them.
- Practise some common scenarios with a partner and listen to constructive feedback on how you behave and sound.
- How might you improve how you react to complaints – both as an individual and the service as a whole?

a system for complaints

Clients will not always want to make a formal complaint. Most people with a grievance want someone to listen to them and to have their concerns treated with seriousness, not belittled or dismissed. Sometimes people want an apology, which, if appropriate, should be given with genuineness. On some occasions, there will be a solution to the problem. Often people want to be reassured that the same problem will not happen again. If their concern is handled with courtesy and the client feels appropriate action will be taken, the complaint may end at that point.

Services should have different levels of dealing with complaints. However, clients should never be pushed into making a more formal complaint than they wish. For example, clients who want to explain what happened and to have the courtesy of your attention will feel ill-used if their explanations are cut off with, 'You have to put all this in writing.' On the other hand, nobody should be dissuaded from taking their complaint to a higher level when they feel sufficiently strongly about their experience.

| ACTIVITY

Find out about the general complaints procedures of your service. It should be clear to you and to the clients of your organisation:

- How to get help, if they are dissatisfied with the initial advice, information or decision.
- How to express their dissatisfaction, including how to make a formal complaint.

sharing information and offering advice: directly and via the Web

4.1 information services for clients

the scope of your information service

possibilities

Providing information may either be the major part of what your organisation offers or just one aspect of a broader service. Helping services can provide information through a number of different channels. Personal callers may be able to:

› Consult with a member of staff.
› Read your information resources in books, articles, leaflets and fact sheets.
› Access the information you have stored in files and databases on the computer.

  Clients may also be able to:

› Ask for written material to be sent through the post.
› Ask their questions or request written material by email.
› Seek information over the telephone, perhaps through a dedicated information helpline.
› Consult your service's website on the Internet.

quality and appropriateness

Any service needs to ensure the quality of their information:

› Be clear about the nature and boundaries of your service. This understanding will help to shape what kind of material you need available and to identify the gaps in your current information base. You will need to find material to close that gap or you may consider writing some original material (see page 80).
› Be clear about what your clients want and need. Without making restrictive assumptions about your client base, you should be able to pinpoint key features to ensure that information is useful to clients, and that they can and will use it.

- For instance, you may judge accurately that many of the young people who drop in to your service are not enthusiastic readers. So, you will need short fact sheets, lots of graphics and posters with lively informative pictures. Consider a CD-ROM or DVD and video displays as a source of information.

You need to ensure the accuracy of any information:

- Make sure that any of the available material is suitable and accurate, including material from outside your service. If it is sitting on your display shelf, or on your mail order list, then clients will feel that you are endorsing the publication – and you are.
- Make sure that at least one person, preferably two, reads any leaflet or book that could go on your shelves, and any reading list or mail order. Even if books or pamphlets are given to your service, check them before they go on display. You want to be sure both of the accuracy of any information and that it carries a supportive message to your clients.

updating information

Your range of material needs to be checked on a regular basis to ensure that it is still accurate:

- Information on local or national organisations and services needs to be updated on a regular basis. Organisations do change their actual address and telephone number, and their website and email addresses. Contact names change, as can the name of the organisation itself. New useful contacts will develop.
- Web pages, fact sheets, information and advice packs should always be dated, so that clients can see how recently the information has been prepared.
- Leaflets or information sheets may have new versions, especially on topics where research and the practical application of new ideas is in a state of change. Handbooks may be revised and you should have the latest edition.
- Resist the temptation to keep old material unless you are confident it is both accurate and still used by clients.

The regular updates may be the particular task of one member of the team, but some might also be appropriate for volunteers or young people on work experience to complete.

is the information useful?

Another important way of updating your information base is to ask your clients about its usefulness. This exercise can be part of a more general monitoring of your organisation's work (see page 7). You may be in a position to ask clients directly about the usefulness of the information you have offered or to find out if another recommended service has been of value and in which ways. It is important to:

- Ask more than just a few clients. With reactions from a very small proportion of your client base, you may get views that are biased in the positive or negative direction.
- Explain your reasons for asking: that your aim is to improve the service and not to check up on particular referral agencies or to encourage gratitude from your clients.

helping clients to access information

Personal callers need a straightforward system of access to material. Some organisations will provide Internet access for their clients through dedicated computers. At least, a small selection of leaflets or booklets can be effectively displayed on an open stand or a table. Even a limited array of these will benefit from some thought as to how you will present it to clients:

- Someone needs to tidy the display from time to time.
- It may be useful to put the copies of the different leaflets or sheets into containers so they do not become muddled or torn.
- Consider notices that invite clients with, 'Please take a free leaflet', or, 'Information on careers – please help yourself'.

If you have more than a small range of resources, you need a logical system of organising the material and labelling the different sections to support clients as they browse or look for something in particular. You may have:

- Labelled sections or headings.
- An alphabetical system within sections.
- Logical collections of leaflets or booklets, so that similar material is placed together.
- Clear labels on boxes or files.
- Visual images or pictures that will support a written label. Relevant pictures or graphics can help clients whose eyesight is not sharp for reading or who have limited literacy skills.

Clients need to be able to see the information and be attracted to the idea of browsing. If you have a range of information leaflets to which you refer in conversation, depending on the client's expressed needs, then you need a straightforward system for finding the one(s) you want.

A relevant explanation by a member of staff and clear notices should let clients know:

- Which material they can borrow and which can only be consulted on site
- Whether leaflets or booklets are free or whether there is a charge and how much
- Whether they can photocopy material, or print out or download information from the computer, and any cost or restrictions on this service.

offering direct help to clients

A few leaflets on a table may not need much explanation. Broader information resources will benefit from a positive approach to help clients access the information. Clients should be made to feel welcome because you communicate a sense of generosity and openness with information. It has been collected precisely to be shared with clients. Avoid the idea of the information base as a precious possession to be guarded. Such an outlook can be communicated, not deliberately, by notices like, 'No food and drink in the reading area', or, 'Please do not tear pages out of the magazines', let alone, 'Clients who abuse these facilities will be banned'.

a positive approach

Clients usually welcome clear directions for where they can get help: either a clear sign for the 'help desk' or immediate help from the first member of staff they approach:

- If your service has a help desk or an information officer for personal callers, then make sure that these are easily found and available.
- If you are asked about the information resources and this is not your main responsibility, then respond with, 'I'll find out', or, 'I'll take you to someone who can help you with that.' Clients do not want to hear, 'I don't know', or, 'I'm only a volunteer.'
- Make an active approach to clients who look uncertain. You can offer, 'Would you like some help?', or, 'Can I help you find anything?' If you are uncertain what a client wants, you might start with, 'Have you used our information service before?', or, 'What sort of material are you looking for?'
- Have some written material in the main community languages and, ideally, some bilingual staff.

TO THINK ABOUT

Draw on some of your own experiences of asking for information and help, not necessarily in information services:

- For example, how does it feel in your local supermarket or DIY warehouse if you go up to a member of staff to ask the whereabouts of an item and are told, 'It's not my section', or, 'I only work here Saturdays'?
- How does it feel in a large library or other information resource centre to wander about uselessly, uncertain whom to ask for help?

> What kind of response do you want to your requests for basic help and direction? What would make you pleased or relieved?

> How can you help to bring your service close to the ideal?

Involve clients in the use of the information base and work to boost their confidence and feelings of competence. Your skills can be used to create a feeling of joint problem-solving with the client and not an unequal buzz of being the person with all the answers:

> Be seen to explore with clients what information will be helpful to them, rather than having set packages given out after a very short conversation.

> Ask clients what they feel could be helpful in the context of explaining what you can offer. Offer a range of options to help focus on what they need.

> Often clients will appreciate more help than, 'It's over there', or, 'All you have to do is press a few buttons'. Be ready to show clients how to use displays of pamphlets and which topics are covered in what section.

limits to literacy

Some clients of your service will have limits to their ability to read and write. They will not necessarily be illiterate but have very limited ability and confidence with the written word and a low interest in exploring information in this way. See page 73 for some ideas.

help with computer access

Even clients who are fully computer-literate will appreciate some guidance on what they can access on the computer terminal and in what way. Many clients will need practical help, patience and guidance on the first and perhaps subsequent times when they access files and databases on your computer.

Some clients will be at ease with a computer, but perhaps wary of unfamiliar systems. Some young clients may have a superficial knowledge of computers, but this experience is restricted to a few types of files and plenty of games. Some clients will not know where to start with a keyboard, mouse or screen. Although the schools are now full of computers, and some have their own network, this situation is relatively new. Older adult clients will not have encountered information technology in school. So, unless they have had other reasons to learn, clients may be starting from scratch. It's always worthwhile to check.

You can help all clients by clear communication and patience as they learn:

> Explain at a steady pace, but not with patronising slowness, and check on clients' understanding step by step. Be ready to repeat your words and actions.

> Show clients how to get in and around the files and then invite them to try. The combination of 'tell-show-do' is the most effective way of teaching.

- It is unhelpful to lean over someone's shoulder and press buttons yourself or to grab the mouse. Clients will not learn easily under these circumstances and it is an invasion of personal space.
- Boost a wary client's confidence with, 'Well done', 'You're getting the hang of it', or, 'You only forgot the last bit. You remembered everything else.'
- If there are several clients who want to access information through the computer, you could organise a group session.
- Some clients may find it helpful to write down the instructions. Consider making a basic notice of instructions on the location of particular files.

sharing information in conversation

Sometimes you will make information available to clients through a conversation, either face to face or over the telephone. Good communication skills are covered in Chapter 2, but the main points are summarised here:

- Listen to what clients say and what they ask.
- Avoid assumptions about what clients need to know or are likely to ask about because of their age, gender, ethnic background, apparent social class or any other broad description of them as individuals.
- Answer clients' questions and concerns before you consider exploring what may be related questions or concerns which they have not yet expressed. Resist giving more information than clients want or need.
- Be alert to clients' feelings about asking for help, even for information. They may be concerned that you will think they are asking foolish questions or should know the answers already.
- Sometimes it will be important to explain the consequences of different options to clients: what will most likely happen if they take a particular route or what are the advantages and disadvantages of a course of action. The pros and cons can be especially important to explain with medical decisions but many life options have an element of, 'What will probably happen if . . .', or, 'Does this choice effectively close down your taking this other option?'
- Be aware that an individual client may be standing in front of you, but behind what she or he says can be a network of family and friends that matter to the client and may be his or her direct responsibility.

how you share information

You can pass on information to clients in more or less helpful ways.

- Clients are more likely to listen to and be motivated to take in information that addresses the questions that they want to ask.
- If you definitely need to convey new information then it helps to flag up that the conversation is changing direction. You might say, 'If you would like to

take that option, then I need to explain this', or, 'I would like to let you know that, if you do . . . , then . . .'

> Give information to clients in manageable amounts; nobody manages well with a long stream of facts and options.
> Pause and allow the client to comment or ask questions about what you have said. Sometimes it will make sense for you to ask, 'Am I being clear in how I explain?', 'Do you see what I mean?', or, 'What questions would you like to ask me?'

ask the client appropriate questions

Sometimes you have to ask specific questions in order to give useful information, to guide the client towards the appropriate source of information or to an alternative service:

> You might need to ask, 'How old is your mother now?', 'How is the school trying to help with your son's dyslexia?', or, 'What kind of child care are you looking for?'
> Ask open-ended questions that invite the client to comment. For example, 'How do you feel about that?', 'Does that sound like a possibility?', or, 'How do you think this service might suit your elderly mother?'
> Sometimes clients seek information or advice on behalf of someone else or in order to help them to support a family member or friend. You may have to ask questions to draw out information about another person who is not present in the conversation. Although this information is second-hand, you could still be in a better position to help. You might ask, 'How does your mother feel about attending a day care centre?', or, 'What does your son feel are the main problems that dyslexia creates for him?'

clients in crisis or distress

You may work within a service where you cannot simply pass on relevant information and leave clients to absorb the impact. For example:

> Health professionals have had to learn a great deal about the inappropriateness of announcing diagnoses to individuals and then leaving, whether this information is about individuals themselves, their children or other people about whom they care deeply.
> Educational services sometimes pass on information about children's learning or behaviour problems without any sense that this communication is more than just information. The emotional impact can be high and has to be recognised by responsible professionals.
> Work-related changes in the quest for competitiveness can have a substantial impact on employees. For example, in the 1990s many organisations undertook substantial redundancy exercises, or 'downsizing', with great variety in the consideration and extent of the information and advice services associated

with the event. The term 'survivors', used to describe those employees left in the organisation, highlights the power and emotional impact of major changes at work.

Clients who are under stress or in shock are not in a receptive state to take in and understand large amounts of information, especially if that information tends to add to their stress and confusion. If you work in an organisation where clients may be under personal stress, then your communication skills need to be fine-tuned to clients' immediate feelings and their ability to hear and understand. Some possibilities are:

‣ Giving information in small amounts, and pausing regularly, so that clients have time to take in the facts and ask questions if they wish.
‣ Not trying to press information and understanding beyond the point where clients can cope. Offer a chance for them to return in the near future. You can explain with, 'In this situation, people often think of questions to ask later on. Please call me if you would like', or, 'I would be happy to talk it through with you again, or to answer any questions.'
‣ Being sensitive to clients and their dignity. They may wish to show their distress in private. But do not use their discomfort as an excuse to leave, or bustle about producing tea or glasses of water. You need to attend well to the client and be ready to ask, if it seems likely, 'Would you rather be alone for a while?', or, 'Would you and your partner like some time together and then we can talk some more?'
‣ Showing clients, even those you do not know very well, a calm presence. You can be supportive without claiming to know more about their feelings than is possible. You might say with consideration, 'I appreciate this may be hard to take in', or, 'I do understand that news like this can be a shock.' Adjust what you say to the situation, the client(s) and the information that you have given.
‣ Avoiding set phrases of sympathy or condolence. If you say almost exactly the same words to all clients, the phrase will soon sound like a cliché, empty of genuine feeling.
‣ Being aware that clients may not share important information with you if they are still coming to terms with bad news, or have been unable to accept a diagnosis of disability or serious illness for them or somebody about whom they care a great deal.

When information is very unwelcome or a shock, clients may grasp at one bit of what has been said. The possibilities for misunderstanding then multiply. For instance, a surgeon who lacks confidence in dealing with 'patients' as real people with feelings may stress that 'the operation was a success'. This apparently positive message may hide the more important communication that, 'I have removed the cancer in your breast, but I am sorry to say that it has moved into your lymphatic system.' Sometimes, information must include an honest admission of ignorance. One of us was told the case of the parents of a blind child informed by a consultant, that, 'There is nothing physically wrong with your son's eyes.' They took this to mean that the child's sight would improve with time. In fact, the specialist meant that he could find nothing damaged in the physical apparatus of the eyes. It was a confused way of admitting, 'I don't know why your son is blind.'

4.2 developing your own material

A website, newsletters, flyers, posters or even telephone answering are part of the public image of your organisation and also an important way to assist potential clients or anyone who refers clients. It is worth taking time and care, so that the end result gives an accurate and positive image of your service. Some resources will be written and published by other organisations or individuals. However, usually you will need to prepare your own original material.

planning a publication

You need to plan in detail, with the help of colleagues, the aim and content of any publication, be this electronic (DVDs or web pages) or hard copy (leaflets, brochures or posters). If you have sole responsibility for the writing then make sure that you consult with colleagues and ask for feedback on your drafts.

the basic information

What do you want to say?

) What are the main messages you want to include? What do you want readers of the leaflet or someone who looks at your poster to take away? Unless you are clear about your five or six main points, then you will not draft them clearly.

) You can think about the content in terms of what *must* go into this publication and what you and your colleagues *would like* to go in if there is space. Whilst electronic media often give considerably greater opportunity to show more, discipline is still required to ensure that the material is focused and relevant to your audience.

your audience

Whom do you want to notice and read your publication?

) Are you clear about the groups of people with whom you wish to make contact?

) Do you know whether some of these groups prefer different media? For example, younger people may be more comfortable using the Internet than the older. Should you cater specifically for special needs?

figure **4.1** **RNIB Helpline publication**

> Is this publication for clients who have already made contact with your organisation, one that needs to reach potential clients or both?
> What are the implications for the level of language in the publication, the kind of examples or appropriate illustrations?
> What do you want your readers to notice? What would you like them to believe and feel about your service?

practical limitations

You need to know the available budget for this publication. Consider which media to use. Financial limits will affect what you can do – whether you can use colour printing, how many pages, the quality of paper, illustrations or how many copies can be made.

Are there any overall design constraints? For example, many organisations

figure **4.2** **Relate publication**

have a 'house style' governing the use of particular typefaces and logos which must be borne in mind. If your organisation is funded only to offer a service to a particular group of people or in a limited geographical area, then make this clear in your publicity information.

Although any organisation has to operate within the limits of its budget, it is worth noting that the general public has expectations about the quality and readability of material. Especially now that good quality print can be produced from a personal computer, clients are unlikely to be impressed with badly photocopied information sheets or leaflets that are full of spelling mistakes. All materials affect the public's view of your service.

clear messages

Your publications should describe the service you offer in everyday language. Information booklets or fact sheets should be written clearly and simply.

- Most areas of expertise have some shared professional language. The words and phrases used regularly in discussion may seem ordinary to you and your colleagues. However, not all of these are used between people who do not share your background.
- Material for clients should be straightforward to read. It often helps to imagine that you are talking with clients. Be guided by spoken language rather than a more formal written style.
- Watch out for clichés and buzz words. The general public is familiar with organisational claims that 'We care' or 'We listen to you' and has become cynical. Avoid generalities and be specific about what your service offers.
- Use headings and bullet points to break up text and guide readers through different parts of the content. Keep sentences and paragraphs relatively short, so that the information or explanations are clear.

choices

Your budget may limit more expensive ideas ('All our clients should have a professionally produced DVD') that you would like to implement. However, continue to aim for the best quality affordable.

- In print there will be choices about the quality of paper. Choose one that is not too thin and consider the colour and texture.
- Can you produce something in-house with word processing or desktop publishing software or will you need a commercial printer?
- Will colour printing justify its higher cost?
- If you have a budget for illustrations, then choose appropriate images that will support your messages. Any illustration should add to your publication and not be used just to break up text. Some illustrations will need a caption.
- Photographs or line drawings should be consistent with the image of your organisation, as well as sometimes being a means to reach out to new client groups. For instance, perhaps your service is more heavily used by particular age groups or ethnic groups. Without being misleading, your illustrations could send the message, 'We're here for you too.'

Be careful about the match between content and illustrations:

- Amusing cartoons can be suitable for a leaflet about healthy eating but are inappropriate for a booklet about coping with bereavement.
- Clip art that comes with popular software such as Microsoft Office or Corel Draw may be easy to access but some images are seen so often that they are already visual clichés.
- Eye-catching images on the cover of a leaflet may grab clients' attention but will confuse the message if the images are inconsistent with the content.

draft and redraft

Thorough planning at an early stage will ensure that your first draft covers the points that must go into the publication and subsequent drafts can focus on style and other features. It is a truism that you cannot improve a first draft until it is actually written. Somebody has to put it down. However, it is very unlikely that a first draft will go forward unchanged. Good publications typically have several drafts before everyone judges that the message is clear and accurate, both in terms of the words themselves and overall design. The first writer may work on future drafts but other opinions should also be invited.

Feedback from colleagues can be helpful so long as it is specific and constructive. A comment like 'This leaflet is confused' is less helpful than 'I can't understand this section because . . .' or 'There seem to be two possible meanings to this sentence.' The criticism of 'Needs more information' or 'Not very user-friendly' is far less use than 'We need something on opening times' or 'I think our clients will be confused by words like "agencies" or "quality assurance".'

feedback from clients

It is worth asking for the opinions of some of your clients at the planning and drafting stage. Having experience of using your service, clients are well-placed to offer informed comments.

- On a leaflet about your service, clients might suggest, 'You really ought to explain the difference between your drop-in advice sessions and the appointments part', or, 'Perhaps you could have some older women in the illustrations. I nearly didn't come because I thought that you only saw teenagers and young women.'
- On a booklet about activities to support young children's play and learning, a client may suggest, 'You keep going on and on about how this is "fun" with your child. That's true enough, but I think you should admit to some of the difficulties. What if you're tired, what if you've got older children who want you? Be realistic.'
- On a web page, clients may say, 'When I clicked on this, I expected to be taken directly to a new section – I wasn't', or, 'It would help to have a tab at the top of the screen showing me how to contact you – there wasn't one, and I had to spend time finding out how to do this.'

If they have the time and are willing to make comments, clients can give you useful insights about use of language or layout which are muddled from their viewpoint, even though they seem clear to you.

final checks

A useful check on any final draft is to read it out loud, either to yourself or in a group of colleagues. If you read silently, it is possible to miss oddities of language. Once you say the words aloud, you hear the slightly odd phrase, pick up any repeated words or phrases and directly experience a very long sentence, as you struggle to make it through without taking a breath.

Ensure that any material, however long or short, is thoroughly proofread. Drafts on a computer can be spell-checked, but the word processing package will not tell you that your correctly spelled word does not carry your intended meaning. It may just be the difference between 'form' and 'from', but it could be the more serious difference between 'public' and 'pubic'. Proofreading is also necessary to pick up any factual inaccuracies. For instance, your computer will not tell you that the opening times for your service are wrong. Read posters very carefully and ideally have more than one person do this checking. Spelling errors and wrong punctuation make materials look sloppy and some mistakes can create real embarrassment.

different versions

Some material may be suitable for different subgroups of clients, though will need to be expressed in different ways. With care, it is possible to tailor the same basic information and key messages for different readers. You will find a very effective example in material from the Child Accident Prevention Trust. CAPT undertook a study into the emotional after-effects of accidents to children. The project team wrote up their findings in four different practical booklets: 1) for children under eight years, 2) for children and young people over eight years, 3) advice for parents and carers and (4) a set of guidelines for professionals. Contact CAPT at 4th Floor, Cloister Court, 22–26 Farringdon Lane, London EC1R 3AT. Tel.: 020 7608 3828; website www.capt.org.uk.

different languages

Ideally, any written material would be produced in the languages spoken and written within the population of your potential clients. However, this task requires thought and planning as it is not simply a matter of translation. It is unwise to distribute leaflets or posters about your service in a number of different languages unless you are able to offer these languages within your service. If you offer telephone help or face-to-face counselling, make sure that you do not imply this service is available in any more languages than you can genuinely offer within your team. If your service offers further written information, then it should be readily available in the languages into which any general leaflet has been translated.

review and reprints

The costs of commercial printing mean that it would be unwise to change written materials frequently. When your organisation is running low on leaflets or posters this is a sensible time to review whether the written content needs changing. Material developed on your in-house computer can be revised and printed on a more regular basis.

ACTIVITY

1 Look with a fresh eye at any written material that is produced by your own organisation.

  ▷ Is it really clear to people outside your area of work? Ask for the reactions of friends or family.
  ▷ Helpful leaflets are concise whereas long and wordy material tends not to be read in its entirety. Is your material about the right length?

2 Send off for some free material or information leaflets from several organisations that are in a different area of helping to your own.

  ▷ How clear is the material to you? Are there areas which you find confusing?
  ▷ What lessons could be learned by your own organisation?

4.3 using the Web for yourself and your service

Many helping organisations now use electronic communications within their service. There are various options:

▸ An email address, as well as a telephone and fax number, for handling questions and requests for information.
▸ Online Internet discussion groups relevant to topics covered by the service. This option is most feasible if your service has a very clear focus of concern.
▸ A website dedicated to the concern of your service – which could include an online counselling provision.

Using computer technology in these ways is a reality for potential users of your service. However, it is easy to overlook the fact that many people still have no access to a computer, at home or at work. Although your organisation should consider these possibilities, communication and information search via computer certainly has not taken over from personal contact by telephone or face to face. Electronic communication is an addition and not a replacement.

hacking and security

Some organisations are wary of using the Internet because of the threat of hackers. Unauthorised entry in computer systems and files is an issue, but the risks can be overstated. Steps taken within your organisation about confidentiality, for instance passwords and effective firewall systems, help to protect against intrusion. You can also consult your Internet Service Provider (ISP) about the measures they can offer. It is possible to become too concerned about hackers. After all ordinary telephone lines are not completely secure and apparently private face-to-face conversations are sometimes overheard.

Make sure that you have a regularly updated virus checker on your organisation's computers that operates automatically on start-up. Viruses can be transmitted from infected disks and from electronic transfer. So viruses cannot pass between computers just with email, but they can be imported with files attached to the email. Increasingly it is also sensible to protect computers against spyware and email scams or 'phishing'. Software is available from a number of vendors like Symantec (Norton), Webroot or MacAfee, and some well-reviewed software is free (for example, the AVG free edition at www.grisoft.com for viruses, and ZoneAlarm Basic for a firewall (www.zonelabs.com)).

In terms of confidentiality, it is almost impossible to completely erase files from a computer. There are many software packages which are designed to recover deleted files (for example Win Undelete). Such a package is instructive to run in order to see just how much material that you thought you had deleted is still hanging around on your hard disk. Software is available which 'shreds' deleted files (for example Webroot's Window Washer) by overwriting data a number of times (typically seven, but can be as high as 24 with the Guttman option) which provides a high level of protection from prying eyes.

your own website

A website, otherwise called a *domain*, is a location on the Internet where people can go to get information about a given topic. Websites are accessible to anyone who has an Internet link, either of their own or through buying time on a computer, for instance in a public library or Internet café. Many helping organisations are now using a website to promote their service. In this way, you can reach an increased number of interested callers without having to take on more people to answer telephones or post out fact sheets.

The first page of a website is called the home page. This gives information about your organisation: what you do and how you can be contacted by email, address or telephone. Pages behind the home page are typically used to give further information about your organisation, extracts from any of your publications, updates on issues that affect clients of your service and links (called *hyperlinks*) to other websites. Your pages may, of course, be animated and include video or audio clips. They may or may not use *pop-ups* to load pictures or other information. The website should meet the same standards as any other service that you offer but has some additional elements as well:

› A website needs to be updated on a very regular basis and it is good practice to show the date when you last updated the site. An out-of–date website will give a poor impression of your service. So it needs to be clear who, in your organisation, is responsible for the website. This person is called the Site Editor.

- As Internet information can be downloaded and printed out, users may change what is written, so it is useful to include a disclaimer on the site that the organisation cannot guarantee the accuracy of information that has been downloaded. This point is equally true for emails.
- Make sure that your professional indemnity insurance covers the Internet. You are providing a service of information and possibly advice, or implied advice.
- Consider how long your site may take to load on a conventional dial-up connection. Many sites assume the existence of a broadband connection and whizzy new computers, and can try the patience of those without the new kit. Further, whilst it is safe to assume that most users will access your site using Microsoft's Internet Explorer, will it work as well with alternative browsers such as Mozilla's Firefox?
- Consider using standard protocols (such as the Adobe Acrobat .pdf files) to help users to print off any documents or publications offered. You may even allow users to download software for free to read your documents or view your videos by providing a hyperlink to the vendor's site. For example, Age Concern offers a free download of Browsealoud software to allow users to have the written word on their site spoken out loud.

Websites can be made more or less difficult for visually disabled users. For instance, moving images or flashing graphics can be hard for Internet users with visual disabilities. The Royal National Institute for the Blind has a website: www.rnib.org.uk that explains how to design an accessible site.

developing your own website

Broadly, website development is in four main stages:

1 Planning – determining your objectives.
2 Building – creating your site.
3 Promotion – helping the right people to reach you through the Web.
4 Evaluation – ensuring that your site works to give you what you want.

Once you have agreed the goals of your site, you will need to build it. Developing a website can be done yourself – it need not be a hugely expensive process if the site is relatively simple. Software is available to help you to build your own site quite economically, and many ISPs now offer a website address (or addresses) as part of the package. A good place to start if you are considering the do-it-yourself option is http://buildit.sitesell.com/main/home.html or Site Studio (www.dotsw.com/sitestudio) as these offer free downloadable software. Others include the Mr Site takeaway (www.mrsite.co.uk) or www.eden.co.uk. Some ISPs offer design help too. You may, of course, choose a professional website designer to meet your requirements.

- In building your site, the best websites use *keywords* to help users find the topics they are interested in. Examples of keywords most of us are familiar with include 'contact us', 'shop' or 'about us'. Each keyword should have its own page. Using keywords to help users navigate your site, and an effective internal search engine using hyperlinks, will help users' visits to be pleasurable and to use their time well.
- If an objective is to increase the number of visits your site receives, then seriously consider linking it to search engines such as Yahoo or Google – particularly if your organisation has a commercial element.
- You may wish to develop reciprocal links with other related sites to broaden the coverage that you offer, and to receive referrals to your site from them. For example, both Age Concern and Help the Aged link to relevant government departments, but choose not to link to each other(!) The Action for Sick Children site (www.actionforsickchildren.org) features the Child Line number in its 'Children and Young People' section. Such links improve the visibility and use of a website.
- You may choose to have areas of your site that have restricted access, for example to users who sign up and give contact details. These 'members' could also form the basis of an email list that could be used for informing them of new developments through a regular newsletter, for example. You may also wish to form a discussion group to allow these members to chat (see below).
- You may require high levels of security in an area of your site (for example for users to buy materials from you, and for which 'https' pages will be required so that credit card details and the like can be safely encrypted).
- A website is organic, and should change in response to user feedback and your own objectives. Today, applications such as Microsoft Word allow the easy saving of documents as web pages to assist the updating process. Continual evaluation and improvement will keep your site relevant and easy to use. Whatever your initial website design budget is, reckon that updating it will cost about the same amount in the first year of operation.

online counselling

In recent years the growth of the Internet has been paralleled by a growth in counselling through both websites and email. Virtually all of these use the written word. It is safe to say that such counselling is not designed to replace traditional ways of helping, rather that it can be complementary to them. Online counselling companies say that they provide a valuable service to people too busy or nervous to seek a therapist in person. The primary disadvantage of web-based counselling is the loss of non-verbal communication. As Paul Appelbaum, the former head of the American Psychiatric Association, commented, 'Even instant messages can be tidied up before they are sent, so you don't know if you are getting the patient's real feelings' (www.telegraph.co.uk/news/main.jhtml?xml=/news/2006/05/07/wangst07.xml). In the future, the growth of broadband and webcams is likely to overcome this problem – at least partially – but this development is still a way off.

Online counselling can be helpful in a wide range of circumstances, but those in need of intensive or extremely urgent assistance (such as feeling actively suicidal, being psychotic or using drugs excessively) are strongly advised to seek help by telephone or in person.

your role and online counselling

Your organisation may wish to provide online counselling for your clients, either through email or possibly interactive messaging – essentially a written conversation. More typically, however, you may wish to offer your clients advice as to whether or not using online counselling may be to their benefit, and by so doing broaden the range of your offer. This may even include a referral (see section 4.5 below).

the pros and cons of online counselling

Apart from the general security issues of using the Internet, the person seeking help is limited by the constraints of the vendor or site, and the charges levied. Email counsellors will typically limit the size of requests – either per email (as low as 100 words) or to no more than 500 words per week.

The most obvious benefits of using the Internet for counselling help are time (the Web is available 24 hours a day) and accessibility (people may seek help when, and how frequently, they like). Furthermore, some people actively appreciate an opportunity for counselling which does not involve meeting someone face to face – and value being able to write down their own issues and reflect upon them. Such reflection can have a therapeutic value in itself, particularly when it is easy to record the written dialogue over time.

Broadly, online helping falls into three categories:

> Information and advice sites – these are typically free, and are usually email only. A good example is the Samaritans (www.samaritans.org.uk).
> Immediately interactive counselling sites – usually with a charge, these offer a chat-room-style real-time conversation using the written word and responded to by an online counsellor.
> Email counselling – also with a charge (usually between £25 and £40 per response), and involving a longer gap between the request and the response (sometimes as much as a 72-hour delay).

Some traditional agencies have expanded their offer to include the Web, for example, Relate (www.relate.org.uk), Gordon House (www.gordonhouse.org.uk) and the Samaritans (www.samaritans.org.uk). However, there is now a large number of individual therapists (and groups) offering services to augment their income – either through email or interactively. For example, amongst others, these include providers with backgrounds in medicine (www.therapy.net); psychology (www.psychologyonline.co.uk); general therapy (www.promis.co.uk and www.7basicneeds.co.uk); hypnotherapy (www.innermind.co.uk); and Christian orientation (www.restoration.co.uk). Whilst providers of online counselling can, of course, be anywhere (and some UK users prefer to use US sites like www.psychcafe.net), many small sites are very clear that they are based locally, for example in the South East (www.therapycures.co.uk) or in London (www.gumtree.com). It does appear to be important, even on the Web, that users can choose virtual counsellors who are physically local.

In short, there are as many offers and orientations for counselling on the Web as anyone could wish. The difficulty is separating the wheat from the chaff. As a guide, individuals should seek therapists who:

‣ Detail and show evidence of their professional qualifications. These may be centred on the subject area of expertise (such as medicine or psychology) or focus (such as bereavement, gambling or addiction) as well as therapy per se. For counselling, the British Association for Counselling and Psychotherapy (BCAP) is a major accreditation body (www.bcap.co.uk).
‣ Show evidence of their experience – including, as appropriate, testimonials.
‣ Respond sooner rather than later to user requests, and be clear about the time delay involved.
‣ Offer the security of the Counselling Code of Conduct (CCC) which carries an independent complaints procedure.
‣ Offer actual, as well as virtual, counselling in case this may be needed.

use of email

Some organisations prefer to deal with enquiries by post, even though many have one or more published email addresses. Others prefer to use email. However, if you do not currently offer email, this should only be added to your information service with a clear understanding of the practical details involved. Almost inevitably today, expect some spam, and it is worthwhile to use spam filters to remove at least the majority of these unwanted emails. Such filters can either be provided by your ISP, your email program or specific spam-removal software such as McAfee's Spam Killer.

increased pressure to respond?

Your service does not want to raise expectations beyond your ability to reply:

‣ You may not know whether an email address will bring in a significantly increased number of queries. You could contact an organisation similar to your own which has offered email, and ask how their level of enquiries altered.
‣ In some ways, using the Web and email is a natural extension to seeking information or advice by letter. However, people who use the Internet on a

regular basis tend to expect a prompt reply, faster than they would expect a reply through conventional post. They may work in organisations where it is usual for email to be checked and a reply sent within a day. Unless your service has the staff to answer all emails promptly, you should let clients know the likely delay in response. The easiest way to do this is by using an email facility with auto-reply. This should thank senders (instantly on receipt of their request) for their email and tell them by when they can expect a reply.

‣ Many email counselling sites make clear expected response times on their home pages. If your response time is predictable, you may choose to do the same on your own website.

confidentiality

Many points from page 11 about confidentiality also apply to email but additional practical points arise.

‣ Many users regard email as part of a confidential system, rather like a private conversation. On the contrary, email can be fairly public. If enquirers email from their place of work, colleagues may be able to access their mail, perhaps not with any intention to pry.

‣ Email service providers sometimes store past emails, although not in a very obvious file, and not on your computer. The sender may assume wrongly that the email has been completely deleted.

‣ Some helping organisations offer information and advice on highly personal issues and senders may need confidentiality. In this case you can suggest that enquirers email you with their name and address for further contact, but do not recount personal details and experiences within the email itself.

‣ Emails can be tagged with levels of urgency or confidentiality. However, this facility helps to inform the recipient but does not offer greater security.

‣ Emails that fall outside the scope of your own service should never simply be passed on to a more appropriate place. Check with clients for permission to redirect the email or suggest an alternative contact or service directly to them.

‣ As well as conventional email, it is possible to use a system that removes the emailer's address. The communication between enquirer and service passes through a third party on the Internet. The Samaritans, for instance, offer the option of ordinary email or an anonymous system.

‣ Services need to develop a system for who deals with emails. Access should be carefully considered and can be restricted by use of passwords to establish different access levels for different staff on computers within a network.

discussion groups

The Internet offers a great variety of online groups and some helping organisations have set up discussion or news groups. Some groups are set up primarily for professionals within a field to communicate, for example Co-Counselling UK (www.co-counselling.org.uk) for counsellor personal development, peer support or stress management. But many online groups are for service users to exchange information and ideas. Some operate like a self-help support group in virtual space. If a group is established under your service's name, you may wish to organise it with a moderator, to vet contributions before they reach the discussion site. This serves to block misleading information or unsuitable comments from entering the forum. If your discussion group allows free access, it will be important to post a notice to the effect that your organisation is not responsible for the accuracy of the information posted.

searching the Web

Do not forget to be a user too! Increasingly, searching the Internet is the first port of call to access information you need, for a vast amount of information is in this one place. The provision of search engines such as Google or Ask.com has made it much easier to find what you want, while specific sites' own search tools can help focus. For example, if you would like to read more on counselling, entering 'counselling' in the search box on www.amazon.co.uk will offer a huge range of books, often including a short synopsis and review of each. Similarly the BBC website (www.bbc.co.uk) gives up-to-date news, www.business.com is focused on managing and growing a business, whilst children and teenagers may find Yahooligans offers a focus they find helpful. Not only can you extend your knowledge base and track down new ideas that become part of your service, but you can also see what works best for you as a user. You could then apply this knowledge to improve the way your own website works.

However, and importantly, do not simply trust information obtained from the Internet; double-check it as you would for any other source of data. Look for reputable websites, and be clear on the suffixes. Educational organisations' suffix typically is '.edu', whilst '.org' (organisation) is not usually a commercial operation and will be a non-profit making or charitable. For psychological (and health) information the sites with '.org' in the address are likely to be more objective than '.com' (commercial) or '.co.uk', both of which are more sales orientated. Be careful of sites 'sponsored by' in the small print somewhere – the site may be full of good information, but may equally be biased in favour of the sponsor(s).

4.4 from information to advice

the boundary between information and advice

It is not always easy to draw the line between a service that offers only information and one that also gives advice. Some helping organisations offer a service in which information is made available, clients are helped to access that information, but are then left to use the information as they wish. Some services have judged it would be irresponsible to offer clients only information with no further guidance. Two examples are:

> The careers guidance service for young people takes the approach that clients will need some active help on how to use the substantial resources on further education, training and careers options.
> Some helping organisations concerned with health issues have also developed an advice service. For instance, organisations for clients who are HIV-positive or who have developed Aids take the approach that clients need active guidance on their options and what these will mean.

The policy decision to move to advice rather than just information sharing should not be left to individual practitioners. A whole service or organisation needs a clear and agreed framework for how all its team should operate. When the philosophy of a service leads to some kinds of advice and precludes other options, the organisation must state this bias honestly and publicly. For instance, a support service for young women uncertain about their pregnancy should not imply that all options will be considered if the avowed aim of the service is to persuade clients to continue the pregnancy rather than consider abortion.

.... responsible advice ....

In practice there is often a shifting balance between giving information and giving advice. You need to be clear where you are in a helping relationship with clients and alert them when you are moving beyond information to advice. You might say:

> 'If you take that route, I'd like to explain what comes next.'
> 'The usual consequences of taking that option are . . .'
> 'This alternative is unlikely to be possible, unless you also . . .'
> 'This possibility won't go easily with what you said earlier about . . . Would you like to talk that through a bit?'
> 'If you want to consider that . . . it almost certainly means that you'd have to . . .'
> 'Sometimes people don't fully realise what . . . means. Can I explain please?'

In none of these possibilities are you necessarily directing a client in one direction or another. You are not saying to clients 'you should' or 'you ought not to' in terms of what they finally decide to do. You are advising them how to think further, to consider more broadly the likely consequences of their actions. For example:

- A parent may be very disappointed that her child has not been accepted by her first choice of school. You can share the information that the parent can make an appeal and how this is done. As well as giving the parent relevant forms or contact addresses, you might also explain that parents who have made successful appeals have spent some time thinking through their case and writing a persuasive argument. Your contribution to the conversation is close to advice in that you alert a parent, who believes the process is simple, to what is really involved in an educational appeal.
- Responsible health information often needs to be blended with advice, so that clients can make informed decisions. You might offer a client, with a serious and possibly terminal health condition, the available information about possible treatments. However, you must also balance this with honest information about the likely impact, short-term and long-term, of these alternatives, from the best knowledge of you and your service. The client may need to be alerted to the possibility that experimental treatments have unpleasant side-effects. Clients who continue to think in terms of possible cure may need advice that helps them to consider the quality of their remaining months.
- Services that advise students in secondary school or sixth form college can share information with students about the gap year between A levels and taking up a university place. An advisor might explain how applications work with a gap year and that the majority of university departments are now favourable to the idea. However, advice would also be appropriate so that students understand that their required personal statement on the UCAS application should give positive reasons for postponing university entry. Young people studying Maths and Physics should also be advised that these departments do not look positively on students who want a gap year, because apparently students in these subjects are seen to 'go off the boil'.

| ACTIVITY

- Note down some examples from your own service that illustrate the difference between giving information and giving advice to clients.
- In what ways do you take care about responsible advice and leaving the choice or decision up to clients?

clients make a final choice

The final decision must rest with the client. Helping services are not in the business of telling clients what to do. It has to remain the clients' choice, as they have to live with the consequences of their decisions. Clients' friends and family can be considerably less inhibited about telling and directing; they do not share your obligation to be impartial. Understandably some clients will push you to tell them what to do and to go several steps beyond advice. You may be pressured with, 'Do you think I should . . .?', 'What do you think I ought to do?', or,

'Come on! What would you do in my position?' There are several positive approaches to this kind of pressure. For instance:

> 'I appreciate that this cannot be a simple decision. You are weighing up . . . against . . .'
> 'Perhaps you need to consider what matters most to you . . . the chance to . . . or the possibility that . . .'
> 'I may be able to help if we go through your options together. Shall we do that?'
> Some clients appreciate the logical approach of 'Let's take each possibility in turn and see what's on the plus and the minus side for each one.'
> Some clients respond better to comments like, 'What feels like the better option to you?'
> Often it is helpful to explain, 'My role isn't to tell you what to do, but I will help you all I can to think through your decision.'

Inexperienced helpers can be tempted to offer clients quick solutions, but responsible advice involves listening and showing respect for what clients have tried already. Telling clients what they should do is rarely helpful. For example, parents of wakeful children are often on the receiving end of blunt 'do this' prescriptions. Specialist sleep clinics, rather like clinics for enuresis (older children's inability to become toilet-trained), are often the first places where anyone has really listened to the parents and worked towards advice that is realistic and respectful.

written advice

Before the telephone, let alone the Internet, people often sought advice from friends and relatives through letters. There is also a tradition of problem pages in newspapers and magazines stretching back to Victorian times. Many helping organisations respond to requests for information through the post or email. A few, for instance Cruse in its work with bereaved clients, offer a facility for exchange of letters. Asking for and receiving written advice can be especially appropriate:

> For clients living in sparsely populated parts of the country, where there is no realistic way to offer face-to-face conversations. Not everyone has an Internet connection.
> When clients prefer the written form. They can start, write and complete a letter at times convenient to them. They can think about what they write, without the sense of having to reply instantly that even a sensitive telephone conversation can create. A letter or draft email can be put to one side for a while, whereas clients might feel that they will not as easily re-establish telephone contact.

- For clients with hearing loss or who are deaf and who may prefer to write or fax. Not all services have a text-telephone facility.

I ACTIVITY

Make a collection of problem pages from a range of newspapers and magazines. Consider whether the answers:

- Seem to address the main issues expressed by the writer.
- Make some assumptions that are not expressed in the letter.
- Acknowledge the feelings that emerge through the letter.
- Seem to miss, or misunderstand, the feelings expressed.
- Use the letter to make a point relevant to the problem page but possibly not to the writer of the letter.

the difference between advice and persuasion

There is a fine line between information-giving and advice and there is also a boundary between offering advice and trying to persuade a client. There is a place for your own views, but these have to be shared carefully and, in many instances, your personal opinion will not be appropriate for sharing.

For example, a local authority drop-in or telephone service for parents might offer information on the different kinds of child care available locally. Informative leaflets and the chance to talk with an advisor could help parents to understand the different options and to consider how they can find a good childminder or nursery. However, it is not within the role of the advisor to challenge whether the parent should be seeking child care at all, nor to attempt to persuade a mother or father to stay at home on the grounds that the practitioner thinks the child is too young to be left. People who fail to recognise the boundary between advice and persuasion sometimes speak of 'counselling clients out of a decision'. However, such an approach is a dishonest way to cover up a persuasive exercise with a client, which can rapidly approach bullying.

I ACTIVITY

- Consider how far you have a clear boundary in your service between advice and persuasion.
- Discuss the issues and risks with a colleague.

4.5 referrals

responsible referral

You may be able to offer a wide range of helping services within your organisation but the possibilities will not be endless. Good practice is to know the boundaries of your service – as well as any limits set by your resources and budget. Clients may approach you on an issue that is not within your area or expertise and then a referral is a positive option:

> Listen carefully to clients so that you can make a useful referral.
> Explain your reasons for suggesting the referral, by linking what clients have said to what you know this other person, group or organisation offers.
> Referrals should be made positively, to benefit the client, rather than in the context of 'We can't do that' or 'I don't know anything about . . .'

informed consent

You should never refer someone on without their knowledge and their informed consent. It does not matter how much you believe the client might benefit from the referral, service or product. See also the comments about email on page 91 and holding a database on clients on page 18.

Clients have the right to choose whether they want to take up a referral. Sometimes previous experience may lead clients to be very wary or to reject potentially useful help. If you listen, you will then be able to understand the source of clients' current resistance. You can reassure clients if their experience was not typical and it may help to say honestly that you feel they experienced indifferent or bad practice.

It is important that everyone involved in your service understands that people must be asked if they would like to have their details passed on to a different but potentially appropriate service. This clarity and consistency is doubly important if clients usually reach your service via a different profession, who may perhaps make different assumptions from your own. Everyone needs to understand that there is no automatic referral without consent. The Victims' Code of Practice is a good example of joint working – in this instance between the police force and the organisation Victim Support. It is fully understood that the police officer, who is in contact with someone who is the victim of crime, must explain that the victim's personal contact details will be passed to the local branch of Victim Support, unless the person says they do not wish for this referral. You can read the code in detail on http://press.homeoffice.gov.uk/documents/victims-code-of-practice?view=Binary. For more general information about Victim Support, see www.victimsupport.org.uk.

internal referrals

An appropriate option can be to refer clients to a colleague in your own organisation. The first-contact person in your organisation may have the responsibility to listen to clients and so could make an appropriate suggestion as to how a client moves on within your organisation. The first contact should make this role clear to clients.

Obviously, in order to make sensible internal referrals, you need to know your own organisation: who offers what kind of expertise, their title or how they are described and their availability face to face or over the telephone. A referral should always be offered with confidence. For example, 'My colleague Zainab will be the best person to help you on that issue', rather than, 'It's no good asking me, that's not my area.' The best person to help may not be available at the time and, again, this situation should be communicated to clients in a positive way. There is a great difference on the receiving end to hearing, 'Sam is our continence specialist' followed by 'he's in every Wednesday from 9 to 5', in contrast with, 'There's nobody here now.'

external referrals

It is good practice to ensure that any organisation does cover the concerns or information enquiries that you believe they do. You could call them yourself and explain how you anticipate referring clients to them on the basis of suggestion, rather than formal referral. It is also worthwhile checking from time to time that the organisation continues to cover the same concern or information and that their contact address and telephone number remain the same. Find out the range of local organisations and groups that offer a service to defined groups of clients and update these regularly. Some national organisations have a network of local branches and it will be useful for you to know whether there is one in your vicinity.

informal suggestion

You may know a number of organisations that are appropriate for questions or concerns that are frequently put to you, but which are outside the scope of your service. Clients are helped by being told that 'We don't cover that issue, but I think that [named organisation] would be able to help you.' Sometimes you may be able to suggest more than one potentially helpful contact.

referral directories

Sometimes, you may use referral directories and databases to help clients to find an organisation that appears to be well-suited to their needs. In particular, you should be aware of Internet support groups that function in your area of expertise. A good starting point is HM Prison Service's 'A–Z of Support Groups' (www.hmprisonservice.gov.uk/adviceandsupport/azofsupportgroups). Explain that you are not making a personal recommendation but that from your knowledge the organisation you recommend looks appropriate. Make sure that you know what kind of entries are in the database and how they are organised. Clients will not expect you to have total recall of a large directory, but they will be less confident in your help if you seem to have no idea how to find a type of entry.

monitoring your referrals

Responsibility needs to be taken within your organisation to ensure that any referrals are based on reliable information, in the same way that your information sources are updated (see page 73).

‣ Does an organisation or self-help group still exist at the same address and telephone, fax or email?
‣ If you are referring to an individual, a counsellor, for example, does this person still undertake the same kind of work and can she or he take more referrals?
‣ Is the service free, or still free? If fees are involved, then what kind of cost is likely?

Sometimes you will be in a position to meet clients again and can ask, in a general way, about the helpfulness (or not) of the referral. Ensure that clients believe that you genuinely want to know. Some social or cultural groups, including some older age groups within British culture, have an approach of 'mustn't complain' and may not volunteer that they have been poorly treated by the referral agency or individual. It is valuable to gain feedback on how your clients are received at the referral agency.

If you are unlikely to see the client again, then consider asking some of your client group if you (or a colleague) could contact them later to hear their views.

‣ You could offer a short feedback sheet, easy for clients to complete and send back to you. Stress that you are not checking up on the clients themselves, perhaps by saying, 'We often suggest that people in your position make contact with this organisation and we have no way of knowing whether it is useful without your help.'

ways of making contact

Referrals are made in different ways. Your approach will almost certainly be part of your service's overall way of working, not a matter of personal decision. For instance:

‣ You may give the information to clients who choose whether to make contact themselves.
‣ Alternatively, you may offer to make the first contact on behalf of clients. Clients who lack confidence may want your help with the referral. Some clients with disabilities affecting communication may appreciate your making the first contact. It is also possible that the other person or organisation works in such a way that they prefer you to contact them on behalf of a client.

Be sure that your client has made an informed choice for you to start a referral; there must be no sense of pressure. Clients should be able to say 'No thank you' just as easily as 'Yes, go ahead' to your offer of, 'Would you like me to contact . . .?', or, 'Would you like to talk with . . .?' Clients have the right to make their own decisions, and not necessarily to explain those choices to you. However, in a good working relationship, clients will usually do so.

Referrals should not be rushed. Give clients a chance to think matters over if they want. Reassure them that they can sit and view the material about another organisation or look through the directory in a relaxed way. You can also offer clients the choice to come back and talk with you at another time. Assertive help through pressured referrals will never be genuinely helpful. This approach can develop either dependency or resistance in clients who are told, 'You really should . . ', 'You'll be sorry if you don't . . ', or the equally disrespectful, 'Well, do you want help or not!'

Discuss with clients the information that you will pass over to the referral agency if you make the contact.

If you contact the referral agency by letter or email, it is good practice to give clients a copy. If you speak over the telephone, tell clients what you have said and communicate the reply of the referral agency to them promptly.

easing the handover

Sometimes you will support clients in their move to the suggested referral:

> Young people or adults who lack confidence may appreciate some basic help at the 'what do I say to them?' level. You are not rehearsing entire conversations, but uneasy clients may be reassured to know that they simply go to a reception desk and say, 'I'm Maggie Pearson and I've got a 10 o'clock appointment with Jan.' They may be uncertain about how much they should say and to whom.

> Manage clients' expectations of what is likely to happen if they call a telephone helpline or try a local self-help group. Some clients have very little idea of what is involved or have unfounded worries which you can allay.

> There should be a gradual and more explicit handover when you have spent some time with a client offering your counselling skills. It may be that new problems have emerged that are not within your area or that a client has taken a long time to disclose what is troubling him or her.

FURTHER RESOURCES

> Mark Gillespie *The Internet Guidelines for Helpers* (2007). Tel.: 0845 1203767 or see: www.helplines.org.uk/publications.

> www.rider.edu/~suler/psycyber/psycyber.html offers John Suler's 'hypertext book' *The Psychology of Cyberspace* (1996) on the development of psychology and therapy via the Internet.

help over the telephone

5.1 telephone helping services

permanent helplines

In numbers of client contacts made each year, telephone help and counselling lines undertake more work than any other type of counselling agency. The *Telephone Helplines Directory* (see page 118) runs to over 200 pages in an A4 format. Some organisations offer their help mainly through a telephone helpline. For example:

‣ The Samaritans pioneered the service of help over the telephone (in the UK, 08457 90 90 90). Their aim is to have helpers available 24 hours a day to befriend callers who feel they have nobody else to whom they can turn for understanding and acceptance with any problem. They offer textphone service for the hard of hearing and also email counselling through their web site (www.samaritans.org.uk).
‣ ChildLine (www.childline.org.uk) offers a 24-hour service for children and young people in danger or distress (0800 1111). Callers are offered support, advice or counselling and children can be helped with a referral to other helping agencies.
‣ The London Lesbian and Gay Switchboard (www.llgs.org.uk) offers a 24-hour nationwide service for lesbians and gay men seeking advice, information or counselling (020 7837 7324).
‣ Message Home Helpline (0800 700 740) offers a national service to people, especially young people, who have left home suddenly and wish to send a message to their families. The helpline also offers advice and can support callers in finding a place of safety. Their website is www.missingpersons.org.

Some organisations offer telephone contact with clients as part of a choice of services. For instance:

- Help the Aged (020 7278 1114 and www.helptheaged.org.uk) runs SeniorLine, a national advice and information service, and they also publish advice leaflets, lobby government on issues that affect older people and provide support services through projects or in partnership with local groups.
- The Children's Legal Centre (www.childrenslegalcentre.com) has an advice line for anyone to ask about legal issues affecting children and young people (0845 120 2948). The centre also produces pamphlets, information sheets and the newsletter *Childright.*

temporary helplines

Some telephone services are a time-limited response to a specific situation. Serious health concerns have sometimes arisen from irregularities in local screening such as cervical smears. A temporary helpline is then established so that people can call for specific information and advice if they think they may be within the affected group. You may be familiar with information helplines set up in the event of a serious motorway traffic accident or air crash and provided after a television news report. Helplines are also regularly offered for a short period of time after a relevant television documentary or when serious problems have been raised through a fictional programme. (There is more about this kind of line on page 107.)

boundaries of the service

Services offering a telephone helpline need to be very clear, as in any helping service, about what is being offered and what is not. The telephone help may focus mainly on information, although there may also be an element of advice. Some lines are set up to offer support through listening and attention. Many helplines offer a service to specific groups of people defined by a similar experience, or by the social or ethnic group that they all share. You need to have a clear understanding of the boundaries of your service. For example:

- BLISS (Baby Life Support Systems) is a charity established for the families of sick, newborn or premature babies (www.bliss.org.uk). The Parent Support Helpline (Freefone 0500 618140) supports parents or other carers affected by the birth of a baby with special-care needs. Callers can be put in touch with support groups but are not given medical advice.
- The Muslim Women's Helpline (0800 032 7587) offers an information and counselling service specific to women and girls in the Muslim community on family, marriage, emotional problems and other personal issues (www.mwhl.org).
- There are many rape and sexual abuse helplines. Some, like the London Rape Crisis Centre (020 7916 5531), offer a nationwide coverage to all callers.

figure **5.1** **helping over the telephone**

However, some have a local remit and limit their service to female callers, or to males.

› The Advisory Centre for Education (www.ace-ed.org.uk) runs a helpline for adults with concerns about children and young people in the state school system. Their general helpline (0808 800 5793) deals with a wide range of questions, but the specific school exclusions helpline is dedicated to that single topic (0808 800 0327).

helping over the telephone

Conversations over the telephone focus on talking and listening but, in this context and with current technology, there is no visual element. A great deal of information is gained and transmitted through the medium of body language (see page 38) so telephone communication can be at a potential disadvantage. Your full attention is necessary to ensure that you listen carefully to what callers say and how they say it, and are not distracted by the appeals of what you may be looking at as you talk.

Some helplines offer reliable information and straight answers to callers' questions. All the skills of listening are required to ensure that callers are heard properly and their questions are taken seriously. However, straightforward answers are possible, including suggestions for someone else whom the caller could contact. The messages that could be gained from the caller's body language are far less important under these circumstances, since emotional issues are not to the forefront.

For example, ScienceLine (Freefone in the UK 0808 800 400, Monday to Friday 1–7pm) gives answers to a very wide range of questions from the general public about any matters of science. The aim of the helpline is to promote the approachable and friendly face of science for the many non-scientists who feel intimated by the subject. So it is important that the science information officers who answer the helpline take the questions seriously, as well as giving clear and accurate answers. Some callers are children with questions that can sound odd or amusing, but which matter to them. Adults and young people will genuinely want to know the answer to their questions, but it may be equally valuable that they feel respected by the scientists who provide answers. Their equivalent website is Science Net (www.sciencenet.org.uk).

easy access

The great advantage of telephone helping services is that they are available simply at the end of the line. Apart from the cost of the call, which is not always borne by the caller, limitations to this easy access are twofold: the times when the helpline is available and the pressure of the number of callers trying to make contact. Callers who have access to their own telephone can just pick up and dial when they want to ask questions or talk. Some callers may need to build up the confidence to call or to be in the right mood. Callers may not want to wait for an appointment to see someone to talk, although some may move to that point after a supportive telephone call.

welcome anonymity

The loss of visual information in telephone communication can be an advantage when callers prefer to talk in relative anonymity. They might not want to take up the offer of more personal counselling, even if this is available. Callers may be more comfortable not being seen and able to respond to a sympathetic voice on the end of the telephone line. The helper may be imagined in a way that the caller wants and needs to envisage: perhaps as a friend, an older sibling, or a parent or grandparent figure.

control of the call

A further advantage of telephone helplines, when callers are uncertain or experiencing mixed emotions, is that callers are in control of the conversation. The telephone call can remain a very brief exchange, if callers want, or because they have changed their mind about talking. They can hang up. It is a very different situation from having arranged a counselling appointment which the client wishes to leave after a very short period of time.

intimacy of the telephone

Telephones are so much a part of everyday life that talking on a helpline can feel very personal to callers. Despite the availability of email contact, some callers want to hear a voice and appreciate:

- A one-to-one conversation in which they have the full attention of the helper.
- Speaking directly into the telephone, with the sense of the helper's ear just at the other end of the line, can give a feeling of closeness.
- The visual privacy offered by a telephone conversation, along with its fewer distractions from the surroundings, may make the exchange seem more personal.

Callers are likely to place the call from a place where they feel comfortable, or at least their preferred location for calling. They do not have to become accustomed to new surroundings which they visit for advice or counselling. A sense of familiarity and the ease of being in your chosen surroundings, possibly your own home, can be crucial for some callers.

relative cost of service

Telephone communication may the best way of making contact for the service offered by many organisations. However, another issue has to be the higher real costs of offering a face-to-face counselling service. Some organisations offer this personal time and attention to a small proportion of clients, but it would be prohibitive in terms of time, space and cost to try to offer the service to everyone.

text telephones

People with severe hearing disabilities need a text telephone (Minicom) to communicate with your service. This system includes a telephone, keyboard and screen. It is possible to have the text option built into the same telephone number used for speaking calls. Callers type in their messages which they can check on their screen and the receiver sends back replies. The system takes no longer than the speed of typing and so is closer to immediate two-way, interactive communication than either faxing or email. There are simple codes of communication that avoid interrupting each other, for example callers show that they have finished this part of the message by typing in 'ga' (go ahead). The end of the conversation from the caller's perspective is signalled by 'sk' (stop keying) but you can add a reply if you have not finished. The complete end of the exchange is signalled by 'bi bi' (goodbye) and 'sk' (stop keying).

Today, particularly among the young, texting to and from mobiles is seen as a normal, daily channel of communication. Some landline phones (for example the BT Diverse series) now offer a text facility which should be particularly considered by services focusing on young people.

5.2 good practice for telephone helplines

access and availability

With the high penetration of mobile phones, most people are able to call almost anytime and from anywhere. However, some callers may have limited opportunity to contact your telephone service, especially if they wish to ensure privacy by making the call when they are alone at home or using a public call box (to guarantee anonymity). Few telephone helplines can offer 24-hour, 7-day-a-week availability, so most organisations have to decide how much time they can realistically offer. Good practice is to ensure that:

› The availability of the helpline is given in any information about your service.
› Details are also communicated clearly on a friendly answering message in operation when the helpline is closed. It is potentially distressing for callers with a pressing concern to fail to get any answer or to hear an insensitive message.
› If the regular volume of callers significantly outweighs your resources, then any written material or queuing message should encourage callers to keep trying.
› The Telephone Helplines Association (www.helplines.org.uk) offer their *Quality Standard* publication. This is a useful resource designed for helpline operators to assess, monitor and improve the quality of service offered.

publicity and increase in potential callers

You need to think about the limits of your helpline coverage if your organisation is offered publicity. It might be an entry in a local free magazine or else you may be invited to join a local radio phone-in or a television programme. It can be very tempting to feel that free publicity should not be refused. Yet, it is wiser to make a considered judgement about how your organisation will become involved and seen by potential clients.

Helplines and television programmes have become such a developing area that the topic was discussed by Maxine Rosenfield in an article in *Exchange*, the newsletter of the Telephone Helplines Association (No. 4, February 1998). This is still available on their website. Some practical suggestions include:

› Helplines operating at Broadcasting Support Services after documentaries or soap operas covering serious illness can experience 400–500 telephone calls in the three hours following the programme. Even 20 live lines do not necessarily enable all callers to make contact.
› It is unwise to encourage a level of calls to your helpline that will overwhelm your ability to answer. Potential callers may develop a negative view of your organisation and communicate the criticism to others.

- An alternative is to have your address (email or actual) given after a programme and then you respond to written queries. Be prepared to cope with a substantial number of responses, which should be handled promptly.
- Another possibility is to work alongside the producers of a programme, offering information and advice, on the clear understanding that your organisation will be mentioned in the credits but not including the helpline number.
- There are rules for broadcasters about the quality of support services offered as part of a programme. It is worth obtaining a copy of the *BBC Producers' Guidelines* from BBC bookshops or from www.bbc.co.uk/worldservice/specials/1715_reporters/page2.shtml.

calls deserve your full attention

pay attention

While you are on your organisation's helpline, you should not attempt to do anything else at the same time, whether this is to check your diary, write notes irrelevant to the call or allow your mind to wander. The caller will not be able to see you scribble or wave across the room to a colleague, but such inattention will almost certainly sound in your voice or through your missing something that the caller says.

You will be far more able to concentrate if you remove distractions:

- Organise comfortable seating arrangements with everything you need close to hand.
- Be in a quiet place. Helplines should offer privacy. Even callers who ask factual questions can be distracted by background noise from your end. Callers who want to discuss something very personal will feel increasingly uneasy if they sense that other people can listen to the call.
- In large organisations several practitioners may be on the helpline at the same time. You will need headsets for privacy and convenience, and, ideally, separate cubicles or work stations.
- In small organisations the helpline room may double as a resource room or similar. You need a team agreement about silence, or avoiding the room when the helpline is operational.
- Small, specialised helplines sometimes depend on volunteers working from home. You must be sure that volunteers only take calls at agreed times when they are not torn between the needs of callers and domestic responsibilities. It is also crucial that other members of the household respect the privacy of callers. Young children, who cannot be expected to understand, should not be able to pick up the telephone or interrupt.

Callers to a telephone helpline should be welcomed through an initial greeting. Your organisation should have some suggestions for what is said: the name of the organisation, your own name and an invitation for the caller to start (see also page 64). You can use phrases such as, 'What can I do to help you?', or, 'How may we help?' You would usually avoid questions like 'What is your problem?' or 'What are you worried about?', even if callers usually want to discuss something that is worrying them.

reflective listening

Support and advice over the telephone use all the skills that are discussed in Chapter 2. When the helpline service requires the use of counselling skills, you will work through the progression described in Chapters 7 and 8. These are the main points.

> Callers cannot see your face, so you have to demonstrate that you are listening by the way in which you audibly respond to what is said. This may mean using more animation in your voice than when face to face.
> The caller will begin to doubt your attention if you make no sounds at all. Use simple verbal encouragement to enable a caller to continue. You might use words and sounds like 'okay', 'yes' or 'uh-uh' slightly more than when face-to-face, as these have to replace the combination of sounds, nods or encouraging looks and smiles unavailable on the phone.
> Callers often want somebody to listen to them and hear their story without rushing to give advice. They want someone to listen because non-judgemental attention is precisely what their family, friends or other professionals have been unable to give.
> The skills of reflecting back and summarising (see page 47) will help you understand what the caller wants to communicate. These skills also show callers that you are concerned and interested in what they want to tell you or ask.
> Some callers may have very strong feelings that they want to express.

dealing with silences

You need to tolerate silences, as you would in a face-to-face conversation, but not allow them to go on too long. It will be a considered judgement as to what is 'too long'. Be ready with some non-specific comments to encourage the caller back into conversation. Depending on the conversation so far, you might say:

> 'What's going through your mind?'
> 'What are you thinking about now?'
> 'You were telling me about . . .'

Telephone conversations that start with silences will often be with a caller who is finding it hard to get started. It is important to give more than one invitation for a caller to speak and to offer encouragement patiently. If the silence continues, then it is not going to be a good use of the helpline for you to hang on indefinitely. You can end the call with a comment like, 'Please call back when you feel more able to talk.'

Sometimes a silent call will be an inappropriate caller. You should have team discussions in your service about how to deal with such callers (see also page 116) but, in general, the same pattern of an invitation to talk, followed by an active closure, will be more useful than expressing frustration or anger.

children and young people

Offering telephone support to children and young people draws on the same range of skills. Children can be experienced users of the telephone, but this may be the first time they have called someone whom they do not know personally. They may lack confidence in how to start such a conversation or be uneasy about how they will be treated.

- When you use respectful communication skills, the younger callers will be reassured, just as with wary adult callers.
- Young callers are maybe unused to being asked for their own perspective, ideas or feelings, but your genuineness will encourage them to talk.
- They should be treated with the same courtesy as adults. For instance, young people should not be addressed by terms like 'dear', when these would not be considered polite for adult callers.
- You may appropriately adjust your language to talk with young callers but do not attempt to make major changes towards what you perceive to be 'teenage-speak'. You will not sound genuine and there is a high chance you will get any street slang wrong, because it changes quickly and differs between social and ethnic groups.

opening up a call

Your task is to find out what callers want or need, without making them feel that you want them to hurry. You need to keep a conversation open, so that it does not rush quickly to some end point that makes sense to you but not necessarily to the caller. You should be guided by the caller because helpline calls are a telephone conversation in which you have no direct investment in where the conversation goes.

- You can use open-ended questions (see page 48) which are non-directive and encourage callers to say more.
- Sometimes it makes sense to open up the call in an active way. You can flag up the shift in the conversation with permission-asking questions like, 'Can I ask you about . . .?', or, 'Do you mind if I ask you a question about . . .?'

figure **5.2 ChildLine poster**

› Using questions well will not feel intrusive to callers and some specific queries may be necessary if possible advice depends on the caller's exact experience.
› Open-ended questions and asking permission communicate respect and show callers that you want to address their personal situation.

information

Some helplines specifically offer information but advice lines will often give information too.

- The helpline needs to operate close to any information resources that you might need. You need to be able to reach or stretch across easily.
- If you regularly suggest that callers make contact with other, specific organisations, then have those details close to hand.
- If you need to stop to find something out for a caller, do not just go silent. Tell the caller what you are doing. For example, 'I'm just going to check that for you. Could you hold on a moment', or, 'The programme's just loading, bear with me for a moment.' If finding out takes longer than you expect, then reassure the caller with a comment like, 'I'm sorry to keep you. I'm going through the directory now.'
- Avoid putting the caller on hold with taped music. People frequently experience this technique with commercial organisations and usually find it impersonal – if not irritating.
- If callers are in a queue, it is helpful for them to know at which point they are in this queue (for example, 'you are third') or how long it is likely it will be before they connect to a real person.

ACTIVITY

Even one or two minutes can feel like a long time if you are left on hold for a telephone call. Start a record of your experiences of being put on hold by commercial organisations.

- Use a stopwatch, or an accurate watch with a seconds facility, to time how long you wait to talk with a real voice or to have a real person come back to talk with you.
- How much time actually passes before you start thinking, 'Where are they?' How long before you feel nobody is bothering with your call?
- How do you feel about taped music, inserted adverts, or recurring automatic messages?

Sometimes you will not be able to help directly yourself. Positive approaches could include:

- 'I would like to check the answer to your question with my colleague.' Ask to put the caller briefly on hold, offer to call the person back or arrange for him or her to call you.
- 'Now that goes outside my area of expertise. But my colleague Michael is experienced with . . .'
- 'I would be pleased to put you through to our specialist in . . .'
- 'I think that [named organisation] would be able to guide you on . . .'
- 'Your GP [or some other specific kind of person] would be the best place for you to start with that kind of query.'

Such suggestions combine honesty about the limits to your knowledge and experience with a practical suggestion. You are then opening doors for the caller rather than closing them.

It is not unusual for callers to start with a request for information. But then what they say may indicate that their feelings, perhaps overwhelming anxiety, are more crucial than a logical question-and-answer exploration. Alternatively, a caller may start with general worries and be pleased and reassured to pass on to solid information. The communications hierarchy in Chapter 2 may help you to move the conversation between levels.

You should neither push callers to talk about their feelings, nor insist that the caller is probably experiencing a particular emotion. Always be guided by callers in how far they want to go in talking about their feelings. You do need to remain aware that telephone conversations can be especially sensitive and hence it is particularly important to avoid leaving a caller feeling raw. Callers may be alone at home, without support or possibly using a small period of time to call, knowing that soon they have to appear strong for someone else.

It is possible to check out feelings with callers in a way that gives them a choice. When the issue could well generate strong feelings or anxiety, you might ask, 'How are you coping with this?' You cannot see the caller, so you have to be alert to the following clues:

▸ What callers say, including their use of words.
▸ Their tone and the level of energy, or lack of it, in their conversation.
▸ The pace of their speech.
▸ Their pauses and silences.

Such clues help you to respond sensitively and flexibly and enable you to offer callers a further choice with, 'You sounded worried when you said . . . do you want to talk about that?'

Sometimes you need to gauge to what extent the worries are central to the caller's concern. You may even be able to ask directly, 'How important is this to you on a scale of 1 to 10?', to get your perceptions aligned, or even offer your own rating for checking. Hopefully you will be able to explore the possible source of strong anxiety. Perhaps a caller to your health line has previous experiences of ill health or distressing medical investigations. Callers may have a friend or relative with the disease that they fear. Alternatively, the caller may have all-purpose fears about his or her health or a particular condition.

After you have listened carefully, you can offer specific comments such as:

▸ 'What makes you think that your son may have a drink problem?'
▸ 'What do you think of the possibility that you might be depressed?'
▸ 'Have you considered that your parent's health problems could be affected by how little he seems to be eating?'

- 'You sound very concerned about the downside of going in to speak with your child's teacher. I wonder if you have thought about what may happen if you don't say anything.'

You will also have a sound basis to make suggestions about how a caller might proceed next, perhaps with respectful comments like:

- 'Have you thought about asking for help with . . .?'
- 'If you want help on . . . then you could . . .'
- 'You probably need to see your GP first, but the sort of person you need is a . . .'
- 'The kind of person who covers this area is called a [named professional such as a clinical psychologist, speech therapist, urologist and so on].'
- 'There is help with . . . from [name of organisation].'

You can offer more information if callers wish, but it is crucial that they retain their own choice about taking action now, later, or doing nothing at all.

the end of a call

length of time taken by calls

Helplines that combine information, advice and support may receive calls that vary considerably in length. For instance:

- Some callers are clear about what they want to know. They ask their questions and you can answer fully in a matter of minutes.
- Some callers need more time to recount an experience or details of what has led up to their current confusion or uncertainty. You can help callers feel heard, perhaps for the first time, in a distressing or confusing sequence of events. You will support callers as they move to a clearer idea of what they want to know or how they can move their situation forward. Such calls will definitely be more than a few minutes, but callers can experience real progress within 20–30 minutes.
- Some callers have difficulty in expressing their concerns or communicate a number of interlocking events or anxieties. Such calls can last for a considerable amount of time and you will need to consider bringing them sensitively to an end at some point.

Helpline teams need to discuss and agree some working time limits for calls. Limits may not be an issue if you work on a helpline that is mainly information, but support helplines deal with calls that can become very long. Some organisations have a working limit of about 50–60 minutes for the longest calls. The limit is usually held for two main reasons:

1 The most experienced helpline practitioner cannot hold concentration indefinitely and 50–60 minutes is the point at which most people need a break.

2 A helpline aims to offer a service to a wide range of callers. Opportunities will be restricted if every caller is allowed to talk for a very long time.

Helpline practitioners sometimes feel uneasy about closing a conversation with a caller who appears to want to continue. However, apart from the two practical reasons given already for time limits, it is useful to remember that:

‣ Even 15–20 minutes of uninterrupted attention will be a luxury for many callers. Most people in their daily lives do not have someone else who really listens to what they want to say.
‣ You will have offered the respect of taking callers' concerns seriously, without pushing advice and judgement.
‣ Within 50–60 minutes a skilled helpline advisor can often support callers in moving away from feeling miserable and being unable to see any way forward. You can help them to a point where they are more able to gain some perspective on the problem and a practical focus.

Unless you genuinely have a very good sense of time passing, it is useful to have a watch or clock in view so you know accurately how long the call has continued.

closing a call

Some helplines experience short calls which have a natural close once the caller's questions are answered. Other helplines deal with many callers whose issues and worries do not have a natural end point. The close of a call may happen in different ways:

‣ Callers themselves end the call, by indicating that their question has been answered.
‣ Callers may end the call by just hanging up.
‣ You sense that the call is finishing and help it to close by asking, 'Does that answer your question?', or, 'Can I help you with any other query?' Avoid standard finishing phrases as discussed before.

When you are initiating a close be sure to use your skills to ease the caller towards the end of the conversation.

‣ You may use phrases like: 'Our conversation must draw to a close now . . .' 'Is there anything else you would like to say/ask?' or 'I can't deal with that now but . . .' (and offer some option).
‣ You can affirm that he or she is welcome to call back at another time or day.
‣ Some callers may need to be orientated to the present and back to very simple actions. You might ask, 'What are you going to do today?', or suggest to the caller, 'Make yourself a cup of tea and call us back if you want'. You could encourage a shift in a caller's emotional state by returning to something positive that she or he raised earlier in the conversation.

- Callers may apologise for talking so long and it can be appropriate to reassure them with, 'You were very welcome to talk', or, 'I was glad to listen.'

realistic expectations

It is important that practitioners on helplines develop realistic expectations for the work. You need a positive outlook both for your own well-being and in order to be of value to the callers.

- Sometimes you will just share useful information. Callers may now know what steps to take to tackle a problem or perhaps that they have legal rights to exercise when they had believed they had none.
- The main benefit of your time to callers is that they now feel that somebody cares and will listen.
- However, you will not solve people's problems or make everything fine in complex or long-running difficulties. Some callers appreciate help in how to cope with a situation which they know cannot be changed. They want support in expressing their feelings and learning to live with the circumstances more easily.
- You open some doors and reassure callers that they are not making a fuss about nothing. You may make a difference today, at the time of this call.

Helpline staff need to accept that they will most likely never know what happens to the callers, especially those taking callers who express strong feelings or recount distressing events. Opportunities for team discussion and supervision are important for dealing with these issues.

inappropriate calls

Any organisation, just like individuals on their own telephone, can be targeted by inappropriate calls of different types. Some services and groups, by the nature of the topic they cover, attract more than their fair share of offensive or obscene callers. The name of your organisation may, for instance, attract racists or callers who have especially offensive attitudes towards your client group, perhaps because they are women or you address the needs of lesbians and gay men.

repeat callers

Callers who want help that your organisation does not offer need to be told courteously the boundaries of your service. They may be given, several times, a suggestion of a more appropriate service to call. Your team needs some agreement about the point when helpline practitioners say firmly, 'Please do not call us again. We cannot help you.'

Return callers who repeat what they have said on previous occasions can be given some latitude, depending on the nature of your helpline. Disorientated callers may be unaware of their repetitions and depressed callers may continue to circle around the same issues as part of their emotional despair. However, it will not be helpful to the caller, and will be wearing for you, if the conversation endlessly revisits the same stories. Your first step to preventing repetition is to summarise the issues, which shows that you have listened and understood. However, you may need to interject with courtesy through comments like, 'Sally, I remember what you've told me about your neighbour. Now let's see where we can go with this', or, 'Dennis, I recall the details about your benefit situation. You remember we talked about . . . now what happened over that?'

hoax and offensive calls

Hoax calls can be hard to identify, since genuine callers sometimes recount unusual or unlikely events. Some may have difficulty in shaping what they want to say and initially sound incoherent or slightly bizarre. Of course, some callers who think they are being funny are recognisable quickly. Depending on the circumstances, you might say sharply, 'The helpline is not set up for this', or you can just hang up the phone.

Some genuine callers habitually use considerably more swear words or sexually related language than you would choose yourself. It is their style, and a real concern to them lies underneath. The content of the conversation, as well as the exact words used, will soon indicate whether the caller's intention is obscene. This intention is not always immediately obvious because obscene callers may engage you in a sequence of conversation that circles slowly towards the intended focus.

As soon as it becomes clear that the caller wishes to offend, shock or distress with no legitimate concern, then you should terminate the call. There is little or no value in trying to remonstrate with such callers. Indicating that you are distressed by the content of what they say will only encourage some of them. Your options are to hang up or place the receiver down for a short while before hanging up. The second option may induce confusion in the caller who is left wondering how long he or she has been talking into thin air.

There is no point in continuing a call once it becomes clear that the caller's sole intention is to gain personal sexual satisfaction. They take up your valuable time and would do better to spend their money on commercial sex lines.

Persistent offensive, threatening or obscene calls may need further action. Even frequent nuisance calls from silent callers can be seriously wearing for the team. Talk through possible options with your telephone supply company, who should have someone who deals with the problem. If the calls have a very disturbing content or include threats to the organisation or its staff, then you should consult the police.

positive attitudes for practitioners on helplines

Basic training should prepare people for work on the helpline but should also select out individuals who are not suitable. The qualities necessary for a good helpline teamworker contribute to the central goal of helping the caller, whatever their information, advice or support needs. Helpline staff need:

‣ An outlook on callers that is respectful of their concerns and leads to listening to callers, not telling or pushing unrequested advice on them. As in face-to-face counselling, helpline practitioners need to hear what the caller is saying rather than rush to shape the conversation in a direction that makes sense to the advisor.
‣ Warmth expressed through their words, their respectful listening and the replies they give. Purely informational helplines still need practitioners who show a human interest in their callers and their questions or confusions.
‣ Patience in helping a caller to express a request for information or advice and in listening in order to understand a problem. Callers will not be helped, and vulnerable callers could be undermined, by practitioners who take a cold, over-intellectual approach or who refuse to accept that an issue concerning the caller is a genuine problem.

The more a helpline is likely to have callers with emotional issues, the more the staff on helplines must have an empathetic approach, a willingness to tune into the feelings of the caller and to respect those feelings.

Helpline practitioners will not be appropriate if they want to make judgements, offer solutions prematurely, dismiss expressed feelings or are unable to deal with the expression of strong emotions from callers. Some helplines deal with callers in extreme crisis and practitioners cannot be helpful if they frequently become overwhelmed with the experiences and emotions they hear.

Staff with very strong philosophical or religious beliefs will not be appropriate if those beliefs cause them to pressurise callers or to judge them negatively. If your helpline has a religious orientation, then this must be absolutely clear in any publicity, including any entries in directories.

⋮FURTHER RESOURCES

▸ The Telephone Helplines Association was established to meet concerns about the quality of helpline services. The organisation offers support to members, a newsletter, *Exchange*, and a range of publications. Contact them at 4th Floor, 9 Marshalsea Road, London SE1 1EP, tel.: 020 7089 6320, website: www.helplines.org.uk. In particular you can get *Telephone Helplines: Guidelines for Good Practice* (2007, 3rd edn) and the 2006 edition of *The Telephone Helplines Directory*, which gives details of more than 1,100 national, regional and local helpline services in the UK.
▸ The Royal National Institute for the Deaf (www.rnid.org.uk), the Royal National Institute for the Blind (www.rnib.org.uk) as well as www.withandwithoutwires.com, offer advice on phones for the disabled.

- Maxine Rosenfield, *Counselling by Telephone* (Sage, 1996).
- The charity Ricability tests products and services for older and disabled people. Their booklet *Stay in Touch* can be downloaded free from www.ricability.org.uk.
- Pete Sanders, *An Incomplete Guide to Using Counselling Skills on the Telephone* (PCCS Books, 1996). Tel.: 01989 763 9000, website: www.pccs-books.co.uk.

a positive framework for helping others

6.1 background briefing on counselling skills

counselling – three broad traditions

- **Psychodynamic counselling** has its origins in the work of Freud and the psychoanalysts, from which it has drawn basic assumptions about people's development and the importance of the unconscious mind in determining the ways we behave.
- **Cognitive behavioural counselling** has evolved from behavioural psychology. This has three key elements: a respect for the contributions of science; a problem-solving and change-focused approach to working with clients; and a focus on individuals' perceptions, thoughts and beliefs through which behaviour is managed.
- **Humanistic counselling** evolved in the 1950s from psychologists (such as Carl Rogers and Abraham Maslow) who were concerned that the preceding approaches were too limited in their view of human nature and its potential. Counsellors following this approach are concerned that clients develop towards a more creative and fulfilling life as well as coping with problems. In the humanistic approach, the client is more of an equal partner in the counselling relationship, not one in which the counsellor is the expert and knows best.

Psychodynamic therapy mainly took the view that everyone was unhealthy psychologically. The resultant process seemed to offer an expensive, lengthy discovery of personal insight but little action. On the other hand, the behavioural, hard-science-based approach (developed originally from animal studies by B. F. Skinner and John Watson) was seen as potentially cold towards clients, who were treated as behavioural symptoms, rather than as individuals with thoughts and feelings.

It is important to realise that since the 1950s both the psychodynamic and behavioural traditions have diversified beyond recognition. However, at that time Rogers's humanistic approach was optimistic and seemed to be more respectful of clients as people, and particularly of their feelings. Rogers emphasised essential core conditions of helping: that the helper had to offer empathy, warmth (also called unconditional positive regard) and genuineness (sometimes called authenticity). The approach was described as person-centred because the aim was to support clients in becoming the person they aspired to be (often called self-actualisation).

Naturally, criticisms were soon voiced about the humanistic approach. Two main concerns were that:

‣ An undiluted person-centred approach may fail to go anywhere. It can create a cul-de-sac of being and not doing.
‣ The tradition can avoid ethical issues; for instance, what if the person whom the client wishes to become is grossly selfish and damages others?

A further concern was that, like any tradition, the person-centred approach is a child of its time and place. It emerged from California in the 1950s and 1960s, which was largely an affluent and optimistic setting within the American culture of individualism. Without adjustment, the approach does not transfer to cultures and communities who believe that appropriate limits need to be placed on individual wants and personal development. Self-actualisation as a goal does not make much sense to clients who face serious practical problems and realistic limits to what they can do with their lives.

A more practical focus was offered by Gerard Egan, who has been extremely influential in the field of counselling. Egan developed a staged approach which charted the possible movement in a helping relationship (therefore using elements of the cognitive behavioural approach) whilst staying true to the core humanistic conditions of empathy, warmth and genuineness. Egan's approach is directed towards helping clients to set and achieve goals in agreed areas of their life. His book *The Skilled Helper*, first published in 1975, has continued through revised editions. His collaboration with Michael Cowan, co-author of *People in Systems: A Model for Development in the Human-service Professions and Education* (Brooks-Cole, 1975), was the basis for our own practice and the model we share in this book.

therapy or counselling

There is an unresolved discussion about the differences, if any, between psychotherapy and counselling. Some writers try to make a very clear distinction, but there are no consistent differences, especially given the great variety of help practised under the two umbrella terms.

A historical distinction was that therapy was a long-term process, whereas counselling was always short-term. This no longer holds now that some forms of therapy are intentionally time-limited. Some counsellors help clients in serious distress, so it is inaccurate to claim that this approach is limited to basic coping skills or temporary problems. However, it is generally true to say that psychotherapy training tends to take longer (four or five years) and involves a higher number of therapy hours than that required for counselling. Typically, psychotherapists encourage a deeper and more fundamental change in clients than is the case in counselling.

Undoubtedly, some therapists (particularly taking the psychodynamic approach) focus strongly on events earlier in clients' lives, especially in childhood, and on bringing so-called unconscious thoughts to the surface. However, all effective counsellors can help clients to acknowledge and resolve the impact of past experiences on both their current behaviour and ways of facing their problems.

counselling or using counselling skills

On page xiii we explained that this book was addressed to readers who will use the skills of counselling but were unlikely to be a full-time counsellor. Your clients will benefit from your counselling skills but will not be likely to regard you as their counsellor. The same professional and ethical issues apply whether you use the skills within your job or are specifically employed as a counsellor. The relevant professional organisation is called deliberately 'The British Association for Counselling and Psychotherapy' and not just 'for counsellors' and the BACAP codes of practice are broadly applicable.

6.2 essentials of counselling

All the points made on page 4 about myths in helping are equally relevant when you use counselling skills. Some more specific issues are raised in this section.

helping is centred on the individual

An essential perspective is that clients are people, not problems. Individual clients may view the 'same' life experience in very different ways, and will show personal reactions and perspectives. One person's problem may be another individual's opportunity; one person's minor irritation may be another's serious problem, and vice versa. Take the example of being made redundant:

› Louisa is devastated. She has worked hard for her position and invested time and considerable energy into her work. She cannot see how she can use her qualifications and skills in any other job that she would want to do.
› Kashif is angry. His firm kept him on long enough so that he made the rest of his department redundant and then, a week later, he received his notice of redundancy. He believes he could get another, similar job but cannot see how he will ever trust any senior management again.
› Erin is cautiously optimistic. She knew redundancy was a possibility and she had been thinking about a possible change in her line of work. She wants a chance to talk through practicalities and boost her confidence.

> Jack is delighted. He wanted to be made redundant and had just bided his time for the best conditions. He has plans to set up his own business with the redundancy money and cannot wait to get started.

| ACTIVITY

On the basis of your own experience and that of people you know, note the different possible reactions to the following life events:

▷ An offer of promotion at work.
▷ A long-term next-door neighbour moves away.
▷ A teenage daughter leaves home to go to college.
▷ A couple break up after a ten-year relationship.
▷ A young woman finds out she is pregnant.
▷ The family pet dies.
▷ The company lottery pool wins a considerable amount.
▷ Any other examples you would like to imagine.

individual life experience

People's experiences will affect how they see themselves as potential clients of a service that encourages them to talk about problems.

▸ In a number of cultures, including the British, women seem to find it easier to ask for help, whereas boys and men have usually been socialised towards appearing strong, not showing softer feelings and in many cases not talking much about problems. Boys and men can be enabled to talk through problems and share feelings but helpers, for instance in youth services, need to consider carefully how to make the experience safe and acceptable to clients.

▸ Talking may not be seen as potentially useful by clients who have limited experience of working through different options verbally. Talking about feelings may be especially resisted and this wariness should be respected. Clients may feel that airing their feelings is self-indulgent, 'navel-gazing' or even potentially dangerous, 'because who knows what might come out'.

▸ People from communities with a strong sense of cultural and religious identity can be doubtful about seeking external help. They may have explicit pressure to keep any problems within the family or immediate local community, supported by clichés like, 'We don't wash our dirty linen in public'. Some helping organisations respond to this preference by establishing a service that draws on skills within the relevant community.

▸ The social position of some potential clients may make them reluctant to ask for help. For instance, people within the helping professions may feel, 'I'm someone who gives help to other people; I should be able to cope'. Specialist networks and telephone helplines have been established in recognition of the stress for professions like doctors, dentists or religious leaders.

priorities in facing problems

Clients' experiences may lead them towards a different order of priorities than you. Helpful interventions have to walk a delicate balance between respecting the client's view of what is most important and encouraging alternative perspectives, especially when clients' priorities put them or someone else at risk.

| CASE STUDIES

1 Lisa did not like being hit, but her past experience and childhood told her that men hitting women was a normal part of life and did not count as a real problem unless the domestic violence became excessive. Although Michaela at the community centre was very concerned about the violence, Lisa's perspective was that other family problems, especially her son's bed-wetting, were a much higher priority at the moment. Lisa could see absolutely no way to change the violent situation, but hoped for some help with her children's behaviour. Michaela recognised that if Lisa developed trust in her, it might later be possible to offer support for the domestic violence. However, Lisa was likely to back away if Michaela insisted on tackling the violence as a priority when Lisa clearly stated that she wanted help with her child.

comments

▷ In your service, what kinds of different priorities emerge between the perspective of clients and the helpers? How do you handle these?

▷ Reflect on personal experiences, with public services or commercial organisations, when your priority was different from that of the person trying to help you. What happened if your priorities were overlooked?

2 Different kinds of help can be more supportive at the different stages of a long-term problem. Thomas developed terminal cancer and he and his wife Olivia knew that he had no more than about a year to live. They were offered support from the local hospice and from the community health visitor. During the remission months when Thomas's health seemed to be back to normal, he and Olivia most welcomed the visits of the hospice support worker who listened and encouraged them in plans to make the most of the time remaining. At that point they found the community health visitor much less useful. Her conversation was mostly of people who had died from cancer and she was negative about Thomas's wish to seek a second opinion on his prognosis. However, in the last months, when his symptoms returned and worsened, the community health visitor became the most helpful as her practical ability to respond to symptoms was now appropriate.

comments

▷ Helpers whose background encourages them to do something can feel at a loss if supportive conversation is required more than action. In what way is this distinction an issue in your service?

▷ If your service offers different kinds of help, how do you ensure that clients are asked what would be most helpful and when?

social and cultural traditions

Clients bring assumptions grounded in the social and cultural background of their childhood and current life. If you do not share this background, then you have to listen very carefully to understand perspectives that you do not share and that may be very different to your own.

In recent decades, Western culture has developed a new tradition of criticising social targets that were previously above criticism. Open complaint is more usual about family, older people, or professionals like the police, teachers or doctors. However, for many people, particular targets remain off-limits. A client may not feel anything like relief if she is encouraged to unload feelings of anger about her parents. She may feel a painful sense of guilt and disloyalty. Emotional conflict may arise for any client, but it is likely to be especially sharp for clients from communities in which family loyalty and commitment are highly valued.

The Western view of growing up is that young people break their ties to the family and set up their own life. Maturity is defined through independence, which means leaving home, establishing new loyalties and a separate life from parents. However, this view is alien to many other cultures. In African, Asian and Far Eastern cultures, maturity is seen more as the growing ability to take on adult responsibilities and to become part of a family network of interdependence. Couples from two different cultures may face serious misunderstandings. What to one partner is a mature loyalty to the family, which may involve financial contributions, is to the other partner an inability to become independent and show loyalty to the new relationship or young family.

clients own their problem

However much help you can offer, remember that clients own their personal problem, family dilemma or difficult career choice. In the end, it is their decision how to view the issues and what, if anything, to do. Clients live with the consequences of decisions or their reluctance to make a decision. The counsellor's role is to help the client to solve his or her problem, not to solve it for the client.

If you work with individuals or families who have serious problems, then it is possible to feel a heavy sense of responsibility to relieve the pressure. The cliché 'A problem shared is a problem halved' can be misleading in these circumstances. If you take someone else's problem entirely upon yourself, the result will be two people weighed down. Some of the stress in the helping professions is caused by difficulties in finding a balance between caring and objectivity – between compassion and detachment.

A clear view of 'Whose problem is this?' should not lead to lack of support for clients, or a cold 'You get on with it' approach. The perspective on ownership is important to ensure that clients feel enabled, that what you offer has helped the client to feel more competent and confident to do something constructive. In brief, ownership of the problem is faced through:

- Your positive outlook communicated to clients.
- Encouragement to help clients to take problems one step at a time.
- Encouragement to focus on what can be changed or, if not, managed better.
- Resisting explicit demands from clients to sort out their problems for them.
- Regular supervision and support within your team when clients' problems weigh you down and you find it hard to maintain an appropriate distance.

caring detachment

Counselling skills should be offered in a way that creates mutual trust and respect, so that clients feel safe to disclose and explore their concerns. Clients need to feel that what they are saying matters to you and that you are genuinely concerned for their welfare, that you care about them and their lives. However, your caring has to be tempered with a level of detachment because this approach enables you to be a better helper by providing an alternative, ideally more objective, view of the reality of the client.

You cannot help if you feel overwhelmed by the complexity of clients' problems. The last thing that distressed or confused clients need is any sense that their supposed helper is now distressed as well. You need to be able to stand back from what clients tell you and to consider other perspectives and possibilities. You need to be able to support clients as they move on from their current position and you will find this hard to manage if you become a part of the problem by being over-absorbed in clients' current concerns.

A safe balance between caring and detachment can be especially difficult in helping services where helpers share common experiences with clients or when helpers have strong beliefs. For example:

- Men who have been separated from their children through custody disputes can be a great support to fathers who contact them. But clients have to be approached as individuals and a situation avoided in which any automatic assumptions are made about where responsibility or blame lies.
- When a client describes a problematic work situation in which he or she differs from the other people involved by ethnic group identity (or sex), an impartial helper does not quickly assume that the situation is obviously shaped by racism (or sexism). Social or cultural groups who regularly experience inequalities in society include individuals who are badly behaved or selfish and share responsibility for a negative situation.

warmth

Your words and body language should communicate a welcome to clients and an invitation to talk with you. Warmth can continue to be expressed even when you encourage clients to work hard on their problem and consider perspectives that are not easy for them.

respect

It is not possible to help other people unless you feel respect for them. You may not agree with clients' decisions, but you need to respect their right to make them and to run their own lives in the way that best makes sense to them. You need to find respect for the efforts that clients have made, for the issues that they have faced and for their choice to seek help.

genuineness

An effective helper behaves in an open way, without hidden agendas or desires to manipulate clients in any way. Helpers should be honest and never pretend to agree or understand. Genuineness is most easily seen through a convergence – or match – between what you say and do as a helper.

Genuineness, sometimes called being *authentic* with clients, is not possible if counselling skills are diverted to an unspoken objective of the helper. The term 'counselling' is sometimes used inappropriately to cover behaviour that is designed to persuade. You may have heard phrases like, 'Counsel Priyash out of taking this course. It's not suitable for him but he won't listen to me', or, 'Somebody's got to counsel Caitlin from taking her complaint further.' In either of these examples, somebody may well need to have a conversation with the individual but they are not counselling.

emotional needs of helpers

Wanting to help other people is a natural and legitimate motivation for anyone within a helping service. There can be a great deal of pleasure in seeing clients become more confident and able to face a situation effectively. Work that gives personal satisfaction will also meet your emotional needs in some ways, but that is not the main objective in offering counselling skills to clients:

> Helpers are there for their clients. At no point should the balance shift so that clients are primarily meeting your emotional needs.
> Unaware or irresponsible helpers may want to feel indispensable to clients, make friends or be tempted to rework problems in their own lives through the choices they suggest to clients.
> Clients are often appreciative and express thanks for help. But it is not their responsibility to ensure that you feel needed or affirmed in your practice.
> Clients are certainly not there to support a helper's perspective on life, philosophical beliefs or to prove a pet theory.
> Employed staff or volunteers in a helping role need other sources of emotional satisfaction in their lives besides time with clients. You need a personal life which provides a respite, opportunities for you to receive as well as give and, frankly, to help avoid the risk of delusions of grandeur.

6.3 personal styles in helping

Everyone brings some personal biases to their helping and it is essential to become aware of your own inclinations. Personal bias in style will affect how you learn your counselling skills and to an extent what you will need to unlearn. Self-awareness remains important because your own tendencies will creep into your work, particularly when you feel at an impasse with clients.

Before anyone learns counselling skills, she or he will have some ideas about how best to help and what to say. You will have learned from what you have observed when other people have tried to help, as well as your own experience of what is genuinely helpful or not. Look at the following general descriptions and honestly consider which approaches are closer to your own style. The word 'client' is not used here because we describe ways of helping that are common before people have learned counselling skills.

Seeking more information

One tendency in talking with someone seeking help is to probe for further information. You might ask questions like, 'How often does this happen?', and, 'What did you say next?' Or you might direct the other person towards, 'Tell me some more about your family', or, 'Why do you think taking a year off will make things better?'

Questions and invitations for more information have a place in helping others when you use counselling skills (see page 152). However, people who have a strong bias towards questioning run a number of risks:

▸ You shift a potentially helpful conversation to a narrow channel of communication: one person takes the role of asking the questions and the other person of answering.
▸ You cannot know what will be useful questions until you have listened carefully to another person's concern; you can only guess.
▸ Without this understanding, your questions can feel intrusive to the other person. She or he may go quiet, answer your questions but not find them useful or challenge you with, 'Why do you want to know all this?'
▸ You may ask questions because you are personally interested in the answer or have decided that the topic you wish to probe is important. The focus is on your curiosity or personal judgements rather than the view of the other person.

Are you someone who is comfortable with a questioning style? Maybe other parts of your work role require the ability to find out information within a limited time period. You may need consciously to hold back on questions and concentrate on listening to counsel more effectively. Trust that the information will come because most people will tell you what they need to say when given the space. You will soon learn enough about the perspective of the other person to ask useful questions.

interpreting

Some people's first inclination for helping is to offer an explanation or interpretation of what is happening, how someone is feeling, or why he or she is acting in a particular way. You might offer comments very early in a conversation like, 'Don't you think this is all linked up with being a middle child?', 'Sounds like the male menopause to me', or, 'If you're honest, don't you mean it's you that wants your son to go to college nearby?'

Are you keen to shape up another person's problem or concern in a way that makes sense to you? Perhaps you find it useful to look for possible explanations in your own personal life and perhaps you are genuinely insightful, but there are risks in interpretation as an early approach:

› Without listening and working to understand someone else, you will not have a sound basis for any tentative links or suggestions.
› With support, other people will often come to their own views of what is happening underneath the obvious and their insight will be stronger for having reached it themselves.
› Swift explanations and interpretations run the risk of being wrong and annoying the other person.
› On the other hand, your insights may be uncomfortably close to the truth and the other person is not yet ready to hear that viewpoint.
› The drawback of pushing an interpretation is that you are implicitly trying to teach, without clarifying whether the other person needs or wishes to learn.

supporting

Some people's first inclination is to support and reassure when faced with confusion or distress. If this is your inclination, you may offer comments like, 'I'm sure it will all work out', 'Your child's behaviour is perfectly normal for his age. It's just a phase', or, 'Everyone goes through this, there's nothing serious to worry about.' Supportive comments are sometimes meant to affirm the other person, for instance, 'I'd be angry too in your position', or, 'I think we could all do with showing our feelings more.'

People who have a strong inclination to offer general reassurance often genuinely wish to help and may be affected themselves by the distress or worries of others. There is a place for support and reassurance, but only within the context of hearing about what concerns another person:

› You cannot offer an optimistic outlook without some grasp of the situation. There may be real cause for concern.

- Uninformed reassurance can very easily be experienced as patronising or dismissive. The other person is distressed or confused and you appear to be saying that there is no sound basis for their feelings.
- It is usually better to acknowledge someone's feelings and explore them in ways helpful to the other person, rather than stopping with the message that you agree with their feeling this way.
- You may be correct that the other person's experience falls within the normal range of children's or adults' behaviour in a similar situation. However, that other person still wants some help on how to deal with the situation personally.
- You best show support by giving time and attention. Your helpful presence demonstrates support and earns the right to help.

evaluating

Some potential helpers want to shape up a problem or issue in an evaluative way, by making a judgement about right and wrong, or 'ought' and 'should'. Evaluative comments may direct the other person in a different direction with, 'Isn't it about time you looked at this from your partner's point of view?', or, 'You can't keep on trying to be a big success like your elder brother.' Some evaluative judgements are about how the other person experiences the situation, for instance with, 'Don't you think you're making too much of this', 'You don't really mean that', or even, 'When are you going to tell me what the real problem is?'

You will have opinions about people to whom you offer help, but evaluative comments are rarely, if ever, helpful.

- Such comments usually come across as if you are playing the expert and the moral authority. The other person may well feel that you are reprimanding them and being patronising, and perhaps you are.
- Denial of people's feelings will close down a potentially helpful conversation because it is disrespectful.
- It is not your business in using counselling skills to tell other people what they should do or how they should feel. If you have listened and worked to understand, then you will earn the right to suggest alternative perspectives to another person.

telling

Telling is really a combination of interpretation and evaluation. Some people feel a great pressure to offer solutions to problems, to have something to suggest that the other person does. It can feel very satisfying to hand out quick advice, but this approach is not usually helpful. Examples of the telling approach are, 'You need to get out more. Try a local evening class', 'Stop breast-feeding your baby, then she'll stop waking you up in the night', or even, 'You're just going to have to learn to live with this.' One telling approach is to focus on the personal experience of the supposed helper, to the exclusion of the concern raised by the first individual. An example would be, 'I know exactly what you mean. When my mother died . . . Let me tell you . . .'

Many television programmes, radio phone-ins and some of the magazine problem pages take the approach that helping is the same as telling people what to do, and telling them quickly. You may be lucky with your suggestion but the risks are high:

- Experienced helpers recognise that they have no way of knowing what might be useful until they have listened properly to the other person.
- Telling often proposes that people do something they have already tried and that failed to work. The helper loses credibility for not exploring the issue fully first.
- There is a strong possibility that keen tellers create dependence in others. If your idea is both new and it works, then the expectation is that you will produce an easy answer next time. It does not help the other person to be able to solve his or her own problems next time.
- If the advice does not work, you will have little understanding of why and may well be blamed with, 'You told me that would work. Well, it didn't! It made things worse!' Without deeper understanding and exploration the commitment of people seeking help to the solution proposed is likely to be low, and hence they are unlikely to put in the effort required to make even the best solution work.
- There will be times when you have no idea what to suggest and, if you are not in the habit of listening, then you will feel bad about saying, 'I don't know what to tell you to do.'
- There are rarely neat solutions or even a way to remove a problem completely. For some people, help comes through finding ways to live with a situation that they cannot change, or learning how to prevent past experience from distorting their approach to the present. The positive focus is on the other person's learning to live with particular circumstances and not on your telling them they will 'have to shape up'.
- Sharing your own experience prematurely may be offered with sympathy but you cannot know if it will be helpful to the other person and certainly not whether you really do 'know exactly how you feel'. The recounting of an important part of your life will push away the other person's experience unless it is directly relevant to their needs.

Part of helping other people is working with them to the point where they feel able to consider options in what to do about a problem or concern. Counselling skills will enable you to help them to reach that point and to gain personal satisfaction in what they have learned and managed, not what you have told them to do.

understanding

The initial approach of experienced helpers is most often to attempt to understand what the other person is saying and to show that they are working to grasp that perspective. Until people have experienced ideas and practice in counselling skills, this approach is less common than the others described in this section. Some people are more natural listeners, but many have one or more of the tendencies to shape up and drive a conversation faster than is genuinely helpful.

| ACTIVITY

Read through the three examples one at a time. Consider each of the possible responses that the potential helper has made.

▶ What do you think the response has contributed to the exchange?
▶ How might it lead the conversation?
▶ Is it helpful? If so, in what way?
▶ Which response(s) would you be more likely to offer? Be honest with yourself – what is your first inclination?

Discuss one or two examples with a colleague and exchange ideas. You will find comments on this activity after example three.

example one

Simon is talking with you about his home situation and says, 'It's getting beyond a joke at home, my mother lives with us and she and my wife just can't get on. My mother says she's trying to help out with the children and cooking – that sort of thing. But my wife thinks she's being criticised and I suppose Mum has always been keener to tell people what they're doing wrong than to praise. Now I dread going home at night; I'm pleased if I have to work late. But then I don't see much of my wife and the boys have gone to bed. When my father died, I felt we had to ask Mum to live with us, but my wife said it would cause trouble. It's not her family's way.'

1 'Can you tell me more about the arguments between your mother and your wife?'
2 'You're torn between your loyalty to your mother and your feelings for your wife and sons.'
3 'It sounds as if you're in the middle of some sort of culture clash. You and your wife's families have different traditions.'
4 'Perhaps you should consider sheltered accommodation for your mother.'
5 'You can't expect your wife to do everything. It is your mother after all, not hers.'
6 'I'm afraid daughters and mothers-in-law often don't get on. It's very normal you know: two women – one kitchen.'

example two

Yan-Ling is talking with you about her career: 'I don't know what to do for the best. I've done well in publishing and I've found it very interesting up until recently. I've got a good salary, but I feel I'm not

132 | **MASTERING** counselling skills

going to go much further. No, that's not really true. It's that I'm fed up with all the new qualifications in the area I cover and next year they're going to change them all again. I keep thinking is this all there is to my life? I always wanted to develop my photography and I didn't have the courage. I can see some openings and a friend is interested in starting a business. But, I'm not sure.'

1 'You sound a very sensible individual to me. I think you'll sort out what you really want, if you put your mind to it.'

2 'What's happening with the new qualifications next year? I hadn't heard anything about yet another lot of changes.'

3 'It sounds like a tough decision. Do you stay in a job that doesn't interest you so much any more? Or do you take the risk of starting out in something new?'

4 'In the current economic climate I'd have thought you'd be grateful to have a regular job and a good salary.'

5 'It's obvious that you're the kind of person who always goes for the safe option, but then regrets what could have been. You lack the courage of your own convictions.'

6 'I suggest we draw up a list together. I find it helps to put all the pluses of an important life change on one side and the negatives on the other. Then we can talk about each one in turn.'

example three

You have been asked to speak with ten-year-old Clement because several of the primary school staff say he is surly and aggressive. Clement has said very little in the conversation, then towards the end of your time he bursts out with, 'It's not fair! The teachers say "This is a telling school". They keep on about "Don't hit them back, it only makes things worse". But I've tried to tell Miss a million times and she just says, "Don't tell tales". And I tried to tell the helpers in the playground and they said, "You're a big boy. Sort it out for yourself". I have to hit Harry and his gang; they won't leave me alone.'

1 'I'm afraid your teachers are right. However badly you feel, hitting people never solves anything.'

2 'I think you're especially stuck because you're a boy. We adults haven't been very good at helping boys to talk about things.'

3 'You need some other options. I can help you with ways to deal with these boys without hitting. We call it assertiveness.'

4 'Life does seem very unfair when you're young. I was young once, you know. It does get better, trust me.'

5 'You feel you've got no choice. You've tried to "tell" like the teachers say and that didn't help. So, you can't see how else to defend yourself'

6 'Can you tell me more about what Harry and his friends do? You know the school has an anti-bullying policy.'

comments: different personal styles

The responses to the examples have been kept short. Responses are often longer and combine more than one of the approaches. The types of responses given are as follows, with examples one, two and three in order.

Understanding: 2 3 5

Interpreting: 3 5 2

Seeking more information: 1 2 6

Evaluating: 5 4 1

Telling: 4 6 3

Supporting: 6 1 4

A staged model creates a framework for helping that grows with the relationship between client and helper. Egan returned to a three-stage model after working for some years with four stages. Richard Nelson-Jones explains helping through five stages. We use a four-stage model because we have found that this framework works best for the public services and businesses with whom we have been involved in applying the skills in practice.

The staged model places counselling skills in a framework that is progressive, and focuses on problem-solving in which the helper and the client together work towards what the client can do. The process of helping is one of sharing expertise, building trust and a joint commitment to the way of working on the issues and to the end result of change for the client. Consequently, helping can only happen if helpers value clients for themselves as individuals and accept clients' rights to make decisions for themselves. The model assumes that helping will be a relatively short-term intervention with a client: a series of sessions stretching over weeks or at most a few months, certainly not years.

When you use counselling skills within a staged framework, you are far more likely to be guided by what you have learned by listening to the client. There is a sense of growth in each individual helping relationship, however brief. The four stages are as follows:

- Stage One: understanding the client's perspective, the problems as she or he views them and the current situation for the client.
- Stage Two: exploring alternative perspectives with the client, working in greater depth on a problem and establishing how the client would like his or her situation to change.
- Stage Three: exploring with the client the different possible ways of achieving his or her preferred goals and making definite plans for action.
- Stage Four: the client puts plans into action, evaluates to what extent the goals have been achieved and revises plans if appropriate.

The diagram of the diamonds (Figure 6.1) shows how each stage has an opening-out phase of gathering information and then a closing-down phase of decision-making. The opening up and exploration in each stage sees the helper drawing out or contributing information and the closing-down phase moves to an interim decision with the client. Figure 2.5 is an appropriate model for basic questioning, particularly within the context of clients' needs for information. However, that model fails to stress the need for a broad exploration of a client's issues and concerns that lies at the heart of counselling. As such, the image of the four diamonds becomes a much better symbol for the process of communication developed as you use counselling skills.

Task goals	Understanding your client's perspective	Stimulating the client to greater understanding	Designing change programme	Changing, supporting and measuring progress
Model	Exploration / STAGE 1 / Focusing	New perspectives / STAGE 2 / Goal-setting	Programme census / STAGE 3 / Programme choice	Implementation / STAGE 4 / Evaluation
Process goals	Earns the right to help	Uses right to help and tests commitment	Jointly commits with client to change actions	Earns right to finish, or recycle

figure **6.1** **the counselling model**

source: adapted from Egan and Cowans (1979)

Each of the stages is only successful to the extent that you have communicated effectively in earlier stages. So, making a psychological contract with a client at the very beginning of helping at Stage One is especially important. Unless you do this you might fail to manage expectations about what will happen and how. The skills of Stage One are crucial, because a helper who fails to see the issues through a client's eyes will not have a firm basis for any further helping.

The counselling skills build upon one another. So the skills of Stage One remain important throughout the helping process. The skills of Stage Two are more complex and can feel more challenging to the client than those of Stage One. It is important that you understand and remain aware of the helping process. Then, you will be conscious that you are moving into stronger interventions because it is justified by what and how the client is speaking with you. No new behavioural skills are required for Stages Three and Four, although a range of approaches can be used to help clients in action planning. The stages are *not* rigid. You will sometimes return to an earlier stage, for instance when a client shares a new concern or trusts you with a sensitive experience. You are aware of the stage of helpful interaction and that guides your use of skills.

The helping relationship described in this chapter and Chapters 8 and 9 assumes that you spend uninterrupted, private time with a client. Sometimes you move through the stages fairly quickly; helping is not always a long, drawn-out process. At other times you and a client may spend several sessions exploring within Stage One. It is not unusual that clients first surface a less important problem and are only prepared to talk about more worrying concerns when they feel able to trust you. A helping conversation will often have a circling quality as you return to Stage One skills if the client discloses a new concern. The staged approach is flexible and will help you to focus on the client, rather than on your initially preferred helping style. We want to stress that the stages are to guide you towards the most helpful interventions and to avoid premature comments or suggestions.

Counselling skills will be useful in the following types of work situation:

> Offering help to clients who ask for time and attention, either in face-to-face conversation or over the telephone.
> In services primarily for one set of clients, for instance children, young people or elderly people, but where you aim for partnership with parents or other carers who may ask for your time.
> Offering help and support to colleagues who ask for time to discuss a work issue that concerns them.
> In your role as a supervisor who gives time to team members to talk about their work, not necessarily serious problems.
> The examples used in Chapters 8 and 9 are all two-person conversations, but counselling skills are also relevant to working with groups (see Chapters 10 and 11).
> Application of the skills will also support you in short conversations within your work. You will be able to make the most of short periods of time, but realise that genuine helping cannot be rushed.

reservations about a staged approach

We have talked with some potential helpers who have expressed doubts about a staged approach. Reservations include the claim that stages can be rigid and helpers are able to judge when clients need more confronting interventions at an earlier point than the model would suggest. In fact the staged model has considerable flexibility. Most doubters that we have encountered have been under unrealistic pressure over how many clients they can see in a working day. Some have also been within a professional framework that has failed to develop a tradition of respect for clients.

These two factors, unless acknowledged and addressed by the potential helpers, run a high risk of perpetuating an unhelpful service in which clients are seen as names on a list that can be sorted out promptly and pushed, if necessary, into accepting what the helpers think they should do for the best. Such a service, whatever those delivering it may want to believe, is not genuinely helpful to those on the receiving end.

It is not, of course, the client's responsibility to 'keep within the stages' of the model. The value and flexibility of this staged model is to enhance the helper's awareness of what clients are saying and the extent to which they are currently comfortable about handling their problem or concern. Nor is there *any* sense of driving the helping conversation in a particular direction.

the use of agreements

Many people think of the word 'contract' in terms of legal agreements like hire purchase or buying your home. A firm, 'sign on the dotted line' agreement would not be appropriate for helping others. However, you will find non-legal examples of a contract in agreements between parents and their children's school or between students and their college. Children's and family centres have long worked with contracts for families about their children's attendance and any planned work with parents. The growth in customer charters is another example of less formal contracts. Such agreements tend to cover two broad areas concerning the relationship between individuals or groups of people:

- Practical issues about the service being offered and accepted: where, when, how often and similar questions.
- Bringing expectations and assumptions out into the open. An effective contract covers both sides of the relationship: 'What you can expect from us as service providers' and 'What we expect of you as users of our service.' The more personal contracts, for instance with children and young people, are more about, 'You agree to work towards these objectives', and, 'I agree to support you in these specific ways.'

ACTIVITY

Collect examples of contracts and customer charters from a range of services.

- In your opinion, how well does each example communicate the two main areas – the practical details and clarity about expectations and assumptions – for both sides?
- Compare the examples with any explicit agreement within your own service.

agreements in helping

There has to be some flexibility in how you establish an agreement with a client. You would sensibly take different approaches with a colleague who says, 'Have you got five minutes to talk with me?', a wary, young person brought to you by his parents, a client who has asked for help in making his career change or a client who wants someone to listen to her worries about her teenage daughter. There will be no ideal form of words that you should use with everyone but you need to cover:

- Practical issues of time and place.
- Your approach to helping and the client's expectations.
- Confidentiality.

time and place

You need to know and be clear with clients about how much time you can offer, where and when.

- Depending on the circumstances, your response might be, 'Yes, I have five minutes, but that's really all I have at the moment. Do you think that will be enough?'
- You may work in an informal service, where clients or colleagues ask for your time without warning. You will need to learn to say, 'I'm busy right now, but I can talk with you this afternoon at 2.30.' You may prefer other words such as 'involved with', 'fully booked until' or other alternatives.
- If your service has an appointments system, then clients should know the time of their slot and how long they will have. It is a fair expectation that clients should arrive on time, but it is equally fair that they expect to see you promptly and not be left waiting.
- If you see clients more than once, then you should discuss at the first session when you will next meet or, if appropriate, how many times you will need to meet. You might suggest (and the client agrees) that you will book in, say, three meetings at given dates and times. Alternatively, it might make sense to say that you can offer more sessions, but that the client can make a decision about taking up that offer at the end of the first session.

privacy

It is not appropriate to use counselling skills in the corner of a busy room or reception area, nor to depend on snatched conversations in hallways. Your time with a client should not be interrupted for anything less than a genuine emergency. So you need to ensure that you and a client are not interrupted, either by the telephone or colleagues sticking heads around the door. If you allow such interruptions, you communicate disrespect to the client – that other activities take priority over your attention to him or her.

- Use a suitable space appropriate for counselling and freed from distractions.
- If necessary, switch your telephone through to someone else or place it on answerphone mode with the shortest number of rings and the sound turned low.
- Put a 'Do not disturb' or 'Occupied' notice on the outside of the door.
- You will need to speak firmly with colleagues who act as if clients are always interruptible.

It is unethical to encourage clients to talk if you do not have the time to listen properly. It is your responsibility to create a more realistic schedule, as hard as this may be, because it is unfair to raise expectations of attention to the client that you cannot fulfil.

figure **6.2**   **privacy**

expectations and assumptions

Clients will come to you with some prior expectations about the way in which you will help them. At the beginning of your first conversation you need to manage clients' expectations, to give some idea of how you will behave in the helping role.

listening and talking with the client

Clients may expect you to tell them what to do or that you will direct them with a series of questions. Clients' assumptions about your behaviour as a helper will emerge throughout your conversation and you can deal with issues as they arise. It would be unrealistic to try to lay every assumption to rest at the beginning. However, at the outset it is useful to explain your approach in brief.

You might say something like, 'I want to understand what is happening from your point of view and then we'll talk together about what might help.' Depending on what clients have said to you or the way in which they approached you, you might say, 'Let's start with you telling me about your current issue and how you feel about it. I'll be in a better position to help you if I understand what's going on.' You may even wish to discuss the four-stage model with your client, so that the process is clear and shared.

the conversation is confidential

Clients may have differing expectations about the boundaries of the conversation. Some may fear that you will repeat everything to colleagues or report back to the client's doctor, employer or whoever has made the referral. On the other hand, some clients may believe or hope that you can keep secrets, even if what they tell you means that someone else is at serious risk.

In most organisations there will be some limits to how complete the confidentiality can be. You need to explain the situation briefly to clients before they disclose personal information (see also page 11).

assumptions that become clear later

You cannot realistically explore all assumptions before you start to listen and talk with clients. Your contracting should not last for ages and some clients will not express their expectations at the beginning. They may feel that questioning what you are likely to do will be impolite. Alternatively, clients may wait to see how you interact with them before stopping you with, 'But I thought what would happen is ..', or, 'When are you going to start helping me?' In some cases, clients may not be clear that they have expectations of what you will do until you obviously are not behaving in that way.

At any point in a helpful exchange, be ready to deal with clients' assumptions and expectations, because they have become important here and now. You might remind clients of the conversation you had at the very beginning, explain how you work when clients did not understand, or maybe listen and explore, as necessary, how clients expect you to help and how they view themselves in this process. Certainly, though, it is a good idea to spend some time contracting and reaffirming expectations at the end of each stage. The coming together of the diamonds indicates a point to take stock and to ensure that helper and client are working together to a shared agenda.

Many of these points are equally applicable to contracting in group work (see Chapters 10 and 11).

ACTIVITY

1 Practise a few sentences that could set the scene when you start to talk with a client. How will you address:

▶ Practical issues?
▶ Your approach to helping?
▶ Confidentiality?

2 Consider how you could reply to clients' assumptions expressed in the following examples.

▶ 'Aren't you going to tell me what to do?'
▶ 'What kind of things do you want me to say?'
▶ 'My friend said you were good at sorting out what was the matter with children.'
▶ 'You're the expert, you tell me what I should do about . . .'
▶ 'You've got to help me.'
▶ 'When are you going to give me some ideas about what to do?'
▶ 'I've been to people like you before. I don't know why I've bothered, you won't understand.'

reluctant clients

It may become clear early on that some clients are not confident that you will be able to help. Clients may have been encouraged, even pushed, to talk with you. In some settings, you may find that clients are told they have to come to you ('I've been sent'), for instance school pupils may be left in little doubt that they should keep the appointment that has been made for them. You will need to address issues with colleagues in the broader setting, if you become aware of pressure on potential clients. However, there is no need to abandon the session just because a client is less than enthusiastic.

You need to acknowledge clients' reservations as they show them and then open the door to the possibility that their time could be well spent with you. For instance:

› To a reluctant 14-year-old student, you might say, 'I hear what you say, Marsha. That Mr Arkwright told you to come, that it wasn't your choice. On the other hand, I understand there's a long-running problem with your Maths teacher. You've got 30 minutes of my time and my job is to listen to your side of it. And I don't report back to Mr Arkwright.'
› To an angry young man who has diabetes and is careless about his medication, you might say, 'I know that talking won't take your diabetes away. But talking with me, and me listening to you, might help you to deal with what you feel diabetes is doing to your life.'

You may work with clients who have first been seen by a colleague or referred by another part of your organisation. It can be useful, and sometimes crucial, to know how your part of the service is described. What do colleagues, or other people, say to anyone whom they think could benefit from your counselling skills? How do they start to shape the potential clients' expectations of you? For example:

› A counsellor available for parents of newborn infants realised that the ward staff described his work as being 'with problem families'. The medical team did not use this phrase in direct conversation with parents, but they said it within the parents' hearing. The ward team meant that the counsellor helped 'families who had any kind of worries about or problems with their newborns'. However, the shorthand 'problem families' gave a negative message to parents who would have welcomed a chance to talk.
› A psychologist involved with several children's centres realised that the teams described her work in different ways. The practitioners in one centre highlighted parents' problems with phrases like, 'Trish is good with difficult children', or, 'You need to talk with someone when you can't cope.' Other centres gave more positive and inclusive messages like, 'We find it helps to bounce ideas off Trish and she's here for parents as well.'

Do your clients pass through even an informal referral system to reach you?

▷ How do your colleagues, or any other involved parties, describe your work to potential clients? What do they call you, by title or informal description?

▷ Take the opportunity to ask and listen to how others introduce you into the conversation.

▷ In what ways could a different introduction through others create a more positive start or accurate expectations for the client?

Several good gateways exist on the Web that focus on counselling. These include:

▷ www.intute.ac.uk/socialsciences (and /psychology) offers thousands of high quality resources, selected by academic librarians and subject specialists.

▷ www.psywww.com/resource/selfhelp.htm is a gateway to a huge number of self-help resources on a big range of health and psychological disorders.

The UK's leading advocate association for counselling professionals is the British Association for Counselling and Psychotherapy (www.bacp.co.uk). This site offers the opportunity to find a therapist accredited by BACP, a listing of specific helplines, as well as its own divisions targeting such areas as counselling at work, children and young people and pastoral/spiritual care.

publications

The Skilled Helper: A Problem-management and Opportunity Development Approach to Helping (8th edn) by Gerald Egan (Wadsworth, 2006). This is the most recent version of *The Skilled Helper*, with Egan and ourselves sharing the same philosophy of helping.

For overall coverage of the various approaches we recommend:

▷ *Theory and Practice of Counselling and Therapy* (4th edn) by Richard Nelson-Jones (Sage, 2005). This is a comprehensive introduction to all of the major therapeutic approaches. It uses a common structure for each approach, hence the book allows easy comparison between them.

▷ *Handbook of Individual Therapy* (4th edn) edited by Windy Dryden (Sage, 2002).

Standards and Ethics for Counselling in Action, (2nd edn) by Tim Bond (Sage, 2000) focuses on the counsellor's responsibility to the client and explores issues of confidentiality, respect for the client's freedom to choose as well as avoiding client exploitation.

understanding and extending the perspective of clients

7.1 Stage One: using counselling skills to understand clients

empathy

Nobody can help by jumping to conclusions, so your entire aim at this stage is to manage, as far as possible, to look through the client's eyes.

▸ What is the difficulty, confusion or hard choice from her point of view? How is it affecting her life; how does she see it all?
▸ Where does he want to start? What is he ready to talk about at the moment and what does he think is important?

Stage One counselling skills build empathy. The term 'empathy' means the state of feeling *with* someone, of being in tune with their viewpoint, seeing the world through their eyes.

Empathy is *not* the same as sympathy. If you feel sympathetic towards someone, you feel for them and maybe sorry for them or agree that life is rough. You can feel sympathy for someone and not understand much of how he or she experiences the situation. In contrast, you can feel empathy with another individual if you have taken the time to listen and to explore with the whole objective of understanding better the feel of this person's world. Building empathy does not necessarily take hours of time. If you focus on a client, then you remove the background noise of how you would feel in this situation, what would be the main problem for you or possible ideas to suggest. Most clients will experience that they have your full attention and will talk. You will learn a great deal about this individual's perspective in a relatively short period of time.

basic understanding

You have three aims within Stage One of using counselling skills. To:

- Understand your client's perspective
- Show to your client that you are working to understand his or her frame of reference
- Help clients to become more concrete about their concern or problem.

In Stage One you work to understand, and show the client that you have noticed and understood, this individual client's experiences, behaviour and feelings. You let the client know that you understand what he or she has explicitly told or shown to you. At this point, you should not try to probe into what the client is half-saying or implying. Stay with what he or she has chosen to share with you. By listening and exploring in a respectful way, you gain the understanding and earn the right to look deeper in Stage Two through skills that support advanced understanding (see page 158).

You work within basic understanding by showing the qualities of warmth, respect and genuineness that are discussed on page 126. Your careful use of the Stage One skills also communicates these qualities through:

- Attending, including listening and looking carefully.
- Being genuine – showing a match between what you say and do.
- Reflecting back and paraphrasing.
- Helping the client to be specific, to share examples of experiences or reactions
- Summarising.
- Careful use of questions.

The following rules of thumb will guide your use of the skills:

- Attend carefully all the time to the messages communicated by word and body language by your client.
- Listen especially for the basic messages, rather than giving energy to thinking, 'I wonder what she really means by that.' Focus on changes in emphasis and energy from the client to help flag his or her key issues.
- Respond to your client fairly frequently and keep your responses fairly brief. If you speak for too long, the balance of talking passes from the client to you and you then have to work to pass the focus back to the client.
- Be flexible and tentative so that the client has room to move: to agree, deny, explain, add more or shift the emphasis.
- Be gentle but not so much that the client remains vague, rambles or consistently avoids following through on issues or topics that she or he raised in the first place.
- Respond to the feelings communicated by words as well as the specific content, unless there is a good reason for emphasising one over the other.
- After you have responded, attend carefully to clues from the client to confirm or deny the accuracy of your response. Some clients will tell you clearly,

'That's not what I meant', or, 'No, you're not getting my point here', others may not.

- Make a mental note of apparent stress or resistance from clients. Time will tell whether these are because your response was inaccurate or uncomfortably accurate.
- Move gradually to the exploration of what emerge as key topics or feelings for this client.

CASE STUDY: AN EXAMPLE OF POOR PRACTICE

A year after Thomas's death (see the case study on page 124), Olivia was offered counselling within her health practice. Her GP was aware that Olivia had difficulty in coming to terms with her loss and continued to miss Thomas deeply. She agreed to see the clinic counsellor, feeling that perhaps she could be helped by someone outside her family, who were very supportive but in distress themselves.

Olivia was uncertain how to talk in the counselling session and the male counsellor said very little initially, leaving Olivia uncertain about whether he understood what she was saying or somehow believed she was making a fuss about nothing. At one point he asked her, 'Why do you think you are so upset?' She replied, 'Because I loved my husband very much', and felt that the counsellor looked surprised, as if older people should not have such feelings. The counsellor started to tell Olivia that she was going through particular 'phases of bereavement' and suggested that she was 'in denial' at the moment. Olivia said she was not denying her loss, 'I know my husband is dead. He died in my arms.' The counsellor went silent at that point.

Eventually, Olivia asked the counsellor if he had lost someone very close to him. She felt he simply did not understand the feelings she had expressed. His response was non-committal and Olivia decided there was no point in continuing with the session. The counsellor gave her a leaflet on bereavement and she later realised from the wording that he had been reading aloud from this leaflet to her during part of the session. The poor quality of Olivia's session not only increased her distress but it led her not to seek any further outside help because, 'If that's counselling, I don't want any more of it'.

comments

It is crucial that any organisation that offers use of counselling skills to clients is effectively monitored so that the quality of the service is ensured.

- In what ways does your service prepare and support helpers who offer counselling skills?
- What additional training is given to enable helpers to support clients in distressing situations such as bereavement?

attending

Careful attention uses your senses of vision and hearing (see page 32). You need to listen carefully to what the client says, trying your very best not to label or interpret what you hear. Accuracy is key. You also need to be alert to the client's body language which can convey vital messages alongside the words:

- Active listening is hard work, because all your attention is on the other person's experiences and expressed feelings. You need to quieten your internal dialogue that otherwise will distract.

- Listening, combined with the other skills of Stage One, communicates respect for the other person. It is a reliable way to prevent swift assumptions such as, 'It's this kind of problem, then.'
- As well as the actual words, also listen to how the client speaks and the feelings that emerge through tone of voice, choice of words and emphasis. These are usually more valuable in fully understanding the client's perspective.
- Use the evidence of your eyes, noticing the client's body language and how it may change with what is said. At an early stage of talking with a client, you will make a mental note of your observations. Sometimes it may be appropriate to share them with the client but only tentatively (see page 157).
- It is just as important not to draw conclusions about body language alone as it is not to depend just on spoken words. If a client's body language suggests to you that she is tense about the issue she has raised, you file this in your mind as a possibility, not a certainty.
- You cannot just listen and look in a helping session. You will have to say something yourself as well. The other skills of Stage One will help you to make appropriate responses within the helping conversation.

helping yourself to attend

How you sit when you speak with a client can help you to attend and also show a client that you are focusing on him or her. Ideally, remove any barriers between you, like tables, and sit at the same level. SOLER is a shorthand used to describe a good attending position. The letters stand for:

- Square: sit facing the client, square on. If your seating arrangements mean that you have to sit slightly to one side, then make sure that you turn well towards the client.
- Open: use your body language to communicate that you are open to what the client has to say. Avoid crossing your legs and arms in any way that shuts down on your body. If you do not know what to do with your hands, experiment with holding them in your lap or on each side of you.
- Lean forward: as you sit, lean slightly towards the client. If you lean back in your chair, you may communicate reserve, trying to create a distance between you and the client or an inappropriate laid-back outlook. If you lean too far forward, clients may feel you are invading their personal space, or placing pressure on them. Leaning forward is the body language equivalent of 'Come on, tell me!' A useful rule of thumb is that the top of your back should not be touching your chair.
- Eye contact: looking does not mean staring, which can be disconcerting for clients. The best approach is to make regular direct eye contact with the client and to break that contact occasionally, best by looking down.
- Relax: within an attentive posture, that avoids distracting gestures, try to relax. Really this is about not being immovable, wooden and holding a pose.

This suggestion can feel hard at the outset but with practice you will be able to have an attentive posture and be relaxed. Finally, like everyone, you need to become aware of your own habits, such as fiddling with your hair that may distract the client as evidence of a lack of attention. You may be unaware of such mannerisms, so remain open to feedback from colleagues or friends (see also page 41).

listening and assumptions

It does not matter how experienced you become in using your counselling skills, you will never become a mind reader. Careful listening, combined with the other Stage One skills, is the only safe, practical way to avoid making assumptions about what a client is about to say or the meaning that she or he places on an event. For instance:

> You know that Nathan's son was recently involved in a road traffic accident. You assume that he wants to talk with you about how Michael is coping with his injuries and the aftermath of the accident. By listening, you quickly realise that Michael is coping well. Nathan is worried about his other son, Jamie, who witnessed his younger brother's accident. Jamie has flashbacks and nightmares and tries to keep Michael safe from harm in ways that are seriously annoying to his brother.

> Tamar says that 'something awful' happened on the train today. You look expectant and she says, 'This young man offered me his seat.' You are confused about the meaning of this event and reflect back in a neutral way, 'A young man offered you his seat on the train and you felt awful.' Tamar goes on to explain that for her this was a watershed event because she felt the seat was offered to her as 'an older woman.' There have been other recent incidents that have added to Tamar's very mixed feelings about approaching her fortieth birthday.

> Yasmin says to you, 'I think a lot of my problems come from being the youngest of six children.' You hold back your expectation of what being the youngest in a big family means. In your own experience it meant being the last in line, no new clothes and very few photographs of you in the family album. Yasmin continues with, 'I look back now and I can see that I was completely spoiled. There were ten years between me and my next brother. Everybody indulged me: Mum, Dad, all my older brothers and sisters. It was lovely at the time but . . .'

| TO THINK ABOUT

As you practise your Stage One counselling skills, after a session make a personal note of the times when you successfully hold back on your assumptions and what the client tells you is very different from what you were expecting. Be pleased with yourself for not jumping in with your own assumptions.

As with any notes about your use of counselling skills, ensure that you keep such records in a secure and confidential way.

One helpful pattern of response is to reflect back to the other person what you have just heard. Sometimes, but not always, you will reflect back almost the client's exact words. On other occasions you put the ideas or reactions into your own words, because continuous repetition sounds odd and is likely to irritate clients. However, you should not add your own words to change a client's meaning so that what is said makes more sense to you.

There are a number of different ways to start a paraphrase of what the other person has told you. For example:

> 'You are finding it hard/frustrating/tiring to deal with . . .'
> 'So, what happened was that . . .'
> 'You're pleased that . . . but you wish that . . .'
> 'You sound very excited about the prospect of . . .'
> 'You say you are uneasy about . . .'
> 'You were telling me earlier about . . .' (when a topic has been left, possibly unfinished)
> 'If I've got it right, you most want that . . .'
> 'Can I see if I understand you? You started to . . . but then . . .'
> 'So far, you've managed to . . .'

You can reflect back to clients what they have said about experiences, what they did in a particular situation and how they felt. When clients voice their feelings, it is appropriate to reflect them back because those emotions have been shared with you. Listen for nuances in what clients say and acknowledge mixed emotions that take clients in two directions at once, for instance:

> 'It sounds as if you've got mixed feelings about the promotion. Part of you is excited at the prospect, but you're also wary about the increased workload.'
> 'Sometimes you're half-pleased that your parents say "no" to your plans and then at other times you're annoyed about their interference.'
> 'You're fond of your cousin and you feel a strong sense of loyalty to her, but you still think she's put you in a difficult position over this secret.'

You should reflect back with some caution, especially as you are learning about the client and not delivering an instant interpretation. You should not overdo the tentative phrases or else you will sound too doubtful, but there are times to use expressions like:

> 'It seems . . .'
> 'It looked like . . .'
> 'I think . . .'
> 'Perhaps . . .'

- 'So what you seem to be feeling is . . .'
- 'I sense you feel that . . .'

You can also, with care, reflect back what the other person is telling you through body language combined with what the client has said. You should not reflect back your observations of non-verbal communication until the client is relatively comfortable with you. Some people are unnerved by the idea that their body betrays feelings and reactions that they have chosen not to voice out loud. Examples of a careful comment could be:

- 'When you were telling me about your neighbour, you shivered. It seems that Tuesday's incident has left you very uneasy.'
- 'You looked so pleased when you told me about your media project with Jamal. You and he seem to be getting along better now.'

At Stage One in a helping relationship, you should only reflect back to clients what they have said or clearly shown you. As the conversation progresses, you may feel justified in taking a considered guess, even if the feeling words are not said by the client. You have to have a good reason, from what you have heard and seen, to step even a little further than what the client says. It is not your role in Stage One to probe under the surface of what has been said.

A NOTE ABOUT WHAT YOU SAY

Some courses on basic counselling skills start by telling participants to use a specific phrase as their response to clients during the course practice, usually organised with other participants as clients. The phrases told to us have included, 'What I hear you saying is . . .', and, 'How do you feel about that?' Some people with whom we have spoken had emerged with the idea that they could only ever use this single phrase in talking with clients. They said that such an approach was rigid and could never appear as genuine to clients. We agreed completely with them, though, presumably, the course tutors had not intended this result.

In teaching basic counselling skills we sometimes restrict participants to a limited choice of phrases in the early stage of learning. We have found that this temporary measure helps people to resist their own personal biases and to focus on the client. When people have learned to be still, to listen and to rein in their desire to question, interpret or be supportive, then they are ready to drop the interim restrictions on what they say.

reflection to help clients be more specific

Unless clients are able to talk through their concerns in a fairly specific way, the discussion stays at a vague level. You have two main ways of helping clients to become more concrete about their concerns: the skills of reflecting back and questioning (see page 47).

finding 'I'

Sometimes it is useful to restate what the client has said in more specific terms. Many people use their words, at least sometimes, to distance themselves from what is happening; their 'I' becomes lost in the words they say. You may experience some clients who frequently take this approach. For example:

- 'Anyone would be upset when . . .'
- 'It's so annoying when he . . .'
- 'You feel worthless when your husband does this kind of thing.'
- 'I know one shouldn't feel this way, of course, but . . .'
- 'People shouldn't do this to you.'
- 'We're all fed up about . . .'

You could reflect these examples back in a way to bring out the client as the 'I' in the statement: by using slight changes, for instance:

- 'You feel upset about . . .'
- 'You feel annoyed when he . . .'
- 'When Greg contradicts what you've said to the children, you feel like you're worthless.'
- 'You feel angry with your mother and you believe as well that you shouldn't feel this way.'
- 'You feel sure that your supervisor should not go through your files without asking you.'
- 'You feel fed up and you believe that the rest of the team share your feelings.'

Sometimes clients describe a situation in a way that places the emphasis on other people, for instance:

- 'She should stop . . .'
- 'They've got no business . . .'
- 'He should understand that . . .'
- 'They shouldn't make me feel . . .'
- 'Don't you think it would be better if I . . .?'

You could paraphrase these comments with:

- 'You'd like Anna to stop interrupting you in meetings.'
- 'You feel that your neighbours should not ask you to wait in for their deliveries because you're at home.'
- 'You'd rather that Damian understood that . . .', or, 'You believe it would make a difference if Damian understood that . . .'
- 'When your parents ask if you've done your homework, you feel they're suggesting you can't keep track without being nagged.'
- 'It sounds like you believe it would be better if you . . .'

highlighting choice

Some clients describe situations in such a way that they appear to have no choice or are stuck between two impossible options. They may say:

- 'I can't get up on time. I've always had this problem with punctuality.'
- 'I have to keep the shared kitchen clean, it's disgusting otherwise.'
- 'You have to learn to be hard or else other people take advantage of you.'
- 'What's the point, I know it's not going to work out.'
- 'I want to lose weight but I've always eaten too much.'
- 'I'd like to stop smoking but I can't.'

You could paraphrase each example with:

- 'You find it hard to get up on time and so you're often late.'
- 'You believe that if you don't clean the kitchen, nobody else will.'
- 'You feel you have no choice but to be hard with other people.'
- 'You believe this idea can't work.'
- 'You want to lose weight and you think you eat too much.'
- 'You want to stop smoking and you find it hard', or the tougher version, 'You want to stop smoking and you choose not to stop.'

When clients use words like 'can't', 'won't', 'have to', 'ought to' or 'should', they are telling you that they feel some sense of compulsion or of having no real choice. A similar message comes when they join together two thoughts with 'but' rather than 'and'. Changing the words in your paraphrase (as in the last two examples above) highlights the nature of the issue and helps the client to see more clearly the meaning of what she or he has said. Words do not, of course, provide a resolution. Some problems are genuinely difficult to resolve. Clients may also be faced with a dilemma, in which they are torn between two equally unpleasant, or pleasant, alternatives (see page 175).

remember what you have noticed

At Stage One in a helping conversation, you would highlight the client's approach through reflecting back only. Some clients will be more alert to your use of words than others, will listen, stop and think about what they have said and how they talk about this issue. You should not in any sense pursue clients to acknowledge what you have noticed. If clients do not react to your paraphrase, then hold this perspective in your mind, because it may be useful to return to it further in the conversation or in another session. In Stage Two, it will be appropriate to explain what you have noticed about how this client views the problem, with the encouragement to consider this alternative perspective.

Listen to your own use of words as you talk or think about issues and problems in your own life. Experiment with restating comments to yourself and experience how the change of words may give an alternative perspective. For instance:

▶ Practise making 'I' statements out of comments that distance you from an issue – even simple ones like 'It's hot today'. Become aware of the ways that you distance yourself. Do you use 'you', 'people', 'it's' or any of the other ways with words from page 151?

▶ When you face a situation that appears to have few alternatives, try rethinking 'I can't' into 'I don't want to' or 'I choose not to'.

▶ Perhaps you are someone who often says or thinks, 'He makes me feel . . .', or, 'They shouldn't . . .'. Try replacing those phrases with, 'When he . . . I feel . . .', or, 'I should . . .'.

summarising

A good summary is brief and includes not only the facts and the words, but also the feelings that clients have expressed. For example:

▸ 'So, Phil regularly submits his reports at least a week late. You sound annoyed by this, Angie, like it's getting you down.'

▸ 'You've realised that Jamie has frequent nightmares and what sound like flashbacks about his brother's accident. You're sure that Jamie feels responsible for the accident, although you've reassured your son many times that it wasn't his fault. And you feel confused and frustrated, because your family doctor believes that Michael is the only one who should need help, because he was the one injured.'

Put the ideas or descriptions at least partly into your own words. The language should still be primarily in the words, particularly the emotional ones, used by the client.

It is especially important to summarise the main points if the client shifts to another topic, or when the conversation or session is coming to an end. The summary affirms that you have understood and helps the client to focus on the main points as she or he has expressed them. Summaries are also important to link several elements of the problem together, as you and the client move towards a conclusion at the end of Stage One about what the client sees as the issue.

careful use of questions

You can help clients by encouraging them to explore the issue in more detail and to become more specific about elements of the situation. Any questions should be asked within the client's framework and not because of your particular interests or curiosity. Questions have to be used with care, since a long sequence of questions can feel like an interrogation.

The more useful questions are open-ended rather than closed (see also page 48). You invite the other person to explore and explain, rather than give you a one-word or very short answer. For instance:

- 'Would you like to say some more about how you see the possibilities in your career?'
- 'What happened then?'
- 'How did you feel about that?'
- 'Could you give me an example of that?'
- 'What decided you to do that?'
- 'You've gone quiet, would you like to tell me what you're thinking?'
- 'I understand that you're worried about your teenage daughter. Tell me a bit more about what is making you so worried.'

Clients who have been on the receiving end of a great deal of unsolicited advice from friends or family may never have been asked for their opinion of the situation. You could ask:

- 'What do you think is going on with your child's night waking?'
- 'How do you think . . . has come about?'

Clients may be quiet for a moment as they consider their own views and beliefs. Leave a silence so that they can work through their response. They may also feel pleased that you have shown respect in asking for and listening to their views, and waiting for their answer.

rephrasing 'why' questions

Questions that start with 'why' tend to be less useful because they guide clients towards a justification of their position or trying to think up a reason to satisfy you because you appear to want an explanation.

- Instead of, 'Why did you get so angry about . . .?', you could reflect back with, 'You became very angry when . . .'. Or ask, 'What do you think made you so angry about . . .?'
- Often the words 'what for' are an improvement over 'why'. For example, instead of 'Why do you think your son locks himself in his room?', ask, 'What do you think your son locks himself in his room for?' The 'why' question more often brings responses like, 'To stop me getting in', or, 'Because he's a pain.' The 'what for' question is more likely to encourage the client to consider a new angle, and to bring responses like, 'Perhaps to get some privacy', or, 'I suppose he doesn't know what else to do when we've all got so angry.'
- Instead of 'Why do you think Alric's drinking is a problem?', you can ask, 'How does Alric's drinking affect your life?' In addition, this last example helps to keep the discussion focused on the client who is present. You can

only counsel the person who is with you, not his or her absent partner, friend or colleague.

helping clients to be more specific

Some clients will be more concrete in how they talk than others. As you listen, you may have a clear visual image of what the client has experienced and why it troubles him or her. On the other hand, some clients talk more in the abstract and you are left feeling uncertain about what she or he means in practice. It can be helpful to invite the other person to give specific examples or more description of a given event. For example:

▸ 'Lucy, you say that your mother interferes with how you bring up the children. Can you give me an example?'
▸ 'You've told me that sometimes your confidence seems to disappear when you face your boss. You used the phrase, "I feel frozen". Can you describe to me the most recent time this happened to you?' Or you might ask, 'What does "frozen" mean to you?'

Both of the above examples have placed a question after a reflection or paraphrase of what the client has just said. This approach puts your question in a positive context of exploring what the client has said rather than directing with just a question.

Sometimes you will need to ask a question because you are confused. This is perfectly all right, as you need to understand in order to help. For example, perhaps the client is assuming that you know details of her or his personal life when you do not. For example:

▸ Lindsay, who is nominally Christian, is married to Annop, whose background is Hindu. Lindsay says to you, 'It's the time of year. I always feel down in the autumn. It's because Divali is coming up and I know Annop and I will have a row, however hard I try. I'm so relieved when it's over, but I'm sad too because Divali should be a nice family time, more like I feel that Christmas is. It's the same each year; it's got that I call it my Divali time. But only to myself, of course. Annop only sees it his way, never mine.'

You understand that the celebration of Divali leads to rows between Lindsay and Annop but you are confused about how this happens. If Lindsay seems unlikely to explain, you will need to intervene, for example with, 'Lindsay, I haven't understood what happens around Divali time that is linked with the rows between you and Annop.' Lindsay then explains that Annop is convinced she spends much more time and attention on preparing for Christmas than she does for Divali.

Be alert to situations in which you are on the receiving end of questions from someone else:

▷ What kind of questions help you to explore an issue?

▷ What kind tend to narrow down on the conversation?

▷ How does it feel on the receiving end if another person asks you a whole series of directive questions?

moving on from Stage One

Potential helpers often find Stage One the most difficult in the helping model. The emphasis is on the perspective of the client and you may doubt that you are really doing anything. You may be very tempted to fall back into your personal bias (see page 128), with the result that you will not gain a full understanding. The work you then try to do in the later stages of the model will be less effective because you only understand parts of the client's problem rather than the bigger, more complete picture.

Stage One is complete when:

› Clients have explored their situation thoroughly from how they see it or all they are prepared to discuss at the moment. If clients are starting to circle back to the same issues or information, it is very likely to be time to move on.

› You feel you have a good understanding of the client's situation and concerns.

› Your exploration with the client has led to an agreement between the two of you on the problem or the nature of the choice that the client is facing.

In every case, however, Stage One should be completed with a summary to ensure that you and your client have a shared understanding of what the problem is – and what it is not – from the client's perspective. You may even use the end of Stage One to check whether the client wishes to progress further with the issue or not as appropriate.

Your Stage One exploration with a client does not have a fixed time period. Some helpful conversations may last in total, all stages, for 10–15 minutes; others will stretch over several sessions with the same client. Often, you will move into Stage Two skills with the client within the same conversation. You recognise that the time is ready for a different kind of exploration.

making a choice of priorities

Sometimes clients have to decide which of several possible factors or concerns to take further. Other problems are not dismissed, but you cannot explore everything in detail at the same time. If there are several possibilities, then be guided by your client and help him or her to reach a focus for the next part of your conversation. There is no one right way to choose and you will need to guide clients in the light of your understanding of them and their current situation:

- Some clients can be most highly motivated to explore an issue that they could resolve fairly easily alone. Some clients lack confidence or are just now accepting that they could make a difference. Then their success in understanding a smaller problem will boost their confidence to do some painful thinking about more difficult issues.

- Regardless of difficulty, some clients want and need to face the most pressing problem, or the immediate crisis. They will not be able to concentrate on anything else or what they could learn for the future until they have some sense of facing up to the present. This may encourage you to work on addressing a symptom (such as finding it hard to get up in the morning), rather than the cause (worries about problems at work). Be aware of what you are doing and ready to look at deeper issues when the client is ready.

- The client's best priority is to focus on that part of the problem over which they have some control. For instance, Alastair has told you about his long-standing problems with a colleague. You may have helped Alastair to get through his view of, 'My colleague makes me feel mean if I say "no" to her demands for help', or, 'She should stop interrupting my work'. Alastair has begun to acknowledge that he cannot make the colleague change her behaviour but that he could look at his own reactions, feelings and contribution to the difficult situation – in other words, what Alastair can do to make the situation less difficult and more manageable.

- Clients who have several important concerns may only have given you a hint of their deeper worries. You need to respect the priority they give to an issue with which they feel able to trust you for the time being. Clients may choose to return to a more distressing or confusing issue at a later time. If they do, you will need to return to using Stage One skills to explore this issue and its relationship to your previous discussion in more depth.

You may go through a similar process of helping clients to sort out priorities at the end of Stage Two (see page 174) when you work with them to develop goals for action.

AN EXAMPLE OF STAGE ONE EXPLORATION

Wai is an early years practitioner in a nursery. She is having supervision from Leela and they are discussing Wai's frustrations in her working relationship with Monica, the speech therapist who visits the nursery.

Wai: I can't put my finger on it. Monica's got good ideas. I think she's probably a good speech therapist, but the children don't enjoy her sessions.

Leela: So, you don't have worries about Monica's professional abilities?

Wai: No, I don't – well, except that she doesn't seem to be making much difference to the children! And she was all right about giving me some written suggestions in the end – although I had to remind her twice. You know, Leela, it's funny. None of the children are pleased to see her. I honestly don't think they would go to the sessions if I didn't stay as well.

Leela: You're concerned that the children aren't really happy to be with Monica? That and the fact that you can't see much progress from the sessions?

Wai: Yes. So I think, why are we bothering?

Leela: How did you feel about this week's session with Monica?

Wai: Much the same as always. The children don't warm to her. Could you have a word with her, Leela?

Leela: I'm willing to have a chat with Monica but I really need more to go on. Why don't you talk me through this week's session as you remember it? You've noticed something, so let's see if you can put your finger on it. Help me see the session through your eyes, Wai. So, how did Monica start?

question

▷ What skills does Leela use in this short extract?

▷ Wai has a gut feeling of worry but cannot put her concerns in a concrete, specific way. How does Leela help Wai to get closer to the observations that have fed her concern?

ACTIVITY

During the next couple of weeks, make a conscious effort to use some of the Stage One skills in conversations with colleagues, friends or family.

▷ Focus on your attending skills, listening and looking, in everyday exchanges

▷ Try reflecting back and paraphrasing rather than moving swiftly to give advice or shape up a problem for someone else

▷ Ask open-ended questions rather than closed ones

▷ Sometimes use a summary to check that you have understood what another person has said.

Reflect on what has happened in exchanges and what you have learned.

We would add a cautionary note from our experience of suggesting this kind of activity to a wide range of people. First, the most likely consequence of using Stage One skills is that another person will be encouraged to say more. So, please do not practise your skills unless you have the time to listen. Second, you may receive feedback that surprises you from friends or family. We were told the story of a son who stopped his father in his tracks with, 'Dad, why are you listening to me today?'

personal experience

You may have noticed that there has been no suggestion at Stage One to share your own experiences with clients. There is no way of knowing whether a personal experience is appropriate to share until you have listened well to the client. Your unvoiced experience may support the help you offer, but the emphasis in the relationship must remain with the client.

We do not recommend sharing any personal experience in Stage One unless you really know that your experience directly parallels that of the client, in terms of situation, experience and resulting feelings. In addition, even if all of the above is true, sharing your own experience should only be done tentatively and in the spirit of summarising the client's perceptions from your personal experience. In Stage Two, it is far more likely there will be appropriate opportunities for you to share something personal (see page 165).

Can you recall times when someone else, perhaps with a wish to help, gave you a detailed account of their own experience?

▷ To what extent was it helpful and in what ways unhelpful?
▷ How did you feel if you were told, 'I know exactly how you feel', or, 'The same thing happened to me'?
▷ What can you learn from the times when the recounting of other people's personal experiences created a block for you to talk about your own?

7.2 Stage Two: exploring alternative perspectives

advanced understanding

The objective of Stage Two is to help the client to explore new perspectives. The opening-out phase of Stage Two is possible because you have worked hard to see the situation through the client's eyes. You remain focused on the client and certainly moving into Stage Two does not give you permission to direct clients, or to tell them how they should view the situation or what they should do. All the skills described within Stage One are equally important now, but through giving the client the time to understand their issue fully you have earned the right to use the skills differently and in a stronger way. Unless you build all the elements of basic understanding, showing respect for the client, genuineness and helping the client to be specific, the approaches of Stage Two can be at best unhelpful or at worst destructive to a client's well-being.

By the end of Stage One, you should have a thorough understanding of how the client sees and feels the problem, and have checked that your perception is accurate through the summary. You will neither know nor have heard everything, but you have enough observational information to apply your counselling skills in more advanced ways. You can use reflecting back, summarising and questions in ways which are potentially more challenging to the client. Your use of skills should enable the client to think in new ways, to consider the issues from fresh angles. Stage Two is designed to make the subjective view of the client (gathered in Stage One) more objective and realistic, so that achievable goals to address the issue can be agreed.

Your overall objective is to support clients as they consider other perspectives or acknowledge the importance of experiences, feelings and thoughts of which they may be scarcely aware. You are not implying that the client is wrong, just understandably focused on his or her own point of view.

put into words what the client implies

You are only justified in putting the implication into words on the basis of all that you have heard from your client. Perhaps you attempt to express ideas or experiences that have emerged in a confused way from the client. On the basis of all you have heard and noticed, you start to express what clients have not yet said for themselves. For example:

- 'Lucy, you sound torn. I understand that you feel your mother interferes. Yet she sometimes has a good idea – like her suggestion about Alan's eating. It sounds as if you are wary of going with the good ideas because that will make her think she's right about everything.'
- Maryam has spent several conversations with Amy, who is Davy's mother. Amy has wanted to talk about the local primary schools 'so that I can make a good decision', but Maryam has noticed that Amy finds something wrong with all the schools. Amy has also talked sadly about how much she will miss coming to the family centre. Maryam says warmly, 'Amy, I think that a lot of what you're feeling is about leaving here. The decision about schools is important but perhaps it would help to talk about these other feelings. You and Davy have been coming to the centre for a long time.'

making links within the client's disjointed information

Often clients express thoughts, describe events or give hints about personal dilemmas in a disjointed way. Even clients who are confident with their words will not necessarily present a tidy version. It is not a client's role to provide a neat flow of what they wish to communicate; it is your job to help them to sort out the various themes and issues.

Your skills in providing a summary are particularly useful when information has emerged in a fragmented way. Your summary is more extensive or deeper in terms of addressing feelings than in Stage One. For example:

- 'So, you're weighing up several issues that sound as if they are equally important to you, Helen. You want to extend your skills, particularly in information technology. You are undecided whether you get on a part-time course or give up work for a full-time one. Your husband, Robert, has been offered a job in America and you have both always wanted to go there. And neither of you wants to postpone having a family for much longer. Ideally, you would like all these things, but you know they can't all happen at once.'

Under these circumstances it can sometimes help to write down the main points. Offer the client this possibility before you pick up a pen or offer one to the client. Writing down can shift the atmosphere of the exchange, so be sure that it is suitable for the topic and stage of the conversation. For example:

- Saira has been helping Paresh with his study skills in general and with his upcoming student project in particular. Paresh has found it especially difficult to organise all the separate parts of his project. He uses phrases like, 'I'm drowning in the details', and, 'There so much that's possible, I don't know where to start'. Saira suggests that it is exactly the wealth of detail that is central to Paresh's problem at the moment. Paresh agrees they will write down the main headings to get his project into a more manageable shape.

highlight themes and consequences

Sometimes, your attentive listening will suggest that a theme runs through experiences that the client has described. You have listened and contributed in a positive way so that you can see possible connections and consequences. Stage Two is the time to share your observation with the client. You can be helpful so long as you remain tentative, with no sense of, 'It's obvious that . . ', or, 'I'm surprised you haven't realised that . . .' You show respect to the client and leave him or her with space to consider when you describe any theme rather than label the client. For instance:

› You may be able to suggest tentatively, 'Do you see the possible pattern here? You've talked with me about three people: your father, your boyfriend and your colleague. You ask each of them for advice and then you argue whether or not their view is different from yours. You seem to want confirmation of your own view but you're unwilling to volunteer it.'

On occasion, clients talk about issues that are potentially linked as if there is no connection at all. Perhaps recognising the connection may be uncomfortable or lead the client towards a need for action that she or he would rather avoid. For example:

› Sally has had a long conversation with Liam, Sean's father. Liam had wanted to talk about Sean's rough approach to the other children and Sally was pleased since the reception class team have been concerned. Liam is worried that Sean wets the bed and is very upset whenever he has to stay with his grandparents because Liam has a weekend shift. Liam then mentions almost in passing, 'Sean's mother walked out at Christmas. I thought you might wonder why you never see her now.' Sally expresses sympathy and asks a few questions about how Liam is managing with his shift work. She then offers, 'Liam, have you considered that Sean's behaviour may be a reaction to his Mum going?' Liana looks thoughtful, 'It crossed my mind but my mother said that Sean would soon forget all about his Mum if we didn't mention her.' Sally replies with, 'I wouldn't say that has been my experience. Children don't forget that easily.'

Often you can help the client to draw conclusions from what he or she is describing. For example:

› 'You've spoken about arguments with your wife, who you feel is strong and independent. You've also shared issues around working with your new female boss, and problems with your teenage daughter. Is there a pattern here of difficulties with women?'

These may or may not be firm conclusions but a helper can encourage the client to take the issue that bit further. On occasion this carries the sense of, 'Do you see where this approach is leading you? Is that where you want to be?' For instance:

› Moira has spent time with Wesley, whose main concern is to feel more confident. Wesley has talked in detail about how he was so disheartened by criticism from his new art teacher. Wesley dismisses this teacher as a poor artist, yet claims, 'He has destroyed my confidence.' Moira replies, 'Wesley, it sounds as if you're making the opinion of one person, whom you say you don't respect, carry more weight than your previous teacher. Let alone your family who you tell me all admire your artistic ability. Are you really prepared to stop painting because of this one man?'

› Six weeks ago Jane was mugged by someone who ran up behind her on a dark winter afternoon, grabbed her bag and sped off down the street. Jane was very shaken although otherwise unhurt. She prides herself on being able to cope and not worrying anyone else, especially her children. She has not told her daughters about the mugging but her silence has led to some problems. Her older daughter has asked why Jane is no longer using the special pen that was a birthday present from the child. (The pen was stolen with the bag.) Yesterday, Jane reacted dramatically when a jogger ran up behind her and the two girls. She yanked both daughters behind her in a protective gesture and it was impossible for her to hide her fright. In conversation with you, Jane has regularly used phrases like, 'I have to be strong for the girls', and, 'I can't possibly tell them I was mugged. They'll be frightened to go out.' You make the decision to confront some of Jane's convictions with, 'Jane, you say you "can't" tell the girls because "they'll be frightened". But from your description of what happened last night, I'd guess that they know that you're frightened, but not why. We've discussed your choice not to tell them about the mugging, what you felt were the advantages of keeping silent. Perhaps we should talk now about the disadvantages of your silence and some reasons why your daughters need to understand what has happened to you.'

offering other perspectives

Helping is hard work because it requires you to focus on what clients have expressed, in the way that they first wish to express it. Because you have listened, you will now have the basis for offering different views of the issue.

› Morag is trying hard to resolve competing demands: 'I want to give nothing but my best to my job but I can't bear the thought that I might neglect my own family. And I believe so strongly that women should find some time for themselves.' Perhaps it is not possible for Morag to give 100 per cent to everything, and this could be a useful perspective to offer her.

> Andrew organises his life around a goal that he has never questioned: 'I must keep any money problems to myself; I mustn't worry my wife with that.' You may offer another perspective with a comment such as, 'What makes you so certain that you must keep money worries to yourself? What leads you to be so sure that your wife wouldn't rather know? Have you checked? Perhaps she would rather help with the problem.' This intervention has to be offered as a perspective because Andrew may be right, perhaps his wife does not want to know or will panic to such a degree that he will be unable to deal with the problem. You are not saying Andrew should tell his wife; you are offering the space for him to think through the possibility of telling her.

Offering alternative views can also include checking to see whether other people share the same view as your client. For example:

> Matthew has talked extensively about how he is irritated by his dictatorial manager, Pat, and how he feels that his contribution is not rewarded. You might ask, 'Do your colleagues who report to Pat feel the same way as you?' If they do not, this can provide a helpful avenue of exploration, around differences in the way that Matthew and his colleagues work with Pat to give him a new perspective on the issue.

AN EXAMPLE OF USE OF SKILLS DURING STAGE TWO

Kevin (the centre manager) is in the middle of a supervision session with Cathy (a team member).

Kevin: You say that Jon dominates team meetings and won't let you talk. But Cathy, I want you to think over yesterday's meeting. I recall at least three occasions when Jon asked you what you thought. I don't think you replied at any of those times.

Cathy: I don't think it was three times. Once at the most. Well, maybe twice.

Kevin: Okay, let's follow the theme that Jon does sometimes make space for you to talk and you choose not to speak up. What do you think is going on here?

Cathy: If he wasn't so pushy most of the time then I might. It's more his fault than mine.

Kevin: I hear what you're saying about Jon's approach but let's focus on your behaviour and your choices. It takes two to tango.

Cathy: He intimidates me.

Kevin: You're saying you feel intimidated by Jon?

Cathy: Yes, he undermines my confidence. I'm frightened to speak up.

Kevin: I saw your expression yesterday, Cathy. I wouldn't have described you as 'frightened'. To be honest, you looked rather pleased with yourself.

Cathy: (silence)

Kevin: Come on, Cathy. We've worked together for long enough. You looked pleased to put Jon in the hot spot.

Cathy: All right, maybe not frightened.

Kevin: Maybe not frightened. What then?

Cathy (after a short silence which Kevin deliberately does not break): You don't know what Jon was like when he first came here. He thought he knew everything! He talked over the top of everybody, wanted to reorganise everything in sight! He's just one team member like the rest of us; he was never in charge.

Kevin: So, there's some history here?

Cathy: Yes, and I suppose he has tried recently. But he was such a pain in the beginning . . .

comment

Notice how Kevin uses skills of reflecting back Cathy's words and asking open-ended questions, but in a stronger way than in Stage One. It is possible to challenge the client in Stage Two, but this should never turn into a relentless pursuit.

This example shows an informed challenge. The way that Kevin frames his contributions communicates a feeling of, 'Cathy, try looking at it this way', and, 'Hold on a minute.' Kevin does not pronounce judgement on Cathy, nor try to come across as if he can read her mind. He has shared with her what he has heard and seen. In a friendly way appropriate to their working relationship, Kevin communicates that he is not going to let Cathy avoid considering a perspective other than the one that makes her feel comfortable and faultless. He helps her to make her own view more realistic and objective. His careful challenge has been combined with support.

challenge or confrontation

Many of the examples given so far for Stage Two have an element of challenge to the client, of an intervention that still shows respect because your contribution is based firmly on what the client has said so far. Sometimes you would alert clients to contradictions in what they say about the same issue or person at different times. At no point would a good helper say bluntly, 'You're defensive!', or, 'You can't make up your mind about . . .'. Your approach is a more respectful, 'Morag, you say that you really love your children, yet you spend most of your leisure time alone.' Your intervention is stronger and more testing of clients than at Stage One yet not driving clients into a corner. Sometimes, it makes sense to create space for the client by tentative phrases like, 'Does this make sense to you?', 'I suggest we look at this angle', or, 'It sounds to me like', and words like 'perhaps', 'possibly'.

Your summaries or questions may also bring to a client's attention what she or he is not saying, or almost says. For instance:

› Freddy asked to talk with you about the recent death of his father. So far, he has spent most of the conversation complaining about how the hospital phoned him in the early hours of the morning with the news of his father's death. Freddy has insisted on discussing this early hours call in an objective and logical way: why would a hospital do this, why wake people up when they can do nothing until daybreak, what do you think about this kind of practice? You have offered reflections and summaries, but your client has resolutely stayed with practical details and now returns to the phone call for the third time. You sense a rerun of the same litany as before and stop the client courteously with, 'Freddy, let's leave to one side whether the hospital should or shouldn't have called you when they did. How did you feel when the hospital sister told you your father had died?'

Respectful and informed challenge of a client, blended with support, can help him or her to think through the unthinkable in a safe environment.

› Joanne has been telling you about the practical difficulties created around her mother's recent heart attack. Bit by bit, it emerges that her mother had been estranged from Joanne in recent months. After a great deal of thought, Joanne had told her family that she was gay and that the person whom her family believed to be a flatmate was in fact her long-term partner. Joanne's father had seemed neither very surprised nor shocked by his daughter's revelation but was angry that the news had upset his wife. He and Joanne's sister have been on the phone, saying that Joanne caused her mother's heart attack and that nothing would have happened if she had had the sense to keep quiet. Joanne says to you, 'They think it's all my fault, that I put Mum in danger.' On the basis of what you have learned of Joanne so far, you sensitively put back to her, 'And what do you think?', or even the more challenging, 'And do you think this has some justification?'

A client may be very resistant to the perspective that she is making a choice, preferring to place the responsibility elsewhere. Perhaps you tried some paraphrases in Stage One (like the examples on page 148) and the client dismissed them with a firm, 'Yes but . . .'. At Stage Two, as your client circles round the same material with the same perspective, you will judge that the time has come to press her. For example:

› 'Natalie, you've told me all about how your neighbour, Rosie, wants to talk with you frequently. I understand how, if you start to say "no" to her at the door, you say Rosie just stands there and "looks pathetic" and you feel you "have to let her in". You're also concerned that your children often can't talk with you when they want and your husband says that he feels "pushed out" of his own kitchen. Perhaps we should look hard at your real choices in this situation. You say that you "have to talk with Rosie" and so she "makes you neglect your children". Let's see this as "you choose to talk with Rosie and so you choose the consequence that your children often can't talk with you because you're giving time and attention to Rosie rather than to them". These things are not isolated, they affect each other.'

Finally, confrontation can be used to help the client to recognise areas of personal strength that are not being used in this situation. For example:

› 'You have shown lots of skills in dealing with subordinates at work. Can any of these skills be used to help address the problems you're having with your nephew?'

There will be some times in helping relationships when it is appropriate for you to contribute a personal experience. This personal experience should demonstrate that you have experienced something very close to your client's experience – direct empathy. You might share briefly what happened to you, how you felt or what you learned from the experience. This contribution should always be done with the objective of helping the client see that you understand their position. For example:

- 'I don't think people understand what months of broken nights are like, unless they've been there. I know I didn't really understand until I had my daughter. People are very quick to give you simple advice as if you haven't tried everything obvious.'
- You might be able to offer a personal insight in the example of Natalie and her neighbour Rosie. For instance, perhaps Natalie says, 'I'm being stupid, aren't I?', and you reply, 'No, I don't think you're being stupid, Natalie. I got myself into what sounds like a very similar situation with my neighbour. I needed to recognise that I was making a choice, not just see it as all down to her. That's one reason why I put this idea of choice to you.'
- Ciaran has been talking about problems in managing his time at the charity for which he works and his outside life. You reply, 'When I was working for another charity, I found that balancing my time between home and work was very difficult – particularly when my caseload got very high. I really felt guilty sometimes, although I knew how many hours I was working. Is that how you feel too?'

positive self-disclosure

There is sometimes a place for contributing your own experience with clients but it will not always be appropriate to self-disclose. Sharing a personal experience will be helpful if you bear in mind the following points:

- Your contribution should be brief. Clients are there to talk about their concerns, not to listen to the details of yours.
- Your shared personal experience should bring into sharper focus what clients think or feel about their own issue and help them to consider other perspectives.
- If you speak for too long or do not link what you are saying to the client's own issue, then he or she may start to ask you about your experience: what happened, what you felt or what you did. In other words, you have moved the entire focus of the discussion inappropriately away from the client.
- Hence, if the client asks direct questions about you, answer briefly before bringing the focus back with, 'Let's explore how you feel about what's happening to you', or, 'So what does that mean for you?'

- You might introduce short personal experiences with tentative phrases like, 'I felt something similar to that when . . ', or, 'I think I had an experience that was like that.' Avoid saying, 'I know exactly how you feel', or, 'The same thing happened to me', because such phrases deny a client's individuality.
- The way that you coped or what you learned may be useful to the client but it is for him or her to see the potentially helpful links. It is not for you to assume that what worked for you will work for the client, any more than what did not work for you will be no use to someone else.

You should never invent experiences similar to those of your client. There is no need to tell untruths or even to modify your experience to sound more like that of the client. If you bend the truth, you will undermine the genuineness of the helping relationship and respect for the client. You need not have had the same experience in order to understand and help your client.

when you have strong feelings

To be helpful to clients you need to remain alert to your own feelings. Sometimes, the experience or problem that you are talking through with a client stirs up your own painful memories. As a responsible helper you need to keep your own experience and any unresolved feelings clearly separate from that of the client. For instance:

- It is crucial that the client does not begin to feel burdened with your distress, confusion or unresolved feelings of anger and frustration.
- It is not the client's role to help you express your feelings; you should talk with somebody else. Keep your feelings separate from those of your client.
- Be very careful not to rerun your experience with the client, perhaps encouraging him or her to take a line of action that you wish you had followed. You should remain objective but you are not perfect and may travel this route a short way before you realise. Stop yourself and bring the client back into sharp focus.
- If all else fails, you may need to refer the client to another helper who will be able to help when you have become unable to apply your skills. Without going into great detail, you should be honest with your client about the reason for referral. Otherwise clients, especially vulnerable ones, may blame themselves for the breakdown of the helping relationship.

dealing with issues in the helping relationship itself

Sometimes it is important to address the relationship itself. You should carefully raise the issue if you judge that you or the client have unspoken thoughts and feelings that are blocking the helping process. You use your counselling skills to address the here and now of the situation in a way that combines elements of self-disclosure (your feelings and perceptions) and informed confrontation (an element of 'Hold on a minute').

The reasons for a client's silence, reservations or short answers will not necessarily be distress. Until you address what is happening, you can only guess. For example:

> Halfway through a careers guidance session, Sejeeven realises that his client David is scarcely talking. This situation is unusual because David usually has plenty to say. Sejeeven addresses the issue directly with, 'David, you've gone quiet. Is there something on your mind?' David pauses and replies, 'It's what you said about a gap year. I didn't realise I could take a break between my A levels and university. I thought you had to keep going. That's why I said what I did about not being sure I wanted to go to university. I said the same thing to my parents; they weren't very pleased at all.' Sejeeven needs to acknowledge David's fresh perspective, perhaps with, 'I'm sorry, David. I hadn't realised you didn't know about gap years. Perhaps that changes how you'd like to talk about your plans.'

> Over the last month in the family centre, Gareth has been helping Effie to talk through her feelings about her son, Cameron, and difficulties in handling his behaviour. Effie has seemed easy with Gareth until the last two sessions, when she started to talk about Cameron's birth and the long-term consequences of her post-natal depression. Gareth feels that Effie is far less happy talking with him on these topics and she does not seem to be getting any more at ease. She has made several comments about it being 'different for men!' So today he raises the issue by saying, 'Effie, I've noticed that recently it seems harder for you to talk with me. You've looked less comfortable since you started to explain about Cameron's birth and what happened to you. Are you still comfortable to continue with me, which would be fine, or would you rather talk with a female practitioner?'

Addressing immediate issues within the helping relationship is placed within Stage Two because this use of your skills will often be more confronting. However, there will be times when talking with a client about the here and now will be appropriate within Stage One, for instance:

> The example of Sejeeven and David could easily happen within Stage One of a helpful conversation.
> You might need to address the behaviour of extremely quiet clients within Stage One, because you will not be able to progress with almost silent clients. You use all your skills to draw out the client and tolerate silences, but in the end you cannot help if you are mainly listening to silence.
> When for some reason or another, you (or your client) are distracted and miss something.

An immediate issue may arise from your side of the work. For example:

▸ You have continued a session with a client hoping that your growing headache will be controlled by the two paracetamol you took earlier. However, you are now aware that the pounding from inside your head is making it very hard to concentrate. Under such conditions the best course will be to admit the difficulty to the client, bring the session to a close and set another time.

A personal example comes from Jennie's experience of continuing to work with individuals and groups whilst expecting our daughter. In the second half of the pregnancy the baby's repertoire of drop kicks was sufficiently energetic to cause visible winces. Clients needed to be told, briefly, that painful expressions were internally caused and had nothing to do with what they had just said.

setting goals

Stage Two opens out as you encourage clients to consider new perspectives on the issues they first raised with you. This stage reaches a closing-down phase and a new focus when you have helped clients to explore their issues in detail and they have reached a more extensive understanding. Now you and your client need to work towards setting goals that will provide the basis for the client to act on the issue.

This model of helping enables clients to move beyond new ideas or insights and towards what they want to do and can do on the basis of those new perspectives. The client still retains the choice; at no point do you insist that she or he does something and some issues are more orientated to possible action than others. Goal-setting is covered in the following chapter.

goal setting and action planning

8.1 from problems to realistic goals

helping the client towards doing something

You help clients to set specific goals at the end of Stage Two (what they will achieve), when they are motivated to move towards Stage Three of action-planning (how they will achieve it). Vague plans will not help a client move on. For instance, there is not much practical future in the following, 'Now I understand why I get so angry with my colleague. I'll be more patient, starting tomorrow.' The client will benefit from time to discuss possible ways of dealing with the strong emotions that are provoked by the colleague under particular conditions and how the client will deal with these feelings when they arise.

You are looking for a willingness from the client to act and some focus for that action. For example:

▸ Delroy has spent some time with Nancy, whose twin sons attend the family centre. Nancy's initial approach to her problems with her sons was, 'It's hopeless. They run all over me. If only I'd been tougher when they were younger. It's too late now; I can't control them.' Delroy has helped Nancy to focus on the present, not the past, and to recognise some real positives in her time with the boys (some 'can's' and not only the 'can'ts'). Nancy most wants to manage the chaotic evenings, when she finds it so difficult to get her sons to bed, and she is keen to talk over possible ways to handle this time.

▸ Kitty has gained insight into her difficulties within the team. She explains to you, 'I can see now that what I claimed was helpful was exactly what drove people mad. I would do something for a colleague because I wanted to feel needed and I wouldn't even listen if they said not to do it. Then I'd want them to be grateful for all my effort, when it was me that had insisted. I'll never forget that phrase you used, that it was a case of, "Watch out! Here comes the help!" [Kitty laughs]. I have this picture in my mind, that people duck when I throw my help at them. But I've also realised that I'm going to find it hard to stop; I'm not sure what to do instead.'

clearing the way for clients to set goals

In order to set workable goals, you have to identify and clarify the problems and issues faced by the client. Most of this work should have been covered within Stage Two so far, but clients also need to view their problems in such a way that they can see it is actually possible to do something positive. It is crucial that clients:

› Have been enabled to describe the situation in such a way that it is possible for it to be solved, or at least improved. Goals have to be worded so that it is possible to achieve them. Some clients may see a benefit in holding on to the problem. For example, other people are sympathetic to them and it gives them something to talk about. If you have explored the issues and the client resolutely does not want to solve the problem, you should respectfully end the counselling process (see page 185).
› Take responsibility for their problem – or can sort out which parts of a problem they are prepared to own. Clients cannot set goals and resolve any issues that they still insist are somebody else's responsibility.
› Are able to describe their problem in concrete terms so that the goals can be made specific.
› Work with you to break any large problem into smaller, more manageable units on which you can work together to produce realistic goals.

problems can be solved

Some clients may create harder work for themselves because they actively block any possible route forward. Clients create blockages in different ways, and for understandable reasons, but in order to help you need to use Stage Two skills to bring the blockages into the open. For instance:

› Brian feels he has no way out of applying to train as a lawyer. He says, 'It's been part of my childhood. I'm the bright one, my sister isn't academic at all, so she's off the hook. My father always wanted to be a lawyer but his parents couldn't afford it. Then he got married and we were born. So he gave up his dream so that we could have the best possible education. Gran keeps on about how guilty she feels but I'm going to make it all right. It's no good, I don't have a choice. They're all depending on me.'

There is no way out as Brian describes his situation. The helper will need to bring out the different parts of the problem and highlight Brian's possible choices while acknowledging how he feels about the blocks. Brian will also need to get in touch with what he would like to do, given a choice, and the helper will be important in supporting him beyond 'Ah but . . .' You will find more on page 175 about dealing with apparently insoluble dilemmas.

Some clients will seek to avoid working towards achievable goals on one problem through the tactic of introducing another concern. You should respect clients' wishes to explore broadly but you will realise with some clients that an interjection of 'Before we do that, I'd really like to talk about . . .' can be a pattern of avoidance. Use your counselling skills to confront the client with the pattern, for instance:

› The example of Amy from page 159 might reach this point before Maryam as a helper fully realises the pattern. Amy finds different strategies to avoid Maryam's help in deciding on schools for Davy. Without putting her feelings into words, Amy is postponing her leave-taking from the family centre where she has been so happy. Her goal cannot be finding a way to freeze time because that is not possible. She needs to face goals in two areas: to make an informed decision about her son's school and to find ways to meet her own emotional needs that have so far been met through involvement in the centre.

Some clients may resist discussing a problem in ways that make it open to resolution because they want to avoid the consequences that will follow For instance:

› Perhaps Wesley (page 161) has enjoyed the attention of Moira's helping him with his lack of confidence. It is the first time that anyone has given him this kind of non-judgemental attention. He feels that if his problem with confidence is resolved, there will be no more reason to talk with Moira. A respectful helper would not label Wesley as 'attention-seeking'. Moira needs to address the issue in the here and now of her helping relationship with Wesley and explore the extent to which he needs other goals to address his social and emotional needs.
› Parents, sometimes whole families, strongly resist specific goals about handling one child's behaviour. You may realise that the child's problematic behaviour is the front of other family dynamics. The focus on this child as a difficult and dramatic 'case' gives family members a focus that distracts everyone from other serious problems in the family.

Problems can also be presented in an insoluble way if clients resist owning their problem or insist on keeping the description vague; these are discussed in the next two sections.

problems are owned by the client

Some clients are resistant to moving from what may be a long-standing way of coping, sometimes because of their fear of the unknown. For example:

› Graham recognises that his pattern of being aggressive disrupts his relationships with friends and at work. However, he has experience of dealing with the consequences of being aggressive; the situation feels familiar to him. Graham has no experience of the likely consequences of acting in an assertive way, and he finds this uncertainty scary. In this case you would need to work through specific issues for Graham in choosing assertion rather than aggression and be ready to help him to own and if necessary to confront the feelings that block a new option.

Some clients may have coped so far by placing responsibility or blame with other people. For instance:

› Perhaps Lucy (pages 154 and 159) has continued difficulty in talking about specific examples of how her mother 'interferes' in the upbringing of the children. Lucy appears happier describing her domestic difficulties as something that her mother should solve, as shown by repeated phrases like, 'Mum should realise that I feel . . ', and, 'If she wasn't such a busybody, all these problems wouldn't arise.' An effective helper has to use Stage Two skills to confront Lucy over her unwillingness to focus on her own behaviour – the resistance to talking with her mother and preference that the latter should read her mind – and then on how Lucy behaves in the fraught situations.

You may need to stress with clients like Lucy that your focus on their reactions and possible actions are not an attempt to shift fault and blame. Perhaps the client comes back with, 'So, you think my marriage problems are all down to me then?', and you need to reply, 'No, I'm not saying it's your fault rather than his. I am saying that there are two of you in this situation and so far you seem to be much happier talking about what Jim does.'

Clients may be able to lever a problematic situation through changes in their own behaviour, once they have accepted their area of responsibility.

problems are described in concrete terms

Clients cannot tackle a problem that remains intangible without examples and specific descriptions on which to base goals and then some actions. For instance:

› Paresh (from page 159) does not only have problems with his current project but describes his study problems on a very general level as, 'I'm disorganised. There's so much to do and never enough time and you need some life outside study, don't you? I've never been a good timekeeper. I guess I'm just not a natural student.' Along with possible issues about Paresh owning his study difficulties, Saira may need to work with him towards a more concrete description of how the problem arises. There might be several aspects. Paresh has a chaotic filing system in which it is genuinely difficult to work out what piece of work is due when. He has gone to sixth form college from an all-boys' school, is thoroughly enjoying the company of girls and does not want to turn down even one invitation for social events. He never wears a watch, fails to notice clocks and has never developed the habit of asking others for the time.

Some clients take a broad perspective that makes it harder to home in on what they personally could develop as goals. For example:

‣ Miriam is enthusiastic about what she has gained through involvement in the disability rights movement. 'It's changed my life. I used to feel apologetic about asking for help with my wheelchair and now I think, "Well! This building ought to be changed so that I have easy access!" People see the wheelchair and not me, like I'm invisible. I used to get upset, but now I get angry because they've got no business seeing me as an extension to my wheels; I'm a real person. I say I'm disabled, yes, but disabled by society, not by the cerebral palsy. Society does the disabling and that's what we have to fight. That's what I want to do – change people's attitudes, change society.' As Miriam's helper, you should acknowledge the strength and confidence that she has found. However, you need to work with her on goals more concrete, realistic and relevant to her situation than tackling 'people' in general or society as a whole.

divide large problem areas into manageable units

It is impossible to tackle a problem with clients if it is so large and general that nobody could cope effectively with all the issues.

‣ Simon (from page 132) might present a large and worrying problem of, 'My home life is falling apart.' Through your use of counselling skills in Stages One and Two you may have an overall view of the different parts, although Simon still views the problem as an undifferentiated mass. You can use the skills of summarising to alert Simon to the themes you have identified, checking as you speak that this summary makes sense to him. Simon is unhappy that he and his wife do not talk together as they used to do. He fears that he does not spend enough time with his children and does not know how to deal with their complaints about Granny. He wants his wife and his mother to get along better, but does not know how to make this happen. He wishes that he had not invited his mother to live with the family and guilty about even having such regrets. Each element can then be dealt with specifically, and in turn.

Some clients will be clear about the problem which they want to resolve. However, when clients have several problems and they are possibly motivated to work on any of them, you will need to help the client to make a choice. The process has similarities to the decision-making with some clients at the end of Stage One regarding which of several problems they would like to discuss further. You help the client to make a choice, bearing in mind these broad guidelines:

‣ Choose a problem over which the client has some control.
‣ Give priority to pressing problems or a crisis situation.
‣ Choose problems that could be solved fairly easily and can therefore increase the client's sense of competence.

- Choose a problem that, if it was resolved, could bring about a broader improvement in the client's life
- Start with the less severe problems and move on as the client gains in confidence.

Choose the focus that makes sense to the client, as well as to you in the light of your understanding of this client.

Goals are not in themselves a programme of action; they are the detailed objectives that will guide the actions. There will often be different potential programmes of action that could resolve a problem and those possibilities are explored in Stage Three (page 178).

steps to helping clients set goals

If they are to be of any real use to clients, goals have to include the following characteristics. Goals are:

- Expressed in terms of what the client will do. Some clients may have goals about feelings but even these need to result in some action.
- Related to the problem as described and defined by the client.
- Realistic, that is, they are likely to be achieved by this client, allowing for his or her capabilities and situation.
- Under the direct control of the client, not someone or something else.
- Valued by the client as helpful and useful. In other words, the client is committed to achieving the goal.
- Able to be measured in some way. For instance, goals are described in specific terms so that someone, perhaps only the client and helper, can tell if the goal has been achieved or not.
- Time-bound – in other words the goal includes some element of by when it will be achieved, or a sequence of steps taken. How long might this realistically take? Goals with a long time span can be disheartening. Perhaps the goal needs to be broken down into manageable steps. Similarly, ambitious clients may need to be cautioned that solving the problem is likely to take longer than they anticipate.

You are likely to go through the following steps to help clients to reach specific, realistic and useful goals.

- You summarise the problem, with the client's help, including what she or he has learned so far within this helping relationship.
- You undertake any necessary work with the client to ensure that the problem is solvable and manageable.
- You invite the client to explore possible goals, which may at first be vague, such as, 'Become more organised' (Paresh, page 172), 'Stop worrying to myself and start doing something' (Simon, page 173), or, 'Develop my assertive side' (Miriam, page 173).

- You encourage the client to become more specific. For instance, Paresh agrees, 'I want to reorganise how I time my college work. I don't want to miss another deadline.' Simon decides, 'I want to really listen to my wife and understand how she feels about the situation. And I want to do this within the next week – no later.' Miriam focuses on, 'I want to find a way to deal with unhelpful strangers, so that they are more likely to think of me as a person.'
- Explore some aspects of the goal with clients: is it specific enough or do they need a different time deadline (some clients may need a tighter limit than others)? How will clients know they have achieved their goal: what will they have done, how will they feel, what kind of changes do they expect, will anyone else be able to see the changes?
- Check that clients definitely value this goal and are personally committed. They need to own this goal, not go along with it to please you. What do clients believe they will gain, what is important to them, what difference will achieving the goal make to them? Check that they have considered the consequences – of either going for the goal or doing nothing.

8.2 dealing with dilemmas

Some clients describe problems that seem to have no way out. These situations are dilemmas in which it is easy for you to become as blocked as the client. Dilemmas involve two, or more, equally positive alternatives or at least two equally negative alternatives. Clients express their difficulties in terms like, 'I could do . . . but then that would mean . . . and that's no use', or, 'I really want to . . . , but then I couldn't bear it if I missed out on . . .'. Occasionally dilemmas can involve both a positive outcome, 'I will be able to spend more time with my family', and a negative one, 'I am unlikely to be promoted if I spend less time at work.'

People talk about being stuck on 'the horns of a dilemma' and the image created by this phrase evokes the feelings of being trapped and entangled. You may identify the existence of a dilemma by the client's use of words. Sometimes, two parts of the sentence are joined by 'but' which highlights the client's conviction that she or he must meet the requirements of both parts of the sentence, but this is impossible and so the circle continues. For instance:

- Gemma tells you, 'I've had a fantastic invitation to join Rory in a trip to the Far East but I've landed the holiday job that I really wanted. I worked so hard to get this job and it'll look good on my CV, but I'll never get another chance to go to the Far East and Rory really wants me to go with him.'
- Ayesha and Winston are due to get married in two months' time. They are both having doubts and last night had their first really serious row. They are not sure about getting married, but their families are all excited about the wedding and arrangements are well advanced. Both Ayesha and Winston dread the upheaval and recriminations from the families if they say they are

no longer sure about being married, but it seems wrong to take such an important step without being certain.

In the first example, Gemma is facing a dilemma between two equally positive alternatives and, in the second, Ayesha and Winston feel torn between two equally negative outcomes. As a helper, you will have listened to the various elements in the dilemma; your role is now to help clients to tease out those elements in a logical way and to explore each one specifically. You encourage clients through a logical process and you still completely acknowledge that feelings are both involved and fully legitimate. You help clients step back from the strength of feelings and to talk around and through the blocks that have been created in an objective 'facts and information' way. The example of Ayesha and Winston will be used to illustrate these logical steps. You can practise the same process with the examples on page 177.

an example: the horns of a dilemma

Imagine that Ayesha and Winston talk over their worries with you. Through a relatively short Stage One and Two in helping you are clear about the complex and impossible situation, as they both see it. You realise that a detailed analysis of the options is the most useful route forward now. There are five parts to the dilemma and you encourage Ayesha and Winston to talk about each in turn. You reassure them that you are not trying to persuade them to follow any particular option, but to explore everything thoroughly and get all the assumptions out in the open. Ayesha and Winston work through their options as follows:

1 First option: cancel our wedding.
2 The negative consequences we believe will follow this option are: our parents will be upset and cross, our friends will think we're stupid and they'll take sides, it will be so embarrassing and we'll feel we have to pay our parents back for the money they'll lose by cancelling the arrangements.
3 Second option: go through with our wedding.
4 The negative consequences we believe will follow this option are: our rows will get worse, we'll feel trapped and we'll hate each other, we'll end up getting divorced, we'll feel like failures and our mothers will be heartbroken.
5 Our dilemma: we have to do something, we don't have the choice of doing nothing. Whatever we do will be awful; there is no right thing to do.

You now talk through each part of the dilemma, encouraging Ayesha and Winston to test out their assumptions and judgements. You acknowledge their worries about the expected consequences of cancelling the wedding and encourage them to think further, on the basis of what they have told you earlier in the conversation. With your help the pair allow for other possibilities.

1 First option: cancel our wedding.
2 The consequences we believe will follow this option may not be all negative and we might be able to reduce the negatives. For instance, our parents are kind people, they love us and we are letting them stay ignorant of our worries. They might be sad, they might even be cross with us, but they might also soon be pleased that we are being honest and responsible about a serious decision like marriage. Perhaps we should focus on the marriage part rather than just the wedding day. Perhaps our friends won't think we're stupid; they might think we have courage. We could take some steps, like sticking together and not blaming each other, to stop our friends taking sides. Perhaps the money is less important than our happiness, but we could still find out how much it would actually cost to cancel the arrangements.
3 Second option: go through with our wedding.
4 The consequences we believe will follow this option may not be all negative. We have only started arguing recently and all our rows have been about the wedding arrangements. We can talk together, we have done it today without shouting and we have both become very sad at the prospect of breaking up. We don't want to have a failed marriage, but will that really happen when we want so much to be together?
5 Our dilemma may not be to choose between two equally awful alternatives. Is our problem more about this big wedding that has got out of control rather than getting married? We were very happy together until both families started to take over our wedding day. Do we want to postpone the wedding rather than cancel it completely? Or would we feel happier about cancelling this big wedding and scaling it down to something we would enjoy? Do we want to set up home together without getting married, how do we feel about that, how would our families feel?

By encouraging the exploration of possibilities you have helped Ayesha and Winston to bring in a range of other perspectives and possible goals that can lead to action. Their dilemma is not yet resolved but they have a much greater feeling of control and see much more room for manoeuvre than previously. They have been able to focus far more on themselves, what they feel and would prefer. They can then begin to focus on setting appropriate goals for them and move forward to how they can achieve them.

ACTIVITY

Practise teasing out the logical steps of dilemmas with these examples:

▶ The example of Gemma and Rory from page 175.
▶ Patrick tells you, 'I've been headhunted for this really good job. It's in the area that I want to be in, it's more money and I like the people I've met so far. But I've worked very hard to get where I am with my current firm. We're just about to break through from being a small operator to a big

success. I want to see it happen; I want to be part of what I've set up. If this offer had been in maybe a year's time, it would be ideal. And yet it seems too good to let go. I wish they'd never headhunted me, then I wouldn't know what I could be missing!'

▸ In your day centre for older clients, you are talking with a less experienced colleague who says, 'Rachel has asked to speak with me, I'm seeing her on Friday. I'm worried because she said, "I can trust you, can't I? What I say will stay just between the two of us." But you know we've been concerned about Rachel's elderly mother and all the bruises. Supposing Rachel tells me she's been hitting her mother; the old lady isn't the easiest of people. In my job description it says I must pass on serious concerns. But if I tell Rachel that, she'll probably clam up. And if I let her think I'll keep anything secret and I pass it on to my senior, Rachel is sure to find out and all hell will break loose. But then if I keep quiet and Rachel really hurts her mother, I'd never forgive myself.'

▸ You are offering support to a day nursery team. One team member voices the concerns of all of them with, 'In our day nursery we've made such a strong commitment to partnership with parents, and I really support that, but we've also worked so hard to give good quality care to the babies and toddlers, to make a close relationship with them like they need. Now some of the parents are saying that they don't want us to get close to their babies. They say that they chose a day nursery because they didn't want their babies to get attached to other people. If they'd wanted that to happen, they'd employ a nanny. I don't see how we can win. If we go with what these parents want, I really believe that young children will be emotionally damaged. But, if we continue to make close relationships with the babies, then the parents will say we lied about being ready to listen to them and wanting to work in partnership.'

▸ Do you have a personal dilemma that you are currently facing? Try working it through in a logical way, step by step.

8.3 Stage Three: action planning

a range of ways forward

Stage Two of the helping model closes with a definite goal or goals to which clients are committed. They are motivated to bring about some change in their life and are prepared to give energy to making this change happen. Your work in Stage Three is to help clients explore possibilities for action in order to achieve their goal(s) – in other words how to achieve the goal(s) set. Stage Three cannot progress unless clients are committed to do something.

Some clients may choose to end the helping relationship at the close of Stage Two, because they feel able to plan action on their own. This is a reasonable position at which the counselling can end, so long as you have explored, briefly, that they are able to move forward alone.

By the end of Stage Two most clients should know what they want to achieve, even if they do not yet know how to achieve that goal. You then help them through a systematic discussion to test action possibilities, rather than a haphazard approach. Many people have not experienced a systematic problem-solving approach. So it is important that you explain the need to open up more, rather than fewer, possibilities of how to achieve their goal and not run with the first idea or with one that worked for someone else. All the skills used within Stages One and Two of the helping model are still highly relevant. Some clients may generate ideas more easily than others and your help will support others who need assistance to get beyond the first few ideas. Clients may have tried an approach unsuccessfully in the past but that is not necessarily a reason to abandon the idea. They may now have a greater understanding and be able to take the approach through properly. It may be useful for you or the client to write down the options as you discuss them – maybe even on a flip chart. Your role is to help clients to generate ideas but the final choice of what to use must remain with the client. Any course of action will have to be consistent with the client's values. People will not follow through an idea that leaves them feeling ill at ease or which requires them to go against deeply held beliefs.

This section describes some ways of encouraging ideas for action from clients. Select what you use on the basis of your knowledge of individual clients; it would be very rare to use all the possibilities with a single client. Many of the approaches are also useful in working with groups (see Chapters 9 and 10).

creative exploration

brainstorming

The objective of brainstorming is to encourage plenty of ideas before looking at practicalities and moving towards any decision. There has been concern over whether the term 'brainstorming' causes offence to people who experience seizures or live with brain damage. Epilepsy Action (www.epilepsy.org.uk) takes the clear stance that the term 'brainstorming' is not offensive when it is used to describe this process of generating ideas. It is inappropriate to apply the term to a seizure or the electrical brain activity that provokes a seizure. We agree, but if you work with an organisation that persists in finding a (non-existent) problem with the term, then use the alternative of 'quicklisting'.

The key features of this method are as follows:

▶ Suspend your judgement for a while and ensure that the client backs away from, 'Ah, but . . ', or, 'It'll never work'. Neither you nor the client should try to judge the quality of the ideas yet. Realism and practical issues come later.
▶ Encourage quantity, as many options as possible, because it is easier to reach a practical short list when you start with a longer one.
▶ Relax and help the client to enjoy generating the ideas. Even wild ideas are to be welcomed. Odd suggestions may lead to something more realistic in the end. One idea may 'piggyback' on to another. Clarify ideas with the client in order to reach definite proposals. Do not criticise ideas, just make them clear and not vague notions.

You then work on the resulting list of ideas with the client (reverse brainstorm) to discuss real possibilities. Which ideas might be more practicable? Does one funny or bizarre idea lead to something that is a real option? Perhaps two ideas might be combined together?

Some ideas can also reveal strong feelings about the situation that the client has still not quite expressed. For instance, Natalie (who had a long-running problem with her neighbour, page 164) may surprise herself by generating a few violent solutions to her neighbour's intrusions. Obviously, you should never encourage clients to put irresponsible solutions into action but their expression can sometimes confirm for a client, 'Yes! I do feel that strongly about what has happened.'

positive imagination

The aim of encouraging a step into fantasy is to free clients from blocks such as, 'I couldn't possibly', or, 'It's all too difficult, what's the point?' This technique is not a rush from reality, rather more a useful way to move some clients from an all-too-firm grip on the exact current situation.

You guide the client to talk out loud with themes like:

) 'I would really like to walk into work one day and find that . . .'
) 'In five years time I would love to be . . .'
) 'If I had a magic wand, I would . . .'
) 'What I really want is . . .'

You do not leave clients with unrealistic hopes; the fantasy is just the beginning. You and the client then discuss the practical possibilities that can follow from recognising the message of the imaginary scene. You may also invite the client to draw a picture of what a solution might look like. This option can be particularly useful with less verbally fluent clients, and gives a good opportunity to explore the relationships between the elements and the images themselves as a possible way forward.

prompting

Through this approach you take a more active role by using open-ended questions to direct clients' attention to particular possibilities. You do not answer the questions you pose, it is the client who answers. Prompting is useful with clients who have a narrow view of who or what might be useful to them. You might encourage the client to consider any of the following:

) Who might help in some way?
) Is there anyone who is already managing what this client wants to do? Can this other person, or observation of his or her behaviour, help and how?
) Are there particular places, environments or circumstances that are more helpful, or could support the client to achieve the goal? For example, a

discussion with a colleague with whom the client has difficulty may feel less formal or confrontational in the canteen than in the office.

‣ What about any organisations, self-help groups or sources of useful information that can help?

You can prompt clients to list their own personal resources, abilities or successful experiences. Some clients may need a further friendly push to step back from negative views or perfectionist standards. Some clients may especially need to recognise their own strengths rather than a long list of failings, to acknowledge what they do well rather than when they fall short of their own tough standards.

overcoming blocks

In Stages One and Two, clients may be able to talk about their situation in a detached way as a 'problem'. Stage Three stands on the verge of action and some clients develop a strong resistance to change when actually doing something becomes the focus of attention. Instead of being a theoretical possibility and just a pleasant discussion, the focus becomes more real, tangible and sometimes scary.

clients' outlook on risk

Some clients will be especially fearful of taking risks, believing that, 'If I do this, then there's one chance of success but nine chances of failure.' Such 'catastrophic expectations' are quite common, and often result from giving too much weight to potential negative consequences than is realistic. In contrast, some clients are willing to 'go excessively boldly' and to take on an action plan which has a very high chance of failure. They may find it hard to let ideas settle and to think matters over before a final decision. As a helper, you need to explore the reality of this balance. Some clients may demand too high a level of certainty, 'This will definitely work, won't it?', that is incompatible with the need to take even small risks. On the other hand, some clients are more willing to hazard themselves, perhaps because they genuinely take the view that, 'At least I'll know I tried.'

choices and rejection of choices

Phrases like 'I can't' sum up a perspective that blocks clients from seeing action as a choice. If the action is theoretically possible, then clients have chosen to turn down the option: 'can't' means 'choose not to'. You can help by encouraging clients to explore the reasons they have rejected an option and to make those reasons conscious. At no point do you insist that clients take the option; you are effectively saying, 'Let's at least explore this before you reject the idea straightaway.'

clients' general view of problem-solving

Clients may have fixed expectations about how situations develop and what can be done. Some clients may still have trouble in nailing a problem and return to the safety of vagueness, for instance that, 'My life is just in such a mess.' Alternatively some clients may have difficulty in acknowledging the bigger picture and insist on addressing just one part of a problem with, 'No, no. If I can just beat this insomnia, everything else will be fine', as if that is all there is to consider.

social and cultural background

Everyone learns continually from their environment, including their childhood. Some clients will be more aware than others of how experience has shaped their outlook: what they believe is possible or not really an option, what they feel is normal or out of the ordinary. You, of course, will also be carrying this kind of baggage from your own early and later experiences. Clients may experience general blocks, such as:

> Fantasy or playfulness is for children, not adults, as shown by phrases like, 'Don't be childish!', and, 'Do grow up!' This may get in the way of their exploring creative possibilities, and so limits their options and freedom of action.
> Logic and practicality are positive, intuition and fun are negative.
> Traditional ways are the best, change is risky and often bad.
> The echo of family phrases like, 'If anything can go wrong, it will!'

Clients' background and beliefs may also create limits to options with which they can feel at ease. For instance:

> Clients from some cultural and social backgrounds will place a strong emphasis on family loyalty or duty. Any options will have to respect, and if necessary help to manage, this concern.
> Clients with strong religious beliefs may feel unable to contemplate some options. You may be able to work through, for instance with a Christian client, the consequences of her view that, 'This is the cross that I have to bear', or, 'I must be seen to turn the other cheek.' But any final decisions about action have to respect her beliefs.
> Young people with strong allegiance to their friends may need options that can sit with the shared set of beliefs and priorities of their social group.

During Stages One and Two you should have gained an understanding of the client's concerns and convictions and you may have worked hard to understand a perspective that is different from your own. Your aim is not to force clients to abandon their beliefs but to encourage them to acknowledge how a belief is blocking action and help them to make a more informed and conscious choice. Clients may then decide to live with the consequences of their beliefs and to

choose from a more narrow range of options. They have made their own choice, with an improved awareness of both what they are doing and why.

helping the client towards action

The opening-out phase of Stage Three happens as you and the client consider a wide range of options for action. The closing-down or focusing phase helps the client to choose the best activities to achieve the goal. Using the counselling skills described for Stages One and Two, typically you discuss the following kinds of issues:

> Will this course of action be likely to achieve the goal? Here, you can share experience about the likelihood of success from your informed understanding of this client and your experiences of others.
> Perhaps a different course of action might bring encouraging changes more swiftly, or the actions need to be broken down into smaller, manageable steps so that the client will experience some early success without a disheartening wait.
> What level of uncertainty or risk is this client comfortable with, or can tolerate?
> Which possible courses of action are realistic, given clients' circumstances?
> What factors, both personal and from outside (like other people, organisations or resources), might support this action and how can the client make the most of these positive forces?
> What might work against the client and achieving the goal through this course of action? In what ways can the client anticipate and minimise the negative forces?

The conclusion of Stage Three is the client's agreement to a plan of action. Your helping relationship need not end yet, since it can be useful to clients to meet you after they have put their plan into action. You can support and encourage their efforts and offer help if needed. However, just as at the close of the preceding stages, it is the client's right to choose to act alone.

8.4 Stage Four: plans into action

learning from action

When clients meet you again after putting a plan into action, your role is to support them in learning from what they have done:

> Praise clients for what they have achieved in meeting or making progress towards their goal, be pleased with them. Highlight how far they have moved from where they started to where they are now.

- Help clients recognise how much they have learned and to take pride in their achievements, rather than viewing you as the person who has brought about the progress.
- Explore any setbacks that arose and unexpected difficulties in a positive light. Support clients towards what they can now do to move on rather than looking on the negative side of how 'it all went wrong'.
- Help clients to explore what happened, to take the credit for what they have managed and to find constructive lessons in what did not go as they hoped.

You may need to return to some issues that were covered in Stage Three or even Stage Two if it emerges that such issues were relevant to how the plan went awry. A logical approach called force field analysis is often valuable within Stage Three as well. The earlier points about building positive forces (both within the client and in her environment) and reducing the negative forces are central to force field analysis.

force field analysis

This logical problem-solving approach passes through four steps. With some clients you might focus on only one or two steps, since you realise these are the likely sources of the disappointment in putting a plan into action. You use all the counselling skills to explore with clients the details of what happened this time and how to plan better for next time.

1 Identify and clarify the issue.
  - Have any difficulties arisen or been overlooked?
2 Establish priorities for remedial action.
  - Has the client tried to tackle too many problems at once or lost sight of priorities?
  - Has the partial success of what sounded like a wise programme of action only now thrown up other factors? Talk these through with the client.
3 Establish more realistic objectives.
  - Is it now clear that a goal was not concrete enough, that the client was not really committed or that the goal as stated was too big or unwieldy?
  - Perhaps you need to return to a Stage Two discussion with clients. What was their real level of commitment to this goal? What did they really mean when they put the goal into words? Is it now clear that this goal is in conflict with other goals in their life?
  - Perhaps when clients came very close to action they realised that achieving this goal would bring a mix of consequences, some of which they were not yet ready to face.
4 Choose revised actions to achieve the goal. Perhaps you and the client now recognise in hindsight that parts of the discussion were rushed. You need to

return to consider the possible actions and choose the best in light of the changed circumstances.

 ⟩ Are possible actions within an appropriate time frame or is the deadline part of the problem?
 ⟩ Has the client, or you, overestimated the level of risk that is comfortable for him or her?
 ⟩ Are there blocks (see page 181) that were not resolved effectively or which are only now clear?
 ⟩ Have you and the client properly explored the positive and negative forces operating for this individual client on this problem situation? Have you worked through how best to maximise the positives and minimise the negatives? If not, what can you now do?

On the basis of this discussion you can support the client in a revised plan of action. Clients feel enabled to continue to work on the change they want to make, so long as this conversation is couched in what can be learned and made better rather than focusing on what went wrong.

8.5 the end of a helping relationship

The helping relationship will conclude whether you have offered your skills in a single conversation or a series of sessions to a client. If you use your skills within supervision of other practitioners, then the relationship does not end, but you move on to other issues.

A helping relationship ends when clients feel any of the following. They:

 ⟩ Feel that their needs have been met. They have been able to follow through the course of action and have dealt effectively with the problem. Alternatively, they have been able to find a way to live with the difficulty and to cope with it more positively.
 ⟩ Have decided that they can take control of the issue and the actions needed and no longer want your support.
 ⟩ Choose to stop, whether or not progress has been made. You would then ideally summarise what you feel the relationship has achieved and leave the option for the client to return, if wished.

If the helping relationship has not worked, it can be useful to explore some reasons at least briefly with the client. You may be able to learn about your style and approach or clients may acknowledge that they were expecting a different kind of help or are not yet ready to face this issue.

A helping relationship will also stop if you:

 ⟩ Feel unable to offer any further help. This feeling may result from blocks put forward by the client, which you have been unable to address effectively. This can happen at any time within the stages.

> Judge that the client needs specialist input that is outside your experience or ability. Typically this is most likely in Stage Three, or at the end of Stage Two.

a sense of closure

It is important that a helping relationship does not just stop abruptly. Clients, and you too, need to experience a positive closure and a review of what has been learned and achieved. This kind of closure may still be possible even if you, or the client, feel that not as much has been achieved as either of you hoped. You can use the skill of accurate summarising to alert clients to how far they have come. This message can be especially important when clients lack confidence or attribute changes or success to your ability and not their own. You may need to stress, 'You've done some hard work', 'Remember how you felt when we started', or, 'You were sitting right on top of the problem. It wasn't easy to stand back but you did it.'

A helping relationship should not finish only with a rational summary. Clients may have regrets about ending their time with you that need to be expressed. Feelings may be communicated of warmth and appreciation. Sometimes it will be appropriate for you to express warm feelings, still within the professional relationship with the client. It is important that you give some thought and attention to endings.

if you refer a client

At some point you will work with a client whose needs, when these become obvious, fall outside your expertise. It is a responsible course to admit to yourself that you are unlikely to be able to help and to explain the situation to the client. Ideally, you should ease your client's transition to another person who will offer the specialist help:

> Gather your thoughts and some information about who could be an appropriate referral. If necessary, contact individuals or agencies with general questions that will help you decide if they are suitable. Keep client confidentiality as agreed.
> You may be able to explain the limits to your help in the same conversation that you offer the client some suggestions about people or organisations that are likely to be of more direct help. Sometimes, there might be a break in which you realise the client's needs go beyond your capability and you gather ideas to bring to the next session.
> It will be the client's choice whether to accept any of your suggestions but you need to be honest when they do not have the choice to continue talking with you.
> Depending on the circumstances, you might offer names and telephone numbers with whom the client makes direct contact. Sometimes, it will be

appropriate that you introduce the client personally or by referral to another individual, perhaps within your own organisation or well-known to you.

- Of course, you may continue to have informal contact with some clients and to support them in a general way. Check that any referral has been useful, since the client may appreciate other suggestions if the first has not worked. However, it would not be appropriate to encourage clients to talk with you about the work they are doing with the new helper.

helping through group work

9.1 the nature of group work

some background

With the strong emphasis in society on help offered to individuals, it can be easy to overlook just how much helping is offered in groups rather than one-to-one. Group work was relatively rare until the 1960s when unstructured sensitivity groups developed in the United States. By the late 1960s and 1970s such groups were increasingly used as a method of personal exploration in the UK. This development brought varied reactions throughout the 1970s, with some wariness based on the very unstructured American model. However, approaches to working with groups have diversified and there is now a great variety in how groups are set up and run.

This chapter and Chapter 10 provide a practical framework for working with groups, covering some opportunities and predictable difficulties. Counselling skills are equally valuable for group work, but the dynamics of a group are far more complicated than those of a one-to-one conversation. The ideas here will support you to set up, plan and run relatively straightforward groups. However, group work, like counselling, is often very challenging, especially if you are involved with a client group experiencing complex life problems. Specific training will be necessary to run such groups.

why run groups?

The majority of people spend a great deal of time in groups: family, school and work, religious and other belief groups, chosen social and leisure groups. Groups can:

› Support and help individuals, affirm their sense of identity and acceptance by others and satisfy social needs.
› Create a sense of consistency in individual lives, of predictability.

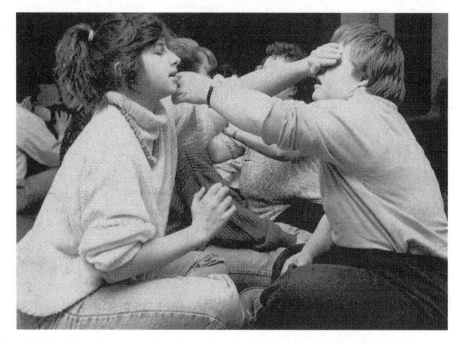

figure **9.1**   **groupwork**

‣ Provide individuals with a context in which to be themselves, to learn and sometimes to relax.
‣ Also exert negative pressures, making individuals doubt themselves or feel coerced into saying or doing what they would not do otherwise.

All groups have to deal with three major elements:

‣ The demands of the tasks to be done: what the objectives are, the level of support or opposition to these and the tasks required. Such needs have to be met within the group structure.
‣ The needs of the individuals in the group: to be included and not rejected, the satisfaction of personal aims and motivations.
‣ The needs of the whole group itself: the dynamics that make the group work well or badly. These include the level of participation, willingness to listen, use of assertiveness and how the group conducts itself.

The group leader needs to manage these three themes to satisfy group members and to work effectively to achieve the aims agreed. These themes affect each other and the emphasis of the group on one or other focus will change over time. Typically groups are most concerned about individual needs early on, and more concerned with achieving the goals later (see also Chapter 10). These themes are shown in Figure 9.2.

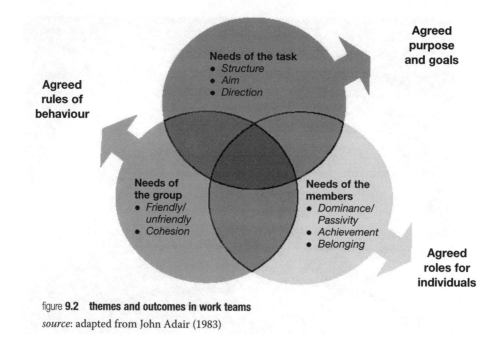

figure **9.2**   **themes and outcomes in work teams**
source: adapted from John Adair (1983)

I ACTIVITY

List the social and other groups to which you belong.

▶ To what extent do the groups overlap?
▶ In what way do different interests or sides to your personality emerge more in some groups than others? How do you think that happens?

different kinds of groups

People come together in groups, or are brought together, because they share a focus: similar objectives, beliefs, experiences or concerns. Groups develop an identity of their own, additional to the separate personal identities of their members. Groups come together to achieve an aim. They share some common characteristics, although their reasons for meeting are varied.

to make contact with people who share similar experiences

Individuals appreciate spending time with people who are now, or have been, in a very similar situation. The objective is to have time to talk, listen and offer support and informed advice through shared experiences. Some groups come together in order to enjoy an activity. So groups may form to play football, share their passion for steam locomotives or go rambling. In the professional context, some examples are:

▸ Groups of professionals in a minority at work: black professionals' groups, male early years practitioners or women in male-dominated professions.

- Young people or adults who have been abused at some point in their lives.
- Parents who have disabled or very sick children and welcome the support of people who understand the reality of their daily life.
- The National Childbirth Trust (www.nct.org.uk) brings together new parents, mainly mothers, with parents of slightly older children. The aim is to build local networks for isolated new parents and offer informal support and advice.
- Support groups for the families of prisoners who face practical and emotional problems arising from the imprisonment of a family member (see www.hmprisonservice.gov.uk/adviceandsupport/azofsupportgroups).

self-help in a support group

Some groups focus on individual self-help with support from other group members who share a very similar difficulty. The aim is to change group members' outlook and behaviour, sometimes by harnessing the challenge from group members who have or have had very similar problems. Examples of such groups include:

- Groups for people coping with addiction: either chemical, for instance alcohol and drugs, or behavioural addictions like gambling, eating disorders and self-harm
- Juvenile or other offenders who wish to avoid re-offending
- Groups for people of any age who have very limited social contacts.

The group itself provides social links and an opportunity for learning social skills. Mainly these groups are actual face-to-face meetings with other people, such as Alcoholics Anonymous or WeightWatchers. Increasingly though, the virtual option (through using chat rooms and groupings on the Web) is being used as well. Many big websites focusing on therapy offer several chat rooms (for example www.psychcafe.net) whilst there are also specific area chats (for example at the Multiple Sclerosis Resource Centre (www.msrc.co.uk)). Some organisations offer different sections appropriate to different age ranges of site users, for example the Teen Spirit section of www.bodyandsoulcharity.org, a support group for families who have a member who is HIV-positive.

Whilst websites offer information and a forum for exchange on a given topic, their orientation is important to recognise. For example, is the website and its associated forum and chat room helping the user to overcome a significant problem, such as anorexia? Or does the content encourage site users in dangerous behaviour, with the group claiming that it is other people who do not understand this 'life style choice'? There is serious concern about the self-described 'pro-ana' and 'pro-mia' websites that celebrate extreme weight loss and the behaviour surrounding bulimia.

to gain skills and knowledge

Other groups focus on the development of skills. Examples include:

, Sessions for parents and other carers on parenting skills.
, Assertiveness for young people or adults.
, Developing the skills of self-care and independence for young people about to leave residential care.
, Physical exercise and health for older people whose situation has led them to be sedentary and out of condition.
, Groups for prospective foster or adoptive parents to help them to understand what is involved in their plans to foster or adopt.

to make change happen

Some groups come together with an action plan specifically for change. They want to make something happen, for instance:

, A job club for unemployed people who want to find ways to improve their prospects.
, A residents' or neighbourhood group that wants to bring about a local change such as better street lighting or a pedestrian crossing.
, A parents' group that wants better play or child-care facilities locally.
, Minority groups of professionals (as mentioned on page 190) may also have the objective to improve their treatment or enhance their status in addition to networking and sharing experiences.

9.2 planning a group

identifying a need

You should be clear about your reasons for developing group work for clients.

, What do you believe a group could achieve?
, What makes you think a group will be helpful? To whom? To what ends?
, What will the group experience offer to the potential members? What are they likely to gain that would not happen without the group?
, What would be the purpose of the group? With an unclear purpose, a group can be chaotic and members regularly return to questions about, 'What are we here for?', 'Why are we talking about this?', or, 'But weren't we going to . . .?'
, Which potential members should be included? How will you find out if people are likely to be enthusiastic about the kind of group that you envisage?

how do you talk about the group?

Even at the early stages of thinking about a group, be thoughtful about what the planned group is called and the way it is discussed.

▸ Is there is a possibility that group membership could create a stigma for members?
▸ In what way could this negative feature be avoided or minimised?

For instance, parenting groups may be linked in people's mind with 'bad' parents and anti-crime initiatives. A group for parents based at their children's school often works well if support and friendly advice about parenting is combined with practical suggestions about 'helping your child with school work'. Young people who are absent from school may consider a self-help group that is known as 'The Tuesday Club' but avoid one that has become known as 'The Truanting Group'. A related issue with this kind of support group is to avoid the situation in which more facilities, or more interesting options, seem to be available for those students who do not behave well.

is there a request for a group?

▸ Do potential members ask for a group? You may have direct requests for a group with a particular focus if you work in a centre with an existing client base. For instance, young people in a residential home may want a chance to prepare for the day they have to leave or a primary school may have requests from parents for informative groups about helping children with reading or maths.
▸ How do the potential group members see this group working? Regardless of what they call the group, what do they expect will happen in group time and what do they hope the group will achieve? How realistic are their expectations?

CASE STUDY

A primary school head sounded out a few parents about what she described as 'groups to help parents get more involved in their children's school learning'. The reaction was enthusiastic and, without further consultation, the head set up a series of monthly evening meetings on themes like 'Home–school links for reading', 'Maths nowadays' and 'Healthy eating'.

Many parents attended the first meeting, less came as the term progressed and very few were at the final meeting. The head sent a letter to all parents saying how much work the teachers had put into the meetings and how disappointed she was that so few parents had bothered to come. Some parents were so insulted by the tone of the head's letter that they wrote back angrily. The deputy started to gather further reactions by talking with many parents in the playground. Several key issues emerged:

▸ Many parents had expected smaller, more focused, groups in which they could discuss the work that their own children were doing and details of how they could help at home.

- Parents felt there was little give and take. Teachers and invited speakers behaved as if parents were there to be told what to do. The final blow had been a very patronising speaker for the healthy eating topic followed, ironically, by refreshments of squash and biscuits.
- The parents confirmed that they would welcome the kind of group that they believed had been offered. They were offended by the head's letter, which effectively accused them of disinterest in their children's education.

questions

- What went wrong here? How might the proposed groups have been better researched and planned?
- What do you think might be done to retrieve the situation?

will the group be open or closed?

Closed groups start and finish with the same group members and are usually run for a pre-agreed number of sessions. If members drop out for some reason, they are not replaced. Individuals who are keen to become involved wait for the start of another group with a new set of members.

In contrast, open groups work on the understanding that members can come and go. The open group may also work for a fixed number of sessions or continue, with reviews of the work, for an indefinite period of time.

There is no simple answer that a closed group is better than an open one, or vice versa. You need to make the decision, sometimes with group members, based on the membership and objectives of the group. Some considerations are:

- Some advantages of open groups are that new members can bring in fresh ideas and perspectives and a different range of skills. They may constructively challenge the habits that have grown in the existing group.
- Like closed groups, open groups can still have subgroups and cliques, perhaps between 'old' members and the 'new' ones. Recent arrivals may become frustrated with the old clique or be cold-shouldered on the grounds that they do not really understand nor have committed to the original purpose of the group.
- An open, and therefore changing, membership is not suitable for groups in which members are working to share deep personal experiences. Trust has to built over time and new members will not be immediately admitted to this trust. New arrivals therefore, by no fault of their own, unbalance the previous group atmosphere. Personal work at depth is not likely to be possible in an open group.
- Closed groups can undoubtedly become inward-looking and may develop favourite ways of dealing with more difficult situations, such as conflict, or develop habits and assumptions about group members. A group leader has to be alert to this disadvantage of a closed group, including the possibility that he or she has also fallen into these habits.

- Closed groups can become very cohesive and intimate, offering considerable support in an atmosphere of trust. The downside is that closed groups are likely to have more difficulty and sadness about the ending of a group, because of the significance of the relationships that have grown over time. The group leader has to be ready and prepare the group for ending and moving on.

| TO THINK ABOUT

In your opinion, what are the issues that arise in the following three groups? How would you resolve the difficulties?

- In an all-girls' secondary school, with many different clubs and societies, agreement has been given for students of African-Caribbean origin to have a closed group to explore cultural and historical issues about their ethnic group identity. Some other students, who are interested in cultural diversity, have challenged the fact that the group has a closed membership. They ask the teacher who plans to lead the group, 'Would you let us have just a white European group? We think not; you'd call us racist.'
- An open group on health issues for young people in residential care has reached the maximum numbers. Recent additions to the group have made the balance three-quarters male and the girls feel in a minority. They say, 'The boys mess about and want to talk about different things.' The girls request that the group be made open only to girls until natural turnover evens up the sex balance.
- An informal drop-in group for childminders meets every Tuesday at a community centre. The under-eights adviser had always envisaged the drop-in as an open group, but on a recent visit she realises that circumstances have changed. Four minders, who have attended since the start and are active in organising events, appear to have closed the group to new arrivals. Nothing explicit is said to the adviser, but she hears along the grapevine that several new childminders had felt very unwelcome in the group and did not return after a first visit.

how do people join the group?

You need to consider how prospective group members are likely to hear about and join a group. Some possibilities are:

- Group members are active themselves in starting up the group.
- They hear about the group and contact the group leader or existing members.
- Someone, either inside or outside it, recommends the group.
- Group members bring along a friend.
- Someone encourages or persuades individuals to join the group. In this case, members may not feel they had a genuine choice.

As a group leader, you need to know about the routes taken to the group by members, whether they are much the same or diverse. Some routes may encourage subgroups and any reluctant group members need to have their wariness acknowledged. There may not be serious problems, but an understanding of how the group has developed will help you to work well with the group dynamics.

Apart from the issue of closed or open groups, there will be other issues about the composition of the group. A good rule of thumb is that groups need to have members similar enough to have a level of shared interests, motivations and concerns, yet different enough to bring varied perspectives to help each other.

The composition of the group will have to be related to the group's objective, which in turn needs to be openly expressed. Almost certainly you will have some limits on who is suitable to join a group. If the interests, skills or concerns of the group membership are too diverse, then it will be practically impossible to have a clear group purpose and at least some of the group will be disappointed in their experience.

| CASE STUDY

A day centre group for promoting physical fitness for older people was set up to involve the regular carers of the members. The group objective was to develop appropriate physical exercises to maintain muscle strength and emotional well-being. The rationale for inviting family carers was that they could better support their relatives in continuing the exercises at home.

By the end of the third session this situation was challenged by several of the older group members. Their rationale was that they preferred to exercise privately with the person they now regarded as their group personal trainer. They asked why nobody had bothered to invite their opinions and felt that this implied they were incapable of showing their carers what they had learned in each session. They also objected to some family carers who 'hijack our training session to moan about their problems with social services'.

questions

▶ What in your opinion has happened with this group? What assumptions appear to be at work?
▶ What would be positive steps now? For the physical training session? For the needs expressed by some carers?

size of the group

You need to decide how large the group can become. Size will be an issue at the planning stage, but can also arise with an open group that becomes more successful than expected. Size is partly determined by the purpose of the group, but groups of over 25 become unwieldy whatever the purpose. Once a group grows beyond eight members, it is very difficult to attend in detail to individuals, and in groups focused on discussion some members will feel it difficult, if not impossible, to contribute.

▸ Groups therefore need to be kept small when the purpose is for members to talk about personal experiences and seek support for what may be distressing events. Such a group cannot function if membership rises beyond seven or eight members. The atmosphere becomes less personal and each individual has considerably less time for expressing his or her own concerns.

- An activity group with a shared purpose might work well with up to 11–15 members. The group work is less personal and so less likely to raise intimate feelings or personal pain. The larger membership then brings the advantage of greater variety in experiences, skills and ideas.
- A group with an educational purpose can function well with up to 25 members. The group leader becomes more responsible for the balance of activity, for ensuring that everyone is enabled to contribute and for managing the subgroups which are almost certain to develop.

how long does each session last?

Again the final decision here needs to be based on the purpose of the group and on the variety and size of group membership.

- Some group members, with family or other obligations, may only be able to organise to attend for a couple of hours at the most.
- Groups will not gather much momentum unless each session has a reasonable amount of time to develop. Between 60 and 90 minutes is usually the minimum time allowed, while some groups work well in sessions of two to three hours.
- Some members may become tired or their attention may wander in longer sessions. It will be the task of a group leader to help members to refocus and to maintain attention through changes in activities. Groups often appreciate and need a short refreshment or comfort break.

9.3 the role of group leader

We use the words 'group leader' to describe anyone who takes primary responsibility for the life of a group. People use different phrases to describe this position and undoubtedly 'leading' has some different connotations, depending with whom you speak. The leader is basically responsible for helping the group to meet its goals through facilitation and to structure activities.

Individual style and temperament affects the way that a group leader operates and there is no absolute set of rules to follow. However, it is a leadership role and the leader has to accept that she or he is in a different position from the other group members. Groups can become very frustrated with leaders who insist that they are 'just another member of the group', when this claim is clearly untrue, or with leaders who give out conflicting messages about how they exercise authority in the group.

rights and responsibilities

Group leaders, whether they are formally called this or not, have obligations to provide direction, boundaries and a safe situation for all group members.

Groups have a right to expect that their leader should be a legitimate source of authority and that he or she should:

- Be consistent, fair and honest with the group.
- Treat all members equally, not have favourites nor form subgroups with individuals.
- Focus on the needs of the group and of individual members and not on the group as a means for the leader to achieve personal goals.
- Be aware of the needs of all members and alert to their welfare and feelings.
- Offer new experiences or activities, appropriate to the group purpose and the members' skills, interests and past experience.
- Offer objective feedback and comment equally to all members.
- Provide and help the group to hold to boundaries and to ensure that the group is a safe and positive experience for group members.

leadership style

Depending on the nature of the group, a leader may be:

directive or structuring

The leader takes a major responsibility for organising what will happen, guiding the group and stimulating ideas and expression of views or feelings. This role of leadership may be important when group members are very low in confidence or have limited experience of organising their time to a purpose. When the group purpose is educational, the leader has a definite responsibility to create and guide a group programme of learning. Typically this leader's primary focus is to fulfil the objectives of the group.

coaching

The leader still has authority; he or she does not simply sit back and do nothing. However, the leader is less directive and gives the group more scope to plan, make decisions and agree a clear purpose. In some groups, the leader's aim may be to support members as they move to a point where they have far less need for leadership. This leadership style works best when members have some experience of working in a group and show willingness to share responsibility with the leader.

facilitative or encouraging

The group leader brings expertise to the group and an alertness to the group process while working to support the responsibility of group members for what happens within the group. The leader offers encouragement and is involved, but with a different role to group members. A facilitative role is usually appropriate in groups where the purpose is for individuals to explore feelings and experiences, and there is not a clear group aim to achieve a defined collective result.

delegative

Here the group leader takes a low profile, perhaps merely arranging sessions, to enable an established group to work in ways that they see fit. The delegative leader's prime role is to monitor what occurs and to ensure that the group continues to fulfil the needs of all the members. This leadership style works best with competent, experienced and motivated group members who can be trusted to make good decisions without interference.

flexible – a combination of styles

None of the above styles is likely to work consistently all the time. As groups develop, a less structured style is typically more productive than in the early days of the group. Hence the work in most groups requires that the leader is flexible and takes up the directive, coaching or facilitating styles in response to events in the group. Flexibility definitely should not mean unpredictability. Groups resent a leader who directs when it suits and stays well back when the group would appreciate some direction. The key is to flex your style to match the needs of the group and the objectives set, and particularly the needs of the members which will change over time. You need to be fully aware of what you are doing in terms of your leadership style and why.

skills

As a group leader you will use your skills towards four broad objectives: the creation of the group, maintenance of the group as a whole, the achievement of group tasks and the development of a positive group culture.

creation

Groups do not simply happen; their creation and development requires work. As a group leader you need to:

▸ Make initial contacts and research the need for a group. What should it achieve? Who should be invited? What are its boundaries?
▸ Work out the practical details of the group. When should it meet? For how long? How frequently? Should it be open or closed?
▸ Establish a suitable and positive role as group leader and start to develop working relationships with the group, either as a new group or one that already exists but where you are a new leader. What do the members seek from the leader? What are you able, and willing, to do?

maintenance

You apply your skills to support and maintain the existence of this group. You need to:

- Communicate your commitment to the group and optimism about what the group will do.
- Talk and listen equally with all group members and find out what each individual within the group wants and can contribute.
- Help group members to communicate with each other and deal with any blocks that arise within the group that affect the group's objectives or the well-being of individuals.
- Be aware of all levels of group working: what happens in the sessions, the emotional dimension, different relationships and subgroups. Use your observational and counselling skills to deal with events within the group and any outside issues that become part of the group's interaction.

achievement of group tasks

All groups should have a purpose, honestly expressed, and a key focus for commitment of all the group members. The purpose is what the group is formed to achieve. Leaders need to:

- Remember and restate the group purpose as necessary, and what this means in terms of specific objectives and tasks to complete.
- Act so as to help the group contribute to the purpose and perform the tasks that need doing.
- Guide the group within agreed boundaries, values and standards for the work. Leaders need to ensure that practical issues such as timekeeping, feedback and follow-up on group tasks are completed. The group may be happy for the leader to delegate some areas for others to do but the leader still has overall responsibility that they are done.

group culture or atmosphere

Groups should operate within some boundaries of behaviour. The expectations of how people will behave may be part of an explicit contract or result from more informal encouragement, or illustration, from the group leader. You need to:

- Develop group rules with the members and remind them of these when necessary. These can involve timekeeping, confidentiality and processes for ensuring that everyone gets a chance to contribute.
- Make sure that you behave as a good example of the group contract and any ground rules (see page 216). For instance, a rule in a group undertaking physical activities may be that individuals are allowed to refuse an activity or to determine their preferred level of risk. The leader has to ensure that nobody is made to feel foolish or bullied for saying no.
- Model positive interaction, for instance, on listening, accepting feedback in a constructive way, being honest about your feelings when appropriate or dealing well with confrontation or distress in the group.

- Behave appropriately for the kind of group with whom you work. For instance, a self-help group needs to be gently dissuaded from looking to you as an expert. A group in which members share personal feelings and doubts will understandably look to the leader to share something of her or himself as well, not just act as an onlooker.

joint or co-leadership

Sometimes co-leadership – two leaders working together – makes sense for the content and purpose of a group. Co-leading is not necessarily easier than leading a group on your own, and in some ways it can become more difficult. The joint leaders need to work together in an integrated way and not compete for the group's attention. Each of the co-leaders' roles needs to be carefully agreed.

co-leadership for a reason

Co-leadership should be decided for clear reasons, linked to the purpose of the group. Two leaders may work well in a large group, when the tasks can be shared between the leaders. Two pairs of eyes and ears increase the chance that no group member will be overlooked. However, it is unwise to take on a second leader just because the group has expanded. Two leaders will not offset the disadvantages of having too many people for the work and purpose of this particular group.

Visible differences between the co-leaders may be an advantage for the purpose of some groups: perhaps one male and one female, they may show differences in ethnic group or one leader is disabled. Male and female co-leaders can act deliberately to cross gender stereotypes. Or it may be very important for a group to see a competent and disabled leader in action. Be clear between yourselves as co-leaders, particularly if your differences are intended to promote a particular message. Be wary that a group might take more than you intend from the difference. Sometimes, co-leaders will simply be different, with no agenda linked to the group purpose. Co-leaders should be seen as equal within the group and any differences in status from outside need to be anticipated and handled constructively.

plan and talk together

Two leaders must plan together so that you face the first and subsequent groups clear between yourselves about what will happen, why and how you will deal with some predictable events of group life, such as conflict, expressions of strong feelings or group boundaries.

Co-leaders need to talk together outside the group during the group's life. You need to discuss what is happening in the group, any issues in the dynamics between group members and how these will be handled. You also need to discuss in an open way the dynamics between yourselves as co-leaders and the relationships between you and individual group members. Does one or both co-leaders feel that subgroups are developing, that one leader is being manoeuvred into supporting a stance that is not appropriate? Are there issues about boundaries or discipline in the group that one leader feels fall disproportionately to her or him?

Typically, joint leaders will have different roles in the group. For example, one may focus on helping the group to achieve the tasks set, whilst the other focuses on ensuring that members are working well together and addresses issues of how tasks are being done. This division is quite appropriate, but both the co-leaders and the group need to be clear of the differences and boundaries of these distinct roles.

work positively together in the group

Co-leaders need to value, trust and respect each other. Some differences in approach or style can be a positive addition to group life, so long as the leaders respect each other. Sometimes it can be appropriate for co-leaders to discuss options or uncertainties outside the group, and sometimes within. Co-leaders both have an opportunity to model, in a natural way, how to manage disagreements, misunderstandings and expression of feelings to other group members, and hence to develop skills within the group.

constructive feedback between co-leaders

If you are to work well with your co-leader, you will both need to draw on the skills of constructive feedback as you talk outside the group. When you wish to discuss issues of your work with your co-leader, the conversation will be more productive if you follow the guidelines on feedback described on page 41. In brief you need to:

- ‣ Describe what happened rather than label or blame your co-leader.
- ‣ Express your feelings honestly rather than trying to put them onto your co-leader.
- ‣ Be even-handed and share what you felt went well in a session, not just what you think went wrong.
- ‣ Make positive suggestions about what you would rather have happen, if appropriate.
- ‣ When the feedback comes from your co-leader, listen and make sure you understand his or her perspective. Ask for clarification, if necessary, and consider what you have been told and how you might make positive changes in your style or reactions.

Think about what is happening in these groups and between the co-leaders. Do you believe the issue(s) should be addressed and, if so, in what way? How might feedback between the co-leaders be made constructive?

▷ Tricia and Roy are co-leading a group for 16–18-year-olds on the skills of independent living. Tricia has become increasingly annoyed with what she sees as Roy's tendency to bond unhelpfully with the boys. She expects Roy to challenge remarks from the boys like, 'Why should we learn to cook? We'll just pull some soft girl to cook for us!', but he does not. After one meeting, Tricia starts to take issue with her co-leader's behaviour. Roy's reaction is, 'I'm glad you've brought this up. I wanted to talk to you about what you're doing. You're lining up with the girls against me. I'm supposed to take cracks about "men who can't even sew on a button" as a joke, am I?'

▷ Shireen and Fazila are jointly running a support group for lone parents. Fazila has a more expressive style than Shireen, who feels pushed into the background with her quieter style with far fewer gestures. Matters come to a head in one session when Fazila's burst of energy leads her to get to her feet and address the group standing up. Shireen is angry that Fazila stood directly in front of her, so that she is now physically blocked from the group. Shireen hisses to Fazila, 'Sit down! For goodness' sake!'

▷ Joseph and Owen jointly run a neighbourhood action group. Over the last few weeks Owen has almost imperceptibly moved into the discipline role: keeping time, bringing the group back to task and reminding members of commitments made to the group earlier. Owen acknowledges that he is better at this role than his co-leader, but Joseph seems to be having all the fun. The last straw for Owen is when one group member calls him 'Owen-the-time' and everyone laughs, including Joseph.

▷ A paediatrician and a researcher are jointly running a series of sessions for parents on positive ways to deal with young children's behaviour. The nursery head who organised the practical arrangements for the group introduces the two group leaders as 'Dr Cartwright and Sarah'. Sarah, the researcher, is not pleased about this inequality and expects her co-leader to intervene with 'Please call me Nadia'. Her co-leader says nothing and Sarah becomes progressively more uneasy and annoyed. The group members appear to listen with more attention to the paediatrician and to ask her more questions than they address to Sarah.

▷ Tim and Clare are co-leaders on an assertiveness skills group. They organised six sessions and group members have a copy of the programme. After two sessions Tim has become frustrated with Clare's tendency to take the group off at a tangent, with the consequence that they are now behind in the agreed programme of activities. Tim tackles Clare before the third session and she agrees to keep to their plan. However, halfway through this session, Clare says in response to a comment from one group member, 'That's a great idea, let's see where that leads us. You'd all like that, wouldn't you?' She glances at Tim and laughs, 'Except my esteemed co-leader. He doesn't like me being spontaneous.'

9.4 learning in the group

planning

Group leaders need to plan for group work. You can leave some flexibility and no plan should be so tight that you are unable to respond at all to group members' wishes. However, you do need to think ahead to what will happen in each session.

- If you are taking on a group that was previously run by a colleague, then part of your preparation is to find out about the work of the group so far.
- If you are not responsible for the practical arrangements then make contact with the person who is. Practical issues include times and dates, the room you will use, enough chairs for the size of the group, any equipment, possible refreshments and advance communication with group members.
- Some groups, for instance those where there is a clear learning purpose, will need detailed planning about activities (see page 230) and some outline plan to be sent to group members to manage their expectations.

the physical setting

You may have limited choice over where you run the group, but it is definitely worthwhile to choose or create as welcoming and physically comfortable an environment as possible. A group leader has responsibilities towards the group's physical needs as well as other aspects of group life. A leader who seems unaware of physical comfort or unwilling to address issues for the group appears uncaring.

practical issues

- Have a room with sufficient, ideally natural, light, not harsh artificial lighting.
- You need to be able to create an environment at an appropriate temperature for the time of year. Over warm or airless settings tend to make people dozy, even send them to sleep, whilst chilly rooms leave people more concerned about how to keep warm than what the group is doing. Remove all the distractions that you can.
- Have seats that will be comfortable for the duration of a normal group session. Consider seating and access issues for any disabled group members.
- Would the group appreciate refreshments? If so, then these need to be organised in advance. Is it appropriate to plan for some non-structured chat time?
- If group members are likely to be very tired, then you need to consider the length of any session and suitable activities. One of us worked with a group of young mothers who were suffering broken nights, and at least one person fell asleep during each session. It was important to be tolerant, since the behaviour arose from exhaustion and not criticism of what the group was doing.

Some groups may be composed of strangers or people who scarcely know each other. However, some groups include members who know each other well outside the group. The physical setting and its practical details may be especially important for such groups. You have the chance to make this group distinct from the rest of the members' working or personal daily life. For example:

- If you want to encourage a health clinic team to talk openly, with less awareness of the usual status hierarchy, then have the group meet somewhere other than the clinic. Perhaps prepare name badges that only give a first name and no titles. You might want to seat people apart from those with whom they normally work.
- You might want to boost the self-esteem of a group of primary school assistants who feel unappreciated. You can start by taking trouble over the comfort of the group setting: perhaps get a vase of flowers and organise some decent refreshments. If the group must happen in the school, then be firm that you are not interrupted by teachers who 'just want a word about . . .'

privacy and security

Individuals need to feel safe both in the group and in the surroundings. If group members feel physically or emotionally threatened within or around a group, they will not be as committed.

- Groups cannot work well unless they are ensured some privacy. Avoid rooms in which group discussion is disturbed by people knocking on a window or staring in on the group.
- You may have to use a room that is a throughway to some other part of the building or doubles as the resource centre for your organisation. Negotiate with the rest of your team, and put up a notice for any service users, that the room is closed for the duration of the group. You need to tackle any colleagues who treat group time as open to interruption.
- Some groups run in buildings where members have to leave through empty corridors or a badly lit car park. Group members may be positive about the group experience but seriously worried about arriving and leaving. Consider practical arrangements to provide company for the times or areas that people find intimidating.

learning is best when active and through doing

Fundamentally all groups are designed to help the members learn something: how to cope better, ways of expressing feelings, what to do, or some new knowledge or skill.

experiential learning – learning through experience

The main ideas underlying experiential learning are that:

- Everyone learns more effectively by doing actively rather than simply being told and listening passively.
- People learn best when they are personally involved in the learning experience.
- Learning is sometimes painful, particularly if it involves unlearning established and unproductive habits or coming to grips with a deep personal issue.

- People really need to discover knowledge and insights for themselves if these are to have meaning. Group leaders therefore primarily support and enable. Telling is minimal. Look also at page 130 about the unhelpfulness of telling in a one-to-one helping relationship.
- People are more committed to learning when they can set their own goals within a framework that they help to determine.

Effective learning involves four phases that repeat within a cycle. These ideas were developed by D. A. Kolb and R. Fry (first presented in C. L. Cooper (ed.) *Theories of Group Processes* (Wiley, 1975)).

- Concrete Experience (CE) – something happens in which you are directly involved. For example, your car breaks down.
- Reflective Observation (RO) – you think about what has happened. If you know something about the workings of a car, you may open the bonnet (to use your Abstract Conceptualisation of the workings of the engine). If you know nothing, this is pointless, so you call an expert like the Automobile Association.
- Abstract Conceptualisation (AC) – you (or the representative from the Automobile Association) use knowledge of the workings of a car engine to do:
- Active Experimentation (AE) – and tinker with the car.
- Concrete Experience (CE) – the car starts (end of cycle) or it does not, at which point further reflection occurs. For instance, the manual may be used to help with alternative ways of experimenting, until the car does start.

Additional learning may have been acquired by reflecting on this complete experience. It may be that the fan belt was the problem and, as the AA representative said this often breaks, you determine to carry a spare in the future. Through watching the expert, your reflection tells you that the repair was straightforward and you could save the lost hour. You are willing to experiment actively with this new strategy next time.

You may start at any point in the cycle, but for best learning to result, you must go through all elements. For instance, a group exploring assertiveness skills may do short interviews with each other (CE). Following the interviews, group members are encouraged to reflect on their own current style and situations in which they find it most hard to be assertive (RO). The leader then briefs the group on how to be more assertive, and gives them a summary in a handout (AC). Individuals then develop plans for how to behave in new ways and practise alternative ways in the group (AE). They experiment in a safe environment by doing another interview (CE) and so on. Alternatively, you may begin the learning process by a briefing from an expert on the behaviour associated with assertiveness (AC). You then plan your practice (AE) and do it (CE) before reflecting on the experience (RO) as the springboard for additional tips from the trainer in response (AC).

Individual differences

Some people are more comfortable in one phase of the learning cycle than others and may have difficulty in moving on to less preferred aspects of learning. For instance, some people may relish trying out new options for action and experimenting but are less keen to reflect on what they have learned. Others may enjoy the discussion of ideas and building theories but are far less enthusiastic to do anything as a result.

Group leaders will also have personal preferences. Become aware of your own inclinations and how these may affect both your choice of activities and how you use these to help the group to learn. Perhaps you value discussion and find it relatively easy to express your feelings. However, some or most of this group may not share your comfort at all. On the other hand perhaps you are enthusiastic about physical games and are confident that such activities always generate energy and throw group dynamics into sharp relief. You need to be aware that some group members may not share your enthusiasm, especially if they feel there is no choice or feelings of physical insecurity are not acknowledged. The cycle must be completed for learning to be most effective, and this means inevitably that both the leaders and group members will experience some aspects which they enjoy less than others.

plan activities

Some groups may spend most of their time talking and listening together. Then the role of the group leader is to support discussion using counselling skills. Further suggestions about talking in the group are made from page 219 onwards. However, some groups do not find it easy to talk fluently about issues, or else the purpose of the group leads to other activities besides talking. You will need to plan ahead, at least to the extent of having ideas up your sleeve, and to prepare activities, some of which will need materials. You will find suggestions for activities from page 230 onwards. In planning to use activities, consider the following:

> A planned activity should help to focus the group and add to the learning of group members. As group leader, you should have a clear purpose in choosing one activity or a series of activities beyond the sense that 'We have to do something otherwise they'll get bored.'

> Sometimes a group will express themselves successfully in words but, on other occasions, even careful interventions by a leader may be met with denial or avoidance. Pushing groups to face or discuss something can be counter-productive. They need an experience which helps them to stand back and to discover for themselves, perhaps something creative which does not primarily involve language.

> An activity can provide a group with direct and shared experience which can be a focus for discussion. Working together on a common task can develop

group feelings of support and achievement. Another advantage is that all group members have taken part in some way in this activity and ideas or feelings can be raised through the activity and the debriefing afterwards.

| TO THINK ABOUT

Focus on a group to which you belong now or recently. (Your notes from the examples on page 203 may remind you of groups.) Reflect on your own experience as a group member:

▶ What were the advantages and disadvantages of the physical setting in which you all met? What did the group leader do to overcome the negative aspects?

▶ What was the purpose of the group (and/or the meeting itself) and how clear was this to everyone?

▶ What kind of role was taken by the group leader or co-leaders (look back at page 198)?

▶ In your opinion, what went well in the life of the group and what did not go so well? Looking back, what would you change and for what reasons?

running a group

10.1 the development of a group

Your aim in running a group is to enable the group members to interact as productively as possible to achieve the aims of the group. As such it will take longer, and require more patience, to help a group share deep feelings with each other than it will to encourage them accurately to share facts or opinions. You constantly encourage members to stretch outside their personal zone of complete safety to learn and to grow, but should never pressure them to move so far or so quickly that they panic or withdraw. The art is to lead, sensitively, where members wish to follow, until they are able to chart their own paths.

Most groups pass through similar stages in their life. Each meeting may also be a mini-version of the entire process too. An awareness of these developments helps you to recognise that some difficulties are part of the inevitable group process rather than events you should have managed to avoid. These are essentially the same as the communications hierarchy discussed in Chapter 2. Groups start with *ritual and cliché*, and over time progress through *facts and information* and so on to *emotions*.

the polite phase

Initially, as groups form, everyone is polite and communication is in the form of a lot of ritual and greeting. At the outset, nothing of any great relevance is aired or discussed.

'why are we here?' – forming

Groups start as everyone gets to know each other and finds out how this group is going to work. It is not unusual that events occur such as:

- People are uncertain what to do and look for clues from you, from the first outspoken person, their past experience of similar groups and any expectations

figure **10.1 running a group**

of this kind of group. The leader's role in the early sessions is to ease people into this group.

- Group members show a mixture of scepticism and cautious commitment to the group. Individuals may wish to protect themselves from making a wrong move, appearing bossy or being given responsibilities. At this stage, members are wary about being rejected.
- If group members do not know each other already, they need to see how they will all work together. If some people do know each other, they may be wary of how their current relationship in the group will fit with life outside. The group leader has the task of establishing this group as distinct from any groups or relationships elsewhere.
- One or two people may be keen to speak up and shape where the group will go. Some may even make a bid for formal or informal leadership.
- In groups who meet to discuss problems or feelings, someone may talk about him or herself at a deeper level than the rest of the group are yet comfortable with. That person may feel exposed or be frustrated that nobody else will follow the lead, whilst the others may feel pressured to reveal more than they wish.

The discussion may ramble and the group may look in a dependent way to you as leader for structure and control, perhaps for a clearer guide than you feel is appropriate. If you do not take an appropriate lead, some members may suspect from previous group experience that you have an agenda which you are not willing to disclose. Needless to say, any hidden agendas that you later reveal will shake the group's trust in you. Be honest with the group.

Open groups often have new members and under these circumstances there will be some re-forming whenever new people join. New arrivals have to find their place and learn how this group runs. Existing members may be welcoming yet wary that the newcomers do not push the group in ways that are contrary to established group norms. Much of the group's energy at this time is spent focused on the individual, each person wishing to feel comfortable and not threatened.

Once members feel more at ease in the group, or judge that they have the measure of this particular group, then leaders have to deal with group events linked with individuals' needs. Individual members trying to fulfil potentially selfish needs from the group is a common characteristic of the storming phase. For instance:

▸ Some people will manoeuvre for position in the group, seeking a preferred role or making a bid for power in some way.
▸ Group members may voice objections: that they did not really want to come to this group in the first place, that it is not the kind of group they expected or that nothing useful is happening.
▸ High hopes that the group task might be easy can move towards disappointment, perhaps that the group leader does not tell everyone what to do or that members are expected to do some work themselves. Some members may become frustrated or angry with the behaviour of others in the group. You have to manage any conflict and balance a constructive confrontation with support. Expectations of the group must be managed constantly: why the group is here, what it is aiming to do, and how it behaves.
▸ Some members may be torn between wanting to belong to and work with the group and yet also retaining their own individuality. Some people may already face conflicts arising from their current group membership, or previous experiences in groups, as well as their relationships or responsibilities outside the group.

A time of reaction and rebellion is very normal in group life and will usually help the group to move on. Instead of being polite (and concerned about being rejected), now that group members have better information, they begin to make judgements about what the group should do, how it should be run and by whom. Group members may now be thinking whether or not they should reject the group! As group leader, you need to communicate clearly what seems to be happening in the group, and explore and bring out the key issues. You should try very hard not to see the events as a direct attack on your own competence or self-worth, even if some members make personal remarks. The group are growing in confidence and are telling you what they think. You need to create an atmosphere where you remain in control of the group but still leave space for disagreements to be expressed and handled.

Storming is the most risky and potentially disruptive time for the group and sometimes a group disbands at this point. The storming phase certainly may result in some people leaving. Some group members may now understand much better that the group is not right for them through the honest and sometimes conflictual sharing of perceptions,. The benefit of storming is that the level of honesty has increased in the group, and the improved candour enables the group to move to agree improved ways of working together to reach their goals, ways which hopefully will prevent storming in the future.

norming

With the help of the leader, groups should be able to work through the issues raised at the storming phase.

‣ The discussion and group activities should have helped to develop greater trust, cohesion in the group and a sense of group identity, of 'our group'.
‣ Stronger norms develop about the way of working in this group. These norms may be formal or informal useful ground rules of communication and support.
‣ However, norms can also be disruptive or impose on some of the group, for example prevailing on one person to take on unwanted group responsibilities or making another the butt of unpleasant jokes. A group leader has to remain aware of these patterns and step in, even at the cost of possible disharmony in the group (see page 224).
‣ Your aim is to harness the group's motivation, members' energy, skills and commitment to work towards the group's task. At this stage, people are more ready to take responsibility as individuals and as a whole group.
‣ During norming, the group devotes quite a lot of time to sorting out issues of functioning as a group, the processes and patterns of behaviour and interaction. Length and frequency of meetings are typically revisited, and membership criteria amended. Only when this discussion is largely completed will the group be able to devote its energy to doing the tasks for which it was formed.

performing

The group settles to work on the agreed objectives. Some groups may have very specific tasks to achieve or actions to complete. Others may have definite learning objectives and yet another kind of group may aim for personal exploration and resolution for individual problems and concerns. The idea of stages in the life of a group does not imply a fixed, forward movement. Many groups have setbacks, unexpected problems or crises. Issues that you thought had been resolved earlier in the group re-emerge and have to be faced.

As group leader you need both to keep the group on task and also to manage the processes that will support their work. You can help by reviewing progress, guiding the group to learn from mistakes and reassess norms as needed. In some groups, an important role will also be to remind people why they are there and why it is important. You may need to stress how group work links with outside life as a means to an end.

In some groups, leaders remain central and help by assigning tasks, helping with problem-solving and supporting members in difficulty. In other groups, the leader may become less and less necessary until the point at which the group manages alone, and the leader becomes fully delegative.

esprit

If you are lucky, sometimes groups experience esprit, in which they reach higher goals than were initially sought, and group members develop very high levels of pride in and commitment to each other. This phase is wonderful when it happens (akin to being in love) and quite rare.

ending

Some theoretical discussions about group life fail to cover endings. Some groups may run with a clear end-time fixed at the beginning but many groups are more flexible and under review. Some groups end prematurely, often through being unable to resolve a storming period. Group members and the leader benefit from a clear end to the life of a group and a review of what has been achieved (see page 236). The ending needs to be recognised, as well as the feelings of loss that this may engender.

10.2 the first session

The opening session of any group is important because it sets the pattern of how the group may well continue. First sessions can be awkward, with long silences. Group members often look to the leader for direction and there is usually uneven participation between group members, some talking considerably more than others. Group members begin to get to know each other or, if they are already familiar, to establish how they will relate in this context. They form their first impressions of the group leader and how this group is likely to work.

Jarlath Benson, in *Working more Creatively with Groups* (Tavistock, 1987), stresses the three Cs, key messages for a group leader to communicate in the first session and afterwards:

- Competency: the group leader communicates, through words and non-verbal behaviour, that she or he is prepared and can be relied upon by the group. Leaders do not imply that they are utterly in control and certain about the group; this would be unrealistic. Show that you are competent to deal with the group's natural concerns at the start.
- Compassion: the leader should act in a way that helps members to feel safe and included. You should show, from the very beginning of the group, a willingness to be considerate of everyone present and to adjust what happens in response to the input of the group. Care and concern will be shown through how you manage expectations and give space to each group member. However, it is not genuine to imply deep feelings for individuals whom you do not yet know.
- Commitment: you show through your words and actions that you are ready to give time and energy to this group, that developing the group matters to you.

welcome to the group

relate to members as individuals

Be at the venue in good time to welcome people personally as they arrive. You may prepare simple name labels for group members in advance to ease the introduction process. Greet them by name, if you know it, or ask their name after you have introduced yourself. Simple refreshments help to show a welcome and give members some informal time to adjust to the new environment without pressure. It also gives new members something to do while waiting for others to arrive.

promote good communication

Work to even out striking differences in participation between group members. Some may talk a great deal or want to shape the group in a direction that makes sense to them. Others may be very quiet and contribute little, although they may show resentment of individuals who are very prominent. Particularly quieter people need to be asked to contribute, but not pressured. (See page 219 on helping groups to listen.)

Communicate clearly and in straightforward language. Avoid professional jargon and any phrases that are unlikely to be part of this group's usual language. However, it is unwise to change your way of speaking significantly in order to appear to be more like the group. You will not appear genuine and anyone who knows you in a different context will probably comment on the discrepancy.

be aware of your body language

Make your voice, tone of voice, gestures and body posture communicate interest in the group, warmth towards them and a level of your own comfort in being there. Remove barriers, such as a desk, from you and the group. Hold an attentive and open posture, whether you are talking or listening. Avoid hunching up, firmly crossed legs or folded arms and any distracting body gestures. Your aim is to model openness and attention to the group (see also Chapter 2).

Consider how you dress since this too carries a message. Do not make yourself uncomfortable, but generally aim to make your dress in tune with the group. For instance, you should not be dressed very formally, in a business suit, if most or all of this group is dressed casually. The difference will create distance between you; members may even think you are trying to be superior. On the other hand, you would give an equally discordant message if you insisted on wearing gardening gear when the group were in smart casual style.

introductions

There are several ways to introduce each other. These include:

▸ Group members simply introducing themselves with some personal information, not necessarily serious, for instance, 'I'm Janine and my favourite film is . . .'
▸ Members can talk briefly in pairs and then introduce each other.
▸ A soft ball or bean bag can be passed between members as one person says, 'I'm Steve and I'm passing the ball to Aaron.' A variation is to run this activity with a ball of wool or string, when everyone holds on to part of the wool but throws on the remaining ball. You create a visible network of links between the group members.

Use people's names regularly during the first session. Ask politely if you have forgotten (or you can't read the name tag). You will help other members of the group to learn names by repeating them and showing that you think it is important.

expectations and contracting

All groups need to discuss the purpose and limits of the group. You need to explore a group contract in a similar way to the contracting process with one person (see page 137). Contracting in a group should not take up the whole first session, but the discussion will take longer than with one person. The objective is to clear away as soon as possible any issues which can get in the way of the group functioning well and to form a basis of sensibly working together. A group contract should establish the appropriate boundaries for this group. It sets out how the group will act and summarises its purpose. Group members' rights and responsibilities are sometimes covered. The contract gives something definite to which to refer later in group life. You should consider writing down the details of the group contract for all members to see. A written version will not always be appropriate, but can definitely help if there appear to be diverse views in the group or any issue has needed a lot of discussion before a conclusion is reached. In this area consensus is important. Each member must feel that they have had the chance to contribute, and that any objections have been fully explored before the contract is drawn.

The contents of the contract will vary slightly with the nature of the group but some or all of the following are often included.

the purpose of this group

- The group needs to discuss why they are all here. You can handle expectations about the group or your role much more constructively if they are expressed early. Clarify any misunderstandings about the nature and purpose of this group before these grow.
- Some groups may have specific or time-bound purposes while others are more flexible – but should still not be vague and confined to 'We'll work it out as we go along.'
- If the group purpose is left undisclosed or unclear, wishes and assumptions of individual group members will still exert an impact on behaviour. Strong individuals may push the group towards their own preferences and less confident individuals may follow, but feel resentful.

hopes and concerns

- Have some members arrived expecting a very different kind of group or approach by the leader? However carefully you plan, there may be people who have an unrealistic idea of what the group will do and how quickly. People who have been sent to the group may be reluctant and uncertain.
- If the group is therapeutic in purpose, you should see each individual before the first group session, to clarify whether the experience will be appropriate for them. Other kinds of groups may well have gathered in such a way that the initial session will be the first time to explore individual hopes, expectations and any concerns.
- Consider an activity that helps everyone to express their personal hopes and concerns for this group. You can ask everyone to note and then express their views one by one, or they can discuss the matter in pairs or small groups and write hopes and concerns on large sheets of paper. Deal with what everyone has expressed.

how this group will work

- Cover the practical details of where, when and how often a group will meet. You can cover timekeeping, breaks and, if it is the nature of this group, the commitment of members to attend all sessions.

- Clarify your role as group leader or how you (and a co-leader if necessary) will work together. Give your personal commitment to attend for every session. If another person or co-leader will join only for particular sessions, then tell the group now, as well as reminding them before the relevant sessions.
- Is the group open or closed and do the members understand what this means? Are group members free to give up the group and can they return if they change their mind? If so, how does this happen?
- With regard to confidentiality rules for group members and the group leader, are there any limits to confidentiality? If so, be clear and honest about what they are. In groups where individuals are likely to share personal experiences, then make the importance of confidentiality especially strong. Ask, and get, an individual 'Yes' commitment from everyone, out loud, before moving on. This is important.
- Deal with any practical issues such as smoking breaks, and the length or frequency of general breaks. This may also include exact start and finish times. It is also wise to gain a commitment that all pagers and mobiles are switched off during group time (unless individuals are genuinely on emergency call).

later contracts and agreements

You may need to return to issues within the group contract later on. Perhaps conflicts have arisen about confidentiality, a subgroup wants to take a different direction from that originally agreed, or a challenge has arisen to you as group leader. Over time you may also realise that this particular group needs further exploration of rights and responsibilities. For example, a very lively group in which members talk over the top of each other may need some group rules to which everyone commits:

- It maybe a simple rule of 'One person speaks at a time', 'Listen, don't interrupt', or, 'Talk rather than shout'. You have to manage this process when individual members have limited experience of holding back and listening rather than raising their voices.
- Some groups need a specific rule to help them follow the general one. A group given to saying 'Yes, but ...' to ideas has a rule of 'Say three good things'. The next speaker has to say three things in support of the previous person's comment before making their own point. An alternative is that everyone has to summarise briefly what the previous person has said (to this person's satisfaction) before adding their bit.
- Groups where interruptions are serious may need to create better habits by literally passing the baton (an object that has to be held in order to speak).
- Another group may need a rule about 'Don't assume how people feel, ask them', or some rules derived from constructive feedback (see page 41).

- Cautious and wary groups may need explicit permission, even a written notice that says, 'It's OK to make mistakes here', or, 'It's fine to say that you don't know', to help them feel able to contribute.

introductions and warm-up games

First sessions often benefit from non-threatening activities that help a group to get started and everyone to know each other. Some suggestions are given on page 231.

TO THINK ABOUT

Consider the following scenarios during and immediately after a first group session. What do you think may be going on in the group? What could be a positive way to handle the situation?

- The contracting phase of a group for juvenile offenders is almost finished. The group leader asks if there are any other issues to raise. One young man says, 'I want everyone to know that I hate groups like this. I didn't want to come, but my social worker said I had to. I'm not going to talk about myself and I want everyone to leave me alone. Is that clear?'
- During member introductions in a group for prospective foster parents, everyone has shared their first name and something personal about themselves. Then the last woman says, 'I'm Mrs Hardcastle and I'm sure everyone knows who I am.' Another group member comments, 'Well, I've never met you before', and is given a cold stare by Mrs H.
- At the end of the first session, two members tackle the group leader and one explains, 'We were told this group was our chance to talk about problems with our children. But we're not sure we can trust the others in the group. Especially Tyrone, I know him from work and he can't keep his mouth shut. How can you promise everything will be kept confidential?'
- As you are packing your bag one group member comes up to you. She spoke a great deal during the first session, encouraging other members to talk and sharing her ideas and own experience in detail. She says to you, 'That was hard work, wasn't it? They need a lot of bringing out of themselves. I think we'll make a good team, you and me.'

10.3 working with group dynamics

Group work inevitably brings more uncertainty than using your counselling skills with one other person. In a group there are a number of people whose actions and words you cannot accurately predict, and in addition there is the further complexity of dealing with subgroups.

- An entire group may introduce a brand new topic, work hard to avoid a topic or bring a wide range of strategies for avoiding a clear focus on the agreed task.
- Group members form relationships with each other as well as with you. These allegiances may support, or undermine, the work of the group. Subgroups may involve you, or conspicuously cut you out of their contribution.
- There are many individuals who may want to talk at the same time and interrupt, ignore or misunderstand each other. Some individuals in a group may

be very quiet, even making an issue out of their obvious silence. You may be faced with an entire group which regularly lapses into long silences or many short staccato statements.

▸ Some group members may say or do something that you know you would not have done. In some cases, the impact will be negative on the group, or on you personally but not the whole group. Your skills as group leader will be important to deal with the consequences effectively.

▸ However, on many occasions in groups, individual members will be constructive and insightful, with the consequence that you do not have to speak. Sometimes an unexpected intervention from a group member, something you know you were very unlikely to have said or done, works out positively and you learn from what has happened.

Group work can be very exciting. It may often be the best way to work with clients with common concerns but it is certainly not easy. All the counselling skills described in Chapters 7 and 8 are valuable within group work. This section provides ideas and suggestions about applying these to groups.

listening and helping group members to listen to each other

You need all the skills of listening, reflecting back, summarising and open-ended questions (see page 47). You also use these skills to promote listening and understanding between group members.

▸ Encourage dialogue between members, rather than a whole series of contributions directed to you as group leader. Suggest that members talk directly to each other, rather than just through you as simply as 'ask Bill, he made that point.' Invite other people into the dialogue with, 'What do you think?', 'How does that strike you?', or, 'Is that close to the point you were making earlier?'

▸ Help members to relate to each other by making links between what individuals say. Demonstrate that you value each contribution and expect that members will have some views and experiences in common.

▸ One way of encouraging links is to build explicitly on what individuals contribute. Help the group to explore shared themes with comments like, 'Let's see if we can build on Jof's idea about ..', 'Supposing we add to Hamid's point by ..', or, 'That sounds as if it links back to what Ruth said earlier about ..'. This approach also counteracts the tendency in early sessions for members to communicate through the medium of the group leader.

▸ Work to encourage an atmosphere in which it is acceptable for members to say that they do not understand what someone has said or are confused. Periodically check out that the group understands what you have said, such as, 'Does this make sense to you?', or, 'Are you following what I'm saying here?' Be ready also to show your own need to be clear on what a group member is saying with, 'Chloe, I'm not sure that I follow what you're point is', 'Are you saying that . . ', or, 'I'm sorry, Ron, I got lost at . . '.

Lively groups that have difficulty in listening to each other may benefit from some agreed ground rules as mentioned on page 217.

helping individuals to communicate better

Your role is to help people to speak as well as to listen to each other. By your contributions, you encourage individuals to express ideas when they are cautious; to voice their feelings, hopes or expectations. You help to increase both the quality and quantity of the communication in the group.

› All groups have to develop some level of trust so that everyone, especially the less confident or more cautious members, feel able to speak.
› Help by establishing clear rules of confidentiality and dealing constructively with any individual concerns or experiences of broken confidences within this group or previous ones.
› Use the skill of reflecting back to deal with the negative reactions that can discourage honesty and sharing of ideas. The putdown of 'That's a stupid thing to feel' can be met with 'Do you understand why Kayleigh feels that way?' The block of 'That idea will never work' may be met with 'Rob, you feel that idea won't work. Tell us what you see as the problem.'

focus on the here and now

An advantage of group life is to enable individuals to focus on what is happening now. In some groups, members may be talking about previous experiences or distress, but the role of the group is to help them to focus on how the experience affects them now, their feelings, assumptions and beliefs about themselves and what is possible.

A focus on the here and now also includes what is happening within the group itself. The discussion may be triggered by something that an individual has brought into the group from outside. Yet, what matters is how individual experiences, actions and feelings are affecting the group right now. The task of a group leader is to help everyone to focus on:

› How are you feeling now?
› What's going on in the group at the moment?
› What do you want to happen now?
› What does this experience (behaviour) mean for you (us) now?

Some groups and individuals find it hard to talk about feelings. A group norm may develop or have been brought in from outside that feelings are irrelevant or soft. You can help by modelling how to raise and talk about feelings.

- Deal with emotions as they arise, do not store them up to be dealt with later. Make space and time to deal with people who get upset or angry. Until the feelings have been dealt with, you cannot continue with a productive session.
- Help the feelings to be expressed without pushing anyone. Recognise feelings as *always* valid and true for that individual. Use individuals' own use of words to describe the feelings they are willing to share and guide the rest of the group to respect how others wish to talk about them. For instance, one individual may find it easier to say that he is 'angry' rather than 'upset'; another group member may have the opposite preference. Words have quite specific meanings for different people.
- Offer a constructive challenge to group members who want to protect others from the hurt of feelings and make everything better. Their protective approach may be far more about their own needs and perceived role in the group than what someone else wants or needs.
- Challenge group members who want to speak up for how someone else is feeling or champion them against some assumed slight. It is the individual's right to defend her or himself, or not.
- Sort out the 'We all feel that . . .' into the separate individual 'I's genuinely included in the 'we' and those which are assumed to agree, but whose views have not been checked first.
- Prevent gossip within the group when members talk, or even argue, about the feelings and reactions of another member as if that person is not present. Encourage direct talk to each other, and use their names as appropriate.
- Allow people to say what they wish and no more. Avoid pressing people to share and self-disclose. A group rule may need to be established that 'Everyone has the right to say "I'm not saying any more about that".' Watch out for a group norm of pressure to give more information to satisfy the curiosity of others. Whose needs are being met by continuing?
- Avoid many 'why' questions. Stay with the more productive 'how' or 'what' questions.
- Watch out for individuals who want to take the floor for their own self-disclosure of experience or feelings, but are unwilling to allow space for others.
- Some people may insist on relating the experience of fellow group members to their own with, 'I know exactly how you feel.' You may need to confront such individuals with care, saying, 'Hold on please, I don't think Felicity has finished yet', or, 'I would like us all to listen to Felicity's own version and then

we'll have a much better idea if our own experiences can help.' With serious interrupters, you may have to repeat your comment in slightly different words and with an assertive tone – even on occasion to ask them to shut up for a while.

your own self-disclosure

The points made on page 157 about self-disclosure in one-to-one counselling are equally applicable to the work of a group leader. You may appropriately self-disclose in several different ways:

▸ You share personal feelings to clarify communication within the group, for instance, 'I feel confused about . . ', or, 'I am uncomfortable over what is happening in this group about . . .'

▸ You share brief personal information to help the group forward, for example, 'Yes, I do have some understanding of how you feel. I've got a job now but a few years ago, I was made redundant and it took me 18 months to get another job.'

▸ You say briefly how you feel about an event in the group, for instance, 'Thank you for telling me about . . ', 'I find it pleasing when you . . ', or, 'When you say . . . I find it hard to . . .'

▸ You express personal values and beliefs, when appropriate, such as, 'I don't believe we should be talking about Mina as if she wasn't here', or, 'I don't think we should do . . . without first checking with . . .'

▸ You share experiences gained from running similar groups in the past, or experiences of other approaches to an issue facing group members – all with respect to boundaries of confidentiality.

The central point is that any self-disclosure by a group leader should help the group, or individual members, to achieve their goals. Your self-disclosure will not move the group forward if you:

▸ Have failed to listen and offer an irrelevant self-disclosure.

▸ Share serious feelings of unease or distress. It is not the group's role to help you with these. Share these outside the group, ideally with a trusted colleague or co-leader.

▸ Allow your personal experience to become a focus for the group's discussion. Your professional experience may well allow the group to discuss this new perspective for some time quite appropriately, but not to take over.

▸ Present your experience or feelings as an expert view when they are not. Leaders have quite a lot of power in a group, and it is important to tell the group when you are offering an expert view and when you are not.

▸ Seek group time to work through your feelings or past experience.

▸ Seem through your self-disclosure to condone doubtful behaviour or poor practice within or outside the group.

dominant individuals or subgroups

The development of groups can be swayed by the behaviour of individuals whose actions begin to dominate others. Some people may:

‣ Talk constantly, being the first to speak at each meeting and filling any silence. They may also interrupt and talk over people.
‣ Have the worst problems, the most dramatic difficulties and strive to top other members' experiences.
‣ Be the nicest person, the one who protects and supports other group members whether they want it or not.
‣ Offer assertive help or advice, pronounce on other's problems or insist on speaking up for the rest of the group with, 'We all think that . . .'
‣ Act aggressively and demand attention, especially from the group leader.
‣ Behave in a cynical way, sceptical of the point of any ideas or the point of activities, dismissive of the enthusiasm of others in the group.
‣ Play the clown, joking with or about other members and perhaps refusing to take group activities seriously: 'It's not real. We're just playing games.'

People may dominate a group for a range of different reasons. Reasons are not, of course, sufficient excuses for behaviour that can disrupt a group or reduce the opportunities for other members to participate fully. However, your decision about how to intervene can be guided by keeping an open mind about what fuels the behaviour. Perhaps:

‣ There are problems within the group, maybe lack of trust or confidence in speaking out, and these leave a vacuum that, as group leader, you have only just recognised (perhaps a bit late!).
‣ The group started with unequal relationships, perhaps status differences imported from outside the group, that leave dominant members able to take a lead and others loath to challenge.
‣ The dominating person may be accustomed to being the centre of attention and usually behaves in this way. He or she feels more competent and superior.
‣ A cynic may be reacting to bad previous experiences. He or she deals with a fear of failure by not becoming involved and so avoids risk. Cynics are sometimes protecting themselves to stop anyone coming close.
‣ An individual feels more worthy of attention, more needy and believes that the group should sort out his or her problems as a priority.
‣ A person is unable to tolerate silences.

quiet individuals or subgroups

It can be just as difficult sometimes to deal with very quiet people who may be reticent to express themselves because they:

- Have little self-confidence, fear making mistakes or looking silly in front of other people.
- Have previous bad experiences in groups when their contributions were belittled or dismissed and the group leader did nothing.
- Are in the habit of deferring to particular kinds of people, some of whom are represented in the group. Quiet, passive, individuals are not necessarily content; they may feel resentful and frustrated and this feeling starts to influence the group.
- Want to be noticed for their silence and to be asked to contribute to the group. People can be silent in ways that intrude, through their body language and facial expression, or heavy sighs, dismissive grunts and cynical half-laughs.

scapegoating in groups

Some groups turn on particular individuals, or subgroups (cliques) target one or more individuals. People may be heavily teased or made the butt of jokes or unpleasant innuendo. Ideas may be proposed in a way that dismisses this person, for instance, 'If Richard can manage it, of course', or, 'I can see I've shocked our little Miss Uptight over there!' Individuals who are keen to belong to a group may tolerate, even seem to encourage, jokes made against themselves, but the pattern is disruptive of broader group working. Frequently those scapegoated are different in some way from other group members and the contrast is as likely to be behavioural, that they are quieter or smarter, for example, as are visible differences in how they look.

ways of intervening

When you are working with a single client your choice is when and how to contribute to the conversation and whether to allow a silence to continue. In a group, you have additional choices and decisions because more people are involved as talkers, listeners and observers of the action. The group can take a direction that does not directly involve you, which is acceptable as long as it does not go off-track for the group purpose. If it does you will need to decide both whether and how you intervene. You can use the skills of both Stage One and Stage Two to handle confrontation within the group, to encourage group members to stand back from what is happening and observe the process of what is happening.

do you allow the situation to continue?

There are no hard and fast rules about when you should intervene and when you should listen and watch. Use your skills to judge how you should act and remain very aware of what you are doing as well as the rest of the group.

- You can wait and watch for a short while to judge whether the situation will be handled by the group.

- You can allow a situation to continue, anticipating from experience of this group that other members will intervene in an appropriate way. You can then join and help the group to examine what has been happening.
- Be aware of your own preferred style; your non-intervention should not be just because you dislike confrontation. On the other hand, keen interventionists need to learn that sometimes groups resolve matters themselves.

Disruptive actions or uneven contribution by group members should not be allowed to continue for long. The pattern will become set and that much harder to shift. Trouble may simmer under the surface and group members will complain, either within the group or outside.

indirect responses

Sometimes you can affect how the group works by changing a process or through an activity without openly confronting the issue with the group. For instance:

- Over-talkative or over-quiet group members may be influenced by changes in how people's contributions are managed. Perhaps suggest going round everybody one by one and courteously insist that each person has an uninterrupted turn.
- Some organised group activities (see ideas from page 231) give an opportunity to place individuals in less usual roles within the group.
- You may physically break up subgroups by suggesting or engineering a change in seating to make it harder for the same people to talk to each other.

direct but implicit response

You have some options to affect the group by direct intervention which does not yet identify individuals or a group pattern. You can:

- Give quieter members a chance to speak without identifying them as quiet ones. You might bring someone in with, 'Sasha, I believe you've had experience of . . ', or, 'Dafydd, you started to say something.'
- Halt a dominant person with, 'Hold on a minute, Lesley, I don't think Dafydd had finished.'
- Invite general contributions beyond the ideas of a dominant member with, 'That's a good point, let's see what other people think.'

Quieter group members usually like the opportunity to make a contribution to the group without feeling in the spotlight, or having excessive attention after their contribution.

direct and explicit response

In some groups it becomes necessary to raise the situation as an issue or a problem within this group. You have three main verbal options. You speak:

1 *Directly to an individual* with a comment that describes the situation: 'Richard, you seem to be blamed for . . ', or, 'Lesley, you give so many ideas at once, it's hard to take them in.' Sometimes it will be appropriate to encourage constructive feedback (see page 41) between particular individuals on how they experience each other's behaviour. You might invite a cynic to express doubts more constructively so as to make her or him responsible for the cynicism. A cynic may have a useful point if expressed more positively.

2 *To the rest of the group*, the ones not directly involved, with, 'Does it concern you that Richard is accepting the blame for . . ', or, 'The rest of you are letting Lesley do most of the talking.'

3 *With the whole group* in a way that does not divide off individuals into subgroups. This option is usually preferable since difficulties will affect the entire group in some way. You can ask the group directly to talk about how they are allowing this situation to develop or continue. For instance, 'I'm sure you've all noticed what's happening with . . . can we explore . . . and agree a way to make the group better for everyone?'

However you proceed, your aim is to free individuals from the unhelpful role that they are taking and enable the group to move forward. Your interventions can be gentle, soft but firm, or challenging, depending on the severity of the problem requiring intervention. Your first and preferred approach should be to speak to the individual within the group. If this tactic fails to effect the change that is needed, you might have to speak privately with the person outside the group. As group leader, your commitment is to the success of the group, and this priority may mean in extreme circumstances that you ask a highly disruptive member to leave.

exploration with the group

Your role is to help the group progress further than they would on their own. You are part of the group, yet as leader you have to offer an objective perspective as well. You choose how to approach the range of situations that can arise. These could include: a developing conflict, the scapegoating of an individual or subgroup, avoidance of an activity or topic for exploration, breaking a previously agreed rule or belittling the purpose of the group. You use skills of observation and counselling to understand what seems to be happening and how you may best intervene:

› You need to work out what is happening. By watching and listening, can you identify who is involved and when? Some variations include: one individual is in conflict with another, two group members are setting themselves against you as the leader, or subgroups have developed who are handling the situation in different ways or who are trying to take the group in different directions.

› If the group, or you, appears to have become confused and lost, you need to identify what is most important at this time. Depending on the group, it may be that you show strong leadership, protect individuals or a subgroup, or bring the group back to the agreed task or to the agreed key values.

- Without trying to second-guess individual motivations, consider the emotional needs that may underlie the actions of individual group members (see page 190). You can disapprove of actions and still appreciate the motivations that underlie them.

- Decide if it is appropriate for you to intervene and, if so, say briefly what you see happening, perhaps also what you feel or how the behaviour is affecting the group. Explain simply why you want to discuss what is happening and focus on the here and now of group life.

- Use counselling skills to make informed confrontation a shared experience, pulling back from aggressive responses or highly personal remarks about individuals. You might say, 'I'd like to tell you something I've noticed', and then explain why you feel it is important to the group and invite members to look at what is happening.

- Encourage the group to look at the issues. Perhaps there is very limited commitment at this point and you may decide not to push. However, if the same situation continues or recurs, then consider making a firmer statement, linked if appropriate to the group contract.

- Any discussion should include as many of the group members as possible. It is your role to invite contributions towards a discussion of the problem or where the group appears to be going. Keep the discussion focused on what is happening and how and do not slip into personal blame or revenge between group members. Individuals need the opportunity and encouragement to voice what they need or what they think is happening.

- You can encourage and help the group to consider the consequences of the behaviour of individuals, including those in the group who sit back and watch disapprovingly but do not risk themselves to say anything.

- Deal with the issues as belonging to the group, not just the problem of one or two members. You need to bring out the feelings of everyone involved, including your own. You can consider whether any existing or new group rules would help. Explore what all group members will do about the situation and work to establish a shared responsibility and not just that the dominant person will stop whatever he or she is doing.

- You might also need to make an intervention which changes the structure of the group temporarily to allow a more open debate, or an exercise to help throw the issue into a different light and help the group to learn.

learn about yourself

You will continue to learn about your own behaviour in groups. You will have to deal with what, with hindsight, you believe to have been a poor judgement or a mistake. Willingness to reflect on what you did and why is part of your own development. Just as much as in one-to-one work with clients, you need to consider your own personal style and any ways in which your inclinations may support or mislead you. For instance:

, Perhaps you dislike confrontation and you become aware that this preference tempts you to smooth over conflict in the group rather than using counselling skills to bring out disagreements safely. Smoothing over is a temporary coping mechanism. It does nothing to address the reasons for the conflict and to deal with them directly so that it does not reoccur. Smoothed conflict merely festers beneath the surface.

, Alternatively, you may place a great value on honesty and expression of feelings, however uncomfortable. Your preference leads you to underestimate how raw some of the group feel about what they have been encouraged to disclose and the blunt reactions of some members. Some of the group can feel resentful and frustrated, increasing the chances of conflict later on.

distress in the group

Sometimes someone in a group will become distressed, perhaps because of an event within the group, but possibly because of concerns that are outside the group experience. You may see this situation coming, having noticed that an individual has gone very quiet or tearful, or it may arise without any warning.

, Stay calm. The rest of the group need to see that you are able to cope and are neither embarrassed, nor showing panic.

, Stop the proceedings of the group since it is inappropriate to carry on as if nothing is happening. Apart from being disrespectful, you will make no progress if you continue.

, Offer space to the person and specific comfort as appropriate. It might be a light touch, a hold or hug, depending on the relationship and circumstances. Sometimes, it may be another person in the group who offers the comfort.

, Do not rush to get drinks or do something active. Tissues may be the most that is required if someone is crying.

, Ask if the person wishes to talk, and respect his or her views. If she or he does want to talk then listen and deal briefly with what emerges.

, See if you can talk through the distress to get the group member back on track. You might say, 'Tell us what is happening to you right now', 'How can we help you with this', and reassure as appropriate, perhaps with, 'It's fine to make mistakes. No, I don't think you're stupid at all.'

, If a distressed individual feels unable to stay while distressed, then offer some time out of the group. Does he or she want or need someone with them? Consider how you will ease the entry back. It might be a brief welcome, 'I'm pleased you came back', or a smile.

- Deal with any issues with other group members who feel responsible for causing the upset and reassure if appropriate. Do not let them discuss the incident as if the distressed person is not there.
- Consider whether this person needs additional help and, if so, whether you can give this time. A serious and stressful personal issue, that is very separate from the group work, cannot be handled within the group. If you offer individual help, respect the individual's right to refuse without taking it personally.

Think through how you might handle these scenarios if you were group leader. Work through ideas of the exact words you could use. If possible, discuss some of these examples with a colleague.

- You are running a group on communication skills for reception and front-desk staff. Use of video feedback is part of the learning and this was made clear in the material sent out before the first session. Martha refuses flatly to join any role play that is being videoed. You make the decision to let her sit out for this session, in the hope that she will feel able to participate fully next week. Each role play is then followed by viewing the video and an exchange of constructive feedback. Martha is highly critical of her fellow participants and laughs out loud at one especially awkward moment. You remind Martha firmly of the agreed rules for constructive feedback. She is silent for part of the next feedback but then starts criticising once more.

- Three group members have been targeting James, a quieter individual, by making jokes about any ideas he contributes and teasing him about his dress style. James looks uncomfortable but has refused opportunities to talk about the situation with the group. He now begins any contribution with words like, 'I expect this is a pretty stupid idea', and laughs nervously at the jokes or heavy teasing. From other comments that James has made, you believe that he has learned to tolerate this kind of behaviour in order to have a role in any group.

- Ian normally contributes to the group but he has been very quiet during this session. Max, another group member, tries to bring him in with, 'You're very quiet today, Ian. Aren't we going to get any of your good ideas?' Ian looks stricken and Max follows up lightly with, 'What's the matter? You look like someone's died.' Ian immediately leaves the room. Max looks stunned and says, 'What have I said? I meant it as a joke.' Harriet speaks up: 'It's the first anniversary of the road accident. Ian's daughter was killed this time last year.'

- During the first two sessions of the group, Kamalini has been highly alert for what she judges to be sexist behaviour from any men present. None of the instances which she has confronted have been directed at Kamalini. She speaks up on behalf of other women in the group with phrases like, 'Donna doesn't seem to have noticed, but I think . . .', and, 'We all feel that . . .'. Before the third session, two female group members speak privately with you as leader. They say that they want you to stop Kamalini, they do not agree that any of her examples were sexist, they feel patronised and resent her claim to speak on their behalf.

10.4 activities in the group

Groups spend a great deal of time talking and listening to each other in rooms. Groups also benefit from working in a different way using activities selected in the light of the group objectives and the range of members. These can speed up learning by placing group members in different situations and using different tools. It is worth developing your repertoire of possible activities for groups, which include work on an individual basis, in pairs, small subgroups or whole group work.

Some groups and individuals become blocked into talking in an exclusively rational way. Tapping into the imagination can free up ideas and bring in new perspectives. Group members who place a strong value on rational discussion may be resistant to flights of imagination, so you need to choose with care. Imaginative techniques can also be very relaxing for a group and introduce some lightness and fun, whilst still tapping into the concerns and feelings of the group, sometimes with surprising depth. Some general points about choosing and using activities include:

› Explain the purpose of any activity to the group and manage their expectations about what they will be doing and how.

› Invite but do not insist on participation. Sometimes there will be a choice between being a participant and an observer.

› Make it clear that group members who do not want to join the activity remain part of the group. Discourage unhelpful criticism or poking fun and prevent group members from talking or behaving in ways unrelated to the group activity.

› Be positive and encouraging; expect the activity to be enjoyable and useful.

› Keep an eye on the time, but do not be restricted to a length of time that has worked before. Some groups may take longer, others less, so be guided by this group and do not prolong activities to a point where a group is bored. However, agreed time boundaries for the end of a group meeting or session should be maintained.

› It is usually valuable to review an activity afterwards. This discussion is usually quite brief. You might explore basic questions with the group like, 'What did you think of the activity?', 'What was it like for you?', or, 'What did you get out of it?' Sometimes, even activities that do not work as well as you hoped may still generate a good discussion.

› Group members often want some feedback as to how they did in an activity. You need to provide such feedback without inappropriately appearing the expert or the only person with any insight. There should never be any sense of 'gotcha', in that the leader has manoeuvred the group into experiencing something that should have been obvious at the outset.

- Activities must be suitable for the skills, interests and relevant past experience of group members. Activities can usefully stretch group members and encourage them to take an acceptable level of risk in a safe environment. However, an activity should never purposely expose individuals or show them in a negative light. Learning from such experiences is not predictable and often limited or counter-productive to the well-being of individuals and the group.

warm-up and energising activities

The majority of groups need some introductions at the first session (see page 214) and reminder introductions of names (or continuing with name badges) can be useful in subsequent sessions until no longer needed.

- Some groups need a warm-up at the beginning of each session and you can use different welcome games to practise everyone's name. A regular check-in start to each session allows everyone, including the group leader, to share something to bring the group up to date with how they are feeling, what they have done since the last session or what they are looking forward to in this session.
- Some activities break the ice in a group or boost a sagging energy level. Possible games are to explore communication without words, a 'sword fight' with fingers or making statues out of each other (see page 233).

creative activities

art

There are many ways of using the group's imagination and ideas through art. You should stress that artistic ability is neither the point nor a necessity for involvement and make any such activities straightforward. Some groups express ideas and emotions through drawing or modelling better than verbally, particularly when they find it difficult to put feelings into words or are not verbally adept.

- Collages can build up an image of individuals, the group, or the group as members think they are seen by others. These can help to build a vision of where the group might go, or parts of history that have affected the group. Have a substantial store of magazine pictures, scissors, paste or clear tape and large sheets of paper.
- A drawn self-portrait, personal badge, a self-designed motto, logo or a coat of arms can help people to introduce themselves to the group or to show what is important to them. Keep the materials simple, with pencils, crayons or felt tips, to avoid much cleaning up.

- Group members can show the different sides of themselves through one or more masks.
- Quick line drawings or stick people can sum up feelings of what is happening in the group.
- Drawings, photographs or sketches can be arranged in patterns or 'family trees' to explore relationships within the group or outside in individuals' work, family or friendships.

As with any activity, you should give enough time to discuss and debrief any drawings, collages or models – this usually takes as long, or longer, than the activity itself. Let people share as much as they want from what they have created and resist the temptation to over-interpret. Ideally prevent, or at least discourage, any criticism on artistic grounds since the meaning of the creation is in what the individual wanted to say, not in its technical artistic competence.

expressive writing

Some groups enjoy writing. Less outgoing people are often more comfortable with the written word.

- People might like to keep a group experience diary, either a personal, private journal or a shared group journal to which everyone contributes.
- A group poem or story can be written line by line by different individuals as a way of bringing the group experience together. Neither of these activities necessarily has to be completed within a single group session.
- Ensure that there are no technical blocks to the writing. For instance, poems do not have to rhyme and stories are for this group, not for commercial publication. A group that is uneasy about the actual writing, because of spelling and other literacy issues, can dictate what they wish to say to the group leader to note down accurately.
- Stories might also be supported by pictures from magazines, art or sculptures and presented together with a storyline.
- Personal stories can also be written as a narrative to help each member of the group understand more about everyone else's life before they joined the group. This can also help new members when joining an open group, and may be part of the contract. Group members should never be pressed to disclose more than they wish.

music

There are a number of possibilities for music in groups:

- Consider playing some background music as the group gathers or during a refreshment break. Choose the music as suitable for this group rather than your personal favourite.

- You can sometimes use background or break music to shift the group's mood: quieter music to calm a noisy or disruptive group, lively music to bring back some energy to a group that has sagged.
- Group members may share musical memories or pieces of music that mean a great deal to them. Individuals' musical choices should be respected just as much as any other self-disclosure.
- The use of music can also develop into dance and movement, even 'show us' by acting out a scene, or role play discussed below.

using imagination further

Many of the activities described in this section draw on the group's imagination but some also involve members' more personal use of images, visual descriptions and symbols to extend the work in the group.

Additional ideas include:

- If you were a fly on the wall, that is, not part of the group at all, how would you describe what has just happened or what sense would you make of what is going on?
- What colour is the atmosphere? Pictures and images in the mind can bring out qualities of what is happening that are hard to put into words.
- If we are all animals, which animal are you, what am I? For instance, 'I'm a fox and I'm in my hole and the dogs are coming to get me.'
- If you were a cartoon character, which would you be?
- If we were all on a ship and you were the captain, what would be your first order to us?
- If you could wave a magic wand (or have three wishes about this situation), what would they be?
- If you were listening to yourself as a good friend, what would be your advice? This activity can free people up from the 'ifs' and 'buts' to get to what matters most in the situation.
- How would you like people to remember you after you have died, what would please you to have live on in people's memories?
- In order to get through this difficult situation, who shall I imagine is standing by my side? A real person, someone from a favourite film or television programme, a mythical hero or heroine?
- Use imagination as part of relaxation techniques with a group. Follow a steady pattern of talking the group into a relaxed state and allow time to bring people out of relaxation.
- The activity of body sculpting is a way to encourage group members to move themselves, or to move others, into a living sculpture or live photograph. This sculpture can bring alive some issue or concern in the group, or symbolise feelings or difficulties that are hard to put into words. A body sculpture can

show feelings of relative closeness or distance between individuals in the group. Sometimes it makes sense to invite the group to repeat the activity in a later session and look for any changes.

Some of the above suggestions may look like lightweight games but, in some groups, the activities can release strong feelings or trigger self-disclosures that need respectful handling. All your counselling skills remain as important as ever as you lead and guide the group.

role play

This kind of activity can be developed in several different ways:

‣ You can plan and guide a briefed role play in which some of the group take on a role as a different person and may have to imagine themselves into a given situation. They are briefed for the situation and characters (if necessary). The aim of role play is to resolve a problem, reach a decision, run a meeting, practise a skill or some other clear purpose. This kind of role play is useful in training groups.
‣ Some groups benefit from a role play in which at least one individual is her or himself. This activity gives a chance for group members to replay a past event in a way they would prefer, perhaps to tell someone something and begin to resolve an issue. Some members find role play an easier way to show the rest of the group how they feel or behave in a given situation. This individual will need to brief the other people in his or her role play.
‣ Role play also works as a real life rehearsal. Perhaps individuals want to prepare for an upcoming event like an interview or to practise how to handle a situation that regularly arises, like how to avoid drinking more alcohol than is safe. Again, one or more individuals will be themselves and they will brief the support roles they want other people to play.

Role play is a flexible activity that can work well if the following points are observed:

‣ The details of the role play should be suited to the current needs of the group, everyone should be briefed appropriately and the role play debriefed properly.
‣ The main advantage of the technique is the direct involvement of everyone. So anyone not given a role to play should be briefed to be an attentive observer. Everyone should be involved in debriefing.
‣ Role play can increase spontaneity and free up individuals to behave in ways that they would not normally and they can learn from this experience. A group member with a passive style can sometimes learn much from playing the role of being a highly assertive person, particularly when he or she wishes to achieve this change, and they find the role play both easy and satisfying.

▸ You (or the role players) can stop a role play at any point, but be aware that some groups may find it hard to restart. Ask people to exchange roles or invite individuals to step into a role to express matters differently, or say something that they feel is not being expressed by the current role-holder, to keep the momentum going.

It is always important to debrief a role play, to discuss what has happened after the completion:

▸ You need to enable individuals to step out of role and back to the present and themselves. When feelings are strong, this adjustment may need more than a few moments.
▸ Invite comments from the people directly involved: how did they feel in role, what did they feel about other people, what do they now understand about the situation?
▸ Turn to the observers for comments. What did they notice, what have they learned?
▸ Encourage a general discussion of issues raised by the role play itself.

do you record group activities?

It is sensible to keep a record of what is agreed and decided. The taking of minutes – if appropriate – should be rotated around group members. In addition, groups may want to keep their drawings or written thoughts. On the other hand they may be keen that these are destroyed. You should respect their wishes in this regard. Some training groups have the option of video recording an activity. For some groups, use of video would be inappropriate and provoke anxiety among group members. However, video recording is useful when the group objective is for individuals to learn how they react in a given situation or to practise skills. Several issues arise over positive and responsible use of video:

▸ Groups should always know that they are being videoed; there should be no covert recording.
▸ If individuals are using video for practice and feedback, everyone who wants to practise on video should be given the opportunity in a 'round robin' fashion.
▸ You should allow time within the group session for the participants to watch the recording together soon after the activity. You will need at least twice the amount of time that the activity took in real time. You can stop the recording for discussion during the playback as well as exploring the issues with the participants and observers at the end. Ensure that any discussion is constructive and there is no blaming of individuals or using the recording as proof that 'You always . . .' or 'He never . . .'
▸ Be ready to give time to individuals who have issues arising from how they have seen themselves.

> Wipe the recording as soon as everyone has seen it, or be explicit that the video becomes the property of the person practising, for example, if no one objects.

⋯⋯⋯⋯⋯⋯⋯⋯⋯⋯⋯⋯⋯⋯⋯⋯I FURTHER INFORMATION

You will find many activities and games in the following:

▷ John W. Newstrom and Edward E. Scannell, *The Big Book of Team Building Games: Trust-Building Activities, Team Spirit Exercises, and Other Fun Things to Do* (McGraw-Hill, 1997).

▷ Edie West, *201 Icebreakers* (McGraw-Hill, 1997).

10.5 the end of a group

Group members have a variety of feelings about ending, depending on its nature and the experience within the group. People may feel satisfied with a job well done, sad about the end of the group and the loss of relationships that have been built, relieved that an uncomfortable or painful experience is now over and so on. Group leaders also experience a range of feelings.

Groups who do not want to end may try to prolong the group's life by:

> Denying that the group can end.
> Trying to find problems or other reasons to continue.
> Dropping out before the end as a form of avoidance.
> Planning reunions rather than accepting the end.

It is usually disappointing to prolong groups artificially. You need to address directly the feelings in the group that prevent letting go. Work through the suggested ways to end the group, given below, and leave members a choice to continue informal social contact without the group leader.

Some groups end prematurely because:

> The group has achieved its task(s) more swiftly than anyone anticipated.
> The group has not been able to attract enough members or has experienced such variable attendance that the group cannot function.
> Serious misunderstandings about the purpose of the group or how it will run have not been resolved and the group is brought to an end.

Ideally, you need to review any progress the group has made and to understand how it has come to an early end when the reasons are anything other than the completion of the group's task.

when group leaders find it hard to end a group

Sometimes a group is ready to end and the group leader is as resistant, or more so, than the members. You need to remain alert and honest with yourself when a group strongly fulfils your needs. Perhaps you enjoy the social contact of a group that is now completely capable of continuing without you. In some groups, the entire purpose is to develop group working skills to a point at which the group leader has worked him or herself out of a job. The aim of group work, as with individual counselling, is that the helper creates abilities and motivation in those who are helped, not a greater or continuing dependency. Some groups may have the confidence and honesty to tell you that your work is appreciated but no longer needed. On the other hand, you may conspire with a group that wants to continue when you, as group leader, should be helping them to review and make an end.

You may need to talk with a colleague or supervisor to come to terms with your own feelings, what this group meant to you or how you need to set yourself new goals rather than hold on to old ones.

It is a fundamental part of the role of group leaders to help groups to end in different ways:

- If appropriate, make it clear at the outset that the group is scheduled for a fixed number of sessions.
- Keep an eye on the completion of individual or group tasks as the end of group time approaches. If appropriate allow group activity to wind down somewhat, but not to the point of boredom. Avoid starting new activities and projects that cannot be completed in the time left.
- Some groups may naturally move towards relationships and links outside the group and you may encourage this shift. In some groups, external speakers may be invited to emphasise a positive movement away from group life.
- Allow the time to review and celebrate progress with the group. You can cover issues such as: 'Where did we start?', 'What was the group like for you?', 'Where are you now and where are you going now?' In some groups it will be appropriate to help members to plan their next move, perhaps through the logical steps of force field analysis (see page 184).
- Express your appreciation to the group of what has been achieved. If positive, and therefore appropriate, share with them what you have learned and enjoyed. An alert and effective group leader usually learns something with each group experience, but it is not suitable to share feelings such as, 'I've learned that I hate group work.'
- Seek to give group members a tangible memento of the group. It may be a copy of a group photograph, a group diary or a certificate of attendance.
- Individual unfinished business or needs still unmet will have to be handled outside the group, by you or through an appropriate referral.
- Some groups want and appreciate a proper ending through celebration. It may be a plate of seriously indulgent cakes, a group trip to the pub, a meal or a party.
- Whatever you do, recognise the importance of a proper ending, and for some members that means an opportunity to grieve.

▷ Allan Brown, *Groupwork* (Gower Community Care Practice Handbooks, 1989).

▷ Kimball Fisher *et al.*, *Tips for Teams: A Ready Reference for Solving Common Team Problems* (McGraw-Hill, 1993)

▷ Marianne Schneider Corey and Gerald Corey, *Groups: Process and Practice* (Brooks Cole, 1997).

specific applications in brief

This chapter provides a brief review of some specific applications of counselling skills and suggestions for further resources.

11.1 mediation or conciliation

Mediation services use a specific application of counselling skills when clients are in dispute or conflict. Mediators help other people by offering the following opportunities:

‣ Each person in a conflict to be heard in turn. Mediators use the skills of reflective listening and non-judgemental questioning, with support skills to enable involved individuals both to express themselves and listen to others.
‣ In an even-handed way, mediators create a conciliation process, in which disputants are enabled to see both sides, to acknowledge each other's feelings and to focus on the main issues.
‣ The parties are helped to explore possible choices and to negotiate and offer compromise between the possibilities.
‣ The end of the mediation process is that all involved individuals agree on a mutually acceptable way forward.

One use of mediation skills is to support couples who are in the process of separation and divorce with the aim of reducing the high levels of conflict and hostility that can arise far too easily. The skills have been successfully taught to children and young people, often as part of the personal and social element of a school curriculum. Primary school children as young as nine and ten years old have become effective playground supporters enabling their peers to deal with conflict in a non-aggressive way.

further resources

‣ For general information about mediation, contact Mediation UK, Alexander House, Telephone Avenue, Bristol BS1 4BS. Tel.: 0117 904 6661, website:

www.mediationuk.org.uk. The project Bristol Mediation at the same address is involved with schools.

- ▸ For information about using mediation skills to help couples who separate, contact National Family Mediation, 7 The Close, Exeter, Devon EX1 1EZ. Tel.: 01392 271610, website: www.nfm.org.uk.
- ▸ For workplace issues, the Centre for Effective Dispute Resolution is an independent non-profit organisation focusing on encouraging and developing mediation and other dispute resolution and prevention techniques. Tel.: 020 7536 6000, website www.cedr.co.uk.
- ▸ Hilary Stacey and Pat Robinson, *Let's Mediate: A Teachers' Guide to Peer Support and Conflict Resolutions for all Ages* (Sage/Lucky Duck Publishing, 1997).

11.2 advocacy

An advocate acts as an objective representative of an individual whose interests and concerns may not otherwise be heard. Advocacy should operate so as to empower clients to have their viewpoint heard, to exert control over their lives and to obtain their legal rights. Advocacy should not be used if it is possible for clients to deal with the situation themselves.

Advocacy on behalf of children can be a valuable addition to the mediation process for separating couples. Agreements at the end of mediation may deal with arrangements for continued contact for children with the non-resident parent. However, mediators are not usually in a position to follow through how such arrangements work in practice. An advocate for children can bring their perspective and their rights to the fore, whilst helping to maintain a friendly relationship with both parents uncomplicated by the adults' continuing frustrations with each other.

A guardian *ad litem* (GAL) is appointed to represent children, their wishes and interests, in a range of legal proceedings. GALs need to establish rapport with a child but will not form a closer relationship since their work ends with the final hearing in court. Independent visitors are appointed for children and young people in local authority care who have little or no contact with their families. The visitors may act as advocates in ensuring children's views are heard and also develop social relationships with the children.

Advocates represent adult clients when they lack the relevant expertise or language to deal with the situation. Advocates are also essential if clients are not permitted to attend the setting in which they need representation.

For advocacy to work:

- ▸ The role of the advocate and the boundaries of that role have to be very clear to all concerned. Clients need to understand both the potential benefits of and the limits to advocacy.

- Advocates must listen to clients and enable them to ask questions and to express their priorities. Advocates are professionals working under their clients' instructions and should never act so as to undermine clients or to encourage dependency.
- An advocate has to reach an agreement with a client about the terms and conditions of the advocacy and this pattern should be consistently applied across the service. As with any helping service, advocacy needs realistic aims and if the client does not agree with those aims then other avenues need to be explored.

further resources

- There is a general discussion of advocacy in Naomi Dale, *Working with Families of Children with Special Needs: Partnership and Practice* (Routledge, 1996).
- The work of guardians *ad litem* is described in Susan Howard, *Guardians ad litem and Reporting Officers* (National Children's Bureau, Highlight, no. 147, 1997).
- NAGALRO is the professional association for children's guardians, children and family reporters and Independent Social Workers and is contactable at NAGALRO, PO Box 264, Esher, Surrey KT10 0WA. Tel.: 01372 818504, website: www.nagalgro.com.
- The work of independent visitors is described in Abigail Knight, *Valued or Forgotten? Disabled Children and Independent Visitors* (National Children's Bureau and Joseph Rowntree Foundation, 1998).
- If you want to know more about advocacy with children and young people, contact the National Youth Advocacy Service, 99–105 Argyle Street, Birkenhead, Wirral CH41 6AD. Tel.: 0151 649 8700, website: www.nyas.net.

11.3 bereavement and loss

British society has lost many of the supportive rituals surrounding death, with the consequence that many people are uncertain how to behave towards friends or acquaintances experiencing a loss. Individuals who have lost someone they loved can find that friends and acquaintances offer clichés that seem to diminish their pain, phrases like, 'It was a happy release', or, 'It's been a year now, surely you're getting over it.'

The 'medicalisation' of death has meant that today many people die in hospital rather than at home. Bereaved relatives sometimes have to deal with brusque reactions from health care staff which worsen their own distress. In contrast, the hospice movement has worked hard to create a caring atmosphere in which terminally ill individuals can feel respected and able to spend time with loved ones. Hospitals or units for very sick or disabled children have also developed good practice in involvement of the whole family through caring concern by staff.

The bereaved cannot change the fact of death, hence the counselling focus is on managing their continuing life. Counselling bereaved clients follows a very similar pattern to work with any client, but there are some special issues:

> When individuals have lost someone very close, they often go through a phase of feeling numb, of shock at what has happened and even a sense of disbelief. It can help to alert bereaved clients that such feelings are not unusual. However, clients should never be given the impression that there are fixed stages in bereavement, nor should their individuality be undermined by comments like, 'Everyone goes through this.'

> Clients may experience a mixed range of emotions. People may feel distress along with feelings of guilt about what was done or not done, anger with other family members or the medical profession who should have done more, and even anger at the person who has died and left them. Your role is to listen in a non-judgemental way and to support your client to move forward.

> Over time clients need to reach acceptance of their loss. You may be able to help by listening as they talk through the circumstances of loss, perhaps many times. However, clients who cared deeply for a deceased partner, close friend or child may never be over that loss completely, because it has changed their life for ever.

> Help them to find their own way of coping and to grieve in a way that best supports them. What worked well for a friend will not necessarily be right for this client.

> Clients may be helped by positive remembrance. Removing all reminders of the person who has died is certainly not the best way forward for everyone. Talking about that person can be a positive part of coming to terms with loss. Finding past happy memories can be especially important when the most recent memories are of a loved one in pain or fading away from illness.

> Children and young people are also bereaved and can be overlooked in the distress of adult family members. Younger children may be particularly left out because of the inaccurate belief that 'They don't understand' or 'It's better not to upset them.' Cruse (see below) has valuable material on supporting children.

> Be aware that working with bereaved clients can arouse your own feelings of loss from the past or fears about losing loved ones. It is unwise to work with bereaved clients when you are still raw from a personal loss. It is too difficult to separate the feelings and offer the caring detachment necessary.

You may work with clients who are themselves terminally ill. Clients should always have the choice whether to talk with someone or not; it should never be forced on them. Realistic goals in using counselling skills in this situation can include to:

- Help clients talk about their situation with someone who does not resort to false hopes or clichés.
- Listen to clients' feelings, preferences and choices. Perhaps help them to action some choices.
- Support clients in coming to terms with their limited time and to consider any actions they wish to take: to complete tasks, say goodbyes or make arrangements. Clients may appreciate a sense of closure and appropriate support for those they leave behind.
- Support older children and young people who may be fully aware that they will not recover and will value talking with someone just as much as a dying adult.

further resources

- Cruse-Bereavement Care, Unit 0.1, One Victoria Villas, Richmond, Surrey TW9 2GW. Tel.: 020 8939 9530, website: www.crusebereavementcare.org.uk.
- Colin Murray Parkes, *Bereavement: Studies of Grief in Adult Life*, 3rd edn (Penguin Books, 1998).

11.4 crisis and trauma

life transitions and crises

Normal adult life involves periods of uncertainty and distress that can be severe enough to be called life crises. Such events include redundancy, divorce, death in the family, children growing up and leaving home – in fact any event that requires people to readjust familiar patterns and established relationships. Counselling skills are very suitable for supporting clients in life changes. The stages described in Chapters 7 and 8 help clients to move from a full understanding of their current situation (Stage One), to an exploration of how they would prefer matters to be (Stage Two), how to make that transition (Stage Three) and making the transition (Stage Four).

- Because Stage One is exploratory, you offer clients the opportunity to tell their story to someone who will listen and contribute in a non-judgemental way. During life transitions and crises the client may be in shock, unable to take in all the events, minimising what has happened or plagued with self-doubt. Acceptance of the client and gentle exploration can be especially reassuring when clients are uncertain. They may also have experienced unhelpful, although well-meant, interventions from friends, family and other professionals.
- You build a relationship of trust and allow the client to acknowledge mixed feelings: excitement, relief, panic, paralysis. Clients can step aside from the

urgency to do something or to control their feelings. You create time for the client 'to look before you leap'.

▸ Clients in transition can become stuck in Stage One, perhaps continually replaying what happened: the children have left home, there is a serious crisis in the partnership, the experience of redundancy or the final blocking of a much desired goal. By moving to Stage Two, you help clients to take stock and move on in a way that makes sense to them.

▸ In a respectful way, you identify and work on issues that will make a difference to this individual client. Clients may have been driven by friends and family to an unhelpful way of trying to move on. You can help them to explore ways to adjust and grow.

Through Stage Two, you can support clients to examine what their better future could look like. They need to accept the reality of change and that there is no going back. Goal-setting can be a watershed for clients, helping them to let go of the past and shift attention through the present to the future.

accident and trauma

Traumatic events destabilise people for weeks, months or even years. Personal feelings of control and the sense of being able to protect yourself and others are undermined by accidents, assaults and the violation of possessions through break-ins and burglaries. Even minor events can create anxieties where there had been confidence, and raise mixed feelings about what has happened and whether the situation could have been avoided.

Anyone who has experienced a potentially traumatic event should be given a choice about whether to talk with someone and when. Individuals do not always want to talk and pushing people against their will only adds to whatever distress they already feel. Counselling can offer an opportunity to talk through feelings and the impact of the event. Some issues that arise include:

▸ Clients who have not been physically hurt can still be unnerved by what has happened and realise that their anxiety or fear is affecting their behaviour. They want help to recognise what is happening and how best to cope.

▸ Clients need support when they have disturbing experiences such as flashbacks, intrusive thoughts about a traumatic event or recurrent distressing dreams. Reassurance that this is normal can be appropriate, since clients may feel they are losing their mind. Effective help then needs to move towards how to cope better.

▸ Children who have minor injuries from an accident can still feel great emotional distress and do not necessarily tell their parents or carers. The extent of upset becomes more obvious through their general behaviour and play. Child witnesses to accidents are sometimes just as distressed as their injured sibling or friend, whose feelings are more likely to have been addressed.

▸ Clients frequently express mixed feelings, not all of which are logical. They may still need to talk through whether they could have avoided what happened. Individuals often need to locate more responsibility with the criminal who attacked them or the driver who caused the accident, rather than revisiting their own actions as if they are to blame. Victims of random violence sometimes seek some rational basis for what happened, when it was just that they were in the wrong place at the wrong time.

post-traumatic stress disorder (PTSD)

PTSD is defined as a specific collection of symptoms that have persisted for more than a month after a traumatic event. Similar symptoms that last less than a month are known as acute stress disorder. Some of the symptoms of trauma-related stress are:

▸ Persistent recollection of the event, through intrusive thoughts or distressing dreams
▸ Reliving the event through vivid flashbacks
▸ Intense psychological or physiological distress reactions to experiences that are linked to the event
▸ Persistent avoidance of memories and blockage of feelings
▸ Children experience similar symptoms, although they may relive a traumatic event through repetitive play, re-enacting parts of the experience and apparently unrelated disturbed behaviour triggered by an inability to talk about or deal with the distressing feelings.

Dealing with PTSD is a specialised area of offering help and, unless you have received appropriate training, you should look towards referral of a client who, it emerges, is experiencing PTSD. (See page 98 about referral.)

further resources

▸ The Child Accident Prevention Trust, 4th Floor, Cloister Court, 22–26 Farringdon Lane, London EC1R 3AJ. Tel.: 020 7608 3828, website: www.capt.org.uk.
▸ Michael Scott and Stephen Stradling, *Counselling for Post Traumatic Stress Disorder*, 3rd edn (Sage, 2006).

11.5 helping children and young people

Good communication with children and young people has much in common with communicating well with adults. However, some points to bear in mind include:

- The younger the child, the more any helper has to adjust appropriately to his or her understanding and language skills. However, adults often underestimate children's ability either to express themselves when someone listens attentively or to understand when someone explains carefully.
- A child's view can be different from that of older people and you need to work that bit harder to look through children's eyes to avoid assuming how they feel or make sense of a situation. Children may use words differently from adults or lack the language to express subtle distinctions. Often, communicating through play and artwork helps. Make sure that you check your understanding and reassure the children that you want to understand clearly.
- Children are often aware of crises, such as serious illness in the family, redundancy or troubles between their parents, but are not given much information. They have to fill in the gaps. As such they may consequently gain an inaccurate idea of what is happening and their role or responsibility in a difficult situation. They may think it is their fault when it is not.
- Children experiencing troubles of their own, for instance over bullying, may not believe that their life could be different. Even more than adults facing problems, children can be burdened with the view that change is impossible and attempts to share their problem will only bring blame or more distress. Children typically do not see themselves as powerful as do adults.
- Since children are less likely than adults to construe problems as something that could be resolved, they are more likely to be referred for help because an adult is concerned about them. Supportive families and schools with an effective pastoral system are more likely to encourage children to speak out on their own behalf.
- Even more than adults, children are inclined to say what they feel is expected or what adults want to hear. This tendency is worsened by experiencing adults' leading questions or demands to know why the children have done something. Open-ended questions and reflective listening is crucially important to establish trust that you genuinely wish to hear what children feel and think.

further resources

- Kathryn Geldard and David Geldard *Counselling Children: A Practical Introduction*, 2nd edn (Sage, 2002).
- Jennie Lindon, *Safeguarding Children and Young People: Child Protection 0–18 years*, 3rd edn (Hodder & Stoughton, forthcoming).
- John McGuiness, *Counselling in Schools: New Perspectives* (Cassell, 1998).

11.6 helping in health-care settings

Although attitudes have improved, helpers within health-care settings may still have to counteract the medical tradition of people as patients, with all the negative overtones that the term entails. Some specific issues arise with work in health care:

▸ Health, illness, diagnosis and treatment are not just physical and physiological processes; feelings are also involved and can often be crucial to a positive outcome.

▸ Ill health cannot just be seen as a person passively reacting to a condition. His or her outlook and confidence and the extent of support all have an influence on the progress and outcome. Anxiety and lack of information can worsen an individual's outlook. The disease is medically treatable, the illness is not.

▸ Frequently, the illness of one person has an impact on others, especially in the immediate family. Continued chronic illness of an adult or a child affects all the workings of family life.

Clients in health-care settings should not be automatically referred for counselling support. It must be a choice for the client. There should be no stigma of referral of people 'who can't cope'. The availability of such support should certainly not relieve medical staff of the responsibility to treat 'patients' well.

In health-care settings you need to allow for the often strong emotional content of information about diagnosis and possible treatment.

▸ Clients need information but also the time to absorb confusing or distressing facts and to ask questions.

▸ Encourage clients to ask questions, showing that you welcome these and will answer to the best of your knowledge.

▸ Clients will not necessarily absorb all the information, especially a distressing diagnosis, all at once. They often need more than one opportunity to hear something or patience and time within one conversation. Always leave the opportunity to come back after a first meeting.

▸ Explanations about possible courses of action need to be clear and honest so that clients can make an informed decision. Clients may be depressed by the medical conclusion that 'There's nothing we can do' and not realise that symptoms can be relieved even though the underlying condition is untreatable.

▸ Be aware that clients will not necessarily share the same priorities as health-care professionals. Parents, for instance, will often have obligations and concerns in addition to the child with whom you are involved. Everyone has to balance life to meet different priorities.

▸ Be honest if the situation is one of 'We do not know yet' or 'We do not know why'.

▸ Consider using more than one way to communicate information about a condition or approach to treatment. Check if a video is available. Talking and listening can be supported by informative leaflets, and there is the possibility of talking with people in a similar position. Clients need to decide for themselves what is best and on what kind of timescale.

> Robert Bor, Riva Millar, Martha Latz and Heather Salt, *Counselling in Health Care Settings* (Cassell, 1998).
> The *Telephone Helplines Directory* is a valuable source of information on organisations with a specific health focus. (See page 118 for full reference.)

support for children and young people

If you work within health care, take account of the age and understanding of young clients and remain sensitive to individual reactions. Normally confident adults are not at their best when worried or confused and in unfamiliar surroundings. Adults may hide the depth of their feelings or find strategies to cope. In contrast, children will often express their distress, panic or pain without reservation. Children experience embarrassment and loss of dignity in a similar way to adults or teenagers and dismissive or rude treatment can greatly complicate any health procedure. The feelings are the same as for adults, but what children do about them is often different.

Children and young people may appreciate and need the company of a familiar adult, but no-one should talk only to the adult as if the child is not there. Parents will be in a better position to help and support their children if they are given information about a service or a condition. It is less effective to depend only on talking; advice is probably best given in written form as well as spoken.

further resources

> Action for Sick Children, 36 Jacksons Edge Road, Disley, Stockport SK12 2JL. Tel. (Freephone): 0800 0744519, website: www.actionforsickchildren.org.
> Richard Lansdown, *Children in Hospital: A Guide for Families and Carers* (Oxford University Press, 1996).

11.7 disability and chronic health conditions

Working with clients with disabilities or chronic health conditions raises some issues additional to usual good practice in using of counselling skills. You may need to examine your own attitudes – especially when first working with disabled clients. The general concerns raised in Section 1.6 on equality and anti-discriminatory practice apply but further, more specific issues include:

> Ensuring a respectful balance between inappropriately ignoring a client's disability or condition and overreacting so that you fail to see the individual person past the disability.

- Being wary of stereotypes of disabled adults or children that persist in society, whether these are backhanded compliments about being 'brave' or 'special', or negative views such that parents of disabled children are 'over-protective'.
- It is crucial to challenge any of your own unquestioned assumptions that somehow disability is incompatible with intelligence, emotional strength or the ability to make important choices.
- It is dishonest, and often unhelpful, to insist on treating disabled or chronically sick clients 'just like anyone else'. Acknowledge the situation in a straightforward way. Some clients may specifically want to talk about how their disability or illness makes an impact on their daily life.

Action planning with disabled clients has to take relevant account of the disability and not create unrealistic hopes or plans. Even if you share your client's condition, you may still experience different levels of severity in that condition. The usual caution must apply about assuming a similar experience means that clients will share your perspective and priorities.

Clients may need attention relevant to their disability:

- Always enquire what a client would like or will find helpful. You can ask, 'How can I help you with . . .?', or, 'How would you prefer to handle . . .?' Some disabled people may be used to being touched as part of receiving assistance but be careful to offer such help with respect.
- Clients with limited mobility may need assistance within your building or it may be considerate to rearrange your work setting or meeting place.
- Clients with visual disabilities may appreciate help in finding their way around an unknown environment. In conversation, bear in mind that visually disabled clients will not be able to see your body language and the extent of their visual disability will determine how much information is lost. Hence, even though you and your client are physically together, your words and tone of voice have to carry most of the message, rather like telephone communication.
- Clients with hearing disabilities need appropriate communication adjustments from you. The organisation Hearing Concern publishes a useful leaflet, *Break the Sound Barrier*, which explains simple ways for hearing people to improve their communication with individuals who are hard of hearing or deaf. Hearing Concern are at 95 Gray's Inn Road, London WC1X 8TX. Tel.: 020 7440 9871, website: www.hearingconcern.org.uk.

Clients will not benefit from an overprotective attitude from a helper:

- Disabled or sick clients may need to be challenged constructively about their behaviour through Stage Two counselling skills.
- Clients may need to recognise the consequences of their care of themselves, for example mismanagement of a diabetic regime which brings serious health risks.

- Unreasonable behaviour towards friends and family is not made reasonable by the client's condition. If you work with the parents of disabled or very sick children, you may well help parents to establish a better balance. The children deserve attention to their special needs but still benefit, like any children, from clear boundaries.
- Some clients, and parents on behalf of their children, become of necessity experts in the disability or condition. Their expertise can easily coexist with yours so long as you have not tried to establish yourself as an all-round expert inappropriately.

further resources

- Naomi Dale, *Working with Families of Children with Special Needs: Partnership and Practice* (Routledge, 1996).
- Peggy Dalton, *Counselling People with Communication Problems* (Sage, 1994).
- Hilton Davis, *Counselling Parents of Children with Chronic Illness or Disability* (BPS Blackwell, 1997).

HIV-Aids

A helping relationship may be established with the adult who has been diagnosed HIV-positive or with the parent or carer of a child or young person with the condition. Working in this area raises particular concerns:

- Clients who are HIV-positive may have many years of healthy living but still face social difficulties because of their condition. Confidentiality is key here, and clients may want support in discussing whether to disclose their condition.
- HIV-Aids brings inevitable uncertainty about the best treatment, contradictory advice, and likely side-effects in known or experimental medication. The area is unusual in that medical professionals have not retained control over facts, options and research. Possibilities are extensively discussed and information disseminated through activist groups, publications and the Internet.
- Individuals, and their loved ones, will face at some point all the problems of chronic ill health and impending death.

Counselling skills are typically offered to clients at different points in the process:

- Before an HIV test takes place
- While clients are waiting for the result
- When they receive the result
- During the healthy period before any symptoms appear, as well as when physical symptoms are apparent, when clients may wish to discuss possible courses of treatment

- When clients want to discuss possible disclosure of their condition and any issues arising from relationships, family or work
- Coping with the terminal stage of the condition and preparing for death.

Counselling may also be offered to clients' partners, family or to anyone who fears they may be at risk.

further resources

- Terrence Higgins Trust, 314–320 Gray's Inn Road, London WC1X 8DP. Tel.: 020 7812 1600, website: www.tht.org.uk.

11.8 work with couples or families

Clients may seek help as a couple because they realise that problems are rooted in their relationship. Alternatively, an individual may want to talk about difficulties in an intimate relationship but his or her partner never becomes involved in the sessions. Relevant organisations often started as agencies focused on saving marriages; now most have developed towards a more general use of counselling to help relationships and to ease separation if necessary.

Working with couples or families is complex:

- As individuals encourage you to take sides, remaining an objective helper can be hard work. Working with a colleague can help but needs just as much care, and discussion outside the situation, as co-leading a group (see page 201).
- It takes effort to work through what is happening and to make clear distinctions between this and what the parties believe to be happening. It is easy to be pulled into the dynamics of a couple or a family.
- Change in either a couple or a whole family has a series of consequences. The change in behaviour of one partner, or family member, usually requires adjustments from others which are not always welcome. Habits are developed in a relationship and how a family runs, and such habits are hard to change.
- You can be provoked, uncomfortably sometimes, into looking at your own close relationships with a partner or within your family.

An understanding of couple relationships and families can be important in the use of counselling skills described within this book. However, specific work with couples or families needs further training.

further resources

- Rudi Dallos and Rosalind Draper *An Introduction to Family Therapy: Systemic Theory and Practice*, 2nd edn (Sage, 2005).

> Mary Pipher, *The Shelter of Each Other: Rebuilding our Families to Enrich Our Lives* (Ballantine Books, 1997).
> Mary Pipher, *Reviving Ophelia: Helping You to Understand and Cope with your Teenage Daughter* (Vermilion, 1996).

11.9 work with older clients

Apart from the wide range of concerns that any clients bring to you, older clients may also have difficulties or issues that arise specifically from being in their later decades of life. It is important for you to remain aware of anti-discriminatory practice because:

> Older clients often experience patronising attitudes from others during their daily life, with disrespectful assumptions that they are unable to make choices, to learn or even to understand unless people raise their voice. Your practice should affirm older clients as individuals and avoid unchecked assumptions based only on age.
> Clients can be very aware of their own failing health and are frustrated over enforced changes to their lifestyle. Some may have difficulty in coming to terms with illness or frailty. Others will appreciate the chance to talk through practical issues such as achieving independent mobility without a car.
> Clients in their 70s and 80s often face the ill health and loss of friends and partners. A shrinking social circle can lead to loneliness – even for the more outgoing clients.
> Some older clients will have carers, either within the family or in a residential home. You may work with older people themselves, with carers or both. You need to focus clearly on who is the client in your relationships with different individuals in the situation. Be careful not to conspire in a situation where older clients are marginalised or talked about as if they were absent from the session.

further resources

> Mike Nolan, Sue Davies and Gordon Grant (eds), *Working with Older People and Their Families: Key Issues in Policy and Practice* (Open University Press, 2001).
> Age Concern England, Astral House, 1268 London Road, London SW16 4ER. Tel.: 0208 8765 7200, website: www.ageconcern.org.uk. Age Concern also publish a Carers Handbook Series with a range of practical titles.
> Help the Aged, 207–221 Pentonville Road, London N1 9UZ. Tel.: 020 7278 1114, website: www.helptheaged.org.uk.

11.10 general resources

The following cover use of counselling skills with a wide range of clients.

- Patricia d'Ardenne and Aruna Mahtani, *Transcultural Counselling in Action*, 2nd edn (Sage, 1999).
- Windy Dryden, *Key Issues for Counselling in Action* (Sage, 1991).
- Windy Dryden and Brian Thorne (eds), *Training and Supervision for Counselling in Action* (Sage, 1991).
- Colin Feltham and Ian E. Horton, *The Sage Handbook of Counselling and Psychotherapy*, 2nd edn (Sage, 2005).
- Dave Robson and Maggie Robson, 'Counselling via the Internet: Is it Ethical?' (*The Ethicomp Journal*, 2.2, 2005) or website: www.ccsr.cse.dmu.ac.uk/journal/articles/robson_d_counselling.html.
- John McLeod, *An Introduction to Counselling*, 3rd edn (Open University Press, 2003).
- Dave Mearns and Brian Thorne, *Person-centred Counselling in Action*, 2nd edn (Sage, 1999).
- Stephen Palmer with Gladeana McMahon (eds), *Handbook of Counselling*, 2nd edn (Routledge, 1997). This book includes full details of the British Association for Counselling's Codes of Ethics and Practice for counsellors, counselling skills, supervisors of counsellors and trainers of counsellors.
- Jan Sutton and William Stewart, *Learning to Counsel: Develop the Skills you Need to Counsel Others*, 2nd edn (How To Books Ltd, 2002).

The following publishers have series on counselling which offer a wide range of titles – worth checking if you want to explore specific applications of the skills:

- British Psychological Society: *Communication and Counselling in Health Care Settings.*
- Palgrave Macmillan: *Basic Texts in Counselling and Psychotherapy.*
- PCCS Books: *Incomplete Guides* (the series title indicates that the books are good for basic skills rather than unfinished!).
- Sage: *Counselling Practice.*
- Sage: *Counselling in Action.*
- Sage: *Professional Skills for Counsellors.*
- Sheldon Press: *Overcoming Common Problems.* The books in this series are written directly to people experiencing the problem but will also be a source of information and insight if you are in a helping role.

safe practice for yourself, your team and your clients

12.1 safety with clients

Even the best-run helping services will sometimes encounter difficulties. A responsible team avoids the assumption that difficulties always arise from what clients do, or do not do. Effective supervision and even counselling of the counsellor helps to manage the stresses and strains that helping involves. In addition, you need a sense of even-handedness and a willingness to look constructively at your own behaviour. Some problems can be calmed and handled by good use of communication skills (see Section 3.3 on dealing with complaints and mistakes). This section focuses on difficulties and safety issues arising in the client–helper relationship.

clients whom you find difficult

positive self-talk

You need to work to achieve a sense of 'I can' rather than 'I can't'. Negative self-talk seeps into your body language and contributes to an exchange going wrong. On the other hand, positive self-talk can help you avoid being pushed to and fro by other people's reactions. Your internal dialogue can support or undermine your overall attitude and therefore your behaviour. You may need to say to yourself:

› 'I will be able to handle this', rather than, 'Oh no, here we go again.'
› 'I can help this woman in some way', rather than, 'It's that impossible woman again!'
› 'I will focus on helping this unique person' rather than 'I'll knock this off fast to avoid more aggravation.'

Focus on what you can do, rather than viewing the situation as one in which clients are imposing on you.

› Be realistic about your ability to control a situation. Avoid negative internal dialogue such as, 'I can't let her get away with this', or, 'I must cope; I mustn't ask for help.'

- It is unhelpful to go on about, 'They have no right to treat me like dirt!', or, 'They shouldn't . . ', and, 'They ought to . . .' Talk these feelings through with a colleague, vent them and lose them rather than leaving them to fester.
- You can only deal with what is and not with a list of 'shoulds' and 'oughts' that focus on other people's behaviour.
- You have choices over your own behaviour; you cannot force people to behave in different ways. Your reactions can nudge clients in a positive direction.
- Take hold of your own feelings; they are yours. You give other people permission to 'make me feel angry/upset/useless'. You do the feeling and most usefully can explore how these feelings are provoked in you, and then how to address them.

a balance in discussion about clients

Teams in helping services need to work to be fair and balanced with clients. It is far too easy to emphasise those clients with whom you find it harder to work, to call them 'difficult clients' and treat them as difficult which then encourages them to be difficult. You need to be aware about how your team talks about the clients of your service:

- Which clients stick in your mind?
- Whom, or what kind of clients, do you talk over most in team meetings or supervision?
- Does a team or individual member thrive on the drama and story-telling potential of the awkward clients?
- Do people ever talk about exchanges with clients that went well?
- Has the team developed an unhelpful stereotype of the 'good client', against which everyone is then measured? Does this mean that some patterns of behaviour, for instance persistence in asking questions or even a mild challenge, are judged to be evidence of a 'bad' client who is causing trouble?
- Is there a risk that the team conspires in negative outlooks on clients? Are there discussions with comments like, 'You daren't let them get away with anything or else they think they've won', often followed by disrespectful phrases like, 'I know these people!'

In a team you need to spend time on being pleased about clients you have helped, happy with those that are not difficult, and potentially tough situations that you handled well. This kind of discussion is just as important – if not more important – than working through current client issues.

consider the clients' perspective

It is far too easy for any team to focus on a situation only as they see it and to label clients in a negative way. So-called 'inadequate clients' may have learned that this service requires clients to have problems in order to receive help; it does not reward their coping skills. 'Demanding clients' may just want the best for their child or family and have been previously frustrated by a series of unhelpful counselling sessions before coming to your service. A genuinely helpful service makes an effort to go beyond the solely professional perspective. For instance:

> The limited professional viewpoint may be that this is a 'hostile client'.
> The client's perspective is, 'I don't feel valued or respected.'
> A more rounded professional view is to ask yourself, 'What is it about me as the professional, what I represent, or the network of which I am a part, that makes this client feel threatened or belittled?'

You can then address your part of the relationship to help clients. You are not necessarily to blame for clients' previous bad experiences with helping services, but it is your responsibility to work on the situation as it now is.

angry or frustrated clients

Some clients may well be angry. However, in any service a proportion of clients become angry because their calmer and more courteous comments were ignored. Some reasons include:

> Their feelings have been directly provoked by the behaviour of people in your organisation towards clients. Specific actions may be worsened by an unwelcoming setting, disorganised waiting systems or a lack of information about how priorities are handled. For instance the triage system in an Accident and Emergency Department is a way of establishing priorities that is not always explained to waiting 'patients'.
> Clients may not feel valued. You are there; they can tell you what they are feeling. But those feelings have been provoked by a series of frustrating experiences and discourteous treatment outside your control.
> Some individuals have a habitually angry or aggressive approach to life. It has been learned from childhood, perhaps from parents who dealt with problems

through anger and argument. Fury and bluster can cover up a basic lack of confidence, but it has worked in getting clients their way in the past. It may never have occurred to these clients that a courteous approach will gain attention from people in authority, or their previous attempts at courtesy they judged to be less effective than confrontation.

dealing with strong emotions from clients

It is important that you acknowledge clients' feelings (including anger) and the strength of these emotions. It is unhelpful to answer emotion with only logic and rational information, because these do not fit (remember the communications process on page 28). Recognise that these feelings are present and that the client has the right to feel them. Communicate to clients that you appreciate their feelings and perhaps that you understand how they can have them.

You can mirror the intensity of a client's emotion, not the emotion itself. As such, adjust your response to a situation in which a client is angry or distressed, but do not show anger or distress yourself. If you start to show anger, the situation will worsen. If you show distress, then the client may be unable to continue to tell you about what has happened or be distracted into feeling anxious because, 'Now I've upset you too.'

If a client feels strong emotions, she or he can be irritated or annoyed by someone who remains apparently unmoved by the emotions shown, often by remaining very calm or speaking very quietly. Use your words, tone of voice and firm expression to use comments like:

- 'I can see that you are very concerned about this.'
- 'You have every right to feel that way. I'd feel like that too if that had happened to me.'
- 'I can hear that this has been very frustrating for you.'
- 'I'm glad that you are telling me about this.'

Clients will not believe that you have understood or care if your emotional intensity is very different to theirs. However, you must remain calm and in control. Single words like 'obviously', 'exactly', 'of course' or 'absolutely' can be delivered with a positive quality of firmness and respect. Used poorly, they can of course come across as patronising or critical.

Clients who are angry will probably need more personal space than usual, so be prepared to sit or stand less close than you might usually. If clients want to leave the area or the room, then do not try to stop them through misplaced beliefs that you have to control the situation or have failed if they leave. Certainly make no attempt to counsel or problem-solve until the client is calm.

With a partner, experiment with saying phrases such as those given in the section above.

▷ Try saying them with different levels of emotion: from very calm and unmoved through to very emotional yourself.
▷ Explore how to say the words and phrases with a positive quality of firmness but not too emotional.
▷ Discuss the exercise together.

potential violence

Much of the rest of the book, including particularly Chapters 1–3, describes good practice that will encourage clients and help them to feel empowered in your setting. Good use of communication skills, attention to the impact of your setting and changes in rigid, client-unfriendly practices will reduce the risk of aggression, but not always to zero. You may work where service users are more likely to be unpredictable, for example when their inhibitions are reduced by the impact of alcohol or drugs. Several practical issues are important:

▸ Your organisation should act so as to protect you. This protection should partly take the form of safety measures within your setting (see the later points) and effective supervision. However, support is also given through a value position that nobody should have to accept verbal or physical aggression or have it excused as an 'occupational hazard' in your line of work.
▸ Everyone should have a range of skills for coping, but they should still have the right to remove themselves from a potentially dangerous situation, for instance in a home visit to a client, or to summon help within the work setting.
▸ You need to balance safe practices for personal security with not making your setting look too intimidating, as if you expect trouble from clients. If you have security doors, a reception desk that screens callers, safety glass at windows or other similar measures, then counter these with welcoming messages.

If your client base or the physical setting creates vulnerability to violence, then seriously consider some practical safety measures.

▸ Nobody works late in the building on their own, nor sees clients, when the rest of the team has gone home.
▸ A system of buzzers and alarm calls in case the worst happens.
▸ Ensure that the whole team is ready to react constructively at the sound of raised voices or to unusual or worrying events. It is better for one or two team members to make a discreet check than to leave a colleague facing a rapidly deteriorating situation.
▸ Keep track of team members who go out to visits and their expected return time. Perhaps you accept that some areas of your patch are only visited by team members in pairs.
▸ Some self-defence skills may help, but should certainly not be seen as an alternative to the measures described so far. The confidence you feel through

being able to defend yourself can communicate itself assertively through your body language and so help to calm a situation.

Create proper boundaries between work and personal life. Do not give clients your personal phone number or address. In some services it is wise that everyone has an ex-directory home telephone number. Helpers have sometimes been harassed at home over the telephone, but directories also give your address, so you may be troubled by callers on the doorstep.

dealing afterwards with an incident

The worst sometimes happens, and you need to address an incident in your service in which a team member was threatened or actually attacked.

▸ Offer support to the individual through informal contact and the supervision system.
▸ Use counselling skills with the individual to work through the feelings aroused by the incident. As well as feeling angry about threat or attack, helpers can also face some sense of guilt: 'Did I do something wrong?', or, 'Would it have made a difference if I . . .?'
▸ There may be lessons to learn from the incident; equally sometimes helpers have to accept that they could not have anticipated what happened.

Groups of practitioners may discuss events immediately following an incident, however, it is also useful to explore, probably in a meeting, what could be learned for the whole team.

▸ This discussion must be constructive and, while recognising what has happened to one team member, not leave that person feeling uncomfortably in the spotlight.
▸ Watch out for criticisms from colleagues such as, 'Why on earth did you . . .?', or implications of, 'I certainly wouldn't have . . .'. Violent episodes unnerve everyone and even colleagues are sometimes unhelpfully self-protective. If you decide that your team member was foolish in a way that you never would be, then you feel safer, but at the cost of undermining your colleague. If the practitioner was at fault, then this is an issue for supervisory help later.
▸ Look for what can be learned for the whole team. Useful lessons are not always about what must be changed. Perhaps your safety measures worked well.

| FURTHER READING

▸ Glynis Breakwell, *Facing Physical Violence* (BPS Books and Routledge, 1989).
▸ Edward Lewis, *Hostile Ground: Defusing and Restraining Violent Behavior and Physical Assaults* (Paladin Press, 2000).

12.2 health and safety issues: policy and practice

Health and safety in the workplace is covered by legislation and enforced by your local authority Environmental Health and Safety Officers or the Health and Safety Executive (HSE). The officers can inspect any workplace premises following a request from an employee, a union representative or a member of the public. If officers identify health and safety problems, they can issue an Improvement or Prohibition Notice that requires some action to be taken. Failure to comply with the notice can lead to substantial fines.

You will find suggested further reading below but the broad issues include:

› Any organisation should have an easily available written health and safety policy. This policy should take account of volunteers and trainees as well as paid employees.
› Organisations and services should have carried out a risk assessment to identify specific areas where there may be hazards to practitioners or clients. The results should be available and any necessary actions clear.
› Health and safety is everyone's responsibility. Within this there should also be named individuals within the team who take particular responsibility and to whom concerns should first be raised.
› All the relevant insurance should be up to date.
› There should be an easily available Accident Book.
› First aid equipment and facilities should be adequate and there should be someone trained in first aid.
› Fire precautions should be adequate, the Fire Certificate up to date and fire extinguishers and electrical equipment regularly checked by someone who is sufficiently qualified to identify any problems.
› Attention should be paid to health and safety issues specific to the kind of work undertaken. There should be proper work breaks and eye tests for staff who regularly use visual display units (VDUs). Hygiene issues arise when helpline teams pass telephones and headsets between them. Comfortable seating is important when practitioners sit for long amounts of time at a VDU or on a helpline. Stress should also be recognised as a potential risk in helping services.

| FURTHER READING

▸ *The Essentials of Safety at Work* (HSE Books, 2006).
▸ *Charity and Voluntary Workers: A Guide to Health and Safety at Work* (HSE Books, 2006).
▸ *Writing a Safety Policy: Advice for Employers* (a free leaflet from HSE Books).

You can also contact the HSE InfoLine on 0845 345 0055, or on their website www.hse.gov.uk.

12.3 handling stress

Working within helping services can provide a great deal of job satisfaction but the work also requires a high commitment that draws on your physical, intellectual and emotional resources.

A manageable level of stress is not negative. When you successfully cope with new issues or difficulties in work with a client or group, the temporary stress can be a source of learning and a boost to your self-confidence. However, excessive pressure and unrelenting demands can lead to an accelerating experience of strain and distress. 'Burn-out' is the term used to describe the effects of this on the practitioner. In the helping relationships covered in this book, helpers give a great deal to clients in terms of support, empathy, full attention and counselling skills. Clients can work very hard too, but that is not an effort that necessarily replenishes your own energy as a helper. It is not your clients' responsibility to support or take care of you; that is a responsibility shared by you and your organisation. You are responsible for ensuring that you manage your life to achieve a positive balance in giving and receiving, so that your personal energy and emotion account does not slip into the red.

figure **12.1 stress**

Consider the following warnings that can let you know that burn-out may be approaching:

- You are about to attend a case conference or a similar important meeting on your client. You feel depressed and think desperately if there is anyone who could go instead of you.
- You are halfway through a session with an individual client and you realise that he or she is looking directly at you. You have no recall of what the client has said in the last few minutes.
- In a group that you lead, you increasingly have intrusive thoughts about the pointlessness of the group's problems and your ability to make any difference to them.
- Increasingly you find yourself thinking, 'Here we go again', and, 'Been here before', when clients start to explain their individual issues and problems.

You are in danger of losing any freshness in your approach and respect for your clients, because you are too overloaded yourself.

Excessive demands on your time, energy and emotional commitment will drain your personal resources. This overload may arise because of unrealistic demands of your organisation about how many clients you can see, in how short a time, or how many groups you can effectively run within your working week. However, some helping professionals, whether paid or voluntary, conspire in their own dangerous overload because they are unwilling to place limits on their work, to ask for support or to delegate to colleagues. In short, helpers often find it hard to say 'No' or to seek help themselves.

Continued stress damages your health and, even if you are beyond caring about yourself (in itself a serious warning sign of burn-out), recognise that stressed helpers are ineffective in their work, perhaps as seriously as to pose a risk to their clients. There are three phases of burn-out, each more damaging than the previous one: physical, psychological and spiritual fatigue.

physical signs of overload

If you are continually tired or lethargic, you must take this condition as a warning sign. Everyone gets tired sometimes or has a dip in the working day, but if you keep going despite exhaustion, you will never allow yourself to replenish your energy. A good night's sleep will no longer be enough and you will catch any minor illnesses that are doing the rounds. Everyone in a team may be expected to keep going through very minor illness, but it is in nobody's interest if you stagger on with the insistence of, 'I can take it. I won't let my clients down.' You are also overriding stress if you increasingly take over-the-counter medication just to get through your day. You may have personal and familiar physical signs of stress like mouth ulcers, breaking nails, trembling limbs, difficulty in sleeping or breathlessness.

psychological signs

You may start with physical signs, but your emotions will soon also reflect the overload you currently experience. You may think to yourself or express out loud feelings like, 'It's all too much', or, 'What's the point anyway?' Helpers under stress sometimes begin to look towards their clients for personal support or explicit gratitude for their efforts. Your increasing emotional strain will start to lead to mistakes in your work and to lack of attention. Increasingly you will have difficulty thinking around problems, and see them more as stark choices, absolutes of right and wrong or even as impossible dilemmas. Attending and listening, in particular, become harder and harder. You become more impatient and intolerant. Job satisfaction and enjoyment decrease markedly and you will no longer feel that you 'want to go' to work, but that you 'have to'. Your life becomes increasingly seen as all duties and responsibilities, with few apparent choices. You feel alone and unsupported, perhaps even rejecting support that colleagues or friends try to offer. You feel disconnected, low in confidence and competence and you slide easily into the next phase.

spiritual fatigue

You become less and less able to give to others and feel increasingly threatened by legitimate requests for help or attention. Your patience reduces to almost zero. Your energy, interest and health worsen and you think about escape from your current life including leaving a job that previously gave you so much satisfaction. You doubt your own effectiveness, values or even the ethics of what you do. However, this is not a normal, positive self-examination but a self-attack that can see no light at the end of the tunnel. Work, and life itself, begin to seem pointless and meaningless. All fun and laughter disappear, tears seem near for no reason, and, apart from anger and irritation, your emotions shut down. Active caring vanishes.

As the level of distress grows it is a downward spiral in which you are increasingly unable to cope and, as a result, can become a serious liability to yourself, your colleagues and your clients.

take care of yourself

recognise your warning signs

There is no magical solution that will ensure that you do not experience serious stress and move towards burn-out as a helper. You can, however, take positive and sensible steps to take care of yourself, and therefore also of your value to your clients.

Recognise the phases of burn-out as you tend to experience them and take note of what is happening before it goes too far. Ask for help. Be ready to learn from your personal warning signs of overload:

- Perhaps a self-indulgent habit like eating chocolate, smoking, shopping or drinking increases a lot as you try to give yourself some compensation for your distress.
- In burn-out, you start to perceive your work as increasingly endless, and clients increasingly ungrateful and grasping.
- Some people react to excessive stress by adding on even more pressure to prove that they can really cope, for instance by taking up a highly energetic physical exercise regime or new work responsibilities.
- Highly stressed working parents sometimes add another organised activity to their time with their children, when those children would much rather the parent just sat with them and relaxed.
- You may notice that you even have particular phrases that you are far more likely to say when you feel seriously under stress. Quite often these are things your own parents used to say.

create boundaries around your work

Address the main reasons for your overload:

- Work for that crucial blend of caring and detachment. (Look again at the discussion on page 126.) Remember that clients own their problems and you will not help them by trying to take responsibility for matters outside your control.
- You may need to reflect on personal beliefs, philosophical or religious, that make you resistant to creating a safe emotional distance from clients or factors in you which make it hard to say 'No' to further excessive demands on your time.
- Keep a perspective on clients' problems. Focus on what you can do and the difference you have made, and not on what is still left and out of your control. Look back to page 4 on common myths about helping, since some of these are a source of undue stress on helpers.
- Be ready to ask for help yourself, in brief conversations with colleagues and through proper supervision time. Recognise when the problems of a client have hit you hard. Perhaps their experience has touched raw or unresolved emotions within your own life, or their issues are outside your world.
- Keep a realistic schedule in terms of the level of your work and the number of sessions with individuals or groups. Make sure you take breaks and create some time to recover, to reflect and write up notes. Learn to say 'No' within work and to calls on your time outside working hours.
- Leave clients' problems behind when you leave work and try not to continue turning them over in your mind.
- Take holidays without fail. It is a serious warning sign when you refuse to take time off, and perhaps also disrupt valuable shared leisure time with a partner, friends or family because you feel your work cannot do without you for a single day. It can, and always will!

- If you work from home, create as clear a division as possible between work and personal life. Ideally have a room that is dedicated to work and do not let work spread throughout the rest of your home. Have a work-dedicated telephone line and put on the answer phone out of working hours.
- If you work hard, play hard. If necessary, schedule activities into your diary that you enjoy and help to recharge your batteries. See friends, go on a walk, go out to dinner, give yourself permission just to sit, read, or watch television.
- Watch out for your health, with good food, enough sleep and a sensible level of exercise. Have other sources of self-esteem besides your work; it is risky to live only for the buzz of helping.

Burn-out can be positive if worked through effectively. It helps you to empathise better with what many of your clients experience and, through learning to manage stress better, you can be better equipped to help them.

the responsibility of your organisation

Helping services and organisations should support you in taking care, with a working atmosphere in which you feel able to limit the amount of work that you accept. Helping services can develop a culture of macho caring in which nobody feels able to say, 'This is too much.' This negative atmosphere can also be fuelled by an understandable reluctance to turn anyone away. However, services or individuals who stretch themselves way beyond their capacity to cope will not only have a conflict-ridden work place, they will also provide an increasingly poor service to their clients.

Responsible senior staff in a helping organisation must be alert to signs of stress, such as individuals who see matters as absolutely right or wrong or a general increase in impatience. As a good manager, you should:

- React sooner rather than later to improve the situation, without assuming that a stressed team member is weak or incompetent.
- Help by being aware of signs of stress in yourself, rather than assuming that stress only happens to other people.
- Be a model of positive behaviour, such as admitting that you are under stress and intend to take action to relieve the situation. Basic actions can be significant. For instance, your team will feel unable to admit to being overloaded, if you, as their manager, insist on working through the flu, keeping very long hours, or never taking a holiday.

I FURTHER READING

▶ Cary Cooper and Sharon Clarke, *Managing the Risk of Workplace Stress: Health and Safety Hazards* (Routledge, 2003).
▶ Stephen Palmer and Cary L. Cooper, *How to Deal with Stress* (Kogan Page, 2007).

Communication and counselling skills can be very positive within friendships and informal help. So the simple answer is that you can use these skills to improve your own personal relationships and help people you know and those whom you care for deeply. However, the additional answer has to be that help will be given in a different way than in your professional life. Blurring work-life boundaries can be a source of stress.

Family, friends, acquaintances or neighbours are not your clients. You may not want to see them that way, nor are they likely to wish to be viewed with professional detachment. You need to be cautious if you offer or agree to help, because both practical and ethical issues arise. You also need to be ready to reflect on what is happening and re-evaluate the direction that any help is taking.

impartiality and detachment

To be an effective helper and use counselling skills to the full, you have to retain some level of detachment. You should be impartial in a way that is unlikely to be appropriate with your family or friends. If you attempt to run a conversation in much the same way as you would in your paid or voluntary work, you may be pulled up by comments such as, 'Don't act the professional with me! I'm your brother, I know you', 'But surely you're on my side. You're my friend!', or, 'Mum, don't go all cool and logical on me. I'm upset!'

You can draw on your counselling skills, and may be able to help a friend or family member to step back from the problem so long as you are not seen to step back from the personal relationship. When your close friends or family are involved, you will often have a vested interest. It is appropriate that you have an emotional commitment that a situation is resolved and in how it is resolved. In a sense, you tend to interact with friends in the spirit of Stage Two (see page 158), and often appropriately use self-disclosure more, and are more confronting. It can be right to say in ways that would not be appropriate in a professional relationship, 'The horrible girls! I'm really cross that they're bullying you', or, 'I know your wife's a pain in the rear end, but . . .'

priorities and choices

An important issue in your personal life is how you balance your responsibilities and priorities. If you allow a friend or neighbour to call on your time with increasing frequency, then you may have very little time or emotional energy left for your partner or your children, let alone yourself. You may feel the pressure to, 'Must give her time, she's so distressed', or, 'He needs to talk, how can I say no?' It can help to reframe what you are doing in terms of stark choices through self-talk. Try telling yourself, 'I chose to talk with Janie on the phone and to make us late for the cinema', or, 'I chose to walk round the common talking with Stefan rather than help my son with his homework.' Often it is helpful to give yourself permission to do what is best for you and your family. You have the right to help yourself too.

confidences and confidentiality

Relationships with close friends frequently involve issues of confidentiality and trust. Personal experiences or problems are usually confided in the expectation that good friends do not gossip about what has been said. If you offer counselling skills to acquaintances or neighbours, you may hear confidences that are highly personal and may involve other friends as well.

The anticipated problem may be because you will face the friend's partner in social situations. On the other hand, a helping conversation may take you into far more intimate territory than you wish, with someone who is otherwise an acquaintance or neighbour. There are times to say, 'Are you sure you want tell me this?', or the more assertive, 'I don't want to hear this because . . .'

boundaries, assertiveness and saying 'No'

Even people who are skilled in setting up and keeping boundaries in their professional work can be unwary in their personal life. Within your work setting you will have hours of work, perhaps someone who answers the phone or deals initially with callers at reception and you will have a working atmosphere that communicates the other professional calls on your time. In contrast, help offered informally in your personal life can incur greater demands than you either planned or wanted. People may knock on your door or phone you at inconvenient times. What you hoped would be a short conversation stretches on and on. People whom you do not know well may turn out to be very needy or to have complex emotional problems that you cannot possibly resolve in this personal sphere even if you would like to.

Assertiveness is key to handling these types of situations, and is important for your own well-being and peaceful personal life. You need to learn to say 'No' courteously and in different ways appropriate to the circumstances. However, it is also a matter of courtesy to friends and acquaintances to be honest with them as soon as you can to avoid their feeling uncomfortable or guilty when it becomes clear that they have disrupted your other commitments.

With assertive responses, you take responsibility for your position, while respecting the other person's right to theirs. It is not shifting all the responsibility, or blame, to the other person. Unless you tell them your real constraints, friends and acquaintances may assume that their requests are fine; you have given them no reason to think otherwise. So, instead of thinking, 'She should stop asking me', or, 'He ought to know this is a thoughtless time to phone me', you need to offer honest, firm responses. If you have agreed to help, to some extent, consider managing the contact with responses such as:

- 'It's not a good time to talk, I could call you back at [time]. Shall I do that?' Keep your promise to return the call and consider addressing issues about times you are happy for this friend to call. Persistent callers may need to be told, 'Sachin, I said before that I can't talk like this in the evening. I want to give time to the children. Please don't call again at this time.'
- You also need to be fair, and firm, about face-to-face requests for a helpful conversation. If you are happy to talk but have constraints, then say so to your friend or neighbour: 'That's fine, but I have to leave the house in half an hour', or, 'We'll have to stop talking very soon. I must pick the children up from school.'
- Ideally you want to avoid reaching the point when you dread the sight of an acquaintance or neighbour arriving to talk or their voice over the telephone. Try to anticipate the situation and be honest with, 'I'm sorry, I have no time to talk.'

It is natural to want to be generous with your time and effort to close friends and family, but there are limits to even strong emotional commitments. You may need to consider and then say, with care for the other person:

- 'I'm sorry you still feel so unhappy about . . . but I don't feel able to talk with you about it any more.'
- 'I'm too close to this situation. I'll support you in whatever choice you make, but I think you should talk with someone else about what you might do. I can't stand back enough to help you.'
- 'I don't feel able to talk about this any more. To be honest, I find it too distressing. And I can't help you when I'm so upset.'
- 'I really think we've circled round this enough. I'll help you when you're ready to do something.'
- 'Debbie, I am uncomfortable working professionally with a friend. I'd much prefer to keep our relationship just as friends. If you'd like me to recommend someone that could help, I would be happy to.'

Without setting limits to what you give, it is as possible to overload on stress within your personal life as in your professional life. There should be colleagues with an eye on your welfare at work; in your personal life you are number one, and perhaps the only protector is you.

12.4 working well together

teamwork and communication

The quality of relationships within a team affects the work with service users, positively or negatively. Respect for clients is central to an effective helping service, so your organisation must develop a work culture that supports this outlook.

Teams feel much more able to respect clients when they feel respected themselves. It is the responsibility of senior practitioners to ensure that everyone within a team is respected. Some teams operate as if volunteers do not count or that the reception staff are less important. Dangerous cracks can appear in the service to clients when people in the team are ignored or undervalued.

When teams, or parts of a team, feel ill-used or overworked, the result is that:

- The team may shift those feelings on to clients: that it is the clients who ask too much, or are impatient or ungrateful.
- New developments in work with a client group may be seen by a team in a competitive way, with remarks like, 'Never mind the clients' rights, what about ours?'
- A team may start to protect themselves by stopping seeing clients as individuals and seeing them as examples of a problem, as a list of demands on their time or as incompetent and inadequate.
- Problems within the team may even be discussed with sympathetic clients. The proper helping relationship has then been distorted, because the team looks inappropriately towards outsiders rather than colleagues as a source of support for themselves.

Problems of this kind need to be tackled sooner rather than later. As a new team leader you may take over disaffected staff. Communication and counselling skills will be important as you, and committed team members, work to re-establish the boundaries of the work and to address the team's legitimate wish for their skills to be affirmed and their needs to be recognised. It is the responsibility of senior team members to ensure time for thorough discussions and expression of feelings within the team as well as a renewed focus on obligations to clients and the service.

support and supervision

informal support

Ideally, any helping organisation has a positive network of informal support between colleagues. Perhaps you all:

- Share ideas with each other, within the bounds of confidentiality to clients.
- Pass on useful information about contacts and helpful resources.
- Give attention to colleagues who look overloaded, puzzled or distressed.
- Support each other so that you are all more able to support clients.

Being busy makes this less easy, but even so some helping organisations fall far short of this ideal. You may be subject to an unrealistic workload which leaves no time for reflection and exchange of ideas. You are also very unlikely to ask for or accept help from colleagues if your work culture fails to tolerate admission of doubt or mistakes. Again it is the responsibility of senior staff to ensure that everyone is enabled to talk appropriately about their work and to create an atmosphere of learning within the service. Time may need to be allotted to ensure that this occurs.

supervision sessions

Regular supervision is especially important when you use counselling skills within your job:

> To ensure that your work, and that of your colleagues, is consistent with the values and objectives of the overall organisation. This kind of supervision can be crucial when individual team members are dispersed between sites or shifts and do not regularly meet each other.

> You need and deserve some personal support for yourself. Helping services, especially counselling and group work, make considerable demands on your energy and creativity.

> Supervision is needed by everyone, not just trainees and not only when there is a problem. There should never be a sense that supervision is only for those helpers who cannot cope. Helpers may also need to retain some humility, in that they can benefit from help, rather than feeling that 'I'm the one who does the helping.'

> You need to be able to talk over your work with a colleague within the appropriate boundaries of confidentiality. You will have many ideas yourself but it also helps to use someone else as a sounding board.

> Helpers who do not have an opportunity to talk within supervision will either keep all their concerns to themselves or may be tempted to talk with friends or family which raises further issues about confidentiality.

> Often in supervision you may want to talk through the difficulties or uncertainties in your work. A good supervisor should also call your attention to what you have done well and learned through your practice.

> In some organisations, for instance on a telephone helpline, different team members might be contacted by the same clients. Supervision and discussion of issues raised by clients might then take place better in a meeting of a group of helpers.

> Supervisors should offer an understanding of the work you undertake and the skills you use as well as providing a degree of independence, to enable you to be more objective about your work. Ideally supervisors are not your line manager as well, but in practice the two roles are often combined.

the skills of supervision

Good supervision draws on the communication and counselling skills described in earlier chapters of this book, although there are differences between supervision and working with a client. Supervisors have an obligation to ensure that your work is consistent with organisational needs. As such, supervisors may sometimes be more directive than you would be with a client.

It is certainly important to recognise when there is a difficulty with a team member's practice. Counselling skills are appropriate for potential problem-solving and for helpers who are open to learning and change. If the serious problem continues, it may become a disciplinary matter. Communicating clearly and unambiguously, as well as following your organisational procedures for such situations, is crucial for success.

I FURTHER READING

▶ Michael Carroll, *Counselling Supervision* (Sage, 2004).
▶ Peter Hawkins and Robin Shohet, *Supervision in the Helping Professions (Supervision in Context)* 2nd edn (Open University Press, 2000).
▶ John Hayes, *Developing the Manager as a Helper* (Thomson Learning, 1995).
▶ Warren Redman, *Counselling your Staff* (Kogan Page, 1995).

professional networks

It is important to develop and maintain an effective network with other services and professionals, since these contacts can help to extend your information base and support effective referrals (page 98).

contributions to inter-professional discussion

If you are in the position to contribute to a discussion or consultation with other helping professionals, then it is crucial that you value your own contribution. It often helps to prepare what you will say. This is essential if you are giving a report, or contributing a summary of your own work when several different individuals or agencies are involved. However, it will often be enough to list for yourself the key points that you wish to make, without detailing every word.

You may experience established differences of status within some meetings and, difficult as it can be, you need to make your own contribution with confidence. Offer your experience and perspective, rather than waiting passively to be asked. Otherwise, you may continue to support some unhelpful traditions that underestimate the value of your contribution to the helping services.

a coordinating role

Several professionals or services are sometimes involved with the same individual or family. Unless one key person takes responsibility to coordinate the various contributions, the client can become understandably confused. For example, parents of sick or disabled children frequently find themselves trying to relate to many professionals and services. Their differing advice is not always compatible and may not allow for others' recommendations. Parents can appreciate the kind of support that affirms the importance their role. This helps them to weigh up conflicting priorities, assess any confusing advice and find out more information as they need it.

Several general issues can arise in coordination:

› Are you in the role of formal or informal coordinator?
› Informality can be appropriate if the client is coping well with different agencies and appreciates discussion with you to clarify any confusion or to weigh up possible courses of action. Someone who is in regular contact with a client, and his or her family, may be the best person to help that client to coordinate different relationships with helping agencies.
› You will probably need a more formal role if clients need you to contact other agencies on their behalf and certainly will do if you are acting as an advocate for clients (see page 240).
› Is your client present at discussions with other agencies? Good practice is to have clients present and there should be a very good reason if clients are not with you. If clients lack confidence in speaking up, then you may speak for them. They still need to be actively involved and no discussion should proceed as if they are not in the room. Work towards enabling your client to ask the questions and to comment.

12.5 personal development

preparation and training

Practitioners in any kind of helping service, including a telephone helpline, should have the opportunity for:

› Basic training or preparation before they start to relate to clients.
› Further training and development.
› A system of support and supervision so that helpers can discuss the kind of enquiries with which they deal and the responses that are needed.

The nature of the preparation and training that is appropriate will vary depending on the exact service but many skills are in common:

› All helpers should have a basic preparation in the skills of greeting clients, listening and asking open-ended questions.
› Information services need helpers who are well-informed about the topic(s) covered, able to judge when they do not know an answer and able to find out or refer as appropriate.
› Helpers need further preparation in counselling skills when services, including telephone helplines, invite clients who are likely to have emotional as well as practical issues.

- Some services and charitable organisations select helpers and volunteers because of their personal experience. This is valuable but helpers must be able to place their own experience in perspective.

personal learning

Most skills are learned while doing the job, not through formal training. Competent helping professionals remain open to learning, however experienced they have become, and are willing to reflect on what they have done and why. This outlook is sometimes called the 'reflective practitioner'. An effective system of supervision and support (see page 269) should help as you work with individuals or groups. It is also valuable learning to think through, and discuss, work that has been completed.

Review for yourself how the sessions with an individual or work with a group progressed:

- Make sure that you consider the strengths of your practice as well as your weaker points. What have you learned about what you do well? How could you develop these strengths further?
- With hindsight, would you now handle particular events or individuals in a different way? What guided your decisions at the time and what can you learn to improve in the future?
- Admitting mistakes to yourself helps you to learn; it is not saying that you are a poor helper. Check that you are not being too hard on yourself. Is a different choice of action only obvious with hindsight?
- Accept feedback in a constructive way. You may be given feedback by the individuals or groups with whom you work, or by colleagues who observe you or work as a co-leader. Ask directly for feedback if you do not receive enough reaction to how you work. Look at page 41 for a discussion on giving and receiving feedback.

Your practice will improve with both experience and your willingness to reflect on what happened. It will not help to strive for unrealistically high standards that do not allow you to make mistakes. Are you:

- Trying to be perfect, refusing to tolerate your own mistakes, even when you encourage an individual or group members to recognise that mistakes happen?
- Aiming to take complete and personal responsibility for your work as the source of all insights and positive interventions?
- Seeking to take an individual or group in a direction further or faster than they are currently ready to accept?
- Accepting the individual or group as they are at the moment? It is usually unhelpful to compare one individual or group with others that you found easier, friendlier or readier to affirm your skills.

Explore your own learning from a recent experience working with an individual or as a group leader. Ideally, with the support of a colleague in discussion:

▶ Identify a specific area in which you would like to modify how you work. Describe to yourself, or to a colleague, the concrete details of what you would like to do. Focus on your own behaviour, feelings or beliefs, as appropriate.

▶ Develop a realistic goal about the change you want to make in how you work. Plan for this change and consider what will help you and what may hinder. (Look at page 174 on goal-setting.)

▶ Prepare to apply this change, appropriately, to your next work with an individual or group.

▶ Evaluate afterwards what has happened and what you have learned.

final thoughts

In one way or another, a considerable number of people in the UK are employed in helping others. Apart from the many paid professionals involved in help, advice and support, there are a considerable number of people working in a voluntary capacity in organisations and centres, many taking their turn giving information or running helplines.

The considered application of good communication skills makes a huge difference to the experience of clients. Being alert to the importance of non-verbal behaviour and use of language is crucial to the effectiveness of any service, not least the important yet often overlooked reception desk or first telephone response. Within our personal and professional experience, we have been struck by the considerable difference brought about in a service when the whole team genuinely recognise that their clients really matter.

A crucial first step is to acknowledge and behave to clients as deserving the kind of courtesy and respect that we all prefer to receive ourselves in interactions with others. This attitude is crucial, yet typically is most useful when important skills are both in place and visibly supported by the organisation. Courteous communication at its most basic and essential level is not technically difficult and is not indeed about 'techniques' as such: it is about caring for, and respecting, clients. This informs and underwrites the practice often needed to communicate well, and to ensure that skills such as reflective listening become part of what soon seems like the 'natural and obvious way' to approach clients.

Some job roles benefit from applying more detailed helping skills, which we covered in the context of counselling skills both in interaction with individuals and in the related skills of working with groups. However, these more detailed applied areas work best for clients when use of counselling skills is grounded in the context of wider communication skills. Particularly people with concerns or in crisis deserve a respectful approach that treats them as individuals and does not try to simplify matters by fitting unique concerns into pre-shaped problem categories or current solutions. The counselling approach enables clients to learn from their experience and to emerge feeling more competent in their daily life and better able to resolve or cope with difficulties themselves.

In many different settings, and with very different professional groups, we have seen over and over again the approaches that we describe in this book working in practice. The difference between those clients emerging from a service, even from a short exchange, feeling affirmed and respected and those feeling dismissed or left with inappropriate help is simply staggering – and is reflected in the relative success of the helping organisations. Often the greatest pleasure for professionals in a helping position is to feel that they have made a difference to clients and this feeling of satisfaction is far more likely to happen regularly in a climate of mutual respect and open communications. Not only does such an experience cheer you, it also helps to reduce your stress, and hence to release more energy to help your clients. It is a truly virtuous, fulfilling, circle.

This book will support your practice and study on a wide range of counselling courses offered in colleges, by hospital trusts or counselling organisations. The academic year 2002–03 saw the introduction of the new National Qualifications Framework (NQF) established by the Qualifications Curriculum Authority. All vocationally related qualifications now meet standard criteria for outcomes and all are matched with NQF at Level 2 and Level 3. There are several awarding bodies including the Assessment and Qualifications Alliance (www.aqa.co.uk), the National Council for Further Education (www.ncfe.org.uk) and the Counselling and Psychotherapy Central Awarding Body (www.cpcab.com). This book will assist you in studying for the following qualifications:

- NQF Level 2 – Certificate in Counselling Skills
- NQF Level 3 – Certificate in Counselling Studies
- NQF Level 3 – Certificate in Advanced Counselling Skills
- NQF Level 3 – Developing Counselling Skills (Diploma) BTEC
- Introduction to Counselling – ASET Level 2
- Counselling Diploma – ASET Level 3
- Life Coaching and Counselling – ASET Level 3
- CMA recognised and registered Counselling Diploma Course
- Level 3 Certificate in Counselling Skills, Level 4 Diploma in the Theory and Practice of Counselling (mapped to ENTO standards)
- AQA Vocationally Related Qualifications (VRQs), Intermediate Certificate in Counselling Skills and Advanced Certificate in Counselling.

Index

The Student's Guide to Becoming a Nurse

This text is dedicated to my brother John Christopher Peate.

The Student's Guide to Becoming a Nurse

Second Edition

Ian Peate

EN(G), RGN, DipN(Lond), RNT, BEd(Hons), MA(Lond), LLM
Professor of Nursing
Independent Consultant
Editor-in-Chief, *British Journal of Nursing*

WILEY-BLACKWELL
A John Wiley & Sons, Ltd., Publication

Library of Congress Cataloging-in-Publication Data
Peate, Ian.
 The student's guide to becoming a nurse / Ian Peate. – 2nd ed.
   p. ; cm.
 Rev. ed. of: Becoming a nurse in the 21st century / Ian Peate. c2006.
 Includes bibliographical references and index.
 ISBN 978-0-470-67270-9 (pbk. : alk. paper)
 I. Peate, Ian. Becoming a nurse in the 21st century. II. Title.
 [DNLM: 1. Nursing. 2. Nurse's Role. 3. Nurse-Patient Relations. 4.
Nursing Care. WY 16.1]
 610.73–dc23

                    2012002554

A catalogue record for this book is available from the British Library.

Wiley also publishes its books in a variety of electronic formats. Some content that appears in print may not be available in electronic books.

Cover image: iStockphoto.com
Cover design by Steve Thompson

Set in 10/12 pt Calibri by Toppan Best-set Premedia Limited, Hong Kong
Printed and bound in Malaysia by Vivar Printing Sdn Bhd

1 2012

Contents

Preface

Many exciting things have happened to nursing and nurses since the first edition of this text was published in 2007. The Nursing and Midwifery Council (NMC) have decreed that, as of 2013, all those who start programmes of education leading to registration with the NMC will graduate at the minimum of degree level – the profession is now on its way to becoming an all-graduate profession. The day that you start your nurse education programme will become the first day of the rest of your life; no two days will ever be the same. The role and function of the nurse are evolving and changing continuously (some changes more obvious than others) and this is how it should be, responding to the needs of people locally, nationally and internationally.

There are so many opportunities available to you that will allow you to practise the art and science of nursing with a wide variety of people whom you serve in a number of new and exciting venues. Nursing careers are changing and have changed; nurses are leading from the bedside and the board room, providing high-quality, effective and above all safe care as sharp-end practitioners, managers, leaders and academics endeavouring to enhance performance.

This new edition provides you with an update of the standards of competence used by the NMC to admit students to the professional register. I hope that it will help you during the 3 years of your programme of study, encouraging you to move from a being a novice nurse through to an advanced beginner, and to register as a competent practitioner with the longing to be proficient at what you do and ultimately to become an expert in the field of nursing that you have chosen.

Regardless of the path on which you continue, the specialist and expert whom you will become, the one thing that should never change is your wish to offer your services to those who need them, ensuring that the person receiving care is always at the heart of all you do – the patient first and foremost.

This text is not meant to be a manual to teach you how to nurse – that would be unacceptable; it is merely meant as a collection of chapters easing you through the most exciting and sometimes challenging job that you will ever do.

Ian Peate
London

Acknowledgements

I would like to thank and acknowledge the help and support offered to me by my partner, Jussi Lahtinen. To Frances Cohen, who has been a constant source of motivation to me for many years. Thank you to the outstanding professional services offered to me by the Royal College of Nursing library staff.

Abbreviations Commonly Used in Health Care

AAA	abdominal aortic aneurysm
ABCDE	airway breathing circulation disability and exposure
ABG	arterial blood gases
ACE	angiotensin-converting enzyme
A&E	accident and emergency
AF	atrial fibrillation
AFB	acid-fast bacillus
AFP	α-fetoprotein
AHP	allied health professional
AP(E)L	assessment of prior (experience/experiential) learning
APL	assessment of prior learning
ARD	adult respiratory disease
ARF	acute renal failure
ASW	approved social worker
BMI	body mass index
BUPA	British United Provident Association
CABG	coronary artery bypass graft
CAMHS	child and adolescent mental health services
CATS	Credit Accumulation and Transfer Scheme
CCF	congestive cardiac failure
CCU	coronary care unit
CDSC	Communicable Disease Surveillance Centre
CHD	coronary heart disease
CHRE	Council for Healthcare Regulatory Excellence
CNM	clinical nurse manager
CNO	chief nursing officer
CNS	central nervous system
COSHH	Control of Substances Hazardous to Health
CPAP	continuous positive airway pressure
CPD	continuing professional development
CPN	community psychiatric nurse
CPR	cardiac pulmonary resuscitation
CQC	Care Quality Commission
CRF	chronic renal failure

CSF	cerebrospinal fluid
CSSD	central sterile services/supplies department
CT	computed tomography
CVA	cerebrovascular accident
CVP	central venous pressure
DIC	disseminated intravascular coagulation
DNA	did not attend
DSU	day surgery unit
DVT	deep vein thrombosis
EBM	evidence-based medicine
EBP	evidence-based practice
ECDL	European Computer Driving Licence
ECG	electrocardiograph
ECT	electroconvulsive therapy
EEG	electroencephalograph
EMG	electromyograph
ENP	emergency nurse practitioner
ENT	ear, nose and throat
ERCP	endoscopic retrograde cholangiopancreatography
ET	endotracheal tube
FE	further education
FPA	Family Planning Association
GFR	glomerular filtration rate
GI	gastrointestinal
GMS	general medical services
GP	general practitioner
HCAI	health-care-associated infection
HCA	health-care assistant
HEI	higher education institution
HFEA	Human Fertilisation and Embryology Authority
HIV	human immunodeficiency virus
HPA	Health Protection Agency
HPC	Health Professions Council
HRT	hormone replacement therapy
HSE	Health and Safety Executive
HV	health visitor
IBD	inflammatory bowel disease
ICN	infection control nurse
ICP	intracranial pressure
ICPU	intensive care psychiatric unit
ICU	intensive care unit
IHD	ischaemic heart disease
IM	intramuscular
IM&T	information management and technology
IPCU	intensive psychiatric care unit
IT	information technology
ITU	intensive therapy/treatment unit
IUD	intrauterine device

IV	intravenous
IVF	in vitro fertilisation
IVI	intravenous infusion
JVP	jugular venous pressure
LFT	liver function test
LVF	left ventricular failure
LP	lumbar puncture
MC&S	microscopy, culture and sensitivity
MI	myocardial infarction
MIU	minor injuries unit
MRI	magnetic resonance imaging
MRSA	meticillin-resistant *Staphylococcus aureus*
MS	multiple sclerosis
NAO	National Audit Office
NBM	nil by mouth
NFA	no fixed address/abode
NGT	nasogastric tube
NHS	National Health Service
NHS(S)	National Health Service in Scotland
NICE	National Institute for Health and Clinical Excellence
NMC	Nursing and Midwifery Council
NSAID	non-steroidal anti-inflammatory drug
NSFs	National Service Frameworks
NTD	neural tube deficit
OA	osteoarthritis
ODP	operating department practitioner
OP	outpatient
OPA	outpatient attendances (appointments)
OPD	outpatient department
OT	occupational therapist/therapy
PAS	patient administration system
PBL	practice-based learning
PCA	patient-controlled analgesia
PCT	primary care trust
PD	peritoneal dialysis
PE	pulmonary embolism
PEG	percutaneous endoscopic gastrostomy
PEJ	percutaneous endoscopic jejunostomy
PHCT	primary health-care team
PHLS	Public Health Laboratory Service
PID	pelvic inflammatory disease
POM	prescription-only medicine
PR	per rectum
PREP	post-registration education and practice
PSA	prostate-specific antigen
PV	per vagina
PVD	peripheral vascular disease
QA	quality assurance

x

RA	rheumatoid arthritis
RBC	red blood cell
RCN	Royal College of Nursing
ROM	range of movement
RTA	road traffic accident
SAH	subarachnoid haemorrhage
SC	subcutaneous
SCBU	special care baby unit
SHAs	strategic health authorities
SIGN	Scottish Intercollegiate Guidelines Network
SL	sublingual
SLE	systemic lupus erythematosus
SOB	short of breath
STI	sexually transmitted infection
TB	tuberculosis
TENS	transcutaneous electrical nerve stimulation
TOP	termination of pregnancy
TPN	total parenteral nutrition
TQM	total quality management
TSO	The Stationery Office
TSSU	theatre sterile supplies unit
TURP	transurethral resection of the prostate
U&Es	urea and electrolytes
UCAS	Universities and Colleges Admissions Service
URTI	upper respiratory tract infection
UTI	urinary tract infection
VF	ventricular fibrillation
VT	ventricular tachycardia
WBC	white blood cell
WHO	World Health Organization

Introduction

This second edition brings with it a number of changes; it is based on the new NMC *Standards for Pre-registration Nursing Education* (Nursing and Midwifery Council or NMC, 2010a) and is arranged under its four domains. In this new edition the reader will find a number of new additions, e.g. case studies, activities, and reference to contemporary literature and new legislation. The layout has changed in response to feedback from readers and colleagues, helping the reader to navigate the content more easily. I hope that you find this edition as helpful as many others found the first edition. I am indebted to Dr Maxine Offredy who contributed to the first edition. The title of the book has also been changed from *Becoming a Nurse in the 21st Century* to *The Student's Guide to Becoming a Nurse*.

The book is primarily intended for nursing students, health-care assistants, those undertaking SNVQ/NVQ level of study or returning to practice, or anyone who intends to undertake a programme of study leading to registration as a nurse. Throughout the text, the terms 'nurse', 'student', 'learner' and 'nursing' are used. These terms and the principles applied to this book can be transferred to a number of health- and social care workers at various levels and in various settings, in order to develop their skills for caring.

A note on terminology

The terms 'patient' and 'person' have been used in this text and refer to all groups and individuals who have direct or indirect contact with all health-care workers, in particular registered nurses, midwives and health visitors. 'Patient' is the expression that is used commonly within the NHS. Although it is acknowledged that not everyone approves of the passive concept associated with this term, it is used in this text in the knowledge that the term is widely understood. For simplicity, 'people requiring care' is shortened to 'people'. 'People' includes babies, children, young people under the age of 18 years and adults.

Other terms could have been used, e.g. service user, client or consumer, but for the sake of brevity patient will be used.

The term 'carer' is also used in this text. It can be used to describe those who look after family, partners or friends in need of help because they are ill, frail or have a disability. Carer can also mean health-care provider, i.e. care workers or those who provide unpaid care. The number of carers is expected to rise from 6.4 million in 2011 to 9 million by 2037 (Carers UK, 2011). It must be noted and acknowledged that unpaid carers can also be young people aged under 18 years.

The phrase 'specialist community public health nurse' is also used in the text. The NMC decided to establish a part of the register for specialist community public health nurses, because it felt that the practice undertaken by these nurses has distinct characteristics that require public protection (NMC, 2004).

2

The nursing and midwifery council and quality assurance (education)

The programme of study on which you have embarked, or are going to embark, must meet certain standards. There are internal standards within your educational institution, e.g. your own university's policies and procedures relating to quality assurance and external influences. The NMC and the Quality Assurance Agency (QAA) standards must be satisfied before a programme of study can be validated and deemed fit for purpose. Other external factors that must be given due consideration are the orders provided in the guise of European Directives.

It is the responsibility of the NMC to set and monitor standards in training (Nursing and Midwifery Order 2001). The NMC has produced a framework for quality assurance of education programmes. The framework relates to all programmes that lead to registration or to the recording of a qualification on the professional register.

The Nursing and Midwifery Order 2001 provides the NMC with powers in relation to quality assurance and, as a result of this, the production of a framework by which those education providers (e.g. universities) who offer, or intend to offer, NMC-approved programmes leading to registration or recording on the register have to abide. There are many provisions in place in the UK that ensure the quality of education programmes. The NMC appoint personnel to ensure that all programmes in the UK are fit for purpose and adhere to the various standards, these people carry out quality assurance services on behalf of the NMC. They are registrants from practice and education who undertake the approval and annual monitoring activities on behalf of the NMC.

The NMC has to be satisfied that its standards for granting a person with a licence to practice are being met as required and in association with the law. It does this by setting standards to be achieved in order to maintain public confidence, as well as protecting them. By appointing agents and visitors it can be satisfied that it is represented during the quality assurance process in relation to the approval, reapproval and annual monitoring activities associated with programmes of study.

Each programme of study (for pre-registration nursing) must demonstrate in an explicit and robust manner that it has included the extant rules and standards of the NMC, so that those who complete a recognised programme of study are eligible for registration. The *Standards for Pre-registration Nursing Education* (NMC, 2010a) are the standards that must be achieved before registration.

Becoming a competent nurse

Those who wish to study to become a nurse, register with the NMC and afterwards practise as a nurse must undertake a 3-year (or equivalent) programme of study. The programme of study must by law comprise 2300 hours of practice and another 2300 hours of theory.

The title 'registered nurse' is a protected title in law. This means that it can be used only by a person who is registered with the NMC and their name must appear on the national register. There are three parts to the professional register:

1. Nurses
2. Midwives
3. Specialist community public health.

Four distinct disciplines, each specialising in its own field of practice, are associated with nursing:

1. Learning disability nursing
2. Adult nursing

3.   Children's nursing
4.   Mental health nursing.

As well as having to satisfy the NMC's requirements, general entry requirements must be satisfied. Educational requirements are set by each educational institution, and there must also be evidence of literacy and numeracy. How these requirements are set is the prerogative of the educational institution; however, the NMC must agree and permit these requirements. Those wishing to practise in Wales must be able to demonstrate proficiency in the use of the Welsh language where this is required. On entry all applicants must demonstrate, on an ongoing basis and on completion of their programme, that they have good health and good character sufficient for safe and effective practice. It is the responsibility of educational institutions to have processes in place to ensure assessment of good health and good character. Any convictions or cautions related to criminal offences that the applicant may hold must be declared. There are several ways in which this can be achieved, e.g. self-disclosure and/or criminal record checks conducted by accredited organisations.

Completion of the programme and successful achievement of the proficiencies means that the student will graduate with both a professional qualification – Registered Nurse (RN) – and an academic one. The academic qualification will be at degree level. The NMC requires a self-declaration of good health and good character from all those entering the register. The good character and good health declaration is made on an approved form provided by the NMC. This must also be supported by the registered nurse whose name has been notified to the NMC as being responsible for directing the educational programme at the university, or his or her designated registered nurse substitute.

Once registered with the NMC the nurse becomes accountable for his or her actions or omissions. He or she is subject to the tenets enshrined in the Code of Professional Conduct (NMC, 2008). Important issues that must be legally undertaken, such as participating in continuing professional development and the maintenance of a personal professional portfolio, are addressed in this book. This text provides you with insight into how to become a competent nurse; the NMC domains (NMC, 2010a) are also considered.

The provision of nursing care in the twenty-first century

There are and will be many opportunities and challenges facing nurses and nursing in the twenty-first century. Care provision is complex and the way in which health and social care is delivered is changing. As a result of this, the knowledge and level of skill that people will expect nurses to possess must change in order to meet these challenges.

Nurses will have to practise differently in the future. Adult and children's nurses will be required to have the knowledge and skills essential to meet the various needs of people who have mental health problems, and mental health and learning disability nurses must be able to demonstrate that they are better able to care for those with a range of physical needs.

If nurses are to rise to the challenges successfully programmes of study will have to prove that nurses, when they graduate in their field of practice, have the essential high level skills central to care safely and effectively for those in their particular field. Nurses must also have the knowledge and variety of skills needed to provide care to other people in other settings.

Nursing students will continue to undertake their learning in hospitals and residential settings. Increasingly this will also take place in the wider community where care will range from fundamental to highly complex. Care delivery will be more and more interdisciplinary in nature.

Changing nursing education in the twenty-first century

Any student completing the programme of study successfully must be able to demonstrate knowledge and competence in practice at degree level; he or she will have to justify actions based on sound evidence. The aim is to ensure that those being cared for are safe.

Learning to be a nurse means that you have the specialised skills to care for certain groups of people, and also the knowledge and skills essential to providing the fundamental aspects of care to all groups of people. The NMC has determined that, in the future, nurse education programmes will have a blend of generic learning associated with learning that is specific to the student's chosen specialism (field), with the proportion of field-specific learning increasing as the programme develops.

Generic and field-specific aspects of the programme will be combined, offering the chance to develop shared learning. Opportunities will also be made available for shared learning with other health- and social care professions. By doing this, it will provide students with an opportunity to meet the required generic and field competencies in a varied range of settings, in the many places where nurses provide care.

The NMC requires students to meet the new competencies successfully and at that point the student may (satisfying all requirements) register as a nurse; students have to be able to demonstrate competence in the skills demanded by the NMC (2010a). These specific skills are included in the essential skills clusters (ESCs) and the student must be deemed competent with regard to the ESCs at various points in the programme.

The programmes of study

All new programmes are still required to last at least 3 years, with 50 per cent of the time spent learning how to give direct care in practice settings. There are two progression points as opposed to one. The progression points usually separate the programme into equal parts, with each part having specific criteria that must be met before the student is allowed to progress from one part of the programme to the next.

The competencies that have to be completed successfully for progression point 1 are associated with achieving the criteria related to the fundamental elements of care and safety, as well as being able to demonstrate the professional behaviour required of a nursing student (NMC, 2010b). Learning outcomes for progression point 2 enable the student to demonstrate an aptitude to work in a more independent and confident manner.

Academic level

In October 2008 the NMC made a decision that the minimum academic level for pre-registration nursing education would be at degree level. From September 2013 there will only be degree level pre-registration nursing programmes offered in the UK.

The NMC made the decision based on a variety of factors including the requirement to prepare nurses to have and develop critical thinking skills in the increasingly diverse and complex sphere of health and social care delivery. Raising the minimum level of nursing education to degree level will bring the UK in line with many other countries; it will also bring nursing in line with a large number of other health- and social care professions. This approach also has the potential to encourage further interprofessional learning across the various pre-registration health- and social care programmes.

It is expected that nursing students will build on their knowledge of basic sciences, social sciences and the fundamentals of nursing to combine and critically analyse new skills required to demonstrate and ensure clinical competence.

This text provides you with the knowledge and skills required to care for people, the emphasis being on the adult, with the aim of promoting health, facilitating recovery from illness and injury, and providing support when the person has to cope with disability or loss. It is essential that all the people for whom you have the privilege of caring receive holistic, individualised care irrespective of their age or racial, cultural or socioeconomic background.

The NMC's competencies

The NMC's *Standards of Competence for Pre-registration Nursing Education* (NMC, 2010a) contains the nursing standards that have to achieved to demonstrate competence to the NMC. The standards require that the public can be confident that all new nurses will be competent when:

- delivering high-quality essential care to all
- delivering complex care to service users in their field of practice
- acting to safeguard the public, and being responsible and accountable for safe, person-centred, evidence-based nursing practice
- acting with professionalism and integrity, and working within agreed professional, ethical and legal frameworks and processes to maintain and improve standards
- practising in a compassionate, respectful way, maintaining dignity and wellbeing, and communicating effectively
- acting on an understanding of how people's lifestyles, environments and the location of care delivery influence their health and wellbeing
- seeking out every opportunity to promote health and prevent illness
- working in partnership with other health- and social care professionals and agencies, service users, carers and families to ensure that decisions about care are shared
- using leadership skills to supervise and manage others and contribute to planning, designing, delivering and improving future services.

The standards of competence identify the knowledge, skills and attitudes that the student has to acquire by the time that he or she reaches the end of the programme, as set out in the degree-level competency framework. This framework is made up of four sets of competencies, one for each field of practice: adult, mental health, learning disabilities and children's nursing.

Each set has both generic competencies and field-specific competencies. The competencies are organised in four domains:

1. Professional values
2. Communication and interpersonal skills
3. Nursing practice and decision-making
4. Leadership, management and team working

The context in which the competencies are acquired in relation to the field of nursing defines the scope of professional practice at the point of registration.

Associated with the standards of competence are standards of education: there are 10 of these. The organisation (the Approved Education Institution [AEI]) offering pre-registration nurse education must satisfy the NMC that they are able to meet these 10 standards of education for programme approval and delivery. They provide the framework within which programmes are delivered and stipulate the requirements that all programmes must meet, which are associated with the teaching, learning and assessment of nursing students.

The chapters

Each chapter of this text addresses the content of each of the domains as prescribed by the NMC (NMC, 2010a). The domains provide a framework for this text, as four sections.

Think points

Each chapter provides the reader with think points. These are included to help encourage and motivate you, as well as for you to assess your learning and progress. They are recognised by this symbol:

Think

Most of the think points provide you with answers or suggestions for responses. You are encouraged to delve deeper and to seek other sources, human and material, to help with your responses.

All chapters offer a selection of top tips to help you along the way, sharing insight and understanding of some of the key issues.

At the end of each chapter you will find an activity section. A number of approaches have been used, e.g. multiple choice questions, fill in the blanks, crosswords, true and false responses. You are asked to attempt the questions that are related to the content of the chapter to test your knowledge. The answers can be found at the back of this book, in the chapter called 'Activity Answers'.

Most of the chapters provide you with four case studies related to each field of nursing. They are there to help relate the theory to practice (where appropriate).

Over to you

The aim of *The Student's Guide to Becoming a Nurse* is to encourage and motivate you and to instil in you the desire, confidence and competence to become a registered nurse. To become a member of the nursing profession bestows on you many demands, and the key demand is the desire to care with compassion and understanding.

All I have done is put the words on the paper; the biggest challenge now is all down to you. You have to demonstrate to so many people that you are fit to be a nurse and to nurse, I hope that the words here can help you to do this.

References

Carers UK (2011) *The Dilnot Commission and Carers*. London: Carers UK. Available at: www.carersuk.org/professionals/
resources/briefings/item/2239-dilnot-commission-briefing last (accessed August 2011).

Nursing and Midwifery Council (2004) *Standards of Proficiency for Specialist Community Public Health Nurses*.
London: NMC.

Nursing and Midwifery Council (2008) *The Code: Standards of Conduct, Performance and Ethics for Nurses and
Midwives*. London: NMC.

Nursing and Midwifery Council (2010a) *Standards for Pre-registration Nursing Education*. London: NMC. Available
at: http://standards.nmc-uk.org/PublishedDocuments/Standards%20for%20pre-registration%20nursing%20
education%2016082010.pdf (accessed August 2011).

Nursing and Midwifery Council (2010b) *Guidance on Professional Conduct for Nursing and Midwifery Students*.
London: NMC.

Nursing and Midwifery Order (2001) Statutory Instrument 2002, No. 253.

References

Part I

Professional Values

1

The Code of Conduct and Professional Practice

Aims and objectives

The aim of this chapter is to enable the reader to begin to understand some of the key professional values that underpin the art and science of nursing.

At the end of the chapter you will be able to do the following:

- Discuss some of the professional attributes that underlie the art and science of nursing
- Demonstrate an understanding of the history of nursing and the historical landmarks
- Outline the key functions of the Nursing and Midwifery Council
- Describe the key issues associated with codes of professional conduct
- Begin to apply the concepts discussed to the practice setting
- Appreciate the Nursing and Midwifery Council's requirements of student nurses

The fundamental basis of nursing is associated with caring and helping; nursing is both an art and a science. One key aspect of the nurse's role is to help people achieve or carry out those activities of living that they are unable to do for themselves. There are many facets associated with the role and function of the nurse. It is a fluid and dynamic entity and this makes it difficult to define.

There are a number of definitions of nursing. One is that of Henderson, which has been used since the 1960s:

> The unique function of the nurse is to assist the individual, sick or well, in performance of those activities contributing to health or its recovery (or to a peaceful death) that he would perform unaided if he had the necessary strength, will or knowledge and to do this in such a way as to help him gain independence as rapidly as possible. (Henderson, 1966)

This definition is succinct and to the point. It attempts to encompass and encapsulate many of the roles that the nurse performs, such as carer and health educator. Such a definition could be seen, although not exclusively, as the nature of nursing. Another definition provided by the Royal College of Nursing (RCN) is:

The Student's Guide to Becoming a Nurse, Second Edition. Ian Peate.
© 2012 John Wiley & Sons, Ltd. Published 2012 by John Wiley & Sons, Ltd.

The use of clinical judgement in the provision of care to enable people to improve, main-tain, or recover health, to cope with health problems, and to achieve the best possible quality of life, whatever their disease or disability until death. (RCN, 2003)

This chapter is concerned with professional values that underpin nursing practice. An overview of the development of nursing, from what was an unstructured, *ad hoc* approach to caring, to what has become a regulated profession, is provided. The student nurse and unregistered practitioners are not subjected to the rigours of professional regulation. However, when you successfully complete your programme of study leading to registration, you will be subject to professional accountability and all that it entails (NMC, 2010a). It is expected that the student nurse will commit to the values of the profession and that he or she accepts and internalises the Code of Conduct as part of the process leading to registration. The code of professional conduct, performance and ethics for nurses and midwives is discussed in detail in this chapter, with emphasis on commitment to the principle that the primary purpose of the registered nurse is to protect and serve society.

A brief overview of the history of nursing in the UK

This brief overview of how the practice of nursing has evolved over the years outlines some key stages in the development of the nursing profession from a British perspective. It must be remembered, however, that the evolution of nursing in the UK did not occur in a vacuum. There are several other international factors that have also helped to focus and shape where we are today and where we may be going tomorrow.

To understand contemporary nursing it is important to have an understanding of where nursing has come from, how nursing has emerged and how it continues to evolve (Craig, 2010). Having an understanding of the way nursing has evolved and developed over the years may help you to appreciate the following:

● Why nursing is regarded as a profession in its own right
● How, by becoming empowered, nurses are in a position to enable others to do things for themselves
● That nurses have become autonomous practitioners
● How nurses are called to account for their actions and omissions.

This aspect of the chapter makes use of a 'time line' in order to frame the discussion about the historical overview. A time line provides you with important dates and events that have occurred over the years and that have had an influence on the evolution of the nursing profession. The discussion centres on the significant events and key characters that have influenced the development of nursing over the ages.

The prehistoric era

The practice of nursing predates history, according to Craig (2010). Those who lived in the prehistoric period suffered similar conditions to those experienced by society today. Tribes in those early years took part in caring for their sick and wounded (Hallett, 2010). Archaeologists have retrieved human remains that demonstrate that fractured limbs have been healed, suggesting therefore that some form of care provision occurred. Healers or shamans used various potions and magical concoctions to heal the sick. Those responsible for feeding and cleaning the sick were predominantly females.

The Bible makes reference to nurses and midwives, e.g. *Genesis* 35 and *Exodus* 1. In *Exodus* 2 there is evidence to suggest that nurses were paid for their services. *Numbers* 11 refers to males who undertook the caring role.

The ancient Greeks

In ancient Greece temples were erected to honour the goddess Hygeia, the goddess of health. Care at the temples was related to bathing and this activity was overseen by priestesses, who were not nurses. The foundation of modern medicine was laid down by Hippocrates during this period. Navel cutters – known as *omphalotomai* – were also practising at this time.

The Roman Empire

The first hospitals were established in the Byzantine Empire, which was the first part of the Roman Empire. As the Roman Empire expanded hospitals were erected. It was Fabiola, a wealthy Roman, who was responsible for the introduction of hospitals in the west; she devoted her life to the sick and made nursing the sick and poor fashionable in Roman society. The primary carers in these hospitals were men, who were called *contubernails*. After the Roman invasion in approximately AD 2 slave girls were known to assist Roman physicians. *Valetudinaria* – civilian hospitals – were kept clean and aired by bailiffs' wives, who would also watch over the sick.

The Middle Ages

Throughout the Middle Ages military, religious and lay orders of men provided most of the health care. Some of these orders of men included the Knights Hospitalers, the Order of the Holy Sprit and Teutonic Knights. Although these men provided care, charlatans and quacks provided treatment for money. The standard of care provided by the latter people often did more harm than good.

Several hospitals were opened during this period, e.g. St Thomas's, St Bartholomew's and Bethlem. Care provision that had been provided by nuns was now provided by local women, whose efforts were overseen by matrons. Their duties centred on domestic chores.

The Enlightenment

The core period of the Enlightenment was the second half of the eighteenth century. Scientific endeavour flourished during the Enlightenment and philanthropists provided the means to open charity hospitals around the UK. In London, for example, the London, Middlesex and Guy's Hospitals provided care to the poor who were ill. These hospitals employed nurses who may have been paid or unpaid. These nurses again predominantly carried out domestic duties. Pay was low and it was not unusual for nurses to drink alcohol and take money from patients in order to pay for their alcohol. Nurses at this time were slovenly and lazy, and reflected characters such as Sairey Gamp and Betsy Prig, caricatures devised by Charles Dickens. Alms houses depended on women to clean floors, make beds and bathe the poor. There were no standards for nurses to work towards.

Medical schools began to emerge as medical knowledge grew. The Royal College of Surgeons was formed in 1800 and at this time doctors were required to carry out some aspects of their training in hospitals.

Florence Nightingale

The founder of modern nursing was born in Italy in 1820 and died aged 90 in 1910. When she was 25 years old she told her parents that she wanted to become a nurse. Her parents were totally opposed to the idea, because nursing was associated with working-class women and had historical links to domestic service and vocational work.

In March 1853, Russia invaded Turkey, and Britain, concerned about the growing power of Russia, went to Turkey's aid. This conflict occurred in and around Scutari and became known as the Crimean War. Soon after British soldiers arrived in Turkey, they began to fall ill with malaria and cholera. Florence Nightingale volunteered her services to the war effort and was given permission to take a group of nurses to a hospital in Scutari based several miles from the front.

Mary Seacole, a Jamaican woman with much expertise in dealing with and caring for those with cholera, arrived in Scutari to offer her services to Nightingale, but these were refused. Undeterred, Seacole set up her own services and provided these to the British and Russian soldiers, often at the battle front (Anionwu, 2005).

In 1856 Florence Nightingale returned to England as a national heroine. She set about reforming conditions in British hospitals (in the first instance this was confined to military hospitals). She published two books, *Notes on Hospital* (Nightingale, 1859a) and *Notes on Nursing* (Nightingale, 1859b). Nightingale was able to raise funds to improve the quality of nursing. In 1860, she used these funds to found the Nightingale School and Home for Nurses at St Thomas's Hospital. She also became involved in the training of nurses for employment in the workhouses.

Nightingale acknowledged the influence of the environment on health. She suggested the environment should be one that promotes health and campaigned for wards to be clean, well ventilated and well lit. She believed that:

- there should be a theoretical basis for nursing practice
- nurses should be formally educated
- a systematic approach to the assessment of patients should be developed
- an individual approach to care provision based on individual patient needs was required
- patient confidentiality needed to be maintained.

Nightingale, together with the philanthropist William Rathbone, set up the first district nursing service in 1861. Queen Victoria gave her support to this venture and district nurses became Queen's Nurses. Caring for the well person was a concept that Nightingale wanted to see developed, and in the late 1800s her thoughts came to fruition when courses were provided to teach women to develop an insight into sanitation in homes. These women, who had a duty to care for the health of adults, children and pregnant women (pre- and antenatal), could be seen as the first health visitors. In 1873 Nightingale wrote: 'Nursing is most truly said to be a high calling, an honourable calling.' She died in London in 1910.

Towards registration

Throughout the 1890s pressure grew for the registration of nurses. In 1887, Ethel Bedford-Fenwick formed the British Nurses' Association, which sought to provide for the registration of British nurses based on the same terms as physicians and surgeons, as evidence of their having received systematic training. Bedford-Fenwick was a staunch supporter of professional regulation. Up until this time nurses remained relatively free from external regulation. In 1902, the Midwives Registration Act established the state regulation of midwives; this Act came about as a response to the concerns about the rising numbers of deaths of women in childbirth (Davies and Beach, 2000). A House of Commons Select Committee was established in 1904 to consider the registration of nurses.

The First World War (1914–18) provided the final stimulus to the creation of nursing regulation, partly because of the contributions made by nurses to the war effort. The College of Nursing (this became the Royal College of Nursing in 1928) was established in 1916.

Eventually, in 1919, the Nurses Registration Acts were passed for England, Wales, Scotland and Ireland. The General Nursing Council (GNC) for England, Wales, Scotland and Ireland and other bodies were established as a result of these Acts. The Councils were established in 1921 with clearly agreed duties and responsibilities for the training, examination and registration of nurses, and the approval of training schools for the purpose of maintaining a Register of Nurses for England and Wales, Scotland and Ireland. The GNC had powers to undertake disciplinary procedures and remove the name of a nurse from the register if she was deemed to have committed an act of misconduct or 'otherwise' – conduct unbecoming of a nurse. The Register of Nurses was first published in 1922. The GNC and the other bodies survived intact until changes were made in 1979. These resulted in the creation of the United Kingdom Central Council (UKCC) and the four national boards.

The establishment of a National Health Service

The National Health Service was established on 5 July 1948. The 1949 Nurses Act allowed that the constitution of the GNC be amended; the general and male nurse parts of the Register were amalgamated.

The Briggs Committee

The Briggs Committee, a working group, was set up in 1976 to review the training of nurses and midwives. The work of this committee led to the Nurses, Midwives and Health Visitors Act 1979, which dissolved the GNC. The GNC was replaced by the UKCC for Nursing, Midwifery and Health Visiting, with four national boards for England, Wales, Scotland and Northern Ireland.

Project 2000

Much of the work of Briggs in the 1970s paved the way for reform in relation to nurse education. In 1984 the UKCC set up a project to consider reforming nurse education, which became known as Project 2000. The UKCC's report, published in 1986 (UKCC, 1986) provided the Council's strategy. The strategy was implemented by the mid-1990s.

The Peach Report

The Peach Report was published in response to the UKCC's desire to conduct a detailed examination of the effectiveness of preregistration nurse education and to determine if students were 'fit for practice' and 'fit for purpose' (UKCC, 1999). The report outlined several recommendations, e.g.:

- A reduction in the common foundation programme from 18 months to 1 year
- An increase in the branch programme from 18 months to 2 years

- To ensure that students experienced at least 3 months' supervised clinical practice towards the end of the programme
- Longer student placements
- The introduction of practice skills and clinical placements early on in the common foundation programme
- Greater flexibility in entry to nursing programmes.

Contemporary nursing practice

Contemporary nursing practice is based on a sound, up-to-date knowledge base, with nurses applying the appropriate skills and attitudes when delivering nursing care. It was Nightingale who suggested that nursing was subordinate to medicine. However, this notion of the nurse as handmaiden to the doctor is changing and the various roles and functions undertaken by the nurse are testimony to this (McGann et al, 2009).

After the number of nurses became substantial and the essential nature of nursing was established in the UK, the need to regulate the practice of nursing under law grew evident. These laws are aimed at the protection of the public.

Nursing as a profession

Professionalism

The term 'professional' is used in many aspects of our society, and often its meaning is taken for granted. When the term 'professional' is used it refers to a process that contains some gravitas, in which a group or individual works in a knowledgeable manner and with understanding. The word professional has other meanings in other contexts. A profession is defined and measured by using several sets of criteria and characteristics.

Etzioni (1969) considered occupations such as nursing, teaching and social work as semi-professional. Nursing, he suggested, was a semi-professional occupation due to the inadequate length of time for training and because of the lack of autonomy and responsibility for decision-making. There has to be a high level of accountability and autonomy in order for an act to be professionally justified (Williamson et al, 2010; Carvalho et al, 2011).

Salvage (2003) states that the nursing profession has often held an uncomfortable social space, because it tends to lie between being a 'true' and being a 'semi'-profession. She described the 'true' professions as male dominated, elitist and powerful, e.g. medicine and law, in contrast to proletarian occupations such as domestic work, health-care assistance and unpaid women's work in the home. However, new professions are emerging and they fit the changing circumstances in which society operates today (Salvage, 2002).

Think

What makes a profession? Many people claim to belong to professions or they say that they are professional. Can you make a list of professionals?

In your list you might have included some of the more obvious professions:

- Clergy
- Doctors
- Solicitors
- Barristers
- Physiotherapists.

But what about others who also profess to be professionals?

- Footballers
- Plumbers
- Teachers
- Engineers
- Architects
- Librarians
- Carpenters.

The terms 'professions' and 'professional' are dynamic and fluid, changing as time passes and technology changes. Burnard and Chapman (2003) state that to be professional the occupation requires a degree of skill and/or specialist knowledge. Knowledge is gained through education and the sharing and development of that knowledge with others.

The characteristics of a profession have changed over time. There are a number of characteristics that may be associated with a profession which are presented in Table 1.1.

New nursing – new ways of working

The role and function of the nurse have changed and developed over the years. The first part of this chapter has demonstrated some of the transformations and the influences causing them. To meet the

Table 1.1   Some characteristics associated with a profession

- Its practice is based on a recognised body of learning
- It establishes an independent body for the collective pursuit of aims and objectives related to these criteria
- Admission to corporate membership is based on strict standards of competence attested by examination and assessed experience
- It recognises that its practice must be for the benefit of the public before the profession
- It recognises its responsibility to advance and extend the body of learning on which it is based
- It recognises its responsibility to concern itself with facilities, methods and provision for educating and training future entrants, and for enhancing the knowledge of present practitioners
- It recognises the need for members to conform to high standards of ethics and professional conduct set out in a published code with appropriate disciplinary procedures
- Its knowledge base is up to date
- Successful completion of recognised programme of study permits entry on to a professional register

Source: adapted from Pyne (1998); Carvalho et al (2011).

health-care needs of the nation, political and professional pressures have transformed the role of the nurse and other health-care professionals involved in the provision of health care, with the aim of developing their full potential. As a result, nursing has seen the creation of a number of new clinical roles, e.g.:

- Family health nurses
- Nurse endoscopists
- Consultant nurses
- Nutritional support nurses
- Nurse prescribers
- Nurse practitioners
- Advanced nurse practitioners.

As society changes, coupled with rapid and important advances in science and technology, so too does the role and function of the nurse and other health- and social care practitioners. Nurses show advances in their skills and practice underpinned by an evidence base and further education.

Hospital at Night is a model of care that has been developed to efficiently and safely deliver care at night and out of hours within the requirements of the Working Time Directive (WTD). It is also a project that supports productivity and efficiency by bringing roles together to ensure a fit-for-purpose multi-professional team (Department of Health or DH, 2006a). Cameron and Masterson (2003) consider the role of the nurse at night and how the traditional role of night sister has changed considerably to become night nurse practitioner. The Hospital at Night project was a project run under the auspices of the Department of Health, aiming to redefine how medical cover is provided in hospitals during the night. The project required a move from cover requirements, defined by professional demarcation, to cover defined by competency – the night nurse practitioner is a competent practitioner. The project advocates that other staff, e.g. nurses, take on some of the work traditionally carried out by junior doctors.

Top tips

Working at night is different to working during the day for a number of reasons and the following are issues that impact on care delivered at night:

- Professional and silo team working
- Sickest patients referred to most junior trainees
- Minimal supervision
- Minimal skill sets and competences
- Staffing levels.

Many of the new nursing roles may not have existed today if the nursing profession had not, over the years, sought to advance its professional practice and status. The key issues of clinical competence, clinical decision-making, and being aware of boundaries and limitations are central to the safety of the patient and the success of such roles.

Hood (2010) suggests that the professional nurse has three intellectual properties:

1. A body of knowledge on which professional practice is based
2. A specialised education to transmit this body of knowledge to others
3. The ability to use the knowledge in critical and creative thinking.

Body of knowledge

Much of the work that nurses carry out on a daily basis has a theoretical underpinning. However, nurses do not always articulate this theoretical basis from which they practise (Burnard and Chapman, 2003). Often the theories cited in Table 1.2, emerging from various disciplines and scientific perspectives, allow nurses to practise effectively and, above all, safely.

The examples cited in Table 1.2 are theoretical examples reflecting a scientific perspective. Limiting caring to the scientific approach and neglecting experience could be detrimental to the care that you provide to people. Professional nursing practice is also based on a body of knowledge that is derived from experience – expertise. The combination of knowledge related to science and experience has the potential to enable the nurse to make reliable clinical decisions.

The use of expertise should never be undervalued, however; having experience may not always be enough to help provide safe care. Nurses derive knowledge through:

- intuition
- tradition
- experience.

Benner (1984) discusses the subject of intuition as a form of expertise. Intuition can be described as just knowing which comes from the individual. It is internal and can occur independently of experience or reason. It can become validated by experience and interaction with other nurses. Kozier et al (2008) suggest that intuition is also described as a sixth sense, a hunch, instinct or feeling of suspicion.

Consider the patient scenario that follows and then list the knowledge bases needed to care effectively for this patient.

Case study 1.1

Mary Samonds, aged 86 years, has had a stroke (cerebrovascular accident). Mrs Samonds is unconscious and totally dependent on the nursing staff for all her care. When providing care for Mary with a registered nurse you find that she is incontinent of urine and faeces, so both you and the staff nurse are going to attend to her hygiene needs. Mary's husband is outside waiting for you to finish. He is clearly upset and seems distressed.

For you to care safely and effectively for Mrs Samonds and to meet all of her needs, she will require much skilled care and you will need to draw on many bodies of knowledge to do this. There are several bodies of knowledge that you could use and these will also include that important perspective – experience or expert practice. Table 1.3 lists some of the things that you might include.

Transmitting the body of knowledge to others

Transmitting the body of knowledge to others occurs at many levels. The educational programmes of study and the educational institutions where they take place are subject to statutory approval and scrutiny. This approval is through the NMC (see below). It is the members of the profession, therefore, who validate the programmes of study that will ultimately lead to registration. Registration conveys a message to the public that the nurse who is admitted to the register has reached and possesses a satisfactory level of competence along with a certain standard of behaviour – good character and good health.

Table 1.2 Theoretical perspectives gained from other disciplines that are used when caring for the patient

Theory basis	Example
Microbiology	Practices associated with aseptic nursing and infection control
Thermodynamics	Performance of duties associated with temperature taking and the care of the patient with a pyrexia or those who may have hypothermia
Psychology	The application of psychological theories when caring for a bereaved relative, or the importance of play in hospitalised children
Pharmacokinetics	Understanding drug therapies and how drugs are metabolised in the body
Physiology	Applying physiological theories to interpretation of nursing observations, for example physiological changes that occur if the patient has diabetes mellitus or a head injury
Sociology	Helping you to understand the patient's needs from a sociological perspective, for example understanding and addressing health inequalities

Source: adapted from Burnard and Chapman (2003); Hood (2010).

Table 1.3 The various bodies of knowledge drawn on to care for a person

Expertise
Psychology
Sociology
Microbiology
Thermodynamics
Physiology
Pharmacokinetics

Using that body of knowledge in critical and creative thinking

Either nurses use their body of knowledge to provide people with care that has undergone critical scrutiny, or a systematic approach has been used to provide that care. Care becomes creative and innovative and provides nurses with new ways of thinking and addressing the problems that people may have.

Advancing nursing practice ensures that nurses have the knowledge base and practical skills to provide specialist nursing care. Critical thinking allows nurses to see different approaches to clinical situations. Critical thinking occurs when nurses are faced with people who have complex needs; the situation provides opportunities for nurses to develop and plan individual care.

Professional nursing

The Hippocratic oath laid down the moral code of conduct for the practice of medicine and the underpinning principle of this code, similar to the underpinning principle of any health-care code, is to treat the patient at all times as you would wish others to treat you.

People receiving the service of nurses must be able to trust nurses with their wellbeing. To justify that trust the nursing profession has a duty to maintain a good standard of practice and care, and to show respect for human life.

Professional nursing practice is judged not only by the recipient of care – the patient – but also by the profession itself. Professionals judge other professionals with regard to the quality and appropriateness of care provided. There are many ways in which this judgement can occur, one way being through the NMC. Deviation from the acceptable standards of practice may result in a nurse's name being removed from the professional register, ultimately resulting in removal of a nurse's licence to practise.

The Nursing and Midwifery Council

In 1998 the government initiated a fundamental review of how the profession was regulated. The outcome of this review resulted in consultation with nurses and midwives regarding professional regulation and areas that needed to be addressed. Recommendations were suggested and acted on with regard to self-professional regulation, regulatory mechanisms and procedural rules. The UKCC and the four national boards were abolished; quality assurance elements were incorporated into the work of the NMC.

The NMC was set up by Parliament to safeguard the public and to ensure that nurses and midwives provide high standards of care to their patients. The Nursing and Midwifery Order 2001 (SI 2002/253) established the Council and it came into being on 1 April 2002. Protection of the public is the key concern of the NMC. Its duties to society are to serve and protect, and this is done as follows:

- Maintaining a register listing all nurses and midwives
- Setting standards and guidelines for nursing and midwifery education, practice and conduct
- Providing advice for registrants on professional standards
- Ensuring quality assurance related to nursing and midwifery education
- Setting standards and providing guidance for local supervising authorities for midwives
- Considering allegations of misconduct or unfitness to practise due to ill health.

The NMC maintains a register of nurses and midwives, setting standards for education and practice and offering guidance and advice to the professions. An overarching aim is to inspire confidence by ensuring that those on the professional register are fit to practise and by dealing speedily and fairly with those who are not.

The Council for Healthcare Regulatory Excellence (CHRE) promotes the health, safety and wellbeing of patients and other members of the public in the regulation of health professionals and has the job of scrutinising the work of the nine health profession regulators:

- General Chiropractic Council
- General Dental Council
- General Medical Council
- General Optical Council
- General Osteopathic Council
- General Pharmaceutical Council
- Health Professions Council
- Nursing and Midwifery Council
- Pharmaceutical Society of Northern Ireland.

Table 1.4   The three parts of the professional register

Nurse's part
Midwives' part
Specialist community public health nurses' part

Under the NHS Reforms and Health Care Professions Act 2002 and the Health and Social Care Act 2008, the CHRE have a number of powers, e.g. they carry out checks on how health-care regulators carry out their work as well as providing advice to the regulators about policy.

The professional register

The NMC maintains a register of over 650 000 qualified nurses and midwives (NMC, 2011a). The nurses' and midwives' names are held on a computer database, including personal details, educational qualifications and registration status. Personal details are never released by the NMC. All nurses and midwives who wish to practise in the UK must be on the NMC register.

The NMC's registration process enables nurses and midwives to be entered on to one or more parts of the register when they have completed an approved programme of study. The registration process begins from the day the student nurse starts a course, be it for initial registration or return to practice. The approved educational institution must ensure that accurate records of a student's progression throughout the course are maintained; this is often known as a transcript of training. There are three parts of the professional register (Table 1.4).

Admittance to the professional register provides the nurse with the privilege of performing certain activities with the public that might otherwise (outside the professional relationship) be deemed unlawful. Members of the public have access to the professional register and can verify whether a nurse is registered with the NMC.

Registration – good health and good character

Amended guidance has been issued for approved education institutions (AEIs) by the NMC concerning good health and good character (NMC, 2010a), with the aim of ensuring consistency in applying the NMC's requirements. The amendments have also been made to ensure that AEIs and the NMC are compliant with current law, e.g. the Equality Act 2010; among other things this legislation protects people who may have a disability or health condition from unlawful discrimination. The NMC state that they do not discriminate against people with disabilities by having a 'blanket ban' on particular impairments or health conditions (NMC, 2010a).

On completion of the approved programme of study, personal details of the applicant and the programme undertaken are transferred to the NMC. The AEI is obliged to make a declaration of good health and good character in support of the applicant. All practitioners must demonstrate that their health and character are appropriate to allow them to register and stay on the register in order to practise. The good health and good character elements of getting on to and renewing an entry on the register are laid down in the legislation. The requirement of good character and good health was introduced by Parliament to enhance the protection of the public after a number of high-profile cases concerning the health and character of nurses and doctors came to light in the past. The nurse must ensure that his or her good character and good health remain just that, 'good', throughout his or her period of time on the professional register. The applicant then pays a registration fee.

Having satisfied the criteria for admission to the professional register, so that the nurse can remain on it (on the 'live' register) he or she needs to abide by the tenets stated within the code of professional conduct. To stay on the professional register, the nurse must renew registration every 3 years – known as periodic renewal. An annual fee is also required at the end of the first and second year of the registration period – the annual retention fee.

Nurses must be able to demonstrate that their skills and knowledge are suitable for their work. Currently, a nurse is required to undertake a minimum of 35 hours of learning relevant to practice over a 3-year period (Webb, 2011). The NMC, along with all the health-care regulators, are exploring the issue of revalidation in response to the Government White Paper on regulation, *Trust, Assurance and Safety: The regulation of healthcare professionals in the 21st century* (DH, 2007). The CHRE are involved in helping to support the regulators with this aspect of their legal duty.

Notification of practice must be made to the NMC and a declaration made that the nurse has met his or her post-registration education and practice (PREP) requirements for continuing professional development (NMC, 2008). He or she must also provide the annual retention fee. The issues of PREP and continuing professional development are considered in more detail in Chapter 14.

Each individual whose name is entered on the register is issued with a unique personal identification number (PIN) in card format and the date on which the registration expires. It must be noted that anyone who is newly qualified and has not yet been registered is unable to practise as a registered nurse until the registration becomes effective. It is a criminal offence for anyone to falsely and deliberately represent him- or herself as a registered nurse. The newly qualified nurse should note that the entire registration process may take up to 3 weeks from the programme completion date. It is important to apply to register within 5 years of the course completion date.

Contemporary nursing

There are a number of key drivers and health- and social care policy initiatives that have and will continue to drive contemporary nursing practice. Issues that must be given serious consideration include changes in demographics and population growth.

Policy

With regard to the demand for health care, the kind and main causes of disease will change. Obesity levels or health inequalities are important factors that must be taken into account. There is a continued need to support the self-care of the growing numbers of people who experience long-term health conditions. The continuing demand to meet health needs remains high, as well as patient demand for choice – on sources of advice, care packages and treatment options as well as access to care provision. The provision of care sees continued growth and an increasingly diverse role for the Third Sector, as well as reliance on the commercial sector to make available considerable inputs for secondary care provision (Longley et al, 2007). Benefits from improved information technology are felt by practitioners and patients; they bring with them information for patients, about patients, and about effectiveness and health-care performance. The increase in understanding of the genetic basis of some diseases continues to grow and develop. In some areas there is growing use of telecare to provide support to those who require care at home, with an increased understanding and use of new applications associated with biotechnology, bioengineering and robotics. Government policy continues to concentrate on measuring effectiveness, ensuring value for money, reducing disparity in performance (locally and nationally, individually and corporately), improving safety and quality, enhancing productivity, and engaging clinicians and recipients of care in all of these aspects. NHS managerial structures are changing and this will continue, as well as provision closer to home of more generalist services and consideration given to specialist services. Regulation of the professions continues to come under scrutiny and focuses on quality and safety.

The current Government has proposed new ways of working in the form of two influential White Papers – *Equity and Excellence: Liberating the NHS* (DH, 2010a) and *Healthy Lives, Healthy People: Our strategy for public health in England* (DH, 2010b). The former sets out the Government's long-term vision for the future of the NHS. The vision builds on the core values and principles of the NHS – a comprehensive service, available to all, free at the point of use, based on need, not ability to pay. The latter provides the Government's long-term vision for the future of public health in England. The aim is to create a 'wellness' service (Public Health England) and to strengthen both national and local leadership.

Nursing workforce

There are future potential workforce difficulties in nursing as a result of an ageing workforce coupled with financial difficulties affecting the commissioning of nurse education. Recruitment and retention continue to have a high profile to ensure that the right type of applicant is attracted to the profession and once in the profession stays; this involves reconsideration of emerging roles and responsibilities for nurses responding to health-care demands which will be dictated by flexibility in the future nursing workforce. There is an increase in specialist and advanced roles and with this comes a blurring of professional and sector boundaries (i.e. health- and social care sectors). Care provision increasingly follow the patient pathway, with an emphasis on community care, closer to home, and multidisciplinary team working. Nurses are enhancing their role in directing and leading care, and are being encouraged to adopt a more entrepreneurial outlook.

Provision of nurse education

As health care changes so too does the role of the nurse, and so must the education required to prepare the student for the new roles and responsibilities (Carvalho et al, 2011). The NMC have introduced (after much consultation) new standards for nurse education (NMC, 2010b); students must meet these standards to be eligible to enter the professional register and the standards help to ensure parity throughout the UK for any field of nursing (fields replace branches). The appropriateness of the four nursing branches has been examined with the concern that future health services may require a more generic worker who is helpful when meeting general health needs. The provision of degree-level programmes has the potential to enhance the status of nursing even further, providing nurses with the skills needed that go beyond diploma level to ensure that the care of the patient is improved and enhanced. These standards replace the NMC's 2004 standards (NMC, 2004). The new standards have been aligned with European Union Directive 2005/36/EC *Recognition of Professional Qualifications.* This sets out the requirements for training nurses responsible for general care and provides the baseline for general nursing in the EU. The Directive includes detailed requirements on programme length, content and ratio of theory to practice, as well as the nature of practice learning and range of experience.

Top tips

Changes occur and will continue to occur that have an impact on the way that nurses work and the career trajectories that they choose:

- Roles and responsibilities of nurses are changing
- The number of people aged over 85 years is projected to rise by almost 75 per cent by 2025
- Over 15 million people in the UK currently have a long-term condition; as the number of older people is projected to increase across the UK by between 18 and 23 per cent, so this number will increase
- Obesity rates have doubled in the last 10 years and will potentially lead to a rise in strokes, heart attacks and type 2 diabetes
- Infant mortality rates vary from 1.6 per 1000 live births in affluent areas to 9.8 per 1000 live births in less affluent areas
- Smoking is still the single greatest cause of illness and premature death in the UK, killing at least 86 500 people per year and accounting for a third of all cancers and a seventh of all cardio-vascular disease

Source: adapted from DH (2006b).

Modernising nursing careers

In 2006 the four Chief Nursing Officers of the UK established the modernising nursing careers initiative and produced a report (DH, 2006b). It forms part of an overarching programme of work covering all the main health-care professionals, setting the direction for modernising nursing careers. The priorities focus on the careers of registered nurses, recognising that nurses do not work in isolation and nursing teams are made up of more than registered nurses. Nursing careers also need to take account of changes in the careers of other professional groups. The report recognises that careers take different forms: some nurses will choose to climb an upward ladder of increasing responsibility and higher rewards, but many others opt for a more lateral career journey, moving within and between care groups and settings.

The modernisation of nursing careers brings with it the opportunity for nurses to take on new and enhanced roles and responsibilities. By undertaking these new roles nursing will be instrumental in delivering the improvements in patient care that are needed to provide a world class health service. Nurses already play a significant part in reducing waiting times, making services more accessible and improving the quality of care.

A career structure is required that will allow nurses to work in different care settings, to take on changed roles and responsibilities, develop a varied mix of skills, pursue education and training when they need it, and develop both generalist and specialist skills as they require them (DH, 2006b).

Provision of services

Various aspects of care are offered and provided by the NHS; however, it must be remembered that it is not just the NHS that provides care – the independent and voluntary sector also provide care and services to people.

There are over 1.3 million staff in the NHS, over 80 per cent of whom are front-line staff. Of these, 60 per cent (675 000) are professionally qualified clinical staff, e.g. 126 000 doctors and 398 000 qualified nurses. They are supported by 454 000 staff in trusts and GP practices. The remainder (209 000) are NHS infrastructure support staff, with almost a half (102 000) of them in central functions, just over a third (71 000) in hotel, property and estates, and just under a fifth (37 000) as managers (NHS Information Centre, 2011).

The provision of care will be influenced by a number of factors including those discussed above, e.g. an ageing population, changing disease patterns, the issue of consumerism and technological advances. Often the provision of care is split between two areas:

- Acute care
- Chronic care.

Care also occurs within the following health-care settings:

- Primary
- Secondary
- Tertiary.

Primary care services

Most care provision is carried out in the primary care sector, with over 95 per cent of care being delivered in this sector. Care is delivered outside hospitals by a range of practitioners, e.g.:

- Teams of nurses
- Groups of doctors
- Midwives
- Health visitors
- Dentists
- Pharmacists
- Optometrists
- Occupational therapists
- Physiotherapists
- Speech and language therapists.

For many patients, the professional health care that they need will be provided in the community setting. In some situations, the care provided by and in the primary care sector may not be appropriate or able to meet the needs of the patient, so referral to other services may be required – the services offered by the secondary care sector.

Secondary care services

This aspect of care provision occurs mainly through the acute hospital setting. The nursing and medical staff who work in this area have more readily available access to specialist and elaborate diagnostic aids and facilities, e.g.:

- Radiology department
- Magnetic resonance imaging (MRI)

- Computed tomography (CT)
- Operating theatres
- Special care baby units (SCBUs)
- Microbiological laboratories.

Those who provide care in the primary care setting, e.g. the community nurse and GP, could be seen as the 'gatekeepers' to care provision in the secondary care sector, because they may make the necessary referrals. The transition from primary care to secondary care should be a seamless move. The distinction between the two is becoming more blurred because the patient may visit the hospital for just a few hours before having follow-up care in the community.

Tertiary care services

In some larger hospitals there may be an opportunity to provide the patient with tertiary care, which is provided by nurses, doctors and other health-care professionals with specialist expertise, equipment and facilities for caring for the patient with complex health-care needs, e.g.:

- Intensive care units
- Burns units
- Oncology centres.

Often staff working in these areas will have undertaken additional courses to enable them to further develop their skills and knowledge. It is important to remember that most patients receive their care and have their needs met in the primary care setting. Only a few will need the services of those who work in the secondary care sector, and even fewer will need to access services provided in tertiary care.

Nurses can be found in all of these care settings. The biggest group of health-care professionals employed by the NHS are the 398 000 qualified nurses. *Modernising Nursing Careers* (DH, 2006b) sets out the establishment of a nursing career framework. The following descriptions of some nursing posts are provided only as a very brief explanation of the potential nursing career that may become available to you.

Chief Nursing Officer

The Chief Nursing Officer (CNO) is the Government's most senior nursing adviser and has the responsibility to ensure that the Government's strategy for nursing is delivered. The CNO leads over 597 625 nurses, midwives and health visitors and other allied health professionals.

Nurse consultant

Nurse consultants are very experienced practitioners. There is now a new range of these posts within all areas of nursing practice, in both the hospital and the community setting. One of the key aims of the post is to strengthen professional leadership, with four main areas of responsibility:

1. Expert practice
2. Professional leadership and consultancy

3. Education and development
4. Practice and service development linked to research and evaluation.

Most nurse consultants will spend approximately 50 per cent of their time in clinical practice, in direct contact with patients; their remaining time may be spent undertaking research, teaching, leadership and evaluation activities.

Clinical nurse specialist

This nurse has acquired extensive specialist knowledge about a specific sphere of nursing. The clinical nurse specialist (CNS) works very closely with doctors who specialise in the same area of health care. There are many CNSs who run their own clinics and take on a caseload of patients, having full responsibility for making decisions about their care. CNSs work across the four fields of nursing in primary, secondary and tertiary care, and the independent and voluntary sectors. The following are some examples of CNSs:

- Skin cancer CNS
- Lymphoma CNS
- Head and neck CNS
- HIV CNS
- Rheumatology CNS
- Community adolescent mental health CNS

Advanced nurse practitioner

An advanced nurse practitioner is defined by the RCN (2010) as a registered nurse who has undertaken a specific course of study of at least first degree (honours) level and who:

- makes professionally autonomous decisions, for which he or she is accountable
- receives patients with undifferentiated and undiagnosed problems, and assesses their health-care needs, based on highly developed nursing knowledge and skills, including skills not usually exercised by nurses, such as physical examination
- screens patients for disease risk factors and early signs of illness
- makes differential diagnosis using decision-making and problem-solving skills
- develops with the patient an ongoing nursing care plan for health, with an emphasis on preventive measures
- orders necessary investigations, and provides treatment and care individually, as part of a team and through referral to other agencies
- has a supportive role in helping people to manage and live with illness
- provides counselling and health education
- has the authority to admit or discharge patients from their caseload, and refer patients to other health-care providers as appropriate
- works collaboratively with other health-care professionals and disciplines
- provides a leadership and consultancy function as required.

Modern matron

This role can be held by a male or female and can sometimes be called the clinical nurse manager. The role was reintroduced to offer support to ward sisters/charge nurses to enhance and focus attention on the patient experience. Veitch and Christie (2007) suggest that the modern matron has three key functions:

1. To provide leadership to staff who provide direct care in order to secure and assure the highest standards of clinical care within their group of wards or within the primary care setting
2. To ensure the availability of appropriate administrative and support services within their group of wards
3. To provide a visible, accessible and authoritative presence in ward settings.

Ward sister/charge nurse

Ward sisters and their male counterparts, charge nurses, are experienced practitioners who have developed extensive skills and knowledge in their chosen area, e.g.:

- SCBU
- Adolescent mental health unit
- Oncology
- Nursing within a general hospital, e.g. acute mental health admissions wards
- Community practice, e.g. community team for learning disability
- Intensive care unit

The ward sister/charge nurse has many responsibilities, including leadership, acting as a role model and facilitating the learning of staff (such as registered nurses, student nurses and health-care assistants).

Staff nurse

The staff nurse has completed a minimum of 3 years' education, usually at a higher education institution, and may be required, as he or she gains more experience, to act as deputy for the ward sister/charge nurse. Usually the staff nurse has his or her own group of patients to care for within the hospital or community setting. More experienced staff nurses can become facilitators/mentors to other junior members of the team.

The code of professional conduct

Codes of professional conduct, also known as codes of ethics, are regularly updated and renewed (Castledine and Close, 2009); an ethical code for nurses in the UK dates back to 1983. Groups recognised as professionals adopt codes of conduct that guide the members of that professional group with regard to their professional behaviour. Nurses are guided with regard to standards for conduct, performance and ethics by way of *The Code: Standards of conduct, performance and ethics for nurses and midwives* (NMC, 2008). The code has been reproduced as Appendix 1.1 at the end of this chapter.

Professional codes for nurses aim to ensure that nurses work within ethical and moral frameworks. Codes of conduct are the collective and prevailing views shared by the profession, so the NMC's code of conduct is the ethical standard that all nurses should be working towards (Fryer, 2004; Clark, 2008; NMC, 2010a). The International Council for Nurses (ICN) has produced its own code. *The ICN Code of Ethics for Nurses* was used to help devise the first *Code of Professional Practice* in 1983 (UKCC, 1983) and is based on ethical principles (ICN, 2000).

Think

Take some time to devise what you think should be contained within a code of professional conduct for nurses. What do you think are the most important standards that nurses ought to aim to adhere to?

You can check your code of conduct against the NMC's code of conduct in Appendix 1.1.

The code of conduct is not law; there is no legal imperative. It is a guide and, according to Kozier et al (2008), it informs the general public and other professionals of the standard of conduct that they should expect from registered nurses. Codes of conduct do not solve problems, but reflect professional morality. They operate in such a way as to remind the practitioner of the standards required by the profession. However, breaching the code of conduct is in effect a breach of registration and may lead to removal of the nurse's name from the register, and consequently of the right to practise.

The purpose of the code of professional conduct is to:

- inform the profession of the standard of professional conduct required of them in the exercise of their professional accountability and practice
- inform the public, other professions and employers of the standard of professional conduct that they can expect of a registered practitioner.

There are a number of key facets incorporated within the NMC's code of conduct and they are arranged, broadly, under the following headings.

Make the care of people your first concern, treating them as individuals and respecting their dignity

- Treat people as individuals
- Respect people's confidentiality
- Collaborate with those in your care
- Ensure that you gain consent
- Maintain clear professional boundaries.

Work with others to protect and promote the health and wellbeing of those in your care, their families and carers, and the wider community

- Share information with your colleagues
- Work effectively as part of a team

- Delegate effectively
- Manage risk.

Provide a high standard of practice and care at all times

- Use the best available evidence
- Keep your skills and knowledge up to date
- Keep clear and accurate records.

Be open and honest, act with integrity and uphold the reputation of your profession

- Act with integrity
- Deal with problems
- Be impartial
- Uphold the reputation of your profession.

The principles enshrined within the code of conduct provide the professional framework from which practice is judged. Practice is judged with regard to professional standards – ethical and behavioural standards – ensuring that public protection occurs and the nurse is called to account for his or her actions or omissions. The code of conduct provides the nurse and the public with a clear message outlining personal accountability and a sense of moral responsibility.

Professional accountability

Whaite (2008) notes that health-care professionals have the potential to do much good as well as much harm to the people for whom they provide care, so the nurse should aim to maximise health and wellbeing. To be accountable the nurse must have up-to-date knowledge and the appropriate nursing skills. For this reason student nurses cannot be expected to be accountable because they may not have acquired the appropriate knowledge and skills.

Professional accountability is unremitting, and means that a nurse is accountable at all times for his or her actions or omissions, when on or off duty. The first section of the code of conduct makes it clear that, as a registered nurse or midwife, you are personally accountable for your practice, which means that you are answerable for your actions and omissions, regardless of advice or directions from another professional.

Carvalho et al (2011) suggest that sometimes the terms 'accountability' and 'responsibility' become confused. There are a number of important links between the two, but they are not the same and should not be used synonymously.

There are four arenas associated with accountability (Dimond, 2011) with which nurses may be faced (Figure 1.1).

Figure 1.1   The four areas associated with accountability. (Source: adapted from Dimond, 2011.)

Public accountability

Public accountability occurs through the criminal courts as defined by criminal law. In an instance where accountability is in question the police are likely to investigate and a decision may be made to prosecute the nurse for a criminal offence. Public accountability is generally associated with a social contract between the public and the profession.

Accountability to the patient

The injured party may seek a civil remedy via criminal law in the criminal courts: the nurse may be sued for her or his actions or omissions – negligence. The person making the complaint or bringing the action for negligence can also, in certain circumstances, sue the NHS for the nurse's negligence (indirect liability). A sum of money in compensation may be paid to the injured party.

Employer accountability

The employer expects the nurse to be accountable through the contract of employment. It is anticipated that every employee will obey the reasonable instructions of the employer and use due care and skill when carrying out his or her duties (Dimond, 2011). In some cases the employee may be in breach of contract if she or he has not acted with due care and skill, and disciplinary action may ensue.

Accountability to the profession

The nurse is professionally accountable to the NMC through its Conduct and Competence Committee. The NMC, through this Committee, will determine if a nurse is deemed incompetent through his or her actions or omissions.

Autonomy

Autonomy can be defined as self-determination, self-rule and being able to make decisions for one's self. It is a complex concept and can be used in a number of different ways (Aveyard, 2000). Dworkin (1988) notes a moral element to the term and suggests that it is about choosing a moral position and accepting responsibility for the kind of person that you are. Hendrick (2010) equates autonomy with:

- integrity
- dignity
- independence

- self-assertion
- critical reflection.

There are two perspectives associated with autonomy: a descriptive aspect and a prescriptive aspect. MacDonald (2002) suggests that descriptive autonomy is the capacity for self-governance and prescriptive autonomy is respect for autonomy, e.g. not interfering with a person's control over his or her own life.

Top tips

The code states clearly that nurses must respect a person's autonomy: '. . . act as an advocate for those in your care, helping them to access relevant health and social care information and support.' When nurses respect a person's autonomy they must be aware of any legal implications. A person's right to accept or refuse treatment and care may change in law, depending on his or her age and health. Specific attention to the legal position of children must be sought, because their right to give consent or refuse treatment and care varies in the four countries of the UK, depending on their age.

Professional self-regulation – the ability of a profession to self-regulate or 'control' itself – will become a reality only if the members of that profession have autonomy to practise. Self-regulation can be seen as an unwritten contract between society and the nurse. Accountability is the primary consequence of professional nurse autonomy. Becoming an autonomous and independent professional is dependent on what the nurse knows and what he or she realises he or she does not know. Nurses need to be aware of their limitations as well as their clinical competence. It is important that nurses understand that, if there are any areas in which they are not clinically competent or they feel that it is unethical to undertake, then it is their duty to decline to undertake them. This is true autonomy – being aware of one's limitations.

There are many new opportunities for nurses to develop advanced roles and skills to improve the quality of patient care. Finn (2001) has demonstrated that there is a direct correlation between job satisfaction among registered nurses and their degree of autonomy. It remains, however, the overriding responsibility of nurses to ensure that they are adequately prepared for any new role and ensure patient safety as the role expands.

Think

Thinking of the role of the nurse (in as many situations as you can), list the skills and the issues that he or she needs to possess in order to perform his or her duties with due care and attention with the ultimate aim of protecting the patient. By being aware of these issues the nurse is better placed to act as an autonomous practitioner.

You must by now have a very long list. Just one nursing action, e.g. feeding a patient, would require the nurse to consider many issues in order to act in the patient's best interests (Table 1.5). These are some of the skills that underpin safe nursing practice with respect to this one activity of living.

Table 1.5 Some of the issues the nurse would need to take into account in order to perform safety and to act in the patient's best interests when feeding a patient

- The patient's likes and dislikes
- Have the patient's nutritional needs been assessed?
- Does the nurse need to consult other health-care professionals such as:
  - nutritional nurse specialists
  - doctors
  - occupational therapists
  - speech and language therapists
  - dieticians?
- The patient's cultural beliefs (e.g. does he or she require a Halal-prepared meal)
- The patient's psychological/emotional status, e.g. does the patient have an appetite disturbance: anorexia nervosa, bulimia nervosa, obesity
- The patient's ability to swallow – his or her physiological status
- The patient's calorific needs – these vary with age
- Does the patient require any aids to eating?
- The nutritional value of the meal being served – your understanding of a balanced diet
- What is the patient's understanding of a balanced diet?
- Does the patient have the financial means to pay for a balanced diet? The patient may be living on a minimum income, if at all
- The level of independence/dependence
- The age of the patient, e.g. is the patient a neonate or an adolescent.
- Where the patient is being fed – eating is a part of social interaction, there may be customary influences
- Is the patient being fed orally or by tube?
- Is a prescription needed for the nutrients that the patient requires?

Confidentiality

There are number of ethical concerns that come into play when the nurse attempts to deal with confidentiality. Ethical debates abound and often there are no right or wrong answers to the questions surrounding this very complicated principle. Confidentiality is closely related to the ethical principles of beneficence (to do good) and non-maleficence (to do no harm). This confirms the often used saying that 'confidentiality is the cornerstone of nursing'. The duty of confidentiality, according to Dimond (2010), arises from a variety of sources, including:

- A duty of care to the patient
- The contract of employment
- The code of conduct
- A number of laws.

Protecting confidentiality can be seen as respect for privacy (Miller and Webb, 2011). The right to a private life is upheld in the Human Rights Act 1998. Patients have a legitimate expectation that the nurse will respect their right to privacy and that he or she will act in an appropriate way when addressing and dealing with privacy and confidentiality.

An element of trust is needed by both the patient and the nurse for confidentiality to exist. In some instances that element of trust may not be agreed by the patient, because he or she may not be competent to enter into a bilateral trust agreement. When this is the case, the duty owed should never be diminished. Mason and Whitehead (2003) point out that there must be an element of trust between both parties if there is to be an honest exchange of information and maintenance of secrecy. Without trust the therapeutic relationship between nurse and patient would be put in jeopardy: the patient may not be open and honest with the nurse. Patients place much trust in nurses and other health-care workers, e.g. doctors, so much so that patients allow nurses to perform intimate procedures on them and ask them personal questions in order to describe and reveal symptoms and problems that they may be experiencing (Hope et al, 2008).

There have been many changes in the ways in which health care has been delivered over the years; this has resulted in devising new ways of protecting patient information. The Department of Health ordered NHS organisations to appoint a Caldicott Guardian who was to be charged with specific respon-sibility for ensuring that confidential information was protected within their organisation (DH, 1997). The Caldicott Report (DH, 1997) led to the production of an NHS code of practice concerned with the issue of confidentiality (DH, 2003).

The NMC code of conduct (NMC, 2008), in relation to confidentiality, states clearly:

- You must respect people's right to confidentiality
- You must ensure that people are informed about how and why information is shared by those who will be providing their care
- You must disclose information if you believe that someone may be at risk of harm, in line with the law of the country in which you are practising.

Although it is commendable for any nurse to seek to ensure that the important ethical principle of confidentiality is maintained, this is often a complex issue and there may be many situations where this will be challenged (Dimond, 2010). Confidentiality is not an absolute principle, i.e. there are certain occasions when exemptions can be applied, and the confidence can be broken and the nurse override individual considerations, particularly when there may be implications for others – these instances are known as qualifications (Mason and Whitehead, 2003). Respect for a person's autonomy is an important component of confidentiality; however, when the confidence is broken the nurse could be said to be acting in a paternalistic manner: 'nurse knows best.' When maintaining a confidence, nurses are using the deontological ethical theory by keeping the patient's secret; conversely, they are acting in a utilitarian manner if they breach a confidence in order, for example, to safeguard the patient or others. In this instance nurses are operating in a maleficent manner (causing harm) as opposed to acting beneficently (the avoidance of doing harm).

If confidentiality is violated an individual has the right to sue through the civil courts. The individual can also make a complaint to the Information Commissioner if there has been a breach of the Data Protection Act 1998 (RCN, 2005). The patient has a right to confidentiality in law:

- Common law
- Data Protection Act 1998
- Human Rights Act 1998.

The patient can also complain about the nurse's alleged breach of confidentiality to the NMC and/or the employer (Figure 1.2).

What is confidential?

This question is not an easy one to answer. Information is provided to nurses in a variety of ways, in a range of situations from many people. Confidentiality is present when one person (the patient) discloses

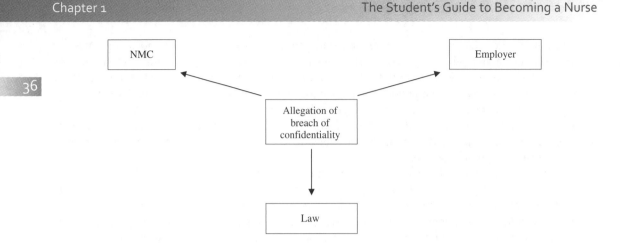

Figure 1.2   Ways in which the patient may pursue a claim alleging a breach of confidentiality.

information to another (the nurse), and the nurse given this information by the patient pledges not to disclose it to a third party without the patient's permission (NMC, 2009; Dimond, 2010). The nurse has already agreed or pledged not to disclose the information by virtue of being on the professional register and adhering to the tenets of the code of conduct.

Think

A nurse goes home after a busy day working on an oncology ward and tells her partner about the events of day. She happens to tell her partner that a patient whom she has been nursing that day has developed a urinary tract infection.

Clearly a breach of confidentiality has occurred: the nurse has disclosed confidential information to a third party without the patient's permission. How serious do you think this breach of confidentiality is?

Now consider this: a nurse goes home after a busy day working on an oncology ward and tells her partner about the events of the day. She happens to tell her partner that a patient whom she has been nursing that day has tested positive for HIV.

Again a breach of confidentiality has occurred. How serious do you think this breach of confidentiality is?

You may have felt that on both counts the confidence breached was serious. You may have thought that telling her partner about a patient developing a urinary tract infection was not as serious as telling her partner about a patient with HIV. Why? Was it because the implications of having HIV may be considered more serious than a urinary tract infection or that there is potential for stigma to arise because of being HIV positive? In both cases a confidence was violated.

Often nurses understand and are aware of the need to maintain confidentiality. Dimond (2010) suggests that challenges occur when issues concerning disclosure arise: what are the exceptions to maintaining confidentiality and the circumstances that would allow the duty to be violated? The NMC (2009) stipulates that improper disclosure should be avoided at all times. Permission needs to be granted by the patient for the nurse to disclose the information to a third party. In practical terms it is not always possible to seek permission to disclose information, but you must make the patient aware that there may be instances when the information obtained may be shared. There are many ways in which this can happen, e.g. by making explicit statements outlining the organisation's policy on the management of confidential information.

The confidentiality model

The Department of Health has produced a model to help health-care professionals provide patients with a confidential service (DH, 2003). The model informs staff that they must inform patients of the intended use of the information that they provide, offer patients the choice to consent to or withhold their consent, as well as protecting the information that has been given (Figure 1.3).

Disclosure of confidential information

There are a number of exceptions to the duty of confidentiality (Dimond, 2010). These are detailed in Table 1.6.

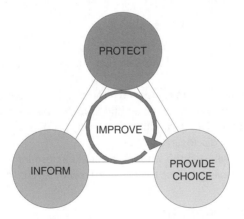

Figure 1.3   The model of confidentiality. (Source: Department of Health, 2003.)

Table 1.6   Seven exceptions that may allow the disclosure of confidential information

- With the patient's consent
- In the patient's interests
- Court order
- Statutory duty to disclose
- In the public's interests
- Police
- Provisions within the Data Protection Act 1998

Source: adapted from Dimond (2010).

The patient's consent

The duty to maintain consent or to provide a confidence is owed to the patient, and as such the patient has the authority to allow disclosures to be made. When the patient provides the nurse with permission to disclose, then there is no obligation to secrecy owed by the person receiving that consent (Mason and McCall-Smith, 2005). The nurse should check with the patient to whom information may be disclosed, e.g. family members and employers.

Think

Martha is the nurse in charge of a gynaecology ward. One of her patients, Jean, has been admitted for a termination of pregnancy. Martha receives a telephone enquiry about Jean from a person saying he is Jean's father and asking how she is after the operation. Martha tells the caller that 'All went well'. He says he will be in later to pick her up and was it the gynaecology ward he needed to come to. Martha responds: 'Yes, the gynaecology ward on the third floor.' When Jean is fully awake Martha tells her that her father has called asking about her and that he will be in later to pick her up. Jean becomes very upset and tells Martha that she has no father and that her partner has threatened her if she goes ahead with the termination of pregnancy. Jean had told her partner that she was away with her mother for a few days. Later it transpires that her partner had thought she would go ahead with the termination despite his objections and he had contacted several clinics and hospitals in the city.

Was confidentiality breached, as Martha only said that 'All went well', she did not say what the operation was for?

Confidentiality has been breached – unauthorised information has been given without Jean's consent. The nurse confirmed (unwittingly) what the partner had thought, that Jean was on the gynaecology ward. Acknowledgement that the patient is on a particular ward or unit, e.g. a psychiatric unit or a breast screening unit, could be deemed disclosure.

Martha should have checked with Jean to whom she could disclose information, if it became necessary. The ward or unit should have a policy in place to help Martha with regard to disclosure of any information.

Disclosure in the patient's interests

If information becomes known that would do the patient harm, then disclosure between the professionals involved in the patient's care would be justified. Dimond (2010) uses the problem of allergy to explain when disclosure in the patient's best interests may be permissible, e.g. if the patient has told a doctor he or she has an allergy to a specific medication, then the nurse and pharmacist would need to be informed of this in order to prevent the administration of a drug that could potentially harm the patient.

Think

Jack is to undergo a right hip replacement. Jack has confided in you that he has a secret: he has hepatitis C and has not told the anaesthetist or the surgeon who have recently been to see him to talk about his operation tomorrow.

Having been given this information by Jack, whom, if anyone, might you tell – who needs to know? Your answer to this question may be 'all those who care for him', or nobody as it has been told to you in confidence. The list of people you may tell could include:

- the surgeon
- the anaesthetist
- the theatre nurses and theatre staff
- the ward nurses.

Would the following people also need to be informed?

- The staff who work in the pathology laboratory who may deal with Jack's body fluids
- The porter who transports his body fluids to the laboratory for analysis
- The domestic who cleans his room
- The phlebotomist who takes his blood for analysis.

Those whom you do decide to tell (and you must only disclose in the patient's best interests) would also be bound by the duty of confidentiality. Disclosure of confidential information to others is justified if it is necessary to protect the health of the patient or the professionals who are to care for him or her. You must decide whom they are and who truly needs to know, as opposed to those who may just be curious.

The response to this dilemma is difficult, because each case has to be considered on an individual basis. Each practitioner must decide on disclosure with regard to the specific circumstances (the context) associated with the individual case. Jack should have been told that information may be discussed and disclosed to other health-care professionals who care for him. The nurse should make every reasonable effort to persuade the patient to allow the information given to be disclosed to those who may need to know (Mason and McCall-Smith, 2005).

Disclosure by court order

A court can demand a nurse to disclose information; this is known as a subpoena, and failure to disclose may render the nurse liable for contempt of court. There are, however, two grounds where the power of the court may fail to ensure disclosure and they are known as being privileged from disclosure. Public interest immunity is associated with national security and disclosure would be contrary to the public interest. Legal professional privilege is the second exception: this exception is associated with communications where litigation may occur or is taking place.

Statutory duty

There are statutory duties that will result in disclosure (regardless of the patient's wishes). Confidential information must be made known by law under the Acts detailed in Table 1.7. The NMC (2011b) note that 'public interest' describes the exceptional circumstances that justify overruling the right of an individual to confidentiality in order to serve a broader social concern.

Staff are permitted under common law to disclose personal information but this must done in order to prevent and support detection, investigation and punishment of serious crime and/or to prevent abuse or serious harm to other people. It is essential that each case be judged on its merits. The NMC (2011b) provide examples where disclosing information in relation to crimes against the person may be

Table 1.7   Statutory requirements to disclose

Act	Requirement
Road Traffic Act 1988	Any person is required to provide the police with information that is related to a road traffic accident that results in personal injury
Prevention of Terrorism Act 2005	Any person who has information that he/she feels may be of assistance in the prevention of terrorism or apprehension of terrorists must make this known to the police
Public Health (Control of Diseases) Act 1984	Any notifiable disease (e.g. plague, typhus, food poisoning), the name and the whereabouts of the person with the notifiable disease must be reported to the medical officer of the district
Abortion Act 1967	Doctors must report to the Chief Medical Officer any information relating to termination of pregnancy
Births and Deaths Registration Act 1953	Authorities must be notified of births and deaths

acceptable, e.g. rape, child abuse, murder, kidnapping, or as a result of injuries sustained from knife or gun-shot wounds.

These are complex decisions and must take account of the public interest in ensuring confidentiality against the public interest in disclosure. Disclosures should be proportionate and limited to relevant details.

Public interest

Disclosure is allowed if this is in the public interest. The major concern with disclosure under the heading of public interest is that there is no definition of public interest in law. Disclosure is referred to in the code of conduct (NMC, 2008); the nurse must disclose information if there is a belief that someone may be at risk of harm, but disclosure must be in line with the law. Disclosure of information must occur only if there is a need to protect the patient or someone else from significant harm and is for the good of society. Often disclosure would be justified if a serious crime had been committed, e.g. murder, child abuse or drug trafficking. Public interest has already been alluded to in the statutory duty to disclose. The DH (2010c) have produced supplementary guidance with regard to public interest disclosure.

Disclosure to the police

During a police investigation there may be instances where the police ask a nurse to disclose information. There is no general legal duty to provide the police with information (apart from the issues described above). It is, however, an offence to obstruct police investigations by providing false or misleading information. No offence will have been committed if the nurse refuses to answer questions posed by police, provided that the nurse has a lawful excuse for refusing, i.e. duty of confidentiality (Hendrick, 2004). A circuit judge can order that medical records be released to the police and the coroner can ask to see the medical records of a dead patient (Hope et al, 2008).

The Data Protection Act 1998 and disclosure of information

Under the Data Protection Act 1998 every living person has the right to apply for access to their health records, including electronic and manual records (Hope et al, 2008). There are nine key principles associated with the Act, which aim to ensure that the data held are:

- accurate
- relevant
- held only for specific defined purposes for which the user has been registered
- not kept for longer than is necessary
- not disclosed to any unauthorised person.

The Act allows data subjects (patients) to be:

- informed as to whether personal data is processed
- provided with a description of the data held, the purposes for which it is processed and knowledge of the people to whom the data may be disclosed
- provided with a copy of the information constituting the data
- given information on the source of the information.

There is also provision within the Act to allow a person to have the information rectified and inaccuracies corrected. As a result of these inaccuracies, the patient may also have the right to receive compensation for the erroneous entries that had been made.

A request, in writing, must be made by the patient to gain access to his or her records and a response to this request is then given to the patient within 40 days of the request being made. Although provisions are made to enable the patient to gain access to medical records, certain information may be withheld in some circumstances. If it is deemed that the information could cause harm to the patient, access can be denied. The following are some of the circumstances:

- Potential physical or mental harm
- If the request is made by some person other than the patient, e.g. a parent
- If access would reveal the identity of another person, unless that other person has given their consent (this does not apply if the other person is a health-care professional who has been involved in the care of the patient, unless serious harm to that health-care professional's physical or mental health is likely to be caused by allowing access).

Case study 1.2

Ms Sarah Orford is a young woman aged 18 years of age with learning disabilities. You are working with Ms Orford and she divulges to you confidentially that she is having some difficulties with her boyfriend, Mark (Mark also has learning disabilities; he is 20 years of age). Sarah and Mark both want to have sex but they are not sure about safe sex and what this means. Sarah and Mark's parents know nothing of their intentions.

What will do you in helping Ms Orford and her partner? You have a duty of care to Ms Orford. You might advise the couple of the various organisations that provide up-to-date information in user-friendly format which might provide them with some knowledge of safe sex, what it is and how to carry it out.

You can also let them know that these organisations often offer support and help in talking over issues associated with safe sex.

Professional misconduct

A breach of the Code may constitute professional misconduct or unprofessional conduct. Anyone can make a complaint about a nurse to the NMC. Complaints come to the NMC via various routes, e.g. the general public, fellow nurses, colleagues in other health-care professions and employers. Most complaints about nurses are usually resolved locally and this is the preferred way of dealing with complaints in the first instance.

Professional misconduct can occur when the nurse has not abided by the rules set by the NMC, often in the form of the code of conduct, bearing in mind that nurses are also subjected to any of the elements of the general law that affect every citizen. The NMC has a legal duty to protect the public and in so doing has the power to exercise disciplinary procedures.

Bringing about disciplinary procedures cannot, and must not, be driven by professional self-interest – the patient first and foremost is the maxim. The key aim is to determine if that unwritten contract referred to earlier has been honoured, by ensuring that any nurse who is deemed to have failed to meet the trust that society places in him or her is not permitted to continue to practise if the allegation is proven.

The NMC will take action whenever a nurse's fitness to practise is impaired because of misconduct, illness, incompetence, criminal conviction or cautions. Professional misconduct can be said to have occurred if a nurse's behaviour has fallen short of what can reasonably be expected of a nurse. If a nurse fails to follow the code, that nurse may be guilty of misconduct and as a consequence may not be fit to practise.

Fitness to practise is the nurse's suitability to be on the register; without restrictions this may mean:

● Failing always to put the patient's interests first
● Not being properly trained, qualified and up to date
● Failing to treat patients with respect and dignity
● Not speaking up for patients who cannot speak for themselves.

Think

 Make a list of what you think might be the most common examples of professional misconduct.

You may have some of the items below on your list. It is not possible to provide a definitive list of complaints that the NMC investigates. However, the NMC (2010c) considers these to be the most common examples of allegations of unfitness to practise (this is not an exhaustive list):

● Physical, sexual or verbal abuse
● Significant failure to provide adequate care

- Significant failure to keep proper records
- Failure to administer medicines safely
- Deliberately concealing unsafe practice
- Committing criminal offences
- Continued lack of competence despite opportunities to improve
- Theft
- Health conditions.

Case study 1.3

 Ms Camille Olabieje, a registered adult nurse, was found to be treating residents in a hostile and inappropriate manner while working at a care home in Edinburgh. Charges including knowingly feeding two residents with dementia contrary to their requirements, pushing a resident forcefully, shouting aggressively at residents and colleagues, and grabbing residents' hands hard enough to cause the skin to redden were made against Ms Olabieje.

The Fitness to Practise panel ruled that Ms Olabieje's behaviour was unacceptable; she fell far short of the behaviour expected from someone in the nursing profession. In order to maintain the good reputation of the profession and public confidence in the NMC, the panel agreed to strike Ms Olabieje off the register.

Lack of competence

A lack of competence relates to a lack of knowledge, skill or judgement of such a nature that the nurse is unfit to practise in a safe and effective manner (NMC, 2010c). Some examples of lack of competence can include:

- A persistent lack of ability in correctly and/or appropriately calculating and recording the administration or disposal of medicines
- A persistent lack of ability in properly identifying care needs and, accordingly, planning and delivering appropriate care
- Inability to work as part of a team
- Difficulty in communicating with colleagues or people in their care.

Conviction or caution

The following may lead to a finding of unfitness to practise in relation to a conviction or caution:

- Theft
- Fraud or other dishonest activities
- Violence
- Sexual offences
- Accessing or downloading child pornography or other illegal material from the internet
- Illegally dealing or importing drugs.

Health conditions

There are certain health conditions that may lead the NMC to question a nurse's fitness to practise:

- Long-term, untreated alcohol or drug dependence
- Unmanaged serious mental illness.

The NMC committees

When a complaint about a nurse is made and all the supporting evidence has been submitted to the NMC, the case is then referred onwards. Three committees handle and deal with all complaints of any allegation of unfitness to practise made against nurses; these are known as policy committees. Other committees make decisions about the governance of the NMC, e.g. the Audit, Risk and Assurance Committee and the Business Planning and Governance Committee.

In the first instance a triage team deal with any referral made to the NMC; this team checks to ensure that the person about whom the referral is being made is on the NMC register and that the nature of the complaint is something that the NMC should be involved with.

A case progression team then receives the referral if the triage team is content that there are grounds for a case. Information about the referral will be collected and then the case is progressed to the independent adjudication committees. The case referral team always send the nurse a copy of the allegations made against them along with supporting information; the nurse is then invited to make a written response. Depending on the case specific information will be required and will include:

- The name of the person making the referral, job title and contact details
- Details about the nurse being referred – name and PIN, the nurse's job at the time of the allegation(s) and key aspects of that post
- Details about the complaint and a clear summary
- Incidents relating to the complaint, when and where the incident took place, the type of place the nurse was employed in at the time, who was there, the context and circumstances of any incident(s)
- Details of any witnesses and copies of their statements
- Previous action – details of any other agency that may have been contacted, e.g. the police, notes and transcripts of any internal investigations
- Other supporting evidence, e.g. an internal investigating report, copies of service users' medical records, sickness record.

The case progression team then refers the case to the Investigating Committee along with all the supporting information.

The Investigating Committee

The Investigating Committee deals with all allegations. This committee meets in private and is made up of nurses, midwives and laypeople outside the two professions. All the evidence is considered by this panel, including evidence from the nurse who has been referred. The panel may seek expert advice. The panel then makes a decision to as to what kind of further investigation is required and whether or not there is a case to answer. In deciding if there is a case to answer, the Investigating Committee must be reasonably satisfied that the facts of the allegation can be proved and if proved those facts could lead to finding that a nurse's fitness to practise is impaired (NMC, 2010e). If this panel determines that there is no case to answer then the case is closed. However, if it finds otherwise the case is then referred to either the Conduct and Competence Committee or the Health Committee. In 2008–2009, 2178 referrals were made to the NMC (this is just 0.3% of all of those on the register) and only 1759 required further investigation (NMC, 2010e).

The Conduct and Competence Committee and the Health Committee

Depending on the type of case, referral is made by the Investigating Committee to either the Conduct and Competence Committee or the Health Committee who then convene a hearing and final adjudication. Just as the Investigation Committee is totally independent from the NMC so are these two committees and the panels are made up of registered nurses, midwives and laypeople (people from outside the two professions). There are a number of allegations that these two committees are requested to adjudicate on, including:

- Dishonesty
- Patient abuse
- Lack of competence
- Failure to maintain adequate records
- Incorrect administration of drugs
- Neglect of basic care
- Unsafe clinical practice
- Failure to collaborate with colleagues
- Colleague abuse
- Failure to report incidents
- Failure to act in an emergency
- Accessing pornography
- Violence.

The panel's convened aim is to determine if the nurse's fitness to practise has been impaired; if this is the case then appropriate action is taken. Conduct and competence cases are usually heard in public; it is unusual for a case that has been referred to the Health Committee to be heard in public.

The panel members of the relevant committee review the information that they have been given; they can take legal advice and question employers as well as the nurse or her or his representative. Witnesses may be called to give their account of the situation; however, this is not always the case. Witnesses are usually called if there is any dispute about the facts of the case. Vulnerable witnesses are protected and there are special provisions. The anonymity of patients and clients is also protected.

Arriving at a decision

The panel may conclude that the nurse's fitness to practise has been impaired (they decide if the nurse is fit to stay on the register). Decisions made are not intended to be punitive; they are made to safeguard the health and wellbeing of the public. The standard of proof used is the civil standard of proof (the balance of probabilities). The decision-making process goes through three stages:

1. Are the facts proven or not?
2. Is the fitness of practise of the nurse impaired?
3. What actions will be needed to safeguard the health and wellbeing of the public?

Before the Committees consider the action that they will take, they have to take into account issues such as:

- Previous disciplinary action taken and how the nurse responded to this
- The availability of training and support
- Staffing issues that may have had an impact on the nurse's performance
- Unreasonable role demands.

There are five options open to the panel if the nurse's fitness to practice has been impaired.

1. The panel can decide not to take any action or to make one of the following four orders
2. Striking off order: the nurse's name is removed from the register for 5 years and he or she is not allowed to work as a nurse in the UK
3. A suspension order: the nurse is suspended from duty for a set period of time
4. A conditions of practice order: this order restricts a nurse's practice for between 1 and 3 years, e.g. he or she may be restricted from working in a particular setting
5. A caution order: the nurse is cautioned for the behaviour but is not prevented from practising. This order can last for between 1 and 5 years.

Interim suspension or interim conditions of practice orders can be made in exceptional circumstances. These orders can be made before either the Conduct and Competence Committee or the Health Committee has heard the case. Such orders usually mean that the allegation is of a serious nature and there may be a risk to the public or to the nurse.

Restoration to the register can and does happen. Any nurse removed from the register has the right to apply to have his or her name restored. The Conduct and Competence Committee or the Health Committee considers cases of restoration. If restoration is to be granted the nurse must be able to demonstrate as a minimum that he or she:

- understands and accepts the reason for removal.
- has undertaken appropriate action to address the problems that led to removal.
- has been working in a related field of care for a significant period of time and has demonstrated exemplary standards of conduct during that time.
- has support for the application for restoration with impeccable references from the current employer and, if deemed appropriate, from a medical practitioner.

Meeting the above conditions, however, does not provide an automatic restoration to the register. In some circumstances appeals to an appropriate court are possible against any of the sanctions stated earlier.

Conclusions

Becoming a competent registered nurse brings with it many privileges, one of which is the privilege of working with the public and providing them with a service that is safe and of a high quality. From a historical perspective nurses and nursing have travelled a long way, and nursing and nurses are now seen as professionals working comfortably and confidently alongside other health-care professionals.

The regulation of nurses has evolved since 1919 when the Nurses Registration Acts were passed. The regulatory framework enhances practice and serves to protect the public. Entry to the professional register also means that the nurse has the right to practise as an autonomous practitioner, but this has to be with the patients' best interests at the core of professional practice. Professional self-regulation, i.e. the ability of the nursing profession to self-regulate or 'control' itself, becomes a reality when nurses embrace the ability to practise in an autonomous manner. Self-regulation can be seen as an unwritten contract between society and the nurse.

Registered nurses are personally accountable for their practice. This means that they are answerable for their actions and omissions, regardless of advice or directions from another professional or any other party. No one else can answer for the actions or omissions and it is no defence for the nurse to say that he or she was acting on someone else's orders.

Students of nursing are never professionally accountable in the same way as they are when they become registered practitioners. It is the registered practitioner with whom the student nurse works who is professionally responsible for the consequences of the student's actions or omissions. Student nurses must always work under the direct supervision of a registered nurse or midwife (NMC, 2010d). The NMC have produced guidance on professional conduct for nursing and midwifery students (NMC, 2010d). This guidance sets out the personal and professional conduct expected of nursing and midwifery students in order for them to be deemed fit to practise. It is based on the standards laid out in the professional code of conduct for registered nurses and midwives – the code that all registered nurses and midwives are required to follow when they register with the NMC. Students work towards these standards during their preregistration programmes of study.

A code of conduct is one hallmark of a profession. It must be remembered that the code of conduct is not law; there is no legal imperative – it is merely a guide. The code of conduct does not solve problems; it reflects professional morality and operates in such a way as to remind the nurse of the standards required by the profession. Furthermore, it guides nurses in the direction of their duties to patients. Breach of the tenets within the code of conduct is in effect a breach of registration and can lead to removal of the nurse from the register and the privileged right to practise.

Self-regulation serves to protect the public. To be seen to be effective those who fall short of upholding the good standing of the profession or bring the professional into disrepute may be found culpable of professional misconduct. Failure to put the patient's best interests first, failing to treat patients with respect and dignity, and not being up-to-date with practice are examples of incompetence that can lead to sanctions being applied. There is a range of sanctions that may be imposed on a nurse whose fitness to practise has been impaired.

When complaints are received about a nurse's fitness to practise the case is referred to the Investigating Committee, which then decides if a case is to be answered. If no case is to be answered the complaint is dismissed. However, if the Investigating Committee considers that the complaint must be investigated further, the case is referred to either the Conduct and Competence Committee or the Health Committee. Interim suspension or interim conditions of practice orders can be made in exceptional circumstances, but this is rare. Such orders usually mean that the allegation is of a serious nature and there may be a risk to the public or the individual nurse.

Restoration to the register can and does happen. Any nurse has the right to apply to have his or her name restored to the register. However, conditions must be met before restoration, as determined by either the Conduct and Competence Committee or the Health Committee. Appeals can be made to an appropriate court in respect to any sanctions applied.

Activities

Attempt the following 10 questions that are related to the code of professional conduct to test your knowledge. The answers can be found at the back of this book, in the section called 'Activity Answers'.

1. What date was the current Code of Conduct published?
   a. 1994
   b. 2001
   c. 2008
   d. 2005

2. Who published the Code of Conduct?
   a. The RCN
   b. The NMC
   c. The Department of Health
   d. The Council of deans

3. The Code of Conduct is:
   a. A legal document
   b. A document produced to protect the nurse
   c. An advisory document
   d. A document used for disciplinary purposes for the student

4. Who does the document concern?
   a. Children and families
   b. Children's nurses
   c. All nurses and midwives
   d. All health-care professionals

5. Where can copies be obtained?
   a. The university learning resource centre
   b. The NMC website
   c. The NMC
   d. All of the above

6. Which of the following are documents that the NMC does not produce?
   a. Administration of medicines
   b. Records and record keeping
   c. National Service Frameworks
   d. Manual removal of faeces

7. The key aim of the NMC is to:
   a. Protect and serve the public
   b. Protect the best interests of the nurse
   c. Provide an annual report to the ombudsman
   d. Generate income

8. How many parts are there to the professional register?
   a. 1
   b. 14
   c. 3
   d. 16

9. Which of the following statements is true?
   a. The NMC is a commercial enterprise.
   b. All doctors must have live registration with NMC in order to practise.

      c. The NMC is an organisation set up by Parliament to ensure that nurses and midwives provide high standards of care to their patients and clients.

      d. Membership to the NMC is open to all health-care professionals.

10. When was the NMC created?
      a. December 2002
      b. April 2003
      c. April 2002
      d. December 2003

References

Anionwu EN (2005) *A Short History of Mary Seacole. A resource for nurses and students*. London: Royal College of Nursing.

Aveyard H (2000) Is there a concept of autonomy that can usefully inform nursing practice? *Journal of Advanced Nursing* **32**: 352–358.

Benner P (1984) *From Novice to Expert*. Menlo Park, CA: Addison Wesley.

Burnard P, Chapman C (2003) *Professional and Ethical Issues in Nursing*, 3rd edn. London: Ballière Tindall.

Cameron A, Masterson A (2003) Reconfiguring the clinical workforce. In: Davies C (ed.), *The Future Health Workforce*. Basingstoke: Palgrave, pp 68–83.

Carvalho S, Reeves M, Orford J (2011) *Fundamental Aspects of Legal, Ethical and Professional Issues in Nursing*, 2nd edn. London: Quay Books.

Castledine G, Close A (2009) *Oxford Handbook of Adult Nursing*. Oxford: Oxford University Press.

Clark J (2008) What is nursing. In: Hinchliff S, Norman S, Schober J (eds), *Nursing Practice and Health Care. A foundation text*, 5th edn. London: Hodder Arnold, pp 18–41.

Craig C (2010) Evolution of nursing practice. In: Daniels R (ed.), *Nursing Fundamentals: Caring and clinical decision making*, 2nd edn. New York: Delmar, pp 2–25.

Davies C, Beach A (2000) *Interpreting Professional Regulation*. London: Routledge.

Department of Health (1997) *The Caldicott Committee: Report on the Review of Patient Identifiable Information*. London: DH.

Department of Health (2003) *Confidentiality: NHS Code of Practice*. London: DH.

Department of Health (2006a) *Hospital at Night. Baseline Report*. London: DH.

Department of Health (2006b) *Modernising Nursing Careers – Setting the Direction*. London: DH.

Department of Health (2007) *Trust, Assurance and Safety: The regulation of healthcare professionals in the 21st century*. London: The Stationery Office. Available at: www.dh.gov.uk/prod_consum_dh/groups/dh_digitalassets/@dh/@en/documents/digitalasset/dh_065947.pdf (accessed May 2011).

Department of Health (2010a) *Equity and Excellence: Liberating the NHS*. London: DH.

Department of Health (2010b) *Healthy Lives, Healthy People: Our strategy for public health in England*. London: DH.

Department of Health (2010c) *Supplementary Guidance: Public interest disclosures*. London: DH.

Dimond B (2010) *Legal Aspects of Patient Confidentiality*, 2nd edn. London: Quay Books.

Dimond B (2011) *Legal Aspects of Nursing*, 6th edn. Harlow: Pearson.

Dworkin G (1988) *The Theory and Practice of Autonomy*. Cambridge: Cambridge University Press.

Etzioni A (1969) *The Semi-Professions and Their Organization: Teachers, nurses and social workers*. New York: Free Press.

Finn CP (2001) Autonomy: An important component for nurses' job satisfaction. *International Journal of Nursing Studies* **38**: 349–357.

Fryer N (2004) Principles of professional practice. In: Hinchliff S, Norman S, Schober J (eds), *Nursing Practice and Health Care*, 4th edn. London: Arnold, pp 27–47.

Hallet CE (2010) *Celebrating Nurses. A Visual History*. London: Fil Rouge Press.

Henderson V (1966) *The Nature of Nursing: A definition and its implications for practice, research and education*. New York: Macmillan.

Hendrick J (2004) *Law and Ethics*. Cheltenham: Nelson Thorne.

Hendrick J (2010) *Law and Ethics in Children's Nursing*. Chichester: Wiley-Blackwell.

Hood LJ (2010) *Conceptual Bases of Professional Nursing*, 7th edn. Philadelphia, PA: Lippincott.

Hope T, Savulescu J, Hendrick J (2008) *Medical Ethics and Law: The core curriculum*, 2nd edn. Edinburgh: Churchill Livingstone.

International Council of Nurses (2000) *The ICN Code of Ethics for Nurses*. Geneva: ICN.

Kozier B, Erb G, Berman A, Snyder S, Lake R, Harvey S (2008) *Fundamentals of Nursing. Concepts, Process and Practice*. Harlow: Pearson.

Longley M, Shaw C, Dolan G (2007) *Nursing: Towards 2015: Alternative Scenarios for Healthcare, Nursing and Nurse Education in the UK in 2015*. Pontypridd: University of Glamorgan.

MacDonald C (2002) Nursing autonomy as relational. *Nursing Ethics* **9**: 194–201.

McGann S, Crowther A, Dougall R (2009) *A History of the Royal College of Nursing 1916–1990. A Voice for Nurses*. Manchester: Manchester University Press.

Mason JK, McCall-Smith RA (2005) *Law and Medical Ethics*, 7th edn. Oxford: Oxford University Press.

Mason T, Whitehead E (2003) *Thinking Nursing*. Milton Keynes: Open University Press.

Miller E, Webb L (2011) Active listening and attending; communication skills and the healthcare environment. In: Webb L (ed.), *Nursing: Communication skills in practice*. Oxford: Oxford University Press, 52–71.

NHS Information Centre (2011) *NHS Staff 1996–2006 Overview*. Available at: www.ic.nhs.uk/statistics-and-data-collections/workforce/nhs-staff-numbers/nhs-staff-1996–2006-overview (accessed May 2011).

Nightingale F (1859a) *Notes on Hospitals*. London: John W. Parker & Sons.

Nightingale F (1859b) *Notes on Nursing: What it is and what it is not*. Glasgow & London: Blackie & Son Ltd.

Nursing and Midwifery Council (2004) *Standards of Proficiency for Specialist Community Public Health Nurses*. London: NMC.

Nursing and Midwifery Council (2008) *The Code: Standards of Conduct, Performance and Ethics for Nurses and Midwives*. London: NMC.

Nursing and Midwifery Council (2009) *Advice Sheet. Confidentiality (A to Z Guidance)*. London: NMC.

Nursing and Midwifery Council (2010a) *Good Health and Good Character: Guidance for approved education institutions*. London: NMC.

Nursing and Midwifery Council (2010b) *Standards for Preregistration Nursing Education*. London: NMC. Available at: http://standards.nmc-uk.org/PublishedDocuments/Standards%20for%20pre-registration%20nursing%20education%2016082010.pdf (accessed July 2011).

Nursing and Midwifery Council (2010c) *The PREP Handbook*. London: NMC.

Nursing and Midwifery Council (2010d) *Guidance on Professional Conduct for Nursing and Midwifery Students*. London: NMC.

Nursing and Midwifery Council (2010e) *Advice and Information for Employers of Nurses and Midwives*. London: NMC.

Nursing and Midwifery Council (2011a) *Statistical Analysis of the Register 1 April 2007 to 31 March 2008*. London: NMC. Available at: www.nmc-uk.org/Documents/Statistical%20analysis%20of%20the%20register/NMC-Statistical-analysis-of-the-register-2007-2008.pdf (accessed May 2011).

Nursing and Midwifery Council (2011b) *Confidentiality*. London: NMC. Available at: www.nmc-uk.org/Nurses-and-midwives/Advice-by-topic/A/Advice/Confidentiality (accessed December 2011).

Pyne R (1998) *Professional Disciplines in Nursing, Midwifery and Health Visiting*, 3rd edn. Oxford: Blackwell Scientific Publications.

Royal College of Nursing (2003) *Defining Nursing*. London: RCN.

Royal College of Nursing (2005) *Confidentiality: RCN Guidance for Occupational Health Nurses*. London: RCN.

Royal College of Nursing (2010) *Advanced Nurse Practitioners – an RCN Guide to the Advanced Nurse Practitioner Role, Competences and Programme Accreditation*. London: RCN.

Salvage J (2002) *Rethinking Professionalism: The First Step for Patient Focused Care*. London: Institute for Public Policy Research.

Salvage J (2003) Nursing today and tomorrow. In: Hinchliff S, Norman S, Schober J (eds), *Nursing Practice and Health Care*, 4th edn. London: Arnold, pp 1–24.

United Kingdom Central Council (1983) *Code of Professional Practice*. London: UKCC.

United Kingdom Central Council (1986) *Project 2000 – A New Preparation for Practice*. London: UKCC.

United Kingdom Central Council (1999) *Fitness for Practice: The UKCC Commission for Nursing and Midwifery Education*. London: UKCC.

Veitch L, Christie J (2007) Evolution of contemporary nursing. In: Brooker C, Waugh A (eds), *Nursing Practice. Fundamentals of Holistic Care*. Edinburgh: Mosby-Elsevier, pp 37–70.

Whaite I (2008) Professional standards and rules: the professional regulatory body and the nursing student. In: Spouse J, Cook M, Cox C (eds) *Common Foundation Studies in Nursing*, 4th edn. Edinburgh: Churchill Livingstone, pp 89–124.

Webb L (2011) Communication for personal and professional development. In: Webb L (ed.), *Nursing: Communication skills in practice*. Oxford: Oxford University Press, pp 300–312.

Williamson GR, Jenkinson T, Proctor Childs T (2010) () *Contexts of Contemporary Nursing*, 2nd edn. Exeter: Learning Matters.

Appendix 1.1

The code: Standards of conduct, performance and ethics for nurses and midwives

Source: reproduced with permission Nursing and Midwifery Council (2008) (www.nmc-uk.org.uk)

The people in your care must be able to trust you with their health and wellbeing.

To justify that trust, you must:

- Make the care of people your first concern, treating them as individuals and respecting their dignity
- Work with others to protect and promote the health and wellbeing of those in your care, their families and carers, and the wider community
- Provide a high standard of practice and care at all times
- Be open and honest, act with integrity and uphold the reputation of your profession

As a professional, you are personally accountable for actions and omissions in your practice and must always be able to justify your decisions.

You must always act lawfully, whether those laws relate to your professional practice or personal life.

Failure to comply with this code may bring your fitness to practise into question and endanger your registration.

This code should be considered together with the Nursing and Midwifery Council's rules, standards, guidance and advice available from www.nmc-uk.org.

Make the care of people your first concern, treating them as individuals and respecting their dignity.

Treat people as individuals:

1. You must treat people as individuals and respect their dignity
2. You must not discriminate in any way against those in your care
3. You must treat people kindly and considerately
4. You must act as an advocate for those in your care, helping them to access relevant health and social care, information and support

Respect people's confidentiality:

5. You must respect people's right to confidentiality
6. You must ensure that people are informed about how and why information is shared by those who will be providing their care
7. You must disclose information if you believe someone may be at risk of harm, in line with the law of the country in which you are practising

Collaborate with those in your care:

8. You must listen to the people in your care and respond to their concerns and preferences
9. You must support people in caring for themselves to improve and maintain their health
10. You must recognise and respect the contribution that people make to their own care and wellbeing
11. You must make arrangements to meet people's language and communication needs
12. You must share with people, in a way that they can understand, the information that they want or need to know about their health

Ensure that you gain consent:

13. You must ensure that you gain consent before you begin any treatment or care
14. You must respect and support people's rights to accept or decline treatment and care
15. You must uphold people's rights to be fully involved in decisions about their care
16. You must be aware of the legislation regarding mental capacity, ensuring that people who lack capacity remain at the centre of decision-making and are fully safeguarded
17. You must be able to demonstrate that you have acted in someone's best interests if you have provided care in an emergency

Maintain clear professional boundaries:

18. You must refuse any gifts, favours or hospitality that might be interpreted as an attempt to gain preferential treatment
19. You must not ask for or accept loans from anyone in your care or anyone close to them
20. You must establish and actively maintain clear sexual boundaries at all times with people in your care, their families and carers

Work with others to protect and promote the health and wellbeing of those in your care, their families and carers, and the wider community.
    Share information with your colleagues:

21. You must keep your colleagues informed when you are sharing the care of others
22. You must work with colleagues to monitor the quality of your work and maintain the safety of those in your care
23. You must facilitate students and others to develop their competence

Work effectively as part of a team:

24. You must work cooperatively within teams and respect the skills, expertise and contributions of your colleagues
25. You must be willing to share your skills and experience for the benefit of your colleagues
26. You must consult and take advice from colleagues when appropriate
27. You must treat your colleagues fairly and without discrimination
28. You must make a referral to another practitioner when it is in the best interests of someone in your care

Delegate effectively:

29. You must establish that anyone you delegate to is able to carry out your instructions
30. You must confirm that the outcome of any delegated task meets required standards
31. You must make sure that everyone you are responsible for is supervised and supported

Manage risk:

32. You must act without delay if you believe that you, a colleague or anyone else may be putting someone at risk
33. You must inform someone in authority if you experience problems that prevent you working within this code or other nationally agreed standards
34. You must report your concerns in writing if problems in the environment of care are putting people at risk

Provide a high standard of practice and care at all times.
  Use the best available evidence:

35. You must deliver care based on the best available evidence or best practice
36. You must ensure that any advice you give is evidence based if you are suggesting healthcare products or services
37. You must ensure that the use of complementary or alternative therapies is safe and in the best interests of those in your care

Complementary alternative therapies and homeopathy.
  Keep your skills and knowledge up to date:

38. You must have the knowledge and skills for safe and effective practice when working without direct supervision
39. You must recognise and work within the limits of your competence
40. You must keep your knowledge and skills up to date throughout your working life
41. You must take part in appropriate learning and practice activities that maintain and develop your competence and performance

Keep clear and accurate records.
  Record keeping: guidance for nurses and midwives:

42. You must keep clear and accurate records of the discussions that you have, the assessments that you make, the treatment and medicines that you give and how effective these have been
43. You must complete records as soon as possible after an event has occurred
44. You must not tamper with original records in any way
45. You must ensure that any entries you make in someone's paper records are clearly and legibly signed, dated and timed
46. You must ensure any entries you make in someone's electronic records are clearly attributable to you
47. You must ensure all records are kept securely

Be open and honest, act with integrity and uphold the reputation of your profession.
  Act with integrity:

48. You must demonstrate a personal and professional commitment to equality and diversity
49. You must adhere to the laws of the country in which you are practising
50. You must inform the NMC if you have been cautioned, charged or found guilty of a criminal offence
51. You must inform any employers you work for if your fitness to practise is called into question

Deal with problems:

52. You must give a constructive and honest response to anyone who complains about the care they have received
53. You must not allow someone's complaint to prejudice the care that you provide for them
54. You must act immediately to put matters right if someone in your care has suffered harm for any reason
55. You must explain fully and promptly to the person affected what has happened and the likely effects
56. You must cooperate with internal and external investigations

Be impartial:

57. You must not abuse your privileged position for your own ends
58. You must ensure that your professional judgement is not influenced by any commercial considerations

Uphold the reputation of your profession:

59. You must not use your professional status to promote causes that are not related to health
60. You must cooperate with the media only when you can confidently protect the confidential information and dignity of those in your care
61. You must uphold the reputation of your profession at all times

Information about indemnity insurance

The NMC recommends that a registered nurse or midwife, in advising, treating and caring for patients/clients, has professional indemnity insurance. This is in the interests of clients, patients and registrants in the event of claims of professional negligence.

Although employers have vicarious liability for the negligent acts and/or omissions of their employees, such cover does not normally extend to activities undertaken outside the registrant's employment. Independent practice would not be covered by vicarious liability. It is the individual registrant's responsibility to establish their insurance status and take appropriate action.

In situations where an employer does not have vicarious liability, the NMC recommends that registrants obtain adequate professional indemnity insurance. If unable to secure professional indemnity insurance, a registrant will need to demonstrate that all their clients/patients are fully informed of this fact and the implications that this might have in the event of a claim for professional negligence.

Appendix 1.2

Guidance on professional conduct for nursing and midwifery students

Source: reproduced with permission Nursing and Midwifery Council (2010) (www.nmc-uk.org)

The four core principles of the code

Your conduct as a nursing or midwifery student is based on the four core principles that we've set out in the code:

- Make the care of people your first concern, treating them as individuals and respecting their dignity
- Work with others to protect and promote the health and wellbeing of those in your care, their families and carers, and the wider community
- Provide a high standard of practice and care at all times
- Be open and honest, act with integrity and uphold the reputation of your profession

Make the care of people your first concern, treating them as individuals and respecting their dignity
    Treat people as individuals

You should:

1. Treat people as individuals and respect their dignity
2. Be polite, kind, caring and compassionate
3. Not discriminate in any way against those for whom you provide care
4. Recognise diversity and respect the cultural differences, values and beliefs of others, including the people you care for and other members of staff

Respect a person's confidentiality
   You should:

5. Respect a person's right to confidentiality
6. Not disclose information to anyone who is not entitled to it
7. Seek advice from your mentor or tutor before disclosing information if you believe someone may be at risk of harm
8. Follow the guidelines or policy on confidentiality as set out by your university and clinical placement provider
9. Be aware of and follow the NMC guidelines on confidentiality (available from our website www.nmc-uk.org)
10. Make anonymous any information included in your coursework or assessments that may directly or indirectly identify people, staff, relatives, carers or clinical placement providers
11. Follow your university and clinical placement provider guidelines and policy on ethics when involved or participating in research

Collaborate with those in your care
   You should:

12. Listen to people and respond to their concerns and preferences
13. Support people in caring for themselves to improve and maintain their health
14. Give people information and advice, in a way they can understand, so they can make choices and decisions about their care
15. Work in partnership with people, their families and carers

Ensure you gain consent
   You should:

16. Make sure that people know that you are a student
17. Ensure that you gain their consent before you begin to provide care
18. Respect the right for people to request care to be provided by a registered professional

Maintain clear professional boundaries
   You should:

19. Maintain clear professional boundaries in the relationships that you have with others, especially with vulnerable adults and children
20. Refuse any gifts, favours or hospitality that might be interpreted as an attempt to gain preferential treatment
21. Not ask for or accept loans from anyone for whom you provide care or anyone close to them

22. Maintain clear sexual boundaries at all times with the people for whom you provide care, their families and carers
23. Be aware of and follow the NMC guidelines on maintaining clear sexual boundaries (available from the advice section on our website www.nmc-uk.org)

Work with others to protect and promote the health and wellbeing of those in your care, their families and carers, and the wider community
   Work as part of a team
   You should:

24. Be aware of the roles and responsibilities of other people involved in providing health and social care
25. Work cooperatively within teams and respect the skills, expertise and contributions from all people involved with your education
26. Treat all colleagues, team members and those with whom you work and learn, fairly and without discrimination
27. Inform your mentor or tutor immediately if you believe that you, a colleague or anyone else may be putting someone at risk of harm

Provide a high standard of practice and care at all times
   Recognise and work within your limits of competence
   You should:

28. Recognise and stay within the limits of your competence
29. Work only under the appropriate supervision and support of a qualified professional and ask for help from your mentor or tutor when you need it
30. Work with your mentor and tutor to monitor the quality of your work and maintain the safety of people for whom you provide care
31. Seek help from an appropriately qualified healthcare professional, as soon as possible, if your performance or judgement is affected by your health

Ensure your skills and knowledge are up to date
   You should:

32. Take responsibility for your own learning
33. Follow the policy on attendance as set out by your university and clinical placement provider
34. Follow the policy on submission of coursework and completion of clinical assessments as set out by your university and clinical placement provider
35. Reflect on and respond constructively to feedback that you are given
36. Endeavour to provide care based on the best available evidence or best practice

Keep clear and accurate records
   You should:

37. Ensure that you are familiar with and follow our record keeping guidance for nurses and midwives (available from our website www.nmc-uk.org)
38. Ensure that you follow local policy on the recording, handling and storage of records

Be open and honest, act with integrity and uphold the reputation of your profession

Be open and honest
You should:

39. Be honest and trustworthy when completing all records and logs of your practice experience
40. Not plagiarise or falsify coursework or clinical assessments
41. Ensure that you complete CVs and application forms truthfully and accurately
42. Ensure that you are not influenced by any commercial incentives

Act with integrity
You should:

43. Demonstrate a personal and professional commitment to equality and diversity
44. Abide by the laws of the country in which you are undertaking your programme and inform your university immediately if, during your programme, you are arrested or receive any caution or warning or similar sanction from the police
45. Inform your university if you have been cautioned, charged or found guilty of a criminal offence at any time
46. Ensure that you are familiar with and abide by the rules, regulations, policies and procedures of your university and clinical placement provider
47. Abide by UK laws and the rules, regulation, policies and procedures of the university and clinical placement providers with regard to your use of the internet and social networking sites
48. Ensure that you are familiar with and follow our advice on the use of social networking sites (available from our website www.nmc-uk.org)

Protect people from harm
You should:

49. Seek help and advice from a mentor or tutor when there is a need to protect people from harm
50. Seek help immediately from an appropriately qualified professional if someone for whom you are providing care has suffered harm for any reason
51. Seek help from your mentor or tutor if people indicate that they are unhappy about their care or treatment

Uphold the reputation of the nursing and midwifery professions
You should:

52. Follow the dress code or uniform policy of your university and clinical placement provider
53. Be aware that your behaviour and conduct inside and outside of the university and clinical placement, including your personal life, may impact on your fitness to practise and ability to complete your programme
54. Uphold the reputation of your chosen profession at all times

2

The Vulnerable Person

Aims and objectives

The aim of this chapter is to provide insight and understanding concerning the care of those who are vulnerable and require safeguarding.

At the end of the chapter you will be able to:

1. Discuss some of the ethical, moral and legal issues that impact on safeguarding those who are vulnerable
2. Understand the role of the nurse in protecting the public, particularly those who are risk
3. Outline the role and function the of the Nursing and Midwifery Council concerning those who are vulnerable
4. Describe the key issues associated with informed consent
5. Begin to apply the concepts discussed to the practice setting
6. Appreciate the Nursing and Midwifery Council's requirements of student nurses

There are some adults in our society who have a right to and a need to be protected from harm and abuse. Michaels and Moffett (2008) suggest that nurses come across vulnerability at a number of levels, e.g. cellular, physiological systems, mind–body, individuals, communities and societies. It is not always the case that adults can protect and care for themselves.

All those seeking to be admitted to the professional register must demonstrate that they understand and can apply existing legislation to all service users, paying particular attention to the safety of vulnerable people; this will include those with complex needs as a result of ageing, cognitive impairment, long-term conditions and those who are approaching the end of life (Nursing and Midwifery Council or NMC, 2010a).

People expect nurses to be able to safeguard those from vulnerable situations, to support and protect them from harm. For the first time in the history of the National Health Service, the NHS Constitution (Department of Health or DH, 2009c) provides in one place details of what staff, patients and the public can expect from the NHS in England. It also explains what we can all do to help support the NHS, help it work effectively and help ensure that its resources are used responsibly. The Constitution sets out people's rights as NHS patients. These rights cover how patients access health services, the quality of care expected, the treatments and programmes available, confidentiality, information and the right to complain if things go wrong. To do this effectively and to work within professional and organisational frameworks, it is essential to understand the fundamental issues associated with ethical theory and the potential impact on nursing and health and wellbeing care.

The Student's Guide to Becoming a Nurse, Second Edition. Ian Peate.
© 2012 John Wiley & Sons, Ltd. Published 2012 by John Wiley & Sons, Ltd.

Ethical issues impinge on all aspects of care. An understanding of ethics will help the nurse when caring for patients and managing their care appropriately. Every aspect of nursing intervention has the potential to impinge on the patient's physical and psychological wellbeing and a constant awareness of this, regardless of how fleeting the interaction with the patient may be, is required. Nurses and nursing students are concerned with the ethical practice of nursing and are confronted with ethical issues, challenges and dilemmas nearly every day. An overview of the various ethical principles is considered.

There are few areas of health care that are untouched by the law and involvement with the legal process. The next section of this chapter briefly considers the legal process in order to develop an understanding of the law and its impact on nursing and health care. In this chapter, the law as applied to England and Wales is the main thrust of the legal debate. The legal systems in Scotland and Northern Ireland have their own traditions and, although different from the English and Welsh arrangements, there is a range of comparisons. The key issues associated with the relevant legislation and health and social policy related to nursing practice are identified and discussed.

You may recall in Chapter 1 that nurses are accountable for their own practice regardless of the advice and directions given to the nurse by another health-care professional, e.g. a doctor. If a nurse acts on the directions of another health-care professional, this does not relieve him or her of personal responsibility, if the act that he or she carried out was unethical or unlawful. It is important therefore that the nurse be aware of the legal and ethical issues surrounding patient care. Nurses need skills in ethical reasoning along with an understanding of the law and the demands made by the nursing profession with the express intention of safeguarding and protecting the public.

Ethics in nursing practice

Several ethical perspectives need to be considered by the nurse when working with patients in any setting. Ethical dilemmas arise when there is or may be conflict between various interests and interested parties. Nurses often need to make decisions, prioritise care, manage resources (both human and material) and address conflict. Carrying out these tasks will involve ethical considerations, and increasingly these decisions transcend technical and professional concerns.

Every individual is important and deserves to be treated with respect. The Royal College of Nursing (RCN, 2009) suggests that this value – respect – is upheld in law and should underpin all aspects of nursing practice.

Defining key terms

Ethics

Defining the term 'ethics' is not easy, just as the definition of 'professional' in the previous chapter proved challenging. Most definitions incorporate the term 'morals', e.g. Kirby and Slevin (2003) in their definition suggest that ethics is the study of moral thinking: it is about the values that we hold and our actions. Dictionary definitions of ethics also incorporate morals – the *New Oxford Dictionary of English* defines ethics as 'Moral principles which govern a person's behaviour or the conduct of an activity' (*New Oxford Dictionary of English*, 2001). Philosophers provide differing explanations of ethics. Hawley (2007) considers ethics in a methodological manner, allowing individuals to offer justification for moral actions and the moral decisions that are made.

According to Hope et al (2008) most of us have gut reactions as to what we think is morally right or wrong in certain situations. Often these reactions are a result of our upbringing. When these rights or wrongs are related to dilemmas that occur during nursing practice, the reasons are sometimes associated with what we have learnt during our professional apprenticeship – our nursing education. These reactions, the reactions that help us decide what is right or wrong, must be examined further.

Ethics and morals applied to nursing practice are primarily concerned with the decisions made about whether something is right or wrong, good or bad. All of this is conducted within the confines of the law and often the issues are complex.

Think

- Are some things always wrong? What are they?
- Why should you be good?
- Is abortion right or wrong?

It may have taken you seconds to respond to the above statements; conversely you might have mulled over them for some time. For many centuries the answers (if there are any) to these questions have been fiercely deliberated and are still being debated today. In your response to the first question you may consider that sometimes some things are wrong depending on the situation, e.g. you may think that murder is wrong. However, there are situations where it may be defensible. You might think that abortion is right or wrong and is related to an individual's particular perspective or point of view, e.g. their religious beliefs or values, cultural values and personal values.

Values

Values are derived from many sources (Figure 2.1). There are several ways of expressing individual or collective values, e.g. in non-verbal and verbal communication, and through codes of professional conduct.

Think

Consider a particular value that your parents or other people have taught you. What kind of an influence did that person or people have on your life and how did that individual (it may have been more than one person) persuade you to think?

Of course, there are many people who have influenced and persuaded you, e.g. your parents, your teachers and your friends. The person or people may have influenced you at an early age or at a period in your life when you were vulnerable or open to persuasion. It is possible to discover how the values that you hold dear today have been formed, shaped and moulded. As you develop and grow as an individual, these values may change – new ideas and influences can affect them and change them. Reflect on some values that you held dear to you: have they changed? Consider why they may have changed.

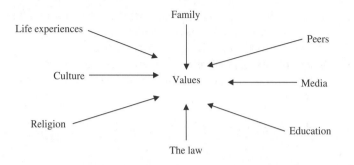

Figure 2.1   Some factors that influence and shape the way that we develop our values systems.

Every nurse will be influenced by his or her own value system, which has been shaped over time. Values are a part of whom you are and what makes you worthwhile (Hendrick, 2004). Values have the potential to motivate and guide a person's choices and decision-making abilities – understanding your own value system may help when making an ethical decision about nursing practice.

Just as nurses have their own value systems so do patients, and often these are informed by the influencing factors outlined in Figure 2.1. As a result of this, they may be similar or differ significantly. There is therefore a potential for conflict. When this conflict arises the nurse must respect the values of others, ensuring that a balance has been achieved in relation to the patient's rights and the nurse's professional duties (Fry and Johnstone, 2008).

Table 2.1 summarises the definitions of ethics, morals and values.

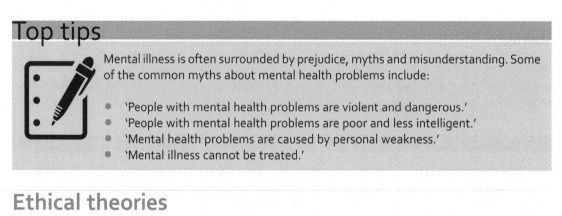

Top tips

Mental illness is often surrounded by prejudice, myths and misunderstanding. Some of the common myths about mental health problems include:

- 'People with mental health problems are violent and dangerous.'
- 'People with mental health problems are poor and less intelligent.'
- 'Mental health problems are caused by personal weakness.'
- 'Mental illness cannot be treated.'

Ethical theories

Ethical theories are complex theories that philosophers use to reflect on moral beliefs and practices. Utilitarianism and deontology are two ethical theories that are briefly discussed here.

Utilitarianism – the greatest good for the greatest number

Utilitarianism is a commonly used ethical theory (Mason and Whitehead, 2003). One of the basic insights into utilitarianism is that the aim of morality is to make the world a better place. It is about producing good consequences, not having good intentions. The emphasis in utilitarianism is on consequences and not intentions: society should do whatever brings the most benefit to all humanity. The most often used

Table 2.1 An overview of morals, values and ethics

Term	Definition	Example
Ethics	• Promotes ideal human behaviour	• Exploration of ethical principles and moral standards related to conduct
	• Considers what ought to be done	• Having high regard to the concept that humans are unique beings who have unique experiences
	• Aims to provide guidance or principles on which to direct human action	
Morals	• Standards of conduct that reflect ideal human behaviour	• An expectation that society will tell the truth and be honest in all situations despite the fact that there may be negative consequences
	• Norms of conduct identified by society	• Behaviours that are judged to be the 'right or correct' thing to do
	• Expected conduct regardless of the consequences of the individual	
Values	• Ideals and beliefs associated with patterns of behaviour that are held dear by individuals	• Personal values
	• Behaviours that have been earned and acquired over a period of time from various influences, e.g. family and peers	• Professional values

Source: adapted from Harkreader et al (2007).

maxim to sum up the utilitarian perspective is 'the greatest good for the greatest number' – always acting in such a way that will produce the greatest overall amount of good in the world. The focus or the moral position emanating from utilitarianism is to put aside our own self-interests for the sake of the whole.

Jeremy Bentham, a legal philosopher (1748–1832), believed that we should try to increase the overall amount of pleasure in the world. However, John Stuart Mill, another philosopher (1806–1873), disagreed with Bentham's philosophy. Despite pleasure being easy to quantify it was of short duration and was associated with the lower levels of our existence (sensual/physical pleasures). Mill felt that the term 'happiness' should be used instead of pleasure. Happiness is associated with the higher levels of human existence (rational/mental pleasures). However, happiness as opposed to pleasure is not so easy to measure and quantify.

There are two types of utilitarianism: see Table 2.2 for an overview of these approaches.

Utilitarianism can be considered as 'cost and benefit' and how alternative courses of action can produce the best overall outcomes. If a nurse uses a utilitarian approach in respect of truth telling, for example, he or she would have to take into account, when making a decision, the consequence or the outcome of truth telling, and whether the act (telling the truth) would produce more happiness than

Table 2.2   An overview of act and rule utilitarianism

Act utilitarianism	Rule utilitarianism
Each individual action a person takes should be assessed in relation to its rightness when the outcome (the utility) has been maximised. There are no moral rules apart from one, and that is that we should always strive to seek the happiness of the greatest number in all situations.	The right actions are those actions that are consistent with outcome. The rules formed are rules that use utilitarian principles, i.e. the greatest good for the greatest number. Deference to predefined rules and exceptions to these rules are acceptable.

unhappiness. In this circumstance, even if a decision is made to tell the truth to arrive at the greatest good for the greatest number, this may not necessarily be the morally correct theory to justify the action. A deontological approach may prove to be more appropriate.

Deontology

Although utilitarianism is concerned with consequences, deontology contrasts with this theory and focuses on the individual's intentions. Immanuel Kant (1724–1804), a German philosopher, argued that an action is morally right only if the individual is motivated by 'good will'. If the proposed action is not motivated by good will then it is wrong, despite the consequences. There are key rules that have to be followed and hence deontologists are concerned with motive as opposed to consequence (Whaite, 2008).

Generally, deontologists are bound by constraints, e.g. the prerequisite not to kill, but they are also given options, e.g. the right not to donate money to a charity if they do not wish to. Strict utilitarians, in contrast, recognise neither constraints nor options, and the aim of the utilitarian is to maximise the good by any and all means necessary.

The above discussion deals with the subject in a superficial manner and the reader should note that the issues are complex. Problems and challenges associated with the philosophical theories have been briefly described. Fry and Johnstone (2008) discuss in more detail the advantages and the disadvantages of both ethical approaches.

Principles of health-care ethics

It is vital to be aware of the various ethical theories, but it is also important to understand that their application to nursing practice can be complicated. Principles of health-care ethics can help to guide and direct our behaviour when ethical issues arise. We choose what principles to apply to what situation depending on the context of care and the situation that has arisen. The following principles are discussed in the next aspect of the chapter:

- Autonomy
- Beneficence and non-maleficence
- Justice
- Veracity
- Fidelity.

Two other issues relating ethical relationships with patients are also discussed:

- Confidentiality
- Consent to treatment.

Autonomy

The term 'autonomy' derives from the Greek and is broadly defined as self-determination or self-rule (Dickenson et al, 2010). Beauchamp and Childress (2008) suggest that the term is often used in a broad manner and is associated with liberty (the qualities of liberty and self-assertion [agency]). An autonomous patient, it could be suggested, is a patient who rules him- or herself and no one rules him or her – an independent person.

You may recall that autonomy was discussed in Chapter 1, but this was primarily in relation to the autonomous practice of the nurse. Patient autonomy and the principle of respect for a patient's autonomy are central to the nurse–patient relationship. It can be seen as the opposite of paternalism, and allows the nurse to practise patient-centred nursing care.

Paternalism can be said to be acting for another person without their agreement or consent. The person acting paternalistically is assuming that he or she knows best and that his or her actions are in the patient's best interests. Autonomy can be overridden or not respected when a person acts paternalistically. In the past paternalistic behaviour towards patients was often accepted as the norm; however, this situation is now changing and it is becoming far less acceptable.

Beauchamp and Childress (2008) suggest that respecting patients' autonomy means that patients are treated as people, as individuals and not as mere objects. The nurse provides the patient with the opportunity to make his or her own decisions related to his or her health-care needs.

Husted and Husted (2008) suggest that being autonomous is about being yourself. Autonomy, they state, allows the nurse to relate to the person – by allowing the patient to experience what he or she wants. Their comments point to the fact that each individual deserves respect and is equal to every other person.

The importance of the freedom of an individual and the freedom to make a decision uncoerced has been discussed by Berlin (1969). He considers that the ability to be free to choose and not be chosen is what makes human beings human beings. This, he says, is an inalienable ingredient of humanness. His definition points to a need for liberty, liberty that is free from unwanted and unwelcome interference.

Seedhouse (2002) states that autonomy is not absolute; it can be found on a continuum ranging from absolute freedom (total control) to no freedom (no control) (Figure 2.2). The degree of freedom, Seedhouse contests, will depend on several circumstances and situations.

Think

 How free are you to make choices? To what extent are you an autonomous person? Think of the last time that you made a choice – did you really have total autonomy or were there other things that stood in the way, 'unwanted interference'?

You may have thought that you had total autonomy to make choices and to do what you wanted. However, this is not always the case because there are often constraints placed on us such as:

- Do we have enough money?
- Are we acting within the law?

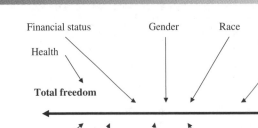
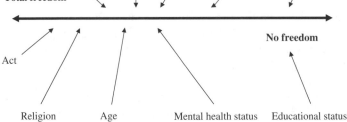
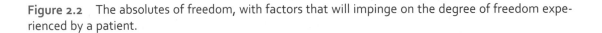

Figure 2.2 The absolutes of freedom, with factors that will impinge on the degree of freedom experienced by a patient.

- Do we know what other choices are out there?
- Do we have the understanding (the mental capacity) to grasp what the consequences of autonomous action are likely to be?
- Do we have the ability to act on the choices that we have made or chosen?

Often it is not easy making choices and acting without unwanted interference if we do not fully understand the choices being offered (or sought) and the options or alternatives available to us. For certain reasons some choices are not available to us, e.g. a 17-year-old may desire or want to act in an autonomous manner in order to purchase alcohol, but the law dictates that he or she is not legally able to do that.

When a patient is admitted to hospital some of his or her ability to make autonomous decisions may be taken away. Often hospital admission can result in a loss of a person's autonomy or some of the autonomous decision-making abilities that person possesses. He or she may no longer be able to decide where and at what time to eat or drink or what clothes he or she wishes to wear, because ward routine may dictate this. Working with the patient and family to ensure that as much autonomous decision-making as possible is retained by the patient is a key aspect of the nurse's role – acting as a patient's advocate.

Case study 2.1

Daksayani Pandit is 35 years of age; she has been diagnosed with a renal condition that requires dialysis. Mrs Pandit is refusing treatment because she is afraid that the treatment is too invasive and may cause her more harm than good; she tells you that she has heard horror stories about people getting 'germs' in hospitals. The renal consultant nurse and the renal consultant have had long discussions with Mrs Pandit about the treatment; it has been explained that because of her condition there are no alternative approaches that would help her. She is competent to make treatment decisions. Mrs Pandit is fully aware of the fact that if she refuses renal dialysis she will die. She has a young daughter aged 12 who lives at home with her and her husband. Despite numerous attempts to encourage and persuade Mrs Pandit that she needs dialysis she still refuses this life-saving treatment.

Issues to consider in relation to this case

Daksayani has been deemed to have competence which means that she has autonomy to make any treatment decisions. Her refusal to undergo renal dialysis has to be upheld if the principle of respect for autonomy is given due regard in spite of the impending harm.

It is essential to determine that she is making an informed decision. The nurse has to determine if any other information could be given to her (despite the fact that she has been given information by the consultant nurse and doctor) it may be appropriate to introduce her to people who are receiving dialysis. As a competent individual respect for her wishes has to take precedence.

Mrs Pandit has capacity to make an informed decision and as such her refusal must be respected (you may have thought about the interests of her daughter and the consequences of Mrs Pandit's actions). To act in any other way could constitute a charge of battery.

Respecting a patient's autonomy can result in conflict, raise ethical dilemmas and may not be straightforward (Hope et al, 2008). Any competent adult patient can refuse treatment; note the word 'competent' – competency is dealt with later in this chapter when considering consent. If a patient is deemed incompetent then the overriding of his or her wishes may be permitted, but this is a serious action and must be fully justified both professionally and legally. Interfering in this manner (unwanted interference) is protected in some circumstances in the law relating to consent. In this instance there is conflict between the issue of autonomy and beneficence.

Top tips

Never ever coerce or trick a person into accepting treatment, e.g. if a person refuses a particular type of treatment. You should always seek advice from a senior colleague. Always document any incidents.

Beneficence and non-maleficence

The term 'beneficence', according to Thompson et al (2006), is associated with a duty to avoid doing harm to others (both physically and psychologically), acting in a way so as not to cause harm; they compare beneficence with the saying 'Do unto others as you would have them do unto you'. On the face of it this seems like a reasonably straightforward statement (Hendrick, 2004); when summed up it is the duty of care (Hendrick, 2004; Thompson et al, 2006). The nurse owes a duty of care to the patient; the nurse is obliged to help others (Edwards, 2009). Beneficence is, therefore, a duty to care or to do good.

Non-maleficence places an obligation on nurses to do no harm to patients in their care (both physically and psychologically). This principle, suggest Hope et al (2008), is the flip side of the coin of the beneficence principle.

Both beneficence and non-maleficence, according to Thompson et al (2006), complement respect for personal rights and justice; they also justify the minimum requirements for a coherent system of ethics. Beneficence and non-maleficence, it could be suggested, are the foundations on which the code of conduct is built.

Employing the principles non-maleficence and beneficence raises the following questions:

- What harm is to be avoided?
- Who judges what is best for the patient?
- What are deemed the patient's best interests and by whom?

Think

Think about giving a patient an intra-muscular injection, while also trying to bring into play the two principles of beneficence (to do good) and non-maleficence (to do no harm).

With all the good will in the world, the administration of an intramuscular injection is going to cause pain, if not hurt, to the patient. By attempting to carry out the principle of doing good (beneficence) you are invoking the principle of doing harm (maleficence). Are you therefore not acting in the patient's best interests?

There are other examples that could also have been used, e.g. when you administer a prescribed drug to a patient, the key aim may be to do the patient good but there may also be side effects associated with that particular medication, which could result in harm to the patient. All nursing interventions have the potential to help and also harm the patient.

The example cited demonstrates how easy it is to harm the patient when attempting to do good. It is important therefore that, during any nursing interaction or intervention that you perform, you balance and weigh up the harm versus hurt equation, considering all the options open to you. The aim should be to take the option that causes the least harm and promotes the most good, ensuring that the risks to be taken are never worse than the potential benefits to be gained.

Olsen (2010) offers suggestions that may minimise the harm that may be caused to a patient (Table 2.3).

Justice

Being fair and right is something for which most people would aim. However, when justice is discussed in a health-care arena there are many other factors that will influence whether we are being fair and right, e.g. inequalities in access to health care. The following are other terms that you may come across that are also associated with justice:

- Fairness
- Desserts (what is deserved)
- Entitlement

It may help to define the term 'justice'. Beauchamp and Childress (2008) suggest that justice is the fair, equitable and appropriate treatment of all people in light of what is owed them. The underpinning principle associated with justice is, therefore, that everyone is valued equally and treated alike. Being

Table 2.3 Issues to be considered when attempting to minimise any harm to the patient

- The treatment must offer the patient a reasonable prospect of benefit
- The treatment must not leave the patient in excessive pain or other inconvenience
- The patient must be fully informed about any side effects, potential consequences of treatment and if appropriate the costs

Source: adapted from Olsen (2010).

fair and equitable will also depend on what we feel is owed to others – it is therefore subjective and can be loaded with values and judgements. Justice to individuals also means non-discriminatory care based on sex, sexual orientation, gender, race or religion, age or illness (physical and psychological).

Seedhouse (2002) states that justice can be understood in more than one way and it can be interpreted in ways that contradict each other. There are three perspectives associated with justice:

- Egalitarian
- Libertarian
- Rights.

Think

In the scenario outlined in Table 2.4, decide to whom you would allocate the resource. Having made your decision you must now justify it.

The egalitarian perspective is concerned with the distribution of health-care resources in association with individual need. From this perspective individual need should be met by equal access to services. The most important tenet of a libertarian perspective is liberty and choice. Justice is associated with how hard an individual has worked in order to earn heath care; he or she is judged on merit. Finally, the rights perspective implies that the state has an obligation to provide care and that the patient should suffer no harm as a result of that provision. People's rights have to be upheld in order to meet the criteria associated with a rights perspective.

Top tips

In order to be fair and just you must respect patients, their unique identity and their individual needs.

The NHS is frequently cited in the media as being unjust in so far as it may not have sufficient resources to meet the needs of all of its patients. Often news stories centre on the number of people on waiting lists and the adverse effects that the wait has on the patient.

Table 2.4   Making a decision with regard to the allocation of resources

- A 10-year-old boy needs to have a lung and heart transplant. He has been waiting for a donor for 18 months now
- A 56-year-old man also requires a lung and heart transplant. He has had heart and lung disease for 20 years despite being advised to cut down on his smoking habits
- A donor becomes available and the opportunity of transplantation is a possibility. However, only one of them will be able to receive the transplant

Table 2.5   Examples of situations that could have consequences for the allocation of scarce resources

- A liver transplantation in a patient who continues to drink alcohol to excess
- A reversal of a sterilisation
- A soft tissue injury as a result of engaging in extreme sporting activity
- A spinal injury as a result of refusing to wear a protective helmet when horse riding
- A patient wanting tattoos removed that she had had done when she was younger

Such a scenario is not unheard of. Table 2.5 provides other examples that may have implications for resource allocation, where patients may need to compete with each other for the use of limited resources.

Veracity

Veracity is the obligation to tell the truth and avoid deception. Thiroux (1995) includes veracity and honesty as part of the principles of ethics that can be applied to any situation. The key principle behind veracity is truth telling or information disclosure. Some health-care professionals often cite the main reason for not telling the patient the truth as disclosure of bad news possibly shattering the patient's hope. However, the disclosure of information and access to that information is the patient's right (see, for example, the Data Protection Act 1998), although there are some exceptions to the right to access information.

At first it may seem easy to uphold the principle of truth telling, because it seems right that the patient should be told the truth. It is, however, difficult to achieve in certain circumstances. Veracity underpins and is a key component of the concept of informed consent. Problems arise, nevertheless, when the nurse needs to decide on how much should be told, to whom and in what circumstances (Olsen, 2010).

Think

In the situation in Table 2.6, should the patient's mother be told the truth?
You must remember that Marie is a minor. Does she have any rights? Do her parents have rights?

Fidelity

The ethical principle of fidelity is concerned with the keeping of promises, the obligation to ensure a trusting relationship and the duty to maintain confidentiality (Hawley, 2007). It is concerned with maintaining the duty of care even when the circumstances in which the patient finds him- or herself are

Table 2.6   To tell the truth and to whom

Marie is 15 years of age and is pregnant. She visits her GP and decides that she wants to have a termination of pregnancy. She refuses to tell her parents and asks the practice nurse to arrange the appointment at the clinic to have the termination. A week later Marie is brought to the GP surgery by her mother complaining of abdominal pain

Table 2.7   Nursing actions that may uphold the ethical principle of fidelity

- The nurse represents the patient's views to other members of the multidisciplinary team
- The nurse avoids letting his or her own values and beliefs influence the ability to advocate for the patient
- Regardless of what decision the patient makes, the nurse will support this even if it conflicts with his or her own preferences or choices

Source: adapted from Olsen (2010).

difficult. Gastmans (2002) suggests that fidelity is the ethical framework on which the nurse–patient relationship is based, because it is concerned with faithfulness. Confidentiality is discussed in detail in the next section of this chapter.

To demonstrate that a nurse is acting in a faithful manner towards the patient, he or she has to function as the patient's advocate. This means that the nurse has to speak up for the patient or act in his or her best interests. Olsen (2010) outlines the acts that he considers would uphold the principle of fidelity (Table 2.7).

Case study 2.2

Lucy Ng is a first year student nurse who has been on her programme of study for 9 months; you and Lucy are friends. Lucy has been diagnosed as having bipolar disorder and was receiving and taking medication to help her cope with her condition. Lucy tells you about her condition and that, when she started her nurse education, she did not declare her bipolar disorder as a disability. Lucy tells you that she has not been taking her medication for the last 6 months because she has been feeling 'great' and is really enjoying the course. In the last few weeks you have noticed that Lucy has been having mood swings; you have observed her having periods of depression and periods of mania where Lucy has been having 'highs'.

Lucy's behaviour can be distressing for family and friends, particularly as you may not have seen her like this before, and this can cause a lot of upset. Knowing Lucy's diagnosis might help because you may understand the behaviour of your friend. Often people with mania usually do not realise that they are ill. So, you can be a great help to Lucy by talking to her, encouraging Lucy to take her medication as prescribed and also to try the 'self-help' measures that she may have been informed about and, if necessary, alerting the university's occupational health nurse if symptoms continue. You will need to be sensitive but, if you continue to be concerned you can speak with the university's counselling/student support services.

Informed consent

Any competent patient has the right to refuse any examination, any investigation or any proposed treatment. An adult patient can refuse any treatment, even if this treatment is considered to be 'life saving'. Every person has the right in law to consent to any touching of their person.

The concept of autonomy has already been considered from the nurse's and the patient's perspective. To uphold consent or to provide the patient with choice, the issue of autonomy is central: the patient has the right to self-determination and what happens to his or her own body. Failure to comply with this

Table 2.8   Three key principles that have to be satisfied if consent is to be valid

- Consent is 'informed'
- The patient is 'competent'
- Consent is 'voluntary'

Source: adapted from Department of Health (2009a).

principle may result in legal action (a charge of battery) by the patient and interference by the NMC; furthermore, should harm come to the patient the nurse may also face a charge of negligence. There are situations where the law recognises that there are exceptions to the common-law requirement to obtain consent.

For consent to be valid three key principles have to be satisfied (Table 2.8).

The patient needs to know in broad terms the nature and purpose of the procedure: failure to provide sufficient information would invalidate consent. The courts (*Sidaway v Bethlem Royal Hospital Governors and others* 1985) have clearly demonstrated that, when a competent individual has given consent (unco-erced) for a procedure to be performed, an action for trespass to the person cannot proceed. The patient should receive information about the procedure in general, e.g. how long it may take, what will happen as a result of the intervention/procedure, any alternatives, and also information about specifics surround-ing anaesthesia, e.g. will it be general, regional or local anaesthesia. If the patient alleges that he or she was not given sufficient/significant information about the procedure, e.g. he or she was not told of the possible side effects and harm that could occur, this may result in an action of negligence as opposed to battery. To ensure that the patient is provided with high-quality care, information is needed to help him or her consent to treatment. However, this raises the question of how much and what information is needed.

There is no precise answer to the above question, although a general principle would be to expect the nurse to follow the reasonable standard of approved practice referred to as the Bolam test (*Bolam v Friern Barnet Hospital Management Committee* 1957). The Bolam test sets the standard that dictates how a nurse should practise in relation to other nurses; a nurse will be deemed negligent if he or she falls short of the standards expected of the 'reasonable' nurse. In summary, the nurse is judged against other reasonable nurses, how those reasonable nurses practise and how they would act in the same or a similar situation. Below is an extract from the Bolam case that sets the expected standard:

> The test is the standard of the ordinary skilled man exercising and professing to have that special skill. A man need not possess the highest expert skill at the risk of being found negligent . . . it is sufficient if he exercises the skill of an ordinary competent man exercis-ing that particular art.

Although this test concerns a doctor, the Bolam test is often used to judge the 'reasonableness' of any health-care professional's actions. The final arbiter of what reasonable means will be the courts (DH, 2009a).

One of the key reasons for providing the patient with information is to enable him or her to make a balanced judgement on whether to provide or withhold consent. The nurse is advised to provide the patient with any information that is 'material' or 'significant' (DH, 2009a) in relation to the risks that he or she may take.

There may be some patients who do not wish to be informed of the treatment proposed, or wish to know only a little about it. In these cases the nurse should offer information and, if the patient declines the offer, this should be recorded in the patient's notes.

Top tips

Giving and obtaining consent is usually a process, not a one off event. People can change their minds and withdraw consent at any time. If there is any doubt, you should always check that the patient still consents to your caring for or treating them.

Patient capacity: is the patient competent?

The NMC (2008) demand that nurses are aware of the legislation regarding mental capacity, ensuring that people who lack capacity remain at the centre of decision-making and are fully safeguarded. The Mental Capacity Act 2005, which came into force in 2007, defines mental capacity. The Mental Capacity Act 2005 applies in England and Wales and is applicable to all those working in health and social care who are involved in the care, treatment and support of those aged 16 or over who may lack the capacity to make decisions for themselves.

Dimond (2009) notes that the Act sets out five principles that apply to situations in which decisions relating to mental capacity have to be made:

1. A person must be assumed to have capacity unless it is established that he or she lacks it
2. A person is not to be treated as unable to make a decision unless all practicable steps to help him or her to do so have been taken without success
3. A person is not to be treated as unable to make a decision merely because he or she makes an unwise decision
4. An act done, or decision made, under this Act for or on behalf of a person who lacks capacity must be done, or made, in his or her best interests
5. Before the act is done, or the decision made, regard must be given to whether the purpose for which it is needed can be as effectively achieved in a way that is less restrictive of the person's rights and freedom of action.

The Act establishes overarching statutory principles governing these decisions, setting out who can make them and when. It sets out the legal requirements for assessing whether or not a person lacks the capacity to make a decision. Where a person lacks this capacity, any decision must be made in that person's best interests.

For a patient to be considered competent or to have the capacity to consent to treatment he or she must be able to comprehend and retain the information that has been given in order to make the decision. More importantly, he or she should understand the consequences of having or not having the proposed treatment. Having demonstrated an ability to do this he or she must then weigh this information in the decision-making process. Hence there are three elements associated with capacity:

1. Comprehend and retain information
2. Understand the consequences of having or refusing the treatment
3. Weigh this information in the decision-making process.

All adults are said to have the capacity to consent. However, there may be situations where there is doubt and an assessment of capacity should be made. There may be some factors that could impinge on an individual's ability to understand, and therefore demonstrate the capacity to consent, including:

- Shock/panic
- Fear/anxiety
- Pain
- The influence of medication (prescribed and non-prescribed)
- Confusion

The Mental Capacity Act 2005 defines a person who lacks capacity as an individual and is unable to make a decision for him- or herself; this may be as a result of an impairment or disturbance in the functioning of their mind or brain. It is irrelevant if the impairment or disturbance is permanent or temporary. A person lacks capacity if:

- He or she has an impairment or disturbance (e.g. a disability, condition or trauma or the effect of drugs or alcohol) that affects the way the mind or brain works
- That impairment or disturbance means that he or she is unable to make a specific decision at the time that it needs to be made.

The nurse must take considerable care not to be influenced by his or her own feelings and beliefs. Some patients may be seen to be making irrational decisions about their treatment. Patients are entitled to make decisions based on their own beliefs and value system, even if this contradicts the nurse's own system of beliefs.

Think

Jamie is a 22-year-old who has anorexia nervosa. His physical condition is failing and he is losing a considerable amount of weight; he is very weak and unable to walk any more. He has been advised that tube feeding is the only alternative left to help his condition, but he is refusing. The team caring for Jamie has explained the situation and how seriously unwell he is.
How might you assess Jamie's capacity?

The three principles alluded to above must be assessed. Does Jamie understand the consequences of refusing to be tube fed? Can he comprehend and retain the information that you have given him? Can he demonstrate to you that he has taken the information given to him and retained it? Does he understand the potential consequences and has he weighed this information in the decision-making process?

If Jamie is able to do this it would be difficult to consider him incapacitated or incompetent to refuse treatment.

The patient must be able to communicate his or her decision to the heath-care team. The nurse should never underestimate the patient's ability to communicate regardless of physical or psychological condition. For example, in the case of a patient with learning disabilities the nurse must make use of all resources available to facilitate communication, and this may include taking time to explain to the individual the issues in simple language, employing visual aids and if appropriate signing. It may be advisable for the nurse to engage the support of those who know the patient, e.g. the family, carers and staff from statutory and non-statutory agencies.

Voluntary consent

Consent must be given freely and voluntarily, without any pressure or undue influence being exerted on the patient. If the nurse feels that the patient is being pressurised into agreeing to (or refusing) treatment by the family, for example, he or she should arrange to see the patient alone to ascertain if the decision is truly that of the patient.

Coercion invalidates consent. If a patient is being treated in an environment where he or she is being involuntarily detained, e.g. a psychiatric hospital, a psychiatric unit or a prison, care must be taken to ensure that the patient is not being coerced (DH, 2009a).

Children and young people

For those under the age of 18 (the age of majority), the situation regarding consent and refusing treatment is different from the position for adults.

Those aged 16–17 are entitled to consent to their own medical treatment (Family Law Reform Act 1969). Gaining consent from this age group will be the same as it is for adults. However, in this age group the refusal of treatment despite the person being aged over 16 and competent can be overridden by a person with parental responsibility or the order of a court. The law may be different in the four parts of the UK.

Those under 16 years of age who have sufficient understanding and intelligence to enable them to fully understand what is involved in the proposed intervention may have the capacity to consent to that intervention (DH, 2009a). Children who possess these abilities are said to be 'Gillick competent'. The term 'Gillick competent' comes from a court case, *Gillick v West Norfolk and Wisbech Area Health Authority* 1985. This concerned a teenage girl's right to consent to medical treatment without her parents' knowledge.

The child should be assessed to determine Gillick competence. Below are some questions that must be asked:

- Does the child understand the proposed treatment, his or her medical condition, the consequences that may emerge if he or she refuses or agrees to treatment?
- Does he or she understand the moral, social and family issues involved in the decision that he or she is to make?
- Does the mental state of the child fluctuate?
- What treatment is to be performed? Does the child understand the complexities of the proposed treatment and potential risks associated with it?

If a young person lacks capacity to consent because of an impairment, or a disturbance in the functioning, of the mind or brain, then the Mental Capacity Act 2005 will apply in the same way as it does to those who are 18 and over.

Case study 2.3

 Danny Jones is 14 years old and has leukaemia; he has been receiving care and treatment for the last 10 months, which involves chemotherapy and a number of other unpleasant treatments as well as their side effects. Danny has told the nurse caring for him and his doctor that he no long wishes to have this treatment because it is a 'nightmare' for him and he would rather just enjoy what is left of the rest of his life. Danny's parents were there when he made this announcement and they are very keen for him to continue on the treatment regimen. Clearly they are upset and anxious.

Children, regardless of their age, have the right to independently seek medical advice and give their own valid consent to or withdrawal of treatment. To do this the child must be deemed to be competent in terms of his or her maturity in understanding what has been requested. As with most ethical and moral issues, it is not always black and white when it comes to these complex issues. In this case study this is an area that requires much careful thought before deciding whether or not Danny's wishes can be accepted without his parents' consent. The nursing and medical staff could try to suggest to Danny that his parents should be involved in the decision-making process.

Giving consent

There are a number of different forms of consent. Consent can be gained in the following ways:

- Written
- Oral
- Non-verbal.

Written consent is thus only one way in which consent can be given. Written consent serves only as evidence of consent. A signature on a consent form does not in itself serve to say that the patient has consented to treatment if the consent did not meet the three elements of valid consent outlined in Table 2.8. A consent form related to a child is provided in Appendix 2.1 at the end of this chapter.

Many aspects of nursing care are carried out with the patient orally agreeing to them. Oral consent lacks the written evidence as identified above, because it may be the word of one person word against another (Dimond, 2011). Where any significant procedure (e.g. an operation) is anticipated it is suggested that written consent be obtained (DH, 2009a).

Non-verbal or implied consent occurs in many situations and Dimond (2011) cites the case of the patient who, when the nurse approaches him or her rolls up his or her sleeve for an injection, or the patient who sees the nurse coming towards him or her with a sphygmomanometer and rolls up his or her sleeve to have his or her blood pressure taken.

Top tips

When a person cannot write, other forms of communication may be sufficient. However, you must ensure that this is clearly documented in the person's notes. Some people may wish to make a mark on the form which should be witnessed and documented in the person's notes.

For those who have visual impairment consent forms can be provided in large print version and Braille.

It is important to note that no one can give consent on behalf of an incompetent adult; however, treatment may still be given if it is considered to be in the patient's best interests. If the person for whom you care needs medical treatment, only he or she can agree to that treatment. No one can legally give or withhold consent to medical treatment on behalf of another adult.

Best interests go further than medical best interests and should include the patient's wishes and beliefs when he or she was competent. In some instances these best interests may have been made known in the form of advanced decisions.

Advanced decisions

Sometimes advanced decisions are also known as advanced directives, living wills or advanced statements; these terms are often used interchangeably. The advanced decision is a legally binding statement in certain situations. Advanced decisions allow people to state (in written form) what type of treatment they would or would not like carried out should they become unable to decide for themselves in the future.

Advance decisions are a way for patients to communicate their wishes to family, friends and health-care professionals in order to avoid confusion later on, should they become unable to do so. Advanced decisions can only be written by those who have reached the age of majority – 18 years.

The Mental Capacity Act puts advance decisions on a statutory basis (National Council for Palliative Care 2009), setting out the requirement that health-care professionals must follow an advanced decision where it is valid and applicable. Health-care professionals must think about what needs to be done if the advanced decision is not valid and what they have to consider if they disagree with a person's right to refuse life-sustaining treatment.

The patient must be deemed competent when making the advanced decision, and only clear refusals of specific treatments will be upheld. If any doubt exists as to the validity of the advanced decision, then a declaration may be obtained or treatment can be given in the patient's best interests. The provision of basic care cannot be refused. Treatment that falls within the remit of the Mental Health Act 1983 treatment provisions cannot be refused by the use of an advanced decision.

Vulnerable people

Those who provide health services have a duty to safeguard all patients, but they also have to provide additional measures for patients who are less able to protect themselves from harm or abuse. Nurses are required to ensure that they safeguard the people for whom they care. The principles of protection are preserved in a number of legislative and policy directives; the Human Rights Act 1998 maintains, in the form of articles, that no person should be subjected to any form of torture or inhumane or degrading treatment or punishment, each person has a right to life, liberty and security and the prohibition of discrimination.

Safeguarding adults covers a wide range of activity from prevention through to multiagency responses where harm and abuse occur; nurses are a part of this multiagency. Multiagency procedures apply if there is concern of neglect, harm or abuse to a patient defined under 'No Secrets' guidance as 'vulnerable'.

Safeguarding adults is an integral part of patient care; it is applicable to all nurses and other health-care professionals. Duties to safeguard patients are required by professional regulators (such as the NMC), service regulators and supported in law (DH, 2011). Safeguarding adults is a fundamental part of patient safety and wellbeing as well as delivering cost-effective care.

A report has been produced by the Parliamentary and Health Service Ombudsman (2011) detailing the poor standards of care and the treatment of 10 older people who received care within the NHS. A number of complaints were made to the Ombudsman about the standard of care that these older people received. The report portrayed a picture of an NHS that is failing to respond to the needs of older people with care and compassion.

We all want to live a life that is free from harm and abuse; this is a fundamental human right of every person and a key requirement for health and wellbeing. Nurses often work with patients who may, for a range of reasons, be less able to protect themselves from neglect, harm or abuse.

Think

Take some time and make a list of those patients whom you think may be less able to protect themselves from neglect, harm or abuse.

Your list must be a very long list because all of us at some stage of our lives are less able to protect ourselves from neglect, harm or abuse. This risk of neglect, harm and abuse traverses the life span from conception to birth to death. As a result of this the definition of 'vulnerable adult' may apply broadly within health care.

In 2000 (in England) guidance was produced on how to develop policies and procedures to protect vulnerable adults from abuse. In Wales the equivalent was also produced in 2000 (Welsh Assembly 2000). The Adult Support and Protection (Scotland) Act 2007 provides legislation to protect vulnerable people from harm. These publications provide protection for those adults who are considered vulnerable in our society, and those who are at risk of abuse and who need safeguarding. Local authorities through their social services are obliged to act and adhere to the general guidance issued in the *No Secrets* publication – procedures must be put in place to protect those who are deemed at risk. *No Secrets* states that there can be no secrets and no hiding places when it comes to exposing the abuse of adults (DH, 2000).

Safe Guarding Adults (DH, 2009b) is a review of *No Secrets*; again this provides guidance on developing and implementing multiagency policies and procedures to protect vulnerable adults from abuse. The review aimed to determine whether and how the *No Secrets* guidance needed to change in order to help society keep adults safe from harm or abuse.

A number of terms are used when discussing adult protection issues and it is important that these key terms are defined. Understanding them can help you help the people you care for.

The Department of Health (2011) suggest that there are some adults who are in vulnerable situations and are less able to protect themselves or to make decisions about their safety. A person's disability or age does not of itself make that person vulnerable. An adult's ability to protect him- or herself and safeguard wellbeing will be affected by a number of things, including:

- Personal circumstances such as physical disability, learning disability, mental health, illness frailty *and*
- Risks arising from the person's environment – social contacts, quality of care, physical environment *counteracted by*
- Resilience factors – personal strength, social supports, environmental supports.

A vulnerable adult is defined as a person 'who is or may be in need of community care services by reason of mental or other disability, age or illness; and who is or may be unable to take care of him or herself, or unable to protect him or herself against significant harm or exploitation'.

Top tips

Beware of myths that may be associated with abuse, such as:

- Abuse and neglect of adults is rare
- Most abuse of adults occurs only in care or nursing homes
- Abuse happens only to those people who are very frail
- Adult abuse occurs to older women, older people, those who are isolated or those with disabilities
- Abuse of adults concerns physical abuse.

Safeguarding when working within health- or social care domains means acting in the best interests of those people who require or are receiving services from those who provide care. It can also mean protecting people from abuse and neglect and actively promoting their welfare. Abuse is defined by the

Department of Health (2000) as a violation of a person's human and civil rights by another person(s). There is a range of activities associated with safeguarding, including the concepts of:

- Prevention
- Empowerment
- Protection.

Both health- and social care teams (all agencies) are required to work together to take action to challenge actual or potential concerns.

'Vulnerable adult' is a term used to describe people who need special attention and protection and this will include those who have complex needs because of age, cognitive impairment and long-term conditions, and those approaching the end of their life. The Criminal Records Bureau (2010) defines a vulnerable person as someone who 18 years or older and who is:

- living in residential accommodation, such as a care home or a residential special school
- living in sheltered housing
- receiving domiciliary care in his or her own home
- receiving any form of health care
- detained in a prison, remand centre, young offender institution, secure training centre or attendance centre, or under the powers of the Immigration and Asylum Act 1999
- in contact with probation services
- receiving a welfare service of a description to be prescribed in regulations
- receiving a service or participating in an activity that is specifically targeted at people with age-related needs, disabilities or prescribed physical or mental health conditions (age-related needs include needs associated with frailty, illness, disability or mental capacity)
- an expectant or nursing mother living in a residential care
- receiving direct payments from a local authority in lieu of social care services
- requiring assistance in the conduct of his or her own affairs.

Another term that requires a definition in respect of the vulnerable person is whistle blowing. This is often used together with protection and vulnerability and can be described as raising concerns with the appropriate authority in the work place (or externally) in the best interests of the public when a worker witnesses wrongdoing or malpractice (NMC, 2010b).

Recognising and responding to people in vulnerable situations

You must act within legal frameworks and the sphere of any local policies related to safeguarding adults who may be in vulnerable situations is a prerequisite. Situations may arise when you need to work with others to implement and monitor any strategies within your workplace, to safeguard and protect people or groups of people who may be in vulnerable situations. The information that is gained in these circumstances must be shared appropriately with other colleagues and advice (from a number of sources) should be sought if there are any concerns. Information sharing can be within your sphere of practice or involve the sharing of information across agency boundaries; the key intention is to safeguard and protect the individual and the public. You may also need to make referrals to others, including social workers or the police. The people for whom you care have a right to confidentiality (this important aspect of care was discussed earlier) and you must ensure that any information disclosed follows local policy and guidance, and that the person concerned has given consent (see earlier). There may be some exceptional circumstances where disclosure can be made without consent, but these situations are usually complex and in this instance you must seek advice before disclosing.

Those people who are, or may be, in vulnerable situations require an advocate who will be needed to help them uphold their human rights. If you are this advocate you must ensure that you are up to date with current legislation and local policy (advocacy was also discussed earlier). If you witness any activity that puts those people in your care at risk of danger or does not safeguard those people, you have a responsibility to challenge this practice. You must also make sure that you have support systems in place that will help you to manage and deal with any emotions that may develop from the situation.

Abuse may happen as a result of calculated intent, negligence or ignorance. The NMC (2009) provide some examples of abuse which can be any of the following:

- Physical – hitting, slapping, pushing, restraining
- Psychological – shouting, swearing, ignoring, blaming, humiliating
- Sexual – forcing a person to take part in any sexual activity without consent
- Financial and material – illegal or unauthorised use of someone's property, money, valuables, theft, fraud
- Neglect – depriving a person of food, clothing, heat, comfort, stimulation, essential care
- Acts of omission – failing to provide medication or treatment, omitting essential aspects of care.

If there are any immediate concerns associated with abuse, these have to be dealt with under local safeguarding policies and procedures in the first instance. Information has been produced by the National Patient Safety Organisation (2009) that may help you if you are worried about patient safety incidents.

Top tips

There are a number of people male or female who may deliberately exploit and abuse vulnerable people and these include family, relatives, professional staff, paid care workers, other service users, neighbours, friends, strangers, a teacher, a member of the clergy.

Making concerns known

Making your concerns known should be done in an appropriate manner; this includes using local policies, clinical governance and risk management procedures. There are times when it is not always easy to report concerns, e.g. you may not know how to go about doing this, you could be afraid of reprisals and you might even feel that you are being disloyal. This may appear even more complex and daunting if you work alone or in remote, small communities. The person for whom you are caring is your first concern; you must not forget this. Raising issues early can prevent them from becoming more serious and as such causing more harm to the person or people being cared for.

Feeling intimidated or isolated can be uncomfortable. A number of sources of advice are available that you can access to seek guidance if you are ever unsure; these include your tutor or your mentor/facilitator, your trade union (e.g. UNISON), your professional body (e.g. the Royal College of Nursing) or the charity Public Concern at Work (this is an independent whistle-blowing charity). These organisations can raise issues formally and in some cases can act on your behalf; they can also provide you with personal support. The NMC (2010b) provide some examples of concern, including:

- Issues associated with health and safety violations where there may be risk to health and safety
- Unprofessional staff behaviour or attitudes
- Concerns about the standard of care being delivered
- Worries about the environment in which care is being delivered
- The health of a colleague and the impact that this is having on his or her ability to practise safely
- A deficiency or lack of the availability of clinical equipment; this can also include a lack of adequate training
- Any criminal acts, fraud and financial mismanagement.

You have to report your concerns to the appropriate person or authority immediately if you suspect or see risk or harm to the safety of those for you whom care.

Silence is not always golden. A normal aspect of your work is to speak up for people for whom you care; failing to do anything and not reporting your concerns are not acceptable. Raising concerns and speaking up show that you are committed to the people for whom you care.

Usually, when you raise concerns with your tutor or your mentor/facilitator, in the most instances this will be dealt with and worked out to a satisfactory conclusion. If this approach fails you may need to take your concerns, through a more formal route; at this stage you might wish to seek support and advice from a professional body or trade union. Figure 2.3 outlines the stages for raising concerns.

The Public Interest Disclosure Act 1998 was established to provide protection to those who raise genuine concerns and may be subjected to victimisation and/or dismissed for raising these concerns about wrongdoing or misconduct observed in the workplace, when this has been done in good faith and with the public interest at heart.

Legal perspectives

Throughout this chapter the law and some legal perspectives have been discussed and how they impinge on nursing practice, including the safeguarding of vulnerable people. A number of legal issues need to be considered by the nurse when working with patients in any setting. There are few areas of health care that are untouched by the law and involvement with the legal process may occur during the course of a nurse's career.

The law

Orderly behaviour in a collective society is governed by rules, and these rules are referred to in this context as laws. Wall and Payne-James (2004) state that the law is an official expression of the formal institutionalisation of the enforcement of these rules through:

- promulgation
- adjudication
- enforcement.

The principal source of law is Parliament. The three points above are operated and organised through the system of the courts.

Sources of law

There are two primary forms of law that emanate through statute and common law:

Stages in raising and escalating concerns

As a nurse or midwife, you have a professional duty to put the interests of the people in your care first and to act to protect them if you feel they may be at risk.

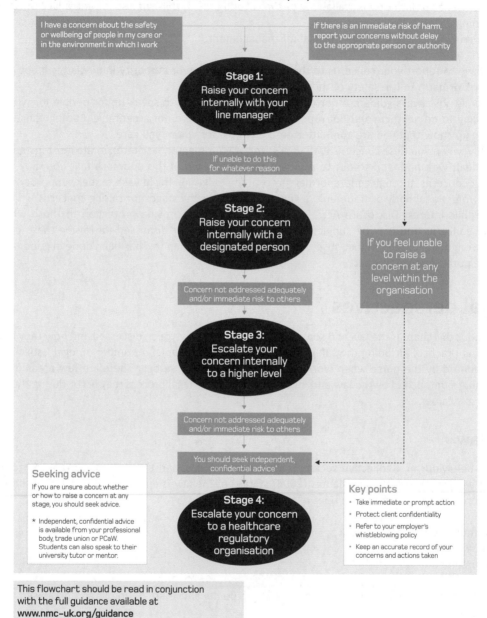

I have a concern about the safety or wellbeing of people in my care or in the environment in which I work

If there is an immediate risk of harm, report your concerns without delay to the appropriate person or authority

Stage 1:
Raise your concern internally with your line manager

If unable to do this for whatever reason

Stage 2:
Raise your concern internally with a designated person

Concern not addressed adequately and/or immediate risk to others

Stage 3:
Escalate your concern internally to a higher level

If you feel unable to raise a concern at any level within the organisation

Concern not addressed adequately and/or immediate risk to others

You should seek independent, confidential advice*

Seeking advice

If you are unsure about whether or how to raise a concern at any stage, you should seek advice.

* Independent, confidential advice is available from your professional body, trade union or PCaW. Students can also speak to their university tutor or mentor.

Stage 4:
Escalate your concern to a healthcare regulatory organisation

Key points

- Take immediate or prompt action
- Protect client confidentiality
- Refer to your employer's whistleblowing policy
- Keep an accurate record of your concerns and actions taken

This flowchart should be read in conjunction with the full guidance available at www.nmc-uk.org/guidance

Figure 2.3 Stages in raising and escalating concerns. Source: NMC (2010b). (Reproduced with permission from the Nursing and Midwifery Council [www.nmc-uk.org].)

- *Primary legislation* is established through Acts of Parliament, also known as statutes. The law-making abilities are given to Parliament by society. There are various stages proposed and legislative law must pass through these before becoming enforceable. An Act of Parliament does not become statute until it has passed through both Houses of Parliament (the House of Commons and the House of Lords) and received royal assent. Secondary legislation is the making of regulation by statutory instruments.

- *Common law*, also known as case law or judge-made law, is law that is decided through the court system. This type of law comes into play when the courts cannot turn to a relevant statute. This may be because a particular Act of Parliament concerning the specific area of law under deliberation has not been made. In case law the courts look to precedent, considering previous cases to determine how a decision has been made and how statute has been interpreted.

The legal system is divided into:

- civil law
- criminal law

and a hierarchical court system exists where different courts administer the two kinds of law (Table 2.9).

A lower court is bound by a decision of a higher court and is obliged to apply the principles of law set by that higher court. Tables 2.10 and 2.11 outline the civil and criminal courts' primary functions.

European law

European law can also influence English law. In the past the greater part of European law was centred on free movement and economic activity; generally this is still the case. However, there are certain areas relevant to health care.

The Human Rights Act 1998

The primary aim of this Act is to give the courts greater powers to protect some fundamental rights; it introduces the European Convention on Human Rights into British domestic law. Articles of the Act can be found in Appendix 2.2. All legislation must be compatible with the rights outlined in this Act. If incompatibility with primary legislation happens, then a declaration of incompatibility must be made.

The principles underpinning human rights apply to all nurses and they are to:

Table 2.9 The criminal and civil courts

Civil law	Concerned with the resolution of disputes between individuals (or in some instances organisations). Remedies in these courts are usually financial
Criminal law	Associated with issues between the state and the individual. The outcome of a prosecution (if the seriousness of the offence warrants a prosecution) of an individual is usually in the form of a sentence or a fine – it is punitive. The outcome of the prosecution depends on the ability to establish a standard of proof that is beyond reasonable doubt

Table 2.10   The civil courts and their key functions

Court	Key function
House of Lords	This is the final appellate court in the UK
Court of Appeal (Civil Division)	Will hear appeals on matters of law
High Court	Generally, hears the more complex cases and often the cases heard here are high monetary value cases. The High Court is divided into three divisions: • Chancery Division: specialises in matters such as company law • Family Division: specialises in matrimonial issues and matters associated with minors • Queen's Bench Division: concerned with issues of a general nature related to civil matters
County Court	Most civil cases are heard in the County Court
Magistrates' Court	The lowest of the civil courts

Note that those under the age of 18 years are tried at special courts – youth courts.

Table 2.11   The criminal courts and their key functions

Court	Key function
House of Lords	This is the final appellate court in the UK. Often cases heard here are associated with important points of law
Court of Appeal	This court will hear appeals on matters of law (Criminal Division)
Crown Court	This court will hear the more serious or indictable offences. In the first instance it also hears any appeals from the Magistrates Court regarding points of law, conviction, or sentences passed
Magistrates Court	The lowest of the criminal courts. The majority of minor criminal cases are heard in this court

Note that those under the age of 18 years are tried at special courts – youth courts.

- maintain dignity
- promote and protect autonomy
- practise in a non-discriminatory manner.

European Directives

The European Union adopts legislation in the form of Directives and Regulations. European Directives require member states to implement their provisions for the benefit of Europe as a whole. Programmes for registration as an adult nurse must comply with the requirements of two European Directives, in particular 77/453/EEC and 89/595/EEC. These requirements are mandatory and require that awards (certificates and diplomas) be granted before registration. Article 1 of 77/453/EEC requires that the qualifications of adult nurses guarantee that the person has acquired:

- Adequate knowledge of the sciences on which general nursing is based, including sufficient understanding of the structure, physiological functions and behaviour of healthy and sick persons, and of the relationship between the state of health and physical and social environment of the human being
- Sufficient knowledge of the nature and ethics of the profession and of general principles of health and nursing
- Adequate clinical experience; such experience should be selected for its training value and should be gained under the supervision of qualified nursing staff in places where the number of qualified staff and the equipment are appropriate for the nursing care of patients
- The ability to participate in the training of health personnel and experience of working with such personnel
- Experience of working with members of other professions in the health sector.

This Directive also specifies that nursing programmes comprise a programme of 3 years with 4600 hours of training, providing a balance between theory and practice. Practical instruction must include nursing in relation to:

- general and specialist medicine
- general and specialist surgery
- child care and paediatrics
- maternity care
- mental health and psychiatry
- care of old people and geriatrics
- home nursing.

Directive 89/595/EEC makes clear the balance of theory and practice and dictates: this must be not less than a third theory and a half practice. The Directive also defines theoretical and clinical instruction. The NMC (2010a), however, has dictated that a programme should contain 2300 hours of practice.

Both Directives cited are related to those students who study in the adult field of a preregistration programme of study.

Conclusions

Nurses have to work in partnership with others to ensure that they safeguard and protect the most vulnerable individuals and to promote high-quality care (Mencap, 2007). To protect the public and those who are deemed vulnerable it is essential to have an understanding of ethical and moral theories, ethical frameworks, and the law that impacts on patient outcomes.

Ethical and legal issues will impinge on all aspects of physical and psychological care. Nurses are faced with ethical and legal challenges on a daily basis, so it is important that they have an understanding of the underlying principles associated with legal and ethical theory when applying this to nursing care.

This chapter has briefly described ethical theories and various ethical principles associated with nursing practice. Key terms have been defined in order to promote a better and deeper understanding of the key issues. Most definitions of ethics include the term 'morals' and suggest that ethics is the study of moral thinking. Ethics and morals can be broadly stated to be concerned with what is good or bad.

Any competent patient has the right to refuse any examination, any investigation or any proposed treatment. If a nurse disregards this right then the patient may seek a remedy in law – a charge of battery. Consent is closely related to the ethical principle of autonomy and self-determination. Three key principles must be present if consent is to be valid: consent must be informed, the patient must be deemed competent and there must be no coercion associated with seeking consent (or refusal). There are separate rules for those who are younger than 18 years. The person aged under 16 years must be Gillick competent if he or she is to consent to treatment. Three key methods of providing consent were briefly outlined. The important point that no one can give consent on behalf of an incompetent adult was stressed, unless (in certain circumstances) there is an advanced decision detailing what events should occur if the patient becomes unable to decide for him- or herself in the future.

A number of key terms have been defined in relation to vulnerability and the vulnerable person; it has been noted that there are challenges when trying to define some terms, e.g. abuse and vulnerability. Furthermore, there are also difficulties when attempting to define who is vulnerable or at risk. The term 'vulnerability' is dynamic and an ever-changing concept; it is often context dependent and relates to all patients in all care settings.

There is a variety of rights that all people can exercise to help ensure that they are safe and free from risk. There is provision for guidance and support to nurses and other health- and social care practitioners which will help them identify, prevent and monitor people who are at risk of abuse and vulnerable. The NMC also provides support, advice and guidance for students and practitioners, helping ensure that the voice of those who are vulnerable is not only heard but also acted upon.

Acting as a patient's advocate means that you have to be knowledgeable and you also need to understand ethical theories and the ways in which these apply to practice. Understanding ethical behaviour and working in an ethical way can have a positive impact on care provision.

A brief overview of the English legal system was provided outlining the two primary sources of law – statute and common law. The impact of European legislation and the Human Rights Act 1998 has been alluded to. Two particular European Directives were cited that impinge on the design and content of programmes of study associated with those students undertaking the adult field.

Activities

Attempt the following 10 true or false questions that are related to vulnerability and vulnerable people to test your knowledge. The answers can be found at the back of this book, in the section called 'Activity Answers'.

True or false

1. The term 'vulnerability' is related only to those people with a learning disability.
2. The standards of good moral conduct or principles are known as confidentiality.
3. An advocate is somebody who speaks up for another person.
4. Empathy and sympathy mean the same thing.
5. Two primary forms of law are common law and statute.
6. The NHS Constitution is a legal document.
7. Abuse can be a criminal offence.
8. You need evidence of abuse before you can report an allegation of abuse.
9. Neglect is a type of abuse.
10. For something to be abuse it has to be deliberate.

Table of cases

Bolam v Friern Barnet Hospital Management Committee [1957] 1 All ER 118.
Gillick v West Norfolk and Wisbech Area Health Authority [1985] 3 All ER HL.
Sidaway v Bethlem Royal Hospital Governors and Others [1985] 1 All ER 643.

References

Beauchamp TL, Childress JF (2008) *Principles of Biomedical Ethics*, 6th edn. Oxford: Oxford University Press.

Berlin I (1969) *Four Essays on Liberty*. Oxford: Oxford University Press.

Criminal Records Bureau (2010) *Definitions FAQs* [online]. Available at: www.crb.homeoffice.gov.uk/faqs/definitions.aspx (accessed May 2011).

Department of Health (2000) *No Secrets Guidance Developing and Implementing Multi Agency Policy and Procedures to Protect Vulnerable Adults from Abuse*. London: Department of Health.

Department of Health (2009a) (2nd Ed) *Reference Guide to Consent for Examination or Treatment*. London: Department of Health.

Department of Health (2009b) *Safe Guarding Adults. Report on the Consultation on the Review of 'No Secrets'*. London: Department of Health.

Department of Health (2009c) *The NHS Constitution: The NHS belongs to all of us*. London: Department of Health.

Department of Health (2011) *Safeguarding Adults: The role of health service practitioners*. London: Department of Health.

Dickenson D, Huxtable R, Parker M (2010) *The Cambridge Medical Ethics Workbook*, 2nd edn. Cambridge: Cambridge University Press.

Dimond B (2009) *Legal Aspects of Consent*, 2nd edn. London: Quay Books.

Dimond B (2011) *Legal Aspects of Nursing*, 6th edn. Harlow: Pearson.

Edwards SD (2009) *Nursing Ethics: A Principle-Based Approach*, 2nd edn. Basingstoke: Palgrave.

Fry S, Johnstone MJ (2008) *Ethics in Nursing Practice: A guide to ethical decision making*, 3rd edn. Oxford: Blackwell.

Gastmans C (2002) A fundamental ethical approach to nursing. Some proposals for ethics education. *Nursing Ethics* **9**: 494–507.

Harkreader H, Hogan MA, Thobaben M (2007) *Fundamentals of Nursing: Caring and clinical judgement*, 3rd edn. St Louis, MO: Saunders.

Hawley G (2007) Making decisions that are ethical. In: Hawley G (ed.), *Ethics in Clinical Practice: An interprofessional approach*. Colchester: Pearson, pp 214–241.

Hendrick J (2004) *Law and Ethics*. Cheltenham: Nelson Thorne

Hope T, Savulescu J, Hendrick J (2008) *Medical Ethics and Law: The core curriculum*, 2nd edn. Edinburgh: Churchill Livingstone.

Husted JH, Husted GL (2008) *Ethical Decision Making in Nursing*, 4th edn. New York: Springer.

Kirby C, Slevin O (2003) Ethical knowing: The moral ground of nursing practice. In: Basford, L, Slevin O (eds), *Theory and Practice of Nursing: An integrated approach to caring practice*, 2nd edn. Cheltenham: Nelson Thorne, pp 209–254.

Mason T, Whitehead E (2003) *Thinking Nursing*. Milton Keynes: Open University Press.

Mencap (2007) *Death by Indifference*. London: Mencap.

Michaels C, Moffett C (2008) Rethinking vulnerability. In: De Chesnay M, Anderson BA (eds), *Caring for the Vulnerable: Perspectives in nursing theory and practice and research*, 2nd edn. Boston, MA: Jones & Bartlett, pp 15–24.

New Oxford Dictionary of English (2001) Oxford: Oxford University Press.

National Council for Palliative Care (2009) *Advanced Decisions to Refuse Treatment. A guide*. London: NHS.

National Patient Safety Organisation (2009) *Being Open: Communicating patient safety incidents with patients, their families and carers*. London: NPSO. Available at: www.nrls.npsa.nhs.uk/resources/?entryid45=65077 (accessed May 2011).

Nursing and Midwifery Council (2008) *Code of Professional Conduct. Standards for conduct, performance and ethics*. London: NMC.

Nursing and Midwifery Council (2009) *Guidance for the Care of Older People*. London: NMC.

Nursing and Midwifery Council (2010a) *Standards for Pre registration Nursing Education*. London: NMC. Available at: http://standards.nmc-uk.org/PublishedDocuments/Standards%20for%20pre-registration%20nursing%20education%2016082010.pdf (accessed May 2011).

Nursing and Midwifery Council (2010b) *Raising and Escalating Concerns. Guidance for Nurses and Midwives*. London: NMC.

Olsen TH (2010) Ethical issues. In: Daniels R (ed.), *Nursing Fundamentals: Caring and clinical decision making*, 2nd edn. New York: Thompson, pp 186–200.

Parliamentary and Health Service Ombudsman (2011) *Care and Compassion? Report of the Health Service Ombudsman on Ten Investigations into the NHS Care of Older People*. London: The Stationery Office.

Royal College of Nursing (2009) *Research Ethics: RCN guidance for nurses*, 2nd edn. London: RCN.

Seedhouse D (2002) An ethical perspective – How to do the right thing. In: Tingle, J, Cribb A (eds), *Nursing Law and Ethics*, 2nd edn. Oxford: Blackwell, pp 150–158.

Thiroux JP (1995) *Ethics, Theory and Practice*. Englewood Cliffs: Prentice Hall.

Thompson IE, Melia KM, Boyd KM (2006) (5th edn) *Nursing Ethics*. Edinburgh: Churchill Livingstone.

Wall I, Payne-James J (2004) Legal institutions and the legal process. In: Payne-James J, Dean P, Wall I (eds), *Medico-Legal Essentials in Health Care*. London: Greenwich Medical Media, pp 1–9.

Welsh Assembly (2000) *In Safe Hands: Implementing adult protection procedures in Wales*. Cardiff: Welsh Assembly.

Whaite I (2008) Professional standards and rules: the professional and regulatory body and the nursing student. In: Spouse J, Cook M, Cox C (eds), *Common Foundation Studies in Nursing*, 4th edn. Edinburgh: Churchill Livingstone, pp 77–112.

Appendix 2.1

Consent form example

Patient identifier/label

Name of proposed procedure or course of treatment (include brief explanation if medical term not clear)

....

....

....

....

Statement of health professional (to be filled in by health professional with appropriate knowledge of proposed procedure, as specified in consent policy)

I have explained the procedure to the child and his or her parent(s). In particular, I have explained:
The intended benefits

....

....

....

Serious or frequently occurring risks

....

....

....

....

....

Any extra procedures which may become necessary during the procedure

☐ blood transfusion..

☐ other procedure (please specify)..

....

I have also discussed what the procedure is likely to involve, the benefits and risks of any available alternative treatments (including no treatment) and any particular concerns of this patient and his or her parents.

☐ The following leaflet/tape has been provided..

This procedure will involve:

☐ general and/or regional anaesthesia   ☐ local anaesthesia   ☐ sedation

Signed:.. Date...

Name (PRINT)... Job title..

Contact details (if child/parent wish to discuss options later)

Statement of interpreter (where appropriate)

I have interpreted the information above to the child and his or her parents to the best of my ability and in a way in which I believe they can understand.

Signed.. Date...

Name (PRINT)...

Top copy accepted by patient: yes/no (please ring)

Statement of parent   Patient identifier/label

Please read this form carefully. If the procedure has been planned in advance, you should already have your own copy of page 2 which describes the benefits and risks of the proposed treatment. If not, you will be offered a copy now. If you have any further questions, do ask – we are here to help you and your child. You have the right to change your mind at any time, including after you have signed this form.

I agree to the procedure or course of treatment described on this form and I confirm that I have 'parental responsibility' for this child.

I understand that you cannot give me a guarantee that a particular person will perform the procedure. The person will, however, have appropriate experience.

I understand that my child and I will have the opportunity to discuss the details of anaesthesia with an anaesthetist before the procedure, unless the urgency of the situation prevents this. (This only applies to children having general or regional anaesthesia.)

I understand that any procedure in addition to those described on this form will only be carried out if it is necessary to save the life of my child or to prevent serious harm to his or her health.

I have been told about additional procedures which may become necessary during my child's treatment. I have listed below any procedures which I do not wish to be carried out without further discussion..

....

....

....

....

Signature.. Date..

Name (PRINT).. Relationship to child..

Child's agreement to treatment (if child wishes to sign)

I agree to have the treatment I have been told about.

Name.. Signature..

Date..

Confirmation of consent (to be completed by a health professional when the child is admitted for the procedure, if the parent/child have signed the form in advance)

On behalf of the team treating the patient, I have confirmed with the child and his or her parent(s) that they have no further questions and wish the procedure to go ahead.

Signed:... Date..

Name (PRINT).. Job title..

Important notes: (tick if applicable)

☐ See also advance directive/living will (e.g. Jehovah's Witness form)

☐ Parent has withdrawn consent (ask parent to sign/date here)

Source: this is Crown copyright material which is reproduced with the permission of the controller of HMSO and the Queen's Printer for Scotland.

Appendix 2.2

Articles of the Human Rights Act 1998

Article 2:   Right to life
Article 3:   Prohibition of torture
Article 4:   Prohibition of slavery and enforced labour
Article 5:   Right to liberty
Article 6:   Right to a fair trial
Article 7:   No punishment without law
Article 8:   Respect for private and family life
Article 9:   Freedom of thought, conscience and religion
Article 10:   Freedom of expression
Article 11:   Freedom of assembly and association
Article 12:   Right to marry
Article 14:   Prohibition of discrimination

3

Inequality, Discrimination and Exclusion

Aims and objectives

The aim of this chapter is to enable the reader to begin to understand the impact of inequality, discrimination and exclusion on the health of people.

At the end of the chapter you will be able to:

1. Define the associated key terms: inequality, discrimination and exclusion
2. Describe how inequality, discrimination and exclusion can impact negatively on health and wellbeing
3. Understand the causes of inequality in health
4. Describe ways in which the nurse can help to tackle health inequalities
5. Reflect the wider dimensions and influences on health
6. Appreciate the Nursing and Midwifery Council's requirements for student nurses

Every person is a unique human being and is entitled to care that is provided in a fair and non-discriminatory manner, acknowledging that there are differences in beliefs and cultural practices between patients and within patient groups. This chapter provides the reader with knowledge with respect to diversity and culture when caring for patients from various communities and with diverse circumstances, e.g. those patients with a disability, however it manifests itself.

This chapter will help to ensure that the student can act in such a way as ensure that the rights of individuals and groups are respected and not compromised. It is important that the values, customs and beliefs of the patient are respected, and that the care provided is sensitive to the diverse needs of the patient for whom the nurse is caring.

Discrimination and disadvantage can obstruct the nurse's aim to provide care and have the potential to lead to inequality. Respecting and valuing the diversity of the people with whom you work, and the patients for whom you care, will help to ensure a quality service.

There are many differences that make us all unique:

- Language
- Religion
- Race

The Student's Guide to Becoming a Nurse, Second Edition. Ian Peate.
© 2012 John Wiley & Sons, Ltd. Published 2012 by John Wiley & Sons, Ltd.

- Employment status
- Class
- Culture
- Physical abilities.

As a result of these differences it is important to recognise that a national, uniform service – a 'one-size-fits-all' approach to health care – cannot work and will fail to meet the needs of diverse populations (Department of Health or DH, 2010).

The greater part of this chapter focuses on inequalities in health care and how to start to tackle them. There remain striking inequalities in health care between groups and areas in the UK. Inequalities are a matter of life and death, health and sickness, wellbeing and misery. The fact that in the UK today there are people in different social circumstances experiencing avoidable differences in health, wellbeing and length of life is quite unacceptable. Building a fairer society is central to improving the health of the nation, ensuring a fairer distribution of good health (Marmot Review, 2010).

Defining key terms

To provide care that respects the patient, is inclusive and takes into account his or her individuality, the nurse has to understand and be able to define key terms.

Culture

Culture is a complex concept and has many facets associated with it. It can be summarised by saying that it describes patterns of learned human behaviour that are transferred from one generation to the next (Anemone, 2011) Culture is not transferred via biological mechanisms. Marsh et al (2009) suggest that culture is related to values, customs and accepted modes of behaviour that characterise a society or social groups within a society. Cesarean (2010) believes culture to be associated with:

- knowledge
- beliefs
- ideas
- behaviours
- habits
- customs
- languages
- symbols
- rituals
- ceremonies
- practices.

All of the above are unique to a particular group of people. Each person is culturally unique. Culture, similar to ethnicity, is fluid and dynamic. People may possess culturally predetermined values and beliefs, but these are subject to change and refinement as new information is gained.

Within particular cultural groups there is much diversity and the differences can come about as a result of individual practices and perspectives. The characteristics of culture, according to Cesarean (2010), are the same for all cultures (Table 3.1).

Table 3.1   Characteristics of culture

- Culture is learned and taught.
- Culture is shared.
- Culture is social in nature.
- Culture is dynamic, adaptive and ever changing.

Source: adapted from Cesarean (2010).

Top tips

Do not make assumptions about the people for whom you care or their families. Always take time to listen to what is being said. Asumptions disrespect the person being cared for and you are in danger of becoming ethnocentric – judging people by your own standards. Refrain from making asumptions or stereotyping people in order to demonstrate cultural competence.

Ethnicity

The term 'ethnicity' is highly contested and its precise meaning remains elusive. According to Ratcliffe (2004) the term in practice tends to be used loosely in the context of health. Ethnicity means a group to which people belong because of shared characteristics, including ancestral and geographical origins, cultural traditions, languages and skin colour. Smart et al (2008) suggest that ethnicity has become a synonym for race.

Ethnicity is a fluid concept and its interpretation will depend on context. Self-assessment of ethnicity allows the individual to choose for him- or herself. It can therefore alter over time: the person's original self-assessment of his or her chosen ethnic group can change depending on the interpretation at that time – and this is his or her privilege. Attempting to measure ethnicity with any degree of accuracy is therefore problematic (Ratcliffe, 2004). According to Giger and Davidhizar (2007) the most important characteristic of ethnicity is that the members of an ethnic group feel a sense of identity.

Race

Although ethnicity can be described as a fluid concept, race has attached to it a variety of meanings that differ significantly from the biological notions associated with it (Anemone, 2011). Humans are one species; there are no biological distinctions between them and little variation in genetic composition. When considering the term 'race' in the pure sense of homogeneous populations, race does not exist in human species – there is only one human species. The term 'race' is often used alongside ethnicity.

The concept of race is scientifically invalid; however, race still retains a central position in contemporary society (Ratcliffe, 2004). Giger and Davidhizar (2007) propose that race can be related to biology, suggesting that members of a particular race share distinguishing physical features such as:

- bone structure
- skin colour
- blood group.

For some, race may merely be a convenient set of descriptors; for others, it may have far more sinister connotations associated with it. The use of the term 'race' can result in making a group feel inferior to the more dominant group, what Ratcliffe (2004) terms 'inferiorisation', in so far as it has the potential to be hierarchical.

Top tips

At all times local policy and procedure must be adhered to.

- Brief the interpreter – when the interpreter arrives check that they are who you are expecting – are they carrying an Identity Card (with photograph).
- Before starting the interpretation session ensure that the interpreter is briefed regarding the purpose of the session/meeting. Provide specific instructions of what needs to be accomplished. Establish/reiterate confidentiality rules.
- Speak directly to the patient – you and the person being cared for should communicate directly with each other as if the interpreter were not there. Speak naturally (not louder) and at your normal pace (not slower); be clear.
- Segments – speak in one sentence or two short ones at a time. Try to avoid breaking up a thought. The interpreter is trying to understand the meaning of what is being said, so express the whole thought if possible. Be ready to slow down or repeat if required. Pause, ensuring that you give the interpreter time to deliver the message.
- Clarifications – if anything is unclear, or if the interpreter is given a long statement, the interpreter may ask you for a repetition of what was said.
- Respect the person – keep in mind that the person's lack of English does not necessarily equate to a lack of education.
- Do not ask for the interpreter's opinion or comments.
- Everything you say will be interpreted – avoid personal conversations with your colleagues. Whatever the interpreter hears will be interpreted.
- The interpreter should not engage in dialogue with the person being cared for, or give advice or opinion – just translation.
- Avoid jargon or technical terms – to help all parties do not use jargon, slang, idioms, acronyms or technical terms. Clarify vocabulary that is unique to the situation and provide examples if needed to explain a term.
- Culture – professional interpreters should be familiar with the culture and customs of the person for whom he or she is interpreting. During the interpretation session, the interpreter might identify and point out a cultural issue of which you may not be aware. Also, if the interpreter feels that a particular question is culturally inappropriate, he or she may ask you to rephrase it.
- Any notes taken by the interpreter during interpretation should be handed to the person who requested the interpretation or destroyed.
- Record the use of an interpreter in the notes.

Gender

Gender and gender roles are closely related to cultural context. Biological sex refers to male or female characteristics. Gender, however, refers to how we are expected to behave as men and women, how society expects men and women to 'be', and the way men and women are expected to be will differ between cultures (Anemone, 2011). Gender is a social construction; both men and women are gendered beings.

The media, schools and religion convey socially constructed meanings related to masculinity and femininity and these constructions can shape people's gender identities. Gender is that which cultural meaning has ascribed to such biological differences. It is a person's concept of him- or herself as male or female. Physical appearance is likely to play a defining role (Bradley, 2007).

Gender can have an effect on the patient's physiological measurements – vital signs. Rayman (2009) states that women experience greater temperature fluctuations than men and this may be as a result of hormonal changes. Males in general have higher blood pressure than females of the same age.

Spirituality

Smith (2006) suggests that spiritual health relates to having a sense of meaning, hope and purpose in life. It is not only about having religious faith. Spirituality does not belong only to those who are dying or suffering; however, it is often situated within the death and dying sections of some textbooks. Spirituality is an aspect of every part of our lives, what we do and how our bodies respond. When faced with illness (but not exclusively) our spiritual beliefs can be threatened. If this occurs the impact or the outcome can be harmful.

Case study 3.1

Siobhán Ryan is a 28-year-old married woman who was involved in a serious road traffic accident and has been admitted to the trauma unit of a large acute trust. She is seriously ill and is being prepared to go to theatre for emergency abdominal surgery. Her next of kin, her husband John, has been contacted and is on his way to the hospital. The surgeon will be performing a laparotomy and it is expected that she will need to perform a splenectomy, until the abdominal contents can be visualised the extent of further surgery will not be known.

You are caring for Mrs Ryan; she is in pain and tells you that she is scared; she is anxious and has been prescribed and given strong analgesia in the form of pethidine. Mrs Ryan is very tired and when awake she cries. Mr Ryan arrives and is comforting his wife; he too is clearly distressed. He informs you that Mrs Ryan is a Roman Catholic.

In the context of attending to Mrs and Mr Ryan's spiritual needs what will you need to do to ensure that her needs are being met in a holistic manner? How can you enhance their spiritual wellbeing? You might have considered the need for prayer, the importance to some Roman Catholics of the presence of a priest to hear a confession or to offer the sacrament of extreme unction (anointing of the sick). The presence of priest may also provide comfort to Mr Ryan during this critical period.

Valuing diversity

Culturally competent nursing care

Wohland et al (2010) suggest that projected estimates of ethnic minorities will make up a fifth of Britain's population by 2051, compared with 8 per cent in 2001. Data estimate that Britain's total population will grow to 77.7 million; predications also indicate that the UK will become less segregated as ethnic groups become more distributed throughout the country.

It is anticipated that there will be noticeable differences in the respective growth rates of the 16 ethnic groups studied. The slowest groups to grow will be white British and Irish groups; those who identify themselves as other white is expected to grow the fastest, much of which, it could be suggested, will result from immigration from Europe, the USA and Australasia. Established groups, e.g. those of south Asian origin (Indian, Pakistani and Bangladeshi) will also grow rapidly (Wohland et al, 2010).

The code of professional conduct (Nursing and Midwifery Council or NMC, 2008) states that you must:

- treat people as individuals, respecting their dignity
- not discriminate against those in your care
- treat people with kindness and consideration
- act as an advocate for those in your care.

The crux of this statement is that nurses should not discriminate against any patient for whom they care; they should promote and protect each patient's diverse needs, respecting them and their dignity as well as being kind and considerate. Discrimination of any kind has no place in professional nursing care.

Culturally competent care has multidimensional facets associated with it. Mold et al (2005) suggest that the provision of culturally competent care is a continuous challenge. Care provision should be built around the individual needs of individual patients. Some aspects of nursing care may be affected and even determined by issues such as religion or ethnic background. High-quality nursing care will recognise and respond in a sensitively effective, empathic and flexible manner, committed to ensuring that these needs are met – care should reflect the patient's life, beliefs and community.

Nurses should aim to preserve and accommodate the cultural beliefs, values and deep-rooted ideologies that some patients may have in this increasingly diverse society. Respecting these values and beliefs is true patient advocacy.

When addressing diversity the nurse needs to concentrate on the care needs of those with differences as well as similarities in beliefs, values and cultures; by doing this the nurse can begin to provide culturally appropriate, meaningful and helpful health care. Nursing care should be provided in a multicultural environment that respects diversity.

The nurse must ensure that, whatever social customs characterise the ethnic group being cared for, these customs are not neglected, but valued and facilitated. These customs may include:

- dietary practices
- religious practices
- dress
- social interactions within groups
- specific rituals enacted during periods of ill health, death and dying.

Think

How would you typify the customs of someone who describes him- or herself as white British?

Your list may have included comments such as:

- Stiff upper lip
- Lover of fish and chips
- Tea drinker
- Celebrates Christmas
- Goes to the pub.

There may be some people who describe themselves as white British who may engage in all of the above; there may also be some who do not. Not all British people like tea; some white British people regard themselves as believing in the Christian God but may never go to church; they may be Jewish and go to the synagogue or could be atheist. Some may be vegans and not eat fish.

Britain is a multicultural and multifaith society. Developments in clinical practice will include cultural awareness about assessment, interpretation and information for patients and the public.

Improved patient care will emerge where there is an increasingly culturally competent workforce. The workforce will be more understanding and better informed about the cultural, economic and social aspects of disease. The next aspect of this chapter considers good practice in relation to culturally competent care and focuses on information about several ethnic and religious groups, including summaries of their beliefs and customs, along with health-care-related advice.

Top tips

Explain every detail to the person being cared for, do not assume that he or she knows what you are talking about or doing to them. The jargon used in health-care provision can be confusing; it may be even more confusing for people whose native language is not English. People may not understand what you are saying and may be too shy to say that they do not understand. Take time to explain everything and use all of your interpersonal skills to actively listen to the person for whom you are caring.

General considerations and good practice guidelines

Every patient should be treated equally, regardless of gender, race or creed. They should have free access to religious support with the opportunity to practise their chosen religion while being cared for.

When first meeting the patient the nurse should establish the patient's ethnic identity and ascertain if he or she has a religious association (do not assume that, if you have a religious faith, others also have one). The information provided by the patient should be noted in the patient's case notes. Early on in the relationship anticipate with the patient if there are likely to be any issues that could arise during the examination, investigation, diagnosis, treatment or medication aspects of his or her care. Discuss with the patient how best you can help to have his or her religious/cultural needs met while caring for him or her. Ensure that the rest of the team caring for the patient are aware of these specific needs.

Admission to a mixed-sex ward may be problematic for members of some cultures where men and women are strictly segregated. Physical examination or investigation being carried out by a nurse of the opposite gender may be unacceptable. As far as possible the patient's needs and wishes should be met. Chaperones should be made available for all patients (Peate, 2007).

Appropriate information and interpretation are essential if the patient is to provide informed consent. Any information booklets or leaflets provided to patients explaining to them what to expect in hospital, or about a proposed investigation or examination, should be translated into several languages, particularly those that are most common in the local community. Translators may be needed if the nurse does not speak the patient's language. However, the use of family members may not always be ideal because they may be unfamiliar with the medical terminology, and both the patient and family member may be reticent about discussing sensitive information with older or younger relatives. Local liaison groups or the Patient Advisory Liaison Service (PALS) may be able to recommend other resources to help translate.

Top tips

Accommodate the needs of the people for whom you care. Whatever the patient's cultural background you have a role to play in accommodating his or her needs, e.g. in helping to preserve beliefs and values. Helping the person in this way can also help with his or her physical and emotional wellbeing. It also demonstrates to the person that you are providing care for him or her in a holistic manner.

When we are unable to communicate with patients because of language difficulties those patients are in danger of becoming disenfranchised. If the patient's first language is sign (British Sign Language) the nurse may need to use facilitators, text telephones and telephone amplifiers. Televisions should have teletext subtitle provision.

Some patients may wish to fast in observation of religious requirements and the nurse may need to make arrangements to have food available outside the fasting period. It may be acceptable to allow the patient's family, friends or community to bring in food; however, the nurse must check hospital policy about this and ensure that if a medical diet is required this is adhered to. Always offer the patient choice, e.g. do not assume that a patient automatically takes milk in a drink. Orthodox Jews will not accept milk mixed with certain foods. Some foods may be prohibited and there may be requirements concerning the way in which other foods are prepared. Avoid using local names for food: some people may not know what is meant by 'Welsh rarebit' or 'Irish stew'.

Table 3.2 provides an overview of some ethnic groups and information that the nurse may find helpful when providing culturally competent nursing care. Care and sensitivity are needed when caring for all patients. The nurse must ensure that he or she preserves the modesty of the patient at all times and, when possible, provide space for the patient to worship as he or she sees fit. Furthermore, the nurse should consult with the patient, and if appropriate the family, when addressing needs at a time when there may be much pain and suffering, e.g. as the patient is dying and when the patient has died. Religious and cultural views must be upheld while caring for the dying person (DH, 2008). The nurse is encouraged to seek advice and help from the appropriate religious organisation if he or she has any queries about the patient's cultural needs.

Think

In the most tolerant of societies, there are many things that should always remain intolerable. Try making a list of the features that you think should have no place in a fair, free and just society.

Table 3.2   An overview of some ethnic groups and information the nurse may find helpful when providing culturally competent nursing care

	Introduction	Health care	Death and dying	Food	Notes
Buddhism	Buddhism is a way of life as opposed to an organised religion; it is intended to be a collection of ways to help individuals seek betterment and enlightenment. It is not a set of ritualistic practices. The Buddha means the Enlightened One	There are no strict dress codes for Buddhists unless they are nuns or priests If possible a separate room should be made available so the Buddhist patient can meditate or chant in private, and without disturbing other patients	**At the moment of death** Tibetan Buddhism explains the process of death in eight clear stages. At the fourth stage, when breathing stops (when the air element dissolves), death has not yet occurred because it is felt that consciousness still exists for up to 3 days **After death and preparation of the body** As death does not occur for up to three days, the body (if in hospital) should be moved to an empty room. Death has occurred when heat is no longer emitted from the heart, the body begins to emit an odour and a small amount of fluid leaves the sexual organs or the nostrils. Mantras can be chanted and prayers read. If the body needs to be touched in order to move it then the crown of the head or the hair on the crown should be touched or pulled. Once this has happened other body parts can be touched	Many Buddhists are vegetarians or vegans as they should not be responsible for the death of any other living organism Buddhists do not condone the consumption of recreational drugs or the use of alcohol	At any stage of the patient's stay or death a Buddhist priest should be contacted to help guide and support care

Continued

Table 3.2 *Continued*

Introduction	Health care	Death and dying	Food	Notes
		Postmortem examination is usually acceptable to Buddhists. However, a postmortem examination occurring within 3 days of death should be avoided		
		Organ donation can be discussed with the family of the deceased. There is much debate about organ donation and therefore the nurse should consult a priest		
		It is normal for cremation to take place several days after the body has lain in state		
		It is not a Buddhist trait to grieve after a person has died		
		The body may be donated to science, so long as time has been allowed for the consciousness to be dispersed (normally 3 days)		
		Suicide is not forbidden but is deeply regretted by the Buddhist community		
		Termination of a pregnancy is believed to be unethical by many Buddhists. Most Buddhists would regard the decision to undergo a termination of pregnancy as a very serious one		

Church of England	The Church of England is the established or state church in England. As the Church of England is the established church, many non-practising Christians cite it as their religion, some as a matter of course, and may or may not seek comfort from it during times of illness	There are no strict dress codes for Christians unless they are nuns or priests	A dying patient may request to see a member of the clergy before death and receive the sacrament of sick people. They, or their visitors may wish to have prayers at their bedside. Routine last offices are appropriate for a dying Christian. More prayers may be said after someone has died	Some Christians may not eat meat on Fridays. They should therefore be offered a fish or vegetarian alternative
	Some members of the Church of England may wish to receive Holy Communion when they are in hospital, and possibly the sacrament of sick people		After death, a Christian should be wrapped in a sheet with their arms and hands placed at their sides. They may be buried or cremated, in accordance with their wishes	
			Christians do not usually have any religious objections to organ donation and postmortem examinations	
			Most Christians view suicide as a rejection not of life itself, but of a particular life, and as a cry for help	
			The Church of England is opposed to abortion	

Continued

Table 3.2 *Continued*

	Introduction	Health care	Death and dying	Food	Notes
Hinduism	Hinduism has developed over thousands of years; it includes a diverse range of customs and beliefs It is difficult to generalise about Hinduism due to its diversity	Generally female Hindus adhere to dress codes. A sari is a common item of clothing. Most Hindu patients would prefer to be examined by health-care staff of the same gender as themselves. A chaperone should be provided; family members may act as chaperones. Young men and boys are often chaperoned by their father or brother and young women and girls by their mother or sister. A married woman may be chaperoned by her husband or sister-in-law	As with most other religious groups Hindus have last rites and religious ceremonies to perform. Often the immediate and extended family make every effort to pay their last respects to a family member who is in the final stages of dying. Most Hindus would prefer to die at home. A dying Hindu may request to be nursed on the floor in order to be as close to Mother Earth as possible The family of the dead patient may prefer to prepare the body. A clean white sheet should be used to wrap the body. There are many rituals that may need to be observed Hindus prefer to cremate the dead body as soon as possible Generally, there is no objection to organ donation. If a post mortem is required this should be conducted as soon as possible so that arrangements can be made for the cremation to take place	Most Hindus are strict vegetarians or vegans. The cow is considered to be a sacred representation of the bounty of the gods. It is important to ensure that all medication is free from beef products such as gelatin Hindus are not permitted to eat meat, drink alcohol or smoke. As with any religion some Hindus may vary in their adherence to such rules	Many Hindus have strong beliefs in Ayurvedic medicines. They may wish to continue using Ayurvedic medicines and prescribed medications

	Specific care must be taken with any sacred objects the patient is wearing for example jewellery, threads or bindi (the holy dot is an auspicious makeup worn by young Hindu females on their forehead). If a man's sacred thread needs to be removed before surgery the nurse must ensure that it is never placed on the floor, close to the feet or shoes or any place where it may become contaminated by body fluids A toothbrush is generally used to clean the teeth but the patient may also use a 'U' wire tool to clean his or her tongue				
Christian Scientists	Christian Science is a Christian religion. Christian Scientists do not believe in medical intervention and are likely to be in hospital for child birth only, for the setting of broken bones or involuntarily	It is not uncommon for Christian Scientists to be cared for and treated by practitioners or nurses who are themselves Christian Scientists, who would only provide food, cleansing and prayer or religious reading Dental care is permitted but it must be preformed without any pain relief Christian Scientists are opposed to all medications and this will include pain relief	When a Christian Scientists is dying no medical intervention is permitted and when a Christian Scientist dies, no rituals or rites need to be performed A dead female body should be handled by female staff Cremation is often preferred to burial; however, the choice is up to each individual Unless it is legally required a Christian Scientist is unlikely to consent to a postmortem examination	Usually no particular diet is followed; however, Christian Scientists do not use alcohol or tobacco, and may not drink tea or coffee	All health-care decisions are up to the individual; some parents may agree to their children receiving life-saving medical intervention

Continued

Table 3.2 *Continued*

	Introduction	Health care	Death and dying	Food	Notes
Jehovah's Witnesses	Jehovah's Witnesses believe in the teachings of the Bible, using their own translation. Jehovah's Witnesses do not use the symbol of the cross because they believe it to be of pagan origin	Jehovah's Witnesses are opposed to taking blood or blood products into the body, preferring to use alternative treatments. For example, bloodless surgery does not involve the use of blood or blood products	There are no particular rites and rituals associated with death and dying. A dying witness patient may request a visit from one of the elders of their faith Individuals can opt for burial or cremation Termination of pregnancy is unacceptable to Jehovah's Witnesses It is unlikely that a Jehovah's Witness will object to a postmortem examination Jehovah's Witnesses may not wish to donate their organs as another person's blood would flow through them. In organs that do not involve blood flow, e.g. corneas, this is acceptable	Issues concerning blood or blood products are also related to food. Anything that contains blood or blood products is unacceptable, as is meat from an animal that has been strangled, or shot and not bled properly. Some Jehovah's Witnesses do not eat meat at all It is believed that tobacco and other recreational drugs are incompatible with Jehovah's Witness principles. Drinking alcohol is allowed but drunkenness is not condoned	Jehovah's Witnesses worship in Kingdom Halls as often as five times per week, and at large gatherings three times a year. Bone-marrow transplants may be acceptable to some individuals as may be albumin, immunoglobulin or clotting factors – each patient must be assessed individually Vaccination is acceptable A special card is carried by most Jehovah's Witnesses that identifies them as such, and directs staff to avoid using blood or blood products in their treatment

Catholics	The Catholic Church (also known as the Roman Catholic Church) is one of the major Christian churches in UK. Patients may request to take regular holy communion and arrangements may also have to be made for them to make a confession	There are no strict dress codes for Catholics unless they are nuns or priests	A priest should always be called when a Catholic patient is dying. Routine last rites are appropriate for all Christians. It is unlikely that a Catholic will have any religious objections to organ donation and the same relates to postmortem examination. The Catholics Church has always condemned the termination of pregnancy	Some Catholics may not eat meat or drink alcohol on Fridays and on Ash Wednesday	There are many rituals associated with Catholic Church. The Catholic Church is opposed to artificial contraception and sterilisation
Sikhism	Sikhism is prevalent in Indian society. There are five signs that Sikhs must wear at all times, known as the five Ks:	Running water is the preferred method of maintaining hygiene. If a shower is not available then a bowl and jug are acceptable. The combing of the hair on a regular basis with the kangha is important for Sikhs and they may need help from the nurse to do this	Prior to touching the body of a dead Sikh the nurse must wear gloves to avoid direct contact. The nurse should not wash the body as the family may wish to carry out this task. Never remove any of the five Ks. The body should be wrapped in a clean white sheet	Sikhs generally do not eat meat, most are vegetarian and some are vegan	The place of worship for Sikhs is called a Gurdwara. It is also seen as a community centre, a teaching room and a kitchen

Continued

Table 3.2   Continued

	Introduction	Health care	Death and dying	Food	Notes
	Kesh: uncut beard and uncut hair **Kangha**: a wooden comb **Kara**: a steel bracelet worn around the right wrist **Kirpan**: a sharp knife with a double-edged blade **Katchera**: specially made long underpants	Unless the patient has given you permission do not touch or remove any of the five Ks. If any of the items are removed they should be treated with respect and never placed on the floor or close to a person's feet. If the turban or head scarf is removed provide the patient with alternative hair covering such as a theatre cap. If hair needs to be removed, e.g. before surgery, then ask the patient for permission and determine if he or she would like it to be returned after it has been removed	There is no Sikh ruling against postmortem examination or the donation of organs The decision to bury or cremate the body is left up to individual choice Suicide is a grave offence and the deceased is expected to serve great penance in a later life Termination of pregnancy is considered taboo		
Judaism	The followers of Judaism are diverse. It is a religion, a way of life and culture, and because of this it is difficult to define Judaism	Some Jews may need help from the nurse with ritual washes they have to perform before eating and praying The nurse should bear in mind that there may be some restrictions placed on the Jewish patient on the Sabbath and other holidays	Death occurs according to the Halachic definition when the body is without heart beat or breath If possible always stay with the body after death until help arrives. It is considered disrespectful to leave the body alone or in the dark before burial. A light should always be left on	Jewish patients should be offered kosher food. Kashrut rules apply equally to both foods and medicines. When available a kosher alternative should be made available	Each Jewish community can have different ways of interpreting the laws of the religion. It is divied into three major categories: Orthodox Reform

Liberal/ progressive		
The nurse should seek the help and advice of a rabbi if there are concerns regarding the care of the Jewish patient	Prior to touching the body of a dead Jew the nurse must wear gloves to avoid direct contact	Some Jewish holidays may require the patient to fast. These holidays do not have a fixed date each year and the nurse needs to bear this in mind when caring for the patient
	Ideally the body should be buried within 24 hours of death	
	The nurse should leave catheters drains and tubing in position; they should be buried with the patient – as they are considered a part of the body	
	As a general rule postmortem examinations are not permittted under Jewish law unless this is legally required	
	Organ donation may be permitted where a transplantation is vital to save a life	
	Generally cremation is forbidden by Jewish law and burial is the preferred method of body disposal	
	Suicide is condemned and forbidden in Jewish law	

Source: adapted from Akhtar (2002); Baxter (2002); Christmas (2002); Collins (2002); Gill (2002); Jootun (2002); Northcott (2002); Papadopoulos (2002); Simpson (2002).

Your list might have included the malevolent violence that destroys young people's lives and families. You might have also have included an often crushing disregard for the rights of children, older people or disabled people by those who should be using their authority to improve lives. Did you cite the complacency that condemns women and men to inevitable roles in life, and the prejudice that confines some to society's dustbin purely because of the colour of their skin? Underpinning all of this is a persistent material, cultural and moral poverty that blights many homes.

Measuring social inequalities

Since 1911 in the UK the most popular method of measuring inequalities has been through occupation. This method, the Registrar General's Social Class scheme, was developed originally to construct the 1911 census. It was the head of the household – the male – whose occupation was used to determine the social class membership of that household.

Using such an approach denied acknowledgement of women's occupations and as such they did not receive their own social class position. The focus when undertaking measurement therefore considered occupation in isolation, neglecting other kinds of social difference.

The system employed may have been appropriate then and possibly did reflect the characteristics of the population at the time. However, in the twenty-first century that may not be the case because it neglects consideration of the many social and economic changes that have occurred over the years, e.g. the increase in the number of women who are employed and the decline of manual work.

Analysis by Registrar General's Social Class has consistently shown social gradients in health, and particularly in mortality at working ages, infant mortality and birthweight. Since 2001, the Registrar General's Social Class has been replaced by the National Statistics Socio-Economic Classification (NS SEC) and this is now used in all official statistics.

The key aspects of the revision include: a tighter definition of managerial occupations; expansion in the field of computing and related occupations; the introduction of specific occupations associated with the environment and conservation; changes linked to the upgrading of skills but the de-skilling of manufacturing processes; and the recognition of the development of customer service occupations and the emergence of remote service provision through the operation of call centres. Most of the major groups of occupations were renamed, and the composition of all major groups changed (Donkin et al, 2002). These changes reflect changes in society. Table 3.3 outlines the current system.

Inequalities concern life and death, are closely associated with health and sickness, and are linked to wellbeing and misery. It is unacceptable that, in the UK today, there are people who find themselves in different social circumstances who will suffer avoidable differences in health, wellbeing and longevity.

To improve the health of the whole population and to ensure a fairer distribution of good health, it is essential that we create a fairer society.

The Marmot Review (2010) notes that inequalities in health arise because of inequalities in society and these are associated with the conditions in which people are born, grow, live, work and age. The link between particular social and economic features of society and the distribution of health among the population is so close that the magnitude of health inequalities is a good marker of progress towards creating a fairer society. Taking action to reduce inequalities in health requires action across the whole of society. The Commission on Social Determinants of Health (2008) concludes that social injustice is killing on a grand scale.

It is erroneous to think that some of the serious health inequalities faced by some members of society arise by chance, and also to think that the inequalities can be attributed simply to genetic make-up, bad, unhealthy behaviour or difficulties in accessing care, although these are important factors social and economic differences in health status reflect, and are caused by, social and economic inequalities within our society.

Determinants of health include all of the non-genetic and biological influences on health and, as such, would include individual risk factors such as smoking. These determinants must also be considered because they have the potential to impinge on a person's health and can modify life chances.

Health inequalities not only are apparent between people of different socioeconomic groups, but also exist between different ethnic groups (House of Commons, 2009). Racial discrimination can also take its toll on the health of these communities.

Although the current occupation approach scheme used to measure social inequalities, health experiences and patterns of mortality has some valid purpose, a concerted effort must be made to produce a measure that encompasses and embraces all of the factors (and more) described in Figure 3.1.

Table 3.3   National Statistics (2005)

Registrar General's social class	National Statistics Socio-economic Classification
I Professional occupations	1 Higher managerial and professional occupations
II Managerial and technical occupations	2 Lower managerial and professional
III Skilled occupations	3 Intermediate occupations
IV Manual (M) and non-manual (N)	4 Small employers and own account workers
IV Partly skilled occupations	5 Lower supervisory and technical occupations
V Unskilled occupations	6 Semi-routine occupations
	7 Routine occupations
	8 Never worked and long-term unemployed

Source: adapted from National Statistics (2005).

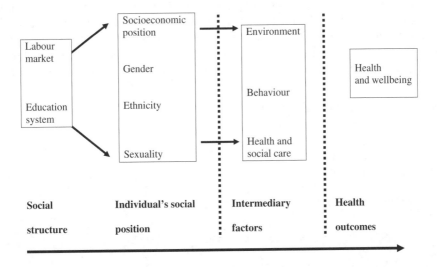

Figure 3.1 Key health determinants and the association they have with health outcomes. *Source*: Graham (2005).

Health inequalities

Equality was the founding principle of the NHS (Ross, 1952). Since its foundation there has been extraordinary progress in a number of spheres: people are living longer and are more prosperous than ever before, and new treatments that could never have been thought possible are saving thousands of lives each year. The overall health of the population in this country has improved greatly over the past 50 years (Sustainable Development Commission, 2010).

Life expectancy and infant mortality indicators demonstrate that the health gap continues and in some cases has increased; however, there are some signs of stabilisation (DH, 2009). There are sections of our society that are still treated unequally with respect to health-care provision.

The cost of these inequalities to individuals, communities and the nation is huge. People who are affected by the inequalities die at a younger age and are likely to spend more of their lives suffering ill health.

Addressing the various problems and inequalities faced by a diverse nation means that we must recognise that the problems are a result of diverse and complex causes. Although at a distance the health inequalities appear to be similar, they are not. This means that they will require diverse solutions, as opposed to identical approaches, to tackle local needs experienced by the most disadvantaged in our society. A mix of national standards and local services is required to meet a diversity of local needs: local solutions for local health inequality problems. Local communities know best what their problems are and how to handle them. Health inequalities can be persistent and difficult to change. There is a need to address both the short-term consequences of avoidable ill health and the longer-term causes.

Health and wellbeing are influenced by several factors, including past and present behaviours, the type of health provision available to treat illness and injury, and provision of care for those with disabling conditions, as well as social, cultural and environmental factors. Income, education, employment, housing and lifestyle must also be considered. Some of these issues have traditionally been considered outside the health domain. However, it is impossible to devise policy and provide meaningful health care if they are not included in the health provision equation (Marmot Review, 2010).

When health inequalities are measured the data used demonstrate that, when measured by occupation, there is a marked difference in health. A top-to-bottom occupational hierarch is used. Using the evidence generated by analysis of the data provides others (e.g. governments) with the information to produce policies that will help to reduce the inequalities in health care. The key aim is to enhance health and decrease health differences between groups occupying unequal positions within society (Graham, 2004a).

Having determined that there are inequalities in health, a response is required to address and tackle these inequalities. Those responsible for the formulation of policy must take into account those members of society:

- who find themselves in the poorest circumstances
- with the poorest health
- who are most socially excluded
- with the highest risk factors
- who are difficult to reach.

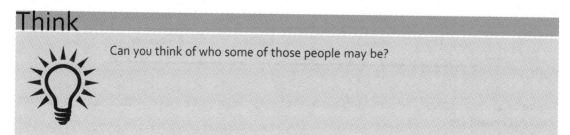

Think

Can you think of who some of those people may be?

Table 3.4   Some members of society who should be given particular consideration when policy and approaches to addressing and tackling inequalities in health are being proposed and formulated

Those at risk	Example
Those who find themselves in the poorest circumstances	Socially and educationally deprived individuals
Those with the poorest health	People with long-term conditions such as HIV, diabetes mellitus
The most socially excluded	Elderly people
	Disabled people
	People with learning disabilities
Individuals with the highest risk factors	People who smoke
	Those who do not exercise
	Some people with specifically genetically inherited diseases
Those who are difficult to reach	Homeless individuals
	People in prison
	Individuals who do not have English as a first language

You might have a list that resembles that in Table 3.4.

Social position

There is a social gradient in health inequalities and social position is related to the position at which people find themselves in the social hierarchy. People occupy many social positions, e.g. a black gay woman in a professional occupation or a heterosexual white man in a non-professional occupation. It could be suggested that social position lies at the root of how healthy a person is. Social position encompasses a person's educational level and employability and the work that he or she does e.g. this links directly to risk factors to which they are exposed, affecting or impacting on health, such as workplace hazards, damp housing and poor diet. Graham (2005) states that there is an enduring association between socioeconomic position and health, both over time and across the major causes of death. This is marked even further in children and adults with learning disabilities, because they are disproportionately represented among the poorer and less healthy sections of society. Figure 3.1 demonstrates how the key health determinants are interconnected and result in the wellbeing of the person.

The association between socioeconomic position and health has endured over the years. In contemporary society changes have occurred, e.g. chronic disease has replaced environmentally transmitted infections. Table 3.5 demonstrates how the association between socioeconomic position and health over the years has changed but still continues.

The following discussions briefly outline some of the inequalities faced by individuals and communities. The reader is encouraged to consult other key texts for a deeper understanding and insight related to inequality and health care.

Table 3.5   Socioeconomic position and health outcomes

Period of time	Health outcome	Social position	Rates
1911	Infant mortality by father's occupation	Higher non-manual occupations	42 deaths per 1000 births
		Semi- and unskilled labourers	171 deaths per births
1959–63	Death rates from suicide by social class (men aged15–64 years)	Social class I	91 deaths per 100 000 person-years
		Social class V	184 deaths per 100 000 person-years
1997–99	Death rates from ischaemic heart disease by social class, men and women aged 35–64 years	Social class I and II	Men
			90 deaths per 100 000 person-years
			167 deaths per 100 000 person-years
		Social class IV and V	Women
			22 deaths per 100 000 person-years
			50 deaths per 100 000 person-years

Source: adapted from Registrar General (1913); Reid (1977); White et al (2003).

Children and health inequalities

In childhood the effects of poverty and disadvantage begin before birth (*in utero*), e.g. a mother's poor nutritional status will have an effect on her unborn child who will be undernourished and vulnerable, potentially leading to serious long-term disease in adult life. Graham and Power (2004) have highlighted how an adult's socioeconomic position (as lawyer or unskilled worker, for example) is impressively shaped by the socioeconomic status of the parents. An increase in child poverty has profound implications for health inequalities in both current and future generations (Stewart, 2009). Ensuring that all children have the best start in life is central to reducing health inequalities across the life course. The basis for almost every aspect of human development, physical, intellectual and emotional, is established in early childhood. What happens during those early years (even in the womb) will have a lifelong impact on various aspects of health and wellbeing, including obesity, heart disease and mental health, as well as educational achievement and economic status (Waldfogel, 2004).

Every child is exposed to the possibility of injury as part of their everyday life. However, the burden is not evenly distributed: injury affects some children more than others. Variations occur in injury mortality and morbidity. These variations reflect a child's age, social and economic factors, gender, culture, ethnicity and the place where they live (Waldfogel, 2004). Socioeconomic gradients are also apparent in birthweight, cognitive and physical development, and range of adult diseases. Children and adolescents who come from poorer families are more likely to experience mental health problems such as emotional and behavioural problems than those who come from better-off families. The relationship between low income and poor health has been discussed in the literature and is well established. There are many ways in which low income can impact on individuals and families. Those who are on low incomes refrain from buying goods and services that can help to maintain or improve their health; they may be forced to buy cheaper goods and services which may result in an increase in health risks. Being on a low income also prevents people from taking part in and contributing to a social life, the consequence of which can leave them feeling isolated, less worthy or having a lower status in society than those who are better off (Marmot, 2004).

The inequalities specifically associated with children, as with other groups, cannot be explained by one single set of risk factors such as smoking or poor diet. The environment in which the child has been raised and family relationships, for example, can also impinge on health outcomes for the child. Among families living with a child with learning disabilities, just under half are living in poverty, compared with 30 per cent of other families (Emerson and Hatton 2007).

Case study 3.2

Jen Marriot was shopping in a department store with her 6-week-old baby, Lara. Jen had breastfed Lara since her birth and was in the process of feeding baby Lara in the restaurant of the department store. The restaurant manager approached Jen and said that she had received a complaint from a customer who felt offended by seeing a woman breastfeed in public; for this reason she asked her to leave the restaurant and go to the ladies' toilet where there was a baby changing area. Ms Marriot was clearly distressed by this and left the shop.

Consider this case. What are your feelings about breastfeeding in public? Think about the Equality Act 2010 which says that it is sex discrimination to treat a woman unfavourably because she is breastfeeding. The law applies to anyone who provides services, benefits, facilities and premises to the public, public bodies, further and higher education bodies, and association. Service providers include most organisations that deal directly with the public and this would apply to the department store. Service providers cannot discriminate, harass or victimise a woman because she is breastfeeding. Discrimination would include refusing to provide a service, providing a lower standard of service or providing a service on different terms; the manager's offer to go to the baby changing facilities could be deemed a lower standard of service. Therefore, the department store manager or store owner cannot ask Ms Marriot to stop breastfeeding her child or refuse to serve her.

Women are protected in public places, e.g. parks, sports and leisure facilities, public buildings and when using public transport such as buses, trains and planes. They are protected in shops, public, restaurants and hotels regardless of size.

Inequalities related to people with learning disability and mental health

Although it has been noted that opportunities for good health are not equally distributed among all people, people with a disability are affected by the broader issues associated with inequality, and also the specific issues that disability brings with it. Living with illness and impairment can make economic hardship difficult to avoid. Issues such as persisting health difficulties and discrimination increase the risk of unemployment, dependency and poverty.

The proportion of disabled people in the population is set to rise (Equalities Review, 2007). Contributing to this increase is the result of greater longevity among both older people with disabling conditions and disabled people as a result of medical advances and other improvements; another factor is that more preterm babies and babies with disabling medical conditions are surviving. This also arises out of the identification of disabilities that previously went unrecognised, for example, emotional and behavioural disorders. Other influential factors include enhanced diagnosis and increasing reporting rates for disability, the stigma of being disabled is gradually declining.

In the Disability Discrimination Act 1995 disability is defined as:

> *A physical or mental impairment which has a substantial and long-term adverse effect on a person's ability to carry out normal day-to-day activities.*

Impairment covers both physical and mental impairments, including:

- Physical impairments affecting the senses, such as sight and hearing
- Mental impairments including learning disabilities and mental illness (if it is recognised by a respected body of medical opinion).

The term 'substantial' means more than minor, e.g.:

- Inability to see moving traffic clearly enough to cross a road safely
- Inability to turn taps or knobs
- Inability to remember and relay a simple message correctly.

Consideration must also be given to the term 'long term'. This means that the condition will have lasted at least 12 months or is likely to last at least 12 months or for the rest of the life of the person affected.

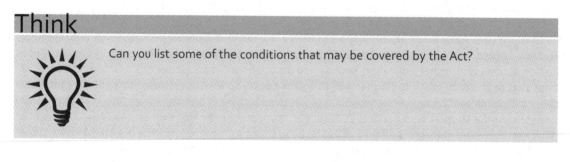

Think

Can you list some of the conditions that may be covered by the Act?

Did you remember to consider conditions experienced by those with mental health problems and learning disabilities as well as physical conditions? For example:

- Cancer
- HIV infection
- Multiple sclerosis
- Muscular dystrophy

There are higher levels of mental health problems associated with being worse off financially. The Marmot Review (2010) notes that insecure and poor quality employment is also associated with increased risks of poor physical and mental health. There is a graded relationship between an individual's status at work and how much control and support he or she has. There are higher rates of psychotic disorders associated with those families who have low income.

Those with a mental illness are expected to have higher than average rates of physical illness. Mortality and morbidity as a result of cardiovascular disease and cancer are higher among people with poor mental health, after controlling for socioeconomic variables. There is a greater prevalence of smoking-related fatal disease among people with mental health problems (Friedli, 2009; Piachaud et al, 2009). It is noted that people who suffer from mental illness have a greater risk of, and higher rates of, heart disease, diabetes, respiratory disease and infections. They also have higher rates of smoking, alcohol consumption and drug misuse. They die younger and have a poorer quality of life. Furthermore, those people who have severe mental illness often experience difficulties accessing services appropriate to their physical health-care, prevention and health promotion needs (NHS Scotland, 2011).

A learning disability is defined in *Valuing People* (DH, 2001) by the presence of both of the following:

- A significantly reduced ability to understand new or complex information, to learn new skills (impaired intelligence)
- A reduced ability to cope independently (impaired social functioning), which started before adulthood, with a lasting effect on development.

115

Case study 3.3

 You are working with people who have varying degrees of learning disability in a community care setting and have been asked by one of the doctors to meet a woman called Maria who will be coming to the unit later that morning. Maria is a researcher undertaking research into how people with learning disability communicate when in a group. You ask the doctor if informed consent has been gained and the doctor says that informed consent from people with learning disabilities is not required as it is with others and anyway Maria will just be observing how people interact.

How might you react to the issues detailed here in practice? Do you think that there is an inequality here? How can people with learning disability give informed consent?

People with learning disabilities have an increased risk of early death when compared with the population in general and those with severe impairments have higher mortality rates (Emerson and Baines, 2010). Early death may also be associated with difficulties that could be prevented. Nearly a third of people with learning disabilities, for example, have a related physical disability; this is commonly cerebral palsy which can put the person at risk of postural deformities, hip dislocation, chest infections, eating and swallowing problems (dysphagia), gastro-oesophageal reflux, constipation and incontinence. Some people with a learning disability tend to have osteoporosis younger than the general population and as a result may have more fractures (Michael, 2008).

The key cause of death for those with a learning disability is respiratory disease associated with pneumonia, dysphagia and gastroreflux disorder. These are followed by coronary heart disease; almost half of the people with Down's syndrome have congenital heart problems (Emerson and Baines, 2010).

Those with learning disabilities have a greater variety of health-care needs. However, these needs go unmet or unrecognised compared with the general population (Kerr, 2004). Unrecognised or poorly managed medical conditions include the following:

- Hypertension
- Obesity

- Coronary heart disease
- Abdominal pain
- Respiratory disease
- Cancer
- Gastrointestinal disorders
- Diabetes mellitus
- Chronic urinary tract infections
- Oral disease
- Musculoskeletal conditions
- Visual and hearing impairments.

There is much inequality among people with learning disability, e.g. issues concerning the availability and uptake of cervical and breast screening need further investigation. Uptake of immunisations against tetanus, poliomyelitis and influenza, according to NHS Scotland (2004), is lower than among the general population. Lack of uptake of influenza immunisation is a concern, because it has already been stated that people with learning disability have a high prevalence of respiratory infection associated with premature deaths caused by pneumonia.

Poorer white families and some ethnic minority families, such as those of Pakistani and Bangladeshi origin, are less likely to use pre-school education for their children. Many disabled children are unable to go to pre-school care because appropriate provision is limited (Equalities Review, 2007).

Older people and health inequalities

The ageing of the British population has been well documented; there were 9.4 million adults over the age of 65 in 2005 (16 per cent of the population) and this figure is predicted to rise to 12.4 million by 2021 (20 per cent). By the middle of this century, the number of people aged 80 or over will be double what it is today (Equalities Review, 2007). The pressures on health and social services provided for older people will increase.

There is a substantial body of research on inequalities in the health of the population as a whole and among working-age people. Much less research is available on health inequalities in the older population, particularly concerning people in late old age. Data from the Health Survey for England (2005) demonstrate that there are inequalities between those people in low and those in high socioeconomic groups for a number of health indicators for older people; data from people with the lowest income report poorer general health, lower consumption of fruit and vegetables, and higher degrees of mobility problems and lower-limb impairment. Likewise, the occurrence of ischaemic heart disease among older people is higher in the most deprived areas. Prevalence of diabetes as well as uncontrolled hypertension are also inversely related to income (Craig and Mindell, 2007).

Winter deaths still occur, despite ongoing government policies and awareness campaigns to reduce the number of cold homes and prevent the risk of ill health due to cold among those who are most vulnerable, e.g. older people and those with a disability or long-term illness. Not being able to afford to keep a warm home is a key factor. Fuel poverty in a household occurs when it needs to spend more than 10 per cent of its income on fuel to sustain satisfactory heating. In 2005–6, 7 per cent of households were spending more than this, over half of which were single-person households. As the cost of fuel changes, so too do the fuel poverty rates. In November 2008 the rising price of domestic fuel resulted in over half of single pensioners and two-thirds of workless households being in fuel poverty (Marmot Review, 2010).

As a person ages the risk of having a collision while crossing the road increases, particularly after the age of 79 years; injuries to those aged over 65 years are inclined to be more serious and more often fatal than injuries to other age groups. Older pedestrians in the UK have particular concerns about crossing busy roads. Although only 35 per cent of roads crossed by older pedestrians were main roads, 85 per cent of this group's injuries were on these roads. Those aged over 65 report traffic as a serious problem that impedes their own travel patterns (Mitchell, 2006).

In England, those people who live in the poorest neighbourhoods, will, on average, die 7 years earlier than those living in the richest neighbourhoods. In London life expectancy for men in Kensington and Chelsea (one of the wealthiest parts of London) was 84 years in 2005–7 but in Greenwich it was 75 years. At a more local level (council ward level) there are greater inequalities, with male life expectancy in Tottenham Green in Haringey (one of the poorest areas of London) being 17 years less than the 88 years in the more affluent Queen's Gate in Kensington and Chelsea (based on 2002–6 data).

Gender inequalities

Many boys and girls have similar experiences throughout childhood, although they are exposed to different risks. As the boys and girls become men and women they are yet again exposed to risks, but different risks associated with the labour market and home circumstances. The incidence of childhood disability differs by gender and class. Boys are twice as likely as girls to be reported as having severe disability. Severe disability affects children and adolescents from semi-skilled manual backgrounds more than any other socioeconomic group. There are systematic gender differences in health outcomes. Lower birthweight, earlier gestation and being small for gestational age are associated with infant mortality. The Marmot Review (2010) reports that, of all infant deaths in England and Wales (excluding multiple births), deprivation, births outside marriage, non-white ethnicity of the infant, maternal age of less than 20 and male gender of the infant were all independently associated with an increased risk of infant mortality. The gender of the infant has an impact on mortality.

Life expectancy at birth in the UK has reached its highest recorded level in both sexes. A newborn baby boy could expect to live 77.7 years and a newborn baby girl 81.9 years if mortality rates remain the same as they were in 2007–9. Females continue to live longer than males; there is evidence that this gap is closing. Although both sexes have shown annual improvements in life expectancy at birth, over the past 27 years the gap has narrowed from 6.0 years to 4.2 years. Based on mortality rates in 1980–2, 26 per cent of newborn males would die before age 65, but this had reduced to 15 per cent based on 2007–9 rates. The equivalent figures for newborn females were 16 per cent in 1980–2 and 10 per cent in 2007–9 (Office for National Statistics, 2010)

There is a vast amount of data available on the poor state of men's health when compared with women's. Table 3.6 outlines some of those inequalities.

Mortality in males is greater at all ages. From 1 year to 14 years the higher mortality rates are in boys who are more likely to die from:

- poisoning and injury
- motor vehicle accidents
- fire and flames
- accidental drowning and submersion.

Most suicides now occur in young men. In men aged less than 35 years suicide is the most common cause of death. In a number of instances suicide is very often an outcome of a complex web of experiences and circumstances, as opposed to a self-contained event.

Wilkins (2010) notes that there are many factors associated with suicide, including:

- Social circumstances
- Biological vulnerability

Table 3.6   Some data comparing certain health outcomes for men and women

- Men are twice as likely as women both to develop, and to die from, the 10 most common cancers affecting both sexes; 70% of men are more likely to die from cancers that affect both sexes
- Men are significantly more likely than women to be overweight or obese and as such are much more likely than women to suffer from the consequences of overweight and obesity including cancer, coronary heart disease and metabolic syndrome; 41% of men and 32% of women are overweight
- Male death rates from circulatory disease are 300 per 100 000 and for women this equates to 190 per 100 000
- 33% of men compared with 16% of women are drinking at a potentiality harmful level
- Three times as many men as women die from suicide; 76% of those who kill themselves are men
- Pedestrian accidents are the leading cause of accidental death and serious injury to children. Boys are twice as likely to be killed or seriously injured in this way than girls
- More sudden infant deaths occur in boys
- Men are much less likely to visit their GP than women; men visit the GP 20% less than women. Under the age of 45, men visit their GP only half as often as women. It is only among elderly people that the gap narrows significantly and even then women see their GP measurably more frequently than men
- Despite the much higher prevalence of overweight and obesity in men, men are massively under-represented in weight management programmes in primary care. Men are also much less likely to have their weight routinely recorded by their GP
- Chlamydia infection is equally prevalent in both sexes but, during the first full year of the National Chlamydia Screening Programme, 13 times as many women were screened and treated as men
- The National Bowel Cancer Screening Programme achieves a much lower take-up among men
- 16% of men in professional work smoke compared with 27% who are employed in manual occupations

Source: adapted from the Men's Health Forum (2011).

- Mental heath problems
- Life events
- Access to means of support.

Women also have serious health problems that are gender specific. Employing an unrefined analytical approach that compares men's health with women's health can mask inequalities for both men and women. Women have more morbidity from poorer mental health, particularly that related to anxiety and depressive disorders. Psychosocial health in women is strongly influenced by socioeconomic status. Some lone mothers have particularly poor psychosocial wellbeing. O'Connell et al (2007) report that women are nearly twice as likely to experience bullying as men, with 10.7 per cent of women compared with 5.8 per cent of men having had this experience.

Women earn less at work than men do and they are over-represented in low paid jobs and part-time employment. Regardless of the growing numbers of women in the workforce, Fine-Davis (2004) in a four-country study of working men and women with at least one child aged less than 6 revealed that women carried out considerably more of the domestic and childcare tasks in the home.

Women can be a minority group whose needs are often overlooked.

Ethnicity and inequality

The reasons for health inequalities among black and minority ethnic groups are, as for other groups, related to a number of factors. However, a number of black and minority ethnic groups face higher rates of poverty than white British groups, with regard to income, benefits use, unemployment, lacking basic necessities and area deprivation (Parliamentary Office of Science and Technology, 2007). A reminder is needed to reiterate that ethnicity is a complex subject and intersects with other ways of defining a person's identity such as religion or language (Burton et al, 2008); it has links with definition and belonging. Some people identify with ethnic groups at a number of levels; they may see themselves as British, Asian, Indian, Punjabi and Liverpudlian at different times and in different circumstances.

Black and minority ethnic older people are more likely to face a greater level of poverty, live in poorer-quality housing, and have poorer access to benefits and pensions than white older people (John Rowntree Foundation, 2004). The poorer socioeconomic position of black and ethnic minority groups is a central factor in driving ethnic health inequalities. As the proportion of older people from minority groups living in the UK increases (Lievesley, 2010), it is important to understand more about how they experience health and wellbeing in order to provide care that is appropriate and responsive to needs.

Large-scale surveys such as the Health Survey for England demonstrate that black and minority ethnic people as a group are more likely to experience ill-health, and that ill-health among these people starts at a younger age than in the white British community. Bhopal (2007) reports that there is more variation in the rates of some diseases by ethnicity than by other socioeconomic factors. However, patterns of ethnic variation in health are diverse, with interlinked and overlapping factors:

- Some black and minority ethnic groups experience worse health than others, e.g. Pakistani, Bangladeshi and African–Caribbean people report the poorest health, with Indian, East African Asian and black African people reporting the same health as white British individuals, and Chinese people reporting better health.
- Patterns of ethnic inequalities in health vary from one health condition to the next, e.g. black and minority ethnic groups tend to have higher rates of cardiovascular disease than white British people, but lower rates of many cancers.
- Ethnic differences in health vary across age groups, so that the greatest variation by ethnicity is seen among elderly people.
- Ethnic differences in health vary between men and women, as well as between geographical areas.
- Ethnic differences in health may vary between generations, e.g. in some that black and minority ethnic groups, rates of ill-health are worse among those born in the UK than in first-generation migrants.

Coronary heart disease is moderately higher in south Asian groups than the population as a whole, and the poorest groups of Bangladeshis and Pakistanis have the highest rates. Mortality ratios for men and women from Scotland and Ireland are also elevated. Table 3.7 provides examples of ethnic health inequalities.

The Maternity Alliance (2004) has identified that ethnic women are twice as likely to die during or immediately after the birth of a child as white women. Poor-quality maternity care is delivered to a fifth of mothers who die during this period.

Consider the following case. This is a case that raised significant questions about the treatment of black people in psychiatric custody, institutional racism within the NHS and the dangers of restraint. It also raised questions about the overdiagnosis of severe mental illness in black people with mental health problems. A number of recommendations were made after Mr Bennett's death; look these up.

Case study 3.4

Mr David Bennett was an African–Caribbean man born in Jamaica in 1960, who came to the UK in 1968 to join his family. He was a Rastafarian. Mr Bennett developed mental health problems and suffered from schizophrenia.

He had been receiving treatment for his mental illness for approximately 18 years before the date of his death. On that evening Mr David Bennett had been in an incident with another patient who was white. During that incident each man struck out at the other. Mr Bennett was also the recipient of repeated racist abuse from the other patient. After this incident, he was moved to another ward.

While in that ward he hit a nurse. He was then restrained by a number of nurses and a struggle developed. He was taken to the floor and placed in a prone position, face down, on the floor. During the prolonged struggle that then continued he collapsed and died. The inquiry into Mr Bennett's death returned a verdict of accidental death aggravated by neglect.

Table 3.7   Some examples of ethnic health inequalities

Cardiovascular disease

Those men born in south Asia are 50% more likely to have a heart attack or angina than men in the general population. Bangladeshis have the highest rates of heart attack or angina, followed by Pakistanis, then Indians and other south Asians. In contrast, men born in the Caribbean are 50% more likely to die of stroke than the general population, but they have much lower mortality from coronary heart disease. Risk factors such as smoking, high blood pressure, obesity and cholesterol fail to account for all these ethnic variations, and there is debate about how much they can be explained by socioeconomic factors. Biological differences between ethnic groups may explain this phenomenon

Cancer

Generally, cancer rates tend to be lower in black and minority ethnic groups. For lung cancer, mortality rates are lower in people from south Asia, the Caribbean and Africa; this equates to lower levels of smoking. The highest mortality is found in people from Ireland and Scotland. Mortality from breast cancer is lower for migrant women than for women born in England and Wales

Mental health

Ethnic differences in mental health are contentious. Most of the data are based on treatment rates, demonstrating that black and minority ethnic people are much more likely to receive a diagnosis of mental illness than white British people. Studies indicate up to seven times higher rates of new diagnosis of psychosis among African–Caribbean people than among white British people. However, surveys on the occurrence of mental illness in the community reveal smaller ethnic differences. There is evidence of ethnic differences in risk factors that impact before a patient comes into contact with the health services, e.g. discrimination, social exclusion and urban living. There is also evidence of differences in treatment. African–Caribbean and African people are more likely to enter psychiatric care through the criminal justice system than through contact with the health services. Some researchers suggest that psychiatrists diagnose potential symptoms of mental illness differently depending on the ethnicity of the patient

Source: adapted from the Parliamentary Office of Science and Technology (2007).

Addressing health inequalities

A society that strives to ensure equality has to recognise the equal worth of each person, as indicated in human rights principles; it is sensitive to both outcomes and opportunities, and recognises the necessary role of institutions (including health- and social care institutions) in removing barriers and ensuring that opportunities to succeed are real. An equal society seeks equality in the freedoms that people have to lead a rewarding and enjoyable life.

Equality is not only about minority groups; policies produced that address or aim to address inequality must be about helping disadvantaged groups, and as such are not just of interest to minorities. Inequality brings with it considerable economic and social costs that are endured by the whole of society. It should be noted that not all deprived groups are minorities, e.g. women make up more than half the population. Older people are a minority group, but most of us will, when we age, become part of that minority. In life, circumstances change and our situation could at any point turn us into one of a minority – if we were to become disabled. Inequality concerns all of us.

The Equalities Review (2007) defines an equal society as one that protects and promotes equal, real freedom and substantive opportunity to live in ways that people value and would choose, so that everyone can flourish. An equal society accepts people's different needs, their situations and goals, and eliminates barriers that restrict what people can do and can be. Nurses are a part of that society and as such should strive to uphold the tenets of equality and fairness.

Health inequalities come about as differences in health status driven by inequalities in society. Health is a complex concept and is shaped by a variety of factors, e.g. lifestyle, material wealth, educational attainment, job security, housing conditions, psychosocial stress, discrimination and the health services. The Parliamentary Office of Science and Technology (2007) suggest that health inequalities represent the cumulative effect of these factors over the course of a person's life. These inequalities can be passed on from one generation to the next through maternal influences on baby and child development.

The reasons for health inequalities are various: there is a link between poverty and illness and the health of those who are worse off; there are differences between those who are better off and those who are poor; there is a health gap between those who are worse off in society and those who are better off; and advantages and disadvantages exist right across the social spectrum. The Health Development Agency (2004) has identified three broad ranges of causes of health inequalities:

- Poor health of poor people
- Health gaps
- Health gradient.

A continued improvement in the constituents of socioeconomic provision occurred from 1970 to 2000: average income rose and the proportion of the population with educational qualifications and in higher non-manual groups also rose. Nevertheless, policies that had been devised to produce the above results failed to reduce inequalities in socioeconomic position. In recent years, understanding about the social determinants, or the causes, of ill-health has deepened (DH, 2009). There is evidence of the following:

- The conditions in which people are born, grow, live, work and age being responsible for health inequalities
- Early childhood, in particular impacts on health and disadvantage throughout life
- The cumulative effects of hazards and disadvantage through life producing a finely graded social patterning of disease and ill-health
- Negative health outcomes being associated with the stress that people experience and the levels of control that they have over their lives, which are socially graded
- Mental well-being having a profound role in shaping physical health and contributing to life chances, as well as being important to individuals and as a societal measure.

Objectives have been set by the Government to tackle the major determinants of health and health inequalities (Wanless, 2004). Understanding what the determinants are that have the potential to influence health outcomes can help address and reduce health inequalities, e.g. being aware of the need to raise educational standards, improve living standards and reduce risk factors (e.g. smoking and obesity).

Improving the health of poorer groups, reducing the health differences between poorer and better-off groups, and raising the levels of health across the socioeconomic hierarchy to those closer to those at the top must be given careful consideration at a local and national level (Graham, 2004b).

Tackling health inequalities requires a commitment to longer time scales. Essential components in delivering reductions in health inequalities, such as community development and capacity building, partnership working, professional development and local institution building, need ongoing investment and time to mature; they need commitment from all health-care professionals including nurses. Regular structural change, staffing shortages, and fragmented and short-term funding streams make improvements harder.

The Health Select Committee (2009) recognise that long-term outcomes of interventions, including those for health, are complex to evaluate and measure. Isolating the impact of a particular mechanism or approach over time is particularly challenging. Political cycles are short and there is a culture of demonstrating quick impact; these challenges and longer time horizons can mean that taking action is a challenge.

Improving the health of poor people requires concerted efforts to achieve positive changes in the poorest of groups. Social conditions and life chances need to be improved; changes must be made in risk-taking behaviours. Attention needs to be focused on the groups of people who have missed out in the general rise in living standards and life expectancy, e.g. the unskilled manual group where life expectancy has yet to reach the level achieved by the professional groups. Social inclusion and regeneration of communities, which may help to ensure life chances and health opportunities of poorer groups, should be promoted.

Targeting specific groups, such as disadvantaged groups including those who are mentally ill or with a learning disability, with specific targets to achieve positive health outcomes, may have an impact on health outcomes. What must be remembered is that health inequalities affect every member of society; they do not and should not concern only those who suffer most – disadvantaged individuals.

There is a health gap between the best off and the worst off. Addressing health gaps means that the health of the poorest needs to be raised the fastest. In an attempt to raise the health of the poorest fastest, there is a need to improve the health of the poorest at a rate that outstrips that of the wider population. Evaluation of policy imposed to reduce the health gaps must demonstrate that the rate of improvement in disadvantaged groups is greater than in the comparison (the advantaged) group. A faster rate of improvement is the vital measure of effectiveness.

At each step up the socioeconomic ladder health improves – health gradients occur. There are health gradients associated with disability and chronic illness as well as most major causes of death, such as coronary heart disease and lung cancer (Health Development Agency, 2004).

The founding principle of the World Health Organization (WHO) is that the highest standard of attainable health is a fundamental right (World Health Assembly, 1998). The standards of health of the better off should be attainable by all. This is implied in the WHO's Constitution (WHO, 1948): there should be no distinction for race, religion, political belief, economic or social condition – good health for all.

Conclusions

Every person is an individual and this therefore extends to every patient. The nurse must respect and recognise the diversity of the population. The provision of culturally competent care will promote equality, thereby enhancing the quality of nursing care.

The nurse can and must act in such a way as to ensure that the rights of individuals and groups are respected and not compromised. The values, customs and beliefs of the patient should be given due consideration and the care that the nurse provides ought to be sensitive to the diverse needs of the patient being cared for.

Discrimination and disadvantage have the powerful potential to hinder the nurse's aim – to provide care – and can lead to inequality. Respecting and valuing the diversity of the people with whom you work and for whom patients you care will help to ensure a quality service.

This chapter provided definitions of the following key terms:

- Culture
- Ethnicity
- Race
- Gender.

It was acknowledged that when attempting to define these terms difficulties arose. They are often fluid terms and can change depending on the context in which they are being used.

The UK is a multicultural society and care provision should be built around the individual needs of individual patients, acknowledging that some aspects of nursing care may be affected and even determined by issues such as religion or ethnic background. A one-size-fits-all approach does not work and if used will result in inequality and discrimination.

An overview of eight different groups was presented in Table 3.2, including information that the nurse may find helpful when providing culturally competent nursing care. Issues surrounding death and dying, dietary requirements and specific material relating to the provision of nursing for these groups were provided in outline format.

Since 1911 the most common method of measuring inequalities in the UK has been through occupation; a similar method is still used today. Despite all of the advances in nursing care and medical technology, there are still members of our society who are treated unequally with respect to health-care provision. There are many factors that have an effect on health outcomes; the most appropriate approach to begin to address these problems is to devise methods that recognise the complexities of the causes and the diversity of the population. Diverse solutions as opposed to identical approaches are advocated, seeking to engage the local population to address local needs.

Social position is seen by some researchers as the basis for health. There are various key determinants that interact and result in good health and wellbeing. Inequality and socioeconomic position will determine health outcomes. Inequalities were discussed and highlighted. The nurse is in an ideal position to identify and address the inequalities, working not in isolation but with others, considering the wider context.

Much has been achieved over the years to address the inequalities seen and felt in health care, but much more needs to be done to ensure that all members of our society are treated with respect, dignity and compassion.

Activities

Attempt the following 10 questions that are related to inequity, discrimination and inclusion and vulnerable people to test your knowledge. The answers can be found at the back of this book, in the chapter called 'Activity Answers'.

1. Equal opportunities means the following:
   a. Giving preference to some people
   b. Giving preference to gays and lesbians
   c. Giving preference to people with a disability
   d. Preferential treatment is exactly what equal opportunity awareness seeks to avoid

2. It is unlawful to ask about a disability at an interview:
   a. No
   b. Yes
   c. Only if the interviewee offers this information
   d. Only if the interviewee's doctors has given permission

3. The most common cause of death in men under 35 years is:
   a. Testicular cancer
   b. Prostate cancer
   c. Diabetes mellitus
   d. Suicide

4. Understanding the determinants of health can help to:
   a. Address and reduce health inequalities
   b. Enhance nurses' pay
   c. Provide data for the census
   d. Provide a baseline for prospective energy consumption

5. The NMC's code of professional conduct (2008) states that you must:
   a. Treat people as individuals, respecting their dignity
   b. Not discriminate against those in your care
   c. Treat people with kindness and consideration
   d. All the above

6. Buddhism is:
   a. A way of life
   b. A political system
   c. A branch of the Christian religion
   d. A system used to differentiate between people

7. Which day of the week is called Shabbat?
   a. 5th
   b. 7th
   c. 6th
   d. 1st

8. What is Ramadan?
   a. The holy book of Muslims
   b. The period when fasting has ended
   c. A month where Muslims fast from dawn to dusk
   d. The period when Muslims can drink but not eat

9. Life expectancy at birth in the UK has:
   a. Reached its highest recorded level in both sexes
   b. Declined

    c. Reached a plateau

    d. Improved

10. The pressures on health and social services provided for older people will:

    a. Be reduced

    b. Increase

    c. Stay the same

    d. All of the above

References

Akhtar S (2002) Nursing with dignity: Part 8: Islam. *Nursing Times* **98**(16): 40–42.

Anemone RL (2011) *Race and Human Diversity. A Biocultural Approach*. Boston, MA: Prentice Hall.

Baxter C (2002) Nursing with dignity: Part 5: Rastafarianism. *Nursing Times* **98**(13): 42–43.

Bhopal RS (2007) *Race, Ethnicity and Health in Multicultural Societies*. Oxford: Oxford University Press

Bradley H (2007) *Gender*. Cambridge: Polity.

Burton J, Nandi A, Platt L (2008) *Who are the UK's Minority Ethnic Groups? Issues of Identification and Measurement in a Longitudinal Study*. Colchester. Institute for Social and Economic Research, University of Essex.

Christmas M (2002) Nursing with dignity: Part 3: Christianity I. *Nursing Times* **98**(11): 37–39.

Cesarean SK (2010) Culture and ethnicity. In: Daniels R, Grendell RN, Wilkins FR (eds), *Nursing Fundamentals: Caring and Clinical Decision Making*, 2nd edn. New York: Delmar, pp 97–127.

Collins A (2002) Nursing with dignity: Part 1: Judaism. *Nursing Times* **98**(9): 33–35.

Commission on Social Determinants of Health (2008) *CSDH Final Report: Closing the Gap in a Generation: Health Equity Through Action on the Social Determinants of Health*. Geneva: World Health Organization.

Craig R, Mindell J (2007) *Health Survey for England 2005*. Vols 1–4: *The health of older people*. Available at: www.ic.nhs.uk/statistics-and-data-collections/health-and-lifestyles-related-surveys/health-survey-for-england/health-survey-for-england-2005:-health-of-older-people-[ns] (accessed May 2011).

Department of Health (2001) *Valuing People: A new strategy for learning disability for the 21st century*. London: The Stationery Office.

Department of Health (2008) *End of Life Care Strategy. Promoting high quality care for all adults at the end of life*. London: Department of Health.

Department of Health (2009) *Tackling Health Inequalities: 10 Years On – A Review of Developments in Tackling Health Inequalities in England over the last 10 years*. London: Department of Health.

Department of Health (2010) *Healthy Lives, Healthy People: Our strategy for public health in England*. London: Department of Health.

Donkin A, Lee YH, Toson B (2002) *Implications of Changes in the UK Social and Occupational Classifications in 2001 for Vital Statistics*. Population Trends 107. London: National Statistics. Available at: www.statistics.gov.uk/articles/population_trends/sococclassifications_pt107.pdf (accessed May 2011).

Emerson E, Baines S (2010) *Health Inequalities and People with Learning Disabilities in the UK: 2010*. London: Department of Health.

Emerson E, Hatton C (2007) Poverty, Socio-economic position, social capital and the health of children and adolescents with intellectual disabilities in Britain: a replication. *Journal of Intellectual Disability Research* **51**: 866–874.

Equalities Review (2007) *Fairness and Freedom: The final report of the equalities review*. London: Equalities Review.

Fine-Davies M (2004) *Fathers and Mothers: Dilemmas of the work–life balance: A comparative study in four European countries*. London: Kluwer Academic.

Friedli L (2009) *Mental Health, Resilience and Inequalities*. Geneva: World Health Organization. Available at: www.euro.who.int/document/e92227.pdf (accessed May 2011).

Giger JN, Davidhizar RE (2007) *Transcultural Nursing: Assessment and Intervention*, 5th edn. St Louis, MO: Mosby.

Gill BK (2002) Nursing with dignity: Part 6: Sikhism. *Nursing Times* **98**(14): 39–41.

Graham H (2004a) Social determinants and their unequal distribution: Clarifying policy understandings. *Millbank Quarterly* **82**: 1010–1124.

Graham H (2004b) Tackling health inequalities in England: Remedying health disadvantage, narrowing gaps or reducing health gradients. *Journal of Social Policy* **33**: 115–131.

Graham H (2005) Socioeconomic inequalities in health: Patterns, determinants and challenges. *Journal of Applied Research on Intellectual Disabilities* **18**: 101–111.

Graham H, Power C (2004) *Childhood Disadvantage and Adult Health: A life-course framework*. London: Health Development Agency.

Health Development Agency (2004) *Health Inequalities: Concepts, frameworks and policy*. London: HDA.

Health Select Committee (2009) *Health Inequalities. Third Report of Session 2008–09* HC286-I. London: The Stationery Office.

Health Survey for England (2005) *Health of Older People*, vol 4: *Mental Health and Wellbeing*. Leeds: National Health Service.

House of Commons (2009) *The Government's Response to the Health Select Committee Report on Health Inequalities*. London: The Stationery Office.

John Rowntree Foundation (2004) *Black and Minority Ethnic Older People's Views on Research Findings*. York: John Rowntree Foundation.

Jootun D (2002) Nursing with dignity: Part 7: Hinduism. *Nursing Times* **98**(15): 38–40.

Kerr M (2004) Improving the general health of people with learning disabilities, *Advances in Psychiatric Treatment* **10**: 200–206.

Lievesley N (2010) *The Future Ageing of the Ethnic Minority Population of England and Wales*. London: Runnymede Trust/Centre for Policy on Ageing.

Marmot M (2004) Social causes of social inequalities in health. In: Anand S, Fabienne P, Sen A (eds), *Public Health, Ethics, and Equity*. Oxford: Oxford University Press.

Marmot Review (2010) *Fair Society healthy Lives*. The Marmot Review [online]. Available at: www.ucl.ac.uk/marmotreview (accessed May 2011).

Marsh I, Keating M, Punch S, Harden J (2009) *Sociology: Making Sense of Society*, 4th edn. Harlow: Prentice Hall.

Maternity Alliance (2004) *Experiences of Maternity Services: Muslim Women's Perspectives*. London: Maternity Alliance.

Men's Health Forum (2011) *Lives Too Short* [online]. Available at: www.menshealthforum.org.uk/21734-why-are-mens-lives-too-short (accessed May 2011).

Michael J (2008) *Healthcare for All. Report of the Independent Inquiry into Access to Healthcare for People with Learning Disabilities*. London: Department of Health.

Mitchell C (2006) Pedestrian mobility and safety: a key to independence for older people topics. *Geriatric Rehabilitation* **22**: 45–52.

Mold F, Fitzpatrick JM, Roberts JD (2005) Caring for minority ethnic older people in nursing care homes. *British Journal of Nursing* **14**: 601–606.

National Statistics (2005) The *National Statistics Socio-economic Classification. User Manual*. London: National Statistics. Available at: www.statistics.gov.uk/methods_quality/ns_sec/downloads/NS-SEC_User_2005.pdf (accessed May 2011).

NHS Scotland (2004) *People with Learning Disabilities in Scotland: Health needs assessment report*. Glasgow: NHS Scotland.

NHS Scotland (2011) *Improving the Physical Health of People with Mental Illness: Mapping and review of physical health improvement activities for adults (16–65) experiencing severe and enduring mental illness*. Edinburgh: NHS Scotland.

Northcott N (2002) Nursing with dignity: Part 2: Buddhism. *Nursing Times* **98**(10): 36–38.

Nursing and Midwifery Council (2008) *Code of Professional Conduct. Standards for conduct, performance and ethics*. London: NMC.

O'Connell P, Calvert E, Watson D (2007) *Bullying in the Workplace: Survey reports: Report to the Department of Environment, Trade and Employment*. London: Department of Environment, Trade and Employment.

Office for National Statistics (2010) *Life Expectancy*. London: ONC. Available at: www.statistics.gov.uk/cci/nugget.asp?id=168 (accessed May 2011).

Parliamentary Office of Science and Technology (2007) Postnote. *Ethnicity and Health* **27**: 1–4. Available at: www.parliament.uk/documents/post/postpn276.pdf (accessed May 2011).

Papadopoulos I (2002) Nursing with dignity: Part 4: Christianity II. *Nursing Times* **98**(12): 36–37.

Peate I (2007) Chaperoning guidelines. *British Journal of Healthcare Assistants* **1**: 406–410.

Piachaud D, Bennett F, Nazroo J, Popay J (2009) *Report of Task Group 9: Social Inclusion and Social Mobility. Task Group Submission to the Marmot Review* [online]. Available at: www.ucl.ac.uk/gheg/marmotreview (accessed May 2011).

Ratcliffe P (2004) *Race, Ethnicity and Culture*. Maidenhead: Open University Press.

Rayman SM (2009) Health assessment. In: Daniels R (ed.), *Nursing Fundamentals: Caring and Clinical Decision Making*. New York: Thompson, pp 545–650.

Reid I (1977) *Social Class Difference in Britain*. London: Open Books.

Registrar General (1913) *Registrar General's 74th Annual Report 1911.* London: Registrar General's Office.

Ross J (1952) *The National Health Service in Great Britain*. Oxford: Oxford University Press.

Simpson J (2002) Nursing with dignity: Part 9: Jehovah's Witnesses. *Nursing Times* **98**(17): 36–37.

Smart A, Tutton R, Martin P, Ellison GTH, Ashcroft R (2008) The standardization of race and ethnicity in biomedical editorials and UK biobanks *Social Studies of Science* **83**: 407–423.

Smith CE (2006) The critically ill patient. in: Alexander MF, Fawcett JN Runciman PJ (eds), *Nursing Practice: Hospital and home: The adult*, 3rd edn. Edinburgh: Churchill Livingstone, pp 989–1010.

Stewart K (2009) A scar on the soul of Britain: Child poverty and disadvantage under New Labour. In: Hills J, Sefton T Stewart K (eds), *Towards a More Equal Society? Poverty, inequality and policy since 1997*. Bristol: Policy Press.

Sustainable Development Commission (2010) *Sustainable Development: The Key to Tackling Health Inequalities*. London: Sustainable Development Commission.

Waldfogel J (2004) *Social Mobility, Life Chances, and the Early Years*. CASE Paper 8. London: London School of Economics.

Wanless D (2004) *Securing Good Health for the Whole Population: Final Report*. London: HMSO.

Wilkins D (2010) *Untold Problems. A Review of the Essential Issues in the Mental Health of Men and Boys*. London: Men's Health Forum.

White C, van Galen F, Chow YH (2003) Trends in social class differences in mortality by cause 1986 to 2000. Health *Statistics Quarterly* **20**: 25–37.

Wohland P, Rees P, Norman P, Boden P, Jasinska M (2010) *Ethnic Population Projections for the UK and Local Areas, 2001–2051*. Leeds: University of Leeds.

World Health Assembly (1998) *World Health Declaration, Health-For-All Policy for the 21st Century*. WHA. 51.7. Geneva: World Health Assembly.

World Health Organization (1948) *Constitution of the World Health Organization*. Geneva: WHO.

4

Partnership Working, Roles and Responsibilities

Aims and objectives

The aim of this chapter is to offer insight and understanding into partnership working across the National Health Service, social services and voluntary and community sector.

At the end of the chapter you will be able to:

1. Understand the importance of effective partnership working and collaboration
2. Explore the meaning of partnership working
3. Describe how partnership working can enhance health and wellbeing
4. Discuss the potential barriers and possible solutions to effective partnership working
5. Begin to apply the concepts discussed to the practice setting
6. Appreciate the Nursing and Midwifery Council's requirements of student nurses

The term 'partnership working' can mean many things to many people in many situations (Glasby and Dickinson, 2008). It can mean effective partnership working with the person being cared for, or partnership working with the NHS trust with which you are working on placement. Tait and Shah (2007) note that there are a number of terms that may be used synonymously when discussing and applying partnership working – joined-up working, joint working and cross-cutting working. Throughout the literature and within policy and practice, partnership is referred to using an assortment of different terms (Dickinson, 2008). Leathard (1994) identified over 52 meanings that signify and refer to partnership as a terminological quagmire. In Table 4.1 Horner and Simpson (2011) discuss three interrelated concepts that should be considered. The concepts are used interchangeably but are different (McKimm et al, 2008).

Defining the concept partnership working can be difficult. Huxham and Vangen (2005) provide a useful definition:

> Any situation in which people are working across organisational boundaries towards some positive end.

This definition is helpful because it resonates with the ways in which nurses work: across and within organisational boundaries. Nurses always have the health and wellbeing of the person for whom they are caring at the heart of all they do, with the intention of providing positive outcomes.

The Student's Guide to Becoming a Nurse, Second Edition. Ian Peate.
© 2012 John Wiley & Sons, Ltd. Published 2012 by John Wiley & Sons, Ltd.

Table 4.1 Interrelated concepts and partnership working

Concept	Description
Cooperation	Often cooperation implies assistance, support and team working. In working environments it is sometimes assumed that cooperative working environments will mean mutual respect for all parties
Collaboration	There is a political imperative to ensure that partnership working delivers, e.g. collaborating with the enemy. From a more positive perspective it may mean working in a unified manner, as a team or forming alliances
Partnership	There are legal overtones associated with this, e.g. working as partner in a firm or company, working together. Whittington (2003) sees partnerships as an activity or relationship that occurs on a number of levels. This relationship has to be maintained and should be reviewed. When used in everyday life the term is usually used with positive connotations in respect to relationships and family

Source: adapted from Horner and Simpson (2011).

Think

Make a list of the people who you think nurses work with within their organisation and external to their organisation, whilst compiling your list consider what might be meant by 'organisational boundaries'.

Most nurses in the UK are employed by the NHS (one organisation) and they work with a number of people members of the multidisciplinary team in that organisation, e.g. paramedics, doctors, physiotherapists, podiatrists, biochemists, and speech and language therapist. Other people with whom who nurses may work in a collaborative manner, but who are external to the NHS (other organisations), include those who work in social services and the voluntary and community sector. This includes social workers, workers in the youth and criminal justice system, teachers, hospice staff and high street pharmacists (the commercial sector). Other organisations may include those that focus on a specific health-related activity, e.g. smoking cessation, safer sex and drinking alcohol wisely.

The Department of Health and Department of Communities and Local Government (2010) have noted that the public want health and social services that are joined up; when this fails to happen a sense of frustration emerges. It is important that integrated services are built around the needs of individuals and not the those of the institutions offering them. Integrated working is essential to developing a personalised health and care system that reflects the health and care needs of the people whom it serves. It is expected that the NHS and local government should work together to integrate resources with the aim of enhancing quality, productivity and efficiency. The impact of world recession on the UK public finances has questioned past approaches to health- and social care unification. Unprecedented productivity and efficiency changes face both social care and the NHS. Changes have to be made in order to make resources go further across organisational boundaries and also within them. The interdependency of NHS and social care resources will emerge forcefully, bringing with it challenges for how these two services work with each other. Humphries (2011) notes that, for closer integration to work, it is important to understand the reciprocal relationship between health- and social care spending.

Case study 4.1

Rhiannon Carrick is a school nurse working in an inner city school. She delivers a variety of services such as providing health and sex education within the school, carrying out developmental screening, undertaking health interviews and administering immunisation programmes. She is employed by the local primary care trust. Given recent concerns about HIV and younger people, the education of students and the content of personal health and social education, Rhiannon has decided to arrange a day's activity concerning sexual health and is now starting to ask a number of external agencies to help her on the day.

What external agencies do you think Rhiannon will invite to take part in the day?

What roles will they be asked to play?

Do they include people from health- and social care sectors, the independent sector, the voluntary and community sector and the commercial sector?

The changing burden of disease, increasing patient expectations and the rise in emergency hospital admissions will see new partnerships between the NHS and other providers of care, e.g. independent providers who will be working to transform new treatments and devise new models of care. There will be an increased need to focus on the prevention of admissions, and the need to speed up treatment and encourage appropriate and timely discharge. There are growing numbers of people with multiple long-term conditions; their needs cross the NHS and social care settings. The NHS has to move from a reactive acute care provider, with an emphasis on episodic encounters for people who use the service, to one that incorporates a proactive wellness service using more widespread preventive approaches.

According to Humphries and Curry (2011) there are three benefits to the integration of social care and health care:

- Better outcomes for those who use services
- Making limited resources go further
- Improve people's experience of health care and support.

Other providers

Other care providers can and are willing and able to enter into greater collaborations to help local NHS commissioners and providers enhance the standard and quality of care. Independent providers often work with the NHS in a number of ways, including the provision of health services as part of a local NHS joint venture. Every available route should be pursued in order to give people the quality of treatment and care that they are entitled to expect.

Case study 4.2

Miss Annabel Cohen is an 83-year-old woman with type 2 diabetes, hypothyroidism, arthritis and renal failure. For the last year Miss Cohen has been at home under the care of the community matron. Although she had limited mobility, she was mentally alert and able to communicate her needs to all those involved in her care. Her family lived abroad, and she relied on carers and a good network of friends to assist her with all activities of living; her needs were regularly assessed and evaluated by the community matron.

Miss Cohen's condition severely deteriorated. The GP and community matron made a joint visit and Miss Cohen was encouraged to be admitted to hospital, but she refused (Miss Cohen had previously made an advanced decision not to go into hospital if her condition deteriorated), stating that she wished to die at home.

Table 4.2   Working together – the role of the independent sector and the NHS

- Provision of specialist services outside NHS service provision
- Development of new technologies, models of care and clinical programmes
- Offering and delivering cost efficiencies for the NHS
- New methods of delivering health care in response to new policy developments
- Offering care and choice to people with health care conditions (i.e. long term conditions)
- Relieving the NHS of backlogs, providing capacity relief
- Offering bespoke health-care solutions for specific local populations
- Providing advanced level skills training for NHS staff, patients and carers
- Offering in-depth knowledge and expertise

Source: adapted from Poole and Wallis (2009).

Can you think of the services that Miss Cohen may require at home now that her condition has deteriorated and in the light of the advanced decision? Did you ensure that you included carers in your list?

The independent sector is made up of a combination of not-for-profit and for-profit providers. These include international and national organisations, as well as a broad base of independent business delivering a wide range of care packages to NHS patients in a number of settings, including hospitals, community, primary care and the person's own home (Poole and Wallis, 2009). Table 4.2 provides an overview of the role of the independent sector and the NHS.

The voluntary and community sector, at local and national levels, has important and meaningful contributions to make to partnership working. Sometimes the views and experience of those being cared for can be expressed more effectively through voluntary organisations. Often the health service fails to acknowledge the valuable role of the voluntary sector, not just as an advocate, but also in providing a range of services for patients and carers. It has already been demonstrated that effective partnerships can be formed among the NHS, social services and the independent sector; there are also useful partnerships involving the voluntary sector. Coe and Barlow (2010) suggest that the voluntary sector is usually independent of the statutory sector, which is usually reflected in the way that it works and its vision. This sector is often small (but not always), locally based, flexible and easy to access. It is sometimes easier for the voluntary sector to connect with hard-to-reach communities (these may include people who are asylum seekers, homeless people, gypsies and travellers, and people with mental health problems). The services provided by the NHS may seem to some people unattractive because of their statutory powers and legal responsibilities. The voluntary sector, although still having to obey the law, acts outside the statutory framework and is independent of Government control. The work of the voluntary sector often focuses on the following:

- Delivering services
- Advocating and or lobbying on behalf of community causes
- Facilitating international, community and economic development
- Advancing religious faith and practice
- Raising funds
- Providing financial support to other voluntary sector organisations.

The voluntary sector may be able to provide resources, expertise and local knowledge to service provision for all (adult, child, mental health and learning disability), which the NHS may not be able to supply. Milne et al (2004) suggest that these features are valued by service users. Services offered may include counselling services, a campaigning role and the provision of information in relation to:

- safer sex
- safer drug and alcohol use

- education
- welfare benefits
- housing and employment opportunities.

There are some voluntary services that provide specialised treatment for young people about their mental health; they act as an advocacy service and also help people overcome the stigma and social exclusion that can be attached to some mental health labels (Lester et al, 2008). As well as filling gaps in specialist service provision that the NHS cannot offer, the voluntary sector, according to Tait and Shah (2007), can provide a means by which hard-to-engage groups can access services as well as providing meaningful community engagement.

People with mental health problems and those with learning disability and their carers are among the most socially excluded and disadvantaged groups in society. They have limited opportunities to engage in their local communities with regard to employment, education, leisure and social activities (Office of the Deputy Prime Minister, 2004). In order to address these complex social and mental health needs will require appropriate responses from a number of agencies which will include the voluntary sector.

Case study 4.3

Mr Arthnott, a 68-year-old man, was admitted to a medical ward after a fall at home; he was already known to community mental health services. After admission to the ward he was referred to the mental health liaison team for assessment of his confusion. Following a conversation with this son, it appeared that the patient should have been prescribed memory drugs, of which the hospital had no knowledge. The liaison nurse who knew Mr Arthnott was able to clarify and provide information about the medications that he usually took; as a result of communication with the liaison nurse these were prescribed.

How can the liaison nurse, the hospital, the patient and the patient's carer work together to ensure a timely and appropriate discharge?

What services do you think Mr Arthnott may need at home?

Engaging the voluntary sector in addressing complex health and social needs of diverse populations can help vulnerable people to negotiate their way through the often complex bureaucracies and multiple agencies that provide care, e.g. people with long-term conditions. For positive outcomes, well-coordinated, seamless services are required from the outset. Table 4.3 provides insight into the possible benefits of the voluntary sector.

Table 4.3   Possible benefits of voluntary sector involvement in partnership working

- Complements the skills of NHS and sectors within it
- Offers practical help and financial advice to people concerning housing and welfare benefits
- Provides an advocacy and campaigning role with aim of improving services
- Helps to combat social exclusion by encouraging local opportunities for employment, education and training, leisure and social networks
- Has the ability to engage hard-to-reach groups
- Uses a person-centred approach to service delivery and responses to service user needs
- Is trusted by people as a result of its independent and advocacy role
- Provides services that are service user led or managed by the users of services
- Can have a positive impact on health and social inequalities

Other providers do not work in isolation when addressing local needs. A local strategic partnership (LSP) brings together important agencies and organisations that work together to identify the long-term priorities needed to sustain and improve an area. Through community planning, the LSP develops a sustainable community strategy where, by working together, key partners can make a big difference. LSPs are made up of many organisations including:

- Local councils
- The police, fire service and health organisations
- Local businesses
- The voluntary and community sector.

Leaders and senior officers represent each of these organisations, ensuring that decisions are made and that the money and resources needed for action are available.

The voluntary sector does and will continue to play an important role in supplementing statutory provision, as well devising innovative and creative responses to ensure that the public receive appropriate and high-quality services. They can, as a result of their close community links and knowledge of local needs, significantly shape national and local policy at a number of levels for service users.

Policy

Collaborative and partnership working is a key concern of government. The Government has proposed new ways of working and has produced two key White Papers – *Equity and Excellence: Liberating the NHS* (Department of Health or DH, 2010a) and *Healthy Lives, Healthy People: Our strategy for public health in England* (DH, 2010b). Both give serious consideration to the important concepts of collaboration and partnership working in ensuring that care at an individual, community and population level is appropriate and effective.

Loveday and Linsley (2011) note that improving the public's health is a key role for all nurses. They acknowledge that this activity does not lie solely in the health domain; it requires a multidisciplinary approach as well as an approach that traverses organisational boundaries. These sentiments are echoed in the tenets of the Nursing and Midwifery Council's Code of Conduct (NMC, 2008). McKimm (2011) asserts that collaborative leadership (and therefore collaborative working) is a key approach to integrating public services such as the NHS where there are complex funding arrangements and increasing accountability. The more joined-up working arrangements there are, the more opportunities as well as challenges will emerge.

Policy-makers have devised and developed a number of approaches for reforming the NHS in the past two decades; in England these included the setting of targets and performance management, regulation and inspection, and choice and competition. The current Government seeks to extend choice and competition and to reduce dependence on targets and performance management as part of their far-reaching programme of reform for the NHS. The aim of this reorganisation is to place the patient at the heart of the NHS and to improve outcomes where, to quote the oft-used refrain, 'nothing about me without me' occurs.

Policy initiatives have been produced to help shape the agenda by successive governments and these incorporated the role of the voluntary sector in delivering health- and social care services with the emphasis on working in partnership with government (and their statutory agencies). Partnership working can be a key way of tackling the complex multifaceted causes of health inequalities. There is a political imperative to ensure that partnership working delivers.

The White Paper *Designed to Care* (Scottish Office, 1997) was the first policy from the then Scottish Office that emphasised the benefits to health improvement from patient focus and community involvement. This was followed in England and Wales by a raft of other policies recognising the value that patients, carers, community members and the wider public play in shaping and implementing services related to health and wellbeing, e.g. *Developing Partnerships in Mental Health* (DH, 1997) and *Making Partnership Work for Patients, Carers and Service Users* (DH, 2004). The policies formulated have emerged from different departments within national government; a departmental cross-cutting approach has been used signalling the Government's support for the significant role that the other sector plays in delivering public services.

Top tips

There are a number of important principles associated with partnership working:

- Openness, trust and honesty between partners
- Agreed shared goals and values
- Regular communication between partners.

The NHS White Paper *Equity and Excellence: Liberating the NHS* (DH 2010a) has set out new roles for local authorities in joining up the commissioning of local NHS services, social care and health improvement. The White Paper brings with it the most significant changes since the inception of the NHS. There are aims to dismantle primary care trusts (PCTs), to create GP consortia and a national commissioning board, and to establish statutory local health and wellbeing boards, led by local authorities, with executive powers to coordinate partnership working and promote integration across health- and social care, children's services, including safeguarding, and the wider local authority agenda. The formation of these boards has not, as yet, been decided on.

In 2000, Victoria Climbié, an 8-year-old child, died and it emerged after this child's death that there were a number of failures at every level and by every organisation that came into contact with Victoria and her family. Services that were provided to Victoria did not work together; instead they were confused and often at conflict with each other. The murder of Victoria led to a public inquiry and resulted in number of changes in child protection policies. Peter Connelly (also known as Baby P) died aged 17 months after being subjected to injuries over an 8-month period inflicted on him by three adults. Another inquiry was held and further recommendations to protect children made. The recommendations called for closer partnership working with organisations and a call was made to ensure that organisational barriers that prevent effective partnership working between health- and social care agencies be removed. A progress report concerning measures in place for the protection of children in England was produced by Lord Laming (2009). Partnership working was made a priority after the Laming Inquiry and the Children Act 2004 for children's services, requiring local public bodies to work together through children's trusts bodies. The Scottish Government (2008) has called for the different agencies that work with children and families to operate more closely in partnership.

Think

Have you been involved in partnerships? Think about these and reflect on if they were a success or not. What would they look like if they were a success, how did you have to work to make the partnership a success? What measures did you use to decide if the partnership was a success or not. Did you come across any difficulties with the partnership? Would you do things differently if so what and why?

Read the following sections of this chapter and compare some of the issues here with your responses to the above.

Benefits of partnership working

The 1999 Health Act places a legal obligation on health- and social care organisations to work together and cooperate with each other in order to improve services, protect the public and improve outcomes. The Act aims to reduce replication of service provision between the various agencies, as well as producing seamless solutions for recipients of services. The Act also includes a need for agencies to be accountable for their actions and omissions.

The National Health Services Act 2006 allows partnership arrangements between NHS partners and local authorities, permitting pooled funds, delegation of commissioning of a service to one lead organisation and integrated provision, where staff, resources and management structures are pooled. Some of these arrangements have been made, and are particularly evident in the areas of learning disability and mental health. This approach enables social and health-care services to be designed and delivered around the needs of users, instead of worrying about the boundaries of the various organisations involved in service provision.

Case study 4.4

People with learning disability need support for their self-care and their families need support to contribute to their care. Self-care includes: 'The actions people take for themselves, their children and their families to stay fit and maintain good physical and mental health; meet social and psychological needs; prevent illness or accidents; care for minor ailments and long-term conditions; and maintain health and wellbeing after an acute illness or discharge from hospital' (DH, 2005).

How can you ensure that people with learning disability and their families are supported in their endeavours to live with a learning disability and a long-term condition?

What services may need to mobilised?

PCTs were legally established statutory bodies that had responsibilities for improving the health of the population, planning, commissioning and delivering services. The PCTs must do this in partnership with local authorities, voluntary agencies and local communities (DH, 2002).

Maslin-Prothero et al (2009) point out that no one organisation, even one as big as the NHS, can meet all the needs of all the people who use it all the time. With economic challenges and the need to manage the long-term demands associated with the increase in chronic disease, the NHS faces increasing challenges (DH, 2008). This is the reason why the NHS is moving towards a plurality of provision based on sound and genuine partnerships with social services and the voluntary and community sector. This move will offer real choice to the people cared for, and services that are equitable and responsive to the diverse needs and preferences of the nation. There are many reasons why partnership work should be advocated; Table 4.4 provides some of these.

There are other benefits associated with partnership working. It will benefit people and their carers and service users by providing them with real alternatives so that they can choose services that best suit their needs, offering them a wider range of services within the community. According to Tait and Shah (2007), professionals can also benefit from partnership working.

The current Government in its White Paper *Equity and Excellence: Liberating the NHS* (DH, 2010a) proposes to devolve commissioning of health care largely to GP commissioning consortia from 2013, and

Table 4.4   Reasons for promoting partnership working

- The delivery of services in a more coordinated way
- Address complex issues and problems that cross the traditional professional boundaries, for example, issues associated with community care and health improvements
- Reduce the fragmentation of local service delivery
- Helps to bid for additional and new resources and to help deciding on priorities in the context of productivity and efficiency
- Adheres to statutory requirements concerning partnership working requirements
- There is a potential for cost-effective and clinically effective care
- When assessing needs, partnership working uses single assessment processes so that people do not need to undergo multiple assessments by different agencies
- Achieving greater efficiency by minimising duplication, improving coordination and sharing buildings and human resources
- Aligning or ring-fencing resources or pooling budgets to achieve efficiencies and better outcomes
- Adopting a holistic, multi-agency approach to the allocation and movement of resources into early intervention and prevention of increasing need.

Source: adapted from National Strategic Partnership Forum (2007).

PCTs will disappear. The Government has made it clear that they are committed to the integration of health and social care; they will start with an undertaking to break down the barriers between health- and social care funding, resulting in proposals for the reform of the NHS and adult social care (HM Government, 2010). For the first time this White Paper brings GPs and local councils together. The relationship between Government and social care will change, providing real opportunities to enhance ways in which these services work together to succeed in achieving better outcomes.

Top tips

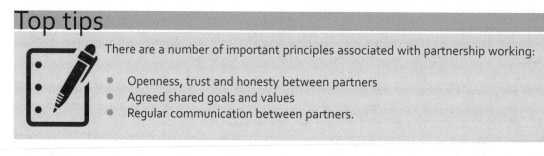

There are a number of important principles associated with partnership working:

- Openness, trust and honesty between partners
- Agreed shared goals and values
- Regular communication between partners.

The white paper promises that Government will simplify and extend the use of powers that enable joint working between the NHS and local authorities. This should enable local authorities to extend their existing partnership arrangements and make new arrangements with GP commissioning consortia. This may result in joint commissioning of pathways, services and systems, and also integration of multidisciplinary staff teams. There will be less reliance on national policy initiatives and central drivers; engagement will be through clinical engagement and local action (Humphries and Curry, 2011). Reforms have done away with top-down targets and performance arrangements to an approach where power will be removed from Government and placed in the hands of people and communities through local democratic accountability, competition, choice and social action (DH, 2010c). Power will shift from a large bureaucratic public service to more local communities and professionals, with devolved power and resources to make decisions.

These proposals provide opportunities for recognising and increasing broader partnerships with other statutory agencies (as well as the independent and voluntary sectors), e.g. leisure, learning, employment, transport, housing and benefits, with the aim of ensuring that people can use these functions for as long as possible and are not forced into segregated health and care services.

Top tips

In order to achieve a coordinated approach to partnership working, all partners need to:

- Communicate
- Coordinate
- Cooperate.

Local authorities and their NHS partners are working in unity to cement relationships and bring together management and delivery structures, including shared chief officers and staff. Structural integration: PCT and local authority care services have formed a single legal entity (care trust) or a combined service (joint primary care and social care department).

The key purpose of partnership working is to improve the experience and outcomes of people who use services. Partnerships and integrated working will thrive only where there is a culture of shared ownership and common working arrangements across organisational and professional boundaries. This is primarily achieved by minimising organisational barriers between different services and ensuring that the individual is at the centre of any initiative, having a voice and being a real partner in health and care decisions. The traditional model emphasises the organisation, service and budget or the professional discipline to the detriment of the person receiving services. Figure 4.1 shows the person receiving care

Top tips

There are several components which – if they are present – will promote successful partnership working:

- The aim of the partnership is agreed and understood by all the partners.
- The partnership has clear, effective leadership.
- The role of each partner is identified and clear to others.
- There is shared ownership of the partnership and all partners feel that there is 'something in it for them'.
- There are dedicated time and resources for the administration and operation of the partnership.
- There is acknowledgement of different organisational cultures within the partnership.
- A supportive atmosphere exists within the partnership where suggestions, ideas and differences are addressed.

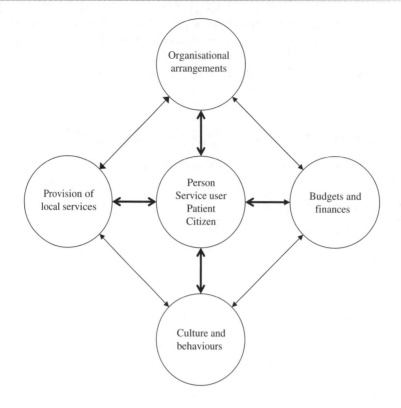

Figure 4.1   A person-centred approach to partnership working.

as the core element. Humphries and Curry (2011) point out that a person-centred approach aspires to the scenario of people experiencing one system of care and treatment, not several disjointed ones.

Barriers to effective partnership working

Translating the theory associated with partnership working into practice is not always easy. There are some potential barriers that may hinder partnership working development. Lymbery (2006) makes the point that it is a retrograde step in effective partnership working to fail to acknowledge actual or potential barriers; it is essential that barriers are recognised in advance.

A number of public bodies experience problems in partnerships and some find the experience of partnership very painful; progress is very slow and occasionally unproductive (Huxham and Vangen, 2004).

Interprofessional conflict can occur and role appreciation can become distorted for a number of reasons (Reeves et al, 2010). Differences in understanding roles, stereotyping and prejudices can have a detrimental effect on partnership working. The Joint Improvement Team (2009) has employed a cause-and-effect approach to recognising the partnership barriers. Table 4.5 provides an overview of the categories identified.

Table 4.5 Barriers to effective partnership working

Category	Barriers	Resolutions
People	This category also includes issues associated with power. The key themes concern: • Power and hierarchy. Problems arise when there are perceived status differences between the individual participants or among occupational groups. Difficulties occur when practitioners think that there are threats to their professional status, autonomy and control when they are asked to take part in democratic decision-making activities. High status professions (e.g. doctors) or higher grade local authority officers are seen to silence others' contributions and have the potential to bias the outcome partnership efforts • The role of the voluntary and community sector, service users and carers are often unclear in partnerships and integrated teams. This lack of clarity is about whether this is to be an advocacy, operational, representative or strategic role • Behaviour is closely related to power and hierarchy and role clarity. Behavioural barriers can compromise trusting relationships. The professional identity, autonomy and interpersonal mistrust of any one profession in relation to others can impede understanding of other professions. Lack of individual knowledge of other professions can result in stereotyping other workers and reinforce prejudice as opposed to enlightening multidisciplinary teams • A perceived lack of commitment from senior managers can lead to poor morale and this includes the morale of service users and community representatives. This will impact on the ability of partnerships to be established and to grow; there may be a failure in meeting predetermined outcomes • A misunderstanding about the aims of partnership and lack of attention to the development of skills of all individuals will result in obstacles that will be difficult to overcome	Learning and innovation are connected to the development of successful partnerships. Education and development can also help individuals to work in partnership, to cope with the stress caused by doubt, complexity and uncertainty, and to bond together teams into an effective whole Several barriers to partnerships working are attributed to behaviour and can be addressed through reducing anxiety, stress, conflicting priorities and loyalties. The behaviours that should be clearly agreed upon and required from partnership participants will include the following behaviours, which are commonly associated with successful partnerships: • Understanding and respect for other partners' points of view, cultures and structures • Shared responsibility with the principal of 'equality around the table' • Consistent, clear communication, intentionally avoiding language that may be specific to individual professions or organisations • Recognising and respecting variations between social and medical approaches, at the same time as trying to unify approaches when possible, through agreement and compromise • Open sharing of information • Hearing the views of those who may have reservations about partnership working and seeking to resolve them • Taking ownership of the agreed strategic direction

Continued

Table 4.5   *Continued*

Category	Barriers	Resolutions
Culture and external influences	These barriers can be the result of external, cultural and political influences. They include issues related to Government policy and political agendas. There may be mistrust and conflict within the group and a history of pre-existing relationships, misconceptions and suspicion	Identify those external matters that partners cannot control, but must be aware of and adapt themselves to – as far as this is possible There will be a number of different organisational and professional cultures; this does not have to be a barrier to effective partnership working if differences are understood and accepted. Important differences should be openly identified and discussed Open acknowledgement of differences and frank exchanges of views should be encouraged with respect to all parties as a prerequisite Developing a shared, corporate culture as a partnership is seen as a necessary ingredient of success. Building trust and taking time to listen can help enhance partnership working
Processes	Poor processes associated with the mechanisms of working together particularly surrounding communications are factors that hinder effective partnership working. Absence of agreed outcomes or outcomes that have not been clearly articulated and not based on the needs of citizens, users of services and patients will jeopardise relationships. There may be conflict or disagreement about the purpose of the partnership, putting the partnership at further risk When there are issues with decision-making mechanisms, i.e. lack of delegated authority, dominating partners and a failure to make decisions this will result in a partnership arrangement that has become stultified.	Provide active, systemic, imaginative and integrated engagement. Make sure user and carer viewpoints are given credence. Appropriate membership on partnership bodies for users, carers and representative groups The vision should be focused on outcomes for service users, patients and citizens, not on process. Working well together or producing a strategy is not an outcome • Assume nothing – discuss openly even the most seemingly obvious goals • Be prepared to compromise • Do not enter a partnership with preconceived ideas • Honest exchange of information, based on sharing, rather than withholding, knowledge • Clear and regular communication of agreed key issues outside the partnership • Shared, simplifed language – being aware of and reducing organisational and professional jargon • Seek clarification from partners who communicate in a language that is not easily understood

Resources	There are three key areas linked with resources: • Money – financial pressures, reluctance to fund partnership objectives and confusion as to who should provide the resources needed to implement decisions will make effective partnership working difficult • Information – failure to provide information, make information sharing work (i.e. communication mechanisms) and a reluctance to share information • Time – this valuable resource must be managed effectively	For partnership to work, it needs money as well as the other skills, time and information There must be a commitment to contribute financial resources proportionate to the problem being addressed Share resources and decision-making Develop information collection and sharing protocols, which address both issues of confidentiality and the needs of individual services and planning functions Fund IT infrastructure and support Involving people effectively using services and community groups requires timescales that enable them to consult their wider membership
Structure	Barriers occur when there is lack of clarity associated with the structure of the partnership and purpose. When wrong or insufficient partners are involved in the partnership and there is failure to look beyond the health- and social care arena, particularly towards voluntary organisations, users of services and carers. Practical issues such as lack of formal structure, accountability and clear roles will hamper partnership working	Involve the right partners. A balance should be made between involving the right breadth of organisations and organisational levels. This means ensuring political and public involvement, and not anticipating all partners to make identical or equivalent financial or staffing contributions (service users, patients and voluntary organisations give contributions in kind – knowledge and networks) Avoid becoming too large for meaningful action Have a universally agreed Partnership Agreement; this should outline: • A clear, shared purpose • Membership of the partnership including how service users and the public are involved • The partnership structure and lines of accountability • Role descriptions for individuals and groups • Financial accountability, performance reporting and audit • A clear protocol for resolving disputes • People attending meetings must have delegated responsibility for making decisions

Source: adapted from Rummery and Glendinning (2000); Hamer and Smithies (2002); Armistead and Pettigrew (2004); Glasby and Lester (2004); Huxham and Vangen (2004); Lymbery (2006); Wistow and Waddington (2006); The Joint Improvement Team (2009); Reeves et al (2010).

Conclusion

Partnership working, integrated care and collaboration are as important to nurses as they are to other health- and social care professionals, and those who work in the independent and voluntary community sectors. Nurses have an important contribution to make to the partnership agenda.

Many benefits have already been found in partnership working and many more to be delivered. By integrating as well as sharing resources in an appropriate manner, the nurse and others can work towards providing care that has the patient at the heart of its delivery.

It is imperative to have a shared understanding of what is meant by partnership, so that all parties are clear about its intended outcomes; however, as this chapter has demonstrated, this is not always easy. The literature contains many references to defining the various aspects of partnership.

Policy initiatives have an enormous impact on how partnership working functions. This chapter has discussed partnership working in the context of NHS reform. The Government is committed to supporting the significant role that the voluntary and community sector, independent sector, and social and health services play in delivering public services that provide safe and effective health and social care in an integrated and appropriate way. The potential benefits of the independent and voluntary and community sectors have been highlighted.

There is much agreement about the characteristics of successful partnership working and the ways to avoid or confront barriers that might impact on partnership; these have been discussed along with strategies that may overcome them. A number of the most important characteristics, e.g. focusing on outcomes for service users, effective communication, competent and confident leadership, and the allocation of appropriate and adequate resources, are closely aligned to effective partnership working. There are challenges to ensuring that these characteristics are present when working in partnership.

There is, however, a need for more research into the outcomes of partnership working and closer examination of the efficiencies of partnership. New ways of working are inevitable and nurses have to be ready to embrace these ways; this can be achieved by approaching them with an open mind and a willingness to learn.

Activities

Attempt the following 10 true or false questions that are related to partnership working and vulnerable people to test your knowledge. The answers can be found at the back of this book, in the chapter called 'Activity Answers'.

1. Stereotyping can be described as generalizations about people that are based on limited, sometimes inaccurate, information.
2. Partnership working only involves those people working on one ward.
3. Multidisciplinary teams are best led by doctors.
4. Partnerships work best when the aim of the partnership is agreed and understood by all the partners.
5. The voluntary and community sector has important and meaningful contributions to make to partnership working.
6. Governments have no interest in ensuring that partnership working delivers.
7. The word collaboration can have sinister undertones.
8. There are growing numbers of people who are living with multiple long-term conditions; their needs are met only by the health service.
9. Improving the public's health should be led by social workers.
10. There are various laws that demand that health- and social care organisations work in partnership.

References

Armistead C, Pettigrew P (2004) Effective partnerships: building a sub-regional network of reflective practitioners. *International Journal of Public Sector Management* **17**: 571–585.

Coe C, Barlow J (2010) Working in partnership with the voluntary sector; early explorer clinics. *Community Practitioner* **82**(11): 33–35.

Department of Health (1997) *Developing Partnerships in Mental Health*. London: Department of Health.

Department of Health (2002) *Shifting the Balance of Power – The next steps*. London: Department of Health.

Department of Health (2004) *Making Partnership Work for Patients, Carers and Service Users*. London: Department of Health.

Department of Health (2005) *Self Care – A Real Choice, Self Care Support – A real option*. London: Department of Health.

Department of Health (2008) *Raising the Profile of Long Term Conditions Care. Compendium of information*. London: Department of Health.

Department of Health (2010a) *Equity and Excellence: Liberating the NHS*. London: Department of Health.

Department of Health (2010b) *Healthy Lives, Healthy People: Our strategy for public health in England*. London: Department of Health.

Department of Health (2010c) *Department of Health Draft Structural Reform Plan*. London: Department of Health.

Department of Health and Department of Communities and Local Government (2010) *Liberating the NHS: Local democratic legitimacy in health – a consultation on proposals*. London: Department of Health.

Dickinson H (2008) *Evaluating Outcomes in Health and Social Care*. Bristol: Community Care.

Glasby J, Lester H (2004) Cases for change in mental health: partnership working in mental health services. *Journal of Interprofessional Care* **18**: 7–16.

Glasby J, Dickinson H (2008) *Partnership Working in Health and Social Care*. Bristol: Polity Press.

Hamer L, Smithies J (2002) *Planning Across the LSP: Case studies of integrating community strategies and health improvement*. London: Health Development Agency.

HM Government (2010). *The Coalition: Our Programme for Government*. London: TSO.

Horner N, Simpson T (2011) Inter-professional practice and education in health and social care. In: Linsley P, Kane R, Owen S (eds), *Nursing for Public Health. Promotion, principles and practice*. Oxford: Oxford University Press, pp 52–63.

Humphries R (2011) *Social Care Funding and the NHS: An impending crisis*. London: King's Fund.

Humphries R, Curry A (2011) *Integrating Health and Social Care. Where next?* London: King's Fund.

Huxham C, Vangen S (2004) Doing things collaboratively: realizing the advantage or succumbing to inertia. *Organizational Dynamics* **33**: 190–201.

Huxham C, Vangen S (2005) *Managing to Collaborate: The theory and practice of collaborative advantage*. London: Routledge.

Joint Improvement Team (2009) *Barriers to Partnership Working*. Edinburgh: Joint Improvement Team. Available at: www.jitscotland.org.uk/search (accessed June 2011).

Leathard A (1994) *Going Inter-professional: Working together from health and welfare*. Hove: Routledge.

Lester H, Birchwood M, Tait L, Shah S, England E (2008) Barriers and facilitators to partnership working between early intervention services and the voluntary and community sector. *Health and Social Care in the Community* **16**: 493–500.

Lord Laming (2009) *The Protection of Children in England: A progress report*. London: TSO.

Loveday I, Linsley P (2011) Implementing interventions: delivering care to individuals and communities. In: Linsley P, Kane R, Owen S (eds), *Nursing for Public Health. Promotion, Principles and Practice*. Oxford: Oxford University Press, pp 134–143.

Lymbery M (2006). United we stand? Partnership working in health and social care and the role of social work in services for older people. *British Journal of Social Work* **36**: 1119–1134.

McKimm J (2011) Leading for collaboration and partnership working. In: Swanwick T, McKimm J (eds), *ABC of Clinical Leadership*. Oxford: Wiley, pp 44–49.

McKimm J, Millard L, Held S (2008) Leadership, education and partnership. Project LEAP: Developing educational regional leadership capacity in higher education and health services through collaboration and partnership working. *International Journal of Public Service Leadership* **4**(4): 24–48.

Maslin-Prothero S, Ashby S, Taylor S (2009) Primary care. In: Glasper A, McEwing G, Richardson J (eds), *Foundation Studies for Caring*. Basingstoke: Palgrave, pp 683–703.

Milne D, McAnaney A, Pollinger B, Bateman K, Fewster E (2004) Analysis of the forms, functions and facilitation of social support in one English county: A way for professionals to improve the quality of health care. *International Journal of Healthcare Quality Assurance* **17**: 294–301.

National Strategic Partnership Forum (2007) *Making Partnerships Work: Examples of Good Practice*. Leeds: Department of Health.

Nursing and Midwifery Council (2008) *The Code: Standards of conduct, performance and ethics for nurses and midwives*. London: NMC.

Office of the Deputy Prime Minister (2004) *Mental Health and Social Exclusion. Social Exclusion Unit Report*. London: Office of the Deputy Prime Minister.

Poole R, Wallis C (2009) Partnership working with independent providers. *British Journal of Community Nursing* **14**(7): 297–300.

Reeves S, Lewin S, Espin S, Zwarenstein M (2010) *Interprofessional Teamwork for Health and Social Care*. Oxford: Wiley.

Rummery K, Glendinning C (2000) *Primary Care and Social Services: Developing new partnerships for older people*. Oxford: Radcliff.

Scottish Government (2008) *Equally Well. Report of the Ministerial Task Force on Health Inequalities*, Vol **2**. Edinburgh: The Scottish Government.

Scottish Office (1997) *Designed to Care. Renewing the National Health Service in Scotland*. London: TSO.

Tait L, Shah S (2007) Partnership working: a policy with promise for mental healthcare. *Advances in Psychiatric Treatment* **13**: 261–271.

Whittington C (2003) Collaboration and partnership in context. In: Weinstein J, Whittington C, Leiba T (eds), *The World Health Report 2006 – Working Together for Health*. Geneva: World Health Organization.

Wistow G, Waddington E (2006) Learning from doing: implications of the Barking and Dagenham experience for integrating health and social care. *Journal of Integrated Care* **14**(3): 8–18.

Part II

Communication and Interpersonal Skills

5

Therapeutic Relationships, Communication and Interpersonal Skills

Aims and objectives

The aim of this chapter is to develop and improve therapeutic relationships, enhance communication and interpersonal skills.

At the end of the chapter you will be able to:

1. Understand the value of safe and effective therapeutic relationships in care contexts
2. Develop communication and interpersonal skills when applied to health- and social care settings in an effective and non-discriminatory manner
3. Appreciate the importance of how to engage, maintain and disengage from therapeutic relationships
4. Understand and respect professional boundaries
5. Begin to apply the concepts discussed to the practice setting
6. Appreciate the Nursing and Midwifery Council's requirements of student nurses

In order to provide an effective therapeutic relationship in a mutually therapeutic environment, it is vital that the nurse uses appropriate communication and interpersonal skills. Effective communication, according to Elton and Reading (2008), is central to the effective delivery of health care.

The thrust of this chapter is to convey to the reader the importance of effective communication skills, e.g. processes and forms of communication, and the importance of establishing, maintaining and disengaging from professional care relationships with patients. In addition, there is discussion about barriers to communication. Effective communication, an appreciation of the therapeutic relationship and an awareness of interpersonal skills can result in improved care outcomes.

Caring for well or sick people is complex and the nurse needs to liaise and communicate with a range of health- and social care professionals from various statutory and voluntary agencies. This chapter describes some of those health- and social care professionals and the various agencies that may be encountered in practice, exploring the skills required to participate effectively as a member of the multidisciplinary team.

Working together as a team for the benefit of the patient has been stressed in the Department of Health's *Confidence in Caring. A framework for best practice* (DH, 2007).

The Student's Guide to Becoming a Nurse, Second Edition. Ian Peate.
© 2012 John Wiley & Sons, Ltd. Published 2012 by John Wiley & Sons, Ltd.

Team working has the potential to enhance the quality of care; furthermore, a growing body of evidence suggests that team working can have a major impact not only on the quality of care but also on the efficient use of resources, and on staff satisfaction. Failure to work as a team can have deleterious effects on patient safety and satisfaction; it can lengthen hospital stay and increase readmissions.

Communicating with health- and social care professionals

Communicating effectively with other health- and social care professionals can be challenging; the nurse and the patient may come into contact with many other professionals. To act as a patient's advocate it is important to understand your own role and the role that others play in health-care delivery.

The Nursing and Midwifery Council (NMC, 2008) require that all nurses work in collaboration with those in their care. Collaborating with those in your care means that you have to:

- listen to the people being cared for and to respond appropriately to their concerns and preferences
- support people in caring for themselves aspiring to improve and maintain their health
- recognise and value the contribution that people make to their own health and wellbeing
- provide resources to meet people's language and communication needs
- share with people, in a manner that they can understand, the information that they request or need to know about their health and wellbeing

This can be achieved only if the nurse works effectively with the person being cared for and others who are a part of the care package, the aim is to enhance and promote high-quality care.

Case study 5.1

Ms Carole Mehta is a 26-year-old who was born with Down's syndrome. She has recently had a chest infection but her condition has worsened and she now has pneumonia. Carole smokes approximately 20 cigarettes a day. She has been living at home with her father and her brothers until this recent admission to hospital.

Carole now requires much nursing support provided by her father and various health-care and social care professionals. Over the last 2 weeks her condition has deteriorated and she was admitted to the ward (an acute care ward) after she had been diagnosed with pneumonia.

Carole and her family will have come into contact with many health- and social care professionals, the voluntary sectors and various nursing staff before and on admission. You might have thought about those listed in Table 5.1.

How will you ensure that Carole's individual differences, capabilities and needs are acknowledged and met?

The following is a list of nursing and medical staff employed within the NHS (this is a broad list). You should familiarise yourself with their various roles and responsibilities:

Nursing staff:

- Chief Nursing Officer
- Nurse consultant

- Ward sister/charge nurse
- Consultant nurse
- Clinical nurse specialist
- Staff nurse
- Student nurse
- Health-care assistant.

Medical staff:

- Chief Medical Officer
- Consultant
- General practitioner
- Registrar general practitioner
- Specialist registrar
- Associate specialist
- Senior house officer (F2)
- Preregistration house officer (F1)
- Medical student.

Table 5.1   Some health-care professionals with whom Carole and her family may have come into contact

• Nursing staff	• Various medical staff
• Health visitor	• Speech therapist
• Community nurses	• Occupational therapist
• Physiotherapists	• Social worker
• Domestic and portering staff	• Social services
• General practitioner	• Technicians
• Voluntary sector	• Dietician
	• Pharmacist

There are of course a number of other staff within the NHS who provide an excellent service and without whom the service would come to a stop, e.g. housekeeping staff, medical laboratory scientific officers, occupational therapists. Remember also the essential input that the voluntary sector play in health- and social care delivery.

Think

Make a list of the voluntary sector organisations that do or could contribute to the health and wellbeing of people. When you have made the list split them into fields (mental health, child, learning disability and adult). You may have found this difficult to do because many services provided by the voluntary sector overlap; think, for example, of the role Mind plays for all members of society.

Jeffrey (2006) notes that effective communication is essential in all clinical care. If professionals fail to communicate effectively with each other, they are less likely to be effective when they interact with patients and carers. However, some nurses find interacting with colleagues more of a challenge than interacting with the patient. There are a number of reasons why this might be:

- Power differences
- Role confusion
- Variations in communication styles
- Variations in philosophies of care.

There are several ways in which these differences may be addressed and the nurse should reflect on the way in which he or she communicates. Open, effective, two-way communication can help to enhance interprofessional communication, thus reducing stress and confusion for both staff and patients. Mutual respect for all parties is a prerequisite.

Boundaries in professional relationships

The only appropriate professional relationship between a patient and a nurse is one that focuses exclusively on the needs of the patient. There is a potential power differential (an imbalance of power) in this relationship that the nurse must be aware of. This is generated by the patient's need for care, assistance, guidance and support. Nurses and patients cannot enjoy totally equal relationships as a result of the contractual relationship in which the nurse and patient are engaged: it is an encounter of necessity, not choice (Horsburgh, 2007). Both patients and nurses, according to Ronayne (2001), must acknowledge these inequalities but implicitly value each other's competencies. At all times the nurse must maintain appropriate professional boundaries within this relationship.

Setting boundaries defines the limits of behaviour that allow a patient and a nurse to engage safely in a therapeutic caring relationship. The boundaries are based on the following:

- Trust
- Respect
- The appropriate use of power.

The relationship between the nurse and the patient is a therapeutic relationship, which has the key aim of focusing on and meeting the health and care needs of the patient. This relationship should not be established in order to build on personal or social contacts for the nurse. An unacceptable abuse of power occurs when the focus of care is moved away from meeting the patient's needs towards meeting the nurse's own needs.

All professional relationships are capable of producing conflicts of interest. There may be occasions when nurses develop strong feelings for a particular patient or family. There is nothing abnormal or wrong with these feelings in themselves, but compromise of the professional relationship occurs if the practitioner acts on them in an improper manner. On occasions personal or business relationships may exist before the professional relationship, and there may be instances where dual relationships exist, e.g. the nurse may already be a personal friend of a patient. The nurse has the responsibility of ensuring that each relationship stays within its own appropriate boundary.

An essential aspect of the therapeutic relationship will involve physical contact. When providing reassurance to a patient, for example, supportive physical gestures are essential in helping that patient. Appropriate supportive physical contact should be maintained in the nurse–patient relationship.

However, abuse can occur within the privileged nurse–patient relationship, often as a result of a misuse of power between the nurse and the patient; the nurse should be aware of this and it could result in physical or emotional harm to the patient, e.g.:

- A betrayal of trust
- A betrayal of respect
- Intimacy between the nurse and the patient.

There are many different forms of abuse. Chapter 2 details those that may be experienced by the person being cared for.

Every incident or allegation of suspected abuse requires a thorough and careful investigation, which must take full account of the circumstances and the context of the abuse. It is the NMC that is charged with this responsibility. To reiterate this important point, if there are any suspicions of abuse this must be made known to your immediate superior or line manager so that the allegation(s) can be dealt with in the most appropriate manner. If the issues concern a doctor it is the General Medical Council (GMC) that deals with these matters; other issues concerning another health-care professional is dealt with by the Health Professions Council (HPC). Go back to Chapter 1 and revisit the section that deals with allegations of misconduct.

Respecting professional boundaries

The relationship between the nurse and people being cared for is based on trust and confidence; however, the nature of this relationship may mean that there is imbalance of power. Professional practice expects the trust not to be violated or abused by the nurse. Respecting professional boundaries also includes respecting sexual boundaries. Breach of sexual boundaries occurs when the nurse displays sexualised behaviour towards the person being cared for, which is unacceptable. Sexualised behaviour includes using words, acts or behaviour in such a way that they intend to generate sexual impulses or desires (Council for Healthcare Regulatory Excellence or CHRE, 2008a). Breaching these sexual boundaries by falling short of the expected standards, the nurse could be acting unprofessionally and breaking the law under the Sexual Offenders Act 2003. Unacceptable sexualised behaviour includes:

- Asking for or accepting a date
- Sexual humour during consultations or examinations
- Inappropriate sexual or demeaning comments
- Requesting details about sexual orientation, history or preferences when this is not necessary or relevant
- Asking for or accepting an offer of sex
- Unnecessary exposure of the person's body
- Unplanned home visits with sexual intent
- Clinically unjustified physical examinations
- Intimate examinations carried out without the person's explicit consent
- Any sexual act induced by the nurse for their own sexual gratification
- Exposure of the nurse's body to the person
- Sexual assault.

Guidance has been produced to help reduce the possibility of patients being sexually abused by health-care professionals (CHRE, 2008a, 2008b, 2008c).

Those who need health and social care are sometimes in a position where their ability to exert power is limited (Horsburgh, 2007). People can feel vulnerable when they have received or are receiving care and treatment. As health-care providers nurses can be in a position of power as a result of the unique knowledge base that they possess; not only are they in position to provide care and offer resources that the person may need, but they are also in a position to withhold these.

Other reasons why this imbalance of power may exist are provided by CHRE (2008a) and include:

- For a person to be diagnosed and treated, he or she may have to share personal, sometimes intimate, information

- The health-care provider initiates the level and degree of intimacy and/or physical contact during the therapeutic and diagnostic process
- The health-care professional knows what it is that constitutes appropriateness related to professional practice. The person being cared for may find him- or herself in an unfamiliar situation and may not know what is appropriate.

Most nurses act with integrity and are dedicated to enhancing the health and wellbeing of the people for whom they have the privilege to care. There is a minority of incidents where some nurses fail in their attempt to uphold the standards required by the profession and serious breaches with respect to maintaining sexual boundaries occur. Displaying sexualised behaviour towards a person being cared for is unacceptable and beaches the trust between the person and the nurse.

Therapeutic nursing interventions

Therapeutic nursing interventions are nursing actions carried out to offer holistic nursing care. Holistic nursing care considers all aspects of the patient – body, mind and spirit – and the nurse using the nursing process in relation to individuals, their families, groups of people and communities. Holistic nursing has been explored many times over the years and continues to be an important aspect of a person's being. Therapeutic nursing interventions have at their heart the caring relationship, and the nurse uses a professional approach in their delivery. The essence of nursing is reflected in the therapeutic relationship that the nurse and patient develop. It is, however, difficult to define and evaluate the impact of therapeutic nursing because the emotional labour often remains hidden (Ronayne, 2001).

To provide effective nursing care the nurse must communicate effectively with the patient, the patient's family (however he or she defines this), and other health- and social care professionals. Effective communication incorporates effective use of your interpersonal skills.

Chapter 3 was concerned with the diverse needs of the patient and it pointed out the diversity of the population; the nurse will meet many patients from various backgrounds and will have to employ interpersonal skills to ensure that effective two-way communication takes place. This next section of the chapter is concerned with the content and the process of communication.

Interpersonal skills

Allender et al (2010) suggest that there are three types of interpersonal skills that build on sending and receiving skills. These interpersonal skills go beyond the simple exchange of messages. To be able to demonstrate a therapeutic partnership with the patient, the nurse must show that he or she possesses the following three skills:

- Respect
- Rapport
- Trust.

Respect

Showing respect means that the nurse must demonstrate a genuine interest in the patient and his or her needs. Addressing the patient in a manner that is respectful, listening carefully without interrupting the patient while he or she is telling his or her story (providing you with his or her history), showing concern for the patient's condition, preserving modesty and promoting dignity are all ways in which the nurse can demonstrate respect. The correct way to address a person is important, e.g. using the courtesy titles of Ms, Mrs or Mr until the patient has given you permission to address him or her in any other manner. Expressing a sincere desire to understand the patient, showing kindness and being concerned for any fears or discomfort are also ways of expressing respect to the patient and the patient's family.

Top tips

Work with the person for whom you are caring; do not think in terms of telling the person what to do. Offer him or her suggestions and choices and then together come up with the best possible solution. The therapeutic caring relationship is a partnership not a dominant paternalistic relationship.

Rapport

Establishing a rapport with the patient or his or her family can be confirmed by showing respect as described above. Possessing communication skills that are effective can instil in the patient a sense of confidence, competence and trust that will validate rapport (Meredith, 2000). See Table 5.2 for ways of establishing rapport.

Trust

Trust must be earned by the nurse; trust generates trust. Often patients will resist expressing their true feelings if they do not trust the nurse. The nurse can lay down solid foundations for trust building, by enhancing this. He or she demonstrates respect and has a rapport with the patient. Trust, similar to respect, is associated with an ability to provide the patient with genuine interest and care. Meredith (2000) suggests that gaining the trust of the patient can be achieved in the following ways:

- Admitting your limitations and seeking appropriate assistance when help is needed
- Remaining non-judgemental and objective
- Taking the patient's fears and apprehensions seriously

Table 5.2   Examples of ways in which the nurse may establish rapport with the patient

- Provision of an open channel of communication. The nurse should endeavour to ensure that he or she has face-to-face interaction with the patient
- Jargon and technological terminology should be avoided and the patient's educational level, culture and any communication impairments should be catered for
- Subtly mirroring the patient's posture can make the patient feel more at ease and helps to establish rapport, e.g. leaning forward when the patient does
- Be aware of your and the patient's body language
- Use paralanguage – the rate of speech, the tone of voice. This approach is powerful and can communicate emotional information to both the patient and the nurse

Source: adapted from Meredith (2000).

- Maintaining the patient's sense of comfort, dignity and privacy
- Acting as the patient's advocate as needed
- Demonstrating genuine empathy and kindness
- Behaving in a professional manner.

Trust can be developed by providing an open, honest and patient-focused approach. As trust develops and grows, so too will free-flowing communication.

Empathy

Empathy is another interpersonal skill. Allender et al (2010) define empathy as the ability to communicate understanding and vicariously experience the feelings and thoughts of others. The British Association for Counselling and Psychotherapy (2010) defines empathy as the ability to communicate understanding of another person's experience from that person's perspective. The nurse demonstrates empathy by reflecting another person's feelings and expressing those feelings to another person. The reflections should be done by using the same terms and phrases that the other person has used.

Empathising with a patient sends him or her the message that you are seeking validation of the messages/issues that have been communicated to you: 'This is how it seems to me' or 'Did I get that right?' The nurse must continue to seek validation in order to ensure that the message received is correct. By empathising the nurse focuses on the patient and this aims to reduce anxieties and fears. The patient should feel that he or she is being listened to and that his or her participation is valued.

Effective communication skills

Effective communication involves the use of many different skills. The Department of Health (2010), in its benchmark statement concerning communication, states that all practicable steps must be taken to communicate effectively with patients and their carers. The effectiveness of communication is mediated by intrapersonal, interpersonal and other factors. Interpersonal skills are skills that are often learnt early on in life, during childhood, for example, and as we grow we tend to refine these skills. When practising nursing, however, these skills can mean the skills or techniques used by nurses in an attempt to produce therapeutic benefit during professional interactions with patients and others, as described above.

Irurita (2000) has identified elements that are present within the helping relationship that patients value, including:

- Genuineness
- Respect
- Being available
- Being honest
- Listening actively
- Being able to empathise.

A person cannot *not* communicate (Smith et al, 2011). Communication is the process of sending and receiving messages via symbols, words, signs, gestures or other actions such as cues.

Figure 5.1 provides a diagrammatic representation of how the process of communication can work. Use of a model to describe communication is helpful, but it is also limited in its value because it does not include, and indeed cannot include, the context of care. There are many factors that can enhance/impinge on the nurse's ability to communicate effectively with his or her patient.

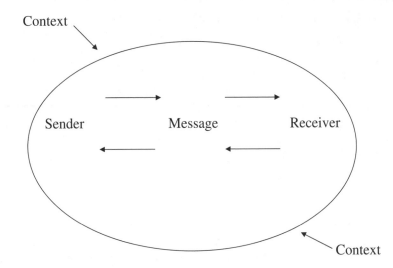

Figure 5.1   A model of communication.

The person sending the message is called the sender; in some models of communication he or she is referred to as the source encoder. The source is concerned with the idea or the event; the receiver, or in some models the decoder, is the person receiving the message and he or she can receive this message through sight, sound or touch. Be aware, however, that the message sent may not be the message received. The three media mentioned here – sight, sound and touch – are also known as the channels through which the message is transmitted. Messages can contain overt and covert communications; although the sender may be aware of the overt meaning of the message, he or she may not be aware of its covert meaning.

Think

Take some time to think about the ways in which people communicate with you and how you communicate with them. Think particularly about the gestures and symbols used.

What message is being given to you when a person kisses you? This gesture is usually associated with kindness.

The messages sent and received can have the potential to define the relationship between the various parties. Communication is required in order to fulfil defined goals, e.g. to transmit facts, feelings and meanings.

Most people would suggest that they can communicate, but in reality that may not be true. The test comes when one word is placed in front of the word communication – 'effectively'. Communication is a process that we undertake on a daily basis; we often do it without thinking and feel that we are successful at both understanding others and being understood. However, most people, including nurses, fail to communicate effectively. Communication appears easy when it is done well. It requires engagement, empathy and the ability to listen to and respond; it also requires time.

Table 5.3   The benefits of effectively communicating with the patient

- Patients' problems are identified more accurately
- Patients are more satisfied with their care and can better understand their problems
- Patients are more likely to comply with treatment or lifestyle advice
- Patients' distress and their vulnerability to anxiety and depression are lessened
- The overall quality of care is improved by ensuring that patients' views are taken into account
- The nurse's own wellbeing is improved
- Fewer clinical errors are made
- Patients are less likely to complain

Source: adapted from Maguire and Pitceathly (2003).

Many health-care workers do communicate effectively, although some patients are unhappy about the information that they are given and the manner in which it is given. When the nurse uses his or her communication skills effectively, both the nurse and the patient may benefit (Maguire and Pitceathly, 2003; Table 5.3).

Effective communication is an essential requirement in nursing. All aspects of the nurse–patient relationship involve some form of communication, e.g.:

- Providing health education to a young person with anorexia
- Listening to the concerns of a worried parent
- Performing a nursing procedure with a patient who has profound learning disabilities.

The modes or forms of communication are varied and include both verbal and non-verbal communication. Some of these are described in the next sections. Effective communication is affected by various factors, including the intrapersonal framework of the person, the relationship between participants and the purpose of the interaction. The communication process is very complex: it is often what you say and how you say it that will have most impact. In order to assess a patient's needs effectively the nurse must employ many skills including:

- communication
- observation
- measurement.

When assessing a patient's needs the nurse should employ the skills associated with interviewing, e.g. listening, talking, recording and documenting. Although listening may appear to be a very passive skill, it is indeed also very complex.

Becoming a better listener means that the nurse listens not only with his or her ears but with his or her whole body. Listening means that you should avoid talking about yourself or your own opinions; keep quiet – listen. There are five fundamental actions hat the nurse can take to ensure that he or she actively listens – summed up by the acronym SOLER (Egan, 2009):

- **S**it squarely, facing the patient: the nurse should adopt a position whereby the patient feels that he or she is being listened to
- **O**pen posture: avoid adopting a defensive position, e.g. arms folded
- **L**ean towards the other person: the nurse when leaning towards the patient will demonstrate that he or she is actively listening

- **E**ye contact should be maintained: avoid excessive eye contact or limited eye contact; you should aim to strike a balance
- **R**elax as much as possible: demonstrating that you are relaxed may encourage the patient to relax.

Verbal communication

The word 'verbal' would suggest that communication in this sense is linguistic, i.e. it is spoken or said. Effective verbal communication will depend on issues such as the tone and the pitch of a person's voice. Just as crucial is the use of language, which is very important in achieving an understanding between the person sending the message and the individual receiving it. According to Sidtis (2004), expression of speech is important and statements used on an everyday basis through slang, sayings, clichés and conventional expressions become a large part of a speaker's competence. Messages transmitted only through a verbal means of communication have to be much clearer than ones that are sent with the aid of other means of communication, so that the recipient receives them effectively. Speakers (the people sending the message) have the potential to control the interaction through the language that they choose to use. Nurses may do this unconsciously by using jargon with the patient.

Open and closed questions

Most of our daily conversation involves either asking or answering questions; we use questions every day. There are a variety of questioning styles available to the nurse and, depending on the context of the interaction, this will result in the nurse choosing one approach over the others in order to have the most impact. The choice of technique will impinge on the efficacy of information gathering.

The use of open questions invites the respondent to elaborate on his or her responses, as opposed to closed questions. When using open questions the nurse aims to understand more specifically what the patient means. Using clarification techniques provides the patient with the opportunity to expand and amplify his or her previous comment. The following are examples of open-ended questions:

- What are your feelings about that experience?
- What thoughts did you have at the time?
- Could you say a little more about what that means for you?

Open questions are designed to give information; they begin with words such as:

- How . . .
- Why . . .
- When . . .
- Where . . .
- What . . .
- Who . . .
- Which . . .

Closed questions can be recognised because they start with words such as:

- Do . . .
- Is . . .

- Can . . .
- Could . . .
- Will . . .
- Would . . .
- Shall . . .
- Should . . .

Closed questions allow the respondent to reply with a single categorical answer to the question posed, e.g. when looking for a straight 'Yes' or 'No'. This type of question can be useful, e.g. if the patient is short of breath you would not seek elaboration to a question because this may exhaust or exacerbate the patient's condition.

Think

With another colleague, ask him or her a question beginning with 'How', 'Why' or 'When'. You may have found it was difficult for him or her to respond with a simple 'yes' or 'no'. That is because you began the question with an 'open' word.

Figure 5.2 demonstrates how, by using various approaches to asking questions, it is possible to filter data down in order to gather the information that is being sought.

Non-verbal communication

Abercrombie (1968) states that we may well speak with our vocal organs, but we converse with our whole body. We place much emphasis on the verbal aspects of communication, e.g. the words used, their sequencing and structure. Non-verbal communication or body language is often unconscious and therefore spontaneous and candid.

Messages can be relayed to others in different ways as well as when we speak, e.g. through the following channels:

- Glances
- Gestures
- Facial expressions
- Posture
- Tone of voice
- Dress
- Body orientation
- Silence.

These modes of communication are known as non-verbal communication and they sometimes do not get noticed when we converse with each other. It is often non-verbal communications that are crucial in the transmission of information and are the prime ways in which we judge or make opinions about others (Smith et al, 2011). Communication is very often a mixture of both verbal and non-verbal messages, sometimes known as metacommunication.

Top tips

If someone's words do not match their non-verbal behaviours, it is important that you pay careful attention. A person may, for example, tell you that he or she is happy while frowning and the eyes are downcast. When words fail to match up with non-verbal signals, people tend to ignore what has been said and focus instead on non-verbal expressions of moods, thoughts and emotions. This is known as incongruence.

159

Non-verbal communications have many functions within the communication process. They have the ability to regulate and influence the processes associated with human interaction; they can also support or replace communications that are verbalised.

Guerrero and Floyd (2006) suggest that 60–65 per cent of meaning is carried non-verbally during social exchanges. Earlier research (often cited) suggests that only about 7 per cent of messages transmitted

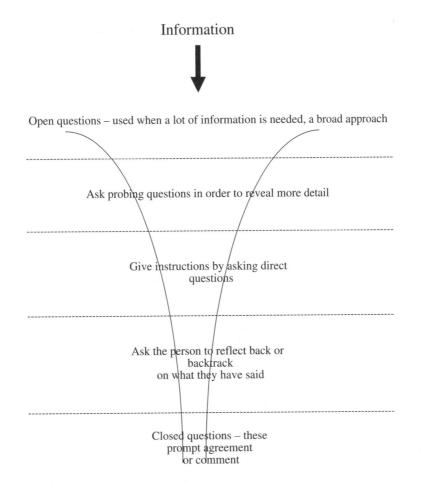

Information

Open questions – used when a lot of information is needed, a broad approach

Ask probing questions in order to reveal more detail

Give instructions by asking direct questions

Ask the person to reflect back or backtrack on what they have said

Closed questions – these prompt agreement or comment

Figure 5.2 The information funnel.

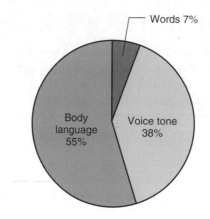

Figure 5.3   The elements of communication.

between people are attributed to words. The other 93 per cent are non-verbal messages (Sherman, 1994). Of this 93 per cent, 38 per cent are transmitted through vocal tones and the remaining 55 per cent are through facial expressions (Figure 5.3).

There are nine types of non-verbal communication:

- Paralanguage
- Kinesics
- Oculesics
- Appearance
- Proxemics
- Haptics
- Olfactics
- Chronemics
- Facial expressions.

Paralanguage

Paralanguage is the vocal cues that accompany language – the way that we say words. Hargie (2011) includes features such as: speech rate and intensity; pitch, modulation and quality of the voice; and articulation and rhythm control. The faster a person speaks the more competent he or she may appear; soft-spoken speakers may be considered timid or shy. Young children (infants) do not understand words and rely on non-verbal communication for information. A raised voice to a child may result in an alteration in the child's behaviour.

Kinesics – communication through body movements

Kinesics is the study of non-verbal communication through facial or body movements. Five categories are associated with kinesics:

- *Emblems* – these are body gestures that translate directly into words or phrases, e.g. the thumbs-up sign for 'a good job'

- *Illustrators* – these types of non-verbal communication often accompany the verbal message. Generally people illustrate with their hands; however, other parts of the body can be used, such as the head. Illustrators can also communicate the shape or size of the objects that you are talking about
- *Regulators* – regulators are behaviours that have the ability to monitor, coordinate, control or maintain the speaking of another person. An example may be when the head is nodded during conversation, which gives the speaker the signal to continue speaking
- *Display of feelings* – sometimes also known as affect display. This is associated with movements of the face or body, e.g. a frown or raising of the eyebrows, which often conveys emotional meaning
- *Adaptors* – an example of an adaptor might be tapping a pen or twisting the hair. Hargie (2011) refers to adaptors as self-manipulative gestures.

161

Oculesics

Oculesics are associated with eye movements and messages conveyed by the eyes. There are many cultural rules associated with eye movements and gaze. There is a balance between how long you engage in eye contact: too long may be threatening and too short a time may convey timidity or shyness.

Eye contact or gaze can play several important roles in face-to-face interaction, e.g.:

- Initiate contact
- Define the relationship
- Regulate the flow of conversation
- Monitor feedback
- Coordinate discussion.

Appearance

The human body reveals much about the person. Tall people are said to be paid more than for the same job done by a shorter person. Attractiveness can also be seen as an artefact. Those who are deemed physically attractive are considered more personable, popular, confident, persuasive, happy, interesting and outgoing. Attractive people fare better in all walks of life, e.g. they do better at school and are more preferred as work mates (Burgoon et al, 2010).

The way an individual dresses can also influence the ability to communicate effectively. People make inferences about the way that you dress. Issues relating to clothing can include uniforms and occupational attire, the style and type of leisure clothes, and the colour of the clothes worn.

Think

Think about the clothes that people around you are wearing. Are there people in leisure clothing, office smart clothing, uniforms? Could you place them in a socioeconomic group, or judge the amount of money that they earn based only on the clothing that they wear?

Often people really do 'judge a book by its cover' and the clothing that we wear (regardless of whether we have chosen to wear that particular type of clothing or it is a requirement of our job) is our 'cover'.

Think, for example, about the inferences that people will make about you if you wear, or do not wear, a wedding ring.

Proxemics

Proxemics or interpersonal space concerns the distance that people maintain while interacting with others. Hargie (2011) points out that there are many factors that shape interpersonal distance:

- Culture/background
- Gender
- Personality
- Interpersonal relations
- Age
- Topic of conversation
- Physical features of the other
- Physical/social setting.

Proxemic distances can be measured in relation to the purpose of the encounter (Table 5.4).

Haptics

The study of touch is known as haptics. Ritualistic touching occurs throughout the day and this can be in the form of handshaking, hugging or kissing. Touch can be seen as an intimate way of communication. Touch can convey many messages: it can communicate positive feelings, reassure patients and comfort them. There are some patients who do not like to be touched because of personal desires or as a result of cultural norms.

Olfactics

Olfactics is the study of smell or in this context olfactory communication. People relate to or disengage with others as a response to smell, e.g. the smell of another person's breath or their aftershave/perfume.

Table 5.4 Interpersonal space and distances

Relationship	Distance	
Intimate relationship	Approximately 45 cm	Usually reserved for very close friends or family
Personal/casual relationship	From about 45 cm to 1.30 m	Used during informal/casual conversations/discussions with friends and associates
Social relationship	1.30 m to approximately 4 m	Used for impersonal business dealings
Public relationship	Over 4 m but within the range of sound and vision	Conferences, large meetings, formal gatherings

Source: adapted from Brody (2004).

Smell is a very powerful memory aid; often it is possible to recall an event that occurred months or years ago when a similar smell is encountered again.

Chronemics

This is the study of time or temporal communication. It is associated with the way people organise and react to time. The communication process is often hindered because of the challenges associated with time.

Facial expressions

As children we learn how to manage facial expressions, e.g. sometimes it is considered rude to yawn openly, so often people attempt to suppress a yawn; we may frown when we are given bad news. Humans have 80 facial muscles that can create in excess of 7000 facial expressions.

There are six main types of facial expression that can be found in all cultures (Table 5.5).

Think

If you were a patient, without using any verbal communication, how might you try to express the following to a nurse who is caring for you?

- I am in pain.
- I need a bedpan.
- I am scared.
- You are not listening to me.

You may have come up with many ways of expressing your needs in the above situations. You might have used the expressions outlined in Table 5.5.

Case study 5.2

Charles Adebayo is applying for a job as a band 5 staff nurse in a mental health foundation trust on an acute admissions ward. Charles did well at university and graduated with a BSc(Hons) Nursing (2.2 classification). He failed one module in his final year and had to retake that; he was successful on his second attempt. There is much competition for this one post; he knows at least three other people from his own cohort have applied for the same post. One of the other candidates graduated with a first class honours and another with an upper 2.1, so the competition is strong.

If you were Charles how would you prepare for this interview?
Thinking only of the issues associated with non-verbal communication:

- Glances
- Gesticulation

Table 5.5 Facial expressions that can be found in all cultures

Expression	Manifestation
Happiness	Round eyes, smiles, raised cheeks
Disgust	Wrinkled nose, lowered eyelids and eyebrow, raised upper lip
Fear	Round eyes, open mouth
Anger	Lowered eyebrow and intense stare
Surprise	Raised eyebrow, wide open eyes, open mouth
Sadness	Area around mouth and eyes lowered

- Facial expressions
- Posture
- Tone of voice
- Dress
- Body orientation
- Silence.

How will Charles use these elements to his advantage at interview?

Is there another advice you would give Charles regarding interpersonal skills and interview technique?

Top tips

When you are communicating with other people, always think about the situation and the context in which the communication occurs. There are some situations that require more formal behaviours that might be interpreted very differently in any other setting. Consider whether or not non-verbal behaviours are suitable for the context. When trying to improve your own non-verbal communication, concentrate on ways to make your signals match the level of formality required by the situation.

Communication skills, counselling and counselling skills

Nurses support and give advice to patients in a variety of ways in their everyday work. Nurses are not counsellors, but they should aim to provide patients with an opportunity to offer their support, as well as allowing patients to refuse that support, and when appropriate giving them an opportunity to work through complex issues relating to their health needs. Providing patients with information may enable nurses to do this.

It should be noted that there are close relationships between:

- counselling
- communication skills
- counselling skills.

Table 5.6   The variety of activities related to counselling

Guidance	Advice	Counselling
Highly directive	Moderately directive	Highly nondirective
Highly structured	Semi-structured	Mainly unstructured
The counsellor determines, the client accepts	The counsellor determines with the client's agreement	The client determines, the counsellor facilitates
Closed – addresses specific issues	Flexible – issues broadly agreed	Open – addresses emerging issues
Information content high	Information content moderate	Information content low
Demands competence in communication skills	Demands competence in interpersonal skills	Demands competence in relational skills
Counsellor is a guide	Counsellor is an adviser	Counsellor is a therapist

Source: adapted from Slevin (2003).

When nurses use counselling skills in an appropriate manner, they provide patients with an opportunity to become more self-aware, and in so doing they gain the ability to make more informed choices.

Slevin (2003) provides another approach to differentiating the variety of counselling activities. He suggests that there is a selection of counselling activities, ranging from guidance, a highly directive and structured approach, to counselling where the approach could be said to be non-directive and unstructured (Table 5.6).

In order to avoid confusion with key terms, Rigazio-DiGlio and Ivey (2006) use the term 'the helping interview' which resembles therapeutic communication as opposed to counselling.

Nurses can develop and use their therapeutic communication and therapeutic nursing interventions to help the patient identify his or her own problems and seek resources to deal with these problems.

The nurse may also be required to communicate with and counsel the patient over the telephone. NHS Direct operates a 24-hour nurse advice and health information service, providing confidential information on:

- What to do if you or your family are feeling ill
- Particular health conditions
- Local health-care services, such as doctors, dentists or late-night-opening pharmacies
- Self-help and support organisations.

There may be other reasons why the nurse needs to communicate with the patient over the telephone, e.g. to provide them with information or instructions, or they may need to speak with other health-care professionals to obtain blood results.

If face-to-face communication is not possible and a telephone call is required, then remember that telephone conversations can be overheard, and confidentiality rules still apply. A telephone call from the patient must be returned as soon as possible. The purpose, content and outcome of the telephone conversation must be documented.

Case study 5.3

Carl Boyd, aged 6, was admitted as a day case to hospital 2 days ago with a phimosis that required circumcision because he was suffering with recurrent balanitis. He was discharged home on the evening of the day of admission with his parents. The staff nurse had provided Carl's parents with postoperative information concerning care after circumcision and contact details of the children's ward. You are working night duty on the children's ward when a telephone call comes through from Mrs Boyd who is concerned and upset about Carl.

What might indicate, over the telephone, that Mrs Boyd is distressed?

How can the nurse use interpersonal skills to alleviate Mrs Boyd's anxiety and stress and to promote her and her son's wellbeing?

What advice would you give Mrs Boyd?

What next steps must you take?

Guidelines for records and record keeping

Most encounters that the nurse has with the patient will potentially involve recording the information that has been exchanged between the two parties. Local policies are in place that will guide the nurse with regard to records and record keeping. Guidelines have been provided by the NMC (2009) on this subject. Record keeping is a fundamental aspect of nursing care. Despite the fact that the NMC (2009) provides guidance, it does not determine the content, nor does it offer a rigid framework for the content of records or record keeping. Ultimately what to include, exclude and the format used are left up to the accountable practitioner and his or her professional judgement.

When the nurse keeps and maintains good records he or she is protecting the interests of the public by doing the following:

- Promoting high standards of nursing care
- Ensuring continuity of care
- Providing enhanced communication and dissemination of information between other members of the interprofessional health-care team
- Maintaining a correct description of treatment, care planning and delivery
- Offering the ability to reveal problems, such as a change in the patient's circumstances, at an early stage.

There may be occasions when a patient's records (or notes) may be used as evidence in a court of law or, at a local level, when following up a complaint. The records may also be requested by the Nursing and Midwifery Council when the Fitness to Practise Committees are investigating complaints made about nurses. In this instance the records may include:

- care plans
- diaries
- anything that makes reference to the patient.

Records must show that the nurse has acted professionally and in the best interests of the patient (Table 5.7).

Table 5.7 Elements associated with documentation, demonstrating that nurses have taken into account their duty of care to the patient

- A full account of the assessment, the care planned and what has been implemented
- Relevant information about the patient's condition at any given time and any measures that have been taken in response to patient needs
- Evidence that the nurse has understood and honoured the duty of care owed to the patient, that all reasonable tasks have been taken to care for the patient and that any actions or omissions have not compromised patient safety in any way
- A record of any arrangements that the nurse has made for the continuing care of the patient

Source: adapted from NMC (2004).

Table 5.8 Some common mistakes recorded in patient records

- Time not included
- Handwriting that is impossible to read
- Use of abbreviations that were vague/unclear
- Use of correction fluid to cover up errors
- Signature omitted
- Inaccuracies, particularly relating to the dates
- Delays in completing the record
- Record completed by a person who did not care for the patient
- Inaccuracies relating to name, date of birth and address
- Unprofessional terminology, e.g. 'dull as a door step'
- Meaningless phrases, e.g. 'nice person'
- Opinion mixed up with facts
- Subjective as opposed to objective comments, e.g. 'slept well'

Source: adapted from Dimond (2011).

Errors do occur in record keeping and Table 5.8 highlights some of these.

The use of abbreviations

The use of abbreviations and acronyms in health care has become an international patient safety issue. There are a number of common problems and these include ambiguous, unfamiliar and look-alike abbreviations as well as acronyms leading to misinterpretation and medical errors (Fenton-Khun, 2007). However, abbreviations may be used to save time, e.g. often nurses use the abbreviations T for temperature, BP for blood pressure and P for pulse; if they did not use them then much more time would be needed for record keeping. If abbreviations are used it may be advisable for NHS trusts to compile a list of approved abbreviations and acceptable symbols to reduce the risk of misinterpretation and misunderstanding.

Uncertainty can arise when abbreviations are used, which can lead to confusion resulting in danger to the patient. Dimond (2005) provides a list of common abbreviations that are sometimes used which may have different meanings (Table 5.9).

Good record keeping is the hallmark of a skilled, competent, confident and safe practitioner and can result in effective communication. However, the message being communicated will only be as good as the nurse who is recording the information. Other health-care workers may depend on the information

167

Table 5.9   Some abbreviations with different meanings

Abbreviated form	Possible meaning
PID	pelvic inflammatory disease OR prolapsed intervertebral disc
DOA	dead on arrival OR date of admission
Pt	patient OR physiotherapist OR part time
NFR	not for resuscitation OR neurophysiological facilitation of respiration
NAD	nothing abnormal discovered OR not a drop
FBC	fluid balance chart OR full blood count

Source: adapted from Dimond (2005).

contained in the records that you make and, as a result of what you have documented (or omitted to document), may act on this.

It is the registered nurse who is professionally accountable for any duties that they choose to delegate to any other member of the interprofessional health-care team, e.g. the student nurse. This includes the delegation of record keeping to preregistration nursing students or health-care assistants. It is imperative that these members of the team are appropriately supervised and that they are capable of carrying out the task. The registered nurse should countersign any such entry and bear in mind that they are professionally accountable for the consequences of such an entry. It is deemed bad practice to use initials in any record; the full signature should be used with the name written alongside it.

Obstructions to effective communication: causes of communication failure

There are many ways in which the message being transmitted never reaches the recipient and messages can become blocked for many reasons. Barriers to communication can occur if the recipient has failed to convey the meaning or the importance of the message.

If sender breakdown occurs, the person transmitting the message may send too much information and as a result the recipient can miss key points. Conversely, too little information can also be a cause of sender breakdown (Kozier et al, 2007). The language or the use of jargon can be difficult for the recipient and sender to understand, or the sender may have limited knowledge concerning the message being sent. The information being transmitted may be the wrong information. The nurse's attitude can convey the message that he or she is not interested in the information. In some instances the sender may be making false assumptions about the recipient (Taylor et al, 2005).

Top tips

When caring for people avoid nursing and medical jargon. Speak plain English, e.g. instead of using the term 'renal' use the 'kidney' instead. Telling a person that he or she has renal lithiasis might sound completely foreign to the patient and may even increase anxiety. However, telling a person that they have stones in the kidney may be much more understandable.

Alternatively, there may be recipient breakdown, when the recipient deliberately makes a choice to misinterpret or refuse to accept the transmitted message. This can be for a variety of reasons. For some the breakdown may be due to reasons beyond the recipient's control, e.g.:

- A speech defect/dysphasia
- Deafness
- Poor sight
- Developmental level
- Poor cognitive skills
- Facial injuries/disorders/dysarthria.

Physical reasons may be only one aspect of communication breakdown. Emotional aspects can also impinge on effective communications (Taylor et al, 2005):

- Perceptions
- Prejudice
- Aggression
- Threat.

Other problems with communication could be related to the following:

- There may be a long chain of command. The message gets passed on to many different people before reaching the recipient, making the process long and offering the possibility that the message may change.
- The reason for the message may be vague, e.g. lacking in detail, more explanation being needed.
- The recipient may be confused or demented.
- The medium used to transmit the message may be inappropriate, e.g. inappropriate written or verbal form.
- Actions can be delayed as a result of the late arrival of the message.
- The status of the two parties, e.g. the patient and the nurse, has the potential to intimidate either party because of their gender, age and knowledge base.
- Distraction, e.g. through pain and anxiety, can cause communication channels to break up.

Generally to reduce the possibility of communication breakdown the nurse should:

- actively listen to the patient
- speak slowly
- ask one question at a time and avoid multiple questioning
- provide only one piece of information at a time – avoid information overload
- use simple language
- consider using gesture
- if possible reduce noise pollution, e.g. from background noise
- check to see if the patient has any aids that he or she uses to enhance communication, such as a hearing aid or spectacles
- not shout
- think about using the written word if appropriate.

Think

How might you attempt to reduce noise pollution on a busy children's ward when you wish to communicate with the parents of a sick child?

To maintain confidentiality, first you would want to conduct the conversation in private if possible, which offers one way in which you can eliminate background noise and interference. However, private areas may not always be available, so you could ensure that communications take place when the ward is less busy, e.g. avoiding meal times, ward rounds or when the ward is being cleaned.

Dealing with patients' complaints

Most nurses and other health-care staff provide an outstanding service but, sometimes, things can and do go wrong. Often complaints arise as a result of poor communication. they can range in severity from dissatisfaction about food to concerns arising as a result of allegations of professional misconduct or inappropriate or incorrect surgical intervention.

Patients who complain about the care or treatment that they have received have a right to expect a prompt, open, constructive and honest response. This will include an explanation of what has happened and, where appropriate, an apology. The nurse must never allow a patient's complaint to prejudice the care or treatment provided for that patient. All complaints should be treated seriously and with respect (McKenna, 2008).

A new approach to dealing with complaints was introduced in England in April 2009 – a single approach that deals with complaints, allowing flexibility to respond and to learn from mistakes that may have been made.

The NHS Constitution (DH, 2009a) makes it clear to people that they have rights when they are unhappy about services provided. The NHS Constitution states that any individual has the right to:

- have any complaint that they make about NHS services dealt with efficiently and have it properly investigated
- know the outcome of any investigation into the complaint
- take the complaint to the Health Service Ombudsman if he or she is not satisfied with the way that the NHS has dealt with their complaint
- make a claim for judicial review if the person thinks that he or she has been directly affected by an unlawful act or decision of an NHS body
- receive compensation when he or she has been harmed by negligent treatment.

Those people who use social care services can take their complaint to the Local Government Ombudsman.

When mistakes occur and a complaint is made people expect an acknowledgement of the error and for it to be dealt with quickly, efficiently and thoroughly (Health Service Ombudsman for England, 2005). When health- and social care providers listen to the experiences of people, mistakes can be resolved faster, learning can occur and actions can be put in place that will prevent the same problem from occurring in the future. If the nurse understands the complaints procedure and how to help deal with complaints more effectively, then services can improve for all concerned (DH, 2009b).

The National Audit Office (2008) notes that people find making a complaint too complicated and that when a complaint has been made it often takes a long time for it to be resolved. The new approach to making a complaint about the NHS and adult social care services is aimed at ending the bureaucracy of the older system (DH, 2009b).

The complaints system should be regarded as a tool for education and not be used as a paper exercise (Norman, 2009). Complaints are important to any organisation's feedback system and are associated very closely with quality indicators. Investigating and dealing with complaints can provide much insight into service provision; nurses should ensure that they are aware of the processes and procedures associated with the complaints system used in organisations where they work, which should enable them to feel confident when addressing complaints, pre-empting situations from arising, as well as learning from those issues.

Armstrong (2009) suggests that those who have been aggrieved (people being cared for and their relatives) when things go wrong are normally only seeking an apology. An apology alone, however, does not in itself make an effective complaints system (Norman, 2009); in England and Wales an apology is not an admission of negligence or a breach of statutory duty (Compensation Act 2006, c 29).

There are six values associated with good complaint management:

1. Getting it right
2. Being customer focused
3. Being open and accountable
4. Acting fairly and proportionately
5. Putting things right
6. Seeking continuous improvement.

In England, Statutory Instrument 2009/309 – The Local Authority Social Services and National Health Service Complaints (England) Regulations 2009 – makes clear the duties and responsibilities concerning complaints and how they should be managed. The Department of Health (2009b) advises that in order to carry out good practice the organisation should:

- make public its complaints procedures
- acknowledge a complaint when it has been made and offer to discuss the matter
- deal with complaint in an efficient way, investigating it properly and appropriately
- write to the person making the complaint once it has been dealt with. Explain how it has been resolved and what appropriate action was taken. Remind the person of the right to take the matter further to the Health Ombudsman or Local Government Ombudsman if they are still not happy
- ensure that a senior member of the organisation takes on the responsibility for the complaints policy and learning from complaints
- offer help to the person making the complaint to understand the procedures associated with making a complaint
- produce a report each year about complaints that have been received and what has been done to improve things as a result.

Listening

By listening to people and what their complaint and their concerns are about can convey the message that the organisation is a listening organisation and it wants to learn from feedback. All NHS bodies and local authorities have to make it clear to people how they can complain. There are several ways in which this may be done. The information provided to help people make a complaint (and a compliment) should be engaging and accessible, offered in such a way that it is effective and meets the needs of all service users, e.g. provided in Braille or large print if this is required.

People usually understand that mistakes can happen. When mistakes happen many people want to know how it happened, that you are sorry and that there have been steps taken to prevent it from happening again. The impression that the organisation makes on the person who is unhappy can have a huge impact on the outcome of the complaint, so it is important that all the information about the complaint is fully assessed, demonstrating that the complaint has been taken seriously; this may provide the basis for a good ongoing relationship. Poor communication is the most common reason people give in relation to being unhappy about how their complaint has been handled.

It must be remembered that for any complaint consent may be needed to check records and access personal details.

When the complaint has been made or the person voices unhappiness, there are a number of things that may help to demonstrate to the person that you are actively listening to them. Start by letting the complainant know the name and details of the person who will be investigating the complaint.

Determine how the person would like to be addressed: Mr, Mrs, Ms or by their first name. If the concern has been raised by telephone you should always ask if they would like you to ring them back, and give them the chance to meet face to face if possible. Ask how they would like to be kept informed about how their complaint is being addressed, e.g. by telephone, email, letter or through a third party – an advocate or support service. If they do wish to be kept informed by telephone then find out when it is convenient to call them and ensure that they are happy for somebody else to take a message if they are not there, or if it is appropriate for messages to be left on their answer phone. If post is the chosen option, check that you have the correct address and that they are happy to receive correspondence at that address.

Enquire if the person has any disabilities that you need to be made aware of, e.g. do they require wheelchair access? Determine the location where it is more convenient for the person to meet and explain that they can have an advocate present to support them throughout the complaint process.

With the person, take time to carefully go through the reasons for his or her unhappiness point by point. This is needed to be able to understand why the person is dissatisfied. Ask the person what he or she would like to happen as a result of the complaint, but it is important from the outset to explain if expectations are unrealistic. The person may respond by saying that he or she wants an apology, a new appointment, reimbursement for costs or loss of personal belongings, or an explanation.

A plan of action is needed and will need to be agreed; this should include when the person will hear back from the organisation. It may be possible to resolve the matter quickly and a plan of action will not be required, but it is important that the person complaining is happy about that and that there is no risk to others.

Making a response

Making the correct response means that the seriousness of the complaint will have to be assessed. A three-step process (DH, 2009b) to gauge the impact of complaints on people is required:

- Step 1: decide how serious the issue is
- Step 2: decide how likely the issue is to recur
- Step 3: categorise the risk.

Using this approach can help to assess the significance of an issue and take the appropriate action.

Table 5.10 Seriousness of the complaint

Seriousness	Description
Low	Unsatisfactory service or experience not directly related to care No impact or risk to provision of care OR Unsatisfactory service or experience related to care, typically a single resolvable issue. Minimal impact and relative minimal risk to the provision of care or the service. No real risk of litigation
Medium	Service or experience below reasonable expectations in several ways, but not causing lasting problems. Has the ability to impact on service provision. Some possibility of litigation
High	Significant issues concerning standards, quality of care and safeguarding of or denial of rights. Complaints with obvious quality assurance or risk management issues that could cause lasting problems for the organisation, and so require investigation. Possibility of litigation and adverse local publicity

Source: adapted from DH (2009b).

Table 5.11 Likelihood of recurrence

Likelihood	Description
Rare	Isolated or a 'one off' – slight or vague connection to service provision
Unlikely	Rare – usual but could have occurred before
Possible	Happens from time to time – not frequently or regularly
Likely	Will most likely occur several times a year
Almost certain	Recurring and frequent, foreseeable

Source: adapted from DH (2009b).

Assessing the significance of an issue, how serious it is, how likely it is to recur and the various categories of risk can be seen in Tables 5.10–5.12.

Addressing and managing complaints in a compassionate, competent and confident manner can help to identify areas of care that may need improving. Health- and social care organisations are required to show how feedback is used to improve the care and services that they provide and organisations must:

- specify the number of complaints received
- highlight the issues that have arisen from these complaints
- state whether the complaints have been upheld
- indicate the number of cases referred to an Ombudsman.

The lessons learnt and actions taken from significant issues by complaints raised have to be recorded by the organisation. The Care Quality Commission requires those registered providers of services to investigate complaints effectively and learn lessons from them.

The Health Service Ombudsman undertakes independent investigations into complaints about the NHS. The results of selected investigations are published in public bi-annual reports.

Table 5.12 Categorising risk

Low (simple non complex issues)	Delayed or cancelled appointments Event resulting in minor harm (e.g. cut, strain) Loss of property Lack of cleanliness Transport problems Single failure to meet care needs (failed to respond to call bell) Medical records missing
Moderate (several issues relating to a short period of care)	Event resulting in moderate harm (e.g. fracture) Delayed discharge Failure to meet care needs Miscommunication or misinformation Medical errors Incorrect treatment Staff attitude or communication
High (multiple issues relating to longer periods of care, often involving more than one organisation or individual)	See moderate list Event resulting in serious harm (e.g. damage to internal organs)
Extreme (multiple issues relating to serious failures, causing serious harm)	Events resulting in serious harm or death Gross professional misconduct Abuse or neglect Criminal offence (e.g. assault)

Source: adapted from DH (2009b).

It is clear that complaints made about services or the care provided by the NHS can be dealt with locally or, if appropriate, go through various processes to ensure that the patient's complaint is addressed fairly and fully. The nurse should always seek advice when providing the patient with details concerned with making a complaint, because it can be a long and tortuous process for all parties.

Case study 5.4

Mrs Dorothy Bragshaw was an 86-year-old woman who was admitted to a medical ward 3 weeks ago; she had sustained a right-sided cerebrovascular accident resulting in a dense left-sided hemiparesis. She was unable to swallow. From the day of her admission Mrs Bragshaw was unconscious, requiring total nursing care to ensure that her needs were met safely and effectively. Mrs Bragshaw had three daughters and two sons who visited her sporadically; two of them lived in Canada. Mrs Bragshaw's condition deteriorated overnight; she was producing reduced amounts of urine via her urethral catheter and she was now displaying Cheyne–Stokes breathing. Her eldest daughter, Kathleen, was called and informed of her mother's deteriorating condition at 09:30. Mrs Bragshaw was confirmed dead at 20:10. Last offices were performed and her body was taken to the mortuary. Her property was sent to the patients' office as per policy and procedure. The next day Kathleen came to the ward to pick up her belongings and was redirected to the patients' office. A call to the ward informed the ward sister that Kathleen said that her mother's purse and two other valuable items were missing.

What might be the next steps?

How is the property belonging to patients in places where you work managed?

Who might Kathleen seek help and support from in attempting to find out what has happened to items she is alleging are missing?

Dealing with compliments

Just as complaints are received, so too are compliments given. Compliments, as with complaints, should help people learn and therefore enhance the quality of care. Compliments should also be recorded. Often compliments are given in writing in the form of thank-you cards or gifts such as chocolates or sweets.

The nurse may be offered gifts, favours or hospitality from patients during the course of or after a period of care or treatment. The Code of Conduct (NMC, 2008) states that the nurse must refuse any gift, favour or hospitality that could be interpreted, now or in the future, as an attempt to obtain preferential consideration from the nurse. The underlying principle is not that the nurse must never receive gifts or favours, but that they must never be interpreted as being given by the patient to the nurse in return for preferential treatment. If you decide to accept a gift or favour you must ensure that you consult local policy and that you adhere to this.

Disengaging from a professional relationship

The final aspect of this chapter deals with leaving or breaking away from a professional relationship. This is in contrast to the preceding aspects of the chapter where the formation and maintenance of the relationship have been promoted. Just as the nurse needs to concentrate on engaging with the patient, he or she must also invest time and energies in leaving the relationship. The nurse may need to consider planning to end the relationship even before it has begun, in order to prepare him- or herself for this potentially upsetting experience. Preparing for the expected outcomes could help to make disengagement easier.

Varcarolis (2010) suggests that ending meaningful relationships that have been created during the time the nurse has spent with the patient can sometimes be difficult because it may evoke feelings of sadness, fear or uncertainty at saying goodbye.

The reason for the termination of the relationship may be a consequence of several things; it may be permanent or temporary:

- The patient has recovered enough to be discharged.
- The patient has deteriorated and may need to be discharged to another unit/institution.
- The nurse may be leaving his or her job
- The patient may have died.

When disengaging from a therapeutic relationship the nurse should be encouraged to reflect on the experience in order to learn and develop. There may be feelings of pleasure – having achieved goals, aims and objectives with the patient and his or her family. There may also be feelings of sadness as a result of having to leave a relationship that had flourished or the deterioration of the patient's health and even his or her death.

Support can be given in the form of facilitative discussion networks at work or the place of study. Opportunities can and should be made for the nurse to speak about his or her feelings.

Ending a therapeutic relationship must be given much thought because the patient may have become reliant on the nurse for many things. Termination of a relationship may leave the patient feeling abandoned and thus vulnerable, so suitable arrangements must be made for the continuation of care/ therapy/treatment where appropriate.

The start and the end of a relationship with a patient or the staff with whom you have worked can provoke many feelings, both positive and negative.

Conclusions

Communication with patients and their families should never be seen as an optional extra; it is a fundamental clinical skill that all nurses, regardless of grade or level, should possess. This chapter has focused on establishing, maintaining and disengaging from professional relationships. When people in therapeutic relationship communicate effectively there is a great potential to:

- improve satisfaction
- foster compliance and control pain
- reduce anxiety
- establish trust and rapport
- support and educate the patient
- establish a plan for treatment.

Caring for people is a complex activity that requires skill. In order to provide a therapeutic relationship with the patient at the centre of the affiliation, the nurse has to work within a team. This chapter has explored the concept of team working and outlined some of the health-care professionals who may be involved in patient care. Effective team working has positive outcomes for patient care.

The nature of the nurse–patient relationship means that this can never be a completely equal relationship. The inequalities should be acknowledged by both patient and nurse; both parties ought to value each other's competencies. The relationship has evolved through mutual trust and respect. Abuses of power can and do occur, and are often the result of a shift in the focus of care, e.g. the needs of the nurse supersede the needs of the patient. These potential abuses have been described in this chapter.

Therapeutic nursing interventions aim to provide holistic nursing care in relation to individual aspects of the body, mind and spirit. Caring is central to therapeutic nursing care. The nurse needs to develop and build on his or her interpersonal skills in an attempt to provide a therapeutic partnership, i.e. respect, rapport and trust. By enhancing skills associated with communication the nurse may then be able to form more elaborate and effective relationships with the patient and other health-care professionals. Applying these skills in an accomplished manner can provide a therapeutic lift to the patient.

To use communication skills effectively there are many competencies that must be brought into play, such as respect, honesty and empathy. There was much discussion in this chapter about communication methods, e.g. active listening is a complex skill that includes the use not only of the ears but also of the whole body. Verbal and non-verbal communications were detailed. Verbal communication accounts for 7 per cent of the messages transmitted between people, with 55 per cent related to the use of body language as a communication medium and the remaining 38 per cent associated with the tone of voice.

Much communication between the nurse and other health-care professionals occurs through the written word – the patient record. Many encounters that the nurse has with the patient will involve some means of recording the encounter, recording the information that has been exchanged. The NMC (2009) has provided advice to the nurse about records and record keeping. Good record keeping is the hallmark of a skilled, competent and safe nurse.

Communication processes are complex and because of this there is the potential for obstructions to occur that will impede effective communications. Some of the causes of communication failure were described.

Despite striving to maintain open, honest and effective communication, complaints can and do occur. Complaints are commonly associated with poor communications, and can range in severity from dissatisfaction about the cleanliness of toilets to allegations of professional misconduct. If complaints do arise they are dealt with (when appropriate) at a local level adhering to local policy. The NHS Complaints Procedure is used to help arrive at a satisfactory explanation of the cause of the complaint. The aim is to deal with the complaint speedily and efficiently, courteously and sympathetically. Advice should always be sought when a complaint has been made, because it can be a long and tortuous process for all concerned.

Compliments are also received by the nurse from the patient. If gifts are given, the principle is not that the nurse must never receive gifts or favours, but that they should never be interpreted as being given by the patient to the nurse in return for preferential treatment.

Although much effort is put into initiating and maintaining a professional relationship, there are skills that are needed to disengage from that professional relationship. Time and energy must be invested into planning the end of the relationship. The reasons for the termination of the relationship are varied, e.g. the patient fully recovers or he or she may die. Ending the relationship can result in feelings of being abandoned and vulnerable, and both parties may need to take part in facilitative discussions in order to deal with and acknowledge these feelings.

Activity

Attempt the following 10 questions that are related to therapeutic relationships and communication and interpersonal skills to test your knowledge. The answers can be found at the back of this book, in the chapter called 'Activity Answers'.

1. The Health Service Ombudsman:
   a. Is employed by the trusts
   b. Is a lay person
   c. Provides a service to the public by undertaking independent investigations into complaints
   d. Works for the Nursing and Midwifery Council

2. In order to assess a patient's needs effectively the nurse must employ many skills including:
   a. Communication
   b. Observation
   c. Measurement
   d. All of the above

3. Respect means:
   a. Being kind
   b. Acting in the best interests of the Nursing and Midwifery Council
   c. Demonstrating a genuine interest in the patient and his or her needs
   d. Responding quickly to a person's needs

4. Empathy means:
   a. Having the ability to communicate understanding of another person's experience from that person's perspective
   b. The same as sympathy
   c. Being compassionate
   d. Using ethical practices

5. How many values are associated with good complaint management?:
   a. 4
   b. 5
   c. 7
   d. 6

6. Paralanguage can be defined as:
   a. The use of a foreign language
   b. Using jargon
   c. The vocal cues that accompany language
   d. The use of semantics

7. Oculesics are associated with:
   a. Eye movements and messages conveyed by the eyes
   b. Listening
   c. Both of the above
   d. The use of dialect

8. When disengaging from a therapeutic relationship the nurse should:
   a. Make arrangements to see the patient after discharge
   b. Forget about the experience
   c. Be encouraged to reflect on the experience in order to learn and develop
   d. Think about the next patient being admitted

9. The Care Quality Commission is:
   a. A branch of the Royal College of Nursing
   b. A Government body
   c. An independent body
   d. A social workers' organisation

10. The use of abbreviations and acronyms in health care:
    a. Should be avoided
    b. Has become an international patient safety issue
    c. Can lead to poor communication
    d. All of the above

References

Abercrombie K (1968) Paralanguage. *British Journal of Disorders of Communication* **3**: 55–59.

Allender JA, Rector C, Warner KD (2010) *Community Health Nursing: Promoting and protecting the public's health*, 7th edn. Philadelphia, PA: Lippincott.

Armstrong D (2009) The power of apology: saying sorry can leave both patients and nurses feeling better. *Nursing Times* **105**(44): 16–19.

British Association for Counselling and Psychotherapy (2010) *Ethical Framework for Good Practice in Counselling and Psychotherapy*. Rugby: British Association for Counselling and Psychotherapy.

Brody M (2004) The nurse–client relationship. In: Daniels R (ed.), *Nursing Fundamentals: Caring and clinical decision-making*. New York: Thompson, pp 68–89.

Burgoon JK, Gurerro L, Floyd K (2010) *Nonverbal Communication*. Boston, MA: Allyn & Bacon.

Council for Healthcare Regulatory Excellence (2008a). *Clear Sexual Boundaries Between Healthcare Professionals and Patents: Responsibilities of healthcare professionals*. London: Council for Healthcare Regulatory Excellence.

Council for Healthcare Regulatory Excellence (2008b). *Clear Sexual Boundaries Between Healthcare Professionals and Patents: Guidance for fitness to practise panels*. London: Council for Healthcare Regulatory Excellence.

Council for Healthcare Regulatory Excellence (2008c). *Learning about Sexual Boundaries Between Healthcare Professionals and Patents: A report on education and training*. London: Council for Healthcare Regulatory Excellence.

Department of Health (2007) *Confidence in Caring. A framework for best practice*. London: Department of Health.

Department of Health (2009a) *The NHS Constitution: The NHS Belongs to All of Us*. London: Department of Health.

Department of Health (2009b) *Listening, Responding, Improving: A guide to better customer care*. London: Department of Health.

Department of Health (2010) *Essence of Care*. London: Department of Health. Available at: www.dh.gov.uk/prod_consum_dh/groups/dh_digitalassets/@dh/@en/@ps/documents/digitalasset/dh_119978.pdf (accessed June 2011).

Dimond B (2005) Abbreviations: The need for legibility and accuracy in documentation. *British Journal of Nursing* **14**: 665–666.

Dimond B (2011) *Legal Aspects of Nursing*, 6th edn. Harlow: Pearson.

Egan G (2009) *The Skilled Helper: A problem management and opportunity approach to helping*, 9th edn. Belmont, CA: Brookes/Cole.

Elton J, Reading H (2008) The needs of the acutely ill adult. In: Hinchliff S, Norman S, Schober J (eds), *Nursing Practice and Health Care. A foundation text*, 5th edn. London: Hodder Arnold, pp 223–243.

Jeffrey D (2006) Communication. In: Falon M, Hanks G (eds), *The ABC of Palliative Care*, 2nd edn. Oxford: Blackwell.

Fenton-Khun I (2007) Abbreviations and acronyms in healthcare: when shorter isn't sweeter. *Pediatric Nursing* **33**: 392–398.

Guerrero L, Floyd K (2006) *Non Verbal Communication in Close Relationships*. Mahwah, NJ: Erlbaum.

Hargie O (2011) *Skilled Interpersonal Communication*, 5th edn. London: Routledge.

Health Service Ombudsman for England (2005) *Making Things Better? A Report on Reform of the NHS Complaints Procedure in England*. London: TSO.

Horsburgh D (2007) The NMC code of conduct and applied ethical principles. In: Brooker C, Waugh A (eds), *Foundations of Nursing Practice. Fundamentals of holistic care*. Edinburgh: Elsevier, pp 163–181.

Irurita V (2000) Preserving integrity: A theory of nursing. In: Greenwood J (ed.), *Nursing Theory in Australia: Development and application*, 2nd edn. Sydney: Prentice Hall.

Kozier B, Erb G, Berman A, Snyder S, Lake R, Harvey S (2007) *Fundamentals of Nursing: Concepts, process and practice*. Harlow: Pearson.

McKenna J (2008) Clinical governanace and accountable practice. In: Hinchliff S, Norman S, Schober J (eds), *Nursing Practice and Health Care*, 5th edn. London: Hodder Arnold, pp 149–174.

Maguire P, Pitceathly C (2003) Key communication skills and how to acquire them. *British Medical Journal* **325**: 697–700.

Meredith PV (2000) Essentials of professional communication. In: Meredith PV, Horan NM (eds), *Adult Primary Care*. Philadelphia, PA: Saunders, pp 91–110.

National Audit Office (2008) *Feeding Back? Learning from Complaints Handling in Health and Social Care*. London: TSO.

Norman A (2009) Involving nurses in the complaints process leads to more effective Care. *Nursing Times* **105**(44) 11.

Nursing and Midwifery Council (2009) *Guidlines for Records and Record Keeping*. London: NMC.

Nursing and Midwifery Council (2008) *The Code: Standards of conduct, performance and ethics for nurses and midwives*. London: NMC.

Rigazio-DiGlio SA, Ivey AE (2006) The helping interview: developmental and counselling therapy. In: Hragie O (ed.), *The Handbook of Communication Skills*, 3rd edn. London: Routledge, pp 481–505.

Ronayne S (2001) Nurse–patient partnerships in hospital care. *Journal of Clinical Nursing* **10**: 591–592.

Sidtis DVL (2004) When novel sentences spoken or heard for the first time in the history of the universe are not enough: Toward a dual-process model of language. *International Journal of Language and Communication Disorders* **39**(1): 1–44.

179

Sherman KM (1994) *Communication and Image in Nursing*. New York: Delmar.

Slevin O (2003) Therapeutic intervention in nursing. In: Basford L, Slevin O (eds), *Theory and Practice of Nursing*, 2nd edn. Cheltenham: Nelson Thornes, pp 533–568.

Smith SF, Duell DJ, Martin BC (2011) *Clinical Nursing Skills: Basic to advanced skills*, 8th edn. Upper Saddle River, NJ: Pearson.

Taylor C, Lillis C, LeMone P (2005) *Fundamentals of Nursing: The art and science of nursing care*, 5th edn. Philadelphia, PA: Lippincott.

Varcarolis EM (2010) Developing therapeutic relationships. In: Varcarolis EM (ed.), *Foundations of Psychiatric Mental Health Nursing: A clinical approach*, 4th edn. St Louis, MO: Elsevier, pp 155–170.

6

Interprofessional Working and Learning

Aims and objectives

The aim of this chapter is to enable the reader to begin to understand and develop the key attributes associated with interprofessional working and learning.

At the end of the chapter you will be able to:

1. Identify members of the interprofessional team
2. Describe the roles and responsibilities of the interprofessional team.
3. Outline the value of interprofessional team working when caring for people
4. Describe the role of the nurse in the promotion of effective interprofessional working and learning
5. Begin to apply the concepts discussed to the practice setting
6. Appreciate the Nursing and Midwifery Council's requirements of student nurses

The focus of this chapter is to encourage the reader to develop an even further understanding of the role that other health-care and social care professionals undertake by participating in interprofessional working practice. The roles and responsibilities of other health- and social care professionals have been discussed in preceding chapters and are disused in this and other chapters that follow. Chapter 4 already started to address the importance of working with others and working in a partnership perspective – an interagency approach. The promotion of the modernisation of the NHS and the production of key, influencing documents, provided by various governments, has promoted the use of interprofessional working practices.

There is little consensus about the term 'interprofessional working'. Several definitions are provided here to help the reader acquire clarity and understanding. It is vital that the nurse understands the terms used if he or she is to engage effectively in interprofessional working and learning, and mutual respect and understanding are common fundamental terms associated with it. Being aware of how each professional group perceives the others may enhance understanding and collaboration. Reinforcing and promoting stereotypes, along with harbouring misconceptions, can hinder and harm good working relationships among health- and social care professionals.

Interprofessional working has much potential to enhance care; it can also produce tensions and concerns within the health-care team. Barriers to effective working relationships associated with interprofessional working and learning are discussed.

The Student's Guide to Becoming a Nurse, Second Edition. Ian Peate.
© 2012 John Wiley & Sons, Ltd. Published 2012 by John Wiley & Sons, Ltd.

To work effectively the nurse must embrace the concept of effective team working. Team working, similar to interprofessional working, is defined in many ways and is often used synonymously with group working. This aspect of the chapter considers both team working and working as a member of a group.

The latter part of this chapter focuses on interprofessional learning, and it is suggested that learning together will lead to more effective and productive working as well an improvement in care provision. Emphasis is placed on the fact that interprofessional learning does not take place in a vacuum. There are many factors that must be taken into consideration, e.g. the needs and interests of the various stakeholders.

Background and underlying principles

The philosophy underpinning interprofessional working lies in the modernisation of the NHS. Referral to various polices and directives has been made previously with the aim of enhancing and improving the patient experience. The interprofessional agenda for health and social care is complex. The interprofessional agenda has the ability to improve cooperation and partnerships and to enhance communications and working practices across professional and organisational boundaries. According to Kenny (2002) interprofessional working provides the vehicle whereby existing power structures (i.e. professional elitism) can be replaced with arrangements that are committed to equality and collective responsibility.

The shift from bureaucratic, centralised service provision to more of a focus on patient centeredness articulates well with current Government policy and the modernisation agenda, a part of which is to enhance interprofessional collaboration. Service users should not become mere recipients of care but should be empowered to become partners in care (Wilby, 2005). The NHS modernisation agenda acknowledges that problems arise when a system that was devised in the 1940s tries to operate in the twenty-first century, with old-fashioned demarcations between staff and barriers to services. Hassmiller and Goodman (2011) note that, globally, we are facing challenges of caring for an ageing population with multiple chronic diseases in a health-care system that is fragmented. It is the fragmentation of care that must be avoided.

It is not only policy development that requires that health- and social care agencies to work together. Glendinning et al (2003) point out that the Health Act 1999 also imposes a duty on all NHS organisations to work in partnership. The key aim of some legislation, e.g. the Community Care Act 1990, is to promote closer and collaborative partnerships with service users. Despite continued increases in health care spending in the UK, sometimes the care provided to people can be too much, too little, too late or too disjointed.

Patients often move from one professional group to another depending on their clinical needs. Collaborative arrangements between health-care groups (health-care professionals) are not new: as far back as 1974 the British Medical Association (BMA, 1974) used the term 'primary care team'. Collaborative arrangements, according to Rushmer (2005), have the ability to unite health provision across disciplines (integrated working), health sectors (intermediate care) and also agencies (multiagency working). The aim is to provide the patient with a service that is seamless and joined up; there is need for coordination and continuity.

Top tips

Before going on to your next placement, take some time to think about the other health and social professionals with whom you may be working. Learn a little about their roles and responsibilities.

What is interprofessional working?

Cowley et al (2002) point out that, despite the fact that partnership working has been widely recognised for a number of years, in a review of over 52 policy documents there was a lack of consensus in terminology accompanied by a paucity of definitions. Lack of clarity about interprofessional working will be reflected in an organisation's philosophy and, as a result, there is a danger that some health-care professionals may dismiss interprofessional working as irrelevant or not needed. It is important to understand what is meant by the term 'interprofessional working'. It is not just the subject of academic debate; it is vital, if the nurse is to engage in interprofessional working (and ultimately learning), that he or she understands the concept.

183

Hassmiller and Goodman (2011) note that when nurses engage with interprofessional working a forum can occur for them to express themselves, and for other health-care professionals to understand and value the role and function of the nurse; nurses are the largest professional health care group in the NHS. Strengthening the professional identity of nursing is seen as a prerequisite if nurses are to collaborate effectively with other health-care professionals. Interprofessional working is one way of strengthening nursing's identity.

Lack of clarity and ambiguity can lead to misunderstandings, which accordingly can multiply, bringing challenges to the full implementation of interprofessional working and learning. Lewy (2010) notes that there has to be more understanding of the key issues to move the agenda forward. The prefixes 'inter' and 'multi' and the adjectives 'disciplinary' and 'professional' are often used. There are several terms that are used interchangeably, e.g. 'multidisciplinary' and 'interdisciplinary' (Wee et al., 2001).

There has been much debate about the terminology associated with interprofessional working and there are many terms, e.g.:

- Multiprofessional
- Interprofessional
- Multidisciplinary
- Interdisciplinary
- Multiagency
- Interagency.

Pirrie at al (1998) state that there is a distinction between 'inter' and 'multi', based on three dimensions:

- Numerical
- Territorial
- Epistemological.

Payne (2000) has attempted to summarise the definition quagmire and suggest that evidence gleaned from the literature indicates that 'multi' denotes activities that:

- bring more than two groups together
- focus on complementary procedures and perspectives
- provide opportunities to learn about each other
- are motivated by a desire to focus on clients' needs
- develop participants' understanding of their separate but inter-related roles as members of a team.

They also suggest that the prefix 'inter' is more appropriate when the activity enables team members to:

- develop a new interprofessional perspective that is more than the sum of the individual parts
- integrate procedures and perspectives on behalf of clients
- learn from and about each other
- reflect critically on their knowledge base
- engage in shared reflection on their joint practice
- surrender some aspects of their own professional role
- share knowledge
- develop a common understanding.

Interprofessional therefore relates to relationships between different professional groups. A third term also needs to be mentioned: 'interagency'. Interagency collaboration refers to relationships between different organisations or agencies. These organisations may be uniprofessional or multiprofessional. Chapter 4 considers interagency working in detail and you may note that much of the emphasis there is associated with health- and social care agencies as well as the voluntary sector. Table 6.1 provides an overview of the three terms.

Table 6.1   A summary of the three terms often associated with interprofessional collaboration

Term	Description
Inter-professional	Relations between different professional groups. Each group will have its own identity and its own professional culture that has been established by professional bodies, e.g. the Health Professions Council (HPC), Nursing and Midwifery Council (NMC) and General Medical Council (GMC)
Inter-agency	Relations that exist between different organisations and agencies. The agencies may consist of representatives from the health, social and voluntary sector. Each agency is likely to have developed its own culture associated with its policies and procedures. There may be, on occasion, competing funding arrangements
Multidisciplinary	This term refers to teams that work in more fluid ways. Members may be from various professional groups but they work towards a focused goal, all aiming to achieve the same outcome. The context is focused, enduring and is often small scale. A shared identity but one with an explicit professional contribution

Source: adapted from Biggs (1997).

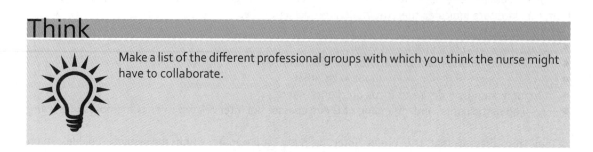

Think

Make a list of the different professional groups with which you think the nurse might have to collaborate.

Did you think broad and wide? Compare your list with the following list and the list of professions that are on the HPC register:

- Physiotherapists
- Paramedics
- Radiographers
- Occupational therapists
- Social workers
- Police
- Doctors
- Probation managers.

Each of the above groups has its own unique professional culture and they have all experienced their own unique educational programme, preparing them for their practice. These professional groups therefore have unique professional identities, yet they are expected to come together to work as a professional group. One common denominator for some of the health-care groups (excluding nursing and medicine) is that they have their own professional regulator – the Health Professions Council (HPC).

Mutual respect, understanding and trust are central components of collaborative working and interprofessional education and are facilitated through open and honest two-way effective communications. This enables the professionals involved in an interprofessional endeavour to develop an understanding of one another's perspectives (Kennison and Fletcher, 2005). Understanding how we perceive other health-care professionals, and being aware of the stereotypes that we hold about them, may help us to work more effectively when engaging in interprofessional working.

Think

What do you think are the stereotypical views that others hold about nurses? Make a list.

Some people have very interesting perceptions, views and clichés about nurses. Did any of the following appear in your list?

- Battle axe
- Angel
- Sex fiend
- All male nurses are gay
- Educated
- Always on the go
- Heavy smoker
- Caring
- Heavy drinker
- Dumb
- Killer

- Overweight
- All female
- Poorly paid.

Do you agree with the stereotypes? Do they annoy you at all?

Now think of some of the other health-care professionals with whom you are required to work and think about the stereotypes that you hold about these other professionals. How do you think they might feel if they think that you perceive them in a particular way?

Stereotyping, prejudging and harbouring misperceptions about other health-care professionals can harm good interprofessional working relationships. Working and learning with other health-care professionals may help to address and correct any misconceptions that you may have about others.

The health professions council

The Government aims to improve the quality of health and social services in many ways. Some of these have already been discussed; one other way is to modernise the systems of professional regulation (Whitcombe, 2005). The Health Act 1999 was the Act responsible for replacing the Council for Professions Supplementary to Medicine (CPSM). The move to a smaller and more unified regulative body – the HPC – was established in 2001 and became operational in 2002.

The Council for Health Care Regulatory Excellence (CHRE) was set up in 2003; they promote the health and wellbeing of patients and the public in the regulation of health professionals. Their job is to scrutinise and oversee the work of the nine regulatory bodies that set standards for training and conduct of health professionals. These nine professional bodies are as follows:

1. General Chiropractic Council
2. General Dental Council
3. General Medical Council
4. General Optical Council
5. General Pharmaceutical Council (PhC)
6. General Osteopathic Council
7. Health Professions Council
8. Nursing and Midwifery Council
9. Pharmaceutical Society of Northern Ireland.

The Health and Social Care Act 2008 gives CHRE a number of powers of scrutiny. The CHRE audit the processes used by the various regulators to receive and screen complaints against individual health professionals.

The HPC maintains a register of health professionals who meet its standards. It also has the power to take action against health professionals who do not meet its standards. The aim of the HPC is to protect the health and wellbeing of the people who use the services of the health professionals registered with it. It monitors standards for professional education and conduct. Currently the HPC regulates 15 health professions:

1. Art therapists
2. Biomedical scientists
3. Chiropodists/podiatrists
4. Dieticians

5.   Hearing aid dispensers
6.   Occupational therapists
7.   Operating department practitioners
8.   Orthoptists
9.   Orthotists
10. Paramedics
11. Physiotherapists
12. Practitioner psychologists
13. Prosthetists
14. Radiographers
15. Speech and language therapists.

The HPC has produced standards of proficiency, standards of conduct and standards of performance and ethics (HPC, 2008).

Think

Take some time to work out which professional body you would need to contact if you wanted to make a complaint about a dental nurse.
   If you had to raise concerns about a social worker ,how would you go about doing this?
   Can you think about ways in which it would be easier for members of the public to raise concerns about health- and social care staff?

Top tips

Always reflect on the patient journey and the various interventions of other professionals. Map or follow parts of that journey to learn about the interventions of others.

Interprofessional working

Pollard (2010) notes that interprofessional working in health and social care is a topic of inertest and importance for each us in our various roles as student, teacher, carer and service user. Many high-profile failures in the health-care system have identified the need for cooperation and collaboration between health- and social care professions (Laming, 2003). These are the negative consequences of a system that has neither cohesive structures for service delivery nor effective interprofessional collaboration (Pollard et al, 2005b). A 'seamless service' is what should occur; however, in reality this may not always be the case, because care and collaboration may be fragmented with potentiality devastating effects for people being cared for. Organisational structures and care environments differ across the UK, adding to uncoordinated care provision.

Before developing interprofessional working it is important to articulate professional identity – nursing's own identity. It is difficult to form collaborative ties when there is uncertainty about one's own professional identity. Once this has been achieved it is possible to establish a team that is based on an egalitarian and cooperative approach to working together, in partnership with patients (Molyneux, 2001).

Making the change from a uniprofessional approach, where traditionally each profession worked in isolation with a rigid hierarchy and a predominant professional (usually medicine), is a challenge. Movement is needed towards a culture that seeks to foster mutual respect as well as shared values, movement away from the concept of silo working. Masta (2003) suggests that egalitarian interprofessional relationships have the potential to alter nursing's status and as a result enhance nursing's professionalisation. It is important to note, however, that by putting people together in groups representing various disciplines will not necessarily guarantee the development of a shared understanding. By consolidating the learning experience, for example, interprofessional learning will reduce stereotyping and segregation of professional groups, and this could pave the way for future developments.

An egalitarian relationship with other professions is a key aim associated with interprofessional working. Traditionally nursing has had a very close relationship with medicine and much focus has been on the nurse–doctor relationship. Other relationships with other health-care professionals occur in both health and social care, and must also be given consideration when proposing an interprofessional working culture.

There are common components between each professional group. However, identity deference, a term used by Newell and Lord (2008), considers some concerns that can arise related to identity and, in particular, the loss of identity as a result of immersing the professions in a wider and less well-defined group. One other concern is the potential problem of one particular professional group (e.g. nursing) being swamped by another professional group (e.g. medicine). Pollard et al (2005a) have demonstrated, in their study, that hierarchies still persist despite some positive moves towards interprofessional working. They note that junior staff, and in particular student nurses, did not contribute as freely as they might during interprofessional meetings. It was identified that the medical staff initiated or sustained the main leader role.

Top tips

When working with other health- and social care professionals try to ensure that you contribute to case management. Do not be afraid to ask questions are seek clarification of key points.

Interprofessional learning

The terms 'interprofessional learning' and 'interprofessional education' are often used interchangeably. Other terms are also used such as transprofessional and interdisciplinary education. Hale (2003) uses the definition of inter-professional education provided by the Centre for the Advancement of Interprofessional Education:

> *An educational activity that uses interactive learning approaches between professionals to cultivate collaborative practice. Multiprofessional education is defined as an education activity where learning is shared passively (e.g. joint lectures).*

Interprofessional learning has become a rapidly developing field as a result of the emphasis on interprofessional practice (Cooper et al, 2004). Interprofessional learning is defined by the Nursing and Midwifery Council (NMC, 2010) as an interactive process of learning undertaken with students or registered professionals from a range of health- and social care professions who learn with and from each other, the aim being to enhance collaborative practice and improve the effectiveness of care delivery. Interprofessional learning is seen by Young et al (2003) as learning that takes place when a mix of disciplines congregate in learning groups. The multidisciplinary group is itself the source of material for learning about interprofessional practice.

Promoting and enhancing the concept of interprofessional working may come as a result of interprofessional learning. Indeed, Cooper et al (2004) suggest that this is the vehicle through which policy goals associated with interprofessional working can be achieved. Interprofessional education is a means of:

- creating positive interactions and modifying reciprocal attitudes and perceptions
- encouraging collaboration and developing mutual respect
- enhancing team work between health and social workers.

Freeth (2001) makes the observation that education and training are crucial to providing the conditions and skills needed for continued collaboration. However, to be able to cross and permeate professional boundaries and feel sufficiently confident enough to share and defer professional autonomy, staff from different disciplines need to feel confident about their own roles as well as their own professional identity. Engaging in interprofessional educational activities has the potential to facilitate learning in relation to gaining an understanding of each other's roles.

Confidence is a key factor in having the ability to influence an individual's capacity to engage with interprofessional working. Freeth et al (2002) have recognised that education plays a key role in the process of encouraging health-care professionals to address their strong uniprofessional focus, as well as their habitual attitudes and ways of functioning in an interprofessional context.

Meeting the Challenge (Department of Health or DH, 2000) over a decade ago provided a strategy for allied health professions. It also places an emphasis on interprofessional education, suggesting that a change is required in the way health- and social care professionals are educated at both preregistration and postregistration/graduate levels.

Student nurses in Pollard et al's (2005a) study are seen as passive participants when considering interprofessional partnerships. Enhancing interprofessional learning opportunities may be one way of encouraging student nurses to participate in a more active manner. This can become a reality only if students develop assertive skills early on in their nurse education.

Preparation (educational programmes of study) for health-care professionals has been addressed in several seminal documents produced by the Government and professional organisations, e.g. the new preregistration nursing standards (NMC, 2010). A review declared that providers of education for health-care professionals, e.g. institutions of higher education, had to develop new common foundation programmes. The aim of these new developments was to enable students (preregistration) and staff (postregistration) to move between careers and educational pathways more easily. A new type of worker is envisaged, one who is flexible, more of a team worker, and who takes on partnership and collaborative activity more easily. A changing workforce programme has already been considered and plans are in place to implement new roles, e.g. *Modernising Nursing Careers* (DH, 2006). The emphasis of this initiative is on the following:

- Team working across professional and organisational boundaries
- Flexible working to make the best use of the range of skills and knowledge that staff have
- Streamlined workforce planning and development that stem from the needs of patients not of professionals
- Maximising the contribution of all staff to patient care; doing away with barriers that say only doctors or nurses can provide particular types of care

- Modernising education and training to ensure that staff are equipped with the skills that they need to work in a complex, changing NHS
- Developing new more flexible careers for staff of all professions
- Expanding the workforce to meet future demands.

Interprofessional learning has also been identified by the General Social Care Council (2002) as a key component of preregistration social work. This requirement is particularly relevant to student nurses who are undertaking a joint social work and registered nurse degree, e.g. in learning disabilities.

There are various models of learning available when implementing an interprofessional learning approach, some of which include common learning. This approach enables students to study topics of common interest whether in single or mixed interdisciplinary groups. Learning takes place both in the classroom and on clinical placements in the myriad of learning contexts available in the clinical field.

Barriers to successful interprofessional working and learning

Barriers to partnership work are evident. Some of these are related to structural and organisational changes, e.g. mergers of trusts, relocation and withdrawal of services.

Salmon and Jones (2001) point out that one of the key reasons for the modernisation of professional education is the need to develop cooperation and partnerships, with the overarching aim of improving communication and working practices across professional and organisational boundaries. Daly (2004) sees poor communication (written or verbal) between professional groups as a potential threat to effective interprofessional working.

It must also be recognised that interprofessional working and learning do not take place in a vacuum. There are several factors to be taken into consideration, such as the needs and interests of the various stakeholders (e.g. professional organisations), the complex power structures, pay disparities among the integrating groups, gender and socioeconomic differentials. The biggest factor associated with positive outcomes in Young et al's (2003) evaluation of multiprofessional programmes was timetabling – various curricula, multisite campuses and uncoordinated clinical placements, which complicated matters and sometimes confused the student. Table 6.2 outlines some barriers to interprofessional collaboration and education.

Table 6.2   Some potential barriers to inter-professional collaboration and education

- Differences in history and culture
- Historical interprofessional and intraprofessional rivalries
- Differences in language and jargon
- Differences in schedules and professional routines (complexities of timetabling)
- Varying levels of preparation, qualifications and status (e.g. A levels, NVQ)
- Fears of diluted professional identity
- Differences in accountability, payment and rewards
- Concerns regarding clinical responsibility and accountability
- An imbalance between student numbers between different professions
- Lack of clinical experience

Adapted from Pirrie et al (1998); Hendrick et al (1998).

Daly (2004) makes recommendations that will ensure multiprofessional collaboration. These recommendations may help to overcome some of the barriers to effective interprofessional working and learning. She suggests, for example, regular multiprofessional team meetings to enhance communication and promote team collaboration.

Finally, there is one question that has yet to be answered: does interprofessional learning help to prepare students to manage and perform better in health- and social care settings? There is currently no evidence to support or refute the value of interprofessional learning. Begley (2008) notes that there is insufficient research to provide a convincing argument either for or against interprofessional learning. There is no published evidence to promote interprofessional education as the vehicle to enhance interprofessional collaboration, or to show that it improves patient outcomes. Freeth et al (2002) emphasise that more research is needed to evaluate the impact of interprofessional education practice.

Top tips

 Avoid using nursing jargon that other members of your team do not understand – this can only lead to frustration and a breakdown in essential communication. If you are unsure about jargon being used, seek clarification.

Team working

Many Government directives or professional edicts frequently require teams to do various things. Often, however, they do not define what they mean by a team. Pollard et al (2005b) state that what is meant and understood by the term 'team' can vary a great deal. Cook (2004) suggests that the label 'team' is being added to any group of people who work together.

He provides a helpful definition of a team and distinguishes between a group and a team. A group, he proposes, is made up of members who want to create a shared view of goals and develop an efficient and effective organisational structure on which to accomplish those goals. A group does not become a team until those shared goals have become established, methods have been developed to accomplish the goals and the goals are in place, with each team member knowing what they are and what their role and function is. Teams, according to Northcott (2003), are different people with different skills all working together towards the same goal(s). Fully functioning, effective teams are committed to a common purpose with skills that complement each other.

Until the purpose of the team has been decided, it will be unable to function effectively. Agreeing on aims, objectives and goals are a central component of team working; this provides focus as well as strategic direction. Clarity is required regarding not only aims, objectives and goals but also responsibilities within the team. The team must also agree on ways in which it will judge its successes or failures.

Teams may be tight-knit units that are composed of individuals who, on a regular basis, work together; alternatively they may be *ad hoc*, loosely woven entities meeting to address or meet specific demands. Teams, according to Pollard et al (2005b), can be formally constituted, with a particular structure or objective, or they can be organic entities that occur with no formal recognition. Depending on circumstances, they may be consensual, democratic or hierarchical, or even all of these. There are a number of different arrangements associated with team structures and processes. The definition of team is not precise, just as the definitions of light and energy are beyond description and explanation; they cannot be reduced to a simple definition (Adair, 1987). Teams and organisations become more concrete when set within a context.

Team values need to come to terms with individual team members, the priorities of the organisation and the needs of the patient. The Royal College of Nursing (RCN, 2003) suggest that, to function as an effective team, the team members need to agree answers to some questions:

- Who are we? What are our unique qualities, qualifications, interests and enthusiasms?
- What do we do? What exactly are we offering and how does our role differ from that of others?
- How do we do it? Consider the technical, interpersonal and educational skills and our commitment to multidisciplinary and multiagency working.

There are structural, historical and attitudinal barriers to effective team working. In some instances individuals working alone may perform better than a team.

Cole (2005) points out that the best teams have the following components:

- Clear objectives
- High levels of participation
- A focus on quality
- Being supportive of innovations
- Using all available opportunities to learn
- Regularly reviewing what they are trying to achieve.

In some NHS trusts some staff feel poorly supported, and only about half of staff say that they are encouraged to suggest ideas to improve care provision, with a third of staff suggesting that they are not involved in important decisions. In NHS organisations where staff work in formal teams, the patient mortality rate was consistently 5 per cent lower, as opposed to those organisations where staff were not part of a formal team (West et al, 2002). The need for effective team working is evident.

Think

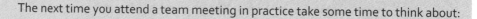

The next time you attend a team meeting in practice take some time to think about:

- What was the purpose of the meeting?
- Was it multidisciplinary in nature?
- Who are the team members?
- Do you know how they were chosen?
- What was their contribution to the meeting?
- What was your contribution; did you contribute?
- What was the outcome of the meeting?
- What could have been done better to enhance the meeting?

Conclusions

A modern NHS is one that provides and delivers care to patients in such a way that it is sensitive and respects their needs and expectations. The NHS provides advice and support to help people manage their own care, quickly and effectively. Care should be streamlined, allowing and facilitating the integration of other services, e.g. social services.

Interprofessional working and interprofessional education are not the panacea for all ills that befall health- and social care provision; they provide many challenges. Disasters such as the tragedy associated with the deaths of Victoria Climbié and Peter Connelly (Baby P) are examples of how lack of collaboration, blurring of roles and responsibilities, and poor communication contributed to ineffective child protection.

The modernisation agenda associated with the NHS is seeking fast and radical changes to the way services are provided. However, if interprofessional teamwork is to be a success, this will require time, because trust building and mutual professional respect are the foundations on which interprofessional working is based. The common goal shared by all who are employed by the NHS is the wellbeing of the patient but, as Daly (2004) suggests, this becomes a singular ideal when each discrete discipline retains its strong and competing dominating identity. Organisations must promote the development of professionalism with independent professional identities and values, and at the same time move towards interprofessional working and collaboration, delivering services to members of the public that they want in response to their needs and expectations.

Nurses are central to interprofessional working. They need to strive to ensure that traditional hierarchies (still evident) are no longer the norm with one profession dominating other(s).

The Centre for the Advancement of Interprofessional Education (2011) has produced a list of principles that underpin effective interprofessional education. This list, reproduced here, aims to summarise some of the key points made in this chapter. Effective interprofessional education:

- Focuses on the needs of individuals, families and communities to improve their quality of care, health outcomes and wellbeing. *Keeping best practice central throughout all teaching and learning.*
- Applies equal opportunities within and between the professions and all with whom they learn and work. *Acknowledging but setting aside differences in power and status between professions.*
- Respects individuality, difference and diversity within and between the professions and all with whom they learn and work. *Utilising distinctive contributions to learning and practice.*
- Sustains the identity and expertise of each profession. *Presenting each profession positively and distinctively.*
- Promotes parity between professions in the learning environment. *Agreeing 'ground rules'.*
- Instils interprofessional values and perspectives throughout uniprofessional and multiprofessional learning. *Permeating means and ends for the professional learning in which it is embedded.*

Although interprofessional working and learning have their merits, there has been insufficient attention paid to the impact that they have on the student experience, and above all patient outcome. More evidence is needed to help guide the way forward. Policies currently formulated must be revisited regularly to determine if they are indeed doing what they say that they should be doing.

Activity

Attempt the following word search related to interprofessional working and learning to test your knowledge. The answers can be found at the back of this book, in the chapter called 'Activity Answers'.

collaboration
egalitarian
flexibility
identity
interdisciplinary
jargon
multiprofessional
objectives
organisations
perceptions
professional
reciprocation
responsibilities
roles
stereotypes
teamwork
transprofessional
uniprofessional
values

s	r	u	c	r	d	o	o	u	o	n	i	e	g	s	n	i	s
e	l	r	s	i	e	r	o	f	k	n	o	g	r	a	j	e	l
p	v	a	n	l	l	l	n	t	f	a	m	i	i	t	i	a	a
y	r	a	n	i	l	p	i	c	s	i	d	r	e	t	n	i	n
t	i	o	l	o	r	g	a	n	i	s	a	t	i	o	n	s	o
o	i	o	f	u	i	d	i	r	e	t	v	l	i	c	r	g	i
e	r	b	n	e	e	s	i	o	i	a	i	s	y	o	p	o	s
r	p	j	r	i	s	s	s	l	g	b	s	s	t	l	r	s	s
e	n	e	i	b	e	s	a	e	i	e	r	l	i	l	i	a	e
t	t	c	r	j	r	g	i	s	f	a	e	s	t	a	s	o	f
s	f	t	r	c	e	v	n	o	p	o	s	m	n	b	t	c	o
i	l	i	c	s	e	o	r	a	n	t	r	c	e	o	a	n	r
e	c	v	i	i	p	p	r	l	a	a	s	p	d	r	i	t	p
e	i	e	b	s	s	p	t	e	p	m	l	l	i	a	s	a	i
i	l	s	e	n	r	e	c	i	p	r	o	c	a	t	i	o	n
b	e	r	a	t	e	a	m	w	o	r	k	s	p	i	l	e	u
o	i	r	m	u	s	n	p	a	f	n	t	t	i	o	f	u	r
y	t	i	l	i	b	i	x	e	l	f	s	r	o	n	u	o	m

References

Adair J (1987) *Effective Teambuilding: How to Make a Winning Team*. London: Pan.

Begley CM (2008) Developing inter-professional learning: tactics teamwork and talk. *Nurse Education Today* **29**: 276–283.

Biggs S (1997) Interprofessional collaboration: problems and prospects. In: Øvretveit J, Mathias P, Thompson T (eds), *Interprofessional Working for Health and Social Care*. London: Macmillan, pp 186–200.

British Medical Association (1974) *Primary Health Care Teams*. London: BMA.

Centre for the Advancement of Interprofessional Education (2011) *Principles of Inter-professional Education*. London: CAIPE. Available at: www.caipe.org.uk/about-us/principles-of-interprofessional-education.

Cole A (2005) Reaping the benefits of teamwork. *Nursing Times* **101**(1): 59.

Cook M (2004) Interprofessional post-qualifying education: Team leadership. In: Glenn S, Leiba T (eds), *Interprofessional Post-Qualifying Education for Nurses Working Together in Health and Social Care*. Basingstoke: Palgrave, pp 79–101.

Cooper H, Braye S, Geyer R (2004) Complexity and interprofessional education. *Learning in Health and Social Care* **3**: 179–189.

Cowley S, Bliss J, Mathew A, McVey G (2002) Effective interagency and interprofessional working: Facilitators and barriers. *International Journal of Palliative Nursing* **8**(1): 30–39.

Daly G (2004) Understanding the barriers to multiprofessional collaboration. *Nursing Times* **100**(9): 78–79.

Department of Health (2000) *Meeting the Challenge: A strategy for the allied health professions*. London: DH.

Department of Health (2006) *Modernising Nursing Careers: Setting the direction*. London: DH.

Freeth D (2001) Sustaining interprofessional collaboration, *Journal of Interprofessional Care* **15**: 37–46.

Freeth D, Hammick M, Koppel I, Reeves S, Barr H (2002) *A Critical Review of Evaluations of Interprofessional Education*. London: Learning and Teaching Support Network Health Sciences and Practice.

General Social Care Council (2002) *Accreditation of Universities to Grant Degrees in Social Work*. London: GSCC.

Glendinning C, Coleman A, Shipman C, Malbon G (2003) Progress in partnerships. *British Medical Journal* **323**: 28–31.

Hale C (2003) Interprofessional education: The way to a success workforce. *British Journal of Therapy and Rehabilitation* **10**: 122–127.

Hassmiller SB, Goodman DC (2011) Interprofessional care and the future of nursing. *Journal of Interprofessional Care* **25**: 163–164.

Health Professions Council (2008) *Standards of Conduct and Ethics*. London: HPC.

Hendrick LA, Wilcock PM, Batalden PB (1998) Interprofessional working and continuing medical education. *British Medical Journal* **316**: 771–774.

Kennison P, Fletcher R (2005) Police. In: Barrett G, Sellman D, Thomas J (eds), *Interprofessional Working in Health and Social Care*. Basingstoke: Palgrave, pp 119–131.

Kenny G (2002) Interprofessional opportunities and challenges. *Nursing Standard* **17**(6): 33–35.

Laming Lord (2003) *Inquiry into the Death of Victoria Climbié*. London: TSO.

Lewy L (2010) The Complexities of interprofessional learning/working: has the agenda lost its way? *Health Education Journal* **69**(1): 4–12.

Masta O (2003) Night cover. *Nursing Standard* **17**(49): 16–18.

Molyneux J (2001) Interprofessional team working: What makes teams work well. *Journal of Interprofessional Care* **15**(1): 29–35.

Newell K, Lord M (2008) A learning and teaching framework for interprofessional learning. In: Howkins E, Bray J (eds), *Preparing for Interprofessional Teaching, Theory and Practice*. Oxford: Radcliffe, pp 13–26.

Northcott N (2003) Working within a health care team. In: Hinchliff S, Norman S, Schober J (eds), *Nursing Practice and Health Care*, 4th edn. London: Arnold, pp 371–389.

Nursing and Midwifery Council (2010) *Standards for Pre registration Nursing Education*. London: NMC. Available at: http://standards.nmc-uk.org/PublishedDocuments/Standards%20for%20pre-registration%20nursing%20education%2016082010.pdf (accessed June 2011).

Payne M (2000) *Teamwork in Multiprofessional Care*. Basingstoke: Macmillan.

Pirrie A, Wilson V, Elsegood J, et al (1998) *Evaluating Multidisciplinary Education in Health Care*. Edinburgh: The Scottish Council for Research in Education.

Pollard KC (2010) Introduction: Background and overview of the book. In: Pollard KC, Thomas J, Miers M (eds), *Understanding Interprofessional Working in Health and Social Care*. Basingstoke: Palgrave.

Pollard KC, Ross K, Means R (2005a) Nurse leadership interprofessionalism and the modernization agenda, *British Journal of Nursing* **14**: 339–344.

Pollard KC, Sellman D, Senior B (2005b) The need for interprofessional working. In: Barrett G, Sellman D, Thomas J (eds), *Interprofessional Working in Health and Social Care*. Basingstoke: Palgrave, pp 7–17.

Royal College of Nursing (2003) *Children's Community Nursing: Promoting effective teamworking for children and their families*. London: RCN.

Rushmer B (2005) Blurred boundaries damage inter-professional working. *Nurse Researcher* **12**(3): 74–85.

Salmon D, Jones M (2001) Shaping the interprofessional agenda: A study examining qualified nurses' perception of working with others. *Nurse Education Today* **21**(1): 18–25.

Wee B, Hillier R, Coles C, Mountford B, Sheldon B, Turner P (2001) Palliative care: A suitable setting for undergraduate interprofessional education. *Palliative Medicine* **15**: 487–492.

West M, Borrill C, Dawson J, et al (2002) The link between management of employees and patient mortality in acute hospitals. *International Journal of Human Resource Management* **13**: 1299–1310.

Whitcombe SW (2005) Understanding healthcare professions from sociological perspectives. In: Clouston TJ, Westcott L (eds), *Working in Health and Social Care: An introduction for allied health professionals*. Edinburgh: Churchill Livingstone, pp 63–73.

Wilby PK (2005) Thinking about teamworking and collaboration. In: Clouston TJ, Westcott L (eds), *Working in Health and Social Care: An introduction for allied health professionals*. Edinburgh: Churchill Livingstone, pp 75–85.

Young G, Mitchell F, Sensky T, Rhodes M (2003) Evaluation of the joint universities multiprofessional programme. *Journal of Inter-professional Care* **17**: 404.

7

Health Promotion, Promoting Self-care and Wellbeing

Aims and objectives

The aim of this chapter is to enable the reader to begin to apply theoretical frameworks for health promotion.

At the end of the chapter you will be able to:

1. Provide definition of key terms
2. Consider a range of strategies that underpin health promotion.
3. Outline the value of interprofessional team working when caring for people
4. Describe the role of the nurse in promoting health
5. Begin to apply the concepts discussed to the practice setting
6. Appreciate the Nursing and Midwifery Council's requirements of student nurses

Understanding the key concepts associated with health promotion will enable the nurse to apply these theories and principles in order to provide high-quality health promotion. Health promotion plays a major part in helping the population maximise their health.

It is not possible in a chapter of this size to address all the complex issues associated with health promotion, so this chapter only starts to address the key issues. The reader is advised and encouraged to delve deeper and become immersed in the topic in order to hone and build on current knowledge and skills.

There are several ways in which the nurse can promote the health and wellbeing of patients; one way is by helping patients gain access to health promotion information. A discussion is provided on how to offer health information in an accessible and effective manner.

One aspect of the nurse's role in relation to health promotion is to support patients. This can be achieved by attempting to empower and educate them, to protect them from illness and to promote and maintain their health; this chapter provides the reader with the knowledge to put this aspect of the nurse's role into action. There are a variety of health promotion models that are discussed in this chapter and the definitions of a range of key terms are provided.

Developing an awareness of the key concepts related to health promotion may allow the nurse to apply these theoretical principles to practice in an attempt to provide patients with opportunities to promote their health. In the past several Government policies have been produced that aim to improve

The Student's Guide to Becoming a Nurse, Second Edition. Ian Peate.
© 2012 John Wiley & Sons, Ltd. Published 2012 by John Wiley & Sons, Ltd.

health, e.g. *Making a Difference* (Department of Health or DH, 1999), *The NHS Plan* (DH, 2000), *Shifting the Balance of Power* (DH, 2001) and *Choosing Health* (DH, 2005a).

There is a growing trend to ensure that the health of the nation continues to be in the forefront of clinicians and policy-makers' minds. More recently, new ways of working in the form of two influential White Papers – *Equity and Excellence: Liberating the NHS* (2010a), and *Healthy Lives, Healthy People: Our strategy for public health in England* (2010b) – have been produced. These set out the Government's long-term vision for the future of the NHS, building on its core values and principles and providing a vision for the future of public health in England. The intention is to create a 'wellness' service (Public Health England).

The Nursing and Midwifery Council (NMC, 2008) requires that the nurse work with others to protect and promote the health and wellbeing of those in their care, their families and carers, and the wider community. There are many ways in which this can occur and one way is by helping patients gain access to information that will enhance or promote their health – health promotion information. The nurse should acknowledge and respect the role of the people being cared for as a partner in their care and the contribution that they can make to it. This points out that the person, where appropriate, should be involved in all aspects of his or her care. The *Standards for Pre-registration Nursing Education* (NMC, 2010) require that all nurses understand public health principles, priorities and practice so that they can recognise and respond to the major causes and social determinants of health, illness and health inequalities. Nurses have to use a range of information and data to assess the needs of people, groups, communities and populations, and to strive to improve health, wellbeing and experiences of health care, secure equal access to health screening, health promotion and health care, and promote social inclusion.

Approaches to health promotion and health promotion developments have been given new status in recent years. There is an increasing focus on health outcomes and investments in the determinants of health through health promotion activity (DH, 2005b). The roots of health promotion and disease prevention are deep, e.g. the ancient Egyptians recorded examples of public health practice such as sewage disposal and how to distribute excess grain to feed the poor. Over 65 years ago Sigerist (1946) noted that health is promoted among other things by providing a decent standard of living and working conditions; this still rings true today. The foundations had been laid down even then to consider health promotion from a holistic perspective.

The nurse's role with regard to health promotion is to support patients by endeavouring to empower and educate, e.g. to protect from infection. There are many characteristics that are shared with good nursing practice and health promotion, e.g. the patient is central and health promotion activities are based on an individual assessment of individual needs, respecting and valuing the patient's own views. When working with the patient and the community the nurse spends time listening to, and talking with, the patient, empowering him or her to make decisions for his or her own health.

Defining key terms

The definitions below provide a useful function in clarifying meaning and relationship across the various terms that are in common usage, as well as helping in practical application. These core definitions are central to the concepts and principles associated with health promotion. The use of the terms defined is often situation specific and guided by social, cultural and economic circumstances. The reader must bear in mind that definitions by their very nature can be restrictive and can provide only a summary of complex ideas and activities. Despite these restrictions and limitations, definitions can help when attempting to understand fundamental ideas and concepts associated with health promotion activities.

The key terms that are associated with health promotion are:

- health
- health education
- health promotion
- public health
- disease prevention.

Health

Think

How would you define health? Make a list of the things that you would include in your definition of health.

There are no right or wrong answers to this question. Your response may have included things such as:

- Free from disease
- The ability to function, e.g. go to university or work and function effectively
- Clean water to drink
- Availability of health services
- Achieving your hopes and ambitions
- A good quality of life.

Your list might have focused on the physical aspects of health, but do not forget that health is about the whole person, mind and body, and often it even extends to the whole community. The way in which you define health could have been guided or influenced by your own personal experiences (Melling et al, 2004); everybody develops a knowledge of what health is or should be through their socialisation in to society. We often use the term 'health', but when asked to define it, it may mean different things to different people. Think how a person who lives on the street may define health – do you think it might be different to your definition?

The term 'health' is therefore complex and broad and there are various definitions available. Health is seen as a fundamental human right, regardless of race, religion, political belief, or economic or social condition (WHO, 1986). Many issues will impinge on and influence health:

- Personal behaviour
- Environment
- Politics
- Social and genetic factors.

A popular definition of health that has not been amended since 1948 is provided by the World Health Organization (WHO, 1948):

> A state of complete physical, mental and social wellbeing and not merely the absence of disease or infirmity.

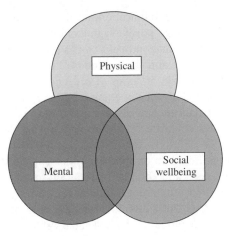

Figure 7.1   The three interrelated aspects associated with the definition of health.

Health in this definition can be regarded as a positive resource that is used in everyday life. This definition will allow the nurse to consider the person from three distinct and, at the same time, interrelated perspectives (Figure 7.1). Health can also have a negative connotation, e.g. the absence of disease or illness.

For the fundamental right to health to become a reality, the Ottawa Charter (WHO, 1986) maintains that particular prerequisites must be in place:

- Peace
- Adequate economic resources
- Food and shelter
- Stable ecosystem
- Sustainable use of resources.

Accepting these prerequisites to health demonstrates the inextricable link between social and economic conditions, the physical environment and individual lifestyles and health. The links described enable the nurse to develop a holistic approach to understanding health, which is at the core of health promotion.

Viewing health as a positive concept encompasses social and personal resources as well as the individual's physical capability. All systems that govern health, including social and economic conditions, should be taken into account and given due consideration when devising and developing health promotion activities.

Health education

Health education is one of the three overlapping spheres of activity making up health promotion:

1. Health education
2. Health protection
3. Ill-health prevention.

Health education can be seen as a communication activity with the key focus aimed at enhancing wellbeing and preventing ill-health through positively influencing people's knowledge, beliefs, attitudes and behaviour. An example of health education might be the promotion of safer sex activities.

Health protection includes the policies and various codes of practice designed to prevent ill-health or positively enhance wellbeing. An example of codes of practice that might be designed to prevent ill-health could be related to cervical and breast screening programmes.

Prevention refers to the initial occurrence of disease and also to its progress and, consequently, the final outcome. Preventive activities could be related to no-smoking policies in the workplace and at leisure venues.

Although the communication of health information is important, health education is also concerned with developing the motivation, skills and confidence required to take action to improve health. It is associated with the conscious construction of opportunities for learning, with the aim to improve health literacy, knowledge and life skills (Abel, 2007). Health literacy is associated with more than the ability to read health education materials; it encompasses an individual's ability to use the information effectively in order to empower. Life skills are the skills that consist of personal, interpersonal, cognitive and physical skills that can help people to control and direct their lives, e.g. decision-making and problem-solving skills (Tones, 2001).

Any measure taken in a planned and premeditated way that aims to enhance health and an individual's awareness of health, leading to empowerment of that individual or the community through learning, can be deemed to be health education. There are many activities that the nurse can use to enhance health and health awareness.

Health promotion

Health promotion is the process whereby people are empowered and enabled to strengthen the control that they have over the determinants of health, and in so doing improving their health. It is a political and social process that has the potential to strengthen the skills and capabilities of individuals and communities. The process can lead to changes in social, environmental and economic conditions, alleviating their impact on public and individual health. Health promotion can, therefore, be influential on many fronts.

Four key health promotion values feature in health promotion practice:

1. Empowerment
2. Social justice and equity
3. Inclusion
4. Respect.

Determinants of health are defined as:

> A range of personal, social, economic and environmental factors which determine the health status of individuals or populations. (WHO, 1998)

These factors are both numerous and interactive. Health promotion has the ability to address the full range of determinants of health that are modifiable and these include the individual's actions, such as lifestyle and chosen health behaviours, as well as working conditions and access to appropriate health services. The determinants of health alone and/or in combination will have an impact on health; changes in the determinants of health will ascertain health status. It follows, therefore, that those who encounter inequalities in health may also experience an impact on their health as a result of the disparity (Chapter 3 discussed determinants of health inequalities in more detail).

There are several definitions of health promotion available. One definition offered by the WHO (1998) is:

> . . . the process of enabling people to increase control over, and to improve their health. Health promotion represents a comprehensive social and political process, it not only embraces actions directed at strengthening the skills and capabilities of individuals, but also action directed towards changing social, environment and economic conditions so as to alleviate their impact on public and individual health.

Public health

201

As with all of the other definitions provided above, the definition of public health will mean different things to different people (Hayes, 2005) depending on:

- their affluence
- their health status
- the environment
- their educational standing
- social, political and cultural contexts.

The description offered by Acheson (1988) is:

> Public health is the science and art of preventing disease, prolonging life and promoting physical health through the organised efforts of society.

Despite the fact that Acheson (1988) used these words over 20 years ago they enable us to pick out and identify a number of relevant features, providing the foundation for further discussion. Public health is concerned with protecting, maintaining and improving health through organised effort in the community. Health and illness are studied in the context of the community as a social group (Sarafino and Smith, 2011). There is a wide range of definitions and descriptions of public health in the literature.

The purpose of public health, according to Hayes (2005), has four essentials associated with it:

1. Improve the health and wellbeing of the population
2. Prevent disease and minimise its consequences
3. Prolong valued life
4. Reduce inequalities in health.

Public health draws on a variety of issues, such as environmental movements, political parties and international agencies, including the United Nations. Public health is as diverse as the public it addresses.

Top tips

Make health service information available through a range of locations including student unions, pharmacies, workplaces, sports clubs, night clubs and other community settings for people of all ages, sexualities and ethnic backgrounds, in culturally appropriate ways.

Disease prevention

Many advances in health over the years are a result of efforts to prevent illness and of improvements in diagnosis and treatments. Recurring themes within current health policy have given increased attention to disease prevention. Naidoo and Wills (2009) suggest that the dominance of the medical model is responsible for health promotion being seen as disease prevention, addressing individuals who have 'high-risk' factors associated with the development of a specific disease. Disease-prevention activities often identify individuals or communities who exhibit identifiable risk factors, e.g. monitoring the health of those people who undertake hazardous activities as a part of their job (Lisle, 2001).

Primary prevention of disease is aimed at preventing the initial occurrence of a disease or disorder and focuses on risk factors and risk conditions. Secondary prevention methods are directed at arresting or slowing down the progression of existing disease, before medical intervention. Reducing the occurrence or relapse of a disease or disorder is associated with tertiary prevention (Sarafino and Smith, 2011). Early detection and appropriate treatment are approaches used to detect and prevent disease (Naidoo and Wills, 2009).

Case study 7.1

Annie Lomax is 36 and has learning disability; she communicates in a number of ways but primarily through the use of Makaton. Ms Lomax lives at home with her father and two brothers. She has been to see her general practitioner because she has been experiencing some heavy painful periods (more so than usually). Ms Lomax has been advised that she will need to have cervical smear performed. An appointment has been made for her to see the practice nurse at the end of the week.

As Ms Lomax's nurse how will you prepare her for this investigation?

What information giving tools will you need to help her understand and, most importantly, give informed consent for the procedure to go ahead?

What information might Mr Lomax, her father, require?

Health promotion theories and models

There are a number of significant theories and models that underpin the practice of health promotion, all with the aim of improving health and wellbeing. When attempting to promote health in an effective way for various individuals, groups and communities, the nurse needs to use multiple, complementary strategies and these interventions must be sensitive to the patient's particular needs. Stand-alone approaches may not be as effective as using multiple methods, so a complementary approach may be more effective.

Nutbeam (2000) suggests that there are three main categories in which health promotion models can be placed: infrastructure, policy and practice. Five influential health promotion approaches or models have been considered by Scriven (2010) and Naidoo and Wills (2009):

1. Medical or preventive
2. Behaviour change
3. Educational
4. Client-centred or empowerment
5. Societal change.

The model or approach chosen will depend on the health promotion strategy that is being considered. Table 7.1 outlines, in brief, five approaches to health promotion. All five models/approaches and the elements associated with them are not mutually exclusive; frequently all five approaches can and are used together and interchangeably. All approaches use different means to achieve their goals; however, they all aim to uphold good health and diminish or avoid the effects of ill-health.

Think

Are there any groups of patients whom you think may be responsible for their own ill-health?

You might have listed the following:

- Smokers
- People who do not exercise or eat a balanced diet, resulting in obesity
- Those who drink more than the recommended amount of alcohol
- People who have contracted a sexually transmitted infection because they have engaged in unsafe sexual activity
- Those who use intravenous drugs recreationally.

Think about what impact this 'blaming' attitude may have on your therapeutic relationship with these patients and your role as health promoter. Your attitude could be different if, for example, you were a smoker or you engaged in unsafe sexual activity.

Although making people aware of their own health and health needs can be seen as a positive approach to empowering them, it may also have negative connotations. Russell (2005) notes that making people responsible can also lead to engendering a culture of blame. Examples of blame culture are often argued and debated within the HIV/AIDS arena, e.g.: 'I have practised safer sex and I am healthy; you have failed to practise safer sex and the reason you have HIV is your own fault.'

In delivering health promotional activities or carrying out health promotion, Scriven (2010) suggests that the nurse needs to possess or to develop some key competencies:

- Managing, planning and evaluating
- Education
- Communicating
- Facilitating and networking
- Marketing and publicity
- Influencing policy and practice.

Despite the competencies being individually listed above they are, and should be, used together to achieve the desired outcomes. The nurse will have to develop and draw on pre-existing skills and knowledge and adapt these to meet the individual needs of the patient who may be in a particular environment, e.g. in a prison.

Table 7.1   An outline of five models/approaches to health promotion

Model/ approach	Principles/characteristics	Comments
Medical	Health is seen as the absence of illness or disease. The traditional view held by many health-care professionals is that health is the 'normal' state, similar to that of a well-adjusted or well-oiled machine (the mechanical metaphor)	The model does not always correspond to an individual's subjective perception of his or her own health. There is an over-reliance on an idea of 'normality' that is far from universally applicable
	There are several practical advantages associated with the medical model. Most of the advances in medical science have been made by scientists who have viewed the human body as a series of systems that follow physical laws. The model takes on the view that there is a mind–body dualism and disease is the result of a disorder that has occurred within the machine (the body). The medical model is closely linked to medical practice and in particular the domain of biomedicine. Power and authority in the form of medical paternalism are a result of the medical model; medicine dominates	Other aspects of health may be ignored that the individual sees as equally, or even more, important to them. Focusing on the machine (the body) and the times it goes wrong could encourage a reactive, as opposed to a proactive, role for the health promoter
	Individuals do not think of their own health in simple terms, such as the presence or absence of physical symptoms. The mental, emotional or social health of the individual can be just as important. Nurses should keep in mind that these things are also important to their patients. When applied to health promotion the medical model emphasises prevention and, in particular, primary prevention. This can result in victim blaming and risk. This model tends to ignore the environmental and sociopolitical factors that impinge on health. The health-care professional becomes the expert and the contribution and responsibility of the individual and community are eroded, which leads to disempowerment. The medical model has much power and those in authority (health-care professionals) are often deferred to, reinforcing this dominance and power. The model is dominated by qualitative, objective fact in contrast to accepting patients' subjective feelings and experiences. The model is always searching for a causative link to ill-health. The medical model remains a popular model	In many instances, health promotion activity that follows and subscribes to the medical model is in danger of viewing interventions as being done to people and communities as opposed to for them. Working in partnership and involving communities, as opposed to being passive recipients of health-care services, will fail to take into account what the expert (the patient) needs. It also has the potential to disempower and to fail to work with the patient and community as an equal partner

| Behavioural change | Models of behavioural change take into account the individual's own attitudes towards health issues and their own health. Individuals contribute to their own health (and the health of others) by avoiding health-damaging behaviours, such as smoking, or by adopting health-enhancing behaviours, e.g. taking regular exercise. The model encourages individuals to adopt healthy behaviours and attitudes towards a healthier lifestyle. This may sound simplistic, but making health-related decisions is a multifaceted process. Health is seen as belonging to individuals – they own it

Individuals make the decision to change their behaviour based on its feasibility and the pros and cons associated with it. The decisions that individuals make are often dependent on whether they feel threatened by the consequences of not taking a health action, if they feel a change would be beneficial and if they feel competent to carry it out. There must be a perceived susceptibility to disease and a perceived seriousness of disease if people are to make a change in their behaviour or attitude, e.g. persuasive education is used in order to promote a change in behaviour, such as in smoking-cessation approaches

In industrialised societies it has been noted that much of the mortality and morbidity is predominantly associated with individual patterns of behaviour, e.g. unsafe sex activities. Interventions that are used to modify risky behaviour such as poor diet must be aimed at changing or influencing lifestyle. The approach chosen will be most successful if it is adapted to individual, specific needs. Although the focus is on behavioural change, other changes, such as an increase in knowledge, are also valid indicators of this model's effectiveness | Changing attitudes, values and beliefs requires the nurse to be highly skilled and knowledgeable. The focus of this model is on the individual, and it could be suggested that it fails to take into account the complexity surrounding health choices and how these choices may be constrained by social factors. The underlying principle of this model is that individuals are rational beings. This is a limitation and it fails to take into account that sometimes individuals do not make rational decisions; they may be fearful or in denial. Being frightened can lead to denial and avoidance of the message. As the model's underlying premise is that the individual is a rational being, it also relies on the provision of information about risk and health hazards. Not all individuals can access or make use of the information often offered through the mass media. The approach appears to use a 'top-down' approach and this may be at odds with community norms, values and practices. This model could be seen as embracing a victim-blaming philosophy |
| --- | --- | --- |

Continued

Table 7.1 Continued

Model/approach	Principles/characteristics	Comments
Educational	This model aims to offer advice and information to encourage the patient to make informed decisions. The fundamental objective of the educational model is to increase autonomy. The information provided relates to the cause and effects of factors that hinder good heath Individuals have a right to choose when they have all the information required to help them make a judgement. The role of the nurse is to assess the needs of the individual. The nurse is seen as either the leader (authority figure) or the facilitator (negotiator) who when appropriate provides educational content. There are several models that define health promotion as a range of interventions, e.g. health persuasion and personal counselling. There is a range of approaches that can make up a programme or intervention and the approach depends on many issues, e.g. views about health as well power and control	As with other approaches assumptions are being made with this model, e.g. does the individual have the capacity or the inclination to learn and take on board the advice given? Furthermore, the model assumes that the nurse or health-care practitioner has the skills and knowledge to implement health education programmes. There are other factors that need to be taken into consideration, e.g. external factors that influence a person's ability to choose and become autonomous
Client centred	Self-empowerment is at the centre of this model and is used to describe health-promotion strategies. The strategies are based on counselling and use non-directive, patient-centred approaches with the key objective of increasing people's control over their live Nurses are often engaged in patient-centred work; they are concerned with facilitating patient autonomy. It is the patient who sets the agenda and the nurse's role is to facilitate, guide, support and empower the patient to make informed choices. The nurse works with the patient on the patient's own terms. The issue(s) that the patient feels are pertinent are addressed, e.g. what choices the patient has and what actions he or she may wish to take (or not). The patient determines what it is he or she wishes to know. In this relationship the patient and nurse are equal partners	This approach is laudable; however, factors outside the control of the patient or the nurse may impinge on fully engaging in client-centred work, e.g. material and human resources. Be aware that the patient may have the intention to carry out a specific behaviour but that intention may not lead to action, e.g. a patient who is overweight or obese may intend to diet but may not actually do so

| Societal change | This approach attempts to address the socioeconomic and environmental causes of ill-health. Individuals group together in order to change their physical and social environments and act collectively. The model recognises that there is a close relationship between an individual's health and the social and material circumstances that they encounter. The social and material aspects become the target for change | The key principle underpinning this approach is the notion of 'community' and what this means. Making change occur has cost repercussions and implications related to the accessibility of the proposed changes. The proposed changes have to be supported by the whole community, who need to be convinced of their importance. There may be an element of social regulation associated with this approach |
| | Self-empowerment, a part of social action, becomes the channel for collective action. The community acts collectively to make attempts to change and challenge determinants that influence ill-health, e.g. health inequalities, often based on class, ethnicity, gender and geography. The model attempts to empower communities. Examples of collective community action may be seen in work that is carried out with those who use intravenous drugs; in this example community outreach approaches are used to achieve subcultural changes in reducing HIV infection by the implementation of needle exchanges. The health-promotion agent must develop skills related to lobbying, policy planning, negotiation and implementation. The remit becomes political in some respects | |

Source: adapted from Illich (1976); Montazeri et al (1998); Tones and Green (2004); Bridle et al (2005); Russell (2005); Naidoo and Wills (2009).

Case study 7.2

 You are working at the local primary care trust and one of your clinical learning placements is attached to the local women's prison. You are working with Staff Nurse Aziz, who is putting together a health promotion package for women who are substance users.

Take some time and think about the implications of introducing a needle-sharing exchange system in the prison.

What do you think may be some of the challenges that Staff Nurse Aziz may face?

How might you overcome these challenges?

The ottawa charter for health promotion: a framework for practice

A world-wide approach to health promotion has been taken up, led by the World Health Organization (WHO). In 1986 the Ottawa Charter was published under the auspices of the WHO (1986). The Charter built on the progress made through the Declaration on Primary Health Care at Alma Ata (WHO, 1978).

The *Ottawa Charter for Health Promotion* (WHO, 1986) is a framework that can be used successfully by nurses in many health-care settings. The primary aim of the Ottawa Charter is to bring about positive long-term changes to the health of communities. The potential role of workplaces, neighbourhoods and schools in improving people's health and reducing health inequalities has been deliberated in the Marmot Review (2010). The Marmot Review potentially derived from the Ottawa Charter, which stated:

> Health is created and lived by people within the settings of their everyday life; where they learn, work, play and love.

It is evident, therefore, that health promotion can and should take place where people congregate and meet when carrying out the activities of daily living. The notion that health cannot be understood in isolation from social conditions (Naidoo and Wills, 2009) is also implicit within the Charter. Therefore, wherever people eat, relax and study this could potentially result in a harmful effect on their health.

Approaches highlighted in the Charter may help address factors that are within the control not only of the individual, but also of those who form society, such as those involved in religion, education and the media. The nurse can adapt and use the structure described within the Charter to address the health-care needs of the patient and the community, thereby promoting health.

When the nurse begins to consider interventions aimed at promoting health, he or she needs to be aware of the strategies and processes outlined in the Charter. These processes – advocating, mediating and enabling – will help to empower the individual and the community to determine their own health promotion activities. They can help place the individual and the community at the centre of any decision-making activities related to their health-care needs. To achieve complete physical, mental and social wellbeing, the individual or community group must be able to identify and achieve ambitions, to satisfy needs and change or manage within the environment.

The Charter (WHO, 1986) identifies three basic strategies for health promotion:

1. Advocacy
2. Enablement
3. Mediation.

These three strategies create the essential conditions for health, enabling all people to achieve their full potential and mediating between the different interests in society.

Advocacy

Good health is a major resource for social, economic and personal development, and also an important dimension of quality of life. Political, economic, social, cultural, environmental, behavioural and biological factors can impact positively or negatively on health. Health promotion aims to make these conditions favourable, through advocacy for health.

Enablement

Health promotion focuses on achieving equity in health. Health promotion action aims to lessen the differences in current health status and ensure the availability of equal opportunities and resources to enable all people to achieve their full health potential. This includes a secure foundation in a supportive environment, and access to information, life skills and opportunities to make healthy choices. People cannot achieve their fullest health potential unless they are able to control those things that determine their health.

Mediation

The prerequisites and prospects for health cannot be ensured by the health sector alone. Health promotion demands coordinated action by all concerned, including governments, health and other social and economic sectors, non-government and voluntary organisations, local authorities, industry and the media.

The three strategies above are supported by five priority action areas. The five priority areas associated with the Charter are (Figure 7.2):

1. Developing personal skills
2. Creating supportive environments
3. Strengthening community action
4. Building healthy public policy
5. Reorienting services in the interest of health.

Developing personal skills

Personal and social development is supported through health promotion by the provision of information, education and enhancing life skills. The choices available to people to take more control over their health and environments are improved, and they are able to select preferences that are beneficial to health. Personal development enables people to adopt a life-long learning approach, by preparing them for all its stages, and to manage and cope with chronic illness and injuries. Opportunities arise for this to occur in schools, homes, workplaces and community settings through actions involving educational, professional, commercial and non-statutory sectors.

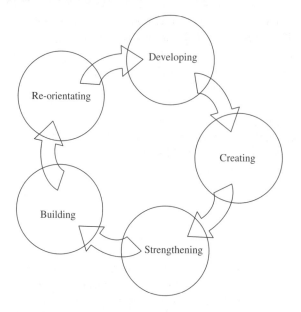

Figure 7.2   The interrelated five priority action areas. Source: WHO (1986).

Top tips

When providing health advice ensure that you know what your role is, your limitations, the subject area and the provision of information that is easy to understand and interesting, and how to make appropriate referrals.

Creating supportive environments

The basis for a socioecological approach to health is noted in the inextricable links that exist between people and their environments. Health promotion encourages people to take care of each other, the community, and the natural and built environments. To achieve this involves creating living and working conditions that are:

- safe
- stimulating
- satisfying
- enjoyable.

   An assessment of the health impacts of technology, work, energy production and urbanisation is needed. This will include the protection of natural and built environments, along with the conservation of our natural resources. Changing patterns of life, work and leisure have a significant impact on health. Work and leisure can and should be a source of health for people. How society organises work can help create a healthy society. Health promotion generates living and working conditions that are safe, stimulating, satisfying and enjoyable.

Strengthening community action

Community action that is associated with the formulation and setting of priorities, decision-making, planning strategies and their implementation to attain improved health can happen through health promotion. However, for this to occur the empowerment of communities, their ownership and the control of their own activities and destinies are needed. This will draw on existing human and material resources within the communities, with the aims of:

- enhancing self-help
- enhancing social support
- encouraging public participation and direction in health matters.

Access to information, various learning opportunities and funding support are crucial if this is to occur in a meaningful manner.

Building healthy public policy

Health is the responsibility of policy makers in all areas, e.g. those in the workplace, the health-care sector and schools. Policy makers must be conscious of the consequences of their decisions and responsibilities for health. Health promotion policy aims to join and bring together legislation, the economy (including taxation, for example) and also changes that occur at an organisational level to meet aims and objectives. This will become a reality only if joint action is taken to guarantee safer and healthier goods and services, healthier public services and cleaner, more enjoyable environments.

Health promotion therefore goes beyond health care. It places health on the agenda of policy makers in all sectors and at all levels, directing them to be aware of the health consequences of their decisions and to accept their responsibilities for health.

Top tips

Health promotion activity can take place anywhere – where people work, where they live, through health and social services that they use, their schools, colleges, universities, social clubs – anywhere where there are people.

Reorienting health services

The health sector has had a tendency to focus on the provision of clinical and curative services. This must be challenged and there must be a concerted effort to move beyond this. The focus should be sensitive to and respectful of cultural needs, be supportive of the needs of individuals and communities, and generate an awareness of the need to enhance relationships between the health sector and broader social, political, economic and physical environment sectors.

It is essential that a change in the attitude and organisation of health services take place, refocusing them on the holistic needs of the individual. If this is to occur it will require specific attention to the health research literature with changes in professional education and training – an interdisciplinary approach is advocated. Health-care professionals must work together toward a health-care system that plays a part in the pursuit of health.

The Ottawa Charter (WHO, 1986) provided a useful framework, to help nurses to provide health promotion activity. The Charter goes beyond the individual in the public health debate and can overcome the problem of victim blaming. It enables and empowers individuals and communities.

The fundamental principles associated with the Charter can be used successfully in many settings and environments and with various client groups, e.g. those with learning disabilities and/or mental health problems (National Health Service Education for Scotland, 2005). The mental health of individuals is influenced by many things, including public policy and the environment in which the individual finds him- or herself.

The vision outlined in the Ottawa Charter was reaffirmed by the Jakarta Declaration (WHO, 1997). The Jakarta Declaration identifies five further priorities that will lead health promotion in the twenty-first century:

- Promote social responsibility for health
- Increase investments for health development
- Consolidate and expand partnerships for health
- Increase community capacity and empower the individual
- Secure an infrastructure for health promotion.

Case study 7.3

 You are working with the school nurse Rohinee. The school is in an area that has been described as socially deprived. Review by the school nurse by the end of the child's first year of school usually includes:

- Check that immunisations are up to date
- Check that children have access to primary and dental care
- Check that appropriate interventions are available for any physical, developmental or emotional problems that had previously been missed, not yet identified or not addressed
- Provide children, parents and school staff with information about specific health issues
- Check the child's height and weight (and obtain body mass index) during the reception year, according to Department of Health guidelines. At the same time, administer the sweep test of hearing
- Selective health interviews.

Foundation Stage Profile – assessment by the teacher with input from the school nurse, to include a child's:

- personal, social and emotional development
- communication, language and literacy
- physical development
- creative development

Health promotion involvement offered in partnership with schools to include: healthy schools and contribution to personal, social and health education (PSHE) programme.

What do you understand by the term 'socially deprived'?

What immunisations will Rohinee be checking?

How can you, working with parents and school staff. enhance the uptake of immunisations

Producing and providing patient information

This section of the chapter provides you with information about the production of patient information to enhance health promotion. The quality of information presented to patients can have an impact on the experience that they have with health-care providers (DH, 2003). The importance of improving information that is given to patients has been cited in some key government publications, e.g. *The NHS Plan* (DH, 2000), the Kennedy Report into the Bristol Royal Infirmary (2001) and *Reference Guide to Consent for Examination or Treatment* (DH, 2009).

Often those who want to lead a healthy life will require information. They may need to know:

- What to do
- When to do it
- Where to do it
- How to do it.

Patient information refers to information that is produced and provided in any medium for the benefit of patients. Information that is produced can relate to information on specific diseases, e.g. diabetes mellitus, or be associated with health services such as going into hospital or related to health promotion activities, e.g. smoking cessation (Duman, 2003).

Crane and Patel (2005) suggest that there are three things that need to be considered when writing information (from a medical perspective):

1. What does the patient want to know?
2. What messages does the medical profession want to get across?
3. What is the most appropriate way to give the information?

Many nurses who provide and produce health information do so in a written form, through pamphlets, leaflets, posters or single sheets of paper. Written materials are often used to support one-to-one interactions with patients. Only 50 per cent of information can be recalled 5 minutes after a consultation with a patient, and patients' recall after a consultation has been demonstrated to be poor (Parkin and Skinner, 2003). Using literature to help patients participate in their own care can therefore be a useful resource.

Top tips

Providing high-quality health information will lead to high-quality care and care outcomes. Remember that the internet can open the door to a wealth of resources, e.g. clinical guidelines and drug compendia.

Hospitals, charities and support groups produce their own literature related to a wide and varied range of topics (Crane and Patel, 2005). Providing patients with written information means that they can take it away and absorb the contents at their own pace and in their own place.

The content of the information must be of a high quality if patients are to use it to enhance their health; there may be times when the standard is inadequate or the material poorly presented, adding to patient anxiety and confusion. Just as it is important to ensure that you employ effective verbal communication with patients, it is important to ensure that written communication skills (remember these are non-verbal communication skills) are also effective. Attention to the information provided is important because it can instil confidence in patients, remind them of what is happening or what is going to happen, and allow them to make informed decisions. The Wanless Report recommends that improved health information be developed to help individuals engage with their own health care in an informed way (HM Treasury, 2002).

The Department of Health (2003) outlines five principles that it considers to underpin good patient communication:

1. Improve health
2. Provide the best care
3. Act professionally
4. Work efficiently
5. Treat everybody equally.

Any written information provided to patients has the potential to hold up these values. Communication should be the following:

- Clear – so that it can be understood
- Straightforward – using fewer words and keeping to the necessary information
- Modern – using everyday language and current images
- Accessible – available to as many people as possible, avoiding jargon, up to date
- Honest – based on current evidence
- Respectful – sensitive to cultural needs and people, avoiding stereotypes.

Duman (2003) provides a process map to help develop patient information resources (Figure 7.3). The reasons for the provision of information are varied (Table 7.2).

Before beginning the process of developing patient information, there are some key questions that must be answered. It is important to determine why the information needs to be produced. There may be corporate or departmental policies that need to be adhered to and these will include issues such as house style. These defined styles ensure that the information produced is consistent with the organisation's (and in some instances national) core values, e.g. there may be a thesaurus covering the use of preferred terms. Any information produced could render the organisation liable in law for the consequences of that information, so advice must be obtained on legal liability.

Think

Imagine that you had to go into hospital for a surgical procedure or for some form of treatment. Make a list of the information that you would like to receive to ensure that you are about to make the right decision for the planned treatment.

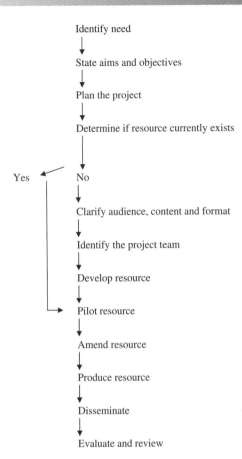

Identify need

State aims and objectives

Plan the project

Determine if resource currently exists

Yes   No

Clarify audience, content and format

Identify the project team

Develop resource

Pilot resource

Amend resource

Produce resource

Disseminate

Evaluate and review

Figure 7.3 The process map for developing patient information resources. Source: Duman (2003).

Table 7.2 Some reasons for providing patients with information

- To understand what is wrong
- To gain a realistic idea of prognosis
- To make the most of consultations
- To understand the process and likely outcomes of possible tests and treatments
- To assist in self-care
- To provide reassurance and help to cope
- To help others understand
- To legitimise help seeking and concerns
- To identify further information and self-help groups
- To identify the best health-care providers

Source: adapted from Department of Health (2003); Crane and Patel (2005).

Your list might include some of the points highlighted below.

If information is being provided that offers the patient advice about any procedure that requires patient to give explicit informed consent, this information must adhere to and comply with the requirements provided by the Department of Health about consent (DH, 2009). The following are required as a minimum:

- The aim of the procedure and the intended benefits
- What the procedure will involve
- What kind of anaesthesia is likely to be used
- Serious or frequently occurring risks if they exist for that procedure and the risks of doing nothing, if applicable
- Any additional procedures that are likely to be necessary
- Any alternative treatments that may be available if appropriate
- How long the patient may be in hospital
- What the patient will experience before, during and after the procedure, e.g. details of the procedure, common side effects and pain relief if appropriate.

Table 7.3 provides questions that need to be considered during the planning stage.

It is vital that the target audience is clearly stated, e.g. it may be patients who are at risk of contracting chlamydia (a sexually transmitted infection); however, one leaflet or resource may not be appropriate for all potential groups, e.g.:

- Women
- Men
- Men who have sex with men
- Women who have sex with women
- Adolescents.

The approach (i.e. the format) used should always be responsive to the target group, taking into account their needs and wishes. It is therefore important to have some insight into the target audience, taking some time to determine their particular characteristics. You should always listen to members of the target audience and their carers, aiming to ascertain how they want the information provided.

Case study 7.4

 A social worker with whom you are working is putting together a range of health promotion activities for homeless people. She is focusing on the safe use of alcohol. She has asked you to see if you can find any images of cancer of the liver or cirrhosis of the liver because she wants to scare the people into stopping drinking – every other method that she knows of has failed. Scare tactics, she feels, 'will shock these guys into stopping'.

How might you react to this approach?
What might be wrong with this approach?
How might you begin to address the issue of safe alcohol use among homeless people?

Table 7.3 Issues to be considered during the planning stage

- Who is the package for (e.g. the target audience)?
- How can an assurance be made that the information provided is relevant to the audience?
- How do you envisage that it will be used?
- What medium would be suited to the target audience?
- What measures will be taken to ensure that the information produced will be easily understood?
- Does it fit with the organisation's corporate image (e.g. its general aims and information policy)?

Source: adapted from Duman (2003).

Producing and providing patient information can be a complex task. The nurse needs to ensure that the medium used is appropriate for the target audience, and the content of the material is factually correct and conforms to the organisation's aims and objectives (corporate image). It is advisable at a draft production stage to show the material to at least one expert in the field (patient and/or health-care professional) to determine the accuracy of its content (Crane and Patel, 2005). Once feedback has been received, it will be necessary to show the information to a group of patients to gain their feedback, after which adjustments and alterations may be needed.

It must be remembered that patient information in the form of leaflets or pamphlets, despite increasing in popularity, is no substitute for spoken communication with the nurse. The written supplementary information provided can be used to expand and reinforce what has been said during a discussion or consultation, but never to replace the need for a face-to-face explanation of issues or concerns.

Crane and Patel (2005) provide some simple advice that may help to enhance the understanding of the information that you may provide. The following may help to ensure that you produce patient literature that will help the patient:

- Break down the information into small chunks – a question-and-answer format may help.
- Begin by stating what information you plan to offer, provide it and summarise it – say what you are going to say, say it and say it again.
- Choose the words that you intend to use carefully.
- Technical terms can be used (Abergavenny, 2003), but you must ensure that you have correctly assessed the needs of the audience.
- Use personal terms such as 'you' (as opposed to patient) and 'we' (as opposed to nurses).
- Take time to consider how much information is needed. Be aware, for example, that not all patients want to know their prognosis, particularly where the condition is serious (Schattner, 2002).

In Table 7.4 you will find a checklist that provides an outline of issues that should be taken into account when producing a leaflet or booklet. The checklist is not a complete list and it may be that not all the items will be relevant. It should be used as a guide only.

When the information has been produced and is being used by the patient (or patient group) it must be evaluated to ensure that it is still current and relevant. Changes within health care and health provision are occurring at an exponential rate: new facts are uncovered, new treatments devised and erstwhile approaches to treatment or care may be discarded, so it is vital that evaluation and review take place. Duman (2003) suggests that evaluation and review take place about a year after the information's inception and at the maximum 2 years.

Table 7.4 Items that should be considered by the nurse when devising leaflets and booklets for operations, treatments and investigations

- What is the leaflet about and who is it for?
- What is the procedure?
- Why are they having the procedure? (Give the benefits and alternatives where appropriate)
- What preparation do they need or not need?
- Do they need a general anaesthetic, sedation or local anaesthetic?
- What happens when they arrive at the hospital/clinic/surgery? Who will meet them?
- Will they be asked to sign a consent form or is verbal consent needed?
- What does the procedure involve? How long does it last? What does it feel like?
- What happens after the procedure – pain control, nursing checks, e.g. observations, stitches?
- How long will they be at the hospital/clinic/surgery?
- Do they need someone with them or any special equipment when they get home?
- What care do they need at home?
- What follow-up care is needed? Do they need to visit their doctor?
- What can go wrong, what signs to look out for and what to do if something goes wrong?
- When can they start their normal activities again, e.g. driving, sport, sex or work?
- Whom can they contact if they have any more questions?
- Tell people where they can find more information, e.g. support groups and websites

Source: adapted from Department of Health (2003).

Conclusions

The role of the nurse is challenging and one aspect of this complex role is to promote the interests of patients. This will include helping them to gain access to health- and social care information and to support their choices related to their health-care needs.

Health promotion cannot be seen as a purely technical activity; it requires a variety of effective communication skills. The nurse must develop and hone his or her skills associated with health promotion. The current health agenda with its focus on health promotion means that the nurse will have to develop and build on a wide range of skills to provide proactive health promotion with the ultimate aim of enhancing patient care.

The nurse should approach health promotion with an acceptance of the existing knowledge and beliefs of the patient. It should be remembered that some patients may be able to adopt a healthier lifestyle only if certain conditions are present and some of the conditions may be outside the immediate control of the patient and the nurse.

When opportunities arise to promote the patient's health the nurse should act accordingly (Whittam, 2008) in order to:

- prevent disease and reduce mortality rates
- reduce risks associated with disease
- promote healthier lifestyles.

The nurse must consider the social factors that contribute to health and ill-health as opposed to locating the cause in the individual. Health promotion activity does not occur in a vacuum. The health of a person, poor or good, is not always that person's fault. Behaviours and the choices individuals make about their health are not always a result of lack of knowledge; other factors may be at play such as fear and denial.

This chapter has provided definitions of some key terms that are used within the health promotion arena. It must be noted, however, that definitions by their very nature can be restrictive and at best can provide only a summary of complex ideas and activities. In spite of these restrictions and limitations, definitions can assist when trying to comprehend the fundamental ideas and concepts associated with health promotion activities. It is important to define key terms that are associated with health promotion, if health promotion is going to be effective,

There are several models of health promotion that help the nurse, patient and community achieve 'health'. The use of these models and the various available frameworks (e.g. the Ottawa Charter and the Jakarta Declaration) provide guidance as well as situating health promotion within the wider social and political domain.

The provision and production of health promotion materials need much consideration if the patient is to receive high-quality advice. This chapter has provided information to help readers understand some important issues that must be considered if they are planning on producing health promotion materials for use with the public.

Finally, the formulation of new public health strategies and the need to orient health services must be a priority for the Government and the nursing profession in order to ensure that health promotion remains high on the political and social agenda.

Activity

Attempt the following cross word, which is related to health promotion to test your knowledge. The answers can be found at the back of this book, in the chapter called 'Activity Answers'.

Across

2. Taking into account all aspects of a person: physical, mental, emotional and social
5. Spreading rapidly and extensively by infection and affecting many individuals in an area or a population at the same time
8. Fairness and the distribution of resources for health on the basis of needs
9. Working together towards agreed goals
11. State of complete physical, mental and social wellbeing and not merely the absence of disease or infirmity
13. To enable others
15. The study of health-event patterns in a society

Down

1. The study of statistics of about a population
3. An abnormal condition of the body or mind that causes discomfort or dysfunction
4. Also known as moral philosophy
6. Variations that are not fair or just
7. Several people
10. One person
12. Small localities with distinct identity
14. Measure of how much illness there is in a population at a particular point in time or over a specific period

References

Abel T (2007) Cultural capital in health promotion. In: McQueen DV, Kickbush I (eds), *Health and Modernity: The role of theory in health promotion*. New York: Springer, pp 43–73.

Abergavenny RD (2003) Patients prefer 'medical labels' to lay language, study finds. *British Medical Journal* **11**: 181.

Acheson D (1988) *Public Health in England*. London: Department of Health.

Bridle G, Riemsma RF, Patthenden J, et al (2005) Systematic review of the effectiveness of health behavior interactions based on the transtheoretical model. *Psychology and Health* **20**: 283–301.

Crane R, Patel B (2005) Producing patient literature. *Student British Medical Journal* **13**: 200.

Department of Health (1999) *Making a Difference: Strengthening the nursing, midwifery and health visiting contribution to health and social care*. London: DH.

Department of Health (2000) *The NHS Plan: A plan for investment, a plan for reform*. London: DH.

Department of Health (2001) *Shifting the Balance of Power*. London: DH.

Department of Health (2003) *Toolkit for Producing Patient Information*. London: DH.

Department of Health (2005a) *Choosing Health: Making healthier choices easier*. London: Department of Health.

Department of Health (2005b) *Delivering Choosing Health: Making healthier choices easier*. London: DH.

Department of Health (2009) *Reference Guide to Consent for Examination or Treatment*, 2nd edn. London: DH.

Department of Health (2010a) *Equity and Excellence: Liberating the NHS*. London: Department of Health.

Department of Health (2010b) *Healthy Lives, Healthy People: Our strategy for public health in England*. London: Department of Health.

Duman M (2003) *Producing Patient Information: How to research, develop and produce effective information resources*. London: King's Fund.

Hayes L (2005) Public health and nurses..What is your role. *Primary Care Journal* **15**(5): 22–25.

HM Treasury (2002) *Securing Our Future Health: Taking a long-term view*. London: HM Treasury.

Illich I (1976) *The Limits to Medicine: Medical Nemesis: The Expropriation of Health*. Penguin. Harmondsworth.

Kennedy Report into the Bristol Royal Infirmary (2001) *Learning from Bristol: The Report of the Public Inquiry into Children's Heart Surgery at the Bristol Royal Infirmary 1984–1995*. Command 5207. London: HMSO.

Lisle M (2001) Organisational health: A new strategy for promoting health and well-being. In: Scriven, A, Orme J (eds), *Health Promotion: Professional Perspectives*, 2nd edn . Basingstoke: Palgrave, pp 222–235.

Marmot Review (2010) *Fair Society Healthy Lives. The Marmot Review*. Available at: www.ucl.ac.uk/marmotreview (accessed June 2011).

Melling K, Gleeson J, Hunter K (2004) Developing health promotion practice. In: Chilton S, Melling K, Drew D, Clarridge A (eds), *Nursing in the Community: An essential guide to practice*. London: Arnold, pp 95–102.

Montazeri A, McGhee S, McEwan J (1998) Fear inducing and positive image strategies in health education campaigns. *Journal of the Institute of Health Promotion and Education* **36**(3): 68–75.

Naidoo J, Wills J (2009) *Foundations for Health Promotion*, 3rd edn. London: Bailliere Tindall.

National Health Service Education for Scotland (2005) *The Right Preparation: The framework for learning disability education in Scotland*. Edinburgh: National Health Service Education for Scotland.

Nutbeam D (2000) Health literacy as a public health goal: A challenge for contemporary health education and communication. Strategies in to the 21st century. *Health Promotion International* **15**: 259–267.

Nursing and Midwifery Council (2008) *The Code: Standards of Conduct, Performance and Ethics for Nurses and Midwives*. London: NMC.

Nursing and Midwifery Council (2010) *Standards for Pre registration Nursing Education*. London: NMC. Available at: http://standards.nmc-uk.org/PublishedDocuments/Standards%20for%20pre-registration%20nursing%20education%2016082010.pdf (accessed June 2011).

Parkin T, Skinner TC (2003) Discrepancies between patient and professionals recall and perception of an outpatient consultation. *Diabetic Medicine* **20**: 909–914.

Russell J (2005) *Introduction to Psychology for Health Carers*. Cheltenham: Nelson Thornes.

Sarafino EP, Smith TW (2011) *Health Psychology: Biopsychosocial interactions*, 7th edn. Hoboken, NJ: Wiley.

Schattner A (2002) What do patients really want to know? *Quality Journal of Medicine* **95**: 135–136.

Scriven A (2010) *Promoting Health: A practical guide*, 6th edn. Edinburgh: Baillière Tindall.

Sigerist HE (1946) *The University at the Crossroads*. New York: Schuman.

Tones K (2001) Health promotion: The empowerment imperative. In: Scriven, A, Orme J (eds), *Health Promotion: Professional perspectives*, 2nd edn. Basingstoke: Palgrave, pp 3–18.

Tones K, Green J (2004) *Health Promotion: Planning and strategies*. London: Sage.

Whittam S (2008) Maintaining a safe environment. In: Holland K, Jenkins J, Solomon, J, Whittam S (eds) *Applying the Roper, Logan and Tierney Model in Practice*, 2nd edn. Edinburgh: Churchill Livingstone, pp 46–100.

World Health Organization (1948) *Preamble to the Constitution of the World Health Organization*. New York: International Health Conference.

World Health Organization (1978) *Report on the International Conference on Primary Health Care, Alma Ata, 6–12th September*. Geneva: WHO.

World Health Organization (1986) *Ottawa Charter for Health Promotion 1st International Conference on Health Promotion. November 17th–21st*. Ottawa: WHO.

World Health Organization (1997) *The Jakarta Declaration on Leading Health Promotion into the 21st Century*. Geneva: WHO.

World Health Organization (1998) *Health Promotion Glossary*. Geneva: WHO.

Part III

Nursing Practice and Decision-making

8

Evidence-based Practice

Aims and objectives

The aim of this chapter is to provide you with an understanding of the key issues associated with evidence-based practice.

At the end of the chapter you will be able to:

1. Understand the importance of using the most up-to-date evidence on which to provide care
2. Discus the meaning of best available evidence
3. Explore the stages of evidence-based practice
4. Describe the steps in literature searching
5. Highlight the factors that have to be taken into account when applying best available evidence to practice
6. Discuss the potential barriers and possible solutions to implementing evidence-based practice

Safe and effective nursing care is based on the best available evidence. As an autonomous practitioner, the nurse will be required to provide essential care to a very high standard and care that is complex using the best available evidence where appropriate (Nursing and Midwifery Council or NMC, 2010). All nurses must be able to use analytical thinking, adopt a problem-solving approach and apply evidence in decision-making. The Code (NMC, 2008) insists that nurses provide a high standard of practice and care at all times, using the best available evidence to deliver that care.

This chapter encourages the reader to apply knowledge and skills indicative of safe and effective nursing practice. The key aspects of the chapter relate to the use of research and best evidence findings that underpin safe and effective care. The stimulus for evidence-based practice has its origins in evidence-based medicine, but its components are appropriate to the practice of all health-care and social care professionals. People in acute and community settings are cared for by multiprofessional teams and nursing interventions can have an impact on patient morbidity and mortality. A competent practitioner must be able to demonstrate the ability to meet the needs of people requiring a range of interventions that support and enhance health and wellbeing.

The start of the evidence-based movement is attributed to the physician and epidemiologist Archie Cochrane, who drew attention to the lack of evidence associated with the effects of health care. He

The Student's Guide to Becoming a Nurse, Second Edition. Ian Peate.
© 2012 John Wiley & Sons, Ltd. Published 2012 by John Wiley & Sons, Ltd.

suggested that there should be efforts to summarise the results of research (specifically summaries arising from randomised clinical trials) available to decision-makers (Cochrane, 1979). The term 'evidence-based medicine' was coined at McMaster University Medical School as a way of describing problem-based learning. Polit and Beck (2011) define evidence-based practice as the best use of clinical evidence when making patient care decisions; this evidence usually comes from research undertaken by nurses and other health-care professionals.

Evidence-based practice is a concept that is used to capture the essence of best evidence used in practice. The primary aim of evidence-based practice is to identify and apply the most effective interventions with the intention of maximising the quality and quantity of life for individuals (Straus et al, 2005). The demand for high-quality care has come from a number of sources, including Government, patients and their carers, the public and the nursing profession. This demand is accompanied by organisational change within health-care provision and the need to ensure that limited resources are used to provide health care that is based on the best available evidence. The chapter starts by explaining the stages of evidence-based practice.

Stages of evidence-based practice

Evidence-based practice has five stages, namely:

1. A clear question is developed arising from the patient's problem.
2. The questions are used to search the literature for evidence relating to the problem.
3. The evidence is appraised critically for its validity and usefulness.
4. The best available current evidence, together with clinical expertise and the patient's perspectives, is used to provide care.
5. The patient outcomes are evaluated through a process of audit and peer assessment, including self-evaluation of the research process.

An explanation of each stage and their subdivisions follows.

A clear question is developed arising from the patient's problem

This stage consists of two aspects: types of questions and finding the answers to your questions. When nursing a patient it is not unusual for you to consider why the patient is being cared for in that way, or whether there is an alternative way to provide that care. How would you find out the answer to your concern or problem? One of the points that you need to be clear about is the question that you want to ask. This may not be as easy as it sounds, because, if you do not ask the right type of question, you will not get the correct answer to your concern or problem.

Types of questions

You will need to decide on the type of information that you require and thus the question that needs to be asked. There are two types of questions: background questions and foreground questions.

Background questions

These questions allow you to find out more about the patient/problem or condition under scrutiny. It is a question about who, what, when, where, why and how, and is related to a problem. For example, what causes vomiting? Note that there are no inclusion or exclusion criteria and this type of search would produce a large amount of information that might be helpful in assisting with your focused question(s). Background questions give basic information about the condition and may help to formulate the specific or foreground questions.

Foreground questions

Unlike background questions, foreground questions ask for specific information about managing the patient or problem (McKibbon and Marks, 2001). Foreground questions can be related to the following:

- *Diagnosis* – selecting the most appropriate diagnostic test, or interpreting the results of a particular test.
- *Treatment* – what is the most effective treatment given a particular clinical problem?
- *Harm or aetiology* – what are the harmful effects of a particular treatment and how can these be minimised or reduced?
- *Prognosis* – what is the likely course of disease in this patient or group of patients?
- *Service redesign* – is it cost-effective to move the care of patients with type 2 diabetes from secondary to primary care?

Straus et al (2009) consider a framework that can be used for asking foreground questions: **p**atient or **p**roblem, **i**ntervention, **c**omparative intervention and **o**utcome. The initials give rise to the mnemonic PICO. In some cases there may be a comparative intervention, but this is not always the case. Table 8.1 provides an example of how PICO may be used. Having devised your question, the next step is to locate the answer; this forms the discussion of the next section.

Think

Consider a patient in your care. Identify the type of patient condition and the current treatment or care, i.e. the intervention. Identify the outcome. Try to formulate a foreground question. You will use your example throughout this chapter.

Top tips

The inability to ask a focused and precise clinical question can be a major impediment to evidence-based practice.

Table 8.1 Components of foreground questions – PICO

Component of the clinical question	Patient or patient's problem/ condition	Intervention	Comparative intervention [(optional) Is there an alternative treatment to compare with the intervention?]	Outcome
Example	In patients with mild hypertension	does anti-hypertensive medication when compared with	exercise and diet	make a difference in the reduction of hypertension?
Example	In premature babies with sickle cell trait	what are the current treatments		in the management of high temperature and infection?
Example	When providing care for patients with type 2 diabetes	does standard care when compared with	primary/community care	make a difference to patient outcomes and reduction in cost?

Finding the answers to your questions

A number of resources may be at your disposal. You could consult a clinical nurse specialist or a nurse consultant, if there are any on your placement. You may also like to consult your knowledge manager or information consultant at your learning resources centre. They may direct you to specialist journals as well as databases such as Medical Literature On-line (Medline) and Cumulative Index to Nursing and Allied Health Literature (CINAHL). You may also like to search the world-wide web for information about your topic. Other sources of information are as follows:

- Peer-reviewed journals, which include research-based articles within their publication range. The research-based articles should provide enough details about the methodology so that informed judgements can be made about the study's validity and the clinical relevance of the findings
- Government publications, which include funded research reports, discussion papers, conference proceedings, Government policies and inquiry results
- Organisations and professional bodies often provide free information and further sources of evidence
- Indexes and abstracts to theses
- Reference collections on past students' work, specific dictionaries and encyclopaedias
- Conference proceedings
- Pharmaceutical company information

- Discussion and networking groups
- Newspapers.

You may be overwhelmed with information, depending on how much research has been done in the area that you are searching. If this is the case, you will need to narrow your search to obtain a manageable number of articles. The second stage of evidence-based practice, searching the literature, provides information about undertaking this procedure, which is discussed below.

The questions are used to search the literature for evidence relating to the problem

Now that you have formulated your question, the next step is to search the literature for evidence. This raises three important questions:

1. What do we mean by evidence?
2. In particular, what do we mean by best evidence?
3. How can we search the literature for evidence?

Having answered these three questions, a decision has to be made on the worth of the material found. A discussion on each of these follows.

What is the meaning of evidence?

Polit and Beck (2011) say that there is no consensus about what is meant by evidence for evidence-based practice (EBP), but there is general agreement that the results from 'robust' or 'best' research studies are of importance. A dictionary definition of evidence (Collins, 1986) includes the following:

- Grounds for belief or disbelief
- Data on which to base proof or to establish truth or falsehood
- To serve to indicate, attest.

The common thread running through the above is that evidence needs to be observed and subjected to scrutiny.

Cochrane's (1979) emphasis on quantitative research, specifically randomised controlled trials, gave rise to a view that quantitative research evidence was more valued than other forms of research evidence. However, qualitative research and quantitative research are equally necessary in the generation of research-based nursing knowledge to inform nursing practice, e.g. if we wish to find out the experiences of a specific group of people living with long-term conditions, a qualitative design may be best suited for this study. On the other hand, if we want to measure the effectiveness of one treatment over another, a quantitative design would be suitable. The evidence-based medicine movement has shifted to include clinically relevant research evidence by all health-care practitioners, whether it is of a quantitative or a qualitative nature (Straus et al, 2005). Higgs et al (2008) consider the view of what constitutes evidence by proposing that evidence is knowledge and is derived from a number of sources; this knowledge has been subjected to testing and is found to be credible. Thus 'evidence' may encompass knowledge broader than research-based information.

What is the meaning of best evidence?

Current best evidence includes clinical practice guidelines, which are usually nationally developed by expert researchers and have undergone research trials. The National Institute for Health and Clinical Excellence (NICE) Scottish Intercollegiate Guidelines Network (SIGN), Guidelines and Audit Implementation Network (GAIN), the Health Quality Improvements Partnerships and National Service Frameworks (NSFs) are examples of authoritative national guidance developed to achieve consistent clinical standards across the NHS.

Clinical guidelines are recommendations by NICE on the relevant treatment and care of people with specific diseases and conditions within the NHS. The guidelines assist health professionals in their work, but they do not replace their knowledge and skills.

The aim of good clinical guidelines is to improve the quality of health care. They can change the way in which health care is delivered and improve people's chances of getting as well as possible. Well-constructed and up-to-date clinical guidelines have the added advantages of:

- providing recommendations for the treatment and care of people by health professionals
- being used to develop standards to assess the clinical practice of individual health professionals
- being used in education and training sessions of health professionals
- assisting patients and carers to make informed decisions, thus improving communication among the patient, carer and health professional.

The clinical guidelines used in nursing should be updated by nurses and other health-care professionals as new empirical evidence becomes available. It is important to bear in mind that not all research is of best quality and practices may be described as research based even when the research process is questionable. Some published research can be of poor quality and result in conflicting evidence. When this is used as a basis for a change in practice, it may mean that patients may not receive the optimum care.

How to search for evidence: steps in literature search

This section provides a guide to the principles of searching the research literature. It is outside the remit of the section to give extensive and detailed information about the art of searching. However, the information given in Figure 8.1 provides good guidance on searching the literature. Conducting a literature search can be a lengthy and complex process, but the time taken is well worth the investment. You will need to be organised and systematic in your approach, because it is important to keep detailed records of the searches made and the information found.

You may wish to use your formulated question to follow the example used in Table 8.2, discussed below. Try to follow the procedures with your own question.

Take the first example in Table 8.1, which is replicated as Table 8.2. Using the PICO example, you will need to set parameters by reviewing the literature in relation to some main themes pertinent to your topic, e.g. you will need to have clear in your mind a definition of mild hypertension. You may wish to use the British Hypertensive Society's guidelines or any other suitable definition. You may also want to specify which type of hypertensive medication you would like to find evidence about. These need to be noted. You may also want to note alternative spellings, synonyms and acronyms for use in your search. As you proceed with your search, you may wish to be more specific by having inclusion and exclusion criteria.

Inclusion criteria

Inclusion criteria are characteristics that are essential to the problem under scrutiny. They are sometimes referred to as eligibility criteria; in other words, the sample population must possess the named characteristics. Examples of inclusion or eligibility criteria include the following:

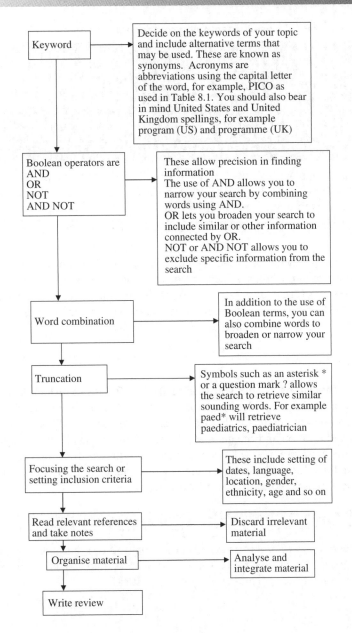

Figure 8.1 Steps in the literature search. Source: adapted from Burns and Grove (2011); Polit and Beck (2011).

- Appropriate age groups
- Language, e.g. English
- Location or geography
- Time period, e.g. between 1995 and 2000
- Evidence-based medicine.

Table 8.2   Illustration of PICO's use in identifying components of a question

Component of the clinical question	Patient or problem	Intervention	Comparative intervention [(optional) Is there an alternative treatment to compare with the intervention?]	Outcome
Example	In patients with mild hypertension	does anti-hypertensive medication when compared with	exercise and diet	make a difference in the reduction of hypertension?

The inclusion criterion of evidence-based medicine will mean that the results of the search will be limited to articles reviewed in databases such as Health Technology Assessment (HTA), Cochrane Database of Systematic Reviews (CDSR) and Databases of Abstracts of Reviews of Effectiveness (DARE). DARE complements the CDSR by providing a selection of quality-assessed reviews in those subjects where there is currently no Cochrane review (Burns and Grove, 2011; Hurley et al, 2011).

Exclusion criteria

Exclusion criteria are characteristics that you specifically do not wish to include in your search, such as white people with diabetes if the problem pertains to African–Caribbean males with diabetes. The inclusion and exclusion criteria are important characteristics of a research study because they have implications for both the interpretation and the generalisability of the findings (Polit and Beck, 2011).

Having obtained the literature, you will need to decide on the worth of the material found. This can be done by assessing the information using a hierarchy of evidence or by appraising the literature using the research process. Discussion of both these follows next.

Top tips

When trying to find the evidence, the ideal source is a systematic review; this summarises the results from a large number of high-quality research studies. The Cochrane Library is an excellent place to start.

The evidence is appraised critically for its validity and usefulness

Hierarchy of evidence

An aid commonly used to assess the worth of the material found, and that is used in clinical decision-making, is the hierarchy of evidence (Table 8.3). Hierarchies of evidence were first used by the Canadian

Table 8.3 An example of the hierarchy of evidence

Rank:	Methodology	Description
1	**Systematic reviews and meta-analyses**	**Systematic review**: review of a body of data that uses explicit methods to locate primary studies, and explicit criteria to assess their quality. **Meta-analysis**: A statistical analysis that combines or integrates the results of several independent clinical trials considered by the analyst to be 'combinable', usually to the level of reanalysing the original data, also sometimes called *pooling, quantitative synthesis*. Both are sometimes called 'overviews'.
2	**Randomised controlled trials** (finer distinctions may be drawn within this group based on statistical parameters like the confidence intervals)	Individuals are randomly allocated to a control group and a group which receives a specific intervention. Otherwise the two groups are identical for any significant variables. They are followed up for specific end points.
3	**Cohort studies**	Groups of people are selected on the basis of their exposure to a particular agent and followed up for specific outcomes.
4	**Case-control studies**	'Cases' with the condition are matched with 'controls' without, and a retrospective analysis used to look for differences between the two groups.
5	**Cross-sectional surveys**	Survey or interview of a sample of the population of interest at one point in time.
6	**Case reports**	A report based on a single patient or subject; sometimes collected together into a short series.
7	**Expert opinion**	A consensus of experience from the good and the great.
8	**Anecdotal**	Something your friend told you after a meeting.

Source: adapted from Mantzoukas (2007); Jolley (2010); Larrabee (2010).

Task Force on the Periodic Health Examination in 1979, and have subsequently been developed and used in assessing the effectiveness of research studies (Canadian Task Force on the Periodic Health Examination, 1979; Petticrew and Roberts, 2003). They allow research-based evidence to be graded according to their design and ranked in order of decreasing internal validity; they indicate the confidence that decision- and policy makers can have in their findings. However, the hierarchy of evidence remains a source of debate, because the use of the term is contentious when applied to health promotion and public health (Petticrew and Roberts, 2003).

Although there is an undeniable necessity for quantitative research, this approach is not suitable for many issues encountered in nursing practice. Patients' views about health care are not always quantifiable, e.g. their experiences of living with a long-term condition, the effects of treatment or their choice of treatment. These need to be considered when delivering health care and the concept of a hierarchy of evidence is often problematic when appraising the evidence for social or public health interventions. These issues cannot be addressed appropriately in a quantitative study; a qualitative approach is more suitable, because this way of conducting research focuses on the meanings and understandings of people's experiences (Burns and Grove, 2011). Another way of deciding on the worth of the material found is by appraising the evidence guided by a systematic process. A number of factors are important in the execution of this process and these are considered below.

Think

Using a research paper found from your literature search of your question/topic, attempt to review as much of the paper by using the process outlined below to appraise the evidence.

Top tips

Often librarians (e.g. those in your university or those at the Royal College of Nursing) can help identify the best resources of evidence and they also provide teaching in effective searching skills. Librarians are exerts in helping you find what you are looking for.

Deciding the worth of the material found

Appraising the evidence

Reviewing the literature requires developing a complex set of skills acquired through practice. A comprehensive review of the literature is important (Gray, 2009) because it:

- provides an up-to-date understanding of the subject and its significance to practice
- identifies the methods used in the research
- helps in the formulation of research topics, questions and direction
- provides a basis on which the subsequent research findings can be compared.

There are a number of ways in which evidence may be appraised. Burns and Grove (2011) and Polit and Beck (2011) suggest that a research appraisal can be divided into several sections. Using the subdivisions and considering the points suggested below will help with this activity.

The structure of the report

- Is the organisation of the report logical?
- Does the report follow the sequence of steps of the process of research?

- — introduction
- — identification of the research problem
- — planning
- — data collection
- — data analysis
- — discussion
- — conclusions
- — recommendation.

   The way in which a report is organised may vary from one researcher to the next. However, in all cases the organisation should be logical. It should begin with a clear identification of what is to be studied and how, and should end with a summary or conclusion recommending further study or application. You should bear in mind that different journals may require a different layout, but the key issue is logical progression.

The abstract

- ● Does the abstract, in a concise paragraph, clearly describe:
   - — what was studied?
   - — how it was studied?
   - — how the sample was selected?
   - — how the data were analysed?
   - — the main findings of the research?

The abstract provides a summary of the question and the most important findings of the study. It outlines how these differ from those of previous studies, and gives some indication of the methodology undertaken. It is usually up to 200–300 words long (depending on the guidelines for specific journals and the thesis formats of the relevant university). The abstract serves to provide the reader with a quick overview of what the research has done and found.

The introduction

The introduction serves to explain 'why' and 'how' the research problem came to be defined in this particular way. It reviews critically previous relevant literature, pointing out any limitations in findings, methodology or theoretical interpretation. It also provides a pathway to the methodology section by clarifying the need for research to be undertaken in the chosen topic, especially with the methodological orientation or techniques chosen by the researcher.

The problem statement/purpose of the research

You should consider whether:

- ● the general problem has been introduced promptly
- ● the problem has been substantiated with adequate background and the need for the study
- ● the general problem has been narrowed down to a specific research problem or to a problem with sub-problems as appropriate
- ● the hypotheses directly answer the research problems.

The literature review and theoretical rationale for the study

- You should aim to consider whether this section is relevant, clearly written, well organised and up to date, and whether the reliability of the methods and data collection is addressed (your reasons should be substantiated).
- Was there a sufficient review of the literature and theoretical rationale to assure you that the author had considered a broad spectrum of possibilities for investigating the problem?
- Is it clear how the study will extend previous findings?

A thesis requires an extensive literature review, whereas in a journal article the author will usually cite the *major* pieces of work that are particularly relevant.

Methodology

The methodology section must fully inform readers of the step-by-step processes undertaken in conducting the study. You should consider the appropriateness of the research methods chosen, including the following:

- Sampling approach
- Data-collection methods
- Validity and reliability of observations or measurements.

Consideration of the following subheadings and questions will help in providing this information.

The population and sample

- Is the study population specific enough so that it is clear to what population the findings may be generalised?
- Is the sample representative of the population defined?
- Would it be possible to replicate the study population?
- Is the method of sample selection appropriate?
- Was any bias introduced by this method?
- Is the sample size appropriate and how is it substantiated?

Instrumentation

- Are the data-collection methods appropriate to the study?
- Do they obtain the data that the researcher seeks?
- Is the author specific about the validity and reliability of the instruments used?

Procedure for data collection

- Were steps taken to control extraneous variables?
- Were collection methods replicable?

Ethical considerations

- The rights of participants
- The impact of ethical problems on the merit of the study and the wellbeing of the participants

- Steps to protect participants
- Indications of violations of ethical principles and suggestions as to how these could have been avoided
- Inclusion in the report of any ethical considerations
- Presentation of evidence that indicates that the rights of the study's participants have been protected.

The pilot study

- Was a pilot study undertaken?
- Were any changes made following the pilot study?

Analysis of data

- Were the analyses reported clearly and related to each hypothesis?
- Is it clear what statistical methods were used and what values were obtained?
- Is there a statement of whether or not the data support the hypotheses?
- Is complete discussion of the data given?
- Has a thorough examination of each hypothesis, including the use of appropriate statistical analysis and the decision to accept or reject the hypothesis, been included?
- Has explanation been given on how missing data were handled?
- Have experts been used to assist in analysis of the data?

Discussion

- Is the discussion critically presented?
- Can the findings be generalised?

Conclusions and limitations

- Has the author related the findings to the theoretical position of the study?
- Did the researcher identify methodological problems?
- Does the author over-generalise?
- Are the implications of the findings for practice identified?
- Are there suggestions for further research?

References and bibliography

- Are references cited relevant to the study?
- Do the reference list and bibliography reflect:
    - the review of the literature
    - search for and/or development of valid and reliable instruments/methodology.

When undertaking or reading a literature review, always be aware of your own value judgements and biases, and try to avoid personalised unhelpful criticisms (Jesson et al, 2011).

The best available current evidence, together with clinical expertise and the patient's perspectives, is used to provide care

The discussion in this section encompasses three aspects: (1) the factors that need to be taken into account when putting evidence into practice; (2) factors affecting the implementation of evidence-based practice; and (3) ways of promoting evidence-based practice. The discussion starts with factors that need to be taken into account.

Factors to be taken into account when putting evidence into practice

Getting research into practice is a complex and time-consuming task and involves behaviour change on the part of the individuals, teams and organisations involved (Straus et al, 2009). Making decisions about care is an iterative process that involves consideration of the potential benefits and harm of treatment and needs of the individual. These factors can create uncertainty about how and whether research evidence can be put into practice. At a time when cost pressures are evident in health-care delivery and there is a need for holistic evidence-based care, evidence of clinical governance as well as quality improvement targets, nurses must be aware of the key factors that should be taken into account when putting evidence into practice, including:

- The need to take into account that there are different types of evidence and that not all research studies provide robust evidence.
- The different sources of evidence, e.g. patient comfort, alteration in lifestyle, evidence from specialist nurses and national guidelines.
- The type of setting, which is key to implementing change. Teaching/learning organisations and those that take part in research, whether at a local or national level, are more likely to be open to introducing evidence-based practice than institutions where nurses are seldom provided with the opportunities for updating their knowledge and skills. Decision-making in the former institutions is bottom-up rather than top-down, as health-care professionals feel valued and are supported to find new ways of working. Leadership has a key role to play in the change process.
- Understanding of cultures, values and beliefs to overcome potential barriers to change.
- The need for nurses to be articulate about the research evidence. Knowledge about the different paradigms is important, because those whom the nurses may be trying to convince for funding to support change may prefer the quantitative approach to research, i.e. their preference is for information in a numerical form, collected and analysed in a systematic, objective and measurable way with definite conclusions. This approach to obtaining data is not always conducive to nursing. It could be tentatively suggested that the qualitative approach, which tries to understand and explain the phenomena under study and is generally seen as less scientific, is often more appropriate to many of the issues central to nursing, and less receptive to policy- makers and decision-makers (Melnyk et al, 2004; Rycroft-Malone et al, 2004).

Overall, nurses need the ability to take into account not just the evidence but also the evidence of case-based knowledge in clinical practice, patient preferences and factors, and the particular clinical scenario before deciding on appropriate management (Rycroft-Malone et al, 2004). This involves assessing the evidence for the appropriate problem, considering the appropriateness of both anecdotal evidence and direct clinical experience in relation to the clinical problem, as well as incorporating the patient's views and deciding whether the patient under discussion is similar to patients addressed by the research or guidelines. Consideration should be given to the issue that similar decision scenarios may not be identical because they may be conducted in different clinical settings and target different patient subgroups. It is also important to note whether or not there is an additional patient problem, because this might influence safety and effectiveness. Further, it should be noted that patients' beliefs about the value of treatment, their assessment of personal risk and their reluctance to change treatment might also influence their treatment preferences (Wulff and Gøtzsche, 2000). In addition, other factors that may affect the implementation of evidence-based practices include individual and organisational factors.

Factors affecting the implementation of evidence-based practice

The barriers to evidence-based practice have been documented in studies by Kajermo et al (1998), Retsas (2000), Jennings and Loan (2001) and McKenna et al (2004), and can be grouped under two subheadings.

Individual factors

- Lack of interest in research
- Lack of confidence in reading and understanding the research process
- Lack of training in research issues and consequently lack of skills required for critical analysis, particularly when there is a plethora of evidence, some of which may be conflicting
- Anticipated outcomes of using research.

Organisational factors

- Cost pressures at work resulting in lack of, or limited, funding for research courses
- Insufficient time within work commitments
- Lack of patient compliance
- Inadequate library and computer facilities
- Inaccessibility of research findings
- Lack of support from peers, managers and other health-care professionals.

McKenna et al (2004) note that identifying barriers to implementing evidence-based practice is only one step to changing practice. Ways that could help in promoting the uptake of research findings are outlined below.

Ways of promoting the uptake of research findings

- Determine that there is an appreciable gap between research findings and practice
- Define the appropriate message (e.g. the information to be used)
- Identify champions to promote the message of change
- Decide which processes need to be altered
- Involve the key players (e.g. those people who will implement change or who are in a position to influence change, such as managers)

- Identify the barriers to change and decide how to overcome them
- Decide on specific interventions to promote change (e.g. the use of guidelines or educational programmes)
- Identify levers for change, i.e. existing mechanisms that can be used to promote change
- Determine whether practice has changed in the way desired; use a clinical audit to monitor change.

Implementing evidence-based practice has become a priority in the NHS, where health-care professionals are urged to use up-to-date research evidence in order to give patients the best possible care. Winch et al (2002) proffer the view that incorporating evidence-based practice principles into nursing requires more than shifting nurses from an oral to a reading tradition. It requires nurses at all levels to embrace practices and attitudes such as interest, professional pride, positiveness and willingness to undertake change as well as a commitment to life-long learning.

Findings from Melnyk et al's (2004) study support the view that knowledge and beliefs about evidence-based practice are important indicators for change in behaviours. However, it is important for nurses to believe that evidence-based practice will result in better patient outcomes in order for changes in practice to occur. Of equal importance was the presence of a mentor who facilitated use of databases, such as the Cochrane Database of Systematic Reviews. Knowledge of learning and searching databases tends to support the use of evidence-based practice as well as support from experts in the field, research departments, library resources and administrators. Melnyk et al's (2004) study supports the findings of an earlier work by Nagy et al (2001), who identified six factors that represent the conditions nurses view as necessary for the development of evidence-based practice:

1. A supportive organisation
2. Nurses' belief in the value of research-based evidence for improvement in patient care
3. Searching, reading and evaluating research studies
4. Clinically relevant research
5. Knowledge of research language and statistics
6. Protected work time for activities related to evidence-based practice.

The final stage in evidence-based process is evaluation.

Top tips

 Resistance to change can be a problem. Involvement of all stakeholders (colleagues, patients, carers, budget holders) can help to ensure that the change is made and sustained.

The patient outcomes are evaluated through a process of audit and peer assessment, including self-evaluation of the research process

This final stage of evidence-based practice will provide a brief discussion on clinical audit, peer and self-evaluation as a means of evaluating the outcomes resulting from implementation of a change in practice. The research process was discussed earlier. The discussion begins with clinical audit.

Clinical audit

Clinical audit is a clinically led initiative that seeks to improve the quality and outcome of patient care through structured peer review, whereby clinicians examine their practices and results against agreed explicit standards and modify their practice where indicated; arguably this is a form of research (Jolley, 2010). The key feature of clinical audit is that it provides a framework to enable improvements in healthcare delivery to be made to ensure that what should be done is being done. Clinical audit has six stages (Clinical Governance Support Team, 2005):

1. Identify the problem or issue
2. Set criteria and standards
3. Observe practice and collect data
4. Compare performance with criteria and standards
5. Implement change
6. Sustain change.

As with the research process, clinical audit follows a systematic process to identify best practice, which is measured against set criteria. Action is taken to improve care based on the data collected and monitoring procedures are implemented to sustain improvement.

Peer assessment and self-evaluation

Peer assessment and self-evaluation (sometimes referred to as self-assessment) constitute a process in which individual practitioners comment on and judge their colleagues' or their own work. It can be used in both formative and summative assessments. It provides the opportunity for the individual to make independent judgements of their own and/or others' work. Practitioners take responsibility for monitoring and making judgements about how the process of implementation has been undertaken, thereby determining their level of knowledge and skills.

The processes of peer assessment and self-evaluation require a high degree of professional ethics with less reliance on subjectivity. There are four main advantages of this type of evaluation:

1. Helping the person become more autonomous, responsible and involved in practices around them
2. Encouraging the person to analyse work done by others in a critical way
3. Assisting in clarifying the assessment criteria
4. Providing a wider range of feedback.

The disadvantages are as follows:

- People may lack the ability to evaluate each other.
- People may not take the process seriously, allowing friendships and entertainment value to influence their marking.
- Peer marking may not be liked by some people because of the possibility of being discriminated against, being misunderstood.

The final aspect of the evaluation is the undertaking of the research process – outlined above.

Some criticisms of evidence-based practice

Evidence-based practice has its critics. Freidson (1970) pointed out many years ago that clinical experience derived from personal observation, reflection and judgement is required to translate scientific results into treatment of individual patients. Building on this view, Armstrong (2002) points out that evidence-based practice reduces professional autonomy by encouraging rigid and prescriptive practices that fail to take into account the complexities of clinical situations. Armstrong (2002) argues that evidence-based practice is in opposition to a patient-centred model of care. Applied programmes in public health are too complex and context driven to be adequately described by evidence-based practice strategies.

Arising from these views is the issue of whether randomised controlled trials (RCTs) should be considered the gold standard for evidence-based practice and the appropriateness of hierarchies that promote meta-analyses as the best available evidence (Petticrew and Roberts, 2003). RCTs inform about which treatment is better, but not for whom it is better; they give an oversimplified and artificial environment that might bear little resemblance to day-to-day reality (Petticrew and Roberts, 2003). The ideal of integrating individual clinical experience with the best external evidence might be realised only by health professionals with a wealth of clinical experience and research knowledge. It should also be taken into account that, when patients are given an active role in their treatment decisions, it may result in a less successful outcome regarding uptake of optimal treatment; particular skills are required of the clinician to maintain a balanced view to convey to the patient why a particular course of action is recommended.

Conclusion

The discussion presented in this chapter offers guidance to help the reader to apply knowledge and skills in obtaining and using the literature to underpin practice. Central to evidence-based practice are the patient, the environment and individuals within that arena in which change is to occur. Evidence is not a static concept; practitioners must make every effort to keep abreast of the latest research data pertaining to their area, bearing in mind that they are accountable for their practice. From the point of view of the organisation, protected time must be set aside for nurses to engage in evidence-based nursing activities. Well-resourced facilities and effective managerial support for evidence-based practice will be seen as a positive step for other members of the health-care professions to regard evidence-based practice as a way of thinking and practising.

Activity

Attempt the following 'fill in the blanks' activity related to the evidence based practice to test your knowledge. Choose from the list of words below. The answers can be found at the back of this book, in the chapter called 'Activity Answers'.

Evidence based practice is a _____ of practitioner _____ and _____ of the best available _____. It involves a careful, clear and thoughtful use of _____ evidence when making _____ about how to _____ and _____ for people. Evidence based practice is a _____ process. The first step in evidence based practice is _____ that there is a need for new _____. This information need has to be _____ into an _____ question. A _____ answer can only be provided in _____ to a precise _____. Carefully _____ the question can also help determine what _____ of _____ is needed. Good clinical questions can be divided into _____ and _____ questions. _____ questions ask for _____ about a disorder. Foreground questions ask for _____ knowledge about a disorder. The foreground question is often referred to as the _____ question structure – _____, _____, _____.

Choose from the following words:

COMBINATION	INFORMATION	FOREGROUND
EXPERTISE	CONVERTED	BACKGROUND
KNOWLEDGE	ANSWERABLE	GENERAL KNOWLEDGE
EVIDENCE	PRECISE	SPECIFIC
UP-TO-DATE	RESPONSE	PICO
DECISIONS	QUESTION	PATIENT/PROBLEM
WORK	FRAMING	INTERVENTION
CARE	TYPE	COMPARISON OUTCOME
CONTINUOUS	EVIDENCE	
RECOGNISING	BACKGROUND	

References

Armstrong D (2002) Clinical autonomy, individual and collective: The problem of changing doctors behaviour. *Social Science of Medicine* **55**: 1771.

Burns N, Grove SK (2011) *Understanding Nursing Research*, 4th edn. Philadelphia, PA: Elsevier.

Canadian Task Force on the Periodic Health Examination (1979) The periodic health examination. *Canadian Medical Association Journal* **121**: 1193–1254.

Clinical Governance Support Team (2005) *A Practical Handbook for Clinical Audit*. London: Clinical Governance Support Team.

Cochrane AL (1979) *A Critical Review, with Particular Reference to the Medical Profession. Medicines for the Year 2000*. London: Office of Health Economics.

Collins (1986) *Collins Paperback English Dictionary*. London: Collins.

Freidson E (1970) *Profession of Medicine: A study of the sociology of applied knowledge*. New York: Dodd, Mead.

Gray DE (2009) *Doing Research in the Real World*, 2nd edn. London: Sage.

Higgs J, Fish D, Rothwell R (2008) Knowledge generation and clinical reasoning in practice. In: Higgs J, Jones MA, Loftus S, Christensen N (eds), *Clinical Reasoning in the Health Professions*, 3rd edn. Oxford: Butterworth Heinemann, pp 163–179.

Hurley WL, Denegar CR, Hertel J (2011) *Research Methods. A framework for evidence-based clinical practice*. Philadelphia, PA: Lippincott.

Jennings B, Loan L (2001) Misconceptions among nurses about evidence-based practice. *Journal of Nursing Scholarship* **33**: 121–127.

Jesson JK, Matheson L, Lacey FM (2011) *Doing Your Literature Review. Traditional and systematic techniques*. London: Sage.

Jolley J (2010) *Introducing Research and Evidence-based Practice for Nurses*. Harlow: Pearson.

Kajermo KN, Nordstrom G, Krusebrant A, Bjorvell H (1998) Barriers to and facilitators of research utilisation as perceived by a group of registered nurses in Sweden. *Journal of Advanced Nursing* **27**: 798–807.

Larrabee JH (2010) *Nurse to Nurse. Evidence based practice*. New York: McGraw Hill.

McKenna H, Ashton S, Keeney S (2004) Barriers to evidence-based practice in primary care. *Journal of Advanced Nursing* **45**: 178–189.

McKibbon KA, Marks S (2001) Posing clinical questions: Framing the question for scientific enquiry. *AACN Clinical Issues: Advanced Practice in Acute and Critical Care* **12**: 477–481.

Mantzoukas S (2007) A review of evidence-based practice, nursing research and reflection: leveling the hierarchy. *Journal of Clinical Nursing* **17**: 214–223.

Melnyk BM, Fineout-Overholt E, Feinstein NF, et al (2004) Nurses' perceived knowledge, beliefs, skills, and needs regarding evidence-based practice: Implications for accelerating the paradigm shift. *World Views on Evidence-Based Nursing* **1**: 185–193.

Nagy S, Lumby J, McKinley S, MacFarlane C (2001) Nurses' beliefs about the conditions that hinder or support evidence-based practice. *International Journal of Nursing Practice* **7**: 314–321.

Nursing and Midwifery Council (2008) *The Code: Standards of conduct, performance and ethics for nurses and midwives*. London: NMC.

Nursing and Midwifery Council (2010) *Standards for Pre registration Nursing Education*. London: NMC. Available at: http://standards.nmc-uk.org/PublishedDocuments/Standards%20for%20pre-registration%20nursing%20education%2016082010.pdf (accessed May 2011).

Petticrew M, Roberts H (2003) Evidence, hierarchies and typologies: Horses for courses. *Journal of Epidemiology and Community Health* **57**: 527–529. Available at: http:///jech.bmjjournals.com/cgi/content/ful/57/7/527.

Polit DF, Beck CT (2011) *Nursing Research: Generating and accessing evidence for nursing practice*, 9th edn. Philadelphia, PA: Lippincott.

Retsas A (2000). Barriers to using research evidence in nursing practice. *Journal of Advanced Nursing* **31**: 599–606.

Rycroft-Malone J, Seers K, Titchen A, Harvey G, Kitson A, McCormack B (2004) What counts as evidence in evidence-based practice? *Journal of Advanced Nursing* **47**: 81–90.

Straus SE, Glasziou P, Richardson WS, Haynes RB (2005) *Evidence-based Medicine: How to practise and teach EBM*, 3rd edn. Edinburgh: Churchill Livingstone.

Straus S, Tetroe, J, Graham ID (2009) *Knowledge Translation in Health Care: Moving from evidence to practice*. Oxford: Wiley.

Winch S, Creedy D, Chaboyer W (2002) Governing nursing conduct: The rise of evidence-based practice. *Nursing Inquiry* **9**: 156–161.

Wulff HR, Gøtzsche PC (2000) *Rational Diagnosis and Treatment. Evidence-based clinical decision making*, 3rd edn. Oxford: Blackwell Science.

9

Assessing, Planning, Implementing and Evaluating Care Needs

Aims and objectives

The aim of this chapter is to describe the nursing process.
  At the end of the chapter you will be able to:

1. Understand the value of applying a systemic approach to care
2. Consider the five stages of the nursing process
3. Describe how to obtain a nursing history
4. Discuss nursing models
5. Begin to apply the concepts discussed to the practice setting
6. Appreciate the Nursing and Midwifery Council's requirements of student nurses

The effective assessment of needs is paramount if the subsequent planning, implementation and evaluatory processes are to be successful. The Nursing and Midwifery Council (NMC, 2010) make clear in the *Standards for Pre-registration Nursing Education* that for entry to the professional register all registrants must be able to demonstrate competency in undertaking a full holistic assessment of needs.

This chapter describes in detail how to undertake and document a comprehensive, systematic and accurate nursing assessment. The patient's physical, psychological, social and spiritual needs are considered. Models of nursing are briefly discussed in order to explain that undertaking an assessment of needs in isolation (the gathering of data) will limit care interventions. A guide or framework (a model of care) will help to enhance the patient's experience, and promote holistic nursing care.

Various assessment strategies are described and a range of assessment tools that are used to guide the collection of data for assessing the needs of the patient is also outlined.

The nursing process

The nursing process is a systematic, patient-centred, goal-oriented approach to caring that provides a framework for nursing practice; it allows the nurse and the patient to work together (Taylor et al, 2011).

The Student's Guide to Becoming a Nurse, Second Edition. Ian Peate.
© 2012 John Wiley & Sons, Ltd. Published 2012 by John Wiley & Sons, Ltd.

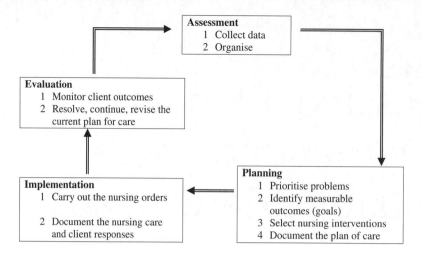

Assessment
1 Collect data
2 Organise

Evaluation
1 Monitor client outcomes
2 Resolve, continue, revise the current plan for care

Implementation
1 Carry out the nursing orders

2 Document the nursing care and client responses

Planning
1 Prioritise problems
2 Identify measurable outcomes (goals)
3 Select nursing interventions
4 Document the plan of care

Figure 9.1   The four-stage nursing process.

The nursing process can be seen as a problem-solving approach to the implementation of nursing, and nursing intervention takes place within the context of the nursing process; it as a systematic inquiry into how the needs of people are assessed, planned, implemented and evaluated.

The nursing process is nursing practice in action. It is a step-by-step approach to the provision of nursing care to patients. The nurse uses various skills to progress through the process in an orderly, systematic manner, with planned actions that are directed or aimed at achieving a particular goal or aim. The aim of the nursing process is to encourage the nurse together with the patient to make decisions and to solve problems in a more holistic manner, as opposed to a task-oriented approach to the delivery of nursing care.

In the UK it is common for theorists and practitioners to describe the nursing process as having four phases or components (Figure 9.1):

1. Assessment
2. Planning
3. Implementation
4. Evaluation.

A five-stage nursing process is now used more widely in the UK. Previously the five-stage or five-component nursing process was used predominantly in the USA (Figure 9.2):

1. Assessment
2. Nursing diagnosis
3. Planning
4. Implementation
5. Evaluation.

The steps of the nursing process are not discrete entities; they are parts of a whole and are interrelated. This chapter discusses the five stages. Table 9.1 provides a summary of the five phases/stages of the nursing process.

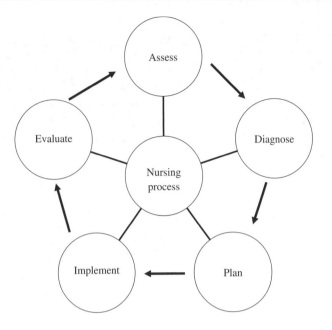

Figure 9.2   The five-stage nursing process.

What is assessment?

Assessment is the first stage or step in the nursing process and is the systematic and continuous collection of facts or data. There are three key features associated with the assessment phase:

- *Communication* – obtaining a health history.
- *Measurement* – physiological measurements, the use of risk-assessment tools (Bird, 2005).
- *Observation* – observing the patient's non-verbal signs of pain; observing the patient in his or her total environment, especially when in his or her own home (Rayman, 2009). Observation of the patient takes place each time the nurse and patient have any contact. The nurse observes many things such as the patient's mood, interactions with others, emotional responses and detecting early signs of health deterioration, e.g. pallor, sweating and cyanosis.

Assessment is crucial to the whole nursing process. When the data have been collected and analysed this will allow the nurse with the patient (if appropriate) to identify the patient's problems and strengths. Assessment can take place anywhere, e.g. in the hospital, the patient's home or the workplace.

Assessment is regarded as the data-collection phase allowing the nurse to make judgements about the patient's health, situation, needs and wishes. Assessment also helps to establish priorities and allows the planning of care. Assessment does not focus solely on the physical aspects of care; it also takes into account the patient's complete social and mental wellbeing.

The purpose of assessment, according to Rayman (2009), is to establish a database about the following:

- Physical wellbeing
- Emotional wellbeing
- Intellectual functioning
- Social relationships
- Spiritual condition.

Table 9.1 An overview of the five stages of the nursing process

Stage/step of the nursing process	Description	Reason	Actions
Assessing	Collection, validation and communication of patient data	Make judgements about the patient's health status, the ability of the patient to manage his or her own health care and determine the need for nursing	Establish a database by: • Obtaining a nursing history • Conducting a physical and if needed psychological assessment • Review of the patient's nursing and medical notes • Seek secondary data from other health-care professionals, the patient's carer(s) Continually update the database Validate the data Communicate data/findings (document findings)
Diagnosing	Analysis of patient data to determine patient's strengths and health problems that nursing interventions can prevent or resolve	Develop and prioritise a list of nursing diagnoses	Interpret and analyse patient data Ascertain patient strengths and health problems Devise and validate nursing diagnoses Develop and document a list of nursing diagnoses that have been prioritised
Planning	Identify measurable outcomes and set goals that can prevent, relieve or resolve the problems identified. Select and describe appropriate nursing interventions. Document the plan of proposed care	To develop an individualised care plan that can be evaluated. To produce evidence that demonstrates an individual assessment of needs has taken place	Determine priorities Document proposed outcomes and put into place an evaluatory strategy Decide on appropriate nursing interventions Communicate proposed plan of care

Table 9.1 *Continued*

Stage/step of the nursing process	Description	Reason	Actions
Implementation	The 'doing' stage. The plan of care is implemented at this stage	Assist and support the patient to achieve the stated goals, to enhance health, prevent disease, illness and deterioration in condition, provide comfort and maintain dignity	Carry out/implement the planned care Continue to gather data and modify the plan of care in response to the patient's condition Document actions and omissions
Evaluation	Monitoring and measuring of patient outcomes and effects of nursing interventions, with reference to interventions that may have helped or exacerbated the patient's condition Consider revision of the plan of care if needed	To continue with plan of care, modify nursing activities or terminate interventions	Refer to original database to determine if there has been a change in the patient's condition as a result of the planned and implemented nursing interventions Measure how well the plan of care has benefited the patient's condition Determine if there are certain interventions that have adversely affected the patient's condition Modify care plan if appropriate Document findings

Source: adapted from Beretta (2008); Kozier et al (2008); Timby (2009); Taylor et al (2011).

It is important to note that data is not collected as a one-off activity. Data collection occurs continuously – it is a continuous process. Ongoing assessment will alert the nurse to any changes in the patient's health as well as any changes in response to nursing intervention; a patient's condition can change quickly.

Kozier et al (2008) note that the activities associated with the assessment phase of the nursing process will include:

- Making a reliable observation
- Being able to distinguish relevant from irrelevant data
- Being able to distinguish important data from unimportant data

- Validating, organising and categorising the data according to a framework
- Making judgements.

Establishing a database means that the nurse has to gather information and this is usually done by interviewing the patient (or his or her carer, family or significant other). This allows the nurse to obtain a nursing history. It is the history that guides the nurse though a series of questions designed to build a profile of the patient and his or her problems. The history-taking event ends with the nurse having a deeper understanding of the patient and the ability to go on and make a diagnosis.

The way in which the nurse can go about obtaining a patient history is described below. More data can be collected by examining the patient if needed. Further information can be gleaned from the patient's nursing/medical notes and other health-care professionals, e.g. a physiotherapist or occupational therapist. A database may contain the information detailed in Table 9.2.

Obtaining a patient history

Chapter 5 outlined the skills that the nurse needs to have to communicate effectively with the patient. This section of this chapter builds on those nursing skills and provides insight into how best to obtain a patient history.

The accuracy of the information that the nurse collects or gathers from a patient during a consultation (clinical interview) has the potential to influence the diagnosis and subsequent treatment of the patient. Obtaining a patient history in a competent manner is crucial to the patient encounter and patient outcome.

The patient and the nurse are partners in care. The clinical interview is at the heart of the nurse–patient relationship and this confirms the bond between the two parties, in order to start to provide care for the patient. The patient needs the help of the nurse, who in turn needs information from the patient to offer that help. A professional relationship needs to be developed and maintained between the patient and the nurse to provide the most effective care.

It is important for the patient to know from the outset how the data will be managed, what the nurse intends to do with the information gathered, what will be written, where this will be stored and who will be able to access it. Being open about the management of the information that the patient wishes to give to the nurse may put the patient's mind at rest that the information collected will be treated confidentially and with respect, kept safe and, when disclosure is to be made to a third party, this will be done with the patient's consent and in his or her best interests.

The clinical interview can be looked at as having three parts:

1. Beginning the interview and introductions
2. Obtaining the history
3. Terminating the interview.

Obtaining a health history from a patient demands a skilled, confident and competent nurse. The more often you undertake a nursing assessment and the gathering of information through the clinical interview, the more proficient you will become (Nusbaum and Hamilton, 2002).

There are no hard-and-fast rules for obtaining a health history; each nurse will have his or her own approach. The nurse should aim to create a comfortable atmosphere with a relaxed, but professional and friendly approach. The way in which the interview is carried out will determine the amount of information that the patient may be prepared to reveal and some patients may have to reveal some very intimate and personal issues. If the patient is to reveal intimate, personal and potentially embarrassing

Table 9.2   Some components of a patient history database

Demographic data
- The patient's name (include here the name he or she wishes to be known by)
- Address
- Age
- Sex
- Marital status
- Occupation
- Religious preferences (if any)

Reason for admission/chief complaint
The reason the patient (or his or her guardian) gives for admission should be documented. The response the patient gives to your question should be documented – verbatim and in inverted commas '. . .' so that the patient's understanding of his or her condition/complaint can be noted in his or her own words.

251

History of present illness
Ask the patient:

- When did the symptoms start?
- Was the onset of the symptoms sudden or gradual?
- How often does the problem occur?
- Where is the exact location of the distress/problem?
- Describe the character of the complaint, e.g. the intensity of pain, the nature of the sputum – colour and consistency, give details about any vomit (colour, quantity) or any discharge (colour, quantity and from where)
- Any activity the patient was performing when the problem arose
- Do any activities aggravate or alleviate the condition, e.g. coughing or passing urine, lying down?

Past history
Ascertain any relevant past history. Ask the patient about:

- Any childhood illness (current or in the past)
- Any immunisations (as a child or/and an adult) and when they were given
- Any known allergies, e.g. allergies to medicines, foods, other agents such as plasters, and the type of reaction that occurs when exposed to the allergen
- Any accidents or illnesses (how, when, where)
- Any hospitalisation or time spent in hospital – reasons, any surgical interventions, any complications
- Medication they may be taking: include here prescribed medications, medications bought over the counter and use of recreational drugs. Note dose, route and frequency

Family history of illness
Spend time with the patient asking about any family history of illness in order to determine if there are any risk factors for certain diseases (e.g. sickle cell anaemia). Ask about the current health of siblings, parents, grandparents, their ages if still alive and, if deceased, the cause of death.

Continued

Table 9.2 *Continued*

Lifestyle

The nurse can use a model of care to help guide this aspect of the assessment process (models of care are discussed later in this chapter). The issues below can help guide the discussion.
   Ask about personal habits such as the frequency and amount of:

- Tobacco use (type)
- Alcohol consumption (type)

Ask the patient to describe their typical diet:

- Any special dietary needs
- Number of meals consumed in a day

Consider asking about leisure activities:

- How much exercise is taken and what type?
- Hobbies or interests

Social history

Social data will help to complete the picture of the patient and will provide information based on the following:

- Family relationships
- Any particular ethnic/cultural beliefs
- Occupational history (current and past occupations)
- Economic status (is the patient self-employed, for example)
- Whether the patient is receiving any social services to help him or her cope at home, e.g. home help or district nursing services

Psychological data
- Is the patient aware of any stressors that impact negatively on his or her health? What is his or her perception of them?

Communication data

Determine how the patient communicates:

- Can the patient verbally respond (e.g. is he or she conscious)?
- What language does the patient prefer to communicate in (is English the patient's first language)?
- Does the patient use eye movements, gestures, touch, posture to interact with others?

Source: adapted from Kozier et al (2008).

information, he or she may find this difficult and hence the nurse must provide a safe environment in which to do this.

Each aspect of the clinical interview is addressed briefly in the following section.

Meeting, greeting and seating

The approach taken will depend on where the interview is taking place, e.g. if it is in the patient's own home then the nurse will need to wait to be invited in and take his or her cues from the patient or family.

If, however, the information-gathering event takes place in a clinical setting such as a hospital ward, a clinic or a GP surgery, the nurse must stand up as the patient enters the room, greet him or her, face the patient and look at him or her directly – smile. Greet the patient verbally (being aware of the non-verbal greeting that you are simultaneously making). Explain to the patient who you are (even though you will have some form of name badge or identity on you) and the reason for the consultation, e.g. 'to obtain a clear picture of the problem/issue'. Ascertain at this stage how the patient would like you to refer to him or her. Using terms that make assumptions about the patient should be avoided, e.g. when enquiring about a patient's sexual orientation it is advised that the nurse use the term 'partner' as opposed to 'boyfriend' or 'girlfriend', 'husband' or 'wife'. Ask about the patient's partner instead of asking if he or she is married. The response that the patient gives may confirm or refute if he or she is married.

Deciding to conduct the interview with the patient alone or with his or her partner present needs much thought. It could be that the patient may not be as open or forthcoming with information if the partner is present; however, joint consultations can provide much important detail. The nurse will need to exercise his or her professional judgement in coming to a decision about this issue.

It may be appropriate to shake the patient's hand, but be aware of cultural values: some cultures may not accept a female touching a male and vice versa. Invite the patient to sit: indicate where clearly by gesture and verbally. The nurse should then sit down in a non-threatening manner. Explain that you will be taking some notes during the interview, reaffirming that the information given will be treated in confidence.

Noise and interruptions can be disconcerting and cause distraction; if possible a quiet room should be sought in which to conduct the interview. Seating and the way that this has been arranged should be given consideration. If possible, the patient's seat should be placed in such a way as to avoid the use of a desk, which could appear confrontational; arrange the seats so that they are at the side of the desk. Doing this gives the nurse an opportunity to observe the patient's body language – remember, however, that this type of arrangement also allows the patient to observe your body language. The nurse must also consider how he or she is dressed for the interview: a dress code may be apparent in some clinical areas and this will dictate how the nurse should dress. The way in which the health-care professional is dressed can have implications for the relationship.

When the interview takes place (the timing of the interview) needs to be given consideration: try to avoid meal times or rest periods. Sufficient time must be set aside by the nurse, and if possible inform the patient of how much of his or her time you may need to conduct the interview. Depending on the reason for the interview, the time required will vary. Cowan and Bell (2011) suggest that when carrying out a sexual health interview, for example, up to an hour may be needed.

Make the patient feel as comfortable as possible; encourage him or her to feel safe, relaxed and to talk openly. On some occasions the patient may reveal information that the nurse may find shocking; however, it is crucial that a non-judgemental approach be taken. Often nurses make use of several techniques to promote comfort intuitively:

- Greeting the patient
- Seating arrangements
- Ensuring privacy (a 'do not disturb' sign, telephones diverted and mobile telephones switched off).

Top tips

Never make assumptions about a patient. Always ensure that you suspend judgement until you have the facts in front of you.

Obtaining the history

When introductions have been performed and the patient feels comfortable, the nurse needs to ask questions to generate more insight into the patient's needs. It may help the patient if the nurse reiterates and explains the reasons why questions are being asked, e.g.: 'I am asking these questions so that I can assess your needs fully and work out the right care for you, so I need to know a bit more detail about your health.'

If the nurse undertakes the history-taking exercise as if he or she is asking questions from a questionnaire or a list that is to be run through with the patient, this approach is in danger of losing all its potential worth. Asking a lot of questions will result in the patient providing a lot of answers. There is a danger that the problem with which the patient presented may not have been identified because the nurse did not hear, because he or she has not allowed the patient to give details. The nurse must listen to the patient and if needed allow or give the patient permission to tell his or her story.

Questioning approaches have been briefly discussed in Chapter 5. However, to reiterate:

- Use appropriate opening questions, e.g.: 'Could you tell me what it was that led to you come here today for help?'
- Use verbal facilitation to encourage his or her patient to tell his or her story in his or her own words, e.g. encourage the patient to continue talking by saying: 'Please go on and tell me some more about it', 'What happened next?', 'You said just then that you felt a pain.'
- Non-verbal facilitation should also be used, e.g. head nodding, looking, attentive posture.
- Listen, allow the patient sufficient time to talk and avoid interrupting too quickly with questions or reassurance.
- Encourage the patient to focus by bringing the patient back to the point if he or she talks about unrelated areas.
- Seek clarification of any issues about which you are unsure and encourage the patient to do the same.
- Avoid the use of jargon, both the jargon that the patient may be using or any that you may be using – seek clarification.
- Avoid bias by the use of leading questions, e.g.: 'Are you depressed?', 'You couldn't breathe very well?' Try instead to use open-ended questions, such as: 'How was your mood at that time?', 'How was your breathing?'
- Take care to avoid using multiple questions, such as: 'How are you and how has your weight been?'
- Encourage the patient to be precise about the issues, such as dates of onset of key symptoms, problems or events, nature of previous treatments. Cross-check key points, e.g.: 'Could I just clarify this. . .?'

- During the physical examination, use all the above communication skills appropriately, being particularly attentive to the patient's responses to your palpation and percussion. Consider incorporating your auditory, tactile and olfactory senses.
- Above all, respect the patient.

Case study 9.1

Shayla is a 5-year-old girl who is admitted to the children's ward at 23:30; she was given a nebuliser in the accident and emergency department to help relieve her asthma. Shayla has experienced asthma before and is being seen by the paediatricians at the same hospital; this is her third admission for stabilisation of her asthma. On arrival at the ward Shayla is accompanied by her non-English-speaking grandmother. Although Shayla's condition is stable, she is still short of breath, wheezing and appears very anxious.

255

How would you begin to assess the needs of Shayla?

What skills are required to ensure that you assess her in a holistic manner and that you are not exacerbating her condition any further?

How would you notice deterioration in her condition? How would you offer support to Shayla's grandmother?

Terminating the interview

The ending of the relationship is just as important as the formulation. At the end of the interview ensure that there is time to summarise what the patient has told you. Make it clear to the patient that you would like to sum up the history with him or her to verify the accuracy of your account of his or her problems/issues, and to determine if anything important has been missed out. Ask if there is anything that he or she would like to add before the interview is concluded. Thank the patient for his or her time.

When a health history is required from children, young people and people with learning disabilities, this may present challenges, because the carer or parents may have accompanied the patient and tend to answer for him or her. Furthermore, the patient may be unwilling to divulge information with a third party present. The use of dolls, puppets and images to demonstrate what is being discussed can help. Wakley et al (2003) suggest breaking each period of communication/interaction into shorter parts, checking after each section that all parties have understood what is being said. The nurse needs to be aware of his or her limitations and be prepared to refer the patient to a more appropriate health-care professional if he or she is feeling out of his or her depth.

Think

Take some time to think about the last time you visited your doctor or a nurse practitioner and reflect on the following:

- How where you greeted?
- Did you feel involved in the process?
- Did you make as much contribution to the consultation as you might have wanted to?
- Do you think any assumptions were made about you?
- How did you feel you were treated overall from the moment you walked into the doctor's surgery/department until you left?

Measurements/risk-assessment tools

The second important feature of the assessment phase is the ability to carry out measurements, e.g. physiological measurements, or risk assessments using recognised risk-assessment tools such as pain assessment or tools associated with the prevention of pressure ulcers.

The skin and the risk of pressure ulcers

The largest and heaviest organ in the body is the skin; this is the primary defence against pathogenic invasion (Doughty, 2010). The skin is a sensory organ and has several physiological functions.

A pressure ulcer or pressure sore can be defined as an area of skin and tissue loss that has been caused by long-standing or extreme soft-tissue pressure. Pressure ulcers often develop because of external pressure that causes an occlusion of blood vessels and endothelial damage to both the arterioles and the microcirculation.

External pressure is a primary causative factor associated with the onset of pressure ulcers, and because of this it follows that some bones that are close to the skin, e.g. shoulders, hips, heels and sacrum, are possible sites for ulcer formation. The pressure sent from the surface of the skin to the bones results in compression of the underlying tissue.

When conducting a holistic assessment of the patient, the nurse must take into account certain intrinsic risk factors that may result in the development of a pressure ulcer, e.g.:

* Reduced mobility or immobility
* Sensory impairment
* Acute illness
* Level of consciousness
* Extremes of age
* Vascular disease
* Severe chronic or terminal illness
* Previous history of pressure-sore damage
* Malnutrition and dehydration.

Extrinsic factors also exist that may cause or predispose a patient to tissue damage, and where possible these should be removed or diminished to prevent injury, e.g.:

* Pressure
* Shearing
* Friction.

If the nurse is to prevent or minimise the effects of pressure ulcers, one important aspect of nursing practice will be to identify those patients who may be at risk of developing them and the nurse does this by conducting an in-depth, holistic assessment of the patient. A pressure ulcer (sore) risk calculator is needed to provide an objective assessment of risk. Risk-assessment tools should, however (e.g. the Waterlow scale – Waterlow, 1985), be used only as an aide mémoire and can never replace clinical judgement. Figure 9.3 describes the Waterlow scale.

There are many risk-assessment tools available to help the nurse make objective (as opposed to subjective) judgements, and each clinical area will choose the tool that best suits the patient's needs. The timing of the assessment of risk should be based on each individual patient, but should be within 6 hours

Build/weight for height	Visual skin type	Continence	Mobility	Sex Age	Appetite
Average **0** Above average **2** Below average **3**	Healthy **0** Tissue paper **1** Dry **1** Oedematous **1** Clammy **1** Discolour **2** Broken/spot **3**	Complete **0** Occasionally incontinent **1** Catheter/incontinent of faeces **2** Doubly incontinent **3**	Fully mobile **0** Restricted/difficult **1** Restless/fidgety **2** Apathetic **3** Inert/traction **4**	Male **1** Female **2** 14–49 **1** 50–64 **2** 65–75 **3** 75–80 **4** 81+ **5**	Average **0** Poor **1** Anorectic **2**
Special risk factors: (1) Poor nutrition e.g. terminal cachexia **8** (2) Sensory depravation e.g. diabetes, paraplegia, CVA **5** (3) High dose antiinflammatory or steroid use **3** (4) Smoking 10+ per day **1** (5) Orthopaedic surgery/fracture below waist **3**			**Assessment value:** At risk = **10** High risk = **15** Very high risk = **20**		
Directions for use: 1 Assess the patient, circling the number in each category in which the patient fits. 2 Add up all the numbers, including 'special risk factors'. 3 If the total places the patient within the 'at risk', 'high risk' areas, turn the card over and read the suggested preventative aids listed on the back. 4 Record the circled numbers in the patient's documentation, giving the total and the date. 5 Assess each patient as per protocol.					

257

Figure 9.3 The Waterlow scale. Source: Waterlow (1985).

of the start of admission and assessment must be ongoing. The importance of ongoing assessment has already been discussed. The NMC (2009) state that all aspects of care must be documented; this is also true of the outcome of assessment and reassessment of a patient who may be at risk of developing pressure ulcers.

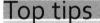

Top tips

Turning a patient who is bed bound is the most important thing you can do to prevent pressure ulcers from occurring. Frequent turning alternates areas of pressure on bony areas, such as the lower back, hips, elbows, and heels.

Think

Can you list and describe any other types of risk-assessment tool you may have seen in use?

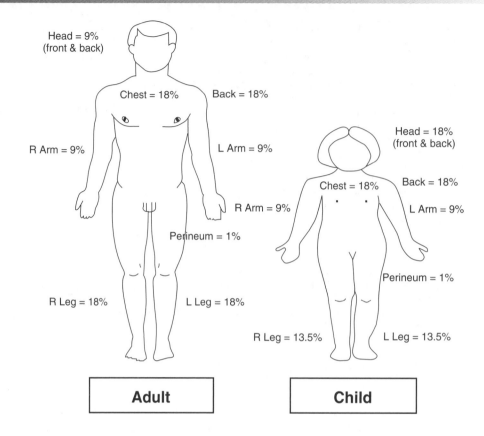

Figure 9.4   The rule of nines assessment tools for both an adult and a child.

The following are tools that are often used in clinical settings:

- The Glasgow Coma Scale (GCS: this tool measures levels of consciousness)
- Pain-assessment scales (there are many of these tools in use and there are specific ones related to specific patient groups, e.g. children)
- The rule of nines, which helps the nurse to assess the extent of a burn (Figure 9.4)
- The Lund and Browder chart (Lund and Browder, 1944) is used predominantly in assessing the extent of a burn in a baby but can be used in children and adults.

Top tips

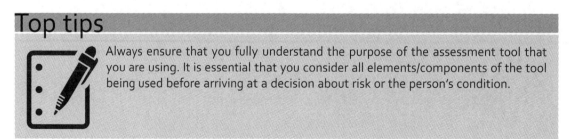

Always ensure that you fully understand the purpose of the assessment tool that you are using. It is essential that you consider all elements/components of the tool being used before arriving at a decision about risk or the person's condition.

Making a nursing diagnosis

Step 2 of the nursing process requires the nurse to make a nursing diagnosis. Having gathered the information, performed a risk assessment and undertaken a physical examination, the nurse then identifies the health-related problem. Analysis of the data gathered is now needed to determine if the findings are normal or abnormal (Timby, 2009). The nurse must now consider carefully the data that have been collected and he or she begins to interpret, analyse and use for diagnosis (Taylor et al, 2011).

The diagnosis can be cited as 'actual' or 'potential', e.g. the patient may have been assessed by the nurse and as a result of his or her condition there may be problems associated with sleep which can be actual or potential. A list will have been formulated by the nurse and statements compiled that reflect the problems identified (Kozier et al, 2008).

Alfaro-LeFevre (2010) states that the diagnosis stage of the nursing process is a pivotal point in the process, because the accuracy and relevancy of the whole nursing care plan will depend on the nurse's ability to be able to identify both the problems and their cause. The creation of a care plan that proactively promotes health and prevents problems before they start will depend on the nurse's ability to recognise risks.

259

Planning

The nurse works with the patient and family (if appropriate) in order to establish priorities, identify the expected patient outcomes, choose interventions to help alleviate or prevent problems, and communicate the plan of care – the planning stage. The identification of measurable goals or outcomes is given much thought at this stage. Once the plan of care is decided on and documented, the nurse, together with the patient and family, must ensure that the goals stated are revised as and when appropriate. The nurse should ask the question: 'How can the patient's needs be met?'

Sibson (2010) suggests that consideration must be given to what nursing care will be undertaken to prevent or manage problems, including:

- Preventing identified problems from becoming actual problems
- Solving actual problems
- Alleviating those problems that cannot be solved and assisting the individual to cope positively with these problems
- Preventing recurrence of a treated problem
- Helping a person to be as pain free and comfortable as possible when death is inevitable.

Some problems with which patients present will require immediate attention and they are given highest priority, e.g. a patient who is liable to self-harm will require help and nursing interventions that will prevent harm. It is imperative that the nurse determines which problems require the most immediate attention.

There are many ways to determine priorities and one way is to use (as a guide) Maslow's (1954) hierarchy of needs. This model is not the only model and different areas of care may employ different methods to establish priorities. Table 9.3 considers this hierarchy.

The plan of care that will be formulated once the goals have been set can be seen as a prescription for care. The goal statements and the interventions required to meet the patient's needs must be documented. The components of a measurable goal should comprise the following, using the mnemonic STAMP:

Table 9.3   An adaptation of Maslow's hierarchy of needs

Self-actualisation
Realising full potential, 'becoming everything one is capable of becoming'

Cognitive needs
Knowledge and understanding, curiosity, exploration, needs for meaning and predictability

Esteem needs
The esteem and respect of others and self-esteem and self-respect. A sense of competence. A sense of worth

Love and belongingness
Receiving and giving love, affection, trust and acceptance. Affiliating, being part of a group (family, friends, work). Relationships with others

Safety needs
Protection from potentially dangerous objects or situations, e.g. the elements, physical illness. The threat is both physical and psychological (e.g. 'fear of the unknown'). Importance of routine and familiarity. Protection from danger or threat

Physiological needs
Food, drink, oxygen, temperature regulation, elimination, rest, activity, sex. These are the basic requirements

Source: adapted from Maslow (1954).

- Specific – the goal must be specific with details, avoid being vague
- Time element – time limits should be applied. The time limits will depend on the goal set, e.g. whether it is a long-term goal or a short-term goal. The target date or time for achievement should be specified when possible
- Achievable – and the goal must be realistic for the patient and the situation in which he or she finds him- or herself
- Measurable – the proposed intervention should be measurable
- Patient centred – 'The patient will. . . . '.

The following is an example of a goal statement that contains all of the components stated above. It is a goal statement for a patient who has asthma:

> *Mrs Jones will be able to perform, using a peak flow meter, a peak flow rate of 400 mL 20 minutes after having had a prescribed bronchodilator nebuliser.*

This goal is specific (S); it is also precise and detailed, and allows Mrs Jones and all who care for her to understand what this goal is trying to achieve in relation to her prescribed medication (the nebuliser). There is a clear time (T) element attached to the goal statement – 20 minutes after the nebuliser has been given. It is achievable (A) and realistic and Mrs Jones should be able to perform a peak flow of 400 mL as the nurse has assessed her condition. It is measurable (M) and the measure is the 400 mL after 20 minutes which she is expected to be able to produce after receiving the drug (a bronchodilator has been given). The goal is patient (P) centred; it is for Mrs Jones because it has been stated that she is the person for whom the goal has been devised.

Producing measurable outcomes can be difficult. The following are some verbs that can help you write measurable outcomes:

- Identify
- Define
- Explain
- Apply
- Demonstrate
- Select.

The following are verbs that are to be avoided when composing measurable outcomes because they are too general and difficult to measure (Taylor et al, 2011). Compare them with the observable and measurable verbs in the list above:

- Know
- Understand
- Become aware
- Learn.

It takes time to write competent goal statements. You must remember that practice makes perfect. Using the STAMP mnemonic may help you to take into account all the important components.

Think

In the following goal statement, can you determine the STAMP components for this patient?

By the end of the week (02/02/12) Mrs Mehta will be able to walk the length of the ward with the aid of one other person twice daily.

'By the end of the week' gives (T), 'Mrs Mehta' gives (P), and (A) and (M) are contained in the goal of walking the ward with another person's help twice daily. You will have to decide if it is specific. A good test for this is: if you had to nurse Mrs Mehta, would you be able to determine the aim of the goal statement?

How might the following statement be rewritten in order for it to become specific and clear?

Encourage fluids.

This statement is not specific; it is ambiguous and in danger of being interpreted differently by different people, and as a result the care provided may be inconsistent and inadequate. You might have considered adding the patient's name and being more specific about the type of fluid, how often the patient is to have the fluid and when. A revised statement might look like this:

Provide Lily with 100 mL of oral fluid of her choice every hour while she is awake.

According to Gega (2009), the language used when writing a problem statement should be:

- user friendly
- non-judgemental
- personalised.

Gega (2009) also provides some helpful points to test if the language used conforms with the above criteria. The nurse can ask him- or herself the following:

- Would this make sense to my patient?
- If this were me, would I mind someone else saying this about me?
- Would I be happy for my patient to read this?
- Does this describe my patient's personal experiences of the problem?

262

Case study 9.2

Peter is a 65-year-old who has been an informal patient on a ward for the last 2 weeks with a diagnosis of dementia. His wife died 6 weeks ago before his admission. He has a daughter and a son who both live locally and would like to take their father home. Peter has attempted on a few occasions to leave the ward, saying that he is going home to see his wife.

Take some time to think about this situation. Think about how you would help Peter regain as much independence as possible.

What other members of the multidisciplinary might you need to work with? How would his care needs be planned short term and long term?

How would you involve Peter in his own care?

How can his children become involved in care delivery and future care planning?

Top tips

Goals must be specific, measurable, attainable, realistic, timed and dated. Collaborate with the patient, to gain cooperation with the goals that are being planned. Goals should also be measurable and include a time frame as well as a date. Goals should conform to the nursing diagnosis. Make them specific to the patient's problem.

Implementation

The penultimate stage of the nursing process is the implementation stage, often referred to as the 'doing' stage. The implementation stage will only be as good as the activity undertaken in the planning stage; here the quality of the goal statements and the ability to communicate them are vital. If the goal statement is written in a nonsensical manner, e.g. if it is not measurable or achievable, then the care that is subsequently provided is in danger of harming the patient. During the planning stage the nurse will have to have documented the proposed nursing interventions for others to read and adhere to.

Reference to the care plan will advise the nurse what nursing interventions are to be performed, how the proposed nursing interventions are to be performed, when they are to be performed and by whom – the what, how, when and who. As with all other aspects of the nursing process the nurse continues to gather and collect data, amending and reviewing care as these new data are gathered, informing the plan of care in an ongoing manner. All care provided (or any that has been omitted) must be documented in line with local policy and in keeping with the tenets associated with the NMC's guidelines (NMC, 2009).

Bulechek et al (2008) define a nursing intervention as any treatment that a nurse performs to enhance patient outcomes. These nursing interventions can include both direct and indirect nurse-initiated care.

The nurse must remember to act in partnership with the family (if appropriate) when implementing care. Always take time to explain to the patient what you are doing and why, and explain this to the patient in a language that he or she understands. Before implementing the proposed nursing actions you must always reassess the patient to determine that the proposed action is still required and appropriate.

263

Think

Thinking about a recent clinical placement you have been on, how would you describe the philosophy of care in that care area?

What is meant by patient-centred care?

When care was delivered, who was the primary care giver – the nurse, health-care assistant, student nurse or family, or all of them?

At any time were the family invited to get involved with care giving? If so how was this initiated?

Case study 9.3

Janine is 20 years old and lives with her parents and two siblings; she has Down's syndrome. Janine has a heart condition and this has become exacerbated recently due to a number of chest infections that she has had. Janine has put on some weight recently, despite her parents' guidance with regard to healthy eating; she is over-weight. Janine has just finished her third course of antibiotics and is to be admitted as a day patient for a bronchoscopy and bronchial lavage in 1 week's time.

Adopting a holistic approach, how will you assess Janine's health before the procedure?

Where will you seek primary and secondary data to inform your assessment?

What do you think may be her actual and potential needs pre-, peri- and post-procedure?

Evaluation

The final stage allows the patient and the nurse to work together to measure and decide if the proposed outcomes that were detailed in the nursing care plan have been achieved. Evaluating the effectiveness of nursing care is necessary for developing a sound knowledge base to guide practice. There has been an increase in the emphasis on evaluation and evidence-based practice in health care (Donaldson, 2004; Swage, 2004). The critical and regular use of evidence as the basis for the provision of nursing care and health-care practice has emerged as a key principle reflecting current health-care provision (see Chapter 8).

Nurses, as members of the health-care team, are concerned with evaluation in a variety of guises. Nurses measure patient outcome achievements and evaluate how they have helped groups of patients achieve specific outcomes, e.g. a nurse may carry out the dressing of a wound with expert skill, but, if that intervention does not help the patient reach his or her desired outcome, then the activity may not be meaningful. Taylor et al (2011) suggest that the aim of nursing evaluation is to assess the overall quality of care.

All five stages of the nursing process need to be seen as ongoing activities as opposed to one-off events. Evaluation is a fluid and dynamic activity. This is also true of the evaluatory stage of the nursing process.

Evaluation affects and is affected by all other aspects of the nursing process (Fitzpatrick, 2002). Freiheit (2009) suggests that, without evaluation, the nursing process has not been completed. Although the evaluation stage is seen as the last stage of the nursing process, it is also the start of the process. Evaluation completes the process and examines the outcome(s).

Smith et al (2011) suggest that evaluation is examination of the outcome of nursing interventions, or the extent to which the anticipated outcomes or goals were achieved. They propose that three questions are asked:

1. Was the goal achieved?
2. What parts of the goal were not achieved?
3. Was client behaviour modified?

They also add that there are five classic elements of evaluation (Table 9.4).

Evaluation, according to Gega (2009), is often associated with outcomes in relation to certain criteria. She states that this is concerned with whether a problem has improved and the goals have been met against certain criteria. The objective of evaluation should be clearly stated in the nursing care plan.

Depending on the response of the patient (and the nurse should be guided by the patient's responses) to the interventions, the patient and nurse may do the following:

Table 9.4   The five classic elements of evaluation

Element	Example
Identifying evaluative criteria and standards	What you are looking for when you are evaluating care, e.g. what was the proposed goal/aim/outcome
Collecting data to determine if these criteria and standards have been met	Measuring, observing and communicating
Interpreting and summarising the findings	Making clinical judgements
Documenting your judgement	Being accountable for your actions
Terminating, continuing or modifying the plan	Reassessment

Source: adapted from Smith et al (2011).

- Discontinue the care plan as each goal has been achieved.
- Alter and amend the plan of care in the light of the evaluation; consider factors that may have prevented the patient from achieving the desired outcomes. Check to see if the care plan is specific and clear, and whether the goals are realistic and achievable.
- Reconsider time frames if more time is needed for the goals to be achieved.

The skills associated with the evaluation stage of the nursing process will be similar to those used in the assessment stage (Freiheit, 2009):

- Communicate
- Measure
- Observe.

Examples of achieving the goals set can be decided, e.g. if a patient has moved along the dependence–independence continuum, demonstrating an ability to become more independent as a result of the nursing interventions.

Situational variables will play an important part in determining if goals have been met as a result of nursing interventions or other variables at play, e.g. the patient's emotional state, medical interventions or the interventions of other health-care professionals such as therapists. There are a number of factors that can influence the achievement or non-achievement of a goal that has been set.

While evaluating the care the patient has received, Alabaster (2003) makes the important point that the evaluation stage also allows the nurse to evaluate him- or herself. She states that all nurses cannot be all things to all people. They may need to develop their own strategies for coping with issues that may arise and give the nurse cause for concern, such as the considerable physical and emotional stressors placed on the nurse in a therapeutic nursing relationship. Evaluation does not only involve a nurse, but also does and should involve the patient and, if appropriate, the patient's family and other members of the health-care team. Overlooking the patient's response to care interventions should be avoided. No area of care provision should be exempt from this, where of course this is achievable. Involving the patient and the family will empower them and allow them to voice their opinions about actual or potential problems concerning their health.

Alfaro-LeFevre (2010) suggests that, when evaluation is carried out beforehand, the nurse is able to 'check out' the interventions and make any alterations or amendments early. This early intervention could be called a formative approach to evaluation. An evaluation that occurs at the end of the interaction, the final aspect (e.g. discharge of the patient) might be deemed summative evaluation.

Although it has been stated that evaluation is an ongoing process, there may be a policy where you work that requires you to evaluate, for example, at the start and end of each shift or every 24 hours. In some long-term facilities, e.g. residential care homes, the interval between evaluations may be extended. You must remember, however, that you should evaluate the care of the patient whenever his or her condition dictates, and in some instances that may be more often than the policy in your place of work suggests.

Critical questioning is needed during the evaluation phase. This would include the following approach: 'How well did the patient accomplish the goal(s) set?' as well as 'What could he or she/we have done differently?' and 'Is this aspect of the care plan now complete and is the problem no longer a concern for the patient?'.

An objective approach is required if care is to be modified in any way, as opposed to an emotional or subjective approach.

Techniques

To evaluate care to the best of your ability, you must be an effective communicator, as already discussed. You have to be able to communicate verbally and non-verbally as well as possessing practised skills of observation. Being in possession of these skills will allow you to work with the patient in order to gain as much important information as you can about the nursing interventions that have been carried out to resolve the patient's problems. Therefore the nurse must use therapeutic communication to encourage the patient to disclose data that are necessary to evaluate care.

Freiheit (2009) alerts the nurse to be sensitive to changes in relation to the patient's physiological condition, emotional status and behaviour. Changes in respect of these issues can often be subtle, so the nurse must be alert and use his or her communication skills to the best of his or her ability to elicit any changes. The judicial use of all five senses – hearing, smelling, feeling, seeing and touching – will be needed when ascertaining clues about the patient's state of health. The nurse should be aware of his or her non-verbal and verbal communication skills. Being conscious of these issues sets a scene that will encourage the patient and his or her family to share comments, be these positive and/or negative.

Both subjective and objective approaches are used when assessing the patient's health status. A description of the patient's feelings and objective data related to measurable facts are required. The nurse must avoid becoming defensive about the feedback that the patient gives him or her about care. Employing such a manner may prevent the patient voicing his or her true feelings and being open. This kind of approach can place patients in a position where they feel that they have to say what they think the nurse wants to hear, or refuse to participate in evaluatory activities.

Subjective and objective methods

Being able to separate information that the patient or his or her family offers you into subjective and objective categories is difficult. It is important, however, to do this because it helps with critical thinking, as each category complements and clarifies the other.

For example, a patient says to you: 'I feel like my heart is pounding, it feels like it is racing.' The data that the patient provides you with are subjective data. When you take the patient's pulse you find that it is tachycardic at 160 beats/min. These data are objective, measurable data.

In the scenario above the two categories, subjective and objective, do indeed complement each other. The data you have observed and measured – a pulse rate of 160 beats/min – confirms what the patient is feeling, 'pounding, racing'.

There are situations, however, where what the patient tells you and what you observe or measure differ.

For example, the patient tells you in response to your question about how they are feeling: 'I feel fine' (subjective data). You observe that the patient has a respiratory rate of 30 breaths/min, is cold and clammy, and is cyanotic (objective data).

In this scenario the subjective data given to you and the objective data observed are at odds with each other; what you are being told is not the same as what you are observing. In this situation you will have to do more investigating to determine why there may be inconsistencies in order to obtain a full picture of all of the issues that might be occurring.

Subjective data

Subjective data can be anything that the patient or the patient's family says or communicates to you, e.g. their main complaint. See Table 9.5 for some examples of subjective data.

Table 9.5   Some examples of subjective data

I feel sick and anxious
I have a headache
I have a gripping vice-like pain across my chest
I feel everyone is talking about me
My tracheotomy tube is burning like fire
I wish my mum were here
I can't manage any more

Table 9.6   Some examples of objective data

Glasgow Coma Scale score 12
Heart rate 82 beats/min
Vomited 120 mL of vomitus
Has a blood pressure of 130/65 mm/Hg
Mucous membranes cyanotic
The patient has a Hb of 8.3 g/dL
Passed 200 mL of diarrhoea

267

Objective data

Objective data are factual – data that you can clearly observe or measure, e.g. vital signs, laboratory test results. Table 9.6 outlines some examples of objective data.

There are some patient groups who may have difficulty expressing their responses to nursing interventions and their treatment, e.g. a child. When this is the case, you may be able to gather objective data only to help you determine if the outcomes or goals have been achieved.

Case study 9.4

Sanna Kovalinen is a 71-year-old who has been admitted to the hospice for end-of-life care. She has one daughter who lives in Finland and is confined to a wheelchair. Sanna has carcinoma of the lung with bony metastases. She is unable to mobilise and is taking very light nutrition orally; she has a red area on the sacrum and is in excruciating pain each time the care staff attend to her needs. Sanna has patient-controlled analgesia delivery and an opioid and antiemetic, which has contributed to her constipation.

Thinking of the pain that Sanna is experiencing, how would you evaluate the effectiveness with regard to the administration of analgesia?

What nursing interventions are needed to help relieve and keep Sanna pain free?

What if any spiritual needs might Sanna have and how can you help her with these?

Nursing models

Nurses can use nursing models in a variety of settings to help guide practice and, in particular, the assessment stage of the nursing process. Nursing models are a collection of ideas, knowledge and values about nursing, helping nurses to make explicit the way in which they work with patients, their families and the communities for whom they care as individuals or groups. A common theme emerges when attempting to define nursing models: they attempt to articulate the reality of nursing and have the potential to enable nurses to work towards common goals.

Conceptual models of nursing attempt to articulate reality, but they can do this by only providing the nurse with a descriptive representation of beliefs about nursing. Central to any nursing model are the following:

- The meaning of nursing
- The individuals receiving nursing care
- The meaning of health.

Several models of care exist that will help nurses provide the patient with consistency and continuity. The choice of model will depend on the patient and the philosophy of care used in the care area. Examples of models are:

- Orem's Self-Care model (Orem, 1995)
- Roper, Logan and Tierney's model (Roper et al, 1996)
- Casey's Partnership Nursing model (Casey, 1988)
- Peplau's model (Peplau, 1988).

One of the most popular and most widely used models in the UK is Roper, Logan and Tierney's model based on a model of living (Roper et al, 1996). Briefly, this model helps guide the nurse, especially during the assessment stage of the nursing process, by encouraging the nurse to consider the following five components or concepts:

1. Twelve activities of living
2. The lifespan
3. The dependence/independence continuum
4. The five factors that influence the activities of living
5. Individuality in living.

Figure 9.5 provides a diagrammatic overview of the model of living.

When the nurse uses Roper et al's model he or she concentrates on the activities of living, basing the assessment on the patient's usual abilities/routine. When the nurse ascertains what the patient usually does in relation to the activities of living, a comparison can then be made based on what the patient is like now. The activities are not assessed in isolation; the nurse must also consider what effect the five influencing factors may have on the patient's abilities to carry out the activities of living, where he or she is in relation to lifespan and the degree of dependence/independence. When carrying out the assessment, the nurse must at all times consider the patient as a unique individual, thereby supporting the notion of a holistic, individual approach to nursing care.

Orem's model is American in origin and is based on the concept of self-care. Orem uses universal self-care requisites on which to base a nursing assessment (Table 9.7).

When using Orem's model the aim of assessment is to determine the patient's ability to self-care (Beretta, 2008). Having identified a shortfall in self-care, the nurse then needs to consider self-care limitations and self-care deficits that have become apparent as a result of the assessment. The nurse's role is to help the patient with the identified deficits.

Casey's Partnership model is used in the paediatric setting. Figure 9.6 provides a diagrammatic representation of the model.

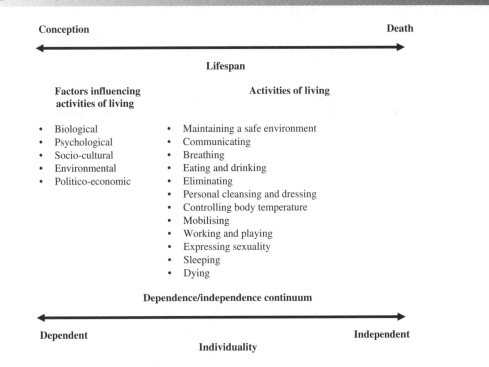

Figure 9.5   A diagrammatic representation of the model of living. Source: adapted from Roper et al (1996); Holland (2008).

Table 9.7   Orem's self-care model and the universal self-care requisites

- Maintenance of sufficient intake of air
- Maintenance of sufficient intake of water
- Maintenance of sufficient intake of food
- Provision of care associated with elimination of processes and excrements
- Maintenance of a balance between solitude and social integration
- Prevention of hazards to life, human functioning and human wellbeing
- Promotion of human functioning and development within social groups in accordance with human potential, known human limitations and the human desire to be normal

Source: adapted from Orem (1995).

The aim of the model is to explain and encourage parental participation in care. Family-centred care in relation to this model considers the needs of the child within the context of the family unit; the family members are seen as the primary carers. The wellbeing of the child is central, but there is a recognition that care, if it is to be effective, will depend on negotiation and partnership between the nurse and the primary carers. Samwell (2005) suggests that each party has an equal part in the relationship.

Conclusions

The concept of the nursing process has been used for many years in both the USA and the UK. It is a systemic, patient-centred, goal-oriented approach to nursing care, providing the nurse with a

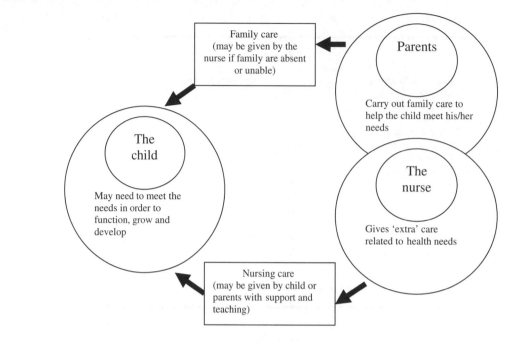

Figure 9.6   A diagrammatic representation of Casey's Partnership model. Source: Casey (1988).

framework on which to deliver nursing care. The nursing process is (when appropriate) carried out with the patient.

A five-stage nursing process is gaining popularity in the UK:

1. Assessment
2. Nursing diagnosis
3. Planning
4. Implementation
5. Evaluation

The first stage of the nursing process is pivotal; this stage involves the continuous collection of data or facts and the nurse uses various strategies to achieve this, e.g. he or she communicates, measures and observes. During this stage judgements are made about the patient's health status. The diagnostic stage demands that the nurse analyses the data in order to determine the patient's strengths and health problems that can be prevented or resolved. Measurable outcomes and goals are set during the planning stage. The purposes of these goals are to prevent, relieve or resolve the problems identified during the diagnostic phase. The outcome of planning is to produce individualised care plans that can be evaluated to determine if care interventions have been successful. Implementation is associated with doing: the nurse implements the care planned. The patient is assisted and supported in an attempt to achieve the stated goals, to enhance health and to prevent disease. Evaluation of the care provided is the final stage of the process. After monitoring and measuring the effects of nursing interventions the nurse, together with the patient, modifies the care plan if needed.

There are several models of care available to the nurse that can help guide practice. They attempt to express the reality of nursing and encourage nurses to work towards common goals. Nursing models are

270

conceptual representations of reality and there are three central components associated with them: the value of nursing, the individuals receiving nursing care and the meaning of health. They are frameworks that help the nurse to make a comprehensive assessment of the 'whole' being. The model chosen cannot be used in isolation: the nurse must also use a systematic approach to care. The nursing process is aimed at providing high-quality, responsive nursing care.

Activity

Attempt the following 10 questions that are related to the assessment, planning, implementation and evaluation of care needs to test your knowledge. The answers can be found at the back of this book, in the chapter called 'Activity Answers'.

1. How many activities do Roper et al (1996) list?
2. What was the additional phase of the nursing process?
3. What is the stage called where the nurse reviews the care plan to determine if the goals set had been met?
4. What is missing: specific, measurable, realistic and time oriented?
5. The data-collection stage is called what?
6. The model of nursing that is commonly used in child health and referred to as the partnership model was devised by whom?
7. What is the most commonly used pressure-sore risk assessment tool used in the UK?
8. What does the MUST tool assess?
9. What does the acronym MUST mean?
10. What does the BMI calculate?

References

Alabaster ES (2003) The chronically ill person. In: Alexander MF, Fawcett JN, Runciman PJ (eds), *Nursing Practice Hospital and Home: The adult*, 2nd edn. Edinburgh: Churchill Livingstone, pp 945–962.

Alfaro-LeFevre R (2010) *Applying the Nursing Process. A tool for critical thinking*, 7th edn. Philadelphia, PA: Lippincott.

Beretta R (2008) Assessment: The foundation of good practice. In: Hinchliff S, Norman, S, Schober J (eds), *Nursing Practice and Health Care*, 5th edn. London: Arnold, pp 290–317.

Bird J (2005) Assessing pain in older people. *Nursing Standard* **19**(19): 45–52.

Bulechek GM, Butcher HK, McCloskey-Dochterman J (2008) *Nursing Interventions Classification (NIC)*, 5th edn. St Louis, MO: Mosby.

Casey A (1988) A partnership with child and family. *Senior Nurse* **8**(4): 8–9.

Cowan F, Bell G (2011) The sexual health consultation in primary and secondary care. In: Rogstrad K (ed.), *ABC of Sexually Transmitted Infections*, 6th edn. Chichester: BMJ Books.

Donaldson L (2004) Clinical governance: A quality concept. In: van Zwanenberg T, Harrison J (eds), *Clinical Governance in Primary Care*, 2nd edn. Oxford: Radcliffe Medical Press, pp 3–16.

Doughty DB (2010) Skin integrity and wound healing. In: Daniels R (ed.), *Nursing Fundamentals: Caring and clinical decision making*, 2nd edn. New York: Thompson, pp 1183–1227.

Fitzpatrick J (2002) The nursing shortage revisited: Focus on patient outcomes. *Applied Nursing Research* **15**: 117.

Freiheit H (2009) Evaluation. In: van Zwanenberg T, Harrison J (eds), *Clinical Governance in Primary Care*, 2nd edn. Oxford: Radcliffe Medical Press, pp 279–290.

Gega L (2009) Problems, goals and care planning. In: Norman I, Ryrie I (eds), *The Art and Science of Mental Health Nursing: A textbook of principles and practice*, 2nd edn. Milton Keynes: Open University Press, pp 637–647.

Holland K (2008) An introduction to the Roper–Logan–Tierney model for nursing, based on activities of living. In: Holland K, Jenkins J, Solomon J, Whittam S (eds), *Roper, Logan and Tierney Model in Practice*, 2nd edn. London: Churchill Livingstone, pp 2–23.

Kozier B, Erb G, Berman A, Snyder S, Lake R, Harvey S (2008) *Fundamentals of Nursing: Concepts, process and practice*. Harlow: Pearson.

Lund CC, Browder NC (1944) Estimation of areas of burns. *Surgery, Gynecology and Obstetrics* **79**: 352–358.

Maslow A (1954) *Motivation and Personality*. New York: Harper & Row.

Nursing and Midwifery Council (2009) *Records Keeping. Guidance for Nurses and Midwives*. London: NMC.

Nursing and Midwifery Council (2010) *Standards for Preregistration Nursing Education*. London: NMC. Available at: http://standards.nmc-uk.org/PublishedDocuments/Standards%20for%20pre-registration%20nursing%20 education%2016082010.pdf (accessed June 2011).

Nusbaum MRH, Hamilton CD (2002) The proactive sexual health history. *American Family Physician* **66**: 1705–1712.

Orem D (1995) *Nursing: Concepts of Practice*, 5th edn. St Louis, MO: Mosby.

Peplau H (1988) *Interpersonal Relationships in Nursing*. New York: Putman.

Rayman SM (2009) Assessment. In: Daniel R (ed.), *Nursing Fundamentals: Caring and clinical decision making*, 2nd edn. New York: Thompson, pp 220–245.

Roper N, Logan WW, Tierney AJ (1996) *The Elements of Nursing: A model based on a model of living*, 4th edn. Edinburgh: Churchill Livingstone.

Samwell B (2005) Nursing the family and supporting the nurse: exploring the nurse–patient relationship in community children's nursing. In: Sidey A, Widdas D (eds), *The Textbook of Community Children's Nursing*, 2nd edn. Edinburgh: Elsevier, pp 129–136.

Sibson LE (2010) Assessing needs and the nursing process. In: Peate I (ed.), *Nursing Care and the Activities of Living*, 2nd edn. London: Whurr, pp 38–59.

Smith SF, Duell DJ, Martin BC (2011) *Clinical Nursing Skills: Basic to advanced skills*, 8th edn. Upper Saddle River, NJ: Pearson.

Swage T (2004) *Clinical Governance in Health Care Practice*, 2nd edn. Edinburgh: Butterworth Heinemann.

Taylor C, Lillis C, LeMone P, Lynn P (2011) *Fundamentals of Nursing: The art and science of nursing care*, 7th edn. Philadelphia: Lippincott.

Timby BK (2009) *Fundamental Nursing Skills and Concepts*, 9th edn. Philadelphia, PA: Lippincott.

Wakley G, Cunnion, M, Chambers R (2003) *Improving Sexual Health Advice*. Oxford: Radcliffe.

Waterlow J (1985) A risk assessment card. *Nursing Times* **81**(49): 51–55.

10

Public Health

Aims and objectives

The aim of this chapter is to introduce the reader to the principles underpinning public health
   At the end of the chapter you will be able to:

1. Provide a definition of public health
2. Describe the origins of public health and emergent public health
3. Discuss the public health needs of specific groups of people and communities
4. Identify opportunities and challenges related to the provision of a contemporary public health service
5. Describe the role of the nurse in relation to public health
6. Appreciate the Nursing and Midwifery Council's requirements of student nurses

The Nursing and Midwifery Council (NMC, 2010) requires that all nurses understand public health principles, priorities and practices so that they can recognise and respond to the major causes and social determinants of health, illness and health inequalities. Nurses are also required to: use a range of information and data to assess the needs of people, groups, communities and populations, and work to improve health, wellbeing and experiences of health care; secure equal access to health screening, health promotion and health care; and promote social inclusion.
   Public health is closely aligned to health promotion and as such there are elements of this chapter that relate to discussions in Chapter 7 and vice versa. This chapter focuses on public health and its definition, the origins of public health and how new public health initiatives have emerged.

Public health

The provision of effective contemporary public health services is essential if the health of the nation is to continue to prosper. Nurses undertake various aspects of public health activity every day when

The Student's Guide to Becoming a Nurse, Second Edition. Ian Peate.
© 2012 John Wiley & Sons, Ltd. Published 2012 by John Wiley & Sons, Ltd.

carrying out their work in a variety of environments with a variety of people. Nursing knowledge is derived from a variety of sources and public health contributes to that knowledge.

Think

Make a list of some of the things that health-care professionals working in the field of public health undertake as part of their job.

Did you think of any of the following in your list?

- Monitor the health status of the community
- Identify health needs
- Develop programmes to reduce risk and screen for early disease
- Control infectious diseases
- Foster policies that promote health plans
- Evaluate the provision of health care
- Manage and implement change.

Case study 10.1

Pueblo DeSouza is 45 years old. He is visiting his general practitioner for a well man's health check; he calls it his MOT. During the visit the practice nurse assesses a range of issues including Pueblo's BMI, blood glucose and blood pressure, and they discuss alcohol use and smoking. During the consultation Pueblo says to the nurse that he has heard of a blood test that will be able to diagnose if he has prostate cancer – the prostate-specific antigen test.

How do you think the practice nurse might react when asked about this?

What are the key issues associated with screening programmes?

How can a screening programme be helpful and detrimental to the health of people?

Just as attempting to define nursing or health is challenging, defining public health is also difficult. The term adopts an umbrella approach for a number of activities that are carried out by a variety of health-care professionals with the intention of influencing health outcomes and patterns of disease. The official definition of public health is attributed to Sir Donald Acheson back in 1988 (Acheson, 1988) and is still relevant today because it reflects the essential focus of contemporary public health:

> . . . the science and art of preventing disease, prolonging life, and promoting health through the organised efforts of society . . .

It is essential to have an understanding of what public health means so that progress in the field can be made. There are many definitions of public health and many of them are context dependent, often related to the issue being discussed or contested.

Wherever nursing takes place there are opportunities for public health activity to take place. Nurses do not work in isolation, and working together is essential in the public health arena. Working together to influence health and to understand disease patterns nurses need to draw up on the work of the following professionals:

- Psychologists
- Doctors
- Anthropologists
- Sociologists
- Epidemiologists
- Economists
- Politicians
- The media
- Environmentalists.

The nurse needs to understand the role of the people who are involved in public health to ensure that the best use of their expertise is made. This is important if the nurse is to influence and be involved in:

- lifestyle choice and changes
- social change
- environmental issues
- empowerment.

Gathering health data, analysing data, making sense of the data and applying them appropriately are known as health intelligence. Health intelligence comes from a variety of sources of data, many of which will include the information and knowledge from a lay perspective; this should be respected and valued as a legitimate source of knowledge. A key source of health intelligence, traditionally concerning mortality and morbidity, surveillance, related to disease and infectious diseases in particular, involves the ways in which diseases spread, the factors contributing to health and disease among populations which is known generally as epidemiology.

Case study 10.2

 Marie is a 20-year-old woman with learning disabilities; she lives in a community home with four other people – two men and two women. Marie and her boyfriend, Peter, who also lives in the community home, get drunk about three times a week. This is causing concern for the community nurse who knows that Marie has diabetes and Peter is obese.

How might you handle this situation?

What do you need to consider to ensure that you respect the choices that Marie and Peter are making?

Are there any opportunities for health improvement with this group of clients and how would you go about implementing them?

Think

What infectious diseases are you aware of? Make a list of them and compare them with the list below.

- Meningitis
- Hepatitis
- Malaria
- Chlamydia infection
- Measles
- Gastroenteritis

- Influenza
- HIV
- Yellow fever
- Diphtheria
- Anthrax
- Polio.

There is a clear move within the National Health Service (NHS) towards the consideration of demographic trends, health improvements and non-communicable diseases, encompassing a growing understanding of socioeconomic and social influences on a person and communities. Before discussing the new approaches associated with the public health agenda, a short historical overview will be presented to contextualise current practice.

Top tips

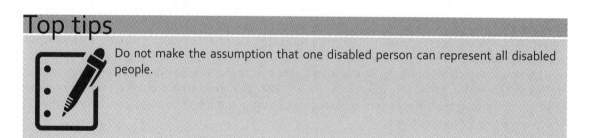

Do not make the assumption that one disabled person can represent all disabled people.

Historical perspective

The many successes associated with the modern NHS should not be played down. People are living longer and living longer with a number of long-term conditions that previously may have killed them. In the list about infectious diseases that you were asked to compile earlier a number of those infections would once have been expected to kill children and adults, and some of those infections, in some parts of the world, have now been eradicated. Immunisation has resulted in the eradication of smallpox, the elimination of polio (in the Americas) and the control of measles, rubella, tetanus, diphtheria and *Haemophilus influenzae* type b.

In the UK there has been an increase in life expectancy. Advances in technology, bacteriology, immunology and pharmacology are considered by Larsen (2009) to have caused a drop in mortality rates. These advances associated with developments in care provision, medicine and technology have also increased the numbers of long-term conditions and, as such, longevity (Table 10.1).

Case study 10.3

Sharmina, aged 12 years, has arrived home from school with a note for her parents from the school nurse. The note informs Sharmina's parents that a vaccine for human papillomavirus (HPV) is available and it is national policy for all 12-year-old girls to receive the vaccine. The HPV vaccine protects against strains of HPV that are behind 70 per cent of cases of cervical cancer. In the note it explains that the immunisation will be given at school to girls in Year 8. School nurses will give the vaccine in three doses, delivered over a period of months by injection in the arm. Parents/guardians are required to give their consent for the procedure. Sharmina's father is unhappy about the vaccine because he has heard that there are several side effects; he is meeting the school nurse to discuss the issue.

Think about the HPV vaccine.

How might you provide Sharmina's father with advice so that he and his daughter can make an informed decision?

What other vaccines are you aware of that raise concerns among some guardians/parents?

Describe the role of the school nurse in relation to Sharmina.

Public health is said to have its origins in the social reformer Edwin Chadwick's report *The Sanitary Conditions of the Labouring Population of Great Britain*, published in 1842. Cholera was rife and Chadwick concluded that the most important measures that could be taken to improve the health of the public were associated with effective drainage systems and the removal of refuse from homes and the streets,

Table 10.1   Contributions to long-term increases in life expectancy

People with bone disease such as osteoarthritis now have the opportunity to have joints replaced
Lung transplantation may extend life and quality of life for those people with cystic fibrosis
People with HIV may now live longer with the condition as a result of advances in pharmacology
Reduction in sexually transmitted infections associated with the advent of antibiotics
Quality of life for some people with Parkinson's disease as a result of advances in technology (e.g. deep brain stimulation)
People who have had a myocardial infarction that in the past might have killed them are living longer with advances in cardiac pharmacology and technology
Performing laparoscopic surgery reduces many risks associated with more invasive procedures
Advances in anaesthesia now allow people who might have been considered unfit for general anaesthetic to undergo surgery
Introduction and development of immunisations
Motor vehicle safety
Safer workplaces
Safer healthier foods, fluoridation of drinking water
Advances in maternal and child health
Recognition of tobacco and alcohol as potential and actual health hazards

Source: adapted from Knai (2009).

277

along with improvements in water supplies. Water companies who had been reluctant to take measures to ensure the purity of their water came under public pressure and the first of the Public Health Acts was introduced in 1848. This Act permitted local authorities to take control of their environment. In 1847 the first Medical Officer of Health, Dr William Henry Duncan, was appointed. Towards the end of the nineteenth century, a central government Department of Public Health, along with local departments of public health, had been established in every local government district.

The Public Health Department headed by the Medical Officer of Health thrived during the first half of the twentieth century. In 1907 the school health service was formed alongside the provision for improving antenatal and postnatal care. The first centre for prenatal care was provided in Edinburgh in 1915. A number of other Acts were introduced that impacted on the public provision of health care, including the National Insurance Act 1911, and by the 1920s and 1930s Medical Officers of Health occupied a central role in the provision of health care to the nation. Their responsibilities included monitoring water supplies, sewage disposal, food hygiene, housing and control of infectious diseases. They also had responsibility for health visitors and midwives as well as the school health service. In 1929 they took on the task of administering municipal hospitals. The Medical Officer of Health had a central role in the public provision of health care as well as in the prevention and monitoring of ill health.

After World War II, the NHS Act 1946 was set up which provided for the formation of three discrete controlling bodies for health care. NHS hospitals were administered by regional hospital boards, public health services were under the responsibility of local authorities and local executive councils administered general medical services providing primary medical care to the population. Reorganisation in the late 1940s occurred, the first of many over the past 60 years, leading to profound changes in the interrelationships of public health, local authorities and clinical services. There has been, and to some extent still continues today, a focus on the curative elements of health care to the detriment of preventive health interventions.

The post of Medical Officer Health was abolished in 1974. Responsibility for monitoring environmental determinants of health was taken over by directors of environmental health, employed by local authorities. Training was available for doctors in public health medicine and they became community medicine specialists employed to monitor the health status of the population and advise health authorities on how best to manage the health problems of their community. Community medicine specialists carried out three basic functions: they were medical administrators who assisted in planning and managing clinical services; they were advisers on the medical aspects of environmental health to the local authority; and they continued to have a role in epidemiology and the evaluation of health status and programmes of health care. The Acheson Committee in 1988 recommended a return to the name public health for the specialty that had been community medicine specialist.

William Rathbone provided the means to set up the first district nursing service in Liverpool in the mid-1880s working with Florence Nightingale. He wanted to ensure that nurses had the necessary knowledge and skills to care for people in their own homes – in a community setting. Since then, public health nurses and doctors have been involved in reshaping health services and are being increasingly involved in the development of evidence-based health care within the NHS. As economic pressures grow, it is important that UK governments do not overlook public health and preventive measures.

Public health nursing

Much of the work of nurses brings them into close contact with the social conditions of the people for whom they care and as a result nurses are able to describe the everyday lived experiences of many of their patients (Royal College of Nursing or RCN, 2010). Plaistow (2009) suggests that public health nursing has its origins in health visiting; the role emerged as a result of societal and political issues of the time

278

and these included poverty, high infant mortality rates and uncontrolled infections. Such issues still remain a challenge for public health nurses (Department of Health/Department for Children, Schools and Families, 2007).

Policy developments concerning the health of the nation are continuing to focus on health inequalities and the need to address and reduce these, as well as ensuring that resources are targeted at the right communities and populations, e.g. the least well off in society, those who are hard to reach and those who are disadvantaged. A population-focused service delivery model led by nurses working in partnership is one way of achieving these aspirations.

In 2004 the NMC published standards related the specialist community public health nursing (NMC, 2004). These standards, according to Plaistow (2009), can help steer the profession towards a wider population-focused public health role. The standards also incorporate the Faculty of Public Health competencies for public health practice. The current NMC register (see Chapter 1) comprises three parts: one for nurses, another for midwives and one for specialist community public health nursing. All health visitors registered on the previous register on part II were automatically transferred to the new part of the register. Migration to the new part of the register also included other discrete groups, such as school nurses, occupational health nurses and sexual health nurses, who have demonstrated competence to practise in the field. In some areas of the UK, the title health visitor is still used; in other areas, the term 'specialist community public health nurse' has been introduced. Health visitors, according to the Department of Health (2011), are public health nurses trained to work at community, family and individual level. There is confusion about the use of titles and the RCN (2011a) has called for consistency with regard to their use.

Specialist community public health nursing is defined by the NMC (2004) as a service that:

> . . . aims to reduce health inequalities by working with individuals, families, and communities promoting health, preventing ill health and in the protection of health. The emphasis is on partnership working that cuts across disciplinary, professional and organisational boundaries that impact on organised social and political policy to influence the determinants of health and promote the health of whole populations.

Coverdale (2009) suggests that this definition offers a different emphasis to the role of the general nurse because the specialist community public health nurse may not necessarily work with individuals; rather they may work more with a community or population group. The elements of public health nursing according to Coverdale (2009) are:

- Planning health promotion and health protecting programmes
- Reducing risky behaviours and health inequalities
- Preventing disease
- Assessing and monitoring the health of communities and populations, identifying risk and those with health problems
- Assessing health needs and identifying priorities for action.

Haggart (2003) notes that the principles of public health nursing focus on equality, collaboration and participation with others, with the intention of strengthening community action. The need for preventive action in the community is essential as services provided in the acute sector become constrained. Ensuring and securing short-term healthy lifestyles has the potential to reap long-term benefits for individuals and society.

Elliott et al (2004) suggest that specialist community public health nurses provide care along a continuum, working with the individual through to the various population groups, working with children and in so doing laying down the foundations of good health, supporting and caring for chronically ill individuals, changing lifestyles, enhancing knowledge or attitudes, empowering people and communities, and influencing policy. The RCN (2009a) discusses the many ways in which nursing contributes to public health, with an emphasis on partnership working. The aims of delivering public health through nursing services can be found in Table 10.2. See Figure 10.1 for a demonstration of the various ways in which nurses can influence the health of communities.

When nurses work with the public they have the ability to influence behaviour as an element of health promotion. Nurses work in partnership with key agencies and a number of community networks; they also have an active role and lead in developing policies and protocols for intersectoral partnerships. Coverdale (2009) suggests that communication and interpersonal skills are essential, along with an understanding of the structure and philosophy of public health practice.

A competency framework has been developed by the Skills for Health and the Public Health Resource Unit (2008); these competencies provide public health practitioners with a career pathway. The framework is a generic framework that can be adapted to meet the needs of the various groups of health-care professionals involved in public health, including environmental health officers, epidemiologists, health promotion staff, pharmacists therapists, dieticians, occupational health practitioners, doctors and midwives. There are nine levels of competence and knowledge within the framework. Level 1 considers those who will have little previous knowledge, skills or experience with regard to public health, and those at level 9 will be responsible for setting strategic priorities and direction and providing leadership to improve population health and wellbeing (Table 10.3).

Loveday and Linsley (2011) note that those nurses working in the public health arena combine community involvement and knowledge of the population with personal clinical understandings of health and illness amassed from the experiences of individuals and families in that population. The knowledge gained can then be used to develop strategies that provide appropriate interventions to meet the needs of the individual family or community.

Public health nurses, along with other nurses, practise nursing within a social, political and economic context. The nurse must consider how culture, economic conditions and overall lifestyle can impinge on an individual's health. Developing skills to understand how these factors can influence a person's health will help the nurse understand the patient (LeMone et al, 2011). All members of society deserve to benefit from the work of the public health nurse and public health nursing, and this includes those who may be considered as marginalised.

Top tips

Poor sexual health can lead to a range of health problems including pelvic inflammatory disease, infertility, ectopic pregnancy, cervical cancer, unintended pregnancies, abortions, neonatal disorders and neonatal death. The nurse needs to provide public health services that can help the reduce the risk of poor sexual health.

Marginalised societies

Three particular groups in society who could be said to be marginalised or oppressed are:

- Homeless people
- People who have offended
- Homosexuals.

Table 10.2   The aims of delivering public health through nursing services

Increasing life expectancy by influencing healthy behaviours
Reducing health inequalities
Improving the health of populations through reducing obesity, smoking, improving sexually health
Increasing the awareness of healthy behaviours in communities
Promoting and developing social capital
Engaging with individuals, families and communities to influence the design and development of services

Source: adapted from Royal College of Nursing (2009a).

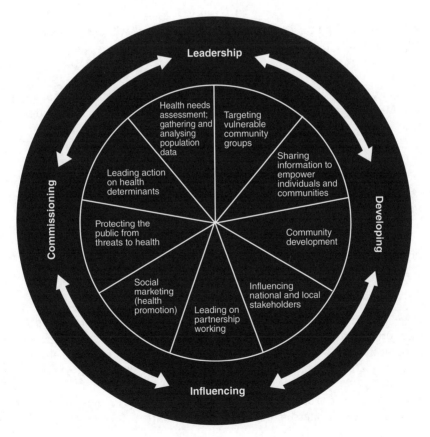

Figure 10.1   The various ways in which nurses can influence the health of communities. Source: Royal College of Nursing (2009a). (Reproduced with kind permission of the Royal College of Nursing from *Nurses as Partners in Delivering Public Health*.)

Table 10.3   Nine levels of competence and knowledge

Level 1
Has little previous knowledge, skills or experience with regard to public health. May undertake specific public health activities under direction or recognise the value of public health in a wider context

Level 2
Has basic public health knowledge through training and/or development. Can perform a number of defined public health activities under direction or may use knowledge to influence public health in a wider context

Level 3
Can carry out a variety of public health activities or small areas of work under supervision. May help in training others and could have responsibility for resources used by others. Might use public health knowledge to set priorities and make decisions in a wider context

Level 4
Takes on responsibility for particular areas of public health work with direction, which may have a breadth and/or depth of application

Level 5
Has autonomy in stated areas, frequently develops own area of work and encourages others to understand it. May contribute to a programme of work in a multiagency or multidisciplinary environment

Level 6
Has autonomy and responsibility in organising complex work, reflecting wider and deeper expertise in own area of work. Is able to develop, facilitate and contribute to programmes of work in multiagency or multidisciplinary environment

Level 7
Is autonomous and has expertise in areas of public health. Leads on areas of work within a defined field

Level 8
Has a high level of expertise in a specific area of work or across an extensive breadth of service delivery and/or programmes. Is accountable for work across boundaries and agencies. Has leadership responsibility and autonomy to act. Sets strategic direction in own area of work

Level 9
Sets strategic direction across organisations and/or areas of work. Provides multidisciplinary or multisectoral public health leadership that determines priorities

Source: adapted from Skills for Health and Public Health Resource Unit (2008).

These groups may have similar yet different sociocultural issues that can have an effect on their health. A person's social position affects health, appearance and chances in life. The World Health Organization (WHO, 2008) note that a person's physical health depends on his or her mental health. There are many complex reasons why people are marginalised by society, e.g. they may feel marginalised because of their difference – physical or otherwise.

Before considering each group, recall the various components or dimensions that affect all humans (Figure 10.2). Remember that health integrates all the human dimensions and as a result the nurse must consider each component in order to provide individualised care.

Think

Consider the following situation.

There are two candidates for a kidney transplantation. One is a homeless unemployed person who has a 95 per cent chance of surviving the operation; the other person is a company manager who has an 85 per cent chance of survival. Who should get the kidney?

This is clearly a difficult case scenario to answer. The example is there to illustrate a point – when decisions are made about many things in life, we can take into account the sociocultural and socioeconomic attributes of a person's life. To make a response or to begin to answer the above scenario, you may need to acquaint yourself once again with the ethical frameworks discussed in earlier chapters. The influencing factors or the criteria used to allocate resources can be medically or socially based. In the decision-making process related to resource allocation, this may hinge on several aspects of the scenario, including the fact that one of the potential transplant recipients is homeless (a social factor).

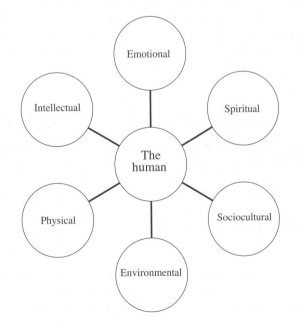

Figure 10.2   The interdependent components of the human being.

If social criteria alone were used to make recommendations for those who required renal transplantations, then aspects such as the person's wealth, marital status, psychological stability and religious affiliation may be taken into the equation and this would be unacceptable. It is easy for us to be disapproving of the idea of using social criteria to make decisions about life and death situations, but often medical criteria merge into social criteria.

The following factors (individually or a collection of them) can be key factors that may lead to marginalisation. Serious deficiencies in any (or all) of the following areas of a person's life may render them susceptible to marginalisation:

- *Accommodation* – the person may live in substandard accommodation that is often unstable or temporary. Renting or owning accommodation depends on income.
- *Income* – often people are on a low income, e.g. those receiving disability allowance or pensions, which is their only source of income. The assets may be some clothes and a small amount of furniture.
- *Diet* – many have a poor and inadequate diet. A number may have no proper cooking facilities and they rely on cheap and unhealthy takeaway food.
- *Social support* – social isolation is a major problem and many marginalised people live alone. Many of them have split away from their families and no longer have contact with them. Few, if any, have close friends. Most of them have no one to turn to if they are facing particular problems.
- *Health* – the general health of many marginalised communities is poor as a result of their lifestyle. Chronic illness is not uncommon.
- *Disabilities and disorders* – disability or other conditions may preclude them from, or limit their opportunities to participate in, regular community activities. Mental illness, behavioural problems, physical disability and learning disability are common among the marginalised people in society. They may also experience some form of substance abuse, e.g. alcohol and nicotine.
- *Self-esteem* – lack of self-confidence is very common among marginalised people. As a result of continuous putdowns in their lives, they may feel that they are of little value and frequently believe that no one is interested in them. Lack of self-esteem is often the hardest thing facing a person who has been marginalised. It is not the lack of material goods such as shelter or food, but being seen as having no worth, being devalued as a person. Feeling as if you are of little worth leads to a loss of dignity as a human. Living a 'dehumanised' existence with few friends and little social contact only exacerbates the situation.

Think

 Thinking about the factors above, make a list of people whom you think could be seen as marginalised.

Your list must be very long; any one of us may have experienced or may experience any of the factors above. Whole societies can be marginalised. Burton and Kagan (2004) state that marginalisation is a multiconceptual, dynamic and fluid idea that can change according to social status; it also has a temporal element attached to it. You might have included the following in your list:

- Elderly people
- People with mental health problems

284

- People who have a stigma (e.g. those with cancer or an infectious disease)
- People who have a physical disability
- People with a learning disability
- Addicted people (e.g. addicted to drugs, alcohol, nicotine)
- People who are travellers
- People who are prostitutes
- People who are refugees
- Uneducated people
- Poor people.

Marginalisation is complex; it is a multifaceted process produced by restricted activity or capacity. Marginalisation leads to exclusion, oppression, discrimination and vulnerabilty. It may be associated with societal attitudes towards a disability, impairment, sexuality or ethnicity. Different people react and respond differently to marginalisation and this frequently depends on the personal and social resources available (Burton and Kagan, 2004).

The literature about marginalisation is limited despite the fact that nurses often work with marginalised members of society, e.g. elderly or mentally ill people and those with a learning disability. Social marginality is defined by Leonard (1984) as:

> *Being outside the mainstream of productive activity and/or social reproductive activity.*

Other dictionary definitions define marginalisation as the social process of becoming or being made marginal (especially as a group within the larger society). Marginalisation refers in general to overt or covert acts and trends within societies, whereby those perceived as lacking function or desirable traits are excluded from existing social systems of interaction.

Those who have been marginalised often have little control over their lives and the resources that are available to them, e.g. health-care resources. The nurse aims to empower people, i.e. help them to make independent decisions with the aim of taking control of their own lives; these are autonomous and informed health-related choices. This, according to Burton and Kagan (2004), is often associated with negative public attitudes towards the marginalised group, leading to stigmatisation and isolation. Isolation can result in withdrawal and this in turn means that the marginalised person will be limited with respect to the contribution that they can make to society, leading to a reduction in self-esteem and self-confidence – a vicious circle begins.

Case study 10.4

 Colin is a 15-year-old who has been admitted under section to the local mental health unit with a diagnosis of anorexia nervosa. He is malnourished and uncommunicative. His mother, a single parent, has accompanied him and is clearly distressed. Colin has been stealing laxatives from a local supermarket and has been seen to purge after eating his food. Colin's mother informs you that Colin and she have been arguing a lot over the last year when she discovered he was being bullied at school. She says he has become obsessed with food over the last 6–9 months and has mentioned to her on a few occasions he would rather be dead than alive.

How might you use your skills to help Colin and his mother during this traumatic period of time?

Think about the role of the nurse and how you can ensure that Colin is safe while in hospital. What other members of the multidisciplinary team might be involved in Colin's care?

What do you understand the Fraser guidelines to be?

Homeless people

Home should not be considered merely as a roof over the head; it is a place that provides security, privacy and links to a community, and has the potential to act as a support network. However, for some, home may also be a place that they associate with fear and anxiety. It may be a threatening environment for them where they feel unsafe and at risk, and this may be detrimental to their health and wellbeing.

It is difficult to estimate how many people in the UK are homeless; this is primarily due to the hidden nature of the problem. Arrivals into large cities and towns make estimating numbers difficult; some people drift in and out of hostels or other accommodation whereas others drift in and out of 'sleeping rough'. Estimating data outside large cities and towns such as London is less robust. The state of 'homelessness' can be temporary and episodic.

In the main, a person is homeless as defined in law (Homelessness Act 2002) if he or she has:

- no accommodation that he or she is entitled to occupy
- accommodation that is available, but it is unreasonable for him or her to continue to occupy, e.g. because of the risk of violence
- accommodation that he or she is entitled to occupy and it is reasonable to continue to occupy, but is not available to occupy.

It is a mistake to think that homelessness occurs or has occurred only to people who live on the streets or to those who are 'sleeping rough'. The scale of the problem extends beyond this common misconception. Most people who are homeless are families or single people. They may be staying with others, e.g. with friends or relatives, or in temporary accommodation. This can also be detrimental to an individual's health and wellbeing (Diaz, 2005).

Despite the difficulties associated with the ability to quantify the numbers of homeless people, there are some data available. Data from various sources are provided on a quarterly basis about the numbers of households that approach local authorities, and those that are given assistance if they meet the requirements stated in legislation that are associated with homelessness, e.g. the Housing (Homeless Persons) Act 1996 and the amended Homelessness Act 2002.

Think

Despite the data that the Government produces, why do you think these data may not reflect a true account of the situation regarding homeless people?

The following are some of the reasons why the data collected may not be a comprehensive measure of all instances of homelessness:

- There may be a number of people who are legally defined as homeless but may not approach their local authority for assistance.
- People may move from one form of temporary accommodation to another.
- Some may stay with friends.
- The collation of data comes from various sources and the reliability of those sources may be questionable.

Problems associated with homelessness

The most comprehensive survey of the problems of homeless people in the UK was published in 2004 (St Mungo's, 2004). This large-scale survey considered the experiences and challenges faced by 1534 homeless people. Table 10.4 provides key data taken from the St Mungo's survey.

Table 10.5 outlines some specific problems associated with the older homeless population and the general homeless population.

Table 10.4   Key data taken from the older and general homeless population

Data from the older homeless population – those who are aged 50 years and over
• One in four (24%) homeless people is aged over 50 years • 36% of the people surveyed are parents and over half of them have no contact with their children • 74% have no next of kin • As well as their homelessness problem 43% have four or more other problems • Over 50% have problems associated with alcohol • 50% have physical problems • Nearly half of them have mental health problems
Data gathered from the general homeless population
• One in four has children and 44% of these have no contact with their children • 50% have no next of kin • 42% have four or more problems as well as being homeless

Source: adapted from adapted from St Mungo's (2004).

287

Table 10.5   Results from data taken from the older and general homeless population in relation to specific issues

Older homeless population	General homeless population
56% have problems with alcohol and 10% with drugs	37% have problems with alcohol and 36% with drugs
48% have mental health problems	40% have mental health problems
47% have problems related to their physical health	23% have problems related to their physical health
4% have learning disability	3% have learning disability
Both groups have problems associated with: • Educational needs • Behaviour (e.g. challenging behaviour, social exclusion) • Relationships (e.g. domestic violence, relationship breakdown) • Employment/unemployment	

Source: adapted from St Mungo's (2004).

The causes of homelessness

Homelessness is often the result of complex interactions between structural and personal factors. They are not exclusively related to housing, and there is no single event that results in homelessness. Events associated with a number of unresolved issues accumulate and this can often result in or lead to homelessness (Shelter, 2007). Structural factors can be related to the state of the economy, legislation, social trends and the state of the national housing system (Diaz, 2005).

Inclination towards homelessness has been shown to be related to having had or experienced an institutional background, e.g. having been in care, the armed forces or prison (approximately a third of offenders lose their housing on imprisonment according to the Office of the Deputy Prime Minister (ODPM, 2005), having experienced family breakdown, sexual and/or physical abuse in childhood or adolescence, or a previous experience of family homelessness. Family conflict is the most common starting point for homelessness (Shelter, 2007). Factors associated with drug and alcohol misuse, difficulties at school, poor educational attainment, poor physical and mental health, and involvement in criminal acts from an early age also play a key role in a person's vulnerability to becoming homeless (Diaz, 2005).

Anderson (2001) points out that low income, unemployment and poverty are universal factors. The unemployed person is unable to pay the mortgage or rent. A result of having a low income can also be an inability to rehouse. Having no fixed address makes finding employment difficult, if not impossible, resulting in further financial hardship – this cycle becomes difficult to break.

The impact of homelessness

Disempowerment, isolation and poverty are the consequences of homelessness. Those who find themselves homeless may find that they are cut off from social support – formal and informal – as well as access to education and health.

Poor housing and homelessness have been recognised as significant causes of ill-health (St Mungo's, 2008) Data have already demonstrated that those who are homeless also have poor physical and mental health (DH, 2010a). Those who sleep on the street experience the most significant effects of poor health; however, the health of children and other adults is also affected by homelessness. The health-related factors in Table 10.6 are associated with being homeless.

Homeless people can often face major barriers in accessing health services, and their life circumstances can mean that they are among those most in need of treatment and care. Homeless people may often leave issues associated with their health untreated until they reach a crisis point, and then they need to rely on treatment and care at accident and emergency departments; alternatively, they may seek assistance at other primary health services, e.g. walk-in centres presenting with multiple and entrenched problems. This combination of events can make health problems more expensive to treat; hospital and accident and emergency waiting lists become longer and can lead to people being less able to support themselves and their families in their accommodation. Local authorities and health services must work together to provide accessible and appropriate services if health inequalities and homelessness are to be tackled. The Department of Health (2011) have provided best practice guidance for those involved in delivering primary health services to homeless and vulnerable people.

Addressing the health needs of homeless people

Traditionally health visitors have been seen as working with families with young children. However, they have a much wider public health role, e.g. working to empower specific groups of people, such as those who are homeless. Health visitors can lead innovative work with homeless people, aiming to assess health needs, improve access to all services, particularly health services, and promote healthy lifestyles.

Table 10.6   Health-related factors associated with being homeless and socially excluded

High prevalence of latent TB among homeless people
A considerable proportion of problematic drug users will have chronic physical health problems such as hepatitis C and cardiovascular pathologies
Self reported chest pain, respiratory problems more prevalent in traveller population 'compared with a similarly deprived comparator sample'
Alcohol misusers are more likely to have diabetes than those not misusing alcohol
63% of women in prostitution experience violence
Being in care leads to 20% higher likelihood of depression at age 33
Malnourished patients stay in hospital for much longer, are three times as likely to develop complications during surgery and have a higher mortality rate

Source: adapted from Department of Health (2010a).

Health visitors work in partnership with a wide range of health and community professionals to evaluate the health needs of individuals, families and communities, and then plan and implement strategies to meet them.

Most health visitors working with homeless people are involved in influencing policy in their local areas. The health visitors' public health approach can enable them to be at the interface between relevant services, such as housing, environmental health and the voluntary sector, being proactive in raising awareness of the difficulties experienced by homeless people in accessing both mainstream and specialist services (DH, 2010a).

When discharging homeless patients, hospitals should have in place formal discharge policies, thereby ensuring that homeless people are identified on admission and relevant health and homelessness agencies notified when discharge is imminent (ODPM, 2005). Good practice can be achieved when there is a clear understanding between hospitals and service providers (e.g. social workers and primary care teams) on how appropriate and timely referral and joint working between agencies can be established.

The vast majority of homeless people in the UK are men (Dandeker et al, 2005). Men in general face a number of problems when attempting to access health-care services. For homeless men this is exacerbated even further. Health provision in its current format needs to be addressed in order to provide appropriate and responsive care for this already marginalised and vulnerable group in society (both male and female).

Stereotyping and prejudice must cease if the marginalisation associated with homelessness is to be reduced. All health-care professionals in all health-care settings must address their own attitudes towards homeless people in society. Service provision, using a creative and innovative approach, needs to reflect the needs of this group of the population.

People who have offended

In 1999 the Government produced a joint policy (the policy was devised by the Joint Prison Services and NHS Executive Working Group, 1999) concerning the development and modernisation of primary care in prisons. The policy set out to place primary care provision for people who have offended within the context of the wider NHS primary care agenda. The transfer of responsibility for the health care of people who have offended in England and Wales to the NHS has now occurred as a result of the joint policy. Some prisons work in clusters, with local primary care trusts making decisions about how best to deliver services locally. Over time the provision of health care has gradually moved from prison officers to registered nurses.

In 2000 HM Prison Service and the NHS Executive produced its deliberation built on the previous work of the Joint Prison Services and NHS Executive Working Group (1999), which led to the establishment of a formal relationship between the NHS and the Prison Service, with the prime aim (in England and Wales) of improving the health of people who have offended (DH, 2000). All three prison services in the UK have made strategic decisions to provide health care that reflects what is provided in the wider community. The main resource for health-care provision within the prison services now relies on the registered nurse (RCN, 2009b).

The prison population

The prison population in England and Wales, including those held in police cells, was at a record high of 85 494 prisoners on 1 October 2010. The Scottish prison population reached a record high of 8214 on 8 July 2009 (House of Commons Library, 2011).

The prison population in England and Wales has increased steadily over the past century and surpassed 80 000 for the first time in December 2006. Of the population in prison custody at the end of March 2011, 79 per cent comprised sentenced males aged 18 or older whereas 14 per cent were on remand either awaiting trial or sentence. A higher proportion of the sentenced female population is now serving sentences for violence against the person offences rather than drug offences, the latter historically being the offence group that accounted for the highest proportion of this population. Approximately 4250 females were in prison at the end of March 2011, 1 per cent lower than the number in prison a year earlier, accounting for 5 per cent of the prison population. Over the past decade the number of female prisoners has increased by almost a third, a slightly higher rate increase than in the male population.

In 2009–10, the average daily population in Scottish prisons totalled 7964, an increase of 1.7 per cent when compared with the previous year, and the highest average annual level ever recorded. The female prison population was 424, 5.3 per cent of the total, an increase of 3 per cent on the previous year. Over the 10-year period, January 2000 to October 2009, the average daily female prison population has doubled.

The health-care needs of people who have offended

The health of the prison population is the concern not only of those who work in prisons, but also of all those who are involved in health care. Each day 10 per cent of the prison population report sick. This is almost eight times more than the numbers of the general population who visit their GP every day. There may be several reasons for this. It may be the result of more general problems, e.g. the inability of some vulnerable offenders to cope with prison life. Two-thirds of inmate consultations involve a nurse or a health-care officer.

The main reasons why offenders seek consultations are associated with self-harm, diabetes, asthma, communicable diseases and drug addiction. Sexually transmitted infections and HIV are far more prevalent in the prison population than in the general population. Patients within prisons have higher than average rates of mental illness and the most common, according to the RCN (2009b), are:

- Psychosis
- Depression

- Suicide
- Self-harm.

Mental health issues

It has been cited by the RCN (2009b) that people who have offended have very high rates of mental ill health; recent estimates suggest that up to 90 per cent of all those in custody will have some form of mental health need. The care of patients with mental health problems in prisons does not always meet the same standards experienced by patients in the NHS. There are a number of inequalities and variations in the standards of health services that offenders receive across the UK and also within the four countries of the UK. Reed and Lyne (2000) have demonstrated that the quality of services for people with a mental illness who have offended fell far below the standards in the NHS. They report that the prisoners' (patients') lives were unacceptably restricted and therapy was limited.

291

Investment in prison health care (and this includes the provision of mental health services) has risen from £118 million in 2002–3 to £200 million in 2006–7 (House of Commons, 2007). Fifty-six per cent of young men and 73 per cent of young women reported that the quality of prison health care was either good or very good (Parke, 2009).

All people who have offended are entitled to the same standard of care as that available to the wider community. Prison Order 3200 (HM Prison Service or HMPS, 2003) states that working in partnership with the NHS the Prison Service have a duty to ensure that offenders are able to access health services equivalent to those that the general public receives from the NHS. Prisons have to develop needs-based health services in partnership with local primary care trusts (PCTs) and other NHS agencies that provide effective evidence-based care to individuals who have offended and the whole prison population.

In England responsibility to ensure that people who have offended receive acceptable health care lies with the Department of Health (services are commissioned by the local PCT). In Scotland the Scottish Prison Service is responsible for prison health. South Eastern Health and Social Care Trust is responsible for prison health care in Northern Ireland. Local health boards in which prisons are located in Wales are responsible for providing health care to people who have offended in Wales.

Providing nursing care in prisons

Adults and young people who are socially excluded experience a high proportion of health inequalities, are in contact more with the criminal justice system, and are more likely to experience mental health problems or learning disabilities or to have difficulties with drugs and alcohol. For many of these people contact with the criminal justice system is their first point of contact with health- and social care professionals (DH, 2009a). Contact at that point with health-care professionals such as nurses is vital in addressing their needs.

A number of advances have been made to achieve better health care outcomes for people who have offended over the last 10 years; the provision of health care in prison has now become a mainstream NHS service. There is a more detailed understanding of the health- and social care needs of the general prison population, but to ensure that the right treatment is given at the right time an offender's health-care needs must be identified as soon as possible (DH, 2009a), and should also include those prisoners with HIV and other diseases linked with HIV, for example, and, in particular, hepatitis C and tuberculosis.

Primary care provision in prisons should comprise the following principles of good practice. These principles provide markers for the development of primary care within prisons:

- *Fairness* – services should not vary widely in range across the country
- *Accessibility* – services should be reasonably accessible to people who need them regardless of their age, sex, ethnicity or health status
- *Responsiveness* – services should reflect users' needs and preferences, and the health and social needs of the local population
- *Efficiency* – services should be based on research evidence of clinical effectiveness and resources should be used efficiently.

Primary care in the prison service should strive to integrate with the development and planning of services that are occurring within the local PCT. Good primary care provision within prisons should eventually become as good as primary care within the community. Just as good primary care in the community integrates with all other health-care activity, so too must primary care in prisons. The interface with other areas of health care is demonstrated in Figure 10.3.

The role of the nurse is complex and multifaceted, and is the same for the nurse working within the prison service. The nurse may need to develop new skills in dealing with the complex needs of the patient in prison. However, he or she must always be cognisant of the fact that the tenets of the professional code (NMC, 2008) apply equally to patients in prisons who, regardless of their conviction, require nursing skills.

As stated above, patients in prisons should be entitled to the same level of health care as that provided to society at large. Those who are physically ill, addicted, mentally ill or disabled have the right to be treated, counselled and nursed to the same standards provided to patients within the NHS.

Top tips

There is overwhelming evidence to support the contention that men's health is much poorer than it need be. Many men die prematurely. Average male life expectancy at birth is just 75.6 years, 5 years less than for women. Public health services must ensure that they are gender sensitive and responsive to the needs of men and women. This is a requirement of the law.

Homosexuals

The term 'homosexual' means a person who is sexually attracted to people of the same sex. Homosexual individuals include males (gays) and females (lesbians). Kinsey et al (1948) used a homosexual rating scale in an attempt to measure sexual orientation (Figure 10.4).

It is evident from the early work of Kinsey et al (1948) that homosexuality can for some be a complex, dynamic and fluid concept. This aspect of the chapter discusses issues that predominantly concern gay men; however, the issues discussed may also apply to lesbians and members of the transsexual and transgender communities.

Health-care needs of gay men do not differ significantly from those of their heterosexual counterparts. However, there are some issues that are specifically related to gay men that the nurse must understand if he or she is to provide effective, high-quality health care, i.e. health care that considers the gay man from a social, physical and emotional perspective (Peate, 2006). The health of men generally is seen as problematic (White and Cash, 2003) and this would also apply to gay men.

The first point of contact with the NHS for many people is with the primary care services; primary care providers are key gatekeepers to health advice and services. Keogh et al (2004) have considered the treatment that gay men receive in primary care – general practice. They have concluded that

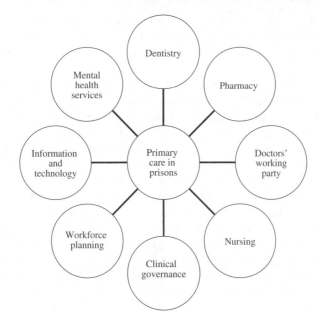

Figure 10.3 Primary care and the wider health-care agenda. Source: Department of Health and HMP (2002).

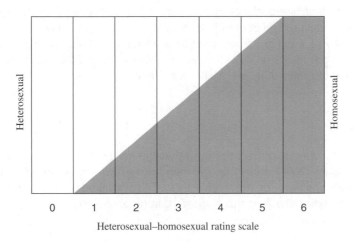

Figure 10.4 The Kinsey scale. Source: Kinsey et al (1948).
0 – Exclusively heterosexual
1 – Predominantly heterosexual, only incidentally homosexual
2 – Predominantly heterosexual, but more than incidentally homosexual
3 – Equally heterosexual and homosexual
4 – Predominantly homosexual, but more than incidentally heterosexual
5 – Predominantly homosexual, only incidentally heterosexual
6 – Exclusively homosexual

approximately a third of gay and bisexual men in that study who were registered with a GP said that the staff did not know that they had sex with men and that they would be unhappy if the practice did know. These findings appear to capture the challenges that some gay men may face in accessing and using health-care provision.

The Department of Health (2007) notes that discrimination, stigma and prejudice exist towards lesbian, gay, bisexual and transgender people. The NMC (2008) points out that each registered nurse, midwife or specialist community public health nurse must respect the patient or client as an individual; to do otherwise would be tantamount to professional misconduct.

Within the gay community there are groups within groups, e.g. gay youths. These youths are a marginalised group, and often there is little opportunity for them to voice their unique needs – they are voiceless. This voicelessness is confounded by the fact that there may be a lack of recognition or acceptance of gay men by some health-care providers, who may harbour homophobic attitudes and are unaware of the health-care needs of the vulnerable gay male adolescent.

It has been suggested that, in relation to health-care needs, lesbians and bisexual women are invisible (Hunt and Fish, 2008). Many gay men do not have the necessary confidence to be open and honest about their sexuality, even if this is relevant to their health care. Some gay men fear that the nurse may react in a hostile and judgemental manner and some gay men have experienced hostile and judgemental care. Harbouring such judgemental and hostile attitudes may marginalise and isolate the patient from experiencing good-quality care and support. The result of the inequalities experienced by gay men include:

- Mental health problems, e.g. higher levels of depression, suicide and self-harm (King and McKeown, 2003)
- Problems associated with sexual health, e.g. a high prevalence and a high incidence of sexually transmitted infections, such as syphilis
- There seems to be a higher incidence of eating disorders among gay men (Bloomfield, 2005)
- Substance misuse, e.g. use and abuse of alcohol (Alcohol Concern, 2004)
- The effects of bullying, e.g. harassment relating to sexual orientation such as homophobic remarks or jokes, offensive comments relating to a person's sexual orientation, threats to disclose a person's sexual orientation to others (King and McKeown, 2003).

Defining terms

From the outset the nurse must respect the term that the male chooses to use in order to identify his individual sexuality. Jones (2004) states that gay men are men who have sex with men, but it must be noted that not all men who have sex with men are gay. This should be borne in mind by the nurse when working with men and when choosing the language that he or she uses.

Attitudes of health-care professionals

Homophobia in the health service can make health-care provision inaccessible to gay people. Douglas-Scott et al (2004) state that there is widespread homophobia among health-care professionals, which has a negative impact on a gay man's health outcomes.

An unwillingness to disclose sexuality to a health-care professional because of a fear of reprisal or disapproval can create difficulties for those gay men who wish to discuss their specific health-care needs in relation to their sexuality. Two barriers to effective communication and possible treatment were noted. First, despite the fact that all the participants in the study had come out – or revealed their sexuality – in many areas of their lives, there was much anxiety and a fear of stigmatisation in relation to doing so, and this was specifically related to primary care. The second barrier was associated with the assumption of practitioners (in the primary care practice environments) that all their patients were heterosexual; there was little evidence of any awareness or understanding of gay and bisexual men.

Nurses must address some of the root causes associated with marginalisation, including accessibility to health-care services. Failure to do this may perpetuate the exclusion of gay men. The everyday occurrence of homophobia, be it implicit or explicit, will affect the gay man's self-confidence, self-worth and emotional wellbeing. Homophobia in nursing can be an extreme violation of the individual's human right to receive care that is adequate, professional and compassionate (Christensen, 2005).

Contemporary public health

Contemporary or new public health adopts a population approach. Jacelon (2009), in an American text, makes a comparison between home nursing and public health nursing (Table 10.7). Jacelon (2009) makes the point that the roles of home visiting nurse and public health nurse are similar, but also have differences; roles and responsibilities are continuing and will continue to blur between both aspects of service

Table 10.7   Similarities between home nursing and public health

Similarities		
Setting		Care is provided in a person's home or in community environment
Control and environment		Nurse is a guest; patient is an active participant in care decisions
		Control is held by the patient
Broad goals		Public health and home nursing services aim to promote, maintain and restore health for individuals and communities
Differences	**Public health**	**Home nursing**
Focus of intervention	Population	Individual/family
Case load acquisition	Case finding in community at large	Referral route
Interventions	Continuous	Episodic
Orientation	Primary prevention	Secondary prevention
		Rehabilitation

Source: adapted from Jacelon (2009).

provision. This could be adapted to the UK where all nurses share the common goals of promoting, maintaining and restoring health (NMC, 2008). Over 10 years ago, Craig and Lindsay (2000) suggested a new 'public health' movement, one that brings together nursing and public health.

There is a desire to ensure a balance between preventive and curative health services and this is becoming evident in policy and protocol. Contemporary approaches are recognising a population approach that contains elements of health promotion, health improvement and health protection each as important as the other.

Naidoo and Wills (2005) consider the two terms public health and health promotion and advocate that it may be appropriate to use them together in the form of a single term. The value in retaining the two terms in the sphere of public health is that it recognises that health promotion is derived from a focus on individuals and public health emerges out of a community/population approach, paying tribute to the broader term 'public health' and its overall role in the new public health.

Think

Take some time to think about your practice learning opportunities and describe some of the specific public health initiatives that you may have seen nurses and other health-care professionals carrying out.

There is a strong possibility that you might have identified some of the following:

- Smoking cessation sessions
- Screening for bowel cancer or other diseases
- Immunisation sessions
- Lifestyle advice
- Involvement in issues related to the effects of poverty
- Working to reduce infectious diseases (advising in infection prevention and control activity in the home and wider environs)
- Providing advice on how to enhance health and wellbeing
- Accident prevention activity with individuals and groups of people.

The current Government's White Paper *Healthy Lives, Healthy People: Our strategy for public health in England* sets out a bold vision for a reformed public health system in England (DH, 2010b). The White Paper establishes a focus on upstream disease prevention and the use of evidence to determine how best to change behaviour, whereby root causes of problems are identified and actions put in place to address them, advocating a preventive, more proactive approach.

The Welsh Assembly Government is working to develop *Our Health Future*, a strategic framework for public health in Wales. The aim is to improve the health and wellbeing of the population, not just by adding to the quality and length of life but also by making the system fairer and by reducing inequalities between different parts of Wales and different groups of people. The Welsh Assembly Government is working with the NHS, local government, voluntary organisations and the education sector to develop *Our Healthy Future*.

Investing for Health (Department of Health, Social Services and Patient Safety, 2002) is the public health strategy of the Northern Ireland Executive and aims to improve the health of the people of Northern Ireland and to reduce inequalities in health. It sets out a broad range of areas where new and concerted action could make a significant difference to health and wellbeing. Three priority groups are identified:

- Very young people and children
- Young people
- Older people.

In line with best practice a settings approach is proposed and homes, schools, workplaces and communities are identified as priority settings. As part of an integrated lifestyle and life skills programme the priority topics identified include the following:

- Smoking
- Physical activity
- Eating for health
- Harm related to alcohol and drug misuse
- Mental health
- Sexual health
- Accidents.

297

Better Health, Better Care (Scottish Government, 2007) is the Scottish Government's strategic public health plan. The aim of the plan is to help the people of Scotland sustain and improve their health, especially in disadvantaged communities, ensuring better, local and faster access to health care. *Better Health, Better Care* is a significant statement by the Scottish Government towards enabling a healthier Scotland; the main components of health improvement in Scotland will focus on tackling health inequality and improving the quality of health care.

Healthy Lives, Healthy People (DH, 2010b) is a new approach to public health and a commitment across local authorities and the public health professions to improving the health of the public across the life span. The aim is to encourage local authorities and public health professionals to plan and build local relationships and partnerships that will be essential to implementing the new public health system; this brings closer the reality of services in health- and social care sectors.

The changes to service provision proposed in *Healthy Lives, Healthy People* are a response to the challenges facing the public's health, e.g. there are increased challenges with obesity with two out of three adults being overweight or obese; also inequalities in health persist and remain widespread, with people in the poorest areas living on average 7 years less than those in the richest areas, and spending up to 17 more years living with poor health. Major health threats are still evident and range from the risk of outbreaks or new pandemics to the potential impact of terrorist incidents. As a result of these challenges a new approach is required that reaches out to local communities, systematically underpinned by public health expertise; these are the central elements of public health nursing.

A reformed public health system for England will see local authorities taking on new responsibilities for public health. This will allow new opportunities for community engagement and to develop holistic solutions to health and wellbeing, embracing the full range of local services, including health, housing, leisure, planning, transport, employment and social care. It will be the responsibility of directors of public health to lead this work. Local authorities will be supported by a new integrated public health service and this will be known as Public Health England, which will drive delivery of improved outcomes in health and wellbeing and protect the population from threats to health.

It is envisaged that Public Health England will bring together in one body the diverse range of public health expertise currently spread across the health system. One of its key functions will be to ensure access to expert advice, intelligence and evidence, providing a focus for the development of new approaches, including adopting insights from behavioural sciences, and provide an expert and responsive health protection service. Public health will be supported by Government, along with the resources to ensure that the focus on public health interventions is maintained. The Government will continue with a commitment to reduce health inequalities as a priority for all parts of the public health system. The Marmot Review (2010) will be the basis on which the wider determinants of health will be addressed; this will complement the role of the NHS to reduce inequalities in access to and outcome from health services.

The Government is currently in the process of setting out how they expect the reformed public health system to work including:

- Clarification of roles – the role of local authorities and the Director of Public Health in health improvement, health protection and population health care
- Identifying who is responsible for commissioning the different public health services
- Addressing issues associated with mandatory service provision and local authorities
- Establishing Public Health England.

There are a variety of other developments that will be required to implement this new public health policy initiative, and engagement with a number of key stakeholders from local government, public health and the NHS will be required to develop realistic policy and implementation solutions.

A comprehensive workforce strategy will need to be published, which will involve working with local authorities and public health professionals to ensure that staff are fit for purpose and prepared in such a manner as to ensure public safety.

The RCN (2011b) has called for sustained and structured nursing involvement during the design, development and delivery of the reforms to health-care services and health-care commissioning. Included in this must be designated nursing posts on commissioning consortia boards, Public Health England, and local health and wellbeing boards, because nurses have a pivotal role to play in helping to close the gaps between hospital and community and health- and social care settings, as the White Paper aims to do. Doing this will ensure the delivery of integrated and seamless care to patients and help to deliver the vision of the Government's new public health policy.

Conclusions

Public health nursing is not a new discipline; it has its origins in the poor laws of the 1800s, and is currently seeing a resurgence. There is a clear commitment by the Government to ensure that the health of the nation is closely aligned with public health initiatives and preventive care. Nurses are seen as partners in delivering public health services. Nursing staff perform public health activities in many contexts and at every level of health care.

Nurses carry out their work in public health departments in primary care trusts, prisons and with homeless people; they have a public health clinical role, such as specialist alcohol nurse, sexual health or travel health, and deliver public health messages as part of their everyday care provision or at 'teachable moments' (i.e. when patients are more open to public health messages in light of their present health condition) (RCN, 2009a). Nurses perform exceptional roles in schools, workplaces, the Health Protection Agency and primary health care settings. The new public health (advocated by the current Government) must ensure that nursing expertise and experience are fully recognised and applied within the new public health system.

There are certain sociocultural determinants or factors that can influence a person's health and wellbeing, in either a positive or a negative direction. Sociocultural factors are wide and varied; they can be considered from a social, economic, environmental and political perspective. What they are and the effects that they have on individuals are also wide and varied. Being aware of these determinants may help the nurse provide care that is individual and holistic.

Marginalised or oppressed societies are societies that nurses come into contact with on a day-to-day basis. Three particular groups have been discussed in this chapter to illustrate the effects of marginalisation on those who are oppressed. Marginalisation and the modes in which it operates are complex. It can result in social isolation and withdrawal, leading to low self-esteem and lack of self-confidence.

In an attempt to reduce the effects of marginalisation on the individual and the wider society, the nurse is encouraged to provide antidiscriminatory care. It has been noted that the provision of such care is complex and always hard to accomplish; however, the nurse should strive to achieve this. One of the root causes of marginalisation and discrimination is an unwillingness or an inability to adapt services to meet the needs of those groups who are marginalised and oppressed.

Marginalised and oppressed individuals deserve good-quality nursing care. This should not depend on whim and fancy; it must be based on a concerted effort by all agencies and health-care professionals involved in the patient's care in an attempt to address the inequalities in health.

The motivation required to provide care to oppressed people should be based on a desire to see them treated fairly and also the knowledge that the care provided is successful, both socially and financially, from an individual and community perspective.

Activity

Attempt the following 10 multiple choice questions related to public health to test your knowledge. The answers can be found at the back of this book, in the chapter called 'Activity Answers'.

1. The study of health-event patterns in a society is called:
   a. Technology
   b. Biography
   c. Epidemiology
   d. Biology

2. Health-care provision in English prisons is the responsibility of:
   a. The prison officers' union
   b. Primary care trusts
   c. The Prison Reform Trust
   d. The Koestler Trust

3. Homophobia is related to:
   a. A hatred of gay men
   b. A hatred of gay women
   c. A hatred of lesbian, gay, bisexual and transgender people
   d. A hatred of transsexuals

4. The Ottawa Charter is:
   a. A European-wide initiative for health promotion
   b. A Canadian-wide initiative promoting healthy lifestyle
   c. A worldwide strategy for global health promotion
   d. A World Health Organization strategy to reduce mortality associated with diabetes mellitus

5. The Acheson Report was produced in:
   a. 1999
   b. 1988

    c. 2001
    d. 1948

6. Health intelligence is:
   a. A term associated with the collection of information about health
   b. A method used by health visitors during developmental testing
   c. The measure that the Government uses to assess the health the nation
   d. The methods employed by practice nurses to assess the needs of a group of patients

7. Life expectancy is:
   a. The age that a person reaches when he or she is able to vote
   b. The number of years that a person is expected to live after major surgery
   c. The time lived free from ill-health or disease
   d. The number of years that a person can expect to live based on statistical average

8. Homeless people are:
   a. Likely to die earlier than the rest of the population
   b. Prone to mental ill health
   c. Marginalised
   d. All of the above

9. Self-determination is:
   a. The ability to make decisions for oneself without external influence
   b. A term used to describe a change in self-esteem
   c. The behaviour displayed by a person who is in a coma
   d. The ability to recover quickly after a major life event

10. A White Paper is:
   a. A statement released by the NMC
   b. The WHO's declaration of intent
   c. The Government's statement of policy intention
   d. All of the above

References

Acheson D (1988) *Public Health in England: The Report of the Committee of Inquiry into the Future Development of the Public Health Function*. Command 289. London: HMSO.

Alcohol Concern (2004) *Gay and Lesbian People's Fact Sheet*. London: Alcohol Concern.

Anderson I (2001) *Pathways through Homelessness: Towards a dynamic analysis*. Stirling: University of Stirling.

Bloomfield S (2005) *Eating Disorders and Men: The facts*. Norwich: Eating Disorders Association.

Burton M, Kagan C (2004) Marginalization. In: Nelson, G, Prilleltensky I (eds), *Community Psychology: In pursuit of liberation and well-being*. Basingstoke: Palgrave, pp 291–308.

Christensen M (2005) Homophobia in nursing: A concept analysis. *Nursing Forum* **40**(2): 60–71.

Coverdale G (2009) Public health nursing. In: Thornbory G (ed.), *Public Health Nursing. A textbook for health visitors, school nurses and occupational health nurses*. Oxford: Wiley, pp 21–45.

Craig PM, Lindsay GM (2000) *Nursing for Public Health: Population-based care*. Edinburgh: Churchill Livingstone.

Dandeker C, Thomas S, Dolan M, Chapman F, Ross J (2005) *Feasibility Study on the Extent, Causes, Impact and Costs of Rough Sleeping and Homelessness Amongst Ex-service Personnel in a Sample of Local Authorities in England*. London: The King's Centre for Military Health Research.

Department of Health (2000) *Report of the Working Group on Nursing in Prisons: Summary and key recommendations*. London: Department of Health.

Department of Health (2007) *Reducing Health Inequalities for Lesbian, Gay, Bisexual and Trans People*. London: Department of Health.

Department of Health (2009a) *Improving Health, Supporting Justice: The National Delivery Plan of the Health and Criminal Justice Programme Board*. London: Department of Health.

Department of Health (2010a) *Inclusion Health: Improving primary care for socially excluded people*. London: Department of Health.

Department of Health (2010b) *Healthy Lives, Healthy People: Our strategy for public health in England*. London: Department of Health.

Department of Health (2011) *Health Visitor Implementation Plan 2011–15 A Call to Action*. London: Department of Health.

Department of Health/Department for Children, Schools and Families (2007) *Implementation Plan for Reducing Health Inequalities in Infant Mortality: A Good Practice Guide*. London: Department of Health.

Department of Health and Her Majesty's Prison Service (2002) *Developing and Modernising Primary Care in Prisons*. London: Department of Health.

Department of Health, Social Services and Paient Safety (2002) *Investing for Health – Report 2002*. Belfast: DHSSPS.

Diaz R (2005) *Housing and Homelessness*. London: Shelter.

Douglas-Scott S, Pringle A, Lumsdaine C (2004) *Sexual Exclusion – Homophobia and Inequalities: A Review*. London: UK Gay Men's Health Network.

Elliott L, Crombie IK, Irvine L, Cantrell J, Taylor J (2004) The effectiveness of public health nursing: the problems and solutions in carrying out a review of systematic reviews. *Journal of Advanced Nursing* **45**: 117–125.

Haggart M (2003) Public health: the professional response. In: Costello, J, Haggart M (eds), *Public Health and Society*. Basingstoke: Palgrave, pp 151–168.

Her Majesty's Prison Service (2003) PSO, 3200. *Health Promotion*. London: HMPS.

House of Commons (2007) *Hansard*. 19th June c1709W.

House of Commons Library (2011) Prison Population Statistics [online]. Available at: www.parliament.uk/briefing-papers/SN04334 (accessed July 2011).

Hunt R, Fish J (2008) *Prescription for Change. Lesbian and Bisexual Women's Health Check*. London: Stonewall.

Jacelon CS (2009) Home healthcare. In: Larsen PD, Lubkin IM (eds), *Chronic Illness, Impact and Interventions*, 7th edn. London: Jones & Bartlett, pp 475–496.

Joint Prison Services and NHS Executive Working Group (1999) *The Future Organisation of Prison Health Care*. London: Department of Health.

Jones M (2004) Working with gay men. In: *The Manual for Sexual Advisors*. London: Society of Sexual Health Advisors, pp 326–338.

Keogh P, Weatherburn P, Henderson L, Reid D, Dodds C, Hickson F (2004) *Doctoring Gay Men: Exploring the contribution of general practice*. London: Sigma Research.

King M, McKeown E (2003) *Mental Health and Social Wellbeing of Gay Men, Lesbians and Bisexuals in England and Wales*. London: MIND.

Kinsey AC, Pomeroy WB, Martin CE (1948) *Sexual Behaviour in the Human Male*. Philadelphia, PA: Saunders.

Knai C (2009) What is public health? In: Thornbory G (ed.), *Public Health Nursing. A textbook for health visitors, school nurses and occupational health nurses*. Oxford: Wiley, pp 1–20.

Larsen PD (2009) Models of care. In: Larsen PD, Lubkin IM (eds), *Chronic Illness, Impact and Interventions*, 7th edn. London: Jones & Bartlett, pp 459–473.

LeMone P, Burke K, Bauldoff G (2011) *Fundamentals of Nursing: The art and science of nursing care*, 11th edn. Philadelphia, PA: Lippincott.

Leonard P (1984) *Personality and Ideology: Towards a materialist understanding of the individual*. London: Macmillan.

Loveday I, Linsley P (2011) Implementing interventions: developing care to individuals and communities. In: Linsley P, Kane, R, Owen S (eds), *Nursing for Public Health. Promotion, Principles and Practice*. Oxford: Oxford University Press, pp 134–143.

Marmot Review (2010) *Fair Society Healthy Lives. The Marmot Review*. Available at: www.ucl.ac.uk/marmotreview (accessed July 2011).

301

Naidoo J, Wills J (2005) *Public Health and Health Promotion: Developing Practice*, 2nd edn. Edinburgh: Baillière Tindall.

Nursing and Midwifery Council (2004) *Standards for Proficiency for Specialist Community Public Health Nursing*. London: NMC. Available at: www.nmcuk.org/Documents/Standards/nmcStandardsofProficiencyforSpecialist CommunityPublicHealthNurses.pdf (accessed July 2011).

Nursing and Midwifery Council (2008) *The Code: Standards of conduct, performance and ethics for nurses and midwives*. London: NMC.

Nursing and Midwifery Council (2010) *Standards for Pre registration Nursing Education*. London: NMC. Available at: http://standards.nmc-uk.org/PublishedDocuments/Standards%20for%20pre-registration%20nursing%20 education%2016082010.pdf (accessed July 2011).

Office of the Deputy Prime Minister (2005) *Homelessness and Health*. Information Sheet Number 4: *Hospital Discharge*. London: ODPM.

Parke S (2009) *HM Inspector of Prisons and Youth Justice Board, Children and Young People in Custody 2006–2008, an Analysis of the Experiences of 15–18 year olds in Prison*. London: HM Inspectorate of Prisons.

Peate I (2006) Caring for gay men 1: Specific health needs. *Practice Nurse* **17**(2): 64–68.

Plaistow L (2009) Public health nursing-strategic direction for future development. In: Sines D, Saunders, M, Forbes-Burford J (eds), *Community Health Care Nursing*, 4th edn. Oxford: Wiley pp 296–310.

Reed JL, Lyne M (2000) Inpatient care of mentally ill people in prison: Results of a year's programme of semi- structured inspections. *British Medical Journal* **320**: 1031–1034.

Royal College of Nursing (2009a) *Nurses as Partners in Delivering Public Health*. London: RCN.

Royal College of Nursing (2009b) *Health and Nursing Care in the Criminal Justice Service. RCN Guidance for Nursing Staff*. London: RCN.

Royal College of Nursing (2010) *Tuppence for the Doctor, Penny for the Nurse. Memories of public health nursing*. London: RCN.

Royal College of Nursing (2011a) *The RCN's UK Position on Health Visiting in the Early Years*. London: RCN.

Royal College of Nursing (2011b) *RCN Response to the Public Health White Paper Healthy Lives, Healthy People: Our strategy for public health in England*. London: RCN.

St Mungo's (2004) *St Mungo's Big Survey into the Problems and Lives of Homeless People*. London: St Mungo's.

St Mungo's (2008) *St Mungo's Health Strategy for Homeless People 2008–2011*. London: St Mungo's.

Scottish Government (2007) *Better Health, Better Care: Action plan*. Edinburgh: Scottish Government.

Shelter (2007) *Homelessness*. London: Shelter. Available at: http://england.shelter.org.uk/__data/assets/pdf_file/0007/66409/Homelessness_factsheet.pdf (accessed July 2011).

Skills for Health and the Public Health Resource Unit (2008) *Public Health Skills and Career Framework. Multidisciplinary/Multi-agency/Multi-professional*. Bristol: Skills for Health.

White A, Cash K (2003) *The State of Men's Health Across 17 European Countries*. Belgium: The European Men's Health Forum.

World Health Organization (2008) *Promoting Mental Health: Concepts, emerging evidence, practice*. Geneva: WHO.

11

Patient Safety

Aims and objectives

The aim of this chapter is to convey the important role that the nurse plays in maintaining and sustaining patient safety.

At the end of the chapter you will be able to:

1. Discuss the complex concept of patient safety
2. Champion patient safety and raise its profile
3. Explore the issues related to safe medicines management
4. Describe the principles of risk management
5. Begin to apply the concepts discussed to the practice setting
6. Appreciate the Nursing and Midwifery Council's requirements of student nurses

Quality assurance, clinical governance and risk management strategies are required to provide the public with protection in order to maintain a safe environment. Clinical governance and risk management strategies are key features of this chapter, which provides an understanding of the principles and policies used to maintain a safe environment. The need to recognise, and the appropriate way to report, situations that are potentially unsafe for patients and others are also discussed.

Clinical governance cannot be achieved in isolation. There are national structures in place that will support local developments and initiatives, e.g. the work undertaken by the Scottish Intercollegiate Guidelines Network (SIGN) and the National Institute for Health and Clinical Excellence (NICE); the role and function of these supporting structures are described. Clinical audit, a quality improvement process that has become a central aspect of clinical governance and the clinical audit cycle, is outlined.

Risk is an unavoidable aspect of all of our lives and this is also true when considering the provision of health care: mistakes and errors do unfortunately occur. The purpose and function of risk management and risk management strategies are briefly described. The safe and effective management of drug treatment is chosen as one aspect of clinical governance. Some practical tips are provided to minimise the likelihood of mistakes occurring when administering medicines.

This chapter draws on some of the content of Chapter 8 and describes the nurse's responsibility to apply relevant principles to ensure the safe and effective administration of therapeutic substances.

The Student's Guide to Becoming a Nurse, Second Edition. Ian Peate.
© 2012 John Wiley & Sons, Ltd. Published 2012 by John Wiley & Sons, Ltd.

Key terms

There is a need to define some of the terms used when discussing quality and risk management in relation to the provision of health-care services. This aspect of the chapter concentrates primarily on terms associated with and used within the field of quality assurance and clinical governance; it also considers the various definitions associated with risk management. Often quality and risk cannot be separated because each has implications for the other – they complement each other. An artificial split is made in this chapter to provide the reader with information.

Clinical governance

Clinical governance is integral to health care and patient safety is a top priority for all staff. There are other terms used alongside it, e.g.:

- Quality assurance
- Clinical audit
- Quality enhancement
- Clinical effectiveness
- Evidence-based practice.

Since its inception in 1948 the NHS has been reinvented in many ways. At its inception the NHS was a state-run entity – bureaucratic with highly centralised systems (Better Regulation Taskforce, 2001). The intention was to provide identical structures and functions for all of the organisations that comprised the NHS. The contemporary NHS aims to move to a more decentralised, innovative service with a clear remit to enhance and improve patient care. The new NHS is concerned with ensuring that structures and processes meet local needs, recognising and respecting diversity, while at the same time working with common definitions of good quality and good clinical care. The Department of Health (DH, 2010), in *Equity and Excellence: Liberating the NHS*, make good clinical care a central requirement and this is to be measured through outcomes.

The ethos of the NHS that was central to its setting up will nevertheless prevail. In 1948 hospital provision (at that stage the NHS was concerned only with hospital care) was to be made available for every citizen. The service was to be made available at the earliest moment, when the necessary provision was to be made regardless of any financial consideration (Beveridge, 1942). The NHS then was to be free to all at the point of provision.

The twenty-first-century NHS aspires to be a service that is responsive to individual and local needs, and as such must therefore decentralise its provision and be devolved. One way of making this move towards devolution is to change the way that health services are managed and run. Centralised services fail to provide care that is patient centred, and do not recognise that patients are individuals with local and individual needs. Care needs to be delivered in a meaningful manner to the people who pay for it – the patients and the public. The current Government are putting patients at the heart of the NHS: through an information revolution and greater choice and control, shared decision-making will become the norm – *no decision about me without me*.

The introduction of clinical governance in the late 1990s was seen as one way of achieving this meaningful approach to health-care provision. In 1997 *The New NHS: Modern and dependable* (DH, 1997) was produced with a plan to modernise health-care provision. Clinical governance was an integral part of the 10-year plan to improve the quality of care (DH, 1999). One key component of this document (a White Paper) was to bring about major improvements in the quality of care delivered to patients from a clinical perspective. For the first time statutory duties were enforced on NHS providers regarding the quality of care that they offer (DH, 2000b). A formal responsibility for quality has now been placed on every health organisation in the UK through arrangements for clinical governance at local level.

Clinical governance is central to quality. There are many different interpretations of what clinical governance means. Clinical governance can be defined as (Scally and Donaldson, 1998):

> A framework through which NHS organisations are accountable for continuously improving the quality of their services and safeguarding high standards of care by creating an environment in which excellence in clinical care will flourish.

Clinical governance can be described as doing the right thing at the right time to the right person in the right way. It is about all that you can do to enhance and make quality better.

The overall aim of clinical governance is to strengthen and build on existing systems of quality assurance across a range of services. Clinical governance has the ability to liberate and enable clinicians to lead the health-care agenda in order for patients to benefit. These opportunities bring with them added responsibility and increased accountability. Hammond (2010) points out that clinical governance aims to set clear standards, monitor implementation and publish results through periodic inspection; she also notes that the key components of clinical governance include the following:

305

- Ensuring patient safety
- Learning from mistakes
- Encouraging openness
- Sharing and maintaining good practice
- Continuing professional development.

Kehoe (2005) notes that clinical governance and the drive for clinical governance arose through untoward incidents, mainly medical in origin, such as the problems at Bristol. The Bristol inquiry was undertaken to investigate children's heart surgery at the Bristol Royal Infirmary between 1984 and 1995, and highlighted the importance of clinical governance (DH, 2002). Further serious incidents have since occurred, e.g. recently a number of deaths at Stepping Hospital, Greater Manchester associated with the issue of patient safety have again revealed breaches in security and safety in hospitals. Reports indicated that ampoules of saline were contaminated with insulin found in a store room close to ward areas at the hospital; it was an experienced senior ward nurse who raised the alarm after she noticed that a higher than normal number of patients had unexplained hypoglycaemia. Other incidents include the severe failings in care provided by Mid Staffordshire NHS Foundation Trust between 2005 and 2008, resulting a number of deaths, the activities of Dr Harold Shipman, a general practitioner, and the deliberations of The Royal Liverpool Children's Inquiry appointed to investigate the removal, retention and disposal of human organs and tissues after postmortem examination at The Royal Liverpool Children's Hospital. These are extraordinary events but they are not unprecedented. The outcome of these improper incidents has led to an increased focus on the competence and performance of health-care professionals.

Clinical governance is a complex activity with a number of key principals underpinning its implementation:

- Clinical governance must be focused on improving the quality of patient care.
- Clinical governance should apply to all health care wherever it is being delivered.
- Clinical governance demands true partnership between all health professionals, between clinical staff and managers, and between patients and clinical staff.
- Public and patient involvement is an essential requirement for effective clinical governance.

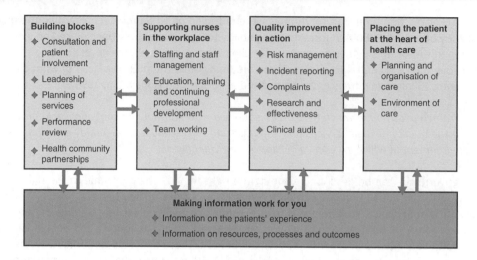

Figure 11.1 Key themes associated with clinical governance. Source: RCN (2003). (Reproduced with the kind permission of the Royal College of Nursing.)

- Nurses have a key role to play in the implementation of clinical governance.
- An improvement-based approach to quality health care creates an enabling culture that celebrates success and learns from mistakes.
- Clinical governance applies to all health-care staff. It needs to be defined and communicated clearly so that all staff understand its relevance to their work.
- Clinical governance does not replace individual clinical judgement or professional self-regulation; it complements these and provides a framework in which they can operate.

Figure 11.1 provides a diagrammatic representation of the key themes associated with clinical governance. Clinical governance places the responsibility for the quality of care on both organisations and individuals working within those organisations. Although the emphasis is on joint responsibility, the nurse must not forget that exercising individual accountability is paramount within a multiprofessional clinical environment. Clinical governance extends to all NHS services and is everybody's business, not just that of those who excel at it or those who are poor at it. Everyone working in the NHS is responsible for contributing to the maintenance of quality and improving it where possible, as an essential part of their role and responsibility, depending on the nature of their post.

In ensuring that the health service is patient focused, the NHS Clinical Governance Support Team (now defunct) produced a seven-pillar model that described clinical governance. The seven pillars are related to five fundamental principles that enhance the aim to be an effective partnership:

1. Risk management: systems used to understand, monitor and minimise the risks to patients, staff and organisations, learning from mistakes.
2. Clinical effectiveness: ensures that the approaches and treatments used are based on the best available evidence as well ensuring that interventions and treatments work.
3. Education, training and continuing personal development: cover the support available to enable all staff to be competent in doing their jobs effectively while developing their skills and the degree to which staff are up to date with developments in their field.

The nurse has a professional duty to remain up to date.

4. Use of information: describes the systems in place to collect and interpret clinical information and to use it to monitor, plan and improve the quality of patient care.
5. Staffing and staff management: describe the recruitment, management and development of staff, and include the promotion of good working conditions and effective methods of working.
6. Clinical audit: describes the continual measurement and improvement by health professionals of their work and the standards that they are achieving.
7. Patient experience (service users and public involvement): describes how patients can have a say in their own treatment and how they, and patient organisations, can have a say on how services are provided. Bases provision of services around the needs of patients, and listens to what the public thinks of services provided.

The additional five principles according to Hammond (2010) are:

1. Systems awareness
2. Team work
3. Communication
4. Ownership
5. Leadership.

It is not possible to achieve clinical governance in isolation. Structures need to be in place to support it, as well as ensuring that there are common standards and a common public ethos. National structures are in place to underpin local clinical governance initiatives.

Top tips

Always ensure that you are familiar with local governance policies and structures in the trust where you are working. Understanding them can help you provide high-quality care as well help you with your university assignments when asked to discuss issues surrounding care provision.

National Service Frameworks

The National Service Frameworks (NSFs) set national standards. They are long-term strategies with the aim of improving specific areas of care and have time frames with measurable goals attached to them. They provide strategies that support their implementation and delivery at local level. The NSFs were launched in 1998 and have so far addressed the following specific areas of care:

- Mental health
- Paediatric intensive care
- Coronary heart disease
- Cancer
- Older people
- Diabetes
- Renal
- Children
- Long-term conditions

- Long-term neurological conditions
- Chronic obstructive pulmonary disease
- Hypertension/blood pressure.

The NSFs were the directories of best practice and standards to be achieved by care providers. There are other documents that provide much more detail than the NSFs, e.g. service standard documents such as paediatric congenital cardiac surgery services (National Specialised Commissioning Group, 2010). These documents draw on range of other policy directives such as the NHS Constitution (DH, 2009). NSFs were created at the same time as NICE in 1999, with the intention of acting as complementary process to establish national standards and guidelines. Littlejohns and Pereira (2010) suggest that the NSFs have provided a solid basis for the standardising care within the areas for which they have been published.

National Institute for Health and Clinical Excellence

The National Institute for Clinical Excellence (NICE), formed in 1999, as it was originally called, is an independent organisation charged with the responsibility to provide national guidance on the promotion of good health and the prevention and treatment of ill-health. In 2005 this organisation merged with the Health Development Agency and is now known as the National Institute for Health and Clinical Excellence (it retains its acronym NICE). Guidance is published on many topics, e.g. generalised anxiety disorder and panic disorder (NICE, 2011a), anaemia management in chronic kidney disease (NICE, 2011b) and food allergy in children and young people (NICE, 2001c). The key role of NICE, when it was formed, was to ensure that health care and safety across the NHS in England was standardised. Although many centres provide high-quality, world-class services, there are pockets of provision that were (and in a minority of cases still are) less than satisfactory. Working with the NSFs (see above), NICE was established to provide strong leadership based on clinical and cost-effectiveness; it does this by drawing on new guidelines and the most up-to-date scientific evidence available. Equity of access to health-care provision and encouraging the uptake of the most clinically and cost-effective (value for money) interventions and the creation of innovative technologies are its key purposes.

The work and co-relationship between NICE and the NSFs were originally seen as a quality improvement model. Littlejohns and Pereira (2010) explain, however, that, due to a number of other institutions providing explicit quality work at the time, the role of quality improvement led to NICE providing guidance on controversial health issues, particularly where there was lack of clarity of consensus resulting in regional variation.

Commission for Health Improvement, Healthcare Commission and Care Quality Commission

CHI (Commission for Health Improvement) was key in ensuring that local clinical governance arrangements were reviewed. It was superseded by the Healthcare Commission in 2004, the legal name for which is the Commission for Health Care Audit and Inspection. One of the significant roles of this body is the ability to intervene if shortcomings and problems have been identified (Roberts, 2005). Its role (in England) is to:

- inspect
- inform
- improve.

In 2009 the Healthcare Commission became the Care Quality Commission (CQC); this commission replaces the Mental Health Act Commission and the Commission for Social Care Inspection. The key aim of the CQC is to ensure that the NHS establish and maintain high standards of quality and safety for patients and staff, focusing on outcomes as opposed to process. The processes undertaken by the CQC can be referred to as regulation, inspection, registration and accreditation (Burgess, 2011). The CQC plays an important role in ensuring that the views of service users are considered when health- and social care policy is being contemplated as well as when decisions are being made about service provision. The explicit use of the word 'quality' in its title focuses the work of this commission on all quality aspects. They ensure that health-care providers are meeting outcomes in response to what people who use services expect. To register with the CQC (a requirement for providers of care services), providers of services must meet the essential standards for registration in Table 11.1.

Top tips

 Go to the CQC website and register with them. In this way you will receive regular updates on developments in relation to the regulation of care services and reports published at www.cqc.org.uk.

Table 11.1   Standards for registration with the Care Quality Commission

Involvement and information:
- Involving, listening to and respecting those people who use services

Personalised care, treatment and support:
- Care and welfare of people who use services
- Meeting nutritional needs
- Cooperating with other providers

Safeguarding and safety:
- Safeguarding those who use services from abuse
- Cleanliness and infection control
- Safe management of medicines
- Safety and suitability of premises
- Safety, availability and suitability of medical devises and other equipment

Quality and management:
- Assessing and mentoring the provision of services
- Managing complaints
- Notification of deaths, incidents or absence of person who has been detained under the Mental Health Act
- Record keeping

Suitability of staffing:
- Requirements associated with workers
- Staffing levels
- Supporting workers

Source: adapted from Care Quality Commission (2010).

Next stage review

This initiative was led by Lord Darzi who worked with others to produce *High Quality Care for all – NHS Next Stage Review* (DH, 2008). Darzi noted that a modern NHS strives to provide high-quality care for all only when it changes to meet the health-care needs of society. Rochford (2010) summarises this as follows:

- Raising expectations
- Demand driven by demographics
- The continuing development of our 'information society'
- Advances in treatments
- The changing nature of disease
- The changing expectations of the health work place.

It was Darzi's desire to give increased control to patients by allowing them to exercise choice. as well as being true partners in their care at the centre of health care. He wanted patients to be encouraged to shape how services were delivered; in effect he strove for patient empowerment giving them a key role to play in determining the standards of care that they expect to receive.

Clinical audit

Clinical audit is a quality improvement process that seeks to improve patient care and outcomes through a systematic review of care against the explicit criteria and implementation of change. Burgess (2011) sees clinical audit as a cycle that addresses issues such as deciding on what to measure, measuring, acting on the findings and re-measuring. Clinical audit is at the heart of clinical governance; it is a multidisciplinary, multiagency and multiprofessional working approach (Sasaru et al, 2005).

To provide the best care in a competent manner it is important that the processes and procedures used by the NHS to deliver care are the most appropriate in relation to the service(s) being delivered. Research and development activity and the evidence gathered in order to provide evidence-based practice (see Chapter 8) aim to increase the sum of academic knowledge. They do this by establishing facts that can then be generalised to a given population and provide the nurse with the information that he or she needs to do the job well – in the best, most effective way possible. Clinical audit has the potential to monitor how well the job is being done and to ensure that standards are being maintained. According to Sasaru et al (2005) clinical audit asks: 'How does the care that we provide compare with established standards for practice?' It cannot increase the sum of knowledge, nor can it provide evidence that can be generalised to a population as research does.

Kehoe (2005) suggests that clinical audit is:

- a tool to assist when implementing clinical governance
- a means of checking that things are being done correctly
- an activity that involves clinicians (nurses) and users of the service (patients)
- a means of ensuring that the treatments used have been shown by research to be effective.

He also adds that audit is not:

- a means of demonstrating that a type of treatment works
- an excuse to collect endless data

- an activity exclusively for the audit department
- an activity that always works.

The audit cycle

Audit as a concept is not new and has been used by the NHS for many years, e.g. nursing audit and medical audit. Quality assurance has also been used in the past and was used in an attempt to decide what should be, and comparing that with reality, identifying gaps and taking action.

Clinical audit is designed as a cycle of change. Actions are taken after a review of existing practices. Several cycles (models) have been suggested over the last decade, which can be very simple or very detailed and complex. The concept of audit is remarkably uncomplicated, but it is also a powerful tool for change. The type of model used will depend on local conditions and requirements. The key to ensuring that audit is successful is to ensure that a systematic approach is used and that planning and preparation are carried out in advance. Kehoe (2005) and Sasaru et al (2005) provide more details concerning planning and preparation for an audit. Audit is a continuous, cyclical process (Figure 11.2).

Set the standard

Some standards already exist and have been predetermined, e.g. the standards outlined in the NSFs. NICE also provides guidance that the nurse can use to formulate standards. Benchmark statements have also been provided that concern aspects of fundamental care such as oral hygiene, which allow nurses

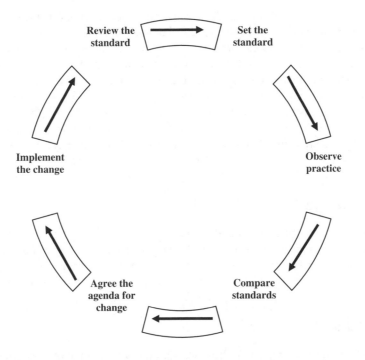

Figure 11.2   Audit cycle. Source: adapted from Sasaru et al (2005).

to compare benchmark statements with current practice. Where no standards have been preset or no guidance exists, standards may need to be formulated locally using a multidisciplinary approach. One approach (and there are several approaches available) to standard setting that has been used before by the nurse is structure (what you need), process (what you do) and outcome (what you expect) (Sasaru et al, 2005).

Observe practice

Current practice is observed by gathering data associated with, for example, everyday or usual practice, nursing and case-notes data, and patient satisfaction surveys. Data-collection tools are often forms or documents and each clinical area/trust will have its own documentation for doing this. This stage of the process must be given careful consideration because the documentation used must yield the data required. Some trusts employ specific individuals to gather these data and then analyse them.

Compare standards

When the data have been collected they need to be analysed. Data collected, according to Sasaru et al (2005), should say with enough accuracy to what extent the care measured matched the standard set. Both standards – the standard set (e.g. the NSF) and the standards being delivered (care being provided) – are compared and contrasted.

Agree the agenda for change

If there is a discrepancy between the standards set (the set criteria) and the care delivered, then an action plan must be formulated to address the shortcomings and improve the service. If care provided is seen as an example of good practice, similarly a plan must be agreed to ensure that good practice is maintained and, where appropriate, replicated. The implementation of change is needed at this stage of the process. Management of change must be done with an understanding of the situation.

Action plans or audit reports are needed; they are best formulated using a multidisciplinary approach. The plan must be written, presented and fed back into clinical practice and to others in a way that is clear and realistic. Dissemination in this manner will help to ensure that whatever new practices or changes are required are understood by all of those involved. Time frames are needed as well as measurable criteria to determine success. This is similar to the setting of goals.

Implement change

This stage requires that the changes needed be implemented. Change is central to clinical audit. Staff may need support or supervision to ensure that this is carried out effectively and there are many interventions that can be used to facilitate the change process. It may be appropriate to provide a programme of staff development to ensure that the action plans are addressed and implemented.

Review standards

The cycle is completed when change, as indicated by audit, has been implemented (Ghosh, 2009). Sasaru et al (2005) see this aspect of the cycle as the closing of the loop. Review should be undertaken to ensure that standards are maintained and are still appropriate – this means that the cycle may need to be repeated and revisited once the action plan has been implemented.

Think

Think about a hotel where you have stayed. How did you measure its quality? How did you decide if it was good quality or poor quality? What do you have to take into account that helped you arrive at a decision concerning good or bad quality? What criteria did you use?

Measuring quality is not easy; however, knowing what is not good quality is much easier.
Did you consider value for money in your response – you get what you pay for?
What about being objective?
Were you able to be objective when you measured quality?
Did the attitude of the staff feature as one of your criteria?
What about cleanliness?

Quality and the independent sector

Although there has been an explicit and concerted effort over the years to enhance the quality of care provided by the NHS, the same applies to the independent sector. The Independent Healthcare Association (IHA) requires that all member organisations demonstrate the quality of their services by achieving a recognised quality award. The Health Quality Service (HQS) is an independent charity that sets organisational standards and makes assessments to determine if the standards have been met.

Assessment of services is conducted by a team of experienced health-care professionals. During the assessment documentation is reviewed, staff are interviewed and practices observed. Successful achievement of the standards set allows the independent facility accreditation for 3 years.

The Commission of Social Care Inspectorate carries out local inspections of all social care organisations – public, private and voluntary – against national standards and publishes reports. The general aims of inspections are to check compliance with standards and regulations (Healthcare Commission, 2005). This role now comes under the auspices of the Care Quality Commission.

The principles applying to clinical governance in the NHS are applied equally across the independent sector. The creation of the Care Standards Act 2000 demonstrated this (Royal College of Nursing or RCN, 2003).

Risk assessments

Most of the care delivered within the NHS is of a high quality. Serious incidents and failures are uncommon when related to the high numbers of patients requiring care provided daily in hospitals and in the community. Clinical governance provides NHS organisations with powerful authority to focus on adverse health-care occurrences. Patient safety is an essential element of nursing care. When ensuring patient safety the nurse and the organisation must establish systems and processes that reduce the likelihood of errors occurring and increase the possibility of intercepting them before any harm can occur. Principle C of the RCN's principles of nursing practice state that nurses and nursing staff manage risk, are vigilant about risk, and help to keep everyone safe in the places they receive health care (Manley et al, 2011).

This demands that all nursing staff must accept responsibility and accountability for any of their decisions and actions associated with the way that care is planned, implemented and evaluated, despite the setting in which care is provide (Currie et al, 2011).

Mistakes and errors do occur and when they occur they can have devastating consequences for patients and their families. Every day over one million people are treated successfully in the NHS (National Patient Safety Agency, 2004). However, it is estimated that in the NHS over 850 000 adverse incidents occur per year (DH, 2000a) (most recent data available). The umbrella term 'clinical governance' includes all things that help to maintain high standards of patient care and this therefore includes the identification and prevention of risks to the welfare of the patient. Patients expect care that is safe and of such quality as is consonant with good practice based on sound evidence.

Improving quality includes a range of activities, and some of these have already been discussed, e.g. providing care that is based on the best available evidence and clinical audit. It also includes the management of risk, the reporting of incidents (actual and near misses) and the management of complaints.

Risk management

Risk management is a central feature of clinical governance. It aims to reduce the risk of adverse incidents by recognising risks, assessing risks, and putting in place strategies to reduce or contain risks that have been identified (Amos and Snowden, 2005). There are several definitions of risk management. Currie et al (2003) suggest that it is seen as a part of a process that aims to raise the quality and safety aspects of service provision; they add that risk management places special emphasis on episodes in which people being cared for are harmed or disturbed by their treatment.

As with several important concepts related to health care, there are many ways to define key terms and the definition of risk is not excluded from this. Risk is often associated with probability or chance, but increasingly it is being linked with danger and hazards. Risk is associated with hazard and is something to be avoided; risk is not only about bad things happening, it is also about good things *not* happening, yet risk must be minimised if harmful and unwanted outcomes are to be avoided. However, risk is an essential aspect of health-care provision, encountered on a daily basis. The provision of health care is a risky activity.

Risk taking occurs on a daily basis for all of us, in our own everyday lives. We gamble with risk daily, and this is the same for nurses.

Think

 Take some time to think of the risks that you take on a daily basis. Think about what they are and how you gambled with the potentially harmful or beneficial results that could be the result of taking those risks.

There may have been several very different things in your list. Did it include any of the following?:

- Crossing the road
- The first time that you decided to taste sushi
- The risks that you took when taking up nurse education

- The risks that you took when having unsafe sex
- The risks that you took when having a general anaesthetic.

The fact is that risks are a part of life. Assessing risk is something people do instinctively. We should aim to contain risks in our personal lives and also when working with patients. It may be impossible and even undesirable, to reduce risk taking to zero (Amos and Snowden, 2005). Risks must be managed and tolerated.

Risk management is about reducing the likelihood of patients coming to harm and creating a safe environment for both patients and staff. NHS organisations must ensure that they adhere to and comply with all applicable legislation. Staff must all feel that they are able to (and encouraged to) report risks, incidents and near misses. Arrangements must be in place for this to occur, and policy and procedures applicable to the reporting of risks, incidents and near misses should be clarified and disseminated among all staff

Some risks may be seen as acceptable risks; these are those that are not significant enough to be considered unreasonable. Good risk management helps to reduce hazards and builds confidence for innovation and creativity to occur (Scrivens, 2005).

Effective risk management addresses all the processes that are involved in the identification, assessment and judgement of risks, as well as the monitoring and reviewing of progress. All activities related to risk can be subjected to risk management. The following are risks that may be subjected to risk management:

- Corporate issues
- Financial matters
- Clinical activity
- Non-clinical activity.

Risk management utilises a systematic approach when identifying and assessing reduction of risk to both patients and staff (Scrivens, 2005).

Amos and Snowden (2005) suggest that there are three stages associated with a dynamic approach to risk management:

1. Risk identification or recognition
2. Risk assessment and analysis
3. Risk management and reduction.

There are several risk-assessment tools available to help nurses and other health-care professionals identify, plan implement and evaluate risk-associated activities. However, risk-assessment tools are only as good as the nurse who is conducting the assessment. The Waterlow scale (Waterlow, 1985) is but one example of a risk-assessment tool. Other tools are also available, e.g. tools that assess the risk of potential malnutrition occurring. Another tool used to predict the possibility of violence occurring was produced in response to an increase in violence associated with patients with a mental illness. Suicide prediction scales have also been published. Murphy et al (2005) describe the use of the dynamic risk-assessment and management system for people with a learning disability and offending behaviours. When risk-assessment tools are used they often predict the probable degree of risk to the patient. When this has been established, the nurse then needs to put into place actions to alleviate the risk, or prevent the risk from becoming any greater. Risk awareness, according to Woodward (2011), is about understanding risk-prone situations and then having the skill to anticipate or predict hazards, risks and incidents, and reduce the consequential personal and organisational risk.

315

Case study 11.1

Kyle is a 14-year-old who has a brain tumour; he has refused to take his chemo-therapy medication despite his parents and other staff encouraging him to allow the nursing staff to give it to him. He said that he has had enough of this; it makes him so sick, sicker than the brain tumour.

The key issue in Kyle's case is his ability to demonstrate that he has the capacity to make the decision to refuse his treatment. The courts have determined that such children can be legally competent if they have 'sufficient understanding and maturity to enable them to understand fully what is proposed'. Fraser competence is a concept used in cases such as this (Gillick competence is also used). Much will depend on the relationship of the clinician with the child and the family, and also on what intervention is being proposed. A young person who has the capacity to consent to straightforward, relatively risk-free treatment may not necessarily have the capacity to consent to complex treatment involving high risks or serious consequences. This is complex case and further guidance must be sought by the nurse and others. If a competent child is refusing treatment, those with parental responsibility can consent if the treatment is deemed to be in the child's interests. These matters often come to court and the court can override the decisions of both those with parental responsibility and the child. The Department of Health (2001) have produced guidance suggesting that the families of children in this age group should be involved in decisions about their care, unless there is a very good reason for not doing so. The nurse must make a clear, accurate and immediate record of all medicine administered, intentionally withheld or refused by the patient.

Top tips

When administering the drug digoxin you must always count the person's heart rate for one full minute before administration. If the pulse is below 60 beats/min you must withhold the medication and inform the doctor. Always inform the patient of what you are doing and why, and ensure that you document the actions that you have taken and the reasons why.

The administration of medicines

It has been said many times in this chapter that improving the quality of care is at the heart of clinical governance. Safe and effective drug treatment is also a part of clinical governance. A prescribed medicine is the most common treatment provided for patients in the NHS. In primary care in England, GPs issue more than over 600 million prescriptions per year; in hospitals this figure is estimated to be as many as 200 million (DH, 2004).

Most medications are prescribed and administered safely in the UK. However, errors do occur and the effects can be upsetting and the consequences serious for all concerned: the patient, his or her family, the prescriber, the dispenser and the administrator. The errors that do occur can be prevented (DH, 2004). Guidance has been issued nationally and locally to help ensure that errors are avoided, e.g. the law (statute), local trust drug policies and the NMC's *Standards for Medicines Management* (NMC, 2010a). Medication errors can render the nurse prone to civil liability and in certain instances criminal prosecution.

The NMCs *Standards for Medicines Management* (NMC, 2010a) is composed of 26 standards with 10 sections (see Appendix 11.1 at the end of this chapter). Interspaced throughout the document are boxes containing guidance. The NMC (20010a) suggest that:

> The administration of medicines is an important aspect of the professional practice of persons whose names are on the Council's register. It is not solely a mechanistic task to be performed in strict compliance with the written prescription of a medical practitioner (can now also be an independent and supplementary prescriber). It requires thought and the exercise of professional judgement.

Legislation

There are a variety of pieces of legislation that impact on prescribing, supplying, storing and administering medicines. The nurse must comply with these elements of legislation as well adhering to local policy and protocol. Dimond (2011) suggests that there are two main sources of law on medicinal products:

1. The Medicines Act 1968
2. The Misuse of Drugs Act 1971.

These elements of statute are supplemented by Statutory Instruments (SIs) that provide a framework for the manufacture, export and import, and supply and control of medicines. The SIs provide more detailed regulation. The following provides a summary of the most relevant legislation – the statutory framework for medicines. The nurse needs to be familiar with these statutory requirements in order to practise as a professional nurse as well as ensuring that he or she is abiding by the law.

Medicines Act 1968

This Act was the first all-inclusive element of law on medicines in the UK. This Act, as well as the variety of SIs (secondary legislation) on medicines produced since 1968, laid the foundation for the legal framework for the manufacture, licensing, prescribing, supply and administration of medicines. One particular SI the Prescription Only Medicines (Human Use) Order 1997, SI No1830, brings together and combines all other secondary legislation concerning prescription-only medicines and lists all the medicines in this category; the SI sets out in its provision who may prescribe them. The Medicines Act 1968 classifies medicines into the following categories.

Pharmacy-only medicines Pharmacy-only medicines (Ps) are those medicines that may be purchased only from a registered pharmacy. Any sales must be by or under the supervision of a pharmacist.

General sales list medicines General sales list medicines (GSLs) do not need a prescription, nor do they need the supervision of a pharmacist and may be obtained from retail outlets.

Controlled drugs Controlled drugs (CDs) and their management are overseen by the Misuse of Drugs Act 1971 as well as its associated regulations.

Misuse of Drugs Act 1971

This Act and its related regulations provide the statutory framework associated with the control and regulation of controlled drugs. The key intention of the Misuse of Drugs Act 1971 is to prevent misuse

317

of CDs. In its provision the Misuse of Drugs Act 1971 makes it illegal to possess or supply a CD apart from where exception or exemption applies. A CD is defined as any drug listed in schedule 2 of the Act. The Health Act 2006 and its associated regulations provide additional statutory measures for the management of CDs.

Misuse of Drugs Regulations 2001 (MDR) and Misuse of Drugs Regulations Northern Ireland (NI) 2002

The Misuse of Drug Regulations (MDR) permits the use of CDs in medicine. The MDR categorise the drugs and organises them into five schedules depending on the various levels of control required. CDs in schedule 1 are subject to the highest level of control whereas schedule 5 CDs come under a much lower level of control.

Misuse of Drugs (Safe Custody) Regulations 1973 Misuse of Drugs (Safe Custody) Regulations Northern Ireland 1973

These Regulations require controls on the storage of controlled drugs. The degree of control depends on the premises within which the drugs are being stored. All schedule 2 and a number of schedule 3 CDs must be securely stored in line with the regulations. The regulations state that such CDs have to be stored in a cabinet or safe, locked with a key. This has to be made of metal, with appropriate hinges and fixed to a wall or the floor with rag bolts that cannot be accessed from outside the cabinet.

Misuse of Drugs (Supply to Addicts) Regulations 1997 and Misuse of Drugs (Notification and Supply to Addicts (Northern Ireland)) Regulations 1973

These Regulations dictate that doctors are prohibited from prescribing, administering or supplying diamorphine, cocaine or dipipanone for the treatment of addiction or suspected addiction unless under Home Office licence. There is no licence needed with such drugs for the treatment of organic disease or injury.

Prescription Only Medicines (Human Use) Order 1997

The order sets out the requirements for a valid prescription. This order permits midwives to possess and administer diamorphine, morphine, pethidine or pentazocine in the course of their professional practice. A variety of health-care professionals are allowed to supply or administer medicines generally in accordance with a patient group direction (PGD) under Medicines Act legislation. Registered nurses are allowed to supply or administer some CDs but only in accordance with a PGD under Misuse of Drugs legislation.

Health Act 2006

Key elements of the act are as follows:

- All designated bodies such as health-care organisations and independent hospitals are required to appoint an accountable officer.

- A duty of collaboration placed on responsible bodies, health-care organisations and other local and national agencies, including professional regulatory bodies, police forces, the Healthcare Commission and the Commission for Social Care inspection, to share intelligence on controlled drug issues.
- A power of entry and inspection for the police and other nominated people to enter premises to inspect stocks and records of controlled drugs.

Controlled drugs (supervision of management and use) regulations 2006

These Regulations came into effect in England on 1 January 2007. They set out the requirements for certain NHS and independent bodies, requiring them to appoint an accountable officer and to describe the duties and responsibilities of accountable officers with the intention of making better the management and use of CDs. There are requirements within the Regulations that demand specified bodies to cooperate with each other, including the sharing of information, making known concerns about the use and management of CDs, and the setting out of arrangements related to powers of entry and inspection.

319

Case study 11.2

Miss Marcia Dhillon is 57 and has had a stroke; she has a dense hemiparesis. She has been progressing well but, she took a turn for the worse last night and when you come on duty today she is unconscious and has a fine-bore nasogastric tube *in situ*. Marcia has been receiving 75 mg enteric-coated aspirin daily. During the drug round where you are working under supervision with staff nurse Coyle, the staff nurse asks you to crush the aspirin in order to put the medicine down the fine-bore nasogastric tube.

There are number of issues in this case study that need to be given consideration. You will need to know what local policy is for the administration of medicines and the use of nasogastric tubes (this is a fine-bore nasogastric tube). The fact that Miss Dhillon's condition has changed means that the nurse administering the medicines must ensure that this has been taken into account before administration (NMC, 2010a). The medication has been prescribed to be given as enteric coated, so to proceed to crush the medicine will take away its enteric-coated properties.

As a student nurse the standards enshrined in the NMC's *Code of Conduct* (NMC, 2008) also apply to you along with the *Guidance on Professional Conduct for Nursing and Midwifery Students* (NMC, 2010b). At all times you must work only within the level of your understanding and competence, and always under the direct supervision of a registered nurse or midwife. This must also apply during the administration of medicines or while assisting with the drug round. As a student you are responsible for your actions or omissions, but as you are not yet registered with the NMC you cannot be answerable for them: the registered nurse or midwife who is supervising your practice is ultimately accountable for your actions or omissions. You must not forget, however, that you are and may be required to be answerable to your educational institution's policies, procedures and rules. Furthermore, you also remain accountable in law for your actions or omissions.

You should not participate in any procedure for which you have not been fully prepared or in which you are not being adequately supervised. Should you ever find yourself in this position, you must make this known to your supervisor as quickly as possible. You must always work within the policies and procedures that apply in the area of care in which you are working (NHS or independent sector, health or social care) as well as follow the advice provided by your educational institution. Additional sources of information and references should be accessed and used as required.

Registered nurses are accountable for their actions and omissions when giving medications and, as such, they take full responsibility for any errors that they may make. Drug errors do occur and there are often many reasons for this, e.g. increasing demands being made on the nurse, overwork and stress (Copping, 2005). Parish (2003) suggests that in some instances drug errors can occur as a result of complacency. Other causes of medication errors are related to distractions and a prescriber's illegible handwriting (Mayo and Duncan, 2004).

Registered nurses are reminded that they must exercise professional judgement and apply their skills and knowledge to the various situations that may emerge during medicine administration. This advice is irrespective of the environment in which the registered nurse is practising.

Case study 11.3

Jemel is a 28-year-old man who has a mild learning disability (he is also epileptic); he lives alone, as part of support living in a house rented from a housing association, which has 24 hours per week from paid careers. Jemel has a number of self-care skills but Mathew, one of the paid carers, informs you that he found six white tables when he was helping Jemel clean his room. Jemel has recently had three seizures and his behaviour has changed – he has become much more subdued.

The immediate concern in this case is Jemel's health. His condition must be assessed and actions taken to ensure that he is safe. The finding of the medication could mean that there has been a breach in the administrations of medicines policy. The nurse has a responsibility when administering medicines to ensure that the medicinal product has been taken even if this task has been appropriately delegated (NMC, 2010a). The nurse must ensure that any errors made must be reported as soon as possible to the prescriber, line manager or employer as policy dictates and any actions taken must be documented. It must never be assumed that, because Jemel has a learning disability, he is unable to make an informed decision to refuse his treatment; further exploration will be needed if this is found to be the case.

Prescribing, dispensing and administration of medicines: an overview

There are many Government and other agencies involved in prescribing, dispensing and administering medicines. These agencies may be concerned with the licensing and manufacturing of medicines for human use. The pharmacist is an invaluable source of advice if the nurse needs to confirm or validate the content of a prescription, but there are other relevant bodies that may be just as resourceful.

Prescribing

Who can prescribe medications? There are a several mechanisms available for prescribing medicines. In certain instances, after consultation with doctors, pharmacists and other health-care professionals, the following registered health-care professionals may, so long as they remain within the confines of the law, prescribe medications using a PGD:

- Nurses, midwives and health visitors
- Paramedics

- Optometrists
- Chiropodists
- Radiographers
- Physiotherapists
- Pharmacists
- Dieticians
- Occupational therapists
- Prosthetists and orthoptists
- Speech and language therapists.

Each of the health-care professionals cited above must be deemed competent, appropriately qualified and educated to use a PGD.

Dispensing

Fewer errors occur with dispensing than with prescribing medications (DH, 2004). Nurses may dispense drugs in exceptional circumstances, but this must be done in line with hospital policy and with the written instructions of a registered medical practitioner – a doctor. In some areas, dispensing of drugs is seen as the nurse's extended role. If this is the case the nurse must practise this activity under the directions of a doctor and with attention to the NMC's (2010a) standards. The public has a right to know that the nurse will carry out this duty with the same reasonable skill expected of a pharmacist.

Administration

Nurses administer medicines in a variety of settings to a variety of patients: those who are mentally ill or those at the extremes of age, e.g. neonates and elderly people. Administration can take place in the patient's home, in residential homes and on hospital wards. The administration of medicines is therefore a fundamental and important nursing activity.

Before administering medications the nurse must ensure that he or she is familiar with policy and regulations, locally and nationally, that govern medicine administration. Principles surrounding medicine administration can be found in the NMC's *Standards for Medicines Management* (NMC, 2010a). Regardless of whether a prescription has been hand written or electronically generated, the nurse must ensure that it contains the details stated in Table 11.2.

Telephone orders are not acceptable for a previously unprescribed drug. However, in exceptional circumstances when the medicine has been previously prescribed and the authorised prescriber is unable to issue a new prescription, but there is a need to alter the dose, telephone alterations may be acceptable. The preferred method is to use other methods of communicating the change, e.g. email or fax. The change that has been agreed must be reflected in the writing of a new prescription within 24 hours (NMC, 2010a).

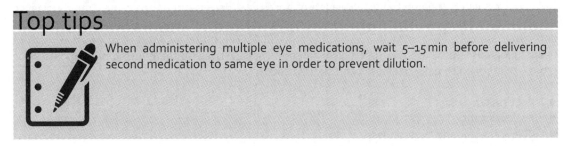

Top tips

When administering multiple eye medications, wait 5–15 min before delivering second medication to same eye in order to prevent dilution.

Table 11.2   Principles advocated by the Nursing and Midwifery Council associated with prescribed medicines

- The prescription is based on informed consent, with the patient's informed consent and awareness of the purpose of the treatment
- Be clearly written, typed or computer generated and be indelible
- Clearly identify for whom the medication is intended
- When the dosage of medication is related to the patient's weight this must be recorded on the prescription sheet
- The substance to be prescribed must be clearly specified and include the generic or brand name of the medication, the form of medication, strength, dose, frequency, start and finish dates, and route of administration
- Be signed by the authorised prescriber
- The prescription must not be for a substance to which the patient is known to be allergic
- Prescribed controlled drugs must state the dosage and the number of dosage units and the total course. If this is a prescription in an outpatient or community setting the prescription must be in the authorised prescriber's own handwriting, signed and dated. There are some exceptions to this handwritten rule

Source: adapted from NMC (2010a).

Reducing risks associated with drug administration

In high-risk areas there is a responsibility to minimise the potential for a drug error occurring, e.g. in paediatric settings such as special care baby units, and in those clinical areas where large quantities of CDs are administrated, e.g. operating theatres, cardiac care units and intensive therapy units.

Medication errors (the terms 'medication error' and 'drug error' are often used interchangeably) are said to account consistently for between 10 and 20 per cent of all adverse events. Aside from the danger to patients, these errors cost the NHS a considerable amount of money. It is therefore of value to make concerted efforts to reduce the numbers and types of errors caused by maladministration

There is no consistent definition of drug error that can be agreed between health-care professionals. A medication error is defined by the Department of Health (2004) as any preventable event that may cause or lead to inappropriate medication use or patient harm while the medication is in the control of a health-care professional, patient or consumer. Medication errors can be the result of professional practice, products, procedures, environment or systems – they are preventable. Errors can occur at all stages associated with the production, prescribing, dispensing and administration of medications, which includes labelling, packaging and the communication that the nurse has with the patient about his or her medication.

Drug errors can be related to miscalculation of doses, overdosing and underdosing. Often, however, drug errors are not the result of isolated incidents: they may be the product of an accumulation of incidents that are complex and multifaceted (Preston, 2004). There are some areas of practice that are deemed high risk and these have been highlighted previously. Likewise there are some particular drug groups that have also been deemed high risk (DH, 2004):

- Anaesthetic agents
- Anticoagulants
- Chemotherapeutic medications

Table 11.3   Most common 'wrong drug', 'wrong strength errors that occur

Amiloride	Amlodipine
Fluoxetine	Paroxetine
Hydralazine	Hydroxyzine
Carbamazepine	Carbimazole
Omeprazole 10 mg	Omeprazole 20 mg
Atenolol 100 mg	Atenolol 50 mg
Morphine sulphate tablets (MST) 10 mg	Morphine sulphate tablets (MST) 30 mg
Paroxetine 20 mg	Paroxetine 30 mg
Warfarin 3 mg	Warfarin 5 mg
Diazepam 2 mg	Diazepam 5 mg
Co-codamol 30/500	Co-codamol 8/500

Source: adapted from Department of Health (2004).

- Any drug delivered via the intravenous route
- Methotrexate
- Opiates
- Potassium chloride.

The nurse should also be aware of drugs that have been involved most commonly in 'wrong drug', 'wrong strength' dispensing errors. These drugs can be found in Table 11.3.

The nurse must ensure that he or she understands the reasons why a particular drug is being given and the therapeutic dose that should be prescribed. The nurse must ensure that he or she is up to date regarding pharmacological developments. Calculation errors occur commonly in paediatric settings where doses used can vary widely according to the weight of the child.

It is essential that, when calculating drug doses for any patient, the nurse should make certain that he or she employs meticulous methods to do this. Any confusion or concerns should be raised and clarified with a senior member of staff before administration. If you are in doubt about any aspect of the prescription or administration of the medication, you must carefully exercise your professional judgement; you may decide not to give the medication.

Good record keeping is also a part of good, safe drug administration. You must ensure that your records are up to date and meet the requirements of your employing authority and that you also adhere to the guidelines and standards produced by the NMC (2010c).

Before the administration of any drug, O'Brien et al (2011) suggest that the nurse must ensure that he or she incorporates the six 'Rs':

- Right drug
- Right dose
- Right route
- Right time
- Right patient
- Right documentation.

Drug errors

To err is human and mistakes do happen. The number of drug errors that are acknowledged and reported are not a true reflection of reality; many more go unreported. The reasons why some go unreported may be associated with a fear of reprisal from managers and worry about how colleagues may react (Dimond, 2011). There may also be loss of self-esteem if a nurse reports an error.

   The nurse who has made a drug error, made known the error and dealt with it promptly should be supported in identifying how the error occurred, and how it may be prevented in the future. A 'no blame' culture should be established in the organisation in order to ensure that learning takes place from the error(s) made.

Some expressions and terms used in relation to medications

- *Independent prescriber*: a prescriber who is legally permitted and qualified to prescribe and takes the responsibility for the clinical assessment of the patient or client, establishing a diagnosis and the clinical management required, as well as the responsibility for prescribing, and the appropriateness of any prescribing.
- *Patient-specific direction*: a traditional written instruction from a nurse prescriber, dentist or doctor for medicines to be supplied or administered to a named person.
- *Patient group direction*: a written instruction for the supply or administration of a medicine where the patient may not be individually identified before presenting for treatment.
- *Nurse Prescriber's Formulary for Community Practitioners*: the formulary used by those nurses who have successfully completed the integrated prescribing component of the SPQ/SCPHN programme may prescribe independently.
- *P*: pharmacy-only medicines – medicines sold or supplied at registered pharmacy premises by or under the personal supervision of a pharmacist. The pharmacist must be present before a P medicine can be sold.
- *POM*: prescription-only medicines – medicines sold or supplied at registered pharmacy premises by or under the personal supervision of a pharmacist *but* in accordance with the authorised practitioner's prescription. The pharmacist must be present before a POM medicine can be sold. This kind of medicine requires a prescription to be produced.
- *GSL*: general sales list medicines – can be sold from a wider range of premises, e.g. general shops and supermarkets, but the premises must be lockable and can be closed to exclude the public. All medicines sold must be pre-packed and are sold in smaller quantities. These medicines are deemed safer than P medicines.
- *OTC*: over the counter, a generic term that covers GSL and P medicines.

Case study 11.4

Gloria Dayford is 71 years old with severe dementia and living in a long-term elderly care facility. She has no family and spends most of her day walking around the ward. Gloria sometimes demonstrates antisocial behaviour, swearing and becoming violent. She has been prescribed a sedative as part of her care pathway. Staff in the care facility are finding it difficult to encourage Gloria to take her medications and as such they hide the medication in her jam.

When nurses disguise medicines in food or drink this involves the fundamental principles of patient autonomy as well as consent to treatment; these principles are set out in common law and statute and underpinned by the Human Rights Act 1998.

Disguising medication without informed consent could be thought of as deception. The NMC (2010a) discuss issues surrounding the capacity to refuse medication and disguising medication in food and drink

Nurses who administer medicines covertly must ensure that they are fully aware of the aims, intent and implications of such treatment. Disguising medication with the intention of saving life, preventing deterioration or ensuring an improvement in the person's physical or mental health must not be taken in isolation from the recognition of the rights of the individual to give consent. In these situations, it may be necessary to administer medicines covertly, however, in some cases; the only proper course of action may be to seek the permission of the court to do so.

Top tips

Ensure that every drug chart has the patient's identification details, either a current patient identification label or the same information printed legibly in black ink, with any known adverse drug reaction recorded on the front. Always and never ever deviate from the policy and procedure with regard to the administration of medicines.

Reporting situations that are potentially unsafe

As a student of nursing it has already been emphasised that you are neither accountable nor answerable to the NMC. You do, however, have a responsibility to make known any situations that you find or consider unsafe in an attempt to protect the patient and others. These situations concern not only medication errors but also any unsafe, or potentially unsafe, practice.

There are local policies and procedures (as well as the policies and procedures that your university produces) that must be adhered to if you wish to make a complaint or raise a concern about the quality, and ultimately the safety, of patient care. You should raise the matter immediately with the person supervising you or another appropriate person, e.g. your trade union representative or tutors at your university.

Being aware of errors that have occurred and taking steps to rectify them will add to current awareness of the cases of medication errors. This, in time, will provide examples of good practice.

If you are asked to write a report or statement about the incident that concerns you, you must seek advice from a more senior member of staff in the clinical area or from staff at your university. Reports and statements must be factual. It is important to be as accurate as possible, use a chronological approach, write the statement as soon after the event has occurred as possible, and always ensure that you keep a copy.

Conclusions

Every day more than one million patients are treated safely and successfully in the NHS. However, the complexity of contemporary health care brings with it risk, and the consequence sometimes, no matter how hard staff work to prevent incidents arising, is harm to the patient.

When the idea of clinical governance was first introduced it challenged traditional ways of thinking, the culture within the health service and the attitudes held by some of those who worked there. It has become an opportunity for nurses and other health-care professionals to improve care provision for all who use health-care services. Clinical governance, described as a framework that provides NHS organisations with the tools to become accountable for continuously improving the quality of their services and safeguarding the public, is central to the 'new NHS'. Today's NHS is moving towards a more decentralised, innovative service with a clear remit that aims to enhance and improve patient care. Central to the new NHS is that structures and processes meet local needs, recognising and respecting diversity, but at the same time working with common definitions of good quality and good clinical care.

Clinical audit is a quality-improvement process that seeks to improve and enhance patient care and outcomes through a systematic review of care against explicit criteria and the implementation of change. It is at the heart of clinical governance and is a multidisciplinary, multiagency and multiprofessional working approach to quality enhancement.

Risk management is a crucial component of clinical governance. It aims to reduce the risk of adverse incidents. Risk taking is evident in most clinical situations and its occurrence is unlikely to be reduced to zero. Risk management is not confined to clinical care only; it also occurs in other areas of the health service, e.g. in health finance and the wider corporate arena.

Clinical governance is about improving the quality of all the services provided to the patient. Quality in this respect is not just restricted to the clinical aspects of care; it also encompasses and includes the quality of life and the overall patient experience.

Activity

Attempt the following questions that are related to patient safety to test your knowledge. The answers can be found at the back of this book, in the chapter called 'Activity Answers'.

1. How many standards are there in the NMC's (2010a) *Standards for Medicines Management*:
   a. 6 standards, 15 sections
   b. 23 standards, 10 sections
   c. 26 standards, 10 sections
   d. 36 standards, 20 sections

2. The acronym SIGN stands for:
   a. Signal Intensified General Notification
   b. Scottish Independent Government Network
   c. Scottish Intercollegiate Guidelines Network
   d. Scottish Interactive Guidelines Network

3. Clinical governance applies to:
   a. Doctors and paramedics
   b. Operating department practitioners and theatre sisters
   c. Mental health nurses
   d. All of the above

4. Risk identification can be:
   a. Active
   b. Passive and latent
   c. Reactive
   d. Reactive or proactive

5. Clinical guidelines:
   a. Help to ensure that patients receive the highest quality care
   b. Help to provide support to staff during appraisal
   c. Provide information about the number of untoward incidents
   d. All of the above

6. The clinical audit:
   a. Is carried out annually
   b. Compares hospital with hospital
   c. Helps to generate income
   d. Is a cyclical process

7. The NMC is responsible for:
   a. The ways in which health-care assistants practise
   b. The amount of money spent on education
   c. The regulation of nursing and midwifery professions
   d. The standards of practice related to dental nursing

8. The Care Quality Commission replaced:
   a. The Health Ombudsman
   b. The Healthcare Commission
   c. The Commission for Sex Equality
   d. The Commission for Racial Equality

9. The first piece of comprehensive legislation in the UK on medicine was:
   a. The Health and Safety at Work Act 1974
   b. The Health Act 1999
   c. The Medicines Act 1968
   d. The Medicines and Foods Act 1968

10. The NSFs are:
    a. National Service Frameworks
    b. National Standard Frameworks
    c. Notional Service Formats
    d. National Service Formulary

References

Amos T, Snowden P (2005) Risk management. In James A, Worrall, A, Kendall T (eds), *Clinical Governance in Mental Health and Learning Disability Services*. London: Gaskell, pp 174–203.

Better Regulation Taskforce (2001) *Annual Report 2000–2001*. London: Better Regulation Taskforce.

Beveridge W (1942) *Social Insurance and Allied Services*. London: HMSO.

Burgess R (2011) Introduction: Foundations, traditions and new directions – the future of clinical audit in a new decade. In: Burgess R (ed.), *New Principles of Best Practice in Clinical Audit*, 2nd edn. Oxford: Radcliffe, pp 1–22.

Care Quality Commission (2010) *Guidance about Compliance. Essential standards of quality and safety*. London: CQC.

Copping C (2005) Preventing and reporting drug administration errors. *Nursing Times* **101**(33): 32–34.

Currie L, Morrell C, Scrivener R (2003) *Clinical Governance Toolkit: An RCN resource guide*. London: Royal College of Nursing.

Currie L, Lecko C, Gallagher R, Sunley K (2011) Safety: Principle of nursing practice C. *Nursing Standard* **25**(30): 35–37.

Department of Health (1997) *The New NHS: Modern and dependable*. London: Department of Health.

Department of Health (1999) *Clinical Governance: Quality in the new NHS*. London: Department of Health.

Department of Health (2000a) *An Organisation with a Memory: Report of an Expert Group on Learning from Adverse Events in the NHS Chaired by the Chief Medical Officer*. London: Department of Health.

Department of Health (2000b) *The NHS Plan: A plan for investment, a plan for reform*. London: Department of Health.

Department of Health (2001) *Seeking Consent Working with 'Children'*. London: Department of Health.

Department of Health (2002) *Learning From Bristol: The Department of Health's Response to the report of the public inquiry into children's heart surgery at the Bristol Royal Infirmary 1984–1995*. London: Department of Health.

Department of Health (2004) *Building a Safer NHS for Patients: Improving medication safety. A report by the Chief Pharmaceutical Officer*. London: Department of Health.

Department of Health (2008) *High Quality Care For All. NHS Next Stage Review Final Report*. London: Department of Health.

Department of Health (2009) *The NHS Constitution*. London: Department of Health.

Department of Health (2010) *Equality and Excellence: Liberating the NHS*. London: Department of Health.

Dimond B (2011) *Legal Aspects of Medicine*, 2nd edn. London: Quay Books.

Ghosh R (2009) *Clinical Audit for Doctors*. Nottingham: Develop Medica.

Hammond S (2010) Clinical governance and patient safety: an overview. In: Haxby E, Hunter D, Jagger S (eds), *An Introduction to Clinical Governance and Patient Safety*. Oxford: Oxford University Press, pp 1–8.

Healthcare Commission (2005) *Inspection Manual: Independent health care*. London: Healthcare Commission.

Kehoe RF (2005) Clinical audit. In: James A, Worrall A, Kendall T (eds), *Clinical Governance in Mental Health and Learning Disability Services*. London: Gaskell, pp 224–236.

Littlejohns P, Pereira AJ (2010) National Institute for Health and Clinical Excellence (NICE) National Service Frameworks (NSFs) and governance. In: Haxby E, Hunter D, Jagger S (eds), *An Introduction to Clinical Governance and Patient Safety*. Oxford: Oxford University Press. pp 87–94.

Manley K, Watts C, Cunningham G, Davies J (2011) Principles of nursing practice: development and implementation. *Nursing Standard* **25**(27): 35–37.

Mayo AM, Duncan D (2004) Nurses' perception of medicine errors. *Nurse Management* **27**(1): 31–34.

Murphy L, Cox L, Murphy D (2005) Users' views of a dynamic risk assessment system. *Nursing Times* **101**(33): 35–37.

National Institute for Health and Clinical Excellence (2011a) *Generalised Anxiety Disorder and Panic Disorder (with or without agoraphobia) in Adults: Management in primary, secondary and community care* (partial update). London: NICE.

National Institute for Health and Clinical Excellence (2011b) *Anaemia Management in Chronic Kidney Disease*. London: NICE.

National Institute for Health and Clinical Excellence (2011c) *Food Allergy in Children and Young People. Diagnosis and assessment of food allergy in children and young people in primary care and community settings*. London: NICE.

National Patient Safety Agency (2004) *Introduction: Seven steps to patient safety*. London: National Patient Safety Agency.

National Specialised Commissioning Group (2010) *Paediatric Congenital Cardiac Surgery Services' National Specialised Commissioning Group*. London: National Specialised Commissioning Group. Available at: www.specialisedservices.nhs.uk/library/30/Developing_the_Model_of_Care.pdf (accessed July 2011).

Nursing and Midwifery Council (2008) *The Code: Standards of Conduct, Performance and Ethics for Nurses and Midwives*. London: NMC.

Nursing and Midwifery Council (2010a) *Standards for Medicines Management*. London: NMC.

Nursing and Midwifery Council (2010b) *Guidance on Professional Conduct for Nursing and Midwifery Students*. London: NMC.

Nursing and Midwifery Council (2010c) *Record Keeping Guidance for Nurses and Midwives*. London: NMC.

O'Brien M, Spires A, Andrews K (2011) *Introduction to Medicine Management in Nursing*. Exeter: Learning Matters.

Parish C (2003) Complacency to blame for transfusion mistakes. *Nursing Standard* **17**(45): 8.

Preston RM (2004) Drug errors and patient safety: The need for a change in practice. *British Journal of Nursing* **13**(2): 72–78.

Roberts GW (2005) The quality agenda in health and social care. In: Clouston TJ, Westcott L (eds), *Working in Health and Social Care*. Edinburgh: Elsevier, pp 119–130.

Rochford (2010) Improving working lives. In: Haxby E, Hunter, D, Jagger S (eds), *An Introduction to Clinical Governance and Patient Safety*. Oxford: Oxford University Press, pp 215–222.

Royal College of Nursing (2003) *Clinical Governance: An RCN resource guide*. London: RCN.

Sasaru R, Sheward Y, Sasaru S (2005) Audit in allied health professional practice. In Clouston TJ, Westcott L (eds), *Working in Health and Social Care*. Edinburgh: Elsevier. pp 145–160.

Scally G, Donaldson LJ (1998) Clinical governance and the drive for quality improvement in the new NHS in England. *British Medical Journal* **317**: 61–65.

Scrivens E (2005) *Quality, Risk and Control in Health Care*. Buckingham: Open University Press.

Waterlow J (1985) A risk assessment card. *Nursing Times* **81**(49): 51–55.

Woodward S (2011) Risk awareness. In: Haxby E, Hunter D, Jagger S (eds), *An Introduction to Clinical Governance and Patient Safety*. Oxford: Oxford University Press, pp 11–18.

Appendix 11.1

Summary of Standards for Medicines Management

This section provides a summary of the standards for easy reference. For further detail you should read, follow and adhere to the standards as detailed later in the document. It is essential that you read the full guidance, and you must follow the advice.

Section 1: Methods of supplying and/or administration of medicines

Standard 1: Methods

Registrants must only supply and administer medicinal products in accordance with one or more of the following processes:

- Patient specific direction (PSD)
- Patient medicines administration chart (may be called medicines administration record MAR)
- Patient group direction (PGD)
- Medicines Act exemption
- Standing order
- Homely remedy protocol
- Prescription forms

Standard 2: Checking

Registrants must check any direction to administer a medicinal product.

Standard 3: Transcribing

As a registrant you may transcribe medication from one 'direction to supply or administer' to another form of 'direction to supply or administer'.

Section 2: Dispensing

Standard 4: Prescription medicines

Registrants may in exceptional circumstances label from stock and supply a clinically appropriate medicine to a patient, against a written prescription (not PGD), for self-administration or administration by another professional, and to advise on its safe and effective use.

Standard 5: Patients' own medicines

Registrants may use patients' own medicines in accordance with the guidance in this booklet *Standards for Medicines Management*.

Section 3: Storage and transportation

Standard 6: Storage

Registrants must ensure that all medicinal products are stored in accordance with the patient information leaflet, summary of product characteristics document found in dispensed UK-licensed medication, and in accordance with any instruction on the label.

Standard 7: Transportation

Registrants may transport medication to patients including controlled drugs, where patients, their carers or representatives are unable to collect them, provided that the registrant is conveying the medication to a patient for whom the medicinal product has been prescribed (e.g. from a pharmacy to the patient's home).

Section 4: Standards for practice of administration of medicines

Standard 8: Administration

As a registrant, in exercising your professional accountability in the best interests of your patients:

- You must be certain of the identity of the patient to whom the medicine is to be administered
- You must check that the patient is not allergic to the medicine before administering it
- You must know the therapeutic uses of the medicine to be administered, its normal dosage, side effects, precautions and contraindications
- You must be aware of the patient's plan of care (care plan or pathway)
- You must check that the prescription or the label on medicine dispensed is clearly written and unambiguous
- You must check the expiry date (where it exists) of the medicine to be administered
- You must have considered the dosage, weight where appropriate, method of administration, route and timing
- You must administer or withhold in the context of the patient's condition (e.g. digoxin not usually to be given if pulse <60) and coexisting therapies, e.g. physiotherapy
- You must contact the prescriber or another authorised prescriber without delay where contraindications to the prescribed medicine are discovered, where the patient develops a reaction to the medicine, or where assessment of the patient indicates that the medicine is no longer suitable (see Standard 25)
- You must make a clear, accurate and immediate record of all medicine administered, intentionally withheld or refused by the patient, ensuring that the signature is clear and legible. It is also your responsibility to ensure that a record is made when delegating the task of administering medicine.

In addition:

- Where medication is not given, the reason for not doing so must be recorded
- You may administer with a single signature any prescription-only medicine (POM), general sales list (GSL) or pharmacy (P) medication.

In respect of controlled drugs:

- These should be administered in line with relevant legislation and local standard operating procedures.

- It is recommended that for the administration of controlled drugs a secondary signatory is required within secondary care and similar health-care settings.
- In a patient's home, where a registrant is administering a controlled drug that has already been prescribed and dispensed to that patient, obtaining a secondary signatory should be based on local risk assessment.
- Although normally the second signatory should be another registered health-care professional (e.g. doctor, pharmacist, dentist) or student nurse or midwife, in the interest of patient care, where this is not possible, a second suitable person who has been assessed as competent may sign. It is good practice that the second signatory witnesses the whole administration process. For guidance, go to www.dh.gov.uk and search for safer management of controlled drugs: guidance on standard operating procedures.
- In cases of direct patient administration of oral medication from stock in a substance misuse clinic, it must be a registered nurse who administers, signed by a second signatory (assessed as competent), who is then supervised by the registrant as the patient receives and consumes the medication.
- You must clearly countersign the signature of the student when supervising a student in the administration of medicines.

Standard 9: Assessment

As a registrant, you are responsible for the initial and continued assessment of patients who are self-administering and have continuing responsibility for recognising and acting upon changes in a patient's condition with regard to safety of the patient and others.

Standard 10: Self-administration – children and young people

In the case of children, when arrangements have been made for parents or carers or patients to administer their own medicinal products before discharge or rehabilitation; the registrant should ascertain that the medicinal product has been taken as prescribed.

Standard 11: Remote prescription or direction to administer

In exceptional circumstances, where medication has been previously prescribed and the prescriber is unable to issue a new prescription, but where changes to the dose are considered necessary, the use of information technology (such as fax, text message or email) may be used but must confirm any change to the original prescription.

Standard 12: Text messaging

As a registrant, you must ensure that there are protocols in place to ensure patient confidentiality and documentation of any text received including: complete text message, telephone number (it was sent from), the time sent, any response given, and the signature and date when received by the registrant.

Standard 13: Titration

Where medication has been prescribed within a range of dosages, it is acceptable for registrants to titrate dosages according to patient response and symptom control and to administer within the prescribed range.

Standard 14: Preparing medication in advance

Registrants must not prepare substances for injection in advance of their immediate use or administer medication drawn into a syringe or container by another practitioner when not in their presence.

Standard 15: Medication acquired over the internet

Registrants should never administer any medication that has not been prescribed, or that has been acquired over the internet without a valid prescription.

Standard 16: Aids to support compliance

Registrants must assess the patient's suitability and understanding of how to use an appropriate compliance aid safely.

Section 5: Delegation

Standard 17: Delegation

A registrant is responsible for the delegation of any aspects of the administration of medicinal products and they are accountable to ensure that the patient, carer or care assistant is competent to carry out the task.

Standard 18: Nursing and midwifery students

Students must never administer or supply medicinal products without direct supervision.

Standard 19: Unregistered practitioners

In delegating the administration of medicinal products to unregistered practitioners, it is the registrant who must apply the principles of administration of medicinal products as listed above. They may then delegate an unregistered practitioner to assist the patient in the ingestion or application of the medicinal product.

Standard 20: Intravenous medication

Wherever possible, two registrants should check medication to be administered intravenously, one of whom should also be the registrant who then administers the intravenous medication.

Section 6: Disposal of medicinal products

Standard 21: Disposal

A registrant must dispose of medicinal products in accordance with legislation.

Section 7: Unlicensed medicines

Standard 22: Unlicensed medicines

A registrant may administer an unlicensed medicinal product with the patient's informed consent against a patient-specific direction but NOT against a patient group direction.

Section 8: Complementary and alternative therapies

Standard 23: Complementary and alternative therapies

Registrants must have successfully undertaken training and be competent to practise the administration of complementary and alternative therapies.

Section 9: Management of adverse events (errors or incidents) in the administration of medicines

Standard 24: Management of adverse effects

As a registrant, if you make an error you must take any action to prevent any potential harm to the patient and report as soon as possible to the prescriber, your line manager or employer (according to local policy) and document your actions. Midwives should also inform their named supervisor of midwives.

Standard 25: Reporting adverse reactions

As a registrant, if a patient experiences an adverse drug reaction to a medication, you must take any action to remedy harm caused by the reaction. You must record this in the patient's notes, notify the prescriber (if you did not prescribe the drug) and notify via the Yellow Card Scheme immediately.

Section 10: Controlled drugs

Standard 26: Controlled drugs

Registrants should ensure that patients prescribed controlled drugs are administered these in a timely fashion in line with the standards for administering medication to patients. Registrants should comply with and follow the legal requirements and approved local standard operating procedures for controlled drugs that are appropriate for their area of work.

Source: reproduced with permission from Nursing and Midwifery Council (2010a) (www.nmc-uk.org).

12

Recognising, Interpreting and Managing Deterioration in Health and Wellbeing

Aims and objectives

The aim of this chapter is to help you recognise, interpret and act appropriately when a person's health deteriorates.

At the end of the chapter you will be able to:

1. Discuss the importance of recognising and responding appropriately to a person's deteriorating condition
2. Consider patient safety as a priority
3. Explore the various early warning system scoring tools available
4. Describe the ways in which nurses can communicate effectively with other health-care staff
5. Begin to apply the concepts discussed to the practice setting
6. Appreciate the Nursing and Midwifery Council's requirements of student nurses

This chapter concentrates on the care of those people who are looked after in acute hospital settings. This is not to say that those who are being cared for in their own homes or other settings are not at risk of deterioration in their health and wellbeing and that the nurse need not be aware of deterioration and instigate actions and provide timely management to ensure their safety. There are people with multiple, long-term, complex conditions being cared for in the community who may be at risk of deterioration.

There is a growing body of evidence suggesting that deterioration in a person's condition is not being recognised or acted upon by hospital staff (National Patient Safety Agency or NPSA, 2007). Failing to act may result in adverse outcomes that can include delayed or avoidable admission to critical care and increased mortality. Boulanger and Toghill (2009) note that hospitals may not consistently be the safe place that patients and their families expect.

There are times when the health of a patient in hospital may get worse suddenly – he or she becomes acutely ill. This is more likely to happen, for example, after an emergency admission to hospital, after surgery or when being discharged from critical care, and can happen at any point of an illness, increasing the risk of the person needing to stay longer in hospital, not fully recovering or dying. Goldhill et al (2005)

The Student's Guide to Becoming a Nurse, Second Edition. Ian Peate.
© 2012 John Wiley & Sons, Ltd. Published 2012 by John Wiley & Sons, Ltd.

note that approximately 25 per cent of patients admitted to an intensive care unit (ICU) who die do so after discharge to a ward. Monitoring patients regularly while they are in hospital and taking action if they show signs of becoming worse can help avoid serious problems.

The nature of health and health care is changing. There are increasing numbers of older people in hospital who have complex and acute problems with multiple comorbidities (Margereson, 2010) and importantly this is complemented by increasingly effective treatments and extremely skilled staff. Enhancing the care of acutely ill patients and ensuring their safety are the responsibility of all staff. This includes nurses, doctors and other health-care staff who provide care for people on general wards, staff on critical care units, the senior management and medical/nursing leadership in trusts, through to those who commission services and those responsible at a national level for the development of policy and guidance.

Patients, their families and carers have a right to believe that when in hospital they will receive the best possible care. They should be able to feel confident that, if their condition deteriorates, they are in the best place for prompt and effective treatment. Sometimes, however, when patients who are, or become, acutely unwell in hospital they may receive poor care. This may occur because the person's condition has deteriorated and this has not been recognised, or because – in spite of signs of clinical deterioration – this has not been appreciated, or not acted upon quickly enough. Communication and documentation are often poor, experience might be lacking and provision of critical care expertise, including admission to critical care areas, delayed (National Institute for Health and Clinical Excellence or NICE, 2007). NPSA (2007) received a number of reports related to serious incidents and identified that 11 per cent of deaths were associated with non-recognition (and subsequently no action) of patients' deteriorating health. Areas noted for improvement included:

- More regular observations
- Earlier recognition of deterioration
- Better communication
- Effective response to concerns.

There are a number of systems currently in use in hospital settings to ensure timely recognition of deteriorating patients. Many of these systems are made up of aggregate scoring systems, e.g. early warning scoring system (often known as modified early warning system). These involve periodic observation of specific vital signs, which are then compared with a simple set of criteria with predefined thresholds (McDonnell et al, 2007).

Think

When you are next working in an acute care setting take some time to look at the various EWSs that are in use. Think about who completes the scores and what happens when the score gives the nurse cause for concern.

Analysis of failures to respond promptly and appropriately to the needs of the acutely ill person are made up of a number of factors, which are often complex and wide ranging. They include challenges in prioritising competing demands, a lack of effective team working and leadership, failure in verbal and written communication, inadequate training to help staff understand the relevance of observations, and a lack of successful implementation of important policies and procedures (NPSA, 2007).

Successful use of these systems depends on appropriate education and training. Emphasis is placed on the importance of training; by making sure that routine measurements are accurately taken and documented by nurses and other staff who can make sense of their clinical relevance and by relating these observations to a graded track-and-trigger system, care can be appropriately escalated. The foundations for patient safety are set out by doing and recording simple measurements well and also having established response strategies in place. NICE (2007) advocate the use of some form of physiological track-and-trigger system that should be used to monitor all adult patients in acute hospital settings. NICE further recommended that physiological observations should be monitored at least every 12 hours and a graded response strategy made up of three levels should be implemented.

Nurses have to be able to demonstrate that they are competent in carrying out a basic assessment of mental health, identifying and assessing deterioration in cognitive function, and recognising deterioration in mental wellbeing so as to be able to refer to an appropriate specialist and to coordinate and support the delivery of the appropriate care. These are skills that are beyond the scope of discussion in this chapter.

It must be recognised that consistently and effectively detecting and acting upon patient deterioration is a complex issue. There are a series of points where the processes can fail and these include not taking observations, not recognising early signs of deterioration, not communicating observations causing concern and not responding to these in an appropriate way.

Patient-centred care

The provision of treatment and care offered to people should always take into account their needs and preferences. If appropriate, those with an acute illness should, if possible, be allowed to make informed decisions about their care and treatment, working in partnership with nurses and other health-care professionals. Where the person does not have the capacity to make decisions, nurses should follow the guidance to consent issued by the Department of Health as well as guidance related to the Mental Capacity Act 2005 in the form of the Mental Capacity Act 2005 Code of Practice (Office of the Public Guardian, 2007). If in agreement with the patient, carers and relatives should have the possibility of being involved in decisions about treatment and care. Carers and relatives will also need to be given the information and support that they need. The Nursing and Midwifery Council (NMC, 2008) urge nurses to ensure that they uphold a person's rights to be fully involved in decisions about their care.

It is essential that there is good communication between health-care professionals and patients, and this should be accompanied by evidence-based written information that has been tailored to meet the needs of the patient. Any information about treatment and care should be culturally appropriate. This should also be accessible to those people who may have additional needs, e.g. physical, sensory or learning disabilities and to those who do not speak or read English.

The unique role of the nurse enables her or him to be in constant contact with patients over a 24-hour period, thus placing nurses in a prime position to identify problems at an early stage when undertaking a systematic approach to patient assessment. This means that appropriate treatment can be identified quickly, possibly saving a person's life. As part of an overall assessment of the person's needs, nurses record baseline observations, e.g. blood pressure, pulse, temperature and respiratory rate. Watson (2006) notes that recording baseline observations is no longer sufficient.

The nurse requires an in-depth and sound knowledge of fundamental anatomy and physiology for them to be able to interpret observations, as well as understanding the pathology and nursing care of commonplace illnesses and injuries. Current preregistration education and the introduction of the NMC's (2010a) *Standards for Pre registration Nursing Education* will help to equip nurses to care for critically ill people, including those outside designated critical care areas. These standards state that the student must be able to respond appropriately when faced with an emergency or a sudden deterioration in a person's physical or psychological condition (e.g. abnormal vital signs, collapse, cardiac arrest, self-harm, extremely challenging behaviour, attempted suicide) including seeking help from an appropriate person. The student must demonstrate competence, have a sound knowledge base and relevant skills before being able to register with the NMC, and this includes the knowledge, skills and competence concerning the acutely ill person. Teaching and assessing methods used to demonstrate competence are varied and will include the objective structured clinical examination (OSCE) through simulation.

Nurses have to be able to critically analyse features of abnormal physiology and understand the principles underpinning accurate physiological and homeostatic measurement when caring for and managing people who may be experiencing an acute deterioration of their condition. Recognition of what can be subtle physiological changes is complex (Johnstone et al, 2007). Analysis and understanding must be based on the best available evidence ensuring the delivery of high-quality, safe and effective care. Care provision has to be undertaken in a holistic way using a multiprofessional team approach. Nurses must recognise the early signs of illness in people of all ages and make accurate assessments and start appropriate and timely management of those who are acutely ill, at risk of clinical deterioration or needing emergency care (NMC, 2010a).

Chapter 9 provided an overview of the nursing process, and discussion in that chapter included the importance of effective patient assessment. The following section of this chapter considers the general skills associated with observing, measuring and acting on your findings, the emphasis being on physical assessment.

Early warning systems: track and trigger

Early warning scoring systems (EWSs), sometimes called early warning scoring systems (EWSSs) or modified early warning systems (MEWSs) have been devised following the publication of a number of studies and reports suggesting that there is often a delay in making an appropriate response to deterioration in a patient's condition. The purpose of assessment and the use of the EWS is to gain accurate information about a person which provides the nurse with a baseline for clinical decision-making. There are a number of tools that have been used (many are constantly under review or modification) which make use of the observation of vital signs to alert the nurse and others to those patients at risk of deterioration and who need an appropriate response. These tools are collectively known as track-and-trigger systems; they are multiple parameter scoring systems and are now an essential part of acute care (Table 12.1). Table 12.2 demonstrates the medical emergency team (MET) scoring system and Table 12.3 shows the patient at-risk team (PART) score. The tools were designed to trigger a response when changes in key physiological data were noted. The Department of Health emphasised the use of EWSs in 2005 (DH, 2005).

When caring for the acutely ill person or the potentially acutely ill person, nurses can be faced with situations where they have to make decisions about intervening as well as when to call for help. Decisions are being made with respect to intervention, timing and communication. EWSs have the potential to support this decision-making; however, according to Johnstone et al (2007) the systems are not always used to their full potential. Using an EWS effectively requires skill and clinical judgement.

When a person's condition deteriorates acutely this is the result of an acute physiological aberration and as such the EWSs reflect this in the type and number of variables that are being used to predict these at-risk patients; other assessment tools also do this, e.g. tools associated with pressure sore formation. When using the EWS the nurse assigns scores to patient observations, e.g. heart rate, blood pressure, temperature, respiratory rate, oxygen and saturations. When the nurse has taken the observations (measurements), an overall score is calculated from the physiological indicators (usually when the score increases this often indicates deterioration) and this acts as a trigger to the nurse to refer to a more

Table 12.1   Early warning system

	3	2	1	0	1	2	3
Heart rate (beats/min)		<40	41–50	51–100	101–110	111–130	
Systolic blood pressure (mmHg)	<70	71–80	81–100	101–199	>200		
Respiratory rate (breaths/min)		<8		9–14	15–20	21–29	>30
Temperature (°C)		<35.0	35.1 0 36.5	36.6–37.4	>37.5		
Central nervous system				A	V	P	U

A = alert; V = responds to voice; P = responds to pain; U = unconscious.

Table 12.2   Medical Emergency Team (MET) Score

Abnormal physiology
- Temperature <35.5 or >39.5°C
- Systolic BP <100 or >200
- Respirations per minute <10 or >40
- Pulse rate < 40 or >120
- Urine output <500 mL/day
- Decreased level of consciousness

Abnormal pathology
- Potassium <3 or >6
- Sodium <125 or >155
- Blood sugar <2 or >20
- Arterial pH <7.2 or >7.55
- Base excess <−15 or >+10

Specific conditions
Cardiovascular
- Cardiopulmonary arrest
- Pulmonary oedema
- New major arrhythmia

Respiratory
- Acute severe asthma
- Acute respiratory failure
- Upper airway obstruction

Surgical
- Excessive bleeding
- Excessive drainage

Shock
- Hypovolaemic
- Anaphylactic
- Cardiogenic
- Septic

Metabolic
- Acute diabetic emergency

Poisoning/trauma
- Near drowning
- Carbon monoxide poisoning
- Severe drug overdose

Obstetric
- Amniotic fluid embolism
- Pre-eclampsia

Neurological
- Status epilepticus
- Acute psychiatric disturbance (aggressive, uncontrollable)

Source: adapted from Hodgetts et al (2002).

Table 12.3   Patient at-risk team (PART) score

Respiratory rate <8 breaths/min or >25 breaths/min
Pulse oximetry <90% on >35% fractional inspired oxygen
Pulse <50 beats/min or >125 beats/min
Systolic blood pressure <90 mmHg, >200 mmHg or >40 mmHg; less than patient's normal values
Urine output >30 mL/h for >2 hours, unless normal for patient
Sustained alteration in level of consciousness or fall in Glasgow Coma Scale score of >2 in past hour
Concerns about the patient

Source: adapted from Goldhill et al (1999).

senior nurse and/or medical staff (Andrews and Waterman, 2005). The collection of data (the indicators) is routinely collected by nursing staff and the level of abnormality and the number of abnormal indicators have the ability to predict subsequent mortality (Goldhill and McNarry, 2004).

Gao et al (2007) have identified 25 distinct EWSs; although they all have variations they also have similarities with regard to the type of data collected and they provide quantifiable evidence of acute change. Many hospitals and even departments within hospitals have developed their own bespoke systems; a national EWS is currently being developed (National Quality Board, 2010). The widespread use of EWSs is constantly under review because evidence may suggest that they are not being used to their full potential. Oakey and Slade (2006) have reported that, in some EWSs on which they collected data, some scores were not being calculated or some of the physiological parameters not recorded; 54 per cent of charts were correctly completed and only 69 per cent of charts had a score recorded. If the EWSs are to achieve their full potential, nurses must use them correctly and report changes in the patient's condition quickly and to the right person with a view to urgent corrective prevention.

Harrison and Daly (2011) note that the aim is to prevent any patient passing through a recognisable yet potentially reversible period of instability and deterioration. The most common events, they continue, preceding a cardiac arrest or transfer to an intensive care unit (ICU), are a falling blood pressure and deterioration in the level of consciousness.

The National Confidential Enquiry into Patient Outcomes and Death (NCEPOD, 2005) reports that patients displayed prolonged physiological instability for more than 12 hours before being admitted to the ICU. In 2000, the Department of Health (DH, 2000) reported that the frequency of not accurately recording the patient's vital signs had become a national concern. The delivery of suboptimal care as a result of failure to record and act upon physiological observations and changes in the person's condition promoted the publication of a clinical guideline by NICE (2007) *Acutely Ill Patients in Hospital NICE Guideline 50*. NICE (2007) have recommended that all hospitals introduce a track-and-trigger scoring system and that physiological observations are performed on all patients on admission to hospital. This was further supported by the Department of Health (2009). Acute illness is intensified by failing to act on recognised changes (Hillman et al, 2001).

Vital signs

The Royal College of Nursing (RCN, 2007) consider vital signs to included temperature, heart/pulse rate, respiratory rate and effort, and blood pressure. Kozier et al (2008) define vital signs as the physiological measures that nurses record when working in clinical situations, with the intention of assessing the clinical status of patients as well as using them to monitor changes. Dougherty and Lister (2011) refer to vital signs as a cluster of physical measurements and these can include pulse, respiration, temperature and blood pressure. There are additions that can be added to vital signs depending on the context of care, e.g. oxygen saturation (pulse oximetry) and capillary refill time may be added in acute or high dependency care units.

It has been noted that the most sensitive indicator of patient deterioration is the respiratory rate (NICE, 2007; NPSA, 2007). Hogan (2006) demonstrated that respiratory rate was the one parameter (vital sign) that was recorded less than 50 per cent of the time. Several reasons for this may exist, e.g. lack of time, lack of understanding and the increasing use of electronic equipment to measure other vital signs.

Measuring vital signs

Nurses play an essential part in influencing patient safety on a daily basis. One key element of the role and function of the nurse is the measurement and recording of vital signs to detect deteriorating patients. Measuring vital signs can be seen as a task, often delegated to the more junior members of the healthcare team, as opposed to an essential duty of gathering clinical data; this is a serious responsibility. Observations, according to Boulanger and Toghill (2009), are a fundamental part of nurses' core skills set. The principal vital signs are as follows:

- Temperature
- Heart rate
- Blood pressure
- Respiratory rate
- Level of consciousness
- Pulse oximetry
- Urine output.

Temperature

The temperature is a vital sign that can help the diagnosis of illness and disease. A patient's temperature can be taken from various sites on the body, using a number of different devices. Core body temperature is the temperature below the subcutaneous tissue. Body temperature is recorded orally, per axilla, per rectum, via the ear canal or by using an infra-red skin thermometer. Changes in body temperature indicate a change in bodily function, e.g. a high temperature may indicate an infection. The nurse records the patient's temperature for a number of reasons, i.e. to determine a baseline, after surgery (postoperatively), to observe response to infection, when a patient has hypothermia, in critically ill patients and when a patient is receiving a blood transfusion.

Heart rate

Assessing heart rate requires the nurse to feel the patient's pulse. All registered nurses, students and other direct care providers are trained to assess a pulse. Often in clinical settings the pulse rate is assessed using an electronic device. This is an accepted method and can provide accurate results, but the automated measurement cannot determine the feel of the patient (i.e. cold clammy, diaphoretic), or the pulse volume, rate or rhythm; only the hands-on touching of the patient can provide this important clinical information.

Blood pressure

Many clinical areas rely on an automated device to assess blood pressure, e.g. Dinamap. This approach can remove the risk of variability which can be present between operators. There are, however, some other issues that could impact on accurate reading, e.g. application of the correct cuff size. An incorrect cuff size using an automated or manual device (i.e. sphygmomanometer) can result in an incorrect recording.

Respiratory rate

This important physiological measure/indicator is frequently absent when staff record vital signs. The nurse must ensure that the respiratory rate, depth and rhythm are counted for a full minute. Other issues associated with respiration, i.e. pain on inspiration or expiration, an audible wheeze and skin colour, should also be noted, recorded and reported.

Level of consciousness

The most common way of detecting the patent's level of consciousness is by using the AVPU (**a**lert, responds to **v**oice, responds to **p**ain, **u**nresponsive) approach:

- A (alert): the person is conscious, alert, eyes open, oriented and is able to answer questions.
- V (responds to voice): the person is not alert, may have the eyes closed, could be semi-conscious. On hearing a voice the person responds when roused.
- P (responds only to pain): the person moves or groans only in response to painful stimuli given by a trained competent person, i.e. a registered nurse or doctor.
- U (unconscious): no response to voice or painful stimuli.

This approach can provide a quick and clear guide concerning the person's level of consciousness, and enables the nurse to identify those patients at risk if they respond only to pain or are unresponsive. A more detailed assessment would involve the use of the GCS; the GCS consists of three parameters: best eye response, best verbal response and best motor response.

Pulse oximetry

This physiological measure must be used alongside other clinical observations and judgements. It is a non-invasive method of recording the pulse and peripheral oxygen saturation. The nurse can confirm or refute clinical assumptions using pulse oximetry. The operator must ensure that he or she knows how to use the device effectively. The pulse oximeter is deemed inaccurate when saturation records below 90 per cent; this requires further investigation. Inaccurate recording can occur if the person has anaemia, arrhythmias, poor peripheral perfusion or has been exposed to carbon monoxide poisoning.

Urine output

To measure the person's urine output hourly will require the insertion of a urinary catheter, which may not always be appropriate or desirable. Oliguria (diminished urine output) is a good indicator of poor perfusion, reduced cardiac output and renal failure. Even when the patient does not have a catheter *in situ* the nurse should, as a matter of course, ask the patient about urine output because this can help detect deterioration.

Top tips

White coat syndrome (sometimes called white coat hypertension) is a phenomenon in which patients exhibit elevated blood pressure in a clinical setting but not in other settings. This is said to be due to the anxiety that some people experience during a clinical visit or when in a clinical setting. You should always allow (if appropriate) the patient to settle in the ward or clinical setting before undertaking observations.

Look, listen and feel

Watson (2006) advocates the use of a systematic look, listen and feel approach when undertaking patient assessment that incorporates an EWS:

- *Look*: look at the patient and see if he or she is pale or peripherally cyanosed. You may notice that the person's skin appears pink and flushed. Observe the chest wall rising and falling. Is it even, regular or irregular? Does the rising of the chest wall look slow or fast? Do you observe the person using the accessory muscles of respiration, assisting them to breathe more easily (the stomach muscles or exaggerated shoulder muscle use)? When observing the person does he or she seem to be confused or agitated? Is there a change in the level of consciousness?
- *Listen*: active listening means really listening not just hearing what the person says. Listen to the responses given to you by the person when you ask them a question, are they coherent, does the person seem to be orientated or disorientated, is the response an appropriate one to the question asked. Does the person make a response? Listen to body sounds, for example, does the patient pass wind, do they have a 'gurgling tummy', is their breathing accompanied by a wheeze, does the wheeze occur on inspiration or expiration? If the person is being electronically monitored is the monitor alarming, what might this tell you, what action must you take?
- *Feel*: therapeutic touch can reveal much about the person being cared for. When you touch the person or attempt to touch him or her does he or she cower away or seem scared of you or other people? Does the person's skin feel cold, clammy, warm? Is the person in pain when touched? When you feel the person's pulse, is it full and bounding, weak and thready, regular or irregular, or does the heart miss a beat?

Top tips

To assess a patient's cardiovascular system use the look, listen and feel approach. Look at the person's skin colour taking into account signs of cyanosis, greyness, flushing. Are there any signs of peripheral cyanosis? Is the person perspiring? Listen for additional breath sounds. Listen to any alarms from any electronic devices that the person may be connected to and act on this. Look at the overall EWS and make a comparison with previous observations. Are there any trends? Feel the patient's skin. Is the person warm, cold, clammy? If you have any concerns report them immediately, act on them and ensure that you document your findings in the most appropriate way.

The systemic use of look, listen and feel is part of the nurse's essential repertoire of nursing skills, along with caring, kindness and compassion. The use of an EWS can help notice deterioration in a person's condition, but the skills associated with look, listen and feel are equally important and should be used to complement the EWS.

Think

All nurses must recognise when people are anxious or in distress and respond effectively, using therapeutic principles, to promote their wellbeing, manage personal safety and resolve conflict. Think about therapeutic touch. What does it mean? It has many meanings. It is suggested that therapeutic touch, when provided appropriately by the nurse in the clinical setting, can promote feelings of comfort, peace, calm and security for patients. Conversely there are times when some patients may feel violated by touch. How could you ascertain that the person for whom you are caring is uncomfortable when touched?

Using an early warning scoring chart

NICE (2007) and the Department of Health (2009) advocated that only those staff who have received training and been deemed competent should undertake and record physiological measurements and observations. There are instances where delegation of the duty to perform and record can occur, e.g. where a registered nurse delegates the duty to a health-care assistant or student nurse. If this is the case, it is essential that the registered nurse ensures that he or she is compliant with the NMC's requirements regarding delegation of duty. The decision whether or not to delegate an aspect of care and to transfer and/or rescind delegation is the sole responsibility of the nurse, and is based on professional judgement. The registered nurse is ultimately accountable for the activity delegated.

Smith and Roberts (2011) provide detailed discussion concerning the completion of an EWS chart. They note that a systematic approach is used, informing staff of important information about the patient as well as ensuring that there are no omissions or failures to document every aspect of the patient's baseline observations. As vital signs are recorded, a score is awarded responding to the parameter measured. When all vital signs have been measured the individual's scores (for each parameter) are added up to provide an overall score. Any patient scoring 3 or more requires the presence of a senior (previously determined) member of the health-care team and the patient's plan of care may need to be revised or interventions escalated. The patient scoring less than 3 will need to have vital signs monitored more frequently. The EWS score should be linked to a trust-wide agreed response or escalation chart where the management of the patient is provided using a visual chart (see Table 12.3). The vital signs that are routinely recorded are awarded a score from 0 to 3. On the left-hand side of the chart are the vital signs being measured; these can vary depending on the context of care. The information that the nurse gains during the assessment process using an EWS can help make a difference to the patient's condition and prognosis initiating a systematic response.

Case study 12.1

Mr Shah, a 60-year-old man, was brought to the accident and emergency department of his local hospital because he had been experiencing increasing shortness of breath. There were no complaints of chest, jaw or arm pain. Mr Shah had a past history of a myocardial infarction and was currently on the waiting list to undergo coronary artery bypass surgery at the regional cardiothoracic centre; he was also known to have asthma. When Mr Shah arrived at the hospital he was alert and able to communicate with staff; his respiratory rate was 30 breaths/min, a pulse rate of 130/min, a blood pressure of 108/60 mmHg, and his temperature was recorded as 38.5°C.

Calculate Mr Shah's EWS and devise a plan of care for him.

Noting a deviation in the score based on a baseline undertaken on admission can help the nurse take further action (Simpson, 2006). It is essential that the nurse ensure that the calculations used to calculate the scores are correct. Oakey and Slade (2006) have noted inaccuracies with scoring and documentation of the score. Some hospitals use hand-held computers at the patient's bedside to enable inputting and subsequent calculation of the patient's score. This is then plotted against other parameters and triggers an alert indicating that there has been deterioration in the person's condition (Tweddell, 2008). It is recognised that technology is now an important aspect of health-care provision and a number of technological devices are in use that assist the nurse in working in an effective manner with patients, for example, the use of Dinamap to assess blood pressure. Lomas and West (2009) have commented on the use of such technologies and the possibility that they may deskill nurses. Nurses provide much more than physical, technological care and this should never be forgotten, the nurse must always demonstrate caring, kindness and compassion when working with patients. If the nurse fails to use the correct skills in order to asses a person's blood pressure or respiratory rate then regardless of the technology there to support the activity the reading may be incorrect and as such the patient may suffer unnecessary harm due to nursing incompetence.

Case study 12.2

Go back to Mr Shah in Case study 12.1. Mr Shah's EWS score was 5. He was assessed by the assistant practitioner and she has prescribed a salbutamol nebuliser and oxygen therapy; both were given. After 15 min and the completion of the use of the nebuliser, on clinical observation the nurse reports that he is looking better. His observations are recorded again and his respiratory rate had dropped to 24 breaths/min, his pulse rate was 124 beats/min, his temperature remained the same, but his blood pressure had dropped to 95/55 mmHg.

Undertake a reassessment of Mr Shah's EWS and revise his plan of care.

Although the EWS has the potential to provide an objective assessment of the person's condition, the nurse must also ensure that he or she uses the tool together with his or her knowledge and skills, making known any deficiency in these. Regardless of the tool being used, the nurse must combine the outcome of the score with a holistic assessment underpinned by sound clinical judgement (Critical Care Stakeholders Forum and National Outreach Forum, 2007).

The important activity of assessing and calculating the EWS score is but one aspect of care required when recognising, interpreting and managing deterioration in a person's health and wellbeing. The nurse must ensure that all incidents and issues are documented as per hospital policy and in line with the NMC's (2010b) *Record Keeping Guidance for Nurses and Midwives*. Griffith and Tengnah (2010) remind practitioners that poor record keeping has legal and professional consequences for nurses and other health-care staff. It is essential that, during all stages of the assessment process, the patient is kept informed and reassured about all activity being undertaken. The patient's relatives or carer will also need to be kept up to date with activities and interventions being undertaken.

NICE (2007) recommend that adult patients being cared for in an acute setting (including those in an A&E setting) should have physiological observations recorded when they are admitted, or initial assessment and a clear written monitoring plan that clearly details which physiological observations should be recorded as well as how often. The plan should take account of the following:

- Patient's diagnosis
- Presence of comorbidities
- Agreed treatment plan.

Physiological observations should be recorded and acted upon by those staff who have been trained to undertake these procedures and understand their clinical relevance.

Track-and-trigger systems should be in place and used to monitor all adult patients in acute hospital settings. Physiological observations should be monitored at least every 12 hours, unless a decision has been made at a senior level to increase or decrease this frequency for the patient. The frequency of monitoring should be increased if there is any abnormal physiology detected.

It is essential that those staff caring for patients in acute hospital settings should have competencies in monitoring, measurement, interpretation and prompt response to the acutely ill patient that are appropriate to the level of care that they are providing.

Graded response strategies for patients identified as being at risk of clinical deterioration should be agreed upon and delivered locally. There are three levels in these strategies:

1. *Low-score group*: increased frequency of observations and the nurse in charge is alerted.
2. *Medium-score group*: there must be an urgent call to the team with primary medical responsibility for the patient. At the same time a call must be made to personnel with core competencies for acute illness, e.g. a critical care outreach team, a hospital at-night team, or a specialist trainee in an acute medical or surgical specialty.
3. *High-score group*: there must be an emergency call to a team with critical care competencies and diagnostic skills. This team should include a medical practitioner skilled in the assessment of the critically ill patient, who has advanced airway management and resuscitation skills. There should be an immediate response.

Figure 12.1 provides a flow diagram detailing responses to acute illness in adults.

If the team caring for the patient believe that admission to a critical care area is clinically indicated, the decision to admit should involve the consultant caring for the patient on the ward as well as the consultant in critical care.

When the patient is to be transferred from a critical care area to the general ward, there are a number of factors that should be taken into account to enhance the patient's safety. NICE (2007) suggest that transfer should take place as early as possible during the day. Transfer from critical care areas to the general ward should be avoided between 22:00 and 07:00 whenever possible. If transfer does occur between these times then this should be documented as an adverse incident.

The critical care area transferring team and the receiving ward team should take shared responsibility for the care of the patient being transferred. Jointly they should ensure the following:

●   Continuity of care through a formal structured handover of care from critical care area staff to ward staff (this should include medical and nursing staff), supported by a written plan
●   The receiving ward, with support from critical care if required, can deliver the agreed plan.

The formal structured handover of care should include:

●   A summary of critical care stay; this includes the diagnosis and treatment provided
●   A monitoring and investigation plan
●   A plan for on-going treatment, which includes drugs and therapies, nutrition plan, infection status and any agreed limitations of treatment
●   Physical and rehabilitation needs
●   Psychological and emotional needs
●   Specific communication or language needs.

Effective communication is the cornerstone of good nursing care. Having noted deterioration in the person's condition, the nurse must communicate this in an effective and efficient manner to other colleagues. The Kaiser Permanente (Institute for Health Improvement) has devised a communication frame-work that can help ensure that communication is clear and appropriate (Haig et al, 2006).

Communicating concerns

Poor communication between and within clinical teams, as well as a lack of communication between different grades of doctors within clinical teams, and between different clinical teams and other health-care professionals, occurs (National Confidential Enquiry into Patient Outcomes and Death, 2005). There are instances where poor decision-making and lack of senior input occur, particularly in the evenings and night. Poor communication can cause delays and waste time.

Case study 12.3

Return to Mr Shah (Case study 12.1). Despite looking better Mr Shah's EWS score has risen to 6; this provides you with evidence that he is still deteriorating. The nurse uses the hospital's escalating concerns protocol and the intensive care outreach team were called; he was admitted to the high dependency unit for observation and treatment. Further analysis reveals that Mr Shah is septic as a result of a chest infection.

347

The outcome of this case study demonstrates that subjective judgements (the nurse felt that he looked better) made on appearance only can be deceptive; there was an underlying chest infection that put Mr Shah's health and wellbeing at risk. The intensive care outreach team can undertake more objective judgements of physiological parameters.

There is a need for better team work, which involves consultants and all medical staff working together with nurses, managers and sometimes patients themselves. Acute and emergency situations may not allow this way of working but, with concerted effort, time and effective communication, specialist groups have the potential to anticipate and plan for the most common presenting scenarios and the associated com-plications. Patients who die in hospital should be provided with the best quality of life until they die. Effec-tive team working and communication with patients, relatives and carers are central to achieving this.

There are two specific tools (SBAR and RSVP) that can be used to help communicate in a more effec-tive way with other health-care colleagues, particularly when a patient's condition has deteriorated. In some hospitals critical care outreach teams or medical emergency response teams are available who are informed of a patient's deterioration in condition and can provide support to ward, and staff undertake a more in-depth or detailed assessment. The additional assessment undertaken by the outreach team may result in a change in care management or a timely admission to a high dependency/intensive care unit.

The SBAR

The SBAR (**s**ituation, **b**ackground, **a**ssessment, **r**ecommendation) system is a framework for communica-tion between members of the health-care team about a patient's condition. It is a situational briefing model. This is an easy-to-remember, distinct tool that is useful for framing any conversation, requiring a clinician's immediate attention and action. The tool provides the opportunity for an easy and focused way to set expectations for what will be communicated and how among members of the team, resulting in enhanced patient safety. There are many types of templates that can be used, some are simplistic and others can be complex (Figure 12.2). The Scottish Patient Safety Alliance (www. patientsafetyalliance.scot.nhs.uk/docs/Toolkit/SPSP_HG%20_SBAR_guide%20(2).pdf) provides a guide

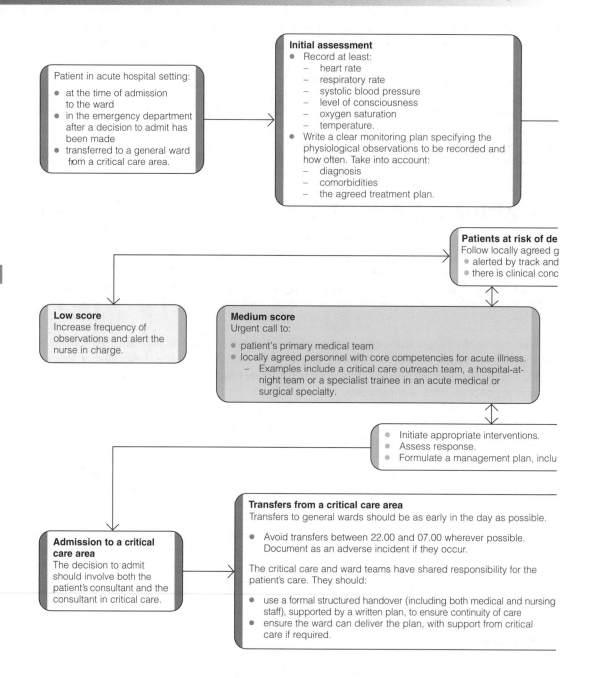

Figure 12.1 Flow diagram concerning the recognition of and response to acute illness in adults in hospital. Source: NICE (2007).

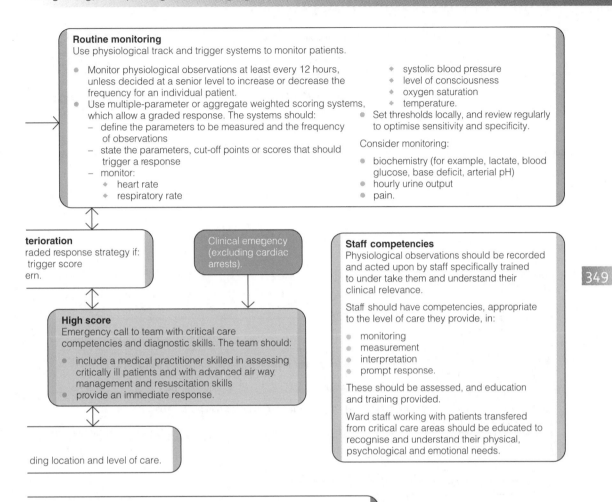

Routine monitoring
Use physiological track and trigger systems to monitor patients.

- Monitor physiological observations at least every 12 hours, unless decided at a senior level to increase or decrease the frequency for an individual patient.
- Use multiple-parameter or aggregate weighted scoring systems, which allow a graded response. The systems should:
  - define the parameters to be measured and the frequency of observations
  - state the parameters, cut-off points or scores that should trigger a response
  - monitor:
    - heart rate
    - respiratory rate
    - systolic blood pressure
    - level of consciousness
    - oxygen saturation
    - temperature.
- Set thresholds locally, and review regularly to optimise sensitivity and specificity.

Consider monitoring:

- biochemistry (for example, lactate, blood glucose, base deficit, arterial pH)
- hourly urine output
- pain.

terioration
raded response strategy if:
trigger score
ern.

Clinical emergency (excluding cardiac arrests).

Staff competencies
Physiological observations should be recorded and acted upon by staff specifically trained to under take them and understand their clinical relevance.

Staff should have competencies, appropriate to the level of care they provide, in:

- monitoring
- measurement
- interpretation
- prompt response.

These should be assessed, and education and training provided.

Ward staff working with patients transferred from critical care areas should be educated to recognise and understand their physical, psychological and emotional needs.

High score
Emergency call to team with critical care competencies and diagnostic skills. The team should:

- include a medical practitioner skilled in assessing critically ill patients and with advanced air way management and resuscitation skills
- provide an immediate response.

ding location and level of care.

The handover of care should include:

- a summary of the critical care stay including diagnosis and treatment
- a monitoring and investigation plan
- a plan for ongoing treatment including drugs and therapies, nutrition plan, infection status and any agreed limitations of treatment
- physical and rehabilitation needs
- psychological and emotional needs
- specific communication or language needs.

Staff should offer patients information about their condition and encourage them to participate in decisions that relate to their recovery.

NHS Greater Glasgow and Clyde

Beatson
West of Scotland Cancer Centre

SBAR Handover Sheet

NHS
Greater Glasgow
and Clyde

ᵀᴴᴱbeatson
WEST OF SCOTLAND CANCER CENTRE

Name: _____

DOB: _____

CHI Number: _____

Affix Patient Data Label

Date: __ __ / __ __ / __ __   Time: __ __ : __ __   Ward: _____

Situation • **What is the issue/concern?** • **What is happening that has changed?**	Diagnosis:_____ Consultant: _____ Admitted On___/ ___/ ___ Reason for Admission: _____ The problem/ concernis: _____ _____
Background **Provide pertinent background information related to the situation or concern.** **For example: -** • **Significant PMH** • **Treatment Modality & status** • **Relevant medication details** • **Symptom control issues and interventions**	**Chemotherapy** Is the patient receiving chemotherapy? Yes ☐ No ☐ Date Last Chemotherapy: ___/ ___/ ___ Chemo Regime: _____ Cycle No:___ **Radiotherapy** Is the patient receiving radiotherapy? Yes ☐ No ☐ Number of Radiotherapy Fractions Received:_____Treatment Room No:_____ **Relevant PMH**:_____ **Symptom Control/Interventions:** O_2 Therapy:_____ l/min **IV Fluids**: Yes ☐ No ☐ Running:_____hrly IV Meds/Antibiotics:_____ **Pain Control**: _____ **What action has been taken already?** _____ _____

Figure 12.2   SBAR. (Reproduced with the kind permission of the Beatson West of Scotland Cancer Centre, NHS Greater Glasgow and Clyde.)

Assessment	**Vital Signs**	**Other Assessment Details**	**Lab Results & Investigations (if known)**
What have you found... • **Vital Signs** • **Symptoms presenting at this time** **What do you think the problem is?**	Most Recent MEWS = _____ Temp = _____°C Pulse = _____ BP= _____ /_____ SaO$_2$ = _____% Resps = _____ GCS/AVPU = _____	Pain Score = _____ Urinary Output: _____ BM Stix:_____ Other Symptoms:	WCC = _____ Neut = _____ Plat = _____ Hb = _____ Other:
Recommendation What needs to be done... • **Review by medical staff** • **Advice and guidance of what to do next and when** • **Referral to the MDT**	**Useful prompts include:** Ask if there is anything which you can do while you are waiting for medical review? Are any further tests needed? How often should observations be done? Are there any other instructions? If the patient does not improve, when would you want us to call you again?		

Handover Given By: _____

Figure 12.2   *Continued*

to using SBAR. The following is an example of SBAR content to be used when communicating with other health-care staff; it is a structured, concise statement of the problem.

Situation

- Identify yourself, your unit, the patient, room number
- Briefly state the problem, what it is, when it happened or started, and how severe
- Give a concise report of the patient's problem.

Background

Provide relevant background information concerning the situation, which might include the following:

- Diagnosis on admission and date of admission
- List of current medications, allergies, intravenous fluid and any laboratory investigations being undertaken
- Most recent vital signs and EWS score
- Laboratory results; give the date and time tests were performed and the results of previous tests for comparison
- Other clinical information
- Code status, i.e. do not attempt resuscitation orders.

Assessment

What do you think is going on? What is your clinical opinion?

Recommendation

What are you requesting or what is your recommended action and when is this required?
   This could include:

- Notification that the patient has been admitted
- The patient needs to be seen now
- Request for a change in order/treatment.

   The nurse must document the change in the patient's condition, that the doctor was notified and also the details of the SBAR.

The RSVP

The RSVP (reason, story, vital signs, plan) tool is also used to enhance communication and was developed by Featherstone et al (2008) (Figure 12.3). The following is an example of good practice that should be used with the RSVP tool when communicating with other health-care staff; it provides a structured, concise statement of the problem.

Reason

1. State your identity
2. Check that you are speaking to the correct person
3. State patient's name and location
4. State the reason for the call.

Story

State:
1. Background information about the patient
2. Reason for admission
3. Relevant past medical history
4. The patient's resuscitation status.

Vital signs

Vital signs are:

- Temperature
- Pulse rate and rhythm
- Blood pressure
- Breathing rate, rhythm and depth

		Good Practice	Experience
R	**Reason**	1. State the identity of caller 2. Check that you are speaking to the correct person 3. State patient's name and location 4. State the reason for the call	I am ….. (Nurse A) Is that ……. (Doctor B?) I am worried about Mrs Jones in bed 3, because… 1. This is what I think the problem is: <the problem seems to be cardiac, infection, etc.> 2. I am not sure what the problem is, but the patient is deteriorating 3. The patient seems to be unstable and may get worse, we need to do something now
S	**Story**	State: 1. Background information about the patient 2. Reason for admission 3. Relevant past medical history 4. The patient's resuscitation Status	Mrs Jones is a 50-year-old woman, who was admitted with a 24-hour history of wheezing and becoming breathless. She has had asthma for 10 years. She has never smoked. She has been improving since admission with nebulisers, but now she seems very tired and unwell and is breathing very fast and shallowly
V	**Vital signs**	Vital signs are: Temperature Pulse rate and rhythm Blood pressure _____/_____ Breathing rate Conscious level, mental state Capillary refill time Sweating? SaO2 FiO2 Urine output Early warning score	Mrs Jones has a respiratory rate of 34, pulse of 110, Sats of 88% on 15 litres of oxygen through a rebreathe mask. She is V on the AVPU scale. Her early warning score has gone up from 3 to 5 in the past hour
P	**Plan**	A. My plan is….. OR B. What is your plan? Say what is required from the receiver of the call	Please… 1. I'm not sure what I should do next and I am concerned about her. Please come to see Mrs Jones now 2. Talk to the patient or family about resuscitation status. 3. Ask the on-call registrar to see Mrs Jones now 4. Transfer Mrs Jones to critical care

353

Figure 12.3 RSVP: a system for communication of deterioration in hospital patients. Source: Featherstone et al (2008).

- Conscious level, mental state
- Capillary refill time
- Sweating?
- SaO$_2$
- FiO$_2$
- Urine output
- Early warning score.

Plan

A. My plan is. . . .
OR
B. What is your plan?
Say what is required from the person who receives the call.

Think

How do nurses in the care area where you work communicate with other members of the multidisciplinary team? There are a number of templates or profomas used in clinical areas that help staff communicate effectively with each other. Can you identify any of these? How do staff ensure that they are maintaining patient confidentiality when using these aides?

Conclusion

The role of the nurse is multi-faceted; one aspect of the role is to ensure that the people for whom they care are safe. The nurse has a duty to recognise and respond to those patients whose condition may be deteriorating. All nurses must recognise when people being cared for are anxious or in distress and make effective responses, using therapeutic principles, to promote their wellbeing and manage personal safety. Nurses must know when to consult a third party and how to make appropriate referrals.

The NMC are clear in demanding that all nurses be able to recognise when a person is at risk and in need of extra support and protection, and take reasonable steps to protect him or her from harm. The nurse has to be able to recognise when a person's physical or psychological condition is deteriorating, demonstrating how to act in an appropriate manner.

The use of EWS tools and a communication framework can help to enhance patient outcomes. It is essential that nurses and other staff work in a collaborative manner with the key goal of assuring safety.

Activity

Attempt the following multiple choice questions related to deteriorating health and wellbeing to test your knowledge. The answers can be found at the back of this book, in the chapter called 'Activity Answers'.

1. When should the nurse undertake an adult patient's observations in hospital?:
   a. Only when the nurse in charge is concerned about the patient's condition
   b. On admission or during the initial assessment
   c. Twice daily
   d. As directed by the matron

2. How would you determine the patient's pulse volume?:
   a. Using a Dinamap
   b. Using a pulse oximeter

c. Using an electrocardiogram (ECG)

d. By manually palpating the pulse

3. What is an early warning system?:
   a. An audit tool
   b. A tool used to predict deterioration in a person's condition
   c. A tool used to detect deep vein thrombosis
   d. A nurse management tool used to calculate the number of staff needed for a shift

4. What does the acronym SBAR mean?:
   a. Salary, benefits, achievements and recognition
   b. Safety, benchmark, awareness, recognition
   c. Situation, background, assessment, recommendation
   d. Situation, background, assessment, regulation

5. What does the acronym RSVP mean?:
   a. Reason, story, vital signs, plan
   b. Respond, safety, vital signs, permission
   c. Reply, story, vision, plan
   d. Respond, satisfy, validate, plan

6. A common method of assessing a person's level of consciousness uses:
   a. AVAD
   b. AVDA
   c. AVUP
   d. AVPU

7. How many minutes must the patient's pulse be counted in order to assess this accurately?:
   a. Two full minutes
   b. One full minute
   c. Thirty seconds divided by two
   d. Fifteen second multiplied by four

8. What does the term cyanosis mean?:
   a. Abnormal pink flushed appearance
   b. Mottled skin over the chin and the cheeks
   c. An abnormal blue discoloration of the skin and mucous membranes
   d. An abnormal rash over the chest

9. In assessing a patient using EWS, a score of 3 or more should alert you to:
   a. Reassess the patient in 30 minutes
   b. Summon help by informing the outreach team/medical team/on-call team
   c. Undertake a 12-lead ECG
   d. Check all electronic equipment

10. The use of SBAR, RSVP and other communication tools can help:
    a. Structure and standardise physiological measurements
    b. Structure and standardise the administration of anticoagulant medications
    c. Structure and standardise communication
    d. Structure and standardise the amount of time a patient is on a waiting list

References

Andrews T, Waterman H (2005) Packaging: A grounded theory of how to report physiological deterioration effectively. *Journal of Advanced Nursing* 52: 473–481.

Boulanger C, Toghill M (2009) How to measure and record vital signs to ensure detection of deteriorating patients. *Nursing Times* **105**(47): 10–12.

Critical Care Stakeholders Forum and National Outreach Forum (2007) *Clinical Indicators Critical Care Outreach Services* [online]. Available at: www.dh.gov.uk/prod_consum_dh/groups/dh_digitalassets/@dh/@en/documents/digitalasset/dh_073187.pdf (accessed August 2011).

Department of Health (2000) *Comprehensive Critical care: A review of adult critical care services*. London: Department of Health.

Department of Health (2005) *Quality Critical Care: Beyond comprehensive critical care: A Report by the Critical Care Stakeholder Forum*. London: Department of Health.

Department of Health (2009) *Competencies for Recognising and Responding to Acutely Ill Patients in Hospital*. London: Department of Health. Available at: www.dh.gov.uk/prod_consum_dh/groups/dh_digitalassets/documents/digitalasset/dh_096988.pdf (accessed August 2011).

Dougherty L, Lister S (eds) (2011) *The Royal Marsden Hospital Manual of Clinical Nursing Procedures*, 8th edn. Oxford: Wiley.

Featherstone P, Chalmers T, Smith GB (2008) RSVP: A system for communication of deterioration in hospital patients. *British Journal of Nursing* **17**: 706–710.

Gao H, McDonnell A, Harrisson DA, et al (2007) Systematic review and evaluation of physiological track and trigger systems for identifying at-risk patients on the ward. *Intensive Care Medicine* **33**: 667–679.

Goldhill D, McNarry AF (2004) Physiological abnormalities in early warning scores are related to mortality in adult inpatients. *British Journal of Anaesthesia* **92**: 882–884.

Goldhill DR, Worthington L, Mulcahy A, Tarling, M, Sumner A (1999) The patient at risk team: identifying and managing seriously ill ward patients. *Anaesthesia* **54**: 853–860.

Goldhill DR, McNarry AF, Manderloot G, McGinley A (2005) A physiologically-based early warning score for ward patients: the association between score and outcome. *Anaesthesia* **60**: 547–553.

Griffith R, Tengnah C (2010) *Law and Professional Issues in Nursing*, 2nd edn. Exeter: Learning Matters.

Haig KM, Sutton S, Whittington J (2006) SBAR – a shared mental model for improving communication between clinicians. *Journal on Quality and Patient Safety* **32**: 167–175.

Harrison R, Daly L (2011) *A Nurse's Survival Guide to Acute Medical Emergencies*. Edinburgh: Churchill Livingstone.

Hillman KM, Bristow PJ, Chey T, et al (2001) Antecedents to hospital deaths. *Internal Medicine Journal* **31**: 343–348.

Hodgetts T, Kenward G, Vlackonilolis I, Payen S, Castle N (2002) The identification of risk factors for cardiac arrest and formulation of activation criteria to alert a medical emergency team. *Resuscitation* **54**: 125–131.

Hogan J (2006) Why don't nurses monitor the respiratory rate of patients? *British Journal of Nursing* **15**: 489–492.

Johnstone CC, Rattray J, Myers L (2007) Physiological risk factors, early warning scoring systems and organizational changes. British Association of Critical Care Nurses. *Nursing in Critical Care* **12**: 291–224.

Kozier B, Erb G, Berman A, Snyder S, Lake R, Harvey S (2008) *Fundamentals of Nursing. Concepts, process and practice*. Harlow: Pearson.

Lomas C, West D (2009) Skills loss as automation takes over. *Nursing Times* **105**(40): 2–3.

McDonnell A, Esmonde L, Morgan R, et al (2007) The provision of critical care outreach services in England: Findings from a aational survey. *Journal of Critical Care* **22**: 212–218.

Margereson C (2010) Trajectory and Impact of Long Term Conditions. In Margereson, C, Trenoweth S (eds) *Developing Holistic Care for Long Term Conditions'* Routledge. London Ch 2 pp 18–33.

National Confidential Enquiry into Patient Outcomes and Death (2005) *An Acute Problem?* [online] Available at: www.ncepod.org.uk (accessed August 2011).

National Institute for Health and Clinical Excellence (2007) *Acutely Ill Patients in Hospital*. NICE Guideline 50. London: NICE.

National Patient Safety Agency (2007) *Recognising and Responding Appropriately to Early Signs of Deterioration in Hospitalised Patients*. London: NPSA.

National Quality Board (2010) *Review of Early Warning Systems in the NHS*. Acute and Community Services [online]. Available at: www.dh.gov.uk/prod_consum_dh/groups/dh_digitalassets/@dh/@en/@ps/documents/digitalasset/dh_113021.pdf (accessed August 2011).

Nursing and Midwifery Council (2008) *The Code: Standards of Conduct, Performance and Ethics for Nurses and Midwives*. London: NMC.

Nursing and Midwifery Council (2010a) *Standards for Pre registration Nursing Education*. London: NMC. Available at: http://standards.nmc-uk.org/PublishedDocuments/Standards%20for%20pre-registration%20nursing%20education%2016082010.pdf (accessed August 2011).

Nursing and Midwifery Council (2010b) *Record Keeping Guidance for Nurses and Midwives*. NMC. London.

Oakey RJ, Slade V (2006) Physiological observation track and trigger system. *Nursing Standard* **20**(27): 48–54.

Office of the Public Guardian (2007) *Mental Capacity Act 2005 Code of Practice*. London: The Stationery Office.

Royal College of Nursing (2007) *Standards for Assessing, Measuring and Monitoring Vital Signs in Infants, Children and Young People. RCN guidance for children's nurses and nurses working with children and young people*. London: RCN.

Simpson H (2006) Respiratory assessment. *British Journal of Nursing* **15**: 484–488.

Smith J, Roberts R (2011) *Vital Signs for Nurses. An introduction to clinical observations*. Oxford: Wiley.

Tweddell L (2008) Computer power on the wards. *Nursing Times* **104**(38):18–19.

Watson D (2006) The impact of accurate patient assessment on the quality of care. *Nursing Times* **102**(6): 34–37.

Part IV

Leadership and Management

13

Leadership and Management

Aims and objectives

The aim of this chapter is to provide insight and understanding of the key concepts that underpin effective leadership and management within the health-care and social care team.

At the end of the chapter you will be able to:

1. Define a range of key terms.
2. Describe the important characteristics associated with an effective leader and manager
3. Explore the issues that may impact on a person's ability to lead or manage
4. Identify the ways in which nurses provide leadership in the management of care
5. Begin to apply the concepts discussed to the practice setting
6. Appreciate the Nursing and Midwifery Council's requirements of student nurses

This chapter provides the reader with insight and understanding associated with two activities that nurses undertake on a daily basis: leading and managing. Nurses need to possess and hone their skills associated with leadership and management in order to provide safe and effective care, be this as a junior nurse or a senior nursing executive. Regardless of career status all registered nurses must ensure that they meet the requirements laid down in the Code (Nursing and Midwifery Council or NMC, 2008) as well as any contractual and legal requirements. For most nurses, clinical practice dominates their working day; however, they are required to work with others as partners and show the necessary leadership to ensure that practice is up to date and able to deliver the best possible care for their patients.

Changing landscapes

There are and there will continue to be a number of changes in nursing and health and social care. Throughout this book reference has been made to demographic and epidemiological transformation, and developments in technology as the environment in which we work and live. The population is living longer, and associated with this increase in life expectancy comes an increase in the number of people living longer with long-term conditions such as HIV, diabetes mellitus, coronary heart disease and respiratory conditions. Developments within the field of cancer, for example, which is the second most common cause of death, means that technologies used to help prolong life will also need to be resourced.

The Student's Guide to Becoming a Nurse, Second Edition. Ian Peate.
© 2012 John Wiley & Sons, Ltd. Published 2012 by John Wiley & Sons, Ltd.

Lifestyle choice associated with health risk is an important issue that needs to be given consideration. The increase in the number of sexually transmitted infections (including HIV), the rise in the number of people who are obese, the rise in the numbers of people who have mental health problems and the increased use of alcohol intake will all take its toll on the health economy.

The population as a whole is increasing in numbers and in a number of ways. The birth rate rises but immigration has decreased; the number of migrants from Europe is difficult to assess because migration in Europe is free and Europeans can choose where they live and work.

These changes will result in changes within the provision of health care reflecting a more complex provision. Those who devise policy and offer care services must take these changes into account, ensuring sensitivity and demonstrating respect and commitment.

The technological revolution, which incorporates mass media, access to the internet through a variety of electronic devices in a variety of places, e.g. the home, work place and places of learning, allows the public access to much more information about issues associated with health and illness. The public are now able to undertake their own literature search and determine options for treatments. This could have an impact on health service resources as the options chosen may be outside the budgets of trusts and other health-care providers. Organisations are challenged to provide the highest quality of care while at the same time ensuring the best use of available resource (Department of Health or DH, 2008a). Creating high quality workplaces are dependent upon great leadership and good management.

To manage the changes in the landscape discussed earlier, the world of nursing has also had to change: nurses and nursing have become more flexible in order to respond effectively and appropriately. The modernisation of nursing careers, an initiative undertaken by the chief nursing officers of the four UK countries, provides a blue print for the potential futures of nursing careers, options and opportunities for progression (DH, 2006). A consultation was undertaken in 2007–8 with regard to a post-registration nursing framework (DH, 2008b) and the outcome proposed that careers in nursing should be structured around care pathways. These changes provide a number of management and leadership opportunities for all grades of nurses, with new roles emerging.

Many of these changes are often seen as challenges, but they can also be seen as opportunities that have yet to be explored and exploited to meet the needs of people for whom nurses care. Weir-Hughes (2011) notes that clinical leadership has always been challenging and this appears to have become even more of a challenge in recent years as a result of changes in global financial climates, change in the way health and social care is delivered, an ageing population, a highly regulated profession and epidemiological developments.

Chapter 6 has specifically considered team work in the context of interprofessional working and learning. Team work, leadership and management can be seen as a triumvirate; this chapter revisits team working. Both concepts – management and leadership – overlap; having one without the other makes it difficult to do either effectively. From early on in their career nurses have the opportunity to develop into exceptional leaders, influencing and shaping practice with the ultimate aim of ensuring safer and effective care provision.

An appreciation of management and leadership

Understanding management and leadership is an essential requirement for those learning to nurse as well as those who are nursing. The Nursing and Midwifery Council's (2010) *Standards for Pre registration Nursing Education* requires students to demonstrate competence in managing and leading teams. Nurses who acquire the knowledge, skills and behaviours that meet the NMC's standards will be equipped to meet present and future challenges, improve health and wellbeing, and drive up standards and quality, working in a range of roles including practitioner, educator, leader and researcher. As autonomous practitioners, nurses will deliver essential care to a very high standard and provide complex care using the best available evidence and technology where appropriate. Nurses have to be able to develop their competence with regard to leadership and management.

Planning, acting as a coordinator, organising and delivering care on a daily basis, along with supporting other staff, are the skills associated with effective and efficient registered nurses. Nurses influence the ways in which patient care is delivered and as such they act as change agents, leading, reforming and improving care delivery. They do this through:

- communicating effectively
- delegating appropriately,
- developing and motivating others
- working with others, addressing conflict and respecting differences
- problem-solving and making decisions underpinned by critical thinking
- embracing change and leading through transitional periods
- managing themselves, their time and their emotions.

Top tips

Good leaders are an enabling force, helping people and organisations to perform and develop, which implies that a sophisticated alignment be achieved – of people's needs and the aims of the organisation. The concept of a leader being the directing chief at the top of a hierarchy is an incomplete appreciation of what true leadership should be.

Management and leadership: key terms

It may help to make a statement about the two key terms in this chapter: leadership and management. It is important to make clear the differences between leadership and management as well as acknowledging the similarities. The two concepts overlap; having one without the other will make it difficult to do either effectively. Rost (1993) offers an explanation of how leadership and management differ (Table 13.1).

Leadership is about setting a new direction or vision for a group of people whom they can then follow, e.g. a leader is at the forefront for setting that new direction. Managers control or direct people and other non-human resources according to principles or values that have already been established in the organisation. Leaders and managers will work toward achieving the strategic aim or vision of the practice.

Managers and leaders accomplish their authority in a variety of ways, e.g. from the formal roles that they occupy in the health-care organisation and the organisation legitimises their power to act when others are told or asked to do something. The managerial relationship with others is a formal relationship; the manager has authority to act or direct other people, it is important that all employees (including the manager) need to know what their role is and who their line manager is. The ability to influence a group or a person is not formally linked to a role and anyone has the potential to influence but may not have the power to force a person to act. Leaders tend to act by influencing and they do this when they persuade others either by word or deed, e.g. leading by example (role modelling). Iles (2006) suggests that real management crosses the division between management and leadership.

Table 13.1 Management and leadership

Leadership	Management
• Influences relationships with others • The intention is to make observable changes in the work environment • The purpose is to make changes that reflect the shared purposes of colleagues and other workers • To achieve the strategic vision • Relationships – leaders and followers	• Has authority relationships with others • The rationale is to produce services and provide goods for consumption and sale • The production of services and goods arises out of the coordinated activity of others • To achieve the strategic vision • Relationships – managers and subordinates

Source: adapted from Rost (1993).

Management and leadership are about working with people – health- and social care staff at all levels, patients, the public and regulatory bodies, e.g. the NMC and the Care Quality Commission. Leaders and managers have to be able to demonstrate their understanding of a number of complex issues, e.g. of being able to have a vision, to work with others in a collegiate and corporate way, to think strategically and to have a wider understanding of health- and social care issues, as well as demonstrating competence and confidence within the sphere of health care.

Thousands of books have been written on various management and leadership theories and styles, and this is how it should be as there is no one definitive model that can be applied to all settings or to all people. Leadership can be demonstrated at a local, national and international level, creating, shaping and forming conclusions. At some time in your life you may be asked to be a leader; many situations require leadership and those roles may be high-profile leadership roles or they may take on a lower-profile role.

Think

Think of the various leadership roles, how and where these may take place and the degree of profile, i.e. high- or lower-level profile.

Your thoughts may have led you to think about acting as a leader in the classroom, e.g. leading a seminar or a discussion, giving a presentation or working as a scout leader coaching younger people. The levels of profile are vast; a high-profile leader could be a prime minister, a president (an elected public office official) or lower level, e.g. leading a local volunteer group

All the roles identified above can be demanding, stimulating, exciting and rewarding; all carry a degree of responsibility

There are a number of different approaches to leadership that can be used in different situations. These approaches have evolved and changed direction and focus and draw from each other. The following approaches/ theories associated with leadership are discussed:

- Trait
- Behavioural
- Situational
- Relational
- New and emerging.

Trait

This approach is associated with the attributes, features and characteristics of the leader. Originally they were known as great man theories, the notion being that leaders are born not made, are destined for a leadership role, had inherited that trait. Trying to understand what it was that a great leader possessed in order to fulfil this role focused on an examination of personality, ability to inspire and commitment, and how these influenced his or her ability to lead. Some leaders are confident and decisive, some outgoing and sociable (these are their traits). The early great man leaders were usually church leaders, royalty or members of the military. These traits are added to continually and additions include the leader's ability to communicate, integrity, degree of emotional intelligence and intelligence.

365

Think

Think of some great leaders of the past. What traits did they possess to help you think of them as a great leader?

Behavioural

The ways in which leaders behave (what they do and how they act) has been studied for a number of years with the intention of determining how behaviour impacts on human relationships. The way in which a person behaves will impact on how others perceive him or her and this can be seen as a reflection of the person's core values and beliefs. Weir-Hughes (2011) suggests that good leaders are often followed because they are deemed trustworthy and committed to their cause. He continues and notes that to be a good leader the person has to be able to fulfil and consciously understand his or her own values and beliefs; this requires self-awareness. Consider the traits associated with trait theory; in this approach the traits may not be observable but in behaviour theory they are, when a person leads the behaviour is what is seen (Northouse, 2012). According to Sullivan and Garland (2010) there are two types of leader who adopt a behavioural approach:

1. Bureaucratic leader
2. Charismatic leader.

Briefly, bureaucratic leaders adopt a highly structured approach; they tend to adhere to policy, process and procedures taking a step-by-step systematic approach to tasks, ensuring that all areas are covered (they exhibit task behaviours); the focus is on getting the job done. The charismatic leader tends to motivate and stimulate others, demonstrating a commitment to the cause. Northouse (2012) sees this as processing behaviours, whereby the leader helps people feel at ease and comfortable with other group members with the intention of helping the process succeed. Leaders often have to combine a charismatic (process) and bureaucratic (tasks) approach in order to lead effectively depending on the organisation in which they work, their role and the situation.

Think

Consider a good leader with whom you have worked. What was it about his or her behaviour that you think made him or her a good leader?

You may have had a very long list. Did your response include any of the following?:

- Ability to inspire
- Commitment to the cause
- Integrity
- Openness.

Situational

Much of the work surrounding situational leadership is attributed to Paul Hersey and has been developed further by Hersey et al (2001). This approach suggests that different types of situations require different types of leadership. Contingency theory is another approach very closely related to the situational approach, which also recognises that different approaches are needed depending on the situation, with the intention of motivating employees to enhance performance and satisfaction. A range of behaviours from authoritarian to permissive is required in response to need and situation. An example might be when a nurse working in a general practice administers a vaccine to a patient and the patient develops a severe life-threatening anaphylactic reaction requiring resuscitation. In this situation the nurse will lead the resuscitation using an authoritarian approach; no other approach would be acceptable. The same nurse working with a group of patients on a smoking cessation programme would adopt a participative approach. Both approaches are acceptable, but they are being used depending on the situation. Contingency theory is more about the leader adapting the leadership style to meet the needs of the organisation. Situational and contingency theories complement each other and are inextricably linked. Effective leaders are those who can adapt their behaviour to meet the demands of the unique situation and the needs of the organisation.

Relational

This approach, as the name suggests, is to do with relationships; a leader can never underestimate the importance of relationships. High-quality relationships will usually generate more positive leadership outcomes (Northouse, 2012). There are many invisible forces that have the potential to shape and drive individuals and teams; effective relational leaders are able to identify those invisible forces using a variety of skills including interpersonal skills. A four 'C' component model devised by Ashridge Business School (2010) considers the following:

1. Change: understanding and working effectively with the dynamics of change. Understanding change theory and reacting to change are essential.
2. Complexity: having the skills to survive and thrive in situations of low certainty and low agreement.
3. Context: understanding key issues and being able to think strategically about how to respond.
4. Connectedness: the ability to understand those who take part in the wider political landscape and to engage and build effective relationships with new kinds of internal and external partners. This concept emphasises the essence of the relational leader.

Think

Think about the relationships that you have with some people with whom you work, e.g. the relationship between yourself and one of your mentors (remember that all relationships are different). What relationship skills did the mentor demonstrate that made your relationship with him or her good (or bad)?

367

Did you identify the following?:

- A good communicator
- A nurturer
- Honesty
- Appreciative
- Knowledgeable
- Confident
- Committed.

New and emerging theories

New and emerging theories are being developed constantly as well as review and revision of the established approaches; this is especially true in the field of health- and social care work, where change is ever present and safety paramount. New partnerships are formed daily with new patients, new teams and new organisations; because of this new approaches may be needed to make a success out of leading and managing people. Sullivan and Garland (2010) refer to the various places where this takes place as a collegiate work environment. Often the older approaches can sit quite comfortably next to the new and emerging approaches.

Top tips

Effective leadership does not necessarily require great technical or intellectual capacity. These qualities might help, but they are not essential. Good leadership requires attitudes and behaviours that characterise and relate to humanity.

Leadership styles

Leadership styles are the methods and approaches of providing direction, implementing plans and motivating people. Managing and leading others will require you to be aware of your relationship with other people. It has already been stressed that positive collegiate relationships with others are essential to achieve high-quality, safe patient care and to ensure that staff are motivated and will feel a respected part of the smaller and wider team. Management styles influence these relationships. Table 13.2 considers four leadership styles that are used when leading and managing others; to reiterate the style used will depend on the given situation – it is context dependent.

Top tips

 Know yourself and which management style you feel most comfortable with. Think about how the team see you and how they react when you ask them to do something. Recognise the different behavioural styles of the team; consider the context in which you work. Build good channels of communication. Work hard to empower team members.

Other elements associated with a good leader are the ability to make decisions and to delegate effectively. Delegation is closely related to accountability; Chapter 1 has addressed the importance of accountability.

Delegation

Before delegating duties to others, the nurse must take into account the role and competence of the person to whom he or she is delegating a duty, because the nurse is ultimately accountable for his or

Table 13.2   Four leadership styles

Style	Characteristics and potential effect
Autocratic (sometimes called authoritarian)	This style is used when leaders need to tell people what they want done and how they want it achieved; the leader alone makes the decisions. This style is associated with tasks and task achievement, when time is short, when there may be possible risk to a person. The leader does not require the employee to be creative or to seek advice from others. There are advantages to using this approach; it provides those people whom you are leading with certainty and clarity, e.g. instructing a member of staff to perform cardiac massage using the correct technique with the correct ratio of breaths to compressions is clear and above all safe and effective. When working with less experienced staff, this approach can provide that person with confidence as well as direction and instil a sense of being facilitated. The leader must, however, know exactly what it is that he or she is aiming to achieve and must be able to command respect from team members; the leader must be able demonstrate authority. Using this approach in all situations can lead to demotivation and inertia, and stifle creativity; it may also cause a degree of dependency

Table 13.2 *Continued*

Style	Characteristics and potential effect
Democratic	This style encourages 'a let's work together approach' involving the leader, including one or more employees in the decision-making process (determining what to do and how to do it). The emphasis is on team working and human relationships; two-way, effective and mutual respect is emphasised with this approach. Often this approach is used when you have some of the information and others have other parts; this results in shared responsibility and accountability, which demonstrates to staff that as a leader you cannot be expected to know everything and that you value their expertise. It can promote team working and team involvement and will ultimately result in better decisions being made. This approach is not suitable in all contexts: the use of a democratic approach during cardiac arrest would result in delay and others may question the leader's competence. When using this style, it is the leader, however, who has the final decision-making authority. Staff often respect a leader who uses this approach
Laissez-faire	In this style, the person leading allows others to make the decisions. The leader does not lead or make decisions; this is why this approach is questioned as a leadership style if the leader does not lead. The approach can be dangerous in some situations in health- and social care settings. Leaders adopt a hands-off approach, allowing others to make the decisions. The approach is characterised by very little guidance from the leader, complete freedom for the group to do as they wish and to make their own decisions. There are situations where a laissez-faire leadership style can be effective, e.g. in situations where group members are highly skilled, motivated and capable of working on their own. However, in health-care settings it is rare for a person to work totally on his or her own. This style of leadership is not suited to situations where group members have little knowledge or experience. This approach can lead to demotivation, lack of consistency in care provision and poor team working, and deadlines can be missed as team members do not receive enough guidance or feedback from the leader
Bureaucratic	The leader depends on rules and regulations and their sphere of influence is through the application of fixed, rigid, inflexible rules. There are few decisions to be made when using this style of leadership and the rules, regulations and policies are adhered to without question. This style of leadership follows a close set of standards, often based on tradition. All that is done is done in an exact, specific way to ensure safety an/or accuracy. The approach is used in situations where the working environment is dangerous and specific sets of procedures are necessary to ensure safety for all concerned. Characteristics of the bureaucratic style include the imposition of strict and systematic discipline on the followers; the leader is empowered by virtue of their office – position or power. Workers are promoted on their ability to be able to demonstrate conformity to the rules and regulations. Caution should be used when applying this style to health-care settings; it can lead to frustration, apathy and high staff turnover

369

her actions or omissions, both professionally and from a legal perspective in relation to a duty of care. The nurse must also remember what the implications are if they accept any delegated duties and responsibilities from other nurses and other health-care professionals. What must be remembered is that accountability can never be delegated.

In everyday life we delegate responsibility to others. In professional practice delegation has the potential to enhance patient care and provide staff with career-development opportunities if it is carried out in an appropriate manner.

There are legal ramifications associated with delegation. Delegation may reduce health-care costs, but this must not be the sole rationale for delegation of responsibility. Modernisation of the NHS has and will continue to demand role changes within the service of all personnel. Before accepting or delegating tasks, the nurse must consider the impact that this may have on patient care. The nurse is legally accountable and there are four spheres of accountability: to the patient, to society, to the profession and to the employer.

The delegation of nursing care must be appropriate, safe and in the best interests of the person being cared for. Before agreeing to delegate, the nurse has the responsibility to understand the issues associated with delegation. If the nurse fails to delegate effectively in the best interest of the person being cared for this may lead to questions being asked about the nurse's fitness to practise. The decision to delegate would be judged against what could be reasonably expected from someone with their knowledge, skills and abilities when placed in those particular circumstances. The NMC (2008) code states:

> You must establish that anyone you delegate to is able to carry out your instructions.
>
> You must confirm that the outcome of any delegated task meets the required standards.
>
> You must make sure that everyone you are responsible for is supervised and supported.

When you become a registered nurse your responsibilities will increase; you will be taking on new duties and people will assume more about you, e.g. they will be aware that you are now deemed a competent nurse. Having undertaken and successfully completed a 3-year period of education, you will now be a professional in your own right registered with the NMC. Delegation is essential for developing nursing practice. With time and practice you will become better at delegating appropriately; you will gain more insight and confidence (Lawrence, 2008).

To reiterate, accountability can never be delegated. At no stage during the delegation process can the nurse hand over accountability (Hansten and Jackson, 2004a). Delegation involves the transfer of authority to another competent person to perform a selected task in a particular situation. However, the person delegating that task to the person deemed competent retains accountability for the outcome. The key factor is the retention of accountability; this makes delegation different from abdication of duty.

Delegation is a management/leadership activity and involves managing your own workload and developing that of other colleagues (Pearce, 2004). Other colleagues may include, for example, other registered nurses as well as health-care assistants, physiotherapists, occupational therapists and operating department practitioners.

Mullins (2010) defines delegation as the process of entrusting authority and responsibility to others; most cases of delegation occur from the top down. Delegation is more than just giving a task to others to perform; it encompasses allowing others to develop understanding and confidence.

Delegation is associated with the handing down of responsibility for action. It is unacceptable to just hand down that responsibility; the person delegating must also ensure that there are necessary resources available to carry out the task, as well as providing the person with the authority to delegate. Delegation plus the encouragement of initiative is empowerment as well as providing a degree of accountability.

Mullins (2010) points out that delegation is founded on three concepts:

1. *Authority*: the right to make decisions and take actions
2. *Responsibility*: the obligation to perform certain duties
3. *Accountability*: this cannot be delegated.

Bergman (1981) provides insight into the various levels associated with accountability. Figure 13.1 demonstrates the component parts related to accountability. Ability, according to Bergman (1981), is associated with the competence to undertake a task or delegated role, having the right knowledge and skills. Responsibility is ensuring that the role or task undertaken is done so in relation to your education and the framework within which you have been asked to work. Accountability – the ability to act and decide on what needs to be done along with being answerable for decisions made – can be achieved only if you have been given the authority to act. Without authority, accountability will not occur. Therefore, to be accountable you must be able, responsible and have authority invested in you. When these are achieved you can provide care in an autonomous and accountable manner.

Responsibility without the authority to achieve things should be avoided. Frustration is the result of this and does little to enhance motivation. Delegation allows people scope to encourage commitment. This comes about because people are motivated by having something more responsible and complex to do (Mullins, 2010).

371

Think

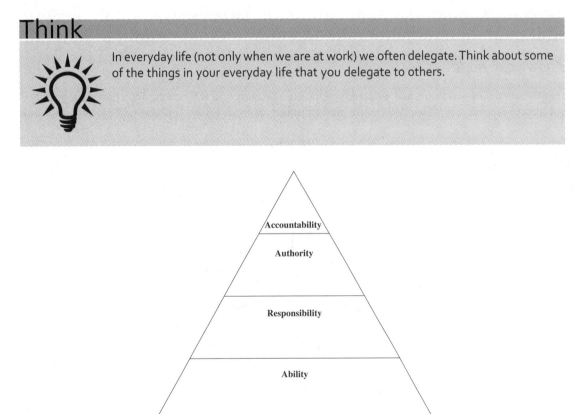

In everyday life (not only when we are at work) we often delegate. Think about some of the things in your everyday life that you delegate to others.

Figure 13.1 The four component parts associated with accountability. Source: Bergman (1981).

Things we often delegate can include:

- Allowing somebody else to go shopping for you
- Ordering your shopping from an online shopping service
- Allowing another person to collect your children from school/nursery
- Permitting someone else to look after your pets while you are away
- Taking your child to the childminder/babysitter
- Ordering food in a restaurant and allowing somebody else to cook it for you to eat.

Hoban (2003) is of the opinion that delegation has a bad name. She considers that delegation tends to be labelled either as a leadership skill needed only by those in charge or as a way of burdening other colleagues with tasks that you would rather not do yourself. Cohen (2004) discusses the difference between delegation and 'dumping'. There is a difference between delegating a task/activity and abdicating that activity. Belbin (2010) considers delegation not as offloading in relation to the volume of work and the responsibility attached to it, but as the choice of that responsibility. There are seven aspects associated with the delegation process. It is suggested that the most important aspect is associated with knowing to whom you are delegating and his or her level of competence.

Delegation: seven associated aspects

Hansten and Jackson (2004a) have suggested that there are seven aspects associated with the delegation process. Similar to the nursing process they are cyclical (Figure 13.2).

Know your world

Health-care delivery systems and ways of working are changing and will continue to change; health- and social care provision is influenced by the modernisation agenda. Porter-O'Grady (2003) notes that one

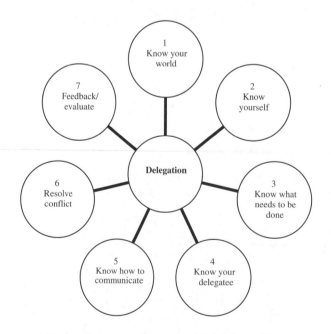

Figure 13.2   The seven aspects associated with delegation. Source: Hansten and Jackson (2004a).

of the biggest areas of change involves the provision of care through others – the delegation of traditional nursing tasks to others.

Increasingly, the nurse is being asked and required to delegate work to care givers such as health-care assistants about whom they may know little. Understanding issues that impinge on your role and your ability to provide quality care – the driving forces leading to the changes above – will help you delegate effectively.

Know yourself

Knowing your own abilities and limitations is an essential component of effective delegation. Self-analysis and self-understanding are prerequisites, according to Hansten and Jackson (2004b). Being able to recognise your own attributes that may impede effective delegation, such as emotions or beliefs, may enable you to understand your actions. Take time also to examine your motivation and the reason why you are delegating the particular task. Determine that you are delegating for the right reasons (Hoban, 2003).

Know what needs to be done

Pressure and the amount of work to be done often result in delegation of duties. Working with others in a successful manner necessitates knowledge of the total picture – knowing what needs to be done. The nurse must ensure that he or she delegates appropriately, effectively and efficiently. Care will need to be prioritised as well as delegating to the right individual based on competence. The key components are an extensive knowledge base and the ability to make sound judgements.

Know your delegatee

Having examined yourself (know yourself) and knowing what needs to be done, it is imperative that you know to whom you are delegating – the delegatee. Perhaps this is the most important aspect of the cycle.

Think

Make a list of those to whom you think you (as a registered nurse) may need to delegate. Here are some of the potential delegatees:

- Student nurses (was this first on your list?)
- New staff nurses
- Health-care assistants (at various levels)
- Speech and language therapists
- Physiotherapists
- Occupational therapists
- Paramedics
- Pharmacists
- Clerical staff/ward clerks
- Volunteers
- Social workers
- Medical students
- Doctors
- Phlebotomists.

You may think that strictly speaking nurses do not delegate to some of the people listed above. Nurses may not ask some of those people to carry out nursing tasks, but they may ask them to do things for the patient and the nurse acts as the coordinator of care. Therefore the same principles associated with safe and effective delegation will apply.

Think

Think about your own family. Who in the family does the cooking and the cleaning? Is that left up to your mother/partner? Is your father/partner responsible for fixing things around the house or on the car? What is your responsibility in the house – do you have any tasks that fall to you to perform?

If this is the case then each person has a role to play and certain things are expected of them – they have their 'job descriptions'. However, family roles and responsibilities are changing, e.g. the father may be the only parent and he may be responsible not only for cleaning and cooking, but also for maintaining things around the house. The family analogy used here can also apply to professional practice: the role of the nurse (and it has been said many times in this text) is changing. Families and family roles are becoming more flexible, fluid and dynamic; so too are nurses' roles. Job descriptions for family members may not be written as a job description is written for your work. Job descriptions at work not only have a written element to them but also an unwritten element attached to them.

Before you delegate to others you must have some insight into their roles. Understanding what their role is (as well as your own) will enable you to be clear about what your expectation of the other is. Whatever you delegate must fall within the remit of the job description of the delegatee; to do otherwise would be inappropriate and potentially dangerous.

Assessing the competency of the person to whom you are delegating is an important activity. The NMC is required by law to establish standards of competency that must be met by applicants to different parts of the professional register. These standards are mandatory and in accordance with statutory legislation and are seen as necessary to provide safe and effective practice. The standards of competency for nursing are the overarching principles of being able to practise as a nurse (NMC, 2010).

Every nurse who appears on the NMC's register will therefore be expected to be able to perform to a particular standard on registration, and at that point he or he is deemed competent. This provides reassurance to the public that the nurse has met the requisite standards of proficiency.

Health-care assistants' standards of competence may be found in their job descriptions or associated with their programme of study, e.g. SNVQ or NVQ. Currently there is no regulation for health-care assistants in the UK, but this may change in the near future. Specific behaviours that might be expected of health-care assistants may also be cited explicitly in their job description, e.g.:

- Reporting and advising the registered nurse of any change in the patient's condition
- Collection of urine, sputum and stool specimens
- Testing urine and stool specimens
- Taking vital signs
- Providing oral hygiene.

In some trusts health-care assistants may be deemed competent to administer enemas, perform venepuncture or apply dressings, and in others this may not be allowed. The lack of consistency provides a challenge for the nurse when considering the delegation of some tasks. It is important, therefore, to know to whom you are delegating. You must fully understand the job description and other organisational policies associated with the role of the people to whom you may delegate; you need to match the job description to the delegated activity. You should never allow a delegatee to perform beyond his or her role and level of competence.

Although much of the above discussion centres on the 'official' role expectations of personnel, there are, as has been suggested, some unofficial expectations. These 'grey areas' can arise when you (or the delegatee) may have inappropriate expectations of the delegatee. Understanding the job description of the delegatee and encouraging effective, honest, open, two-way communication can result in better clarification of role expectations, reduction in conflict and improvement in patient care. The expectations of all parties concerned should be openly expressed in a non-threatening manner.

Table 13.3 summarises some of the important points that you need to consider in an attempt to know yourself and the delegatee better.

Know how to communicate

Open, honest and effective two-way communication is vital if delegation is to work efficiently, as already discussed. Effective communication must be, clear, concise, correct and complete.

When the nurse delegates to another he or she is entrusting another person to act in his or her place for that particular task (O'Neill, 2010). It is important for this reason that the nurse communicate effectively. The person to whom you are delegating is not you, and you must be aware that he or she may not perform the task to your standards. Therefore you must make every effort to ensure that he or she knows exactly what is expected.

It may seem obvious, but you must know what it is you are delegating. If you cannot explain (communicate effectively) to the delegatee what it is you are delegating the task must not be delegated. Ensure that you are specific about the task to be delegated and are able to measure and determine if the task has been completed, be realistic in your expectations and apply a time element to the task being delegated.

Table 13.3   Some points to consider when getting to know the delegatee

- Know your job description and the job description of the delegatee
- Make sure that the person is interested in the task and has the necessary skills and ability to achieve it
- Know the policies and procedures in place in your organisation that may impinge on the delegation process
- Be constantly aware of the concepts of competency and accountability
- Know your own strengths and weaknesses and the strengths and weaknesses of the delegatee
- Know how to motivate and support others
- Continually supervise, monitor and provide feedback to the delegatee
- Be realistic
- You cannot control every action of those to whom you delegate
- Remember that delegatees are also responsible for their actions or omissions
- Be aware of the delegatee's workload

Source: adapted from Hansten and Jackson (2004c); Pearce (2004); Hoban (2003).

At all times during the delegation process allow the delegatee the opportunity to raise any concerns or questions that he or she may have (Hoban, 2003). Listen to any concerns and provide appropriate responses. You may also need to inform other team members of what has been delegated and to whom (Pearce, 2004). However, Mullins (2010) notes that the more specific the instructions and terms of reference, the less stimulating the task, and as a result little learning will occur. The criterion for assessing if delegation has been successful, according to O'Neill (2010), is completion of the task.

Resolving conflict

Conflict is inevitable and the way in which it is managed will determine the outcome of delegation, the ability to move on and enhance nursing practice, and the ability to continue to delegate appropriately. Even before delegating conflict may occur, e.g. the delegatee may be unable or unwilling to accept the delegated task or there may be a shortage of staff, meaning that no one else is available to whom you can delegate (Boswell, 2005). Attempt to resolve conflict before delegating or as soon as there is evidence of conflict arising.

Giving feedback and evaluating

Providing feedback and evaluating processes constitute the final stage of the seven-step approach. This also has the ability to feed into the first stage, 'knowing your world', and starting the cycle over again when the next occasion to delegate arises. Feedback, when given appropriately, can have positive repercussions, enhance working relationships, and encourage reflection and improve self-awareness (Boswell, 2005).

The delegatee should be given the opportunity to self-assess his or her performance, highlighting any difficulties that may have occurred. The outcome of evaluation may provide you with a chance to develop training needs and to enhance and improve your own delegating skills.

Providing the delegatee with feedback and evaluating outcomes – be it a thank-you or a more in-depth discussion – means that you have fulfilled your obligations in association with the cycle. You have monitored, evaluated and followed up on your delegated activity. Feedback and evaluation do not occur as one-off activities; they are continuous activities that enable you to intervene should the need arise. Offering feedback can also be seen as offering support and supervision. Robbins (2005) suggests that providing praise and encouragement when difficulties are being encountered may help ease the situation and restore self-confidence.

Factors associated with delegation

There are many influencing factors that need to be considered regarding delegation: delegation from doctors to nurses, and between nurses and other health-care professionals. The attitude of the person delegating responsibility will enhance or inhibit the level of the task and role sharing.

Effective delegation means that the person delegating delegates with trust and only the minimum of controls. The outcome will depend on the blend of trust and control, the difficulty of the task and the risks associated with it. The delegatee's skills, experience and willingness to take on the task and finally the nurse's skills, experience, willingness to delegate the task and ability to provide constructive feedback will have ramifications for the outcome of delegated actions.

Some of the barriers to effective delegation include lack of confidence, loss of power and loss of authority. Delegation brings with it a degree of risk. The nurse must balance the risks and benefits to the patient before delegating – always acting in the patient's best interests.

Lack of experience, of both the delegator (e.g. staff nurse) and the delegatee (e.g. student nurse), is a factor that needs consideration. Often, when delegating to student nurses, the staff nurse needs to consider the level of the student's education, skill acquisition and experience. Using delegation as a form of coaching can help both the student and the staff nurse to enhance and increase experience and expertise – it is a two-way learning process. Step by step the staff nurse can develop the student's skills and levels of competence as well as his or her own.

Top tips

Is the task you are thinking of delegating suitable for delegating? To whom should you delegate it? Agree the outcome of the activity. Agree the process.

Decision-making

As individuals we make decisions on a daily basis; we are always faced with making decisions, and we approach decision-making in various ways – consciously or subconsciously. Pesut and Harman (1999) provide a definition of decision-making: it is the consideration and selection of interventions from a repertoire of actions that will result in the achievement of a desired outcome. Another, simpler definition is one provided by Etherington (2003), who suggests that decision-making means fitting together the pieces to obtain a full picture in order for the nurse to determine care priorities. Decisions may be made consciously or unconsciously, with or without a framework. We may consider options and then list factors that are important and will enable us to make a choice or a decision, and ultimately opt for what we think is going to be the right decision. There are some decisions that are hurried and others that need time; we may need to deliberate on the decision being made. The right decision is more likely to occur if all options have been thoroughly explored and thought through.

The decision that is being made may be either an individual or a group decision. The outcome of the decision can be almost instantaneous or it may take a little longer or a lot longer. Table 13.4 demonstrates some of the factors that may be involved when making a decision.

Clinical decision-making

It has already been stated that the provision of high-quality, effective nursing care is complex. Clinical decision-making is also a complex process; often nurses are required to make decisions quickly and with information or data that are incomplete.

Table 13.4   Some factors that may be taken into consideration when making a decision

- What is the decision that needs to be made? Make a definition
- What do you need to know in order to make the decision? This is the aim
- What needs to be borne in mind? These are the criteria
- Work out what the options may be
- Are there any decision-making tools that need to be used?
- Review the decision

Clinical decisions and judgements are made concerning the needs of the patient and also about the most appropriate interventions that are required to address these needs and meet goals and outcomes that have been agreed upon. Clinical decisions help nurses to describe how they assign meaning to problems being faced by patients, with the ultimate aim of eliminating or alleviating the problem. Muir (2004) states that nurses make important clinical decisions on a daily basis and that these decisions have the potential to affect on the patient's health and the actions of the health-care professional.

The role and function of the nurse have expanded over the years and as nursing practice continues to expand nurses will be required to take on and make complex clinical decisions. Nurses are taking over work in clinical areas that had hitherto been deemed the domain of the doctor, and as a result they will need help and support when making decisions. Clinical decision-making should also include patients: they should be encouraged to become equal partners. Little research or empirical study has been undertaken into the decision-making role of the patient (Doherty and Doherty, 2005). The nurse of today, and more importantly the nurse of tomorrow, requires autonomous decision-making skills if he or she is to encourage the patient to participate in the decision-making process.

Making a clinical decision is different to making a decision generally, because the consequences of the decision being made must be given much thought. It is imperative, therefore, that the nurse makes the correct clinical decision. As with decision-making in general, the nurse uses several approaches to arriving at the decision.

Nearly every aspect of health care is associated with uncertainty and this is also true when making health-related decisions. Nurses have to be aware of this and deal with this uncertainty in their decision-making. The construction and implementation of evidence-based policies and practice will impinge on how they do this, and also on the quality of decision-making.

What are the clinical decisions that nurses are making?

The decisions that nurses make range from consulting with another health-care professional about a patient's dietary needs to deciding to refer another patient with 'niggling' chest pain to a doctor.

Contemporary nursing practice is expanding. There is a wide range of new and extended nursing roles being developed (RCN, 2005a). This means that nurses are taking on more responsibility and with this comes more opportunity to make more clinical decisions.

To perform as a competent registered nurse, high-level clinical decision-making is required. This is amplified when taking on extended and developing nursing roles. The RCN (2005b) suggest that one aspect associated with the role of nurse practitioner is the ability to make professionally autonomous decisions for which the nurse is accountable.

It is very difficult, if not impossible, to list the clinical decisions that a nurse makes in clinical practice. Attempting to formulate such a list would have to take into account the myriad activities and various contexts of care in which the nurse practises. It is evident that nurses are continually making decisions; often it might be suggested that the nurse may not be aware that he or she is making these decisions.

Top-down and bottom-up approaches to decision-making

The top-down approach to decision-making occurs when there is a centralised management structure in place, and in general decisions are made by senior managers. Those who are further down the chain of command are expected to carry out these decisions, despite having little, if any, input into the process. In the decentralised or bottom-up approach the decisions are formulated by those who are most knowledgeable about the concerns being deliberated, those who are closest to where the impact of the decision is felt most.

The decentralised approach encourages and enhances an individual's accountability, placing the responsibility for the decision-making process at the door of those who have made it – the nurses working with the patient. Nurses are accountable both personally and professionally for any decision that they make and subsequently act on (Muir, 2004).

Most organisations blend both centralised and decentralised approaches, e.g. centralised decisions may be linked with strategic economic issues and personnel planning, and the decentralised approach is often related to clinical issues, such as the introduction of new or innovative procedures (Taylor et al, 2011).

The decision-making process

The nurse needs an understanding of the decision-making process in order to make the most appropriate health-care decisions (Thompson and Dowding, 2002). There are many models available that outline the decision-making process or the steps that are involved in the decision-making process. Models and theories used will reflect the context in which they are being used. One mnemonic that may be used to help remember the various stages is BRAND:

Benefits of the action
Risks in the action
Alternatives to the prospective action
Nothing – doing nothing
Decision.

Tschikota (1993) considers the elements of decision making, and in her study she identifies six elements:

1. Cue
2. Hypothesis
3. Knowledge base
4. Nursing intervention
5. Search
6. Assumption.

Tschikota (1993) describes and defines each element and provides an example – shown in Table 13.5.

Decision-making tools

Sometimes when a nurse makes a decision the outcome is certain. At other times, however, when the nurse makes the decision he or she may not have all of the information available to ensure a good outcome. This certainty versus uncertainty can be improved if the nurse uses a decision-making tool to enhance the potential outcome of a given situation.

Decision-making tools can help and guide the nurse only when faced with complex options and potential outcomes. Decision trees (sometimes referred to as decision analytical models) provide different options, including chance events and potential outcomes. They also include probabilities and likelihoods of a chance event occurring; this is often expressed as a numerical value (Dowding and Thompson, 2002).

There are several advantages to using a decision-making tool such as a decision tree. In complex situations this approach makes explicit the important issues that need to be given consideration; sometimes these considerations are often implicit and may otherwise go unnoticed or ignored. However, the content

Table 13.5   Elements of the decision-making process

Element	Definition	Example
Cue	A piece of information or data	Patients provide nurses with pieces of information all of the time. It may be something they say or do, signs and symptoms, or it could be information gained from the patient when undertaking a nursing history. Other pieces of information might be the information or data provided by the patient's vital signs, e.g. his or her respiratory rate or temperature. Other data may include laboratory values, for example blood results or the results of an investigatory procedure such as renal function tests This element of the decision-making process involves the gathering of preliminary information. It can occur prior to meeting the patient, e.g. the gathering of the patient's name, age and address from records or when meeting the patient. This stage is also known as the cue acquisition stage
Hypothesis	A proposed possibility or a projected likelihood. Often the word 'might' is used at this stage, for example what might it be that concerns the patient? Other words used are 'probably', 'if', 'could be', 'maybe' or 'perhaps'. The hypothesis made is tentative: 'What might be the patient's problems?'	The number of hypotheses generated is generally between four and six: 'Probably croup' 'Could be a chest infection' 'May be paranoid schizophrenia' 'If we increase the rate of oxygen it might change the oxygen saturation'
Knowledge base	The information gained is used to support any statements made by the subject. The information – correct or incorrect – is used as a rationale for proposed action	'As the patient has tachycardia and pyrexia he or she probably has an infection' 'As the patient is hypotensive and tachycardic he or she is probably hypovolaemic' 'As the patient is hypertensive and bradycardic he or she may have raised intracranial pressure'
Nursing intervention	Any proposed nursing activity	'Place the patient flat' 'Elevate the limbs'

Table 13.5 *Continued*

Element	Definition	Example
Search	A desire to search for additional or supplementary information concerning the situation	'I think we need to know what the patient's cardiac enzymes are' 'Do we know what might have exacerbated this condition – what was the patient doing before becoming so breathless?'
Assumption	A conclusion, where there is insufficient information or data to make a definitive judgement. This may lead the nurse to search for more supplementary information concerning the situation	'I believe the patient has a urinary tract infection as she has dysuria, haematuria, proteinuria, is tachycardic and has a pyrexia' 'I think the patient is experiencing hallucinations as his behaviour suggests he is talking to an imagined thing, he has told me he feels he is being followed'

Source: adapted from Tschikota (1993); Thompson and Dowding (2002).

of the decision tree will only be as good as the assumptions that the creator has chosen to include in it. The probability values may not always be based on objective measurement; instead subjective values may be included. The probability of an event occurring (or not) may, therefore, be under- or even over-estimated. Acknowledging the strengths and weaknesses of decision-making trees can help the nurse to decide if he or she needs to use one.

Barriers to effective clinical decision-making

Despite the fact that nurses are involved in making decisions at various levels in various contexts, there are barriers to decision-making in practice. If nurses are to continue to enhance patient care, and it has been demonstrated that one way in which this can occur is through making effective decisions, then it is necessary for the nurse to understand what the barriers to effective clinical decision-making may be. There are many factors that have the potential to influence the decision-making process. It is also true that there are many other factors that are barriers to effective clinical decision-making.

The following could be considered barriers to effective clinical decision-making:

- Inadequate skills
- Emotional difficulties
- Lack of opportunity
- Dependence on others.

As your nursing skills develop and grow, and as you become more competent and confident, the factors listed above may diminish and you will become competent at making effective decisions. Hoffman et al (2004) point out that one of the key barriers to clinical decision-making is lack of participation in the decision-making process. You will become more involved in this process as your nursing career progresses. As a student you must make clear any anxieties or fears that you might have about making clinical decisions.

The dos and don'ts of decision-making

Becoming a proficient clinical decision maker comes with experience and learning. Learning takes place once you have been exposed to various scenarios related to patient care. Table 13.6 provides some dos and don'ts associated with decision-making.

Table 13.6   Some dos and don'ts of decision-making

Dos	Don'ts
Try to gather good pertinent information before making a decision	Make snap decisions
Use all relevant information to the best of your ability; 'think outside the box'	Make decisions for the sake of making them; avoid wasting your time making decisions that do not have to be made
Take time to consider the pros and cons of the issue being dealt with	Feel that there is a right or wrong decision; decisions are choices among alternatives
Try not to allow decisions to be made to build up and accumulate – make decisions as you go along	Procrastinate about making a decision
Delay or revise a decision as you feel necessary – trust yourself and do not be afraid to do this	Regret making a decision
Remember that any decision you make will have consequences and ramifications	Rush, pre-empt and jump to a conclusion
Avoid basing decisions on 'the way things are always done here'	Make decisions in order to justify any decision that you made earlier
	Be forced or coerced into making a decision

Top tips

Do not rush your decision-making. Nothing is worse than rushing to make a decision; the right decision at the wrong time is just as bad as the wrong decision at the right time. So if possible, suspend your decision-making and avoid making snap decisions.

Conclusion

Effective leadership fit for the provision of high-quality effective care for the twenty-first century is essential and this will require the intellectual and practical capacity to work effectively. The nurse of the future will have to develop and hone these skills. Delegation and decision-making are essential skills associated with leading and managing.

The role and function of the nurse will continue to expand in response to the Government's attempts to modernise the NHS. One result of this is a change in the skill mix. Ongoing evaluation is required to determine if the expanding roles undertaken by the nurse and the delegation of roles and duties previously held by the nurse to others are effective.

Effective delegation is the allocation of tasks and responsibilities to those staff who are best suited to do them, providing them with the freedom to perform the activity safely and in the most appropriate and effective manner. Effective delegation is not easy: it is concerned with trusting other people and having confidence in them. The nurse faces challenges when he or she delegates. A balance must be achieved between delegating too much or too little and between over-supervision and under-supervision (Pearce, 2004). Delegation is a useful tool in career development; it can also enhance individual skill development.

There is evidence that nurses can substitute effectively for doctors in some areas, such as arthritis, diabetes mellitus and Parkinson's disease. This evidence, applied in an appropriate manner, has the potential to enhance patient care. This should be the primary aim of delegating responsibility to others. When a task has been delegated the nurse cannot just withdraw from it. The nurse remains accountable for what the delegatee does or does not do.

Clinical decision-making is an essential component of the role of the professional nurse. Nurses who make clinical decisions must also be prepared to accept responsibility and be held accountable for the consequences of those decisions, or the failure to make a decision. To do this the factors that affect the decision-making and decision makers must be understood.

The outcome of effective decision-making results in finding solutions, providing safe and effective nursing care, and an individual, holistic approach to care. There has been an established association between patient outcomes and nurses' decision-making, and as such one way to enhance patient care is to increase and enhance the nurse's ability to make effective decisions.

383

Activity

Attempt the word search that is related to issues surrounding leadership, management, delegation and decision making to test your knowledge.

accountability
approach
assumption
authority
behavioural
charisma
competence
complex
confidence
conflict
cue
delegation
democratic

hypothesis
knowledge
motivation
policy
process
relational
resources
responsibility
situational
task
theory
trait
trust

References

Ashridge Business School (2010) *A Perspective on Leadership: Towards a relational leadership framework*. Available at: www.ashridge.org.uk/website/IC.nsf/wFARATT/Towards%20a%20relational%20leadership%20framework/$file/TowardsARelationalLeadershipFramework.pdf (accessed August 2011).

Belbin RM (2010) *Team Roles at Work*, 2nd edn. Oxford: Butterworth-Heinemann.

Bergman R (1981) Accountability – definition and dimensions. *International Nursing Review* **28**(2): 53–59.

Boswell A (2005) How effective delegation can build better teams. *Nursing Times* **101**(20): 60–61.

Cohen S (2004) Delegating vs dumping: Teach the difference. *Nursing Management* **35**(10): 14–18.

Department of Health (2006) *Modernising Nursing Careers. Setting the direction*. London: Department of Health.

Department of Health (2008a) *High Quality Care for all – NHS next stage review*. London: Department of Health..

Department of Health (2008b) *Towards a Framework for Post-Registration Nursing Careers: Consultation response report*. London: Department of Health.

Doherty C, Doherty W (2005) Patients' preferences for involvement in clinical decision making within secondary care and the factors that influence their preferences. *Journal of Nursing Management* **13**: 119–127.

Dowding D, Thompson C (2002) Decision analysis. In: Thompson, C, Dowding D (eds), *Clinical Decision Making and Judgement in Nursing*. Edinburgh: Churchill Livingstone, pp 131–145.

Etherington L (2003) Nursing the patient in the accident and emergency department. In: Brooker, C, Nichol M (eds), *Nursing Adults: The practice of caring*. Edinburgh: Mosby, pp 923–945.

Hansten RI, Jackson M (2004a) The overall process of delegation. In: Hansten RI, Jackson M (eds), *Clinical Delegation Skills: A handbook for professional practice*, 3rd edn. Boston, MA: Jones & Bartlett, pp 1–9.

Hansten RI, Jackson M (2004b) Know yourself. In: Hansten RI, Jackson M (eds), *Clinical Delegation Skills: A handbook for professional practice*, 3rd edn. Boston, MA: Jones & Bartlett, 113–146.

Hansten RI, Jackson M (2004c) Know your delegate. In: Hansten RI, Jackson M (eds), *Clinical Delegation Skills: A handbook for professional practice*, 3rd edn. Boston, MA: Jones & Bartlett, pp 193–234.

Hersey P, Blanchard KH, Johnson DE (2001) *Management of Organizational Behavior*, 8th edn. Upper Saddle River, NJ: Prentice Hall.

Hoban V (2003) How to..enhance your delegation skills. *Nursing Times* **99**(13): 80–81.

Hoffman K, Duffield C, Donoghue J (2004) Barriers to clinical decision-making in nurses in Australia. *Australian Journal of Advanced Nursing* **21**(3): 8–13.

Iles V (2006) *Really Managing Healthcare*, 2nd edn. Maidenhead: Open University Press.

Lawrence C (2008) The needs of children. In: Hinchliff S, Norman, S, Schober J (eds), *Nursing Practice and Health Care*, 5th edn. London: Arnold, pp 318–346.

Muir N (2004) Clinical decision making: Theory and practice. *Nursing Standard* **18**(36): 47–52.

Mullins L (2010) *Management and Organisational Behaviour*, 9th edn. Harlow: Prentice Hall.

Northouse PG (2012) *Introduction to Leadership. Concepts and practice*. Los Angeles: Sage, in press.

Nursing and Midwifery Council (2008) *The Code: Standards of Conduct, Performance and Ethics for Nurses and Midwives*. London: NMC.

Nursing and Midwifery Council (2010) *Standards for Pre registration Nursing Education*. London: NMC. Available at: http://standards.nmc-uk.org/PublishedDocuments/Standards%20for%20pre-registration%20nursing%20education%2016082010.pdf last accessed July 2011.

O'Neill L (2010) Know how to communicate. In: Hansten RI, Jackson M (eds), *Clinical Delegation Skills: A handbook for professional practice*, 3rd edn. Boston, MA: Jones & Bartlett, pp 235–254.

Pearce C (2004) Honing the art of effective delegation. *Nursing Times* **100**(29): 46–47.

Pesut DJ, Harman J (1999) *Clinical Reasoning: The art and science of critical and creative thinking*. Albany, NY: Delmar.

Porter-O'Grady T (2003) A different age for leadership, Part 1. *Journal of Nursing Administration* **33**: 115–110.

Robbins F (2005) Managing the performance of staff teams and individuals. *Nursing and Residential Care* **7**(4): 148–150.

Rost JC (1993) *Leadership for the Twenty First Century*. Westport: Praeger.

Royal College of Nursing (2005a) *Maxi Nurses: Nurses working in advanced and extended roles promoting and developing patient-centred health care*. London: RCN.

Royal College of Nursing (2005b) *Nurse Practitioners: An RCN guide to the nurse practitioner role, competencies and programme approval*. London: RCN.

Sullivan EJ, Garland G (2010) *Practical Leadership and Management in Nursing*. Harlow: Pearson.

Taylor CR, Lillis C, LeMone P, Lynn P (2011) *Fundamentals of Nursing: The art and science of nursing care*, 7th edn. Philadelphia, PA: Lippincott

Thompson C, Dowding D (2002) Decision making and judgment in nursing – An introduction. In: Thompson C, Dowding D (eds), *Clinical Decision Making and Judgment in Nursing*. Edinburgh: Churchill Livingstone, pp 1–20.

Tschikota S (1993) The clinical decision making processes of student nurses. *Journal of Nursing Education* **32**: 389–398.

Weir-Hughes D (2011) *Clinical Leadership, from A to Z*. Harlow: Pearson.

14

Continuing Professional Development

Aims and objectives

The aim of this chapter is to prepare you for the challenges and opportunities that you may face when you comply with continuing professional development requirements.

At the end of the chapter you will be able to:

1. Understand the value of lifelong learning
2. Understand the various ways of providing evidence of your continuous professional development
3. Explore the various reflective models and the skills required to reflect in a meaningful manner
4. Understand the value and importance of preceptorship
5. Begin to apply the concepts discussed to the practice setting
6. Appreciate the Nursing and Midwifery Council's requirements of student nurses

After engaging in 3 years' nurse education and successful registration with the Nursing and Midwifery Council (NMC), you will have fulfilled the NMC's registration requirements and, as such, be entitled to practise your profession. In order to be cognisant of your own professional development, there will be a need for reflective practice and a commitment to the concept of lifelong learning.

Continuing professional development is a requirement for all registered nurses, midwives and community public health nurses. It is one of the two standards associated with PREP (post-registration education and practice). PREP is a legal requirement that must be met by all those who are on the professional register and who wish to have their registration renewed. Renewal is required every 3 years. An outline of the process as required by the NMC is considered in this chapter.

Reflective practice is introduced and lifelong learning strategies through the development of a personal development plan are discussed. There are a variety of reflective models that may be used; two are mentioned in this chapter. Closely related to reflective practice is clinical supervision. Clinical supervision, what it is and what it is not are described. Reflective practice, clinical supervision and the ability to demonstrate continued professional development are all associated with the concept of lifelong learning.

The way in which the nurse provides evidence of continuing professional development is a personal matter. However, he or she must be aware that the NMC, as part of its audit arrangements, may request and require a nurse to provide evidence of how he or she has maintained his or her professional develop-

The Student's Guide to Becoming a Nurse, Second Edition. Ian Peate.
© 2012 John Wiley & Sons, Ltd. Published 2012 by John Wiley & Sons, Ltd.

ment. Often the nurse chooses to use a professional portfolio to do this – again, there are no set require-ments for how this should look, nor are there any stipulations associated with the content of the portfolio. Advice is provided in this chapter that may help you to devise and develop your own portfolio.

Post-registration education and practice

PREP is a set of standards and guidance produced by the NMC (2010) designed to enhance patient care. PREP can help the nurse keep up to date and be aware of new developments that are occurring in prac-tice. Nursing practice occurs in an environment that is ever changing. PREP has the ability to encourage the nurse to think and reflect, demonstrating to the patient that you are a knowledgeable, up-to-date practitioner who is capable of continuous professional development.

Continuing professional development (CPD), although not a guarantee of competence, is a key com-ponent of clinical governance and affects all health- and social care professionals. CPD is associated with life long learning that will enable nurses to meet the needs of the people whom they serve.

Figure 14.1 provides a useful model of CPD. This model is very similar to the steps used in the nursing process; it is cyclical and ongoing.

387

The NMC and PREP

You may recall that the role of the NMC is to protect the public. This is done through several mechanisms, one of which is to maintain the professional register. As already discussed, registration allows you to

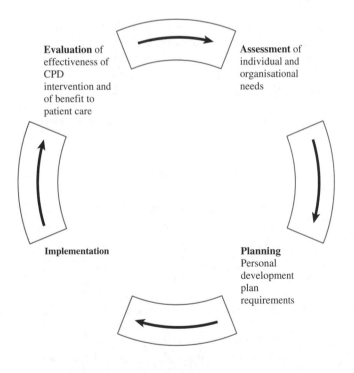

Figure 14.1   A continuing professional development model. Source: Department of Health (1998).

practise legally as a registered nurse in the UK. Every 3 years you are legally required to renew your registration (and pay a fee for this).

One aspect of this renewal process is that you are required to sign a notification of practice form, accompanied by the registration fee. The notification of practice form requires that you make a declaration relating to the details on the form. This declaration in effect states that the information that you have provided is a true and accurate statement of your current practice and CPD status. You also declare that your health and character are sufficiently good to enable you to continue to practise safely and effectively. There is a second section of the form concerned with 'Police cautions and convictions declaration'. Registration (and therefore your ability to practise) will not be renewed until the completed and signed form and payment have been received.

PREP requirements are discussed below.

Top tips

Always ensure you complete all documentation in full when returning any paper work to the NMC. It is essential you comply with the requirements of the NMC's requests for information because failure to do this may invalidate your registration.

PREP requirements

You must demonstrate the ability to meet PREP requirements. These are legal requirements and you will not be able to register unless you meet them. Since 1995 those wanting to re-register have had to provide evidence that they meet the legal PREP requirements. PREP requirements also feature as an important activity with other health-care professionals. The Health Professions Council (HPC, 2009) has produced five standards for continuing professional development (Table 14.1).

For nurses there are two standards associated with PREP: the PREP 'practice' standards and the PREP 'continuing professional development' standards (Table 14.2) that affect registration.

Table 14.1   The five continuing professional development standards produced by the Health Professions Council (HPC)

Registrants must:

1   Maintain continuous, up-to-date and accurate records of their continuing professional development (CPD)
2   Demonstrate that their CPD activities are a mixture of learning and activities relevant to current or future practice
3   Seek to ensure that their CPD has contributed to the quality of their practice and service delivery
4   Seek to ensure that their CPD benefits the service user
5   Present a written profile containing evidence of their CPD on request

Source: adapted from HPC (2009).

Table 14.2   The two standards that must be met in order for registration be renewed

PREP standard	PREP requirements
Practice standard	You are required to have worked in some capacity by virtue of your nursing or midwifery qualification during the previous 5 years for a minimum of 450 hours, or have successfully undertaken an approved return-to-practice course
CPD standard	You must have undertaken and recorded your continuing professional development over the three years prior to the renewal of your registration. All registered nurses and midwives must declare on their notice-to-practice form that they have met this requirement when they renew their registration

Source: adapted from NMC (2010).

The practice standard

This standard aims to ensure that the public are being protected by requiring that the nurse has undertaken a minimum amount of 450 hours in some capacity by virtue of his or her nursing qualification. The 450 hours must have occurred within the last 3 years before renewal of registration. Failure to meet this requirement means that the person wishing to renew registration must undertake an approved return-to-practice programme of study.

Return-to-practice courses

These courses are run in association with approved or accredited institutions, such as a university or other education institution. The programmes often adopt a flexible approach, fitting in with family life and other commitments. Both theoretical and practice experience are provided. The aims are to:

- develop competence
- develop and enhance confidence
- update skills and knowledge
- regain registration
- return to work.

Outcomes have been set by the NMC against which return-to-practice courses are validated. The programme must not be less than 5 days in length. The programme takes into account the needs of the student and previous levels of knowledge and experience. Course outcomes validated by the NMC must include the following:

- An understanding of the influence of health and social policy relevant to the practice of nursing
- An understanding of the law, guidelines, codes of practice and policies that are relevant to the practice of nursing
- An understanding of the current structure and organisation of care, nationally and locally
- An understanding of the current issues in nursing education
- The use of relevant literature to inform the practice of nursing

- The ability to identify and assess need, design and implement care interventions, and evaluate outcomes in all relevant areas of practice, including the effective delivery of appropriate emergency care
- The ability to use appropriate communications, teaching and learning skills
- The ability to function effectively in a team and take part in a multiprofessional approach to the care of people
- The ability to identify strengths and weaknesses, acknowledge limitations of competence, and recognise the need to maintain and develop professional competence.

The PREP practice standard can be met regardless of whether the individual is in paid work, e.g. employed by an NHS trust, working independently or working with a nursing agency, unpaid work, e.g. working for a voluntary organisation, or not working, e.g. the person may be taking a career break, has been on maternity leave or has retired. Whether the person is in part-time or full-time employment is irrelevant.

The continuing professional development standard

This element of PREP is referred to as continuing professional development and is also a condition for re-registration with which the nurse must comply. The nurse is committed to undertaking CPD. The NMC (2010) has decreed that there are three aspects associated with this standard:

1. The nurse must undertake at least 5 days or 35 hours of learning activity relevant to his or her practice during the 3 years before renewal of registration.
2. The nurse must maintain a personal professional portfolio of learning activity.
3. The nurse must comply with any request from the NMC to audit how those requirements have been met.

The way in which this standard is met is up to the nurse. The person who is required to demonstrate CPD activities is the best person to decide what learning activities are needed to comply with the standard. There is no such thing as approved PREP (CPD) learning activity.

What is essential is that you document your learning activities. This is best done in your personal professional portfolio (on which there is more in the next section). There must be evidence that the learning activity you have undertaken has informed and influenced your practice. The important issues associated with the CPD standard are outlined in Table 14.3.

Table 14.3   Important things to remember in relation to the continuing professional development (CPD) standard

- It does not have to cost you any money
- There is no such thing as approved PREP (CPD) learning activity
- You do not need to collect points or certificates of attendance
- There is no approved format for the personal professional portfolio
- It must be relevant to the work that you are doing and/or plan to do in the near future
- It must help you to provide the highest possible standards of care for your patients and clients

Source: adapted from NMC (2010).

You may be asked to demonstrate to the NMC how you have met the CPD standard. You must be able to provide documentation about your learning activities that you have completed within the 3 years before renewal of your registration. You will need to demonstrate where, what and how:

- *Where* you were practising when the learning activity took place.
- *What* the learning activity was concerned with.
- *How* the learning influenced or informed your practice, and how it related to your practice.

The next section of this chapter discusses the personal professional portfolio (your portfolio) and ways in which you can maintain it.

Tops tips

Remember that portfolios can be online, hard copy or a mix; the important thing is to ensure that they are in order, up to date, accessible and relevant. There is no set format for developing your portfolio.

Personal professional portfolios

As a student nurse you may have been required to complete and develop a portfolio during your programme of study. The portfolio might have been used for professional development and assessed as part of your overall academic and practical performance. The portfolio may also have been used as a reflective tool. There are several ways in which this may have been undertaken, depending on your educational institution's preference.

A personal portfolio is your collection of evidence that demonstrates the continuing attainment of skills, knowledge, attitudes, understanding and achievement. The portfolio can be retrospective and prospective, a collection of evidence, as well as reflecting the current stage of development of the individual. It includes a collection of evidence with a particular purpose, for a particular audience

A portfolio is a snapshot in time, outlining where you have come from, where you find yourself now and where it is you intend going, along with the methods you chose to use to get there. Goodfellow (2004) states that the portfolio is a planned and organised collection of artefacts and reflections relating to professional qualities and practices. Compilation of a portfolio can contribute to lifelong learning as part of your CPD. Table 14.4 outlines other ways in which the portfolio can help the nurse.

Table 14.4 Ways in which a portfolio can help you

- Reflect on clinical, academic experiences and personal growth
- Make decisions about the quality of your work and performance
- Encourage reflective thinking
- Provide empowerment to take on responsibility for your own learning
- Develop within you a more critical, reflective practitioner
- Provide documentary evidence of your achievements
- Enhance self-esteem by demonstration of your ability to accomplish activities you have set out to achieve

Source: adapted from Pearce (2003).

Reflection as a tool should feature often in a portfolio. Reflective practice allows the nurse to recognise learning and development that has taken place, either formally or informally, and is a useful tool when developing your portfolio. There are many skills associated with a portfolio and one of the key skills in compiling a portfolio is the ability to communicate with yourself through critical reflection. This critical ability to reflect can occur by seeing yourself and your practice through different lenses or perspectives. There is more on reflection later in this chapter.

The portfolio: the product

The portfolio as a product (how it looks) can come in many guises. Often it is described as a file. This can be a hard-copy folder (often a loose-leaf ring binder) or an electronic file or CD-ROM. There is no definitive requirement for the contents of the folder. The collection of artefacts described by Goodfellow (2004) can be varied and the evidence that you choose to include is up to you.

Below are some suggestions on how to document learning activities that you have undertaken. You may be required to provide evidence of your learning activities to the NMC if it requests you to do so as a part of its auditing procedures (NMC, 2010). The NMC (2010) suggests that the template in Table 14.5 be used, but points out that this is only a suggestion.

Table 14.5   A suggested template for the recording of PREP

PREP (CPD) PERIOD – the 3-year registration period to which this learning applies	
From:	To:
WORK PLACE – where were you working when the learning activity took place?	
Name of organisation:	
Brief description of your work/role:	
NATURE OF THE LEARNING ACTIVITY	
Date:	
Briefly describe the learning activity, e.g. reading a relevant clinical article, attending a course, observing practice:	
State how many hours this took:	
DESCRIPTION OF THE LEARNING ACTIVITY – What did it consist of?	
Describe what the learning activity consisted of – include, for example: why did you decide to do the learning activity or how the opportunity came about; where, when and how you did the learning activity; and what you expected to gain from it?	
OUTCOME OF THE LEARNING ACTIVITY – How did the learning relate to your work?	
Give a personal view of how the learning informed and influenced your work – what effect has this learning had on the way in which you work, or intend to work in the future? Do you have any ideas or plans for any follow-up learning?	
The way in which this activity has influenced my work is . . .	

Source: adapted from NMC (2010).

In the template suggested, the three key attributes of a professional portfolio can be identified: where, what and how. It may help you if you keep records of learning as described in a professional portfolio.

It is not how you present your collection of artefacts that will be assessed or judged. However, you must be able to demonstrate the where, what and how described earlier. A combination of both the process and the finished product is required in order to develop the portfolio. A professional portfolio can help you keep together evidence of your learning and other important facts related to professional development activities.

Portfolios take many forms; you may wish to use a straightforward version, e.g. a folder that includes all your achievements, your development activities, work experiences, specific work or personal activities that have informed or influenced your practice.

Portfolio of evidence

A portfolio of evidence is a collection of important material that you choose to collect to demonstrate some aspects of your professional development, including your evidence of learning. Some students are introduced to the use of a professional portfolio at the start of their studies; others may use a portfolio later on in the programme. If your university requires you to use and compile a portfolio you must follow the guidance provided. The guidelines here are intended to complement that.

The formulation and how you present your portfolio are your responsibility. This approach actively encourages you to take part in your learning as well as emphasising the need for lifelong learning. Regardless of when you begin using a professional portfolio, you will be engaging in a lifelong practice of reflecting, evaluating and recording your professional development.

The portfolio should focus on the process of learning (including evidence of reflective practice), demonstrating, through the collection of evidence, how you have made and can make associations between the theoretical aspects of your programme of study, and what relationship this has to the art and science of nursing practice. This can be seen as an ideal method of relating theory to practice and one way of starting to reduce the practice–theory gap. The portfolio is your own personal record of your achievements.

Organising your portfolio

You can purchase ready-made, commercially produced portfolios. Portfolios are highly personalised and unique to the person producing them; because of this, ownership belongs to you (Hull et al, 2005). The commercially produced portfolios are convenient to use and can help organise your thoughts; they cannot, however, accomplish your achievements.

Think

Make a list of things that you think you might want to include in your professional portfolio.

The list below is not an exhaustive list of what can be included in a professional portfolio, merely suggestions (beware, however, that you do not unintentionally breach confidentiality with any items you choose to include):

- Items related to reflective practice, e.g. critical incidents
- Your curriculum vitae
- Feedback from mentors
- Feedback from tutors
- Letters/cards of thanks from patients/families
- Testimonials
- Certificates of achievement
- Study days attended
- Descriptions of supplementary roles that you may have undertaken, e.g. student ambassador
- Action plans and learning outcomes constructed in response to feedback
- Evidence of achievement
- Learning contracts
- Elective experiences
- Self-assessment of your performance
- Nursing skills/clinical procedures that you have performed, observed or assisted with
- Key documentation produced by organisations such as the NMC, e.g. the code of professional conduct
- Protocols, policies and procedures
- Details from/about appraisals
- Issues concerning and associated with the knowledge and skills framework
- Details related to AP(E)L (assessment of prior [experiential] learning)
- Details about membership of particular professional forums, e.g. the RCN's School Nurses Forum, British Association for Sexual Health and HIV.

Ensure that you organise your information thoroughly, e.g. identify each section of the portfolio clearly. Take some time to ensure that you consider the proposed contents carefully. Construct a contents page and cross-tabulate the pages of your portfolio to this. Use dates to help you recall events; a chronological approach may be appropriate for all or just some of the sections. Try to update the contents of your portfolio on a regular basis, updating items and documents that have been superseded by later materials.

Putting together your biographical details may be the first step towards creating your own portfolio. A part of this might be the creation of your curriculum vitae. You must remember that it is the quality of the evidence you include in your portfolio that matters, not the quantity; bigger does not necessarily mean better. Table 14.6 is an example of a contents list that may be used in a portfolio.

Biographical details

In this section include the following:

Personal details

- Name
- Address
- Email address
- Phone number (work, home and mobile)
- NMC PIN and expiry date
- Membership details for professional organisations, e.g. your RCN membership number.

Table 14.6   A proposed contents list for a professional portfolio

Personal details
Academic and professional achievements
Current role
Employment history
Personal achievements
Learning activities log
Evidence log
Reflective diary
Other information

Source: adapted from NIPEC (2004).

Introduction

In this section provide details about who you are and your reasons are for wanting to develop your professional portfolio. Include your current role and responsibilities. It is up to you what you put here, but try to give the person looking at your profile a 'flavour' of who you are, what you want (career aspirations) and how you intend to get there (action plan).

General education

In this section, and the next two, use a format that is chronological:

- Name(s) of the school(s) you attended and the educational qualifications you gained
- Name(s) of the university you attended and your educational achievements.

Include any specific roles and responsibilities that you held at these educational institutions, e.g. member of the debating society.

Professional education

List here any qualifications that are recordable with the NMC and the qualifications that led to registration with the NMC (on any part of the register). Include the school/college of nursing or university that you attended in order to gain your professional qualification.

Ensure that you include any awards associated with the qualification gained, such as a university prize. Provide details of the classification of your degree (if appropriate).

Include any specific roles and responsibilities that you held at these educational institutions, e.g. member of the curriculum planning group, student ambassador, student rep.

Work experience

A chronological approach must be used. Start with your most recent post and work backwards (as you would on a conventional application form). Include:

- Names of employers
- Position held
- A brief account of the duties and responsibilities associated with the post
- Salary paid (if you wish)
- Any voluntary or temporary posts.

In the next section of the portfolio you will need to include details of your CPD as described above (e.g. reflective accounts, learning activities). You should also list any study activity with dates and venues, e.g.:

- Cardiopulmonary resuscitation updates
- Protecting vulnerable people update
- Moving and handling updates
- Any other statutory requirements such as fire or health and safety-related activity
- Project work
- Clinical supervision activity.

Table 14.7 is a checklist that you may wish to use to ensure that your portfolio is as complete as possible.

There are many skills required of you in an attempt to develop and maintain your professional portfolio. As you become more competent and confident with portfolio development, you will find it easier to maintain.

Reflective practice

Effective reflective practice is crucial to continuing professional practice. The term 'reflection' may be seen by some as a buzzword. Some may feel that they do not have enough time for reflection and others may think it helps them provide safe, high-quality care. Reflective practice has the potential to help the nurse become, among other things, a lifelong learner; reflective practice then becomes reflective learning.

Reflective learning and lifelong learning

Freshwater (2008) notes that there have been many attempts at defining the concept of reflection; she suggests that defining terms proves challenging for anyone who wishes to explain the essence of reflection. Reflective learning is learning from experience formally or informally, allowing the learner to consider his or her practice honestly and critically (Moon, 2004). The outcome may be the development of

Table 14.7 A profile checklist

Item	Tick
Is the table of contents clear with cross-tabulated page numbers?	
Is it well presented and organised?	
Is your portfolio user friendly?	
Could others easily navigate their way around it – do you need more signposts?	
Have you cross-referenced your work?	
Have you used a variety of appropriate sources to support your learning?	
Have you used the most appropriate media to demonstrate learning?	
Can you demonstrate clear reflective action?	
Is your evidence genuine?	
Does the evidence provided do justice to what you claim to have achieved?	
Are the contents true, accurate and your own work?	
Have you ensured that the principle of confidentiality has been respected?	
Are the contents of your profile up to date?	

Source: adapted from NIPEC (2004).

a deeper understanding of personal skills, enhanced self-awareness and individual learning needs. Nurses can develop further and enhance their understanding of practice through reflection.

Continuing professional development is a process of lifelong learning, and as such is an integral aspect of nursing practice. Lifelong learning is a concept that involves the continuous development of skills and knowledge with the intention of enhancing quality of life and employment prospects.

Pre-registration nurse education provides the foundation for lifelong learning. Having experienced this foundation, you are expected to continue as a lifelong learner, especially when related to your professional practice.

To be able to reflect on and in practice this requires the nurse to engage in an active and conscious process when encountering problematic aspects of care provision and making an attempt to make sense of it. Reflective practice is a process that can be used for engaging in lifelong learning.

There are several definitions of reflection available in the literature and because of this there may be confusion about what constitutes reflection. Boud et al (1985) suggest that reflection occurs when individuals engage in activities that aim to explore their experiences in order to lead to new understanding and appreciation of the situation(s). Johns (2000) states that reflection is a window allowing practitioners to view themselves within the context of their own lived experience. By doing this, practitioners can confront, understand and work towards resolving issues that arise in practice.

To maintain competency, Boud et al (1985) suggest that you must learn through practice. Johns (1994) is of the opinion that practitioners, through an active and reflective approach, develop and create their own practice.

Top tips

When undertaking any reflective activity, e.g. in writing or as part of a group, it is essential that you ensure that you maintain patient confidentiality throughout. Breach of patient confidentiality is a serious offence and can have serious ramifications for your career.

Reflective models

Just as there are many definitions of reflection available, there are also a number of models that you may use to help you consciously reflect. There are several techniques available to help you reflect with purpose. They may offer guidance and structure, but no one technique is better than the other. The choice of model may be individual or it may have been dictated to you, e.g. your higher education institution may require you to use a particular model.

Driscoll (2007) considers three stages in his approach to reflection:

1. *What?* describes the event
2. *So what?* analyses the event
3. *Now what?* proposes actions after the event.

Models of reflection with a brief explanation of their use are discussed below.

Gibbs' model of reflection

Gibbs (1988) enables those who engage in reflective activity to consider events in a cyclical manner (Figure 14.2). Gibbs' model is one that promotes a simple approach to refection (Gibbs, 1988). Gibbs (1992) points out that deep learning takes place when reflective practice is used. It goes beyond the memorisation of information, and becomes an active, as opposed to a passive, activity.

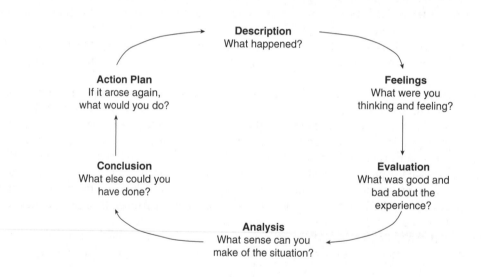

Figure 14.2   Gibbs' reflective model. Source: Gibbs (1988).

Johns' model of reflection

Johns' model of reflection (Johns, 1994) provides a framework that has five components (Table 14.8). His model adapts the theories espoused by Carper (1978) concerning ways of knowing and nursing knowledge as a basis for reflection.

A summary of the overall benefits of reflection are presented in Table 14.9.

Table 14.8   An outline of the components of Johns' reflective model

Component	Description
Description	• Describe the experience, document what happened • What aspects of this experience do I need to pay particular attention to?
Reflection	• What was it that I was trying to achieve? • What was it that made me act the way I did? • What are the consequences of my actions – for myself, the patient and my colleagues? • How did I feel about the experience as it was happening? • How did the patient feel? • How do I know how the patient felt?
Influencing	• What internal factors impinged on my decision making and actions? • What external factors impinged on my decision making and actions? • What sources of knowledge did or should have influenced my decision-making and actions?
Alternative strategies	• Could I have dealt better with the situation? • What other choices did I have? • What would be the consequences of these other choices?
Learning	• How can I make sense of this experience in the light of past experience and future practice? • How do I now feel about this experience? • Have I taken effective action to support myself and others as a result of this experience? • How has this experience changed my way of knowing in practice?

Source: adapted from Johns (1994).

Table 14.9   The benefits of reflection in summary format

- Allows you to consider your practice objectively
- Helps you recognise what you do well
- Improves your professional judgment
- Allows you to learn from your successes and mistakes and as a result enhance your performance
- Helps you to plan for future incidents and respond more positively to change
- It is a critical component of the continuing professional development cycle
- Allows you to resolve uncertainty
- Encourages and fosters independent learning

Source: adapted from Institute of Health Care Management (2004).

Try to set some time aside to write up your reflective accounts on a regular basis. That way they will be fresh in your mind and they will be truer accounts. Try to remember that you are expected to record how you feel and to be honest about this. Keep the reflective account simple; often it is best to be spontaneous, writing, drawing or making a record is the most appropriate way as it happens or occurs to you.

Clinical supervision

Clinical supervision is closely aligned to reflective practice.

Clinical supervision is a term that has been used by nurses and other health-care professionals to provide a purposeful, practice-focused relationship that enables the nurse to reflect on practice with the support of a skilled supervisor. Clinical supervision has its roots in counselling and psychotherapy.

The Royal College of Nursing (RCN, 2003) states that clinical supervision in the workplace has been introduced as one method of using reflective practice as part of CPD. However, there are a number of instances where clinical supervision should and could be used by nurses with regard to critical reflection and innovation, but this is not always the case.

Clinical supervision is said to be a formal process of professional support and learning, enabling practitioners to develop knowledge and competence, assuming responsibility for their own practice and, as a result, improving public safety in complex clinical situations (Jackson et al, 2011). Clinical supervision should be a structured, systematic activity.

As well as providing a relationship between clinical supervision and reflective practice, clinical supervision has the potential to enable the practitioner to contribute in an effective manner to organisational objectives, such as clinical governance (Driscoll and O'Sullivan, 2007). By participating in the clinical supervision process, practitioners are demonstrating commitment to their responsibilities associated with clinical governance. There is a clear symbiotic relationship with the overall framework of clinical governance. Clinical supervision, similar to clinical governance, is not an activity that is carried out in isolation; successful partnerships are developed and maintained through clinical supervision.

Clinical supervision should occur on a regular basis because this will enable facilitated in-depth reflection on clinical practice through focused support and development. The focused support sessions should occur as time-protected sessions. The development and establishment of effective clinical supervision allows the practitioner to:

- reflect on nursing practice
- identify room for improvement
- develop expertise and promote standards of care
- devise new ways of learning
- gain professional support
- develop a deeper understanding of professional issues.

Top tips

Make the most out of your clinical supervision sessions and always plan in advance if possible so that you can make use of the time effectively. A 'one size fits all' approach' does not work. There are many ways you can take part in effective clinical supervision. The session should always be conducted in confidence; however, there may be exceptions to this. At the beginning of the encounter all parties must set and agree boundaries.

What it is and what it is not

Clinical supervision is suited to a variety of areas of clinical practice, e.g. those nurses working in the mental health field, nurses working in the prison service and nurses engaged in activities associated with child protection. Clinical supervision is needed to protect patients from nurses and nurses from themselves. The professional relationships that nurses have with others may seriously affect how the nurse behaves towards those other people. Nursing, by the nature of the role and the relationship that the nurse has with others, has the ability to provoke intimate feelings which, in turn, have the potential to affect the care provided. As a result of this, the nurse must investigate and explore these feelings. One method of doing this in a safe and supportive environment is during clinical supervision.

There are several definitions available that are associated with clinical supervision, but a plethora of definitions can lead to confusion and misunderstanding. It may be more beneficial to state what clinical supervision is *not*, as opposed to what it *is*. It is not psychotherapy or counselling; Cutcliffe et al (2001) state that it is distinct from mentoring. Importantly, clinical supervision is not an opportunity for managers to review staff performance; using clinical supervision in this manner may lead to resistance to the concept. Bond and Holland (2010) note that it is not about managers keeping an eye on staff, nor is it about being looked at critically through a magnifying glass (see Table 14.10 for a summary of what clinical supervision is and what it is not).

When engaging in clinical supervision, opportunities arise that enable practitioners, in either a one-to-one setting or a group context, to discuss areas of their practice that may be problematic or challenging. The encounter should aim to be:

- supportive
- encouraging
- explorative
- reflective.

Table 14.10   What clinical supervision is and what it is not

What clinical supervision is not	
✗	A disciplinary channel
	A route to make complaints
	An opportunity to reprimand poor performance
	An opportunity to criticise other team members
	Time out to chat about things in general
What clinical supervision is	
✔	A chance to openly, safely and honestly examine practice
	An opportunity to consider future development needs
	An opportunity to identify and improve poor practices
	An opportunity to improve the delivery of care to patients (wherever they may be, e.g. institutional settings or within the home)
	A method to feel professionally supported and to minimise professional isolation
	A way of identifying good effective practice

Source: adapted from Department of Health, HM Prison Service and Welsh Assembly Government (2004).

Some practical issues

Before starting clinical supervision an action plan needs to be established. Meetings will be needed to determine the best way forward and, most of all, to determine 'where you are at now'. Decisions need to be made about who will act as clinical supervisor and whether the session will be a one-to-one or group session. These details are important and from the outset they need to be addressed. Local factors will also need to be taken into account. When these issues have been addressed the process can be owned and moved forward. Consider the issues in Table 14.11.

Driscoll (2007) suggests that there are several skills that are essential to the supervisee if effective clinical supervision is to occur. You will become more competent and confident when using the skills listed below as you develop into your role:

- Make the session work for you
- Identify pertinent issues to disclose in the session
- Start to be aware of yourself in clinical practice
- Be open to receiving feedback about your performance in the clinical area
- Write as well as talk about issues that arise during clinical supervision sessions
- Adopt a more proactive approach to problems that you encounter in clinical practice.

Preceptorship

The Next Stage Review (Department of Health or DH, 2008) made a commitment to support a period of preceptorship for all health professionals, including nurses. The provision of support for newly qualified nurses through preceptorship has been advocated as a way of enhancing patient care by assisting new practitioners in developing clinical skills, and encouraging workforce retention by supporting students in the transition to registered practitioners.

Definitions

There are a number of definitions of preceptorship. The Department of Health (2008) defines it as:

> *A foundation period for practitioners at the start of their careers which will help them begin the journey from novice to expert.*

Members of the Modernising Allied Health Professional Careers Steering Group agreed with the Council of Deans of Health (unpublished report) conclusion, reached in 2009 at a national workshop on preceptorship, that:

> *Preceptorship should be seen as a model of enhancement, which acknowledges new graduates/ registrants as safe, competent but novice practitioners who will continue to develop their competence as part of their career development/continuing professional development, not as individuals who need to address a deficit in terms of education and training.*

Bain (1996) considered the role of preceptorship in relation to professional socialisation, suggesting that the concept refers to an individualised period of support under direction or supervision

Table 14.11   Some practicalities for consideration in relation to clinical supervision

Frequency of interactions	Location	Protecting time	Group vs individual sessions	Professional and ethical issues
Determine how often clinical supervision should take place. Often this takes place on a monthly basis. In the initial periods this may be more often and as time progresses this may become less frequent. *Ad hoc* sessions may be required if the need arises	It is important that the location in which clinical supervision takes place is jointly agreed by both the supervisee and the supervisor. The environment must be comfortable, free from interruption and distractions, as well as the possibility of the conversation being overheard. Careful consideration must be given to conducting clinical supervision in the clinical area as this may be counterproductive	When the frequency and location have been agreed it is vital that both supervisee and supervisor are committed to the meetings. You should aim to be punctual and only in absolute emergencies should the session be cancelled	The decision to use group as opposed to one-to-one clinical supervision sessions should be mutually agreed and not prescribed	The content of the discussion must be confidential and all parties must be reminded of this. Boundaries must be established and respected. Documenting that a session has occurred is necessary and this can be done in the professional portfolio. Details of what was discussed will not be necessary although this can be done privately if desired, but the principles of confidentiality must be respected. All nurses must be cognisant of the fact that there may be times when there is a need to disclose records. If this is the case advice must be sought

Source: adapted from Freshwater et al (2002); Driscoll (2007); Bond and Holland (2010).

of an experienced clinician with the aim of easing the transition from student into professional practice or socialisation into a new role.

In the newly developed *Preceptorship Framework* (DH, 2010) preceptorship is defined as:

> *A period of structured transition for the newly registered practitioner during which he or she will be supported by a preceptor, to develop their confidence as an autonomous profes-sional, refine skills, values and behaviours and to continue on their journey of life-long learning.*

All of the definitions provided, as well as the foundation work, have been undertaken by NHS Scotland (www.flyingstart.scot.nhs.uk); these definitions and statements support the assertion that, on com-mencement of preceptorship, newly registered practitioners are safe and competent. They are, however, novice nurses, who will grow, develop and further enhance their competence and confidence as part of their CPD to becoming expert practitioners.

The elements of preceptorship

The newly qualified staff nurse and the employer should work together to ensure that there is a clear understanding of where the boundaries of preceptorship lie. Both parties should understand that there are other processes and systems in place to manage ability and performance with regard to the compe-tency of the newly registered practitioner. Preceptorship is not:

- replacing mandatory training programmes that nurses have to undertake
- an alternative for performance management processes
- intended to replace regulatory body processes that are there to deal with performance
- a further period of training
- a formal coaching activity
- mentorship
- clinical supervision
- replacing induction to employment
- a distance or e-learning package for a newly qualified nurse to undertake in isolation.

The Department of Health (2010) considers the elements of preceptorship from three perspectives:

1. The newly qualified nurse
2. The preceptor
3. The employer

Table 14.12 outlines the three perspectives.

The benefits of preceptorship

When a nurse completes the required 3 years of education or returns to practice after a break, this period of time may be challenging, so good support and guidance during this initial period are essential. Those newly registered nurses who are able to manage the transition from student to staff nurse are success-fully able to provide effective care more quickly, feel better about their role and are more likely to remain

Table 14.12   The three elements of preceptorship

Newly registered practitioner	Preceptor	Employer
Opportunity to apply and develop the knowledge, skills and values already learned in the pre-registration nursing programme	An obligation to develop others professionally to reach their potential	A process that is to be quality assured
Develop specific competences that relate to the preceptee's new role	Conduit to formalise and demonstrate continued professional development – to act a role model	Embedding the knowledge and skills framework at the start of employment
Access support in embedding the values and expectations of the profession	Responsibility to discuss individual practice and provide constructive feedback	Promoting and encouraging an open, honest and transparent culture among staff
Personalised programme of development that incorporates post-registration learning, e.g. leadership, management and effectively working within a multidisciplinary team	Responsibility to share knowledge and experience	Supporting the provision of high-quality efficient health care
Chance to reflect on practice and receive constructive feedback	Demonstrate and possess insight and empathy with the newly qualified nurse during the transition phase	Demonstrates the employer's commitment to the delivery of the NHS Constitution and other key policies
Take and accept responsibility for individual learning and development by learning how to 'manage self'	Receive preparation for the role	Expresses the organisation's commitment to learning
Supports the concept of lifelong learning Enables embracement of the principles of the NHS Constitution	Enables embracement of the principles of the NHS Constitution	Provides evidence of commitment to the NHS Constitution

Source: adapted from Department of Health (2010).

within the profession. This will mean that they make a greater contribution to patient care, as well as ensuring the benefits from the investment in their education is maximised (DH, 2010).

The value of preceptorship has been recognised in policy documents such as *Modernising Nursing Careers* (DH, 2006) and further, in *High Quality Care for All: NHS next stage* review (DH, 2008). The Department of Health has committed funds specifically to support preceptorship. The preceptorship framework also contributes to the delivery of pledges to patients and staff that have been set out in the NHS Constitution (DH, 2009).

The preceptorship framework

The preceptorship framework (DH, 2010), developed in co-production with strategic health authorities (SHAs) and other key stakeholders, indicates what has to be undertaken to ensure that local systems for preceptorship do well, and will further enable a smooth transition for newly registered nurses as they progress in their professional careers and continue on with their journey of life-long learning. The framework. intended primarily as a resource for NHS organisations with responsibility for establishing organisational systems for the management and development nurses, will be of interest to newly registered nurses as well as those directly responsible for preceptorship.

To further support preceptorship the Department of Health has adapted and is continuing to test the Scottish 'Flying Start NHS', web-based, electronic preceptorship programme in a range of NHS organisations in England and also with a higher education institution. This multiprofessional preceptorship programme, designed by NHS Education Scotland (NES), has been used in Scotland since 2006.

It is anticipated that the framework will also contribute to consideration of the introduction of a mandatory period of preceptorship planned by the Nursing and Midwifery Council, with the aim of guiding and supporting all newly qualified nurses to make the transition from student to develop their practice further as staff nurses.

Think

Having read this chapter you should be able to engage in some reflective activity of your own. Think about a recent situation (make it as recent as possible) that you can reflect on. When you have done this, choose one of the models described in this chapter. Follow the model, addressing all aspects associated with it. When you have completed the activity, consider the following:

- How easy was it?
- How hard was it?
- Did you enjoy it?
- Did you feel uncomfortable?
- Did you learn anything?
- Would you do anything differently next time if the same or a similar situation arose?

Conclusions

Most nurse education programmes (pre-registration) require student nurses to use a professional portfolio; this may be assessed or used as an opportunity to develop your skills. Using the portfolio and engaging in reflective practice are preparation for when you become a registered nurse. Becoming a registered nurse confers many things on you, and one of those is to engage in lifelong learning.

It is a legal requirement that the registered nurse update his or her professional development. These mandatory requirements are part of post-registration education practice requirements – the practice component of PREP and the CPD aspect.

Providing evidence to the NMC when it requests and requires it can be done in a variety of ways. Often nurses use a professional portfolio in order to present and organise their CPD activities. Professional portfolios are varied. You may choose to devise your own or use one that has been commercially produced. The choice is yours, but remember that it is not how you arrange and present your portfolio that is important – what it contains will be judged.

Reflective practice is seen as one of the central components of CPD. There are a number of models available and two have been mentioned here; you must choose the one that suits you and your situation. Closely related to reflective practice is the notion of clinical supervision. Clinical supervision provides the nurse with an opportunity to engage in professional debate, to enhance care provision and to voice opinion. This chapter has pointed out what clinical supervision is and what it is not.

Newly qualified nurses are now receiving preceptorship which is seen as central to the successful transition from being a nursing student to a staff nurse. There are, however, some constraints associated with the provision of effective preceptorship programmes, e.g. workload, staffing and relationships. Employers must be committed to preceptorship if positive aspects are to be maintained. Commitment will require workload planning that allows staff the time to provide preceptorship, receive the appropriate training and develop meaningful programmes.

Activity

Attempt the following true or false questions associated with CPD to test your knowledge. The answers can be found at the back of this book, in the chapter called 'Activity Answers'.

1. As a registered nurse it is a legal requirement to ensure that you undertake post-registration education and practice.
2. You must ensure that your personal and professional portfolio is aligned with the NMC's mandatory template.
3. Supervision is one way that your employer can ensure that you adhere to policies and procedures.
4. Preceptorship is a foundation period for practitioners at the start of their careers which will help them begin the journey from novice to expert.
5. You must undertake clinical supervision to remain live on the NMC register.
6. In order to meet the PREP (practice) standard you must have undertaken 450 hours in your capacity as a nurse.
7. Those unable to comply with the practice standard will have to successfully complete an approved return to practice programme.
8. In order to meet the PREP (CPD) standard you must pay.
9. There is no such thing as approved PREP (CPD) learning activity.
10. Lifelong learning ceases when you register with NMC.

References

Bain L (1996) Preceptorship: A review of the literature. *Journal of Advanced Nursing* **24**: 104–107.

Bond M, Holland S (2010) *Skills of Clinical Supervision for Nurses. A practical guide for supervisees, clinical supervisors and managers*. Maidenhead: Open University Press.

Boud D, Keogh R, Walker D (1985) *Reflection: Turning experience into learning*. New York: Kogan Page.

Carper B (1978) Fundamental patterns of knowing in nursing. *Advances in Nursing Science* **1**: 15–23.

Cutcliffe JR, Butterworth T, Proctor B (2001) *Fundamental Themes on Clinical Supervision*. London: Routledge.

Department of Health (1998) *A First Class Service: Quality in the new NHS*. London: Department of Health.

Department of Health (2006) *Modernising Nursing Careers: Setting the Direction*. London: Department of Health.

Department of Health (2008) *High Quality Care for all – NHS next stage review*. London: Department of Health.

Department of Health (2009) *The NHS Constitution for England*. London: Department of Health.

Department of Health (2010) *Preceptorship Framework for Newly Registered Nurses, Midwives and Allied Health Professionals*. London: Department of Health.

Department of Health, HM Prison Service and Welsh Assembly Government (2004) *Clinical Supervision in Prison – Getting Started*. London: Department of Health.

Driscoll J (2007) Supported reflective learning: the essence of clinical supervision. In: Driscoll J (ed.), *Practising Clinical Supervision: A reflective approach for healthcare professionals*, 2nd edn. Edinburgh: Elsevier, pp 27–50.

Driscoll J, O'Sullivan J (2007) The place of clinical supervision in modern healthcare. In: Driscoll J (ed.), *Practising Clinical Supervision: A reflective approach for healthcare professionals*, 2nd edn. Edinburgh: Elsevier, p 326.

Freshwater D (2008) Reflective practice: the state of the art. In: Freshwater D, Taylor BJ, Sherwood G (eds), *International Textbook of Reflective Practice in Nursing*. Oxford: Blackwell, pp 1–18.

Freshwater D, Walsh L, Storey L (2002) Prison healthcare: Developing leadership through supervision. *Nursing Management* **8**(8): 10–14.

Gibbs G (1988) *Learning by Doing: A guide to learning and teaching methods*. Oxford: Further Education Unit, Oxford Polytechnic.

Gibbs G (1992) *Improving the Quality of Student Learning*. Plymouth: Technical and Education Services.

Goodfellow J (2004) Documenting professional practice through the use of a professional portfolio. *Early Years* **24**(1): 63–74.

Health Professions Council (2009) *Your Guide to Our Standards for Continuing Professional Development*. London: HPC.

Hull C, Redfern L, Shuttleworth A (2005) *Profiles and Portfolios: A guide for health and social care*, 2nd edn. Basingstoke: Palgrave.

Institute of Health Care Management (2004) *Developing Through Partnership: CPFD portfolio for health managers*. London: IHCM.

Jackson P, Taylor L, Chambers N (2011) Wound management. In: Hogston, R, Marjoram B (eds), *Foundations of Nursing Practice. Themes, concepts and frameworks*, 4th edn. Basingstoke: Palgrave, pp 238–266.

Johns C (1994) Guided reflection. In: Palmer A, Burns S, Bulman C (eds), *Reflective Practice in Nursing*. Oxford: Blackwell Scientific, pp 110–130.

Johns C (2000) *Becoming a Reflective Practitioner: A reflective and holistic approach to clinical nursing, practice development and clinical supervision*. Oxford: Blackwell Scientific.

Moon J (2004) *A Handbook of Reflective and Experiential Learning*. London: Routledge

Northern Ireland Practice and Education Council for Nursing and Midwifery (2004) *Your Development Framework: Part 1*. Belfast: NIPEC.

Nursing and Midwifery Council (2010) *The PREP Handbook*. London: NMC.

Pearce R (2003) *Profiles and Portfolios of Evidence*. Cheltenham: Nelson Thornes.

Royal College of Nursing (2003) *Clinical Supervision in the Workplace: Guidance for Occupational Health Nurses*. London: RCN.

15

Teaching and Learning in Clinical Practice

Aims and objectives

The aim of this chapter is to explore the opportunities and challenges associated with teaching and learning in clinical practice.

At the end of the chapter you will be able to:

1. Explore the challenges and opportunities associated with teaching in opportunistic settings
2. Understand the key issues associated with teaching and learning in the clinical setting
3. Examine theories of learning and teaching and their relevance related to teaching facilitation in the clinical context
4. Suggest ways of integrating teaching commitments in practice settings
5. Begin to apply the concepts discussed to the practice setting
6. Appreciate the Nursing and Midwifery Council's requirements of a student nurse

Leaders, mentors and teachers are vital for the next generation of practitioners. Nurses are required to enhance the professional development and the safe practice of others (Nursing and Midwifery Council or NMC, 2008a). This can be realised through peer support, leadership, supervision and teaching.

As a student of nursing, 50 per cent of your learning takes place within the clinical environment. In this chapter information and advice are provided to help you get the best from your clinical placement. It is in this environment that you are expected to apply your knowledge, learn new skills, and achieve the required learning outcomes and competencies. As a result of this it is important that things go right when you are in your clinical placement.

As a registered nurse you will be expected to teach as well as update your own knowledge, so teaching and learning become lifelong activities. You are required to be both teacher and learner. Examples of how to provide environments that are conducive to teaching and learning are offered in this chapter, which presents practical and contemporary guidance for the development of teachers in many situations. Several circumstances exist in which the nurse is required to teach, e.g. when teaching more junior members of staff or providing patients with opportunities to learn about their health. The skills and qualities of a successful teacher are outlined.

Emphasis is placed on teaching in the clinical area with a particular focus on teaching nurses and other health-care professionals. The principles related to the teaching of nurses and other health-care professionals can be applied (with care) to the teaching of patients.

The Student's Guide to Becoming a Nurse, Second Edition. Ian Peate.
© 2012 John Wiley & Sons, Ltd. Published 2012 by John Wiley & Sons, Ltd.

It is not possible in a chapter of this size to provide you with authoritative guidelines when it comes to teaching and learning in the clinical area, because there are so many situations that may arise providing you with the opportunity to engage in teaching and learning activities. The discussions in this chapter are offered to whet your appetite with respect to teaching and learning. You are encouraged to delve deeper and seek out more substantial and definitive resources (both human and material) that address the multifaceted issue of teaching and learning in the clinical environment.

Think

Clinical teaching, i.e. teaching and learning focused on, and usually directly involving, patients and their problems, lies at the heart of nurse education. Can you make a list of teaching opportunities when in a clinical learning environment?

Your list may have included the following:

- History taking
- Physical examination
- Ward rounds
- Team meetings
- Assisting patients with their activities of living
- Undertaking clinical procedures such as dressings
- Speaking with relatives and families
- Attending prearranged formal ward teaching sessions.

Teaching and learning in the clinical environment: theoretical frameworks

Teaching and learning in clinical practice can take place anywhere, because health care has many contexts. The terms 'clinical area' and 'clinical practice' are used in this chapter, but in the broadest context. Teaching and learning may occur in many places and can be associated with many situations, e.g. a busy acute mental health ward, a hospice, a patient's own home. There is a range of theories and approaches that you can choose from that suit the situation best; there is no right or wrong way to teach.

Definitions

Definitions of teaching and learning are varied and there is no one 'best' definition. The definition chosen may well reflect the situation in which you find yourself and it is unlikely that there is a definition of teaching that will satisfy all circumstances. Simply put, teaching can be described as a system of activities with the intention of inducing learning. It is a deliberate and methodological activity with a controlling element. This definition is often seen as a mechanistic definition of teaching. Schön (1987) uses a more reflective approach and emphasises the coaching analogy, whereby the learner is encouraged to seek explanations and the teacher provides advice and clarification.

Learning may be defined as a change of behaviour. It is an outcome, an end-product. The assumption with this definition is that learning can be recognised or seen. Learning, in this instance, therefore assumes that a person has to perform in order to learn. This definition is associated with behavioural theory. Nicklin and Kenworthy (1995) move away from this perspective, suggesting that a description of learning when applied to the clinical setting would result in the measurable effect of the sum total of the intended and unintended encounters on the students, in both qualitative and quantitative terms.

The processes by which learning occurs are complex; over time psychologists have tried to describe them. It may help you to gain some understanding of these processes in order to teach and promote learning. Three theories and the theorists associated with them are briefly described. You are strongly advised to gain further insight and understanding of the theoretical concepts associated with teaching and learning.

Behavioural theory

Learning associated with behaviour is linked with early theorists such as Pavlov. In simple terms these theorists, the behaviourists, demonstrated that if a repeated incentive, e.g. a negative stimulus such as an electric shock, or a positive stimulus such as the provision of food, is used enough times to reward or punish, then eventually the individual learns. It could be suggested that this approach does not require the learner, when learning, to engage in thinking and that it is the observed change in behaviour that provides evidence that learning has taken place. The crux of the theory is the reinforcement of punishment or reward and rehearsal of a task over time. If there is a positive outcome, this can result in perfection. Behaviourist theory is associated with the following:

- Activities that aid learning
- Repetitive activity and continued practice that aid learning
- Small bite-size steps that aid learning
- Reinforcement that aids learning.

The approach makes the assumption that the learner is a passive being, responding only when there is some form of environmental stimuli. It may be further assumed that the learner starts off as a clean slate (i.e. *tabula rasa*) and the behaviour is shaped through positive or negative reinforcement. This reinforcement increases the probability that the antecedent behaviour will occur again. Punishing the behaviour, in contrast (both positive and negative), will decrease the possibility that the antecedent behaviour will happen again. Positive implies the application of a stimulus and negative indicates the withholding of a stimulus. Learning is therefore defined as a change in behaviour in the learner. Much of the early work associated with behaviourism was carried out with animals (e.g. Pavlov's salivating dogs) and then generalised to humans. A criticism of behaviourism is that people are not and should not be seen as programmed animals that respond only to environmental stimuli. Humans are usually rational beings who need active participation to learn and whose actions are a result of thinking.

Cognitive theory

This theoretical approach suggests that learning occurs by receiving information, processing it, storing it and retrieving it; the person learning can be perceived as an information processor, similar to a computer. Different to the behaviourists' perspective, this approach, cognitivism, engages with purposeful processing that encourages thinking, perception, organisation and insight. This approach appears to have replaced the behaviourist approach. The term 'cognition', according to Quinn and Hughes (2007), refers to the internal mental processes of humans and encompasses the domains of:

- Memory: allows people to store experience from the past and use these in the present
- Perception: associated with mental organisation and the interpretation of sensory information
- Thinking: a cognitive process comprising internal mental representations of the world; involves problem-solving, reflecting and making decisions.

These are important domains because learning involves all three. Cognitivism seeks to build on the insights of the student by stimulating the development of perception, as opposed to the 'stimulus–response' that is associated with behaviourism.

The psychologist Ausubel uses both educational and psychological theories when considering teaching and learning strategies (Quinn and Hughes, 2007). This approach focuses on the importance of experience, meaning and problem-solving, and the development of insights. Cognitive theory accepts that individuals have different needs and concerns occurring at different times. Those who subscribe to cognitive theory believe that:

- learning comes from understanding
- the organisation of teaching and how this is structured will aid learning
- cognitive feedback aids learning
- individual differences must be considered and taken into account.

412

Cognitivism focuses on the inner mental activities that are valuable and necessary for understanding how people learn. Mental processes such as thinking, memory, knowing and problem-solving need to be explored. Knowledge can be seen as schema or symbolic mental constructions. Learning is defined as change in a learner's schemata.

Humanism

The individual is the crucial component of this theoretical approach. There are two key theorists associated with the humanist approach to teaching and learning: Rogers (1983) and Knowles et al (2011) both support the notion that adults and children learn differently. Adults have:

- life experiences
- prior knowledge
- developed personalities.

The role of the teacher is to facilitate learning; he or she is not seen as the font of all knowledge. Learning (or growth) takes place when feelings and experiences have been taken into consideration. Learning will take place, however, only if the learner feels comfortable and safe. This is related very closely to Maslow's hierarchy of needs (Maslow, 1954).

Rogers (1983) advocated a student-centred approach to learning, believing that the learning that takes place must be significant and meaningful, incorporating both thoughts and feelings. Rogers supports a shift in focus from what the teacher does to what is happening in the student. Knowles et al (2011) suggest that there are five basic assumptions associated with Rogers's thoughts on student-centred learning:

1. We cannot teach a person directly, we can only facilitate his or her learning.
2. A person will learn significantly only those things that he or she perceives as being involved in the maintenance, enhancement or structure of self.

3. In order to learn the learner needs to be ready to learn.
4. Learning can often threaten an individual, so supportive climates that accept the person and enhance student responsibility should be created.
5. If the self is not being threatened and supportive environments are in place, this will promote significant learning.

Much of the theoretical underpinnings associated with humanism can be found in the practice of purposeful reflection.

To summarise the beliefs of the humanist's perspective:

● Learning is a natural process.
● Motivation, purpose and goals are important.
● The social situation can have an effect on learning.
● Choice, relevance and responsibility aid learning.
● Anxiety, discomfort and emotion affect learning.

The humanist approach contrasts with the behaviourist notion of operant conditioning (arguing that all behaviour is the result of the application of consequences) and cognitivism, where the belief is that discovering knowledge or constructing meaning is central to learning. Humanists believe that it is important to study the person as a whole, particularly as the person grows and develops over the lifespan. The study of the self, motivation, goal setting and attainment is an area of specific interest. Humanism can be expressed as the development of self-actualised, autonomous people where learning is student centred and personalised, and the role of the teacher is that of a facilitator. Affective and cognitive needs are central and the aim is to develop self-actualised people in a cooperative, supportive environment.

413

Think

What life experiences do you have that you may bring to nursing? How may they help or hinder your learning?

When beginning to apply the theories to practice, it may be more appropriate to delve into and out of each one of them, adopting a 'pick-and-mix' approach as the situation dictates. All of the above theoretical approaches can be used and adapted for use in any given clinical or classroom setting.

Top tips

Nurses often tend to be practical or experiential learners; they learn best from doing as opposed to reading about something. Remember to relate theory to everyday life, use practice or real-life scenarios, bringing facts and theory to life; where possible allow people to work in groups, sharing ideas and learning from each other.

Table 15.1   The main characteristics of adult learning

- The learning is purposeful
- Participation is voluntary
- Participation should be active not passive
- Clear goals and objectives should be set
- Feedback is required
- Opportunities for reflection should be provided

Source: adapted from Brookfield (1986).

The adult learner

If you are engaged in teaching fellow health-care professionals, the approach that you use will need to acknowledge the specific needs of the adult learner. The methods used will be very different from those employed when teaching children. The following features are associated with adult learners (Quinn and Hughes, 2007; Rogers and Horricks, 2010):

- They are adults by definition.
- Their process of growth is continuing as opposed to just starting.
- They bring in to the learning situation a set of experiences and values.
- The come with intentions and expectations.
- They have competing interests.
- They already hold established patterns of learning.

Table 15.1 provides insight into some of the characteristics of adult learning.

Effective teaching in higher education demands that the individual teacher, organisational culture, and policies and procedures in place meet the needs of the learner. Ramsden (2003) described six key principles associated with teaching in higher education; these beliefs also apply to those who teach in the clinical environment:

1. Teachers should have an interest in the subject and be able to explain it to others.
2. There should be a concern and respect for students and student learning.
3. Appropriate assessment and feedback should be provided.
4. There should be clear goals and intellectual challenge.
5. Learners should have independence, control and active engagement.
6. Teachers should be prepared to learn from students.

By acting as a teacher you also become a role model to other staff (this may include other members of the health-care team, not only nurses) as well as patients. Teaching as a skill, along with all the other skills cited in this text, can be learned and developed. Good teachers are created, not born. Table 15.2 describes the personal attributes of the nurse who also acts as a clinical educator. The skills listed have been adapted to reflect the skills required by the nurse.

The principles above should be taken into account when preparing to teach. The following five steps will be used as a framework to help you with your teaching in the clinical area:

1. Create a positive learning environment
2. Know who your learners are

Table 15.2   Some of the personal qualities required by the nurse with respect to clinical teaching

- An enthusiasm and commitment to high-quality nursing care
- A personal commitment to teaching and learning
- Sensitivity and responsiveness to the educational needs of students
- The capacity to promote development of the required professional attitudes and values
- An understanding of the principles of education applied to nursing
- The command of practical teaching skills and the willingness to enhance these
- A willingness to develop as a good nurse as well as a teacher
- A commitment to evaluation and audit of teaching practices
- The willingness to undertake both summative and formative assessment of student progress

Source: adapted from General Medical Council (1999).

3. Know what it is that you want them to know
4. Prepare
5. Ask for feedback.

Create a positive learning environment

Creating a positive learning environment is paramount. No matter what you intend to teach, or what the learner wishes to learn, it is vital that the learning environment is a positive one. The humanist approach described earlier suggests that the creation of a safe environment will enhance and aid learning. There are some factors that will be outside your control in the clinical environment, e.g. noise and interruptions. Despite these possibilities you should strive to provide an atmosphere that encourages enquiry and is non-threatening.

If you have any control over the physical environment, always try to ensure that the room or area where you are teaching is warm; open windows if it feels stuffy. Observe the learners and suggest a break if they appear to be tiring. Let people know about taking 'comfort breaks' and where the facilities are, and try to provide some idea about how long the session will last. The impact of the room will have implications for learning, so consideration should be directed towards seating arrangements. Issues such as seating arrangements are seen as resources. Poor use of resources can have a substantial impact on the learning experience.

Provide students with evidence that you have their needs at the forefront of your mind, e.g. at the start of the session determine what the students' needs are and when you conclude the session assess if you have met their needs. Student-centred learning means that the teacher must put the needs of the learner at the centre of teaching activities. Emphasis is needed on encouraging the facilitation of learning as opposed to the delivery of teaching. The facilitator should aim to guide the learner towards resources and sources of knowledge (human and material) just as much as being the source of knowledge him- or herself. Bellack (2005) suggests that, when a learning-centred approach is used, the learner learns as much about how to learn as about the specific content. She adds that the teacher's role is to enable students to discover and experiment.

Learning environments are wide and varied and can be the patient's own home, the operating theatre, the clinic and at the bedside. Nearly every activity that the nurse undertakes is potentially a learning opportunity. The nurse may be required to teach in more formal settings such as in a classroom or a lecture theatre. Other venues may be associated with e-learning, e.g. a virtual learning environment.

Know who your learners are

Research your audience. You must have some insight into who you are going to teach, what programme of study they are attending, the academic level and how far they have progressed in the programme so far. How many of them will there be? Find out about previous life experiences (as a professional and as a layperson) and determine what the students already know about the topic that you are teaching. Avoid making assumptions and stereotyping the learners. Find out what they will be going on to learn next.

Think

Once you have started to understand who the learners are, how can that information help you when proving a teaching session?

This can help you to draw up on learners' life experiences and use that experience when teaching; it also helps you to involve the group as well as demonstrating respect for past professional and life experiences.

Know what it is that you want them to know

When using a cognitivist or behaviourist approach you must know what it is you want the learner to know; objectives must be set. Take time considering these carefully: the aims and objectives decided on will result in you applying the correct teaching methods. If you are teaching a rote-based task, e.g. cardiopulmonary resuscitation, you will need to provide instructions to the learners, and this needs to be broken down into smaller chunks. There will be a need to repeat in order to reinforce learning. If, on the other hand, the points that you are trying to convey are concerned with ethics your approach will be different: you may need to seek opinions from the learners, exploring and unravelling these opinions and beliefs, challenging responses in a safe and comfortable manner.

Prepare

Just as with any activity that is undertaken, the outcome of teaching will be more beneficial if it has been prepared. The amount of preparation needed to provide a teaching session that is effective and meaningful cannot be over-estimated. Even opportunist teaching sessions need to have some degree of planning. Preparation of the patient (if appropriate), preparation of the environment and preparation of the teaching tools to be used are some examples of issues that need planning consideration. Determine if there will be any pre-reading materials required for the session: if so, how will the learners access them?

Ask for feedback

Feedback, evaluation and reflection are activities that are synonymous. There are many methods that can be used to provide feedback about performance and how the learners felt about the teaching session, as well as providing the learners with feedback about their performance. Reflective activity has been discussed in detail in Chapter 14; the concepts discussed can be used by the teacher and by the learner.

Table 15.3 Evaluating a teaching session

Aspects of the teaching session	Evidence/comments
Did you experience a positive learning environment? Did you feel that the teacher 'knew' you/the learners? Was he/she aware of your needs? Did you know what was expected of you? Were you aware of the aims and objectives of the session? Was the session adequately prepared? Were you able to provide feedback? How was this done?	

Formal evaluation in the form of feedback questionnaires can be administered and the results analysed; this has the potential to provide both quantitative and qualitative data depending on how the questionnaire is formulated and structured. Peer review is another alternative. This occurs when a colleague is asked to observe your performance. This can be done in a highly structured manner, e.g. if a checklist approach is used and you are graded on the outcome, or alternatively an unstructured approach can be used where you are provided with feedback in a more general manner. Feedback given to you can only help you become even better when teaching in the clinical environment.

Think

Consider a recent teaching session where you were a learner. Provide evidence and make comments on how the session addressed the issues described in Table 15.3.

Do you think the session could have been better? If so, how?

Using resources to enhance teaching and learning

The best resource available to you to enhance and encourage teaching and learning in the clinical environment is you, once you have become an experienced nurse. You should respect students by acknowledging that you are not the font of all knowledge, simply a conduit to facilitate the activity of learning.

It has already been stated that the poor use of resources can have a considerable effect on learning and teaching – hence the importance of dedicating a section of this chapter entirely to teaching resources. The resources discussed here are those that can be used in a variety of settings. Bear in mind the points in Table 15.4 when explaining or facilitating learning.

Overhead projectors

Projectors can be free standing, fixed, permanent or portable. They require the use of transparencies to project the image on to a suitable screen. Their use is not as popular as they once were, but they are still used in a number of settings.

Table 15.4   Some points to be taken into account when teaching or facilitating learners

Point	Action
Be clear	<ul><li>If possible teach in a quiet area</li><li>Speak slowly and clearly – enunciate</li><li>Ensure clarity with your teaching resources and materials, e.g. are your handouts clear and easy to read?</li><li>Use short sentences when speaking</li><li>Do not be tempted to provide too much information</li></ul>
Generate interest	<ul><li>Use a variety of resources and approaches in order to stimulate.</li><li>Be enthusiastic about the topic.</li></ul>
Use logical organisation	<ul><li>Build slowly from one concept to the next</li><li>As with essay writing, ensure that there is an introduction, body and conclusion.</li></ul>
Spell out the relevance	<ul><li>Explain why this topic is important</li><li>Link with the overall assessment strategy</li><li>Explain how patient care can be enhanced by further understanding.</li></ul>
Emphasise important points	<ul><li>Clearly state what the important points are</li><li>Use different emphasis for important points, e.g. different-coloured writing on handouts, use of bold/italics or an increase in font size</li><li>Explain why these points are important</li></ul>
Use examples	<ul><li>Provide clinical examples, e.g. refer to patients who you are currently caring for</li><li>Use anecdotes – but with caution</li></ul>
Avoid unnecessary jargon	<ul><li>Speak plainly</li><li>If jargon is used ensure you provide a definition of the terms used</li></ul>
Check out understanding	<ul><li>Use your skills to determine if learners have understood, be alert to non-verbal communications</li><li>Do not patronise learners</li><li>Listen and respond</li></ul>

Think

Take some time now to reflect on the times when you as a learner have experienced a teacher using a PowerPoint presentation. Think about the size of the font used: was it too small or too large? Was there too much text on the slides?

Table 15.5   Some dos and don'ts when using an overhead projector

Do
- Use permanent marker pens, as water-soluble pens have a tendency to smudge
- Leave space to add to the transparency as the session progresses
- Use large fonts; too small a font and the audience may not be able to read it
- Know how to turn the projector on and what to do if the bulb blows
- Face the audience

Don't
- Use colours that are difficult to read when projected – red, orange and yellow are particularly difficult to read
- Use too much text on the transparency; use key words only
- Use complex diagrams – consider supplementing with hard copies or direct the audience to an electronic source
- Block the audience's view by standing in front of the projection
- Rush through the presentation; the audience may wish to be given time to write down what you have projected

Table 15.5 provides a list of dos and don'ts to be considered when using overhead projectors. Presentation skills are important and can have as much impact as the content that is being provided.

PowerPoint presentations

Before the arrival of PowerPoint as software used in presentations, overhead and 35-mm slide projectors were the tools of choice; however, computer technology brought a new tool to presentations. PowerPoint is a powerful teaching tool enabling the user to prepare a selection of slides for projection via a data projector. The PowerPoint package enables the user to:

- use templates
- add colours to stimulate the audience
- incorporate photographic images and video clips
- use hyperlinks to web pages
- use animation to build up a 'show'
- enhance the presentation by using transitions – a function that provides a variety of ways of changing from one slide to another.

There are also a number of print options that can be used with PowerPoint, including the ability to print either three or six slides to a single A4 page with or without notes. These can be used as handouts for the audience with the key points of your presentation for them to take away.

As with overhead projection, practice makes perfect. Table 15.6 provides some hints and tips associated with PowerPoint.

Video and digital versatile discs

Videotape recorders and the use of digital versatile discs (DVDs) can be used in a variety of ways to enhance teaching in both large and small groups. DVDs makes video images easier to use in the

Table 15.6 Hints and tips for PowerPoint presentations

- Use a sans serif font, e.g. Arial, for slide presentations in order to prevent blurring of the text during projection
- Use different font sizes for main titles and text
- Be judicial with the number of lines used on each slide; seven is a maximum
- A dark-coloured font should be used against a light background (not white)
- Always have a prepared set of overhead transparencies to hand in case of technological failure

classroom, because individual clips can be immediately accessed without the need to search through a length of tape. You can also make video clips available via a website for students to view outside the teaching session. Video and DVDs can be used to provide students with feedback on their performance. A recording is made of a student undertaking some activity, e.g. CPR. Afterwards, this can be reviewed by the student (and teacher) so that the strengths and weaknesses can be identified with the aim of observing the student's skills. Often video and DVD recordings are used in simulation centres in a number of innovative and creative ways.

Flipcharts and whiteboards

These resources are often used when working with small groups, as the participants can be invited to become actively involved in the session. The group could be asked to brainstorm an activity, e.g. the possible causes of urinary tract infection. However, excessive use of this approach may not suit all participants, and therefore needs to be employed with care.

After the session has ended, the teacher must treat the used flipchart sheet with respect. It is advocated that the used sheets are folded up (not ripped off the wall and screwed up) and, if they are not to be retained, they should be disposed of sensitively.

The interactive whiteboard is a newer relation of the whiteboard. The device is attached to a computer and data projector. What is written on the board (with an electronic stylus) may be stored as a computer file, printed and copied to members of the group.

Handouts

The mainstay of teaching for many years has been handouts, which are often used by nurses in many situations and settings. Handouts are normally used to supplement or reinforce learning, and also used as one way of ensuring that all students receive the same information. The creation of handouts should be given much thought if they are to succeed. Students tend to like handouts because they can come away from the lecture with the learning in hand – a record or transcript of learning. Handouts can also be retrieved from the managed learning environment, e.g. blackboard.

Handouts are still used in various clinical settings for health-care professionals and patients, and can be produced as a hard copy or electronically. The better the quality of the handout, the more potential there is for learning to take place. The teacher must remember not only to evaluate his or her teaching on a regular basis but also the use of any resources, including handouts.

When designing handouts, Sakraida and Draus (2005) suggest that the items in Table 15.7 should be considered.

Table 15.7   Some considerations for the preparation of handouts

Type and layout	<ul><li>Font sizes should be 12 to 14, with bold print to promote ease of reading</li><li>Too long a handout can be a distraction</li><li>Brief handouts can enhance attention as a presentation is being made</li></ul>
Purpose	<ul><li>The purpose of the handout will determine when it is distributed to the students</li><li>The following are types of handouts:<ul><li>Complete notes</li><li>Skeleton notes with blank spaces for students to fill in</li><li>Notes that emphasise one aspect of the session, e.g. complex concepts or diagrams</li></ul></li></ul>
Focus	<ul><li>A handout should only be concerned with a single topic</li><li>Key points can be used</li><li>Definitions of key terms may be considered</li></ul>
Visual appeal	<ul><li>Visual appeal can communicate that the teacher has a professional approach</li><li>A creative approach is advocated with the use of various fonts and colours</li><li>Printing on coloured paper is visually appealing</li><li>Spacing of material and design layout must be given some consideration</li></ul>

Source: adapted from Sakraida and Draus (2005).

E-learning

There are many e-learning tools now available. However, not all approaches suit all students and caution should be taken when using them. Some e-learning materials require the installation of specific software packages on computers and not all students (and staff) may have all the necessary software required to run the various e-learning programmes.

Commercial electronic portfolios are becoming popular and specific packages that allow for ongoing records of achievement to be maintained and developed are available, e.g. PebblePad. Whatever learning packages are used, it is essential that all parties (practitioners, students and teachers) are able to use them effectively; training events should be provided.

Learning in the practice placement

The NMC (2010) requires that 50 per cent of your time as a student (2300 hours) be spent in the practice area. As a result of this, it should be noted that there will be serious implications for the student if things do not go well (Royal College of Nursing or RCN, 2005). While undertaking learning experiences in the practice setting, you will be able to apply the theory you have learnt to practice, experiencing the various challenges and issues that occur.

Practice placements

Students have a crucial role to play in ensuring that they get the best from their practice placement. They have responsibilities as well as other key stakeholders in the practice placement relationship.

421

Practice placements can be defined as opportunities where you can undertake practice under supervision. During your time in a practice placement a mentor assesses learning and facilitates achievement of the required learning outcomes and competencies.

The RCN (2006) states that there are several different titles used for nurses who provide support to students in practice, e.g.:

- Mentors
- Preceptors
- Assessors
- Practice educators.

With so many titles there is the potential to cause confusion. To ensure consistency, the NMC's former incarnation – the English National Board (ENB, 2001) – settled on the term 'mentor'. The quality of a clinical placement (including the mentor) has the potential to impinge on your educational experience. You are encouraged to take personal responsibility for directing your own learning and making the best use of human and material resources in order to achieve the competencies required for entry to the professional register.

The RCN (2006) suggests that practice placements that meet the needs of the student can help:

- meet statutory and regulatory requirements
- achieve the required competencies as stipulated by the regulator (NMC)
- provide opportunities to take part in health-care activities in a wide range of rapidly changing health- and social care environments
- make available a full range of nursing care activities to a variety of patients
- offer experiences that will enable the student to appreciate the unpredictable and dynamic nature of nursing care in a clinical setting
- create the feeling of working as a member of a multidisciplinary team
- identify appropriate learning opportunities.

Practice placements must also ensure that the student is provided with opportunities to identify the community focus of care, the continuing nature of care, and the need for acute and critical care, as well as a multiprofessional approach to care. These requirements are cited in the European Directive 77/453/EEC. Placements should, therefore, be varied, reflecting care in the independent sector as well as the NHS and in both health- and social care settings. They must provide the student with the ability to meet the competencies deemed essential by the NMC (2008b).

Key stakeholders associated with the practice placement

The ultimate stakeholder is the patient. There are other stakeholders who will provide support to help students gain as much from their clinical learning experience as possible. All significant stakeholders have a responsibility for ensuring that at the point of registration the nurse is fit for:

- *purpose*: can function as a competent practitioner in the clinical setting
- *practice*: can fulfil the needs of registration
- *award*: has attained the breadth and depth of learning that is commensurate with the award, i.e. degree.

Below is a list of those who could be considered as key stakeholders in the practice placement (the patient has already been mentioned):

- The student
- The NHS and independent sector
- The higher education institution (the university)
- Service providers (those in the clinical placement, e.g. mentors, lecturer practitioners) – these are part of the tripartite arrangements
- The commissioning bodies for education – these are also part of the tripartite arrangements.

Figure 15.1 provides a diagrammatic representation of the stakeholders.

Below are some issues that you may need to consider to get the most out of your clinical placement. Remember that all other members of the tripartite arrangement also have responsibilities to make the experience a valuable and meaningful one. The prospect of a new placement may seem daunting (Harrison, 2006). Preparation before arriving at the placement may help alleviate any anxiety or apprehensions that you may have. Do the following before your placement:

- Ensure that you know about any specific issues related to clinical placements that may be contained in your student handbook. This handbook may include details concerning the assessment of practice and what you are required to achieve while on clinical placement.
- Determine what the purpose of the placement experience is and also what the expectations of the service provider are.
- Contact your link lecturer before the placement starts to find out if there are any specific issues associated with the placement, e.g. whether you have to wear uniform.

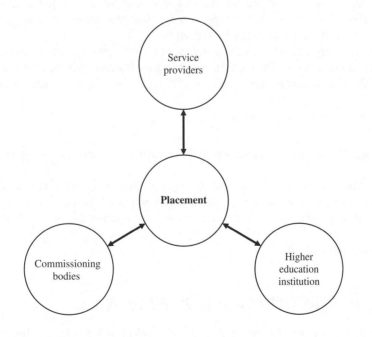

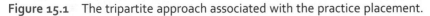

Figure 15.1   The tripartite approach associated with the practice placement.

- Contact relevant people at the placement.
- Ensure that you are aware of how you are to be assessed, what assessment tools are to be used, whether you need to keep a reflective diary, or whether there are any learning contracts that need to be drawn up.

Do the following while on clinical placement:

- Be punctual, maintain confidentiality, be aware of the image that you portray and your attitude, and act professionally at all times.
- Be proactive in seeking out learning opportunities with the help of your mentor.
- Take every opportunity available and be willing to work as a member of the team.
- Express your needs.
- Make use of your named mentor and other resources to achieve your learning outcomes.
- Seek help and advice if you feel that the mentor relationship is not working.
- Work under supervision when achieving clinical skills.
- Take every opportunity to work outside the practice placement to work with specialist practitioners.
- Be willing to provide constructive feedback as well as receiving the same.
- Undertake reflective activity to assess your own confidence and competence.
- If you take time off during your placement, e.g. if you are sick, you may be required to inform the university and the clinical placement with details of your circumstances. You may need to provide self-certification if you are off sick for 3 consecutive days. If your sickness extends and you are off longer than 8 days you may have to produce a doctor's sick certificate. Find out what the requirements are before starting your placement.
- If during placement you are of the opinion that you have witnessed bad practice, you must first inform your mentor or the nurse in charge. You may feel your concerns have not been adequately addressed; if this is the case contact your link lecturer.
- During your placement you will be supernumerary to the placement staffing levels. This means that students are additional to staffing establishment figures. However, you must make a contribution to the work of the practice placement area to enable you to learn how to care for patients.

Do the following after the placement experience:

- Evaluate your achievements – what you have enjoyed and how you have benefited from the placement.
- Evaluate the placement against requirements, e.g. by completing an online evaluation form.
- Participate in classroom discussion regarding the placement if this is required.
- Ensure that you submit on time any placement documentation required as a part of your assessment.
- Reflect on your experiences.

Teaching in the practice placement

Once you are qualified you may be required to act as a resource for teaching junior members of the multidisciplinary team and this may mean teaching student nurses. In time you can choose to become a mentor who holds the relevant mentor qualifications. If you do become a mentor you will be required to have your name placed on an up-to-date mentors' register and undertake a programme of study that prepares you for teaching and assessing in the clinical area.

Top tips

It is absolutely OK to ask for help – learner or registered nurse! If you ever need emotional, educational or practical support, this should always be available to you. Nursing is a demanding job; some things take longer to learn than others and some will be totally new to you, so do not be scared to lean on those who are around you when the need arises.

Mentorship

Mentors and teachers are central to the preparation of the next generation of practitioners. It is vital that student nurses be taught by those with practical and recent experience of their profession; it is equally important that the student be exposed to the experiences of other health- and social care professionals. During your pre-registration programme of study you will have been allocated a mentor. The allocation of a mentor is one way in which the NMC can ensure that the competencies required for registration have been achieved. The mentor, having been prepared to teach and assess in clinical practice, is a key person in ensuring that the student receives clinical education opportunities that are commensurate with achieving learning outcomes associated with the competencies (NMC, 2008b).

The NMC (2008a) states that in order to record a teaching qualification on the NMC register the nurse will need to undertake additional preparation and education that reflects the standards set by the NMC. Originally there were eight advisory standards published by the NMC (2003) for mentors and mentorship (Table 15.8). This was altered in 2003 (NMC, 2003) from 'advisory' to 'required'.

The NMC (2008a) stipulates that mentors must have a current registration with the NMC. They must also have a minimum of 12 months' full-time experience (or a part-time equivalent) before becoming a mentor.

There are several approaches to supporting students in clinical practice and each NHS trust and higher education institution will have its own approved methods of doing this. The use of an appropriately qualified and approved mentor has already been outlined. The terms 'associate mentor', 'co-mentor' and 'secondary mentor' may also be used to identify health-care professionals (not necessarily nurses) who are relevant to the practice experience in which the student is placed. These individuals may be registered nurses who have not completed a recognised programme of study leading to a qualification as a mentor; they may be social workers or teachers. The latter professionals play a significant part in teaching and learning in the practice placement.

Assessment of the student can be undertaken only by a person who is entered on a live register of mentors. The following is a list of those who can carry out the assessment of student performance, although the titles of the programmes of study may vary from institution to institution.

- A registered nurse who has undertaken any of the following programmes of study or their equivalent:
  - ENB 998-approved assessor
  - Mentorship and Support for Professional Practice Module
  - Preparation for Mentorship and Preceptorship in Professional Education

Table 15.8   The standards and expectations required of a mentor

Required standard	Expectations
Communication and working relationships	• Development of effective relationships based on mutual trust and respect • An understanding of how students integrate into practice settings and assisting with this process • Provision of ongoing and constructive support for students
Facilitation of learning	• Demonstration of sufficient knowledge of the student's programme to identify current learning needs • Demonstration of strategies that will assist with the integration of learning from practice and education settings • Creation and development of opportunities for students to identify and undertake experiences to meet their learning needs
Conducting assessment	• Demonstration of a good understanding associated with assessment and ability to assess • Implementation of approved assessment procedures
Role model	• Demonstration of effective relationships with patients and clients • Contribution to the development of an environment in which effective practice is fostered, implemented, evaluated and disseminated • Assessment and management of clinical developments to ensure safe and effective care
Creating an environment for learning	• Ensuring effective learning experiences and opportunities to achieve learning outcomes for students by contribution to the development and maintenance of a learning environment • Implementation of strategies for quality assurance and quality audit
Improving practice	• Contribution to the creation of an environment in which change can be initiated and supported
Knowledge base	• Identification, application and dissemination of research findings within the area of practice
Course development	• Contribution to the development and/or review of courses

Source: adapted from NMC (2003, 2008b).

— Postgraduate Certificate in Education
— A1/2 D32/33.

These qualifications are associated with those who undertake work-based assessments, such as vocational courses and City and Guilds programmes. They are verifiers' qualifications.

You should seek advice from your university if you are unsure about who will be able to assess your performance while on clinical placement.

The growth in the number of terms and roles associated with mentors in relation to teaching and learning may be seen as evidence that practice-based teaching and learning are generally achieving a higher profile in nurse education. This growth in interest will continue, particularly in relation to the expansion of interprofessional education, as well as Government initiatives such as the Knowledge and Skills Framework and *Agenda for Change* (Department of Health, 2004). *Agenda for Change* aims to determine new frameworks for the employment of health-care staff (apart from doctors) and recognises the contribution that nurses are making to the effective delivery of health care.

Top tips

If you are finding things particularly difficult when working in a clinical placement, always try and resolve the problem on the ward before contacting the university. It is best to try to resolve issues locally, e.g. at ward level; staff and mentors will all appreciate this and it may also help to mend relationships. However, you should contact the university if you feel that you need support or the issue has not or is in danger of not being resolved.

Ali and Panther (2008) provide a review of the concept of mentorship: the importance of mentorship in helping students achieve their aims and objectives, the objectives that need to be accomplished as required by a university programme of study and meeting the competencies required by the NMC are discussed.

Conclusions

Half your time as a student nurse is associated with work-based learning and the remaining half is related to theory, e.g. by attending your programme of study at the university. This theory and practice split means that you will be assessed from both a theoretical and a practical perspective. University staff (lecturers) generally assess theory and a recognised and registered practice assessor or your mentor assesses practice. A variety of terms is used to describe those who undertake teaching and assessing roles, and much confusion can occur as a result of this. Some of the terms used have been discussed.

This chapter has addressed several key concepts associated with teaching and learning in the clinical environment. Although the bulk of the chapter focuses on the teaching and learning needs of student nurses and other health-care professionals, the principles outlined can (with care) be applied to the patient in a variety of settings.

The processes associated with learning are complex and much of the theory used to explain and enhance teaching arises in psychology. Three theoretical approaches have been briefly outlined. It is important to gain a fundamental understanding of the theoretical approaches if the teaching of nurses and other health-care professionals in the health-care environment is to be effective. All the approaches discussed can be used and applied simultaneously; the reader is encouraged to pick and mix approaches to suit the situation.

Practical tips and hints have been provided with the aim of helping the student to get the most out of the clinical experience from a teaching and learning perspective, as either a learner or a teacher. A framework is used relating to five areas in order to provide advice, and each aspect of the framework offers the reader pointers to enhance teaching and learning. The use of various resources such as PowerPoint presentations and handouts in order to enhance teaching and learning opportunities is outlined.

Practice placements have the potential to provide students with opportunities to achieve their learning outcomes as well as the competencies required by the regulator (NMC). The mentor is seen as one member of a tripartite arrangement who can help students achieve the statutory requirements. The role and function of the mentor has been described.

Activity

Attempt these multiple-choice questions that are related to issues surrounding teaching and learning to test your knowledge. The answers can be found at the back of this book, in the chapter called 'Activity Answers'.

1. Which of the following is not a part of Maslow's hierarchy of needs?
   a. Safety needs
   b. Physiological needs
   c. Psychomotor needs
   d. Self-actualisation

2. Cognitive theory is associated with:
   a. Learning that occurs by receiving information, processing it, storing it and retrieving it
   b. Learning by change
   c. Learning that occurs through observation only
   d. Learning that involves the whole group

3. Memory is associated with:
   a. The interpretation of sensory information
   b. The internal mental representation of the world
   c. The ability to store experience from the past and use these in the present
   d. Cognitive processes

4. Humanism believes that:
   a. People are able to learn anything
   b. It is important to study the person as a whole, particularly as the person grows and develops over the lifespan
   c. The teacher should be the same age as the group being educated
   d. Only people with previous educational qualifications will succeed in nursing

5. By acting as a teacher:
   a. You are superior to others
   b. You become a role model
   c. You are able make better decisions
   d. You have a higher IQ

6. Feedback in respect to teaching:
   a. Should only be done in the classroom
   b. Can be valid only if over five students provide this
   c. Can help you become even better when teaching
   d. Should never be taken seriously

7. Before going on clinical placement you should:
   a. Find out as much about the placement as possible
   b. Determine details concerning the assessment of practice and what you are required to achieve while on clinical placement

    c. Contact your link lecturer before the placement commencing

    d. All of the above

8. While on clinical placement you should:
   a. Never question the registered health-care professionals
   b. Ask questions only at the end of the shift
   c. Express your needs
   d. Be expected to work as a full-time member of the team

9. If you witness poor practice or practice that concerns you, you must:
   a. Inform your personal tutor
   b. Only discuss this with you mentor when he or she returns for duty
   c. Wait and raise the issue the next time you are in university
   d. Inform your mentor or the health-care professional in charge immediately

10. The allocation of a mentor:
    a. Is one way in which the NMC can ensure that the competencies required for registration have been achieved
    b. Allows the trust to ensure that you meet their standards
    c. Provides a conduit between the union UNISON and the university
    d. Is one way in which the RCN are able to monitor standards of care

429

References

Ali PA, Panther W (2008) Professional development and the role of mentorship. *Nursing Standard* **22**(42): 35–39.

Bellack JP (2005) Teaching for learning and improvement. *Journal of Nursing Education* **44**: 295–296.

Brookfield SD (1986) *Understanding and Facilitating Adult Learning: A comprehensive analysis of principles and effective practice*. Milton Keynes: Open University Press.

Department of Health (2004) *Agenda for Change: Final agreement*. London: Department of Health.

English National Board for Nursing and Midwifery (2001) *Preparation of Mentors and Teachers: A new framework for guidance*. London: ENB.

General Medical Council (1999) *The Doctor as Teacher*. London: GMC.

Harrison P (2006) Perspectives on adult nursing. In: Schrober J, Ash C (eds), *Student Nurses' Guide to Professional Practice and Development*. London: Arnold, pp 35–45.

Knowles M, Holton EF, Swanson RA (2011) *The Adult Learner: The definitive classic in adult education and human resource development*, 11th edn. Oxford: Butterworth.

Maslow A (1954) *Motivation and Personality*. New York: Harper & Row.

Nicklin PJ, Kenworthy N (1995) *Teaching and Assessing in Nursing Practice*, 2nd edn. London: Scutari Press.

Nursing and Midwifery Council (2003) *QA Fact Sheet O/2003: NMC Requirements for Mentors and Mentorship*. London: NMC.

Nursing and Midwifery Council (2008a) *The Code: Standards of Conduct, Performance and Ethics for Nurses and Midwives*. London: NMC.

Nursing and Midwifery Council (2008b) *Standards for the Preparation of Teachers of Nursing and Midwifery*. London: NMC.

Nursing and Midwifery Council (2010) *Standards for Pre registration Nursing Education*. London: NMC. Available at: http://standards.nmc-uk.org/PublishedDocuments/Standards%20for%20pre-registration%20nursing%20education%2016082010.pdf (accessed July 2011).

Quinn FM, Hughes SJ (2007) *Quinn's Principles and Practice of Nurse Education*, 5th edn. Cheltenham: Nelson Thornes.

Ramsden P (2003) *Learning to Teach in Higher Education*, 2nd edn. London: Routledge.

Rogers CR (1983) *Freedom to Learn*. Columbus, OH: Merril.

Rogers, A, Horricks N (2010) *Teaching Adults*, 4th edn. Midenhead: Open University.

Royal College of Nursing (2005) *The Practice Placement Experience: A survey of RCN student members: Executive summary*. London: RCN.

Royal College of Nursing (2006) *Helping Students Get the Best from Their Practice Placements*, 2nd edn. London: RCN.

Sakraida TJ, Draus PJ (2005) Quality handout development and use. *Journal of Nursing Education* **44**: 326–329.

Schön D (1987) *Educating the Reflective Practitioner*. San Francisco, CA: Jossey Bass.

Activity Answers

Chapter 1

1. What date was the current Code of Conduct published?
   c. 2008

2. Who published the Code of Conduct?
   b. The NMC

3. The Code of Conduct is:
   c. An advisory document

4. Who does the document concern?
   c. All nurses and midwives

5. Where can copies be obtained?
   d. All of the above

6. Which of the following are documents that the NMC does not produce?
   c. National Service Frameworks
   d. Manual removal of faeces

7. The key aim of the NMC is to:
   a. Protect and serve the public

8. How many parts are there to the professional register?
   c. 3

9. Which of the following statements is true?
   c. The NMC is an organisation set up by Parliament to ensure that nurses and midwives provide high standards of care to their patients and clients

10. When was the NMC created?
    c. April 2002

Chapter 2

1. The term 'vulnerability' is related only to those people with a learning disability.
   False

2. The standards of good moral conduct or principles are known as confidentiality.
   False

3. An advocate is somebody who speaks up for another person.
   True

4. Empathy and sympathy mean the same thing.
   False

The Student's Guide to Becoming a Nurse, Second Edition. Ian Peate.
© 2012 John Wiley & Sons, Ltd. Published 2012 by John Wiley & Sons, Ltd.

5. Two primary forms of law are common law and statute.
   True

6. The NHS Constitution is a legal document.
   False

7. Abuse can be a criminal offence.
   True

8. You need evidence of abuse before you can report an allegation of abuse.
   False

9. Neglect is a type of abuse.
   True

10. For something to be abuse it has to be deliberate.
    False

Chapter 3

1. Equal opportunities means the following:
   a. Preferential treatment is exactly what equal opportunities awareness seeks to avoid.

2. It is unlawful to ask about a disability at an interview:
   a. No

3. The most common cause of death in men under 35 years is:
   d. Suicide

4. Understanding the determinants of health can help to:
   a. Address and reduce health inequalities

5. The NMC's code of professional conduct (2008) states that you must:
   d. All the above

6. Buddhism is:
   a. A way of life

7. Which day of the week is called Shabbat?
   b. 7th

8. What is Ramadan?
   c. A month where Muslims fast from dawn to dusk

9. Life expectancy at birth in the UK has:
   d. Improved

10. The pressures on health and social services provided for older people will:
    b. Increase

Chapter 4

1. Stereotyping can be described as generalizations about people that are based on limited, sometimes inaccurate, information.
   True

2. Partnership working only involves those people working on one ward.
False

3. Multidisciplinary teams are best led by doctors.
False

4. Partnerships work best when the aim of the partnership is agreed and understood by all the partners.
True

5. The voluntary and community sector has important and meaningful contributions to make to partnership working.
True

6. Governments have no interest in ensuring that partnership working delivers.
False

7. The word collaboration can have sinister undertones.
True

8. There are growing numbers of people who are living with multiple long-term conditions; their needs are met only by the health service.
False

9. Improving the public's health should be led by social workers.
False

10. There are various laws that demand that health- and social care organisations work in partnership.
True

Chapter 5

1. The Health Service Ombudsman:
   c. Provides a service to the public by undertaking independent investigations into complaints

2. In order to assess a patient's needs effectively the nurse must employ many skills including:
   d. All of the above

3. Respect means:
   c. Demonstrate a genuine interest in the patient and his or her needs

4. Empathy means:
   a. Having the ability to communicate understanding of another person's experience from that person's perspective

5. How many values are associated with good complaint management?
   d. 6

6. Paralanguage can be defined as:
   c. The vocal cues that accompany language

7. Oculesics are associated with:
   a. Eye movements and messages conveyed by the eyes

8. When disengaging from a therapeutic relationship the nurse should:
   c. Be encouraged to reflect on the experience in order to learn and develop

9. The Care Quality Commission is:
   c. An independent body

10. The use of abbreviations and acronyms in health care:
   d. All of the above

Chapter 7
Across

2. HOLISTIC
5. EPIDEMIC
8. EQUALITY
9. COLLABORATION
11. HEALTH
13. EMPOWER
15. EPIDEMIOLOGY

Down

1. DEMOGRAPHY
3. DISEASE
4. ETHICS
6. INEQUALITIES
7. COMMUNITY
10. INDIVIDUAL
12. NEIGHBOURHOODS
14. PREVALENCE

Chapter 8
Evidence based practice is a **COMBINATION** of practitioner **EXPERTISE** and **KNOWLEDGE** of the best available **EVIDENCE**. It involves a careful, clear and thoughtful use of **UP-TO-DATE** evidence when making **DECISIONS** about how to **WORK** and **CARE** for people. Evidence based practice is a **CONTINUOUS** process. The first step in evidence based practice is **RECOGNISING** that there is a need for new **INFORMATION**. This information need has to be **CONVERTED** into an **ANSWERABLE** question. A **PRECISE** answer can only be provided in **RESPONSE** to a precise **QUESTION**. Carefully **FRAMING** the question can also help determine what **TYPE** of **EVIDENCE** is needed. Good clinical questions can be divided into **BACKGROUND** and **FOREGROUND** questions. **BACKGROUND** questions ask for **GENERAL KNOWLEDGE** about a disorder. Foreground questions ask for **SPECIFIC** knowledge about a disorder. The foreground question is often referred to as the **PICO** question structure – **PATIENT/PROBLEM, INTERVENTION, COMPARISON OUTCOME**.

Chapter 9

1. How many activities do Roper et al (1996) list?
   12

2. What was the additional phase of the nursing process?
   Diagnosis

3. What is the stage called where the nurse reviews the care plan to determine if the goals set had been met?
   Evaluation

4. What is missing: specific, measurable, realistic and time oriented?
   Achievable

5. The data-collection stage is called what?
   Assessment

6. The model of nursing that is commonly used in child health and referred to as the partnership model was devised by whom?
   Casey

7. What is the most commonly used pressure-sore risk assessment tool used in the UK?
   Waterlow

8. What does the MUST tool assess?
   Nutrition

9. What does the acronym MUST mean?
   Malnutrition Universal Screening Tool

10. What does the BMI calculate?
    Weight status

Chapter 10

1. The study of health-event patterns in a society is called:
   c. Epidemiology

2. Health-care provision in English prisons is the responsibility of:
   b. Primary care trusts

3. Homophobia is related to:
   c. A hatred of lesbian, gay, bisexual and transgendered people

4. The Ottawa Charter is:
   c. A worldwide strategy for global health promotion

5. The Acheson Report was produced in:
   b. 1988

6. Health intelligence is:
   a. A term associated with the collection of information about health

7. Life expectancy is:
   d. The number of years that a person can expect to live based on statistical average

8. Homeless people are:
   d. All of the above

9. Self-determination is:
   a. The ability to make decisions for oneself without external influence

10. A White Paper is:
    c. The Government's statement of policy intention

Chapter 11

1. How many standards are there in the NMC's (2010a) *Standards for Medicines Management*:
   c. 26 standards 10 sections

2. The acronym SIGN stands for:
   c. Scottish Intercollegiate Guidelines Network

3. Clinical governance applies to:
   d. All of the above

4. Risk identification can be:
   d. Reactive or proactive

5. Clinical guidelines:
   a. Help to ensure that patients receive the highest quality care

6. The clinical audit:
   d. Is a cyclical process

7. The NMC is responsible for:
   c. The regulation of nursing and midwifery professions

8. The Care Quality Commission replaced:
   b. The Healthcare Commission

9. The first piece of comprehensive legislation in the UK on medicine was:
   c. The Medicines Act 1968

10. The NSFs are:
    b. National Service Framework

Chapter 12

1. When should the nurse undertake an adult patient's observations in hospital?
   b. On admission or during the initial assessment

2. How would you determine the patient's pulse volume?
   d. By manually palpating the pulse

3. What is an early warning system?
   b. A tool used to predict deterioration in a person's condition

4. What does the acronym SBAR mean?
   c. Situation, background, assessment, recommendation

5. What does the acronym RSVP mean?
   a. Reason, story, vital signs, plan

6. A common method of assessing a person's level of consciousness uses:
   d. AVPU

7. How many minutes must the patient's pulse be counted in order to assess this accurately?
   b. One full minute

8. What does the term cyanosis mean?
   c. An abnormal blue discoloration of the skin and mucous membranes

9. In assessing a patient using EWS, a score of 3 or more should alert you to:
   b. Summons help in informing the outreach team/medical team/on call team

10. The use of SBAR, RSVP and other communication tools can help:
    c. Structure and standardise communication

Chapter 14

1. As a registered nurse it is a legal requirement to ensure that you undertake post-registration education and practice.
   True

2. You must ensure that your personal and professional portfolio is aligned with the NMC's mandatory template.
   False

3. Supervision is one way that your employer can ensure that you adhere to policies and procedures.
   False

4. Preceptorship is a foundation period for practitioners at the start of their careers which will help them begin the journey from novice to expert.
   True

5. You must undertake clinical supervision to remain live on the NMC register.
   False

6. In order to meet the PREP (practice) standard you must have undertaken 450 hours in your capacity as a nurse.
   True

7. Those unable to comply with the practice standard will have to successfully complete an approved return to practice programme.
   True

8. In order to meet the PREP (CPD) standard you must pay.
   False

9. There is no such thing as approved PREP (CPD) learning activity.
   True

10. Lifelong learning ceases when you register with NMC.
    False

Chapter 15

1. Which of the following is not a part of Maslow's hierarchy of needs?
   c. Psychomotor needs

2. Memory is associated with:
   a. Learning that occurs by receiving information, processing it, storing it and retrieving it.

3. Cognitive theory is associated with:
   c. The ability to store experience from the past and use these in the present.

4. Humanism believes that:
   b. It is important to study the person as a whole, particularly as the person grows and develops over the lifespan

5. By acting as teacher:
   b. You become a role model

6. Feedback in respect to teaching:
   c. Can help you become even better when teaching

7. Before going on clinical placement you should:
   d. All of the above

8. While on clinical placement you should:
   c. Express your needs.

9. If you witness poor practice or practice that concerns you, you must:
   d. Inform your mentor or the healthcare professional in charge immediately

10. The allocation of a mentor:
    a. Is one way in which the NMC can ensure that the competencies required for registration have been achieved

Glossary of Terms

Accountability

process that mandates that individuals are answerable for their actions and have an obligation (or duty) to act.

Active listening

listening that focuses on the feelings of the individual who is speaking.

Acute care

short-term hospital care provided to patients with conditions of short duration requiring stays of, on average, fewer than 30 days.

Acute illness

disruption (usually reversible) in functional ability characterised by a rapid onset, intense manifestations and a relatively short duration of illness.

Acute pain

discomfort identified by sudden onset and relatively short duration, mild-to-severe intensity, and a steady decrease in intensity of pain over several days or weeks.

Addiction

the physical and psychological dependence on using a substance, e.g. tobacco or alcohol.

Adverse drug event

harm resulting from medical intervention related to a drug.

Adverse health-care event

an event or omission arising during clinical care and causing physical or psychological injury to a patient.

Advocate

a person who pleads the cause of another.

Aetiology

the cause or contributing factors of a health problem.

Analysis

a mental process that enables a person to gain a better understanding of something.

Antidiscriminatory practice

acknowledging the sources of oppression in a person's life and actively seeking to reduce them.

Anxiety

a vague, uneasy feeling of discomfort or dread accompanied by an autonomic response.

Assumption

something that is taken for granted without any proof.

Attitude

mental stance that is composed of several beliefs. Often involves a negative or positive judgement towards a person, object or idea.

The Student's Guide to Becoming a Nurse, Second Edition. Ian Peate.
© 2012 John Wiley & Sons, Ltd. Published 2012 by John Wiley & Sons, Ltd.

Autonomy	the state of being independent, self-governing, with no outside control; the ability to make one's own decisions.
Bar graph	a chart that displays data by comparing the height or length of bars of equal width.
Behaviour	observable response of an individual to external stimuli.
Beliefs	interpretations or conclusions that are accepted as accurate.
Beneficence	ethical principle regarding the duty to promote good and prevent harm.
Bereavement	period of grieving following the death of a loved one.
Blame culture	an organisational culture that inhibits openness regarding reporting incidents as staff are fearful of being personally penalised for making errors.
Body image	individual's perception of physical self, including appearance, function and ability.
Care Quality Commission	formerly the Healthcare Commission; promotes improvement in quality of the NHS and independent health care. Assesses performance of health-care organisations, awarding annual ratings.
Caring	the intentional action that suggests physical and emotional support and security. A genuine connectedness with another person or group of people.
Categorical imperative	concept that states that one should act only if the action is based on a principle that is universal.
Chronic acute pain	discomfort that occurs almost daily over a long period (months or years) and that has a high probability of ending; also known as progressive pain.
Chronic illness	disruption in functional ability usually characterised by a gradual, insidious onset of illness with lifelong changes that are usually irreversible.
Chronic pain	discomfort that is persistent, almost constant and long-lasting (6 months or longer); or recurrent pain that produces significant negative changes in a person's life.
Client/patient advocate	person who speaks up or acts on behalf of the client/patient.
Clinical decision-making	an organised, sequential reasoning process that includes assessment, analysis, planning, implementation and evaluation.
Clinical governance	a framework whereby organisations are accountable for continuously improving the quality of services and safeguarding high standards of care.
Clinical supervision	a formal process of professional support and learning that enables individual practitioners to develop knowledge and competence.

Closed question	a communication technique that consists of questions that can be answered briefly with yes–no or one-word responses.
Cognition	the mental process of faculty by which knowledge is acquired.
Cognitive skills	intellectual skills that can include problem-solving, critical thinking and decision-making.
Communication	the complex, active process of relating to individuals and groups, which may include health team members, by written, verbal and non-verbal means. The goal is to understand and be understood, and involves the transmission of ideas, messages, emotions and information by various means, between individuals and groups. Therapeutic communication promotes caring relationships between nurses and patients.
Competency	ability, qualities and capacity to function in a particular way.
Compliance	the degree to which the patient follows the recommendations made by nurses and other health-care professionals (this is also sometimes called adherence).
Concept(s)	vehicle of thought. Abstract ideas or mental images of reality.
Conceptual framework (model)	structure that links global concepts together to form a unified whole.
Conceptualisation	process of developing and refining abstract ideas.
Consent	voluntary act by which a person agrees to allow someone else to do something.
Construct	abstraction or mental representation inferred from situations, events or behaviours.
Context	the circumstances in which a particular event or events occur.
Coping	a complex of behavioural, cognitive and physiological responses that aim to prevent or minimise unpleasant or harmful experiences that challenge one's personal resources.
Counselling	the process of helping an individual to recognise and cope with problems that may cause stress. An attempt to develop interpersonal growth with the aim of promoting personal growth.
Criteria	standards that are used to evaluate whether the behaviour demonstrated indicates accomplishment of the goal.
Critical thinking	a purposeful, deliberate method of thinking used in search for meaning.
Cultural competence	process through which the nurse provides care that is appropriate to the patient's cultural context.
Cultural diversity	individual differences among people that result from racial, ethnic and cultural variables.

Culture	dynamic and integrated structures of knowledge, beliefs, behaviours, ideas, attitudes, values, habits, customs, language, symbols, rituals, ceremonies and practices that are unique to a particular group of people; growing microorganisms to identify a pathogen.
Data	pieces of information about health, e.g. the patient's vital signs (also known as cues).
Decision-making	the consideration and selection of interventions that facilitate the achievement of a desired outcome.
Delegation	process of transferring a selected nursing task in a situation to an individual who is competent to perform that task.
Democratic leadership	style of leadership (also called participative style: leadership) that is based on the belief that every group member should have input into the development of goals and problem-solving.
Demography	the study of populations. Statistics related to distribution by age and place of residence, mortality and morbidity.
Deontology	ethical theory that considers the intrinsic moral significance of an act itself as the criterion for determination of good.
Diagnosis	classification of a disease, condition or human response that is determined by scientific evaluation of signs and symptoms, patient history and diagnostic studies.
Disability	a lack of ability to perform an activity that a normal person can perform.
Disease	an alteration in body function resulting in a reduction of capabilities in the ability to perform the activities of living, or contributing to the shortening of the normal lifespan.
Distress	experienced when stressors evoke an ineffective response.
Duty	obligation created either by law or contract, or by any voluntary action.
Efficacy	the extent to which nursing and/or medical interventions achieve health improvements under ideal conditions.
Empathy	understanding another person's perception of a situation. The ability to discriminate what the other person's world may be like.
Emotion	any strong feeling, e.g. joy, hate, sorrow, love.
Empowerment	process of enabling others to do things for themselves.
Epidemic	the situation in which the occurrence of a health problem has increased quickly.
Equity	fair distribution of resources or benefits.

Ethical dilemma	situation that occurs when there is a conflict between two or more ethical principles.
Ethical principles	tenets that direct or govern actions.
Ethical reasoning	process of thinking through what one ought to do in an orderly, systematic manner in order to provide justification of actions based on principles.
Ethics	branch of philosophy concerned with determining right from wrong on the basis of a body of knowledge.
Ethnicity	culture group's perception of themselves (group identity) and others' perception of them.
Ethnocentrism	assumption of cultural superiority and an inability to accept other cultures' ways of organising reality.
Ethnography	a type of qualitative research with an approach involving anthropology, in which a person's culture is examined by studying the meanings of the actions and events of the culture's members.
Ethnomethodology	a type of qualitative methodology in which interpretations of ethnography are made in a particular social world.
Eustress	type of stress that results in positive outcomes.
Euthanasia	intentional action or lack of action causing the merciful death of someone with a terminal illness or incurable condition; derived from the Greed work *euthanatos*, which literally means 'good or gentle death'.
Evaluation	a step in the nursing process; involves determining whether patient goals have been met, partially met or not met.
Express	to manifest or communicate, to make known.
Extended family	family members from previous generations, such as grandparents, uncles and aunts.
Fear	anxiety caused by consciously recognised and realistic danger. It can be a perceived threat, real or imagined.
Fidelity	ethical concept that means faithfulness and keeping promises.
Gender (biology, sex)	biological structure of a person's genitals that designates them as male, female or intersexed.
Gender identity	view of one's self as male or female in relationship to others.
Gender role	masculine or feminine role adopted by a person; often culturally and socially determined.
Goal	aim, intent or end.
Grief	the emotional suffering often caused by bereavement.

443

Group communication	a complex level of communication that occurs when three or more people meet in face-to-face encounters or through another communication medium, such as a conference call.
Group dynamics	study of the events that take place during small-group interaction and the development of subgroups.
Hazard	anything that can cause harm.
Healing	process of recovery from illness, accident or disability.
Healing touch	energy-based therapeutic modality that alters the energy fields through the use of touch, thereby affecting physical, mental, emotional and spiritual health.
Health	process through which a person seeks to maintain an equilibrium that promotes stability and comfort; includes physiological, psychological, sociocultural, intellectual and spiritual wellbeing.
Health and Safety Executive	a statutory body that reports to the Health and Safety Commission, with day-to-day responsibility for making arrangements for the enforcement of safety legislation to ensure that risks to health and safety due to work activities are properly controlled.
Health promotion	process undertaken to increase levels of wellness in individuals, families and communities.
Health Protection Agency	an independent body that protects the health and wellbeing of the population of the UK, particularly with regard to infectious diseases, chemical hazards, poisons and radiation.
Health-seeking behaviours	activities that are directed towards attaining and maintaining a state of wellbeing.
Heterosexism	perspective or assumption that people are heterosexual.
Heterosexual	describes sexual activity between a man and a woman.
Holism	the belief that individuals function as complete units that cannot be reduced to the sum of their parts.
Holistic nursing	nursing practice that has as its aim the healing of the whole person.
Homosexuality	sexual activity between two members of the same sex.
Hopelessness	a subjective state in which an individual sees limited or no alternatives or personal choices available and is unable to mobilise energy on his or her own behalf.
Hospice	type of care for the terminally ill founded on the concept of allowing individuals to die with dignity and surrounded by those who love them.
Hypothesis	statement of an asserted relationship between dependent variables.

Iatrogenic disease	a condition or disease that is caused by medical or surgical intervention, e.g. the side effects of some drugs.
Identity	what sets one person apart as a unique individual; it may include a person's name, gender, ethnic identity, family status, occupation and various roles.
Illness	inability of an individual's adaptive responses to maintain physical and emotional balance which subsequently results in an impairment in functional abilities.
Illness stage	time interval when patient is presenting or manifesting specific signs and symptoms of an infectious agent.
Implementation	a step in the nursing process; involves the execution of the nursing plan of care formulated during the planning phase of the nursing process.
Implied contract	contract that recognises a relationship between parties for services.
Incidence	refers to the prevalence of a disease in a population or community. The predictive value of the same test can be different when applied to people of different ages.
Individualism	a predominant cultural type which focuses on an independent lifestyle that flourishes in urban settings.
Informed consent	the patient understands the reason for the proposed intervention, its benefits and risks, and agrees to the treatment usually by signing a consent form.
Interpersonal	process that occurs between two people in communication: face-to-face encounters over the telephone, or through other communication media.
Intersexed	person born with both sets of or ambiguous genitalia.
Interview	therapeutic interaction that has a specific purpose.
Intrapersonal communication	messages that one sends to oneself, including 'self-talk' or communication with oneself.
Intuition	knowing something without evidence, the learning of things without the conscious use of reasoning.
Justice	ethical principle based on the concept of fairness that is extended to each individual.
Knowledge and Skills Framework	describes the knowledge and skills required by NHS staff to deliver quality services in their work. It also supports personal development and career progression.
Leadership	interpersonal process that involves motivating and guiding others to achieve goals.

Leadership theory	conceptual support framework for leadership.
Leading question	a question that influences the patient to give a specific answer.
Learning	process of assimilating information with a resultant change in behaviour.
Learning plateau	a temporary slowdown in learning.
Lesbian	female who has affectional and sexual tendencies towards females.
Liability	obligation one has incurred or might incur through any act or failure to act.
Life events	major occurrences that occur in a person's life which require some element of psychological adjustment.
Lifestyle	the values and behaviours that have been taken on by a person in daily life.
Line graph	a graph that compares two variables through a line.
Living will	document prepared by a competent adult that provides direction regarding medical care should the person become incapacitated or otherwise unable to make decisions personally.
Locus control	a person's perception of the sources of control over events and situations affecting the person's life.
Measurable	able to be quantified.
Medication error	any preventable harm that may cause or lead to inappropriate medication use or patient harm while the medication is in the control of the health-care professional, patient or customer.
Mentor	a knowledgeable person, someone with insight, someone to trust and confide in, helps a person to clarify thinking.
Minority group	group of people who constitute less than a numerical majority of the population and who, because of their cultural or physical characteristics, are labelled and treated differently from others in society.
Morality	behaviour in accordance with custom or tradition that usually reflects personal or religious beliefs.
Morbidity	the condition, illness, injury or disability in the population.
Mortality	refers to death, often associated with a large population.
Motivation	the internal drive or externally arising stimulus to action or thought.
Mourning	period of time during which grief is expressed and resolution and integration of the loss occur.

National Institute for Health and Clinical Excellence (NICE) — an independent organisation responsible for providing national guidance on the promotion of good health and the prevention and treatment of ill-health.

National Service Frameworks — one of a range of measures to raise quality and decrease variations in service, containing long-term strategies.

Need — anything that is absolutely essential for existence.

Negligence — failure of an individual to provide the care in a situation that a reasonable person would ordinarily provide in a similar circumstance.

Negotiation — a method of conflict management whereby the parties decide what they must retain and what they are willing to give up in order to reach a compromise position.

Non-maleficence — ethical principle that means the duty to cause no harm to others.

Nursing — an art and a science that assists individuals to learn to care for themselves whenever possible; it also involves caring for others when they are unable to meet their own needs.

Nursing leadership — interpersonal process in nursing that involves motivating and guiding others to achieve goals.

Nursing process — systematic method of providing care to patients; consists of four or five steps:

1. Assessment
2. Diagnosis
3. Outcome identification and planning
4. Implementation
5. Evaluation.

Nursing research — systematic application of formalised methods for generating valid and dependable information about the phenomena of concern to the discipline of nursing.

Objective data — observable and measurable data that are obtained through both standard assessment techniques performed during the physical examination, and laboratory and diagnostic tests.

Observation — the skill of watching with thought, using all the senses.

Open-ended questions — interview technique that encourages the patient to elaborate about a particular concern or problem.

Open family system — a family system that interacts with the environment and in doing so maintains growth and balance.

Pain — state in which an individual experiences and reports the presence of physical discomfort; may range in intensity from uncomfortable sensation to severe discomfort. Pain is what the patient says it is, existing whenever he or she says it does.

Paradigm	a pattern of collective understandings and assumptions about reality and the world.
Paraverbal communication	the way in which a person speaks, including voice tone, pitch and inflection.
Paraverbal cue	verbal message accompanied by cues, such as tone and pitch of voice, speed, inflection, volume and other non-language vocalisations.
Participative leadership style	leadership style where every person's viewpoints are considered as valuable and have equal voice in making decisions.
Passive euthanasia	process of cooperating with the patient's dying process.
Paternalism	practice by which health-care providers decide what is 'best' for patients and then attempt to coerce patients to act against their own choices.
Perception	person's sense and understanding of the world.
Personality	the cognitive, affective or behavioural predispositions of people in different situations, over a period of time.
Phenomenon	observable fact or event that can be perceived through the senses and is susceptible to description and explanation.
Philosophy	statement of beliefs that is the foundation for one's thoughts and actions.
Pictograph	pictorial (usually symbols) representation of statistical data on a graph.
Pie chart	a graph that is made up of a circle that is divided into sectors; each sector represents a proportion of the whole.
Planning	a step of the nursing process; includes the formulation of guidelines that establish the proposed course of nursing action in the resolution of nursing diagnoses and the development of the patient's plan of care.
Portfolio	a collection of personal evidence selected for a particular purpose.
Posology	the science of quantity, the science of dosage.
Power	ability to do or act, resulting in the achievement of desired results.
Prejudice	a negative belief that is generalised about a group; this leads to prejudgement.
Prevalence	the total number of cases existing at a given period of time.
Profession	group (vocational or occupational) that requires specialised education and intellectual knowledge.
Professional organisation	members engaged in the same professional pursuit, often with similar goals and concerns.

Professional regulation	process by which nursing ensures that its members act in the public interest by providing a unique service that society has entrusted to them.
Professional standards	authoritative statements developed by the profession by which quality of practice, service and/or education can be judged.
Qualitative research	systematic collection and analysis of subjective narrative materials, using procedures for which there tends to be a minimum of research-imposed control.
Quality assurance framework	traditional approach to quality management in which monitoring and evaluation focus on individual performance, deviation from standards and problem-solving.
Quality improvement	a process for change using a multidisciplinary approach to problem identification and resolution.
Quantitative research	systematic collection of numerical information, often under conditions of considerable control.
Racism	discrimination directed towards individuals who are misperceived to be inferior because of biological factors.
Radiation	loss of heat in the form of infrared rays.
Rapport	mutual trust and understanding in a relationship.
Rationale	explanation based on the theories and scientific principles of natural and behavioural sciences and the humanities.
Reflective diary	a personal aid to reflection, a document used to structure and document reflective accounts.
Relationship	an interaction of individuals over a period of time.
Religion	a system of beliefs and practices that usually involves a community of like-minded people.
Research	systematic method of exploring, describing, explaining, relating or establishing the existence of a phenomenon, the factors that cause changes in the phenomenon and how the phenomenon influences other phenomena.
Risk	the chance of something happening that will have an impact on individuals and/or organisations. Risk is measured in terms of likelihood and consequence.
Risk management	a method of reducing risks of adverse events occurring in organisations by systematically assessing, reviewing and seeking ways to prevent the occurrence of risks.
Role	set of expected behaviours associated with a person's status or position.

449

Role ambiguity	role expectations that are unclear. People do not know what or how to do what is expected of them.
Role conflict	when the expectations of one role compete with the expectations of other roles.
Scattergram	a graph that plots data; however, the points are not joined into lines (sometimes called scatter plot or scatter diagram).
Scope of practice	legal boundaries of practice for health-care providers as defined in statute.
Self-concept	the collection of ideas, feelings and beliefs that one has about oneself.
Self-esteem	a sense of pride in oneself; self-love.
Sexual dysfunction	physical inability to perform sexually, but can also be a psychological inability to perform sexually.
Sexual health	ability to form mutually consensual, developmentally appropriate sexual relationships that are safe and respectful of self and others; includes emotional, physical and psychological components.
Sexuality	human characteristic that refers not just to gender but to all the aspects of being male or female, including feelings, attitudes, beliefs and behaviour.
Sexual orientation	individual's preference for ways of expressing sexual feelings.
Sick role	a set of social expectations met by an ill person, such as being exempt from the usual social role responsibilities and being obligated to get well and to seek competent help.
Socialisation	the ways in which people learn about the ways of a group or society in an attempt to become a functioning partner.
Sociocultural	involving social and cultural features or processes.
Spirituality	relationship with one's self, a sense of connection with others, and a relationship with a higher power or divine source.
Standard of care	delineates the extent and character of the nurse's duty to the patient; defined by organisational policy or professional standards of practice.
Stress	body's reaction to any stimulus.
Stressors	circumstances or events that a person perceives as threatening or harmful.
Subjective data	data from the patient's point of view, including feelings, perceptions and concerns.
Teaching	active process in which one individual shares information with another as a means to facilitate behavioural changes.

Teaching–learning process   planned interaction promoting a behavioural change that is not a result of maturation or coincidence.

Teaching strategies   techniques employed by the teacher to promote learning.

Team   group of individuals who work together to achieve a common goal.

Theory   set of concepts and propositions that provide an orderly way to view phenomena.

Therapeutic   describes actions that are beneficial to the patient.

Therapeutic communication   use of communication for the purpose of creating a beneficial outcome for the patient.

Therapeutic range   achievement of constant therapeutic blood level of a medication within a safe range.

Therapeutic touch   holistic technique that consists of assessing alterations in a person's energy fields and using the hands to direct energy to achieve a balanced state.

Therapeutic use of self   process in which nurses deliberately plan their actions and approach the relationship with a specific goal in mind before interacting with the patient.

Transcultural nursing   formal area of study and practice focused on comparative analysis of different cultures and subcultures with respect to cultural care, health and illness beliefs, and values and practices, with the goal of providing health care within the context of the patient's culture.

Transgender   person who dresses and engages in roles of the person of the opposite gender.

Utility   ethical principle that states that an act must result in the greatest amount of good for the greatest number of people involved in a situation.

Values   principles that influence the development of beliefs and attitudes.

Variable   a characteristic that is measurable on people, objects or events which may change in quantity or quality.

Veracity   ethical principle that means that one should be truthful, neither lying nor deceiving others.

Verbal message   message communicated through words or language, both spoken and written.

Whistle-blowing   calling attention to the unethical, illegal or incompetent actions of others.

Index

454

459